THE
CHANDOS
CLASSICS

THE POETICAL WORKS

OF

PERCY BYSSHE SHELLEY.

THE POETICAL WORKS

OF

PERCY BYSSHE SHELLEY.

REPRINTED FROM THE EARLY EDITIONS,

With Memoir, Explanatory Notes, &c.

LONDON:

FREDERICK WARNE AND CO.

AND NEW YORK.

THE POETICAL WORKS

PERCY BYSSHE SHELLEY.

PREFACE.

THE present Edition of Shelley contains all the poems published by the Poet himself, and those given to the public after his death by Mrs. Shelley, *i.e.*, the "Posthumous Poems" and "Collected Works." It therefore comprises all those which have made his name immortal.

To these have been added the verses and ballad from his boyish novel of "St. Irvyne; or, the Rosicrucian," and the "Posthumous Fragments of Margaret Nicholson," a burlesque production, in which he was assisted by his friend Hogg, and which was published during his first term at University College, under the name of John Fitz Victor.

CONTENTS.

PREFATORY MEMOIR.

PERCY BYSSHE SHELLEY was born at Field Place, Sussex, August 4, 1792. He was the eldest son of Sir Timothy Shelley, of Castle-Goring. Till he was seven or eight years of age he was brought up with his sisters. Sharing their education, and having no boy companion, he never gained a taste for the ordinary sports and amusements of boyhood; and on this account became subject to a good deal of rough usage at school, which may have tended to wake up the spirit of opposition for which he was afterwards remarkable. His first school was that of Sion House, Brentford; from whence, at thirteen, he passed to Eton; from Eton to Oxford in 1810.

Before he entered the University Shelley published two rather silly novels. At Oxford the peculiarities of this wild genius became remarkable. He lived, we are told, chiefly on bread; he carried duelling pistols in his pocket when walking, and would occasionally pause to shoot at some mark he had fixed for himself; he would linger for hours throwing stones into ponds, or sailing paper boats. These harmless and childish eccentricities were, however, destined to be followed by much more objectionable developments.

The "times were out of joint." The French Revolution had unsettled steadier minds than Shelley's; he embraced the wildest dogmas of the day, and actually published a pamphlet entitled the "Necessity of Atheism." For this performance he was (with his friend, Mr. Hogg) expelled from the university.

During his last term at college he had also published a strange burlesque volume of poems, called the "Posthumous Works of Margaret Nicholson," which are reproduced in the present volume. At the time of his expulsion he was only seventeen, but he was already deeply attached to a cousin who had been born on the same day with himself. His expulsion from Oxford and its cause disappointed this affection, and his beloved cousin became the wife of another. Shelley had naturally given great offence to his family, but his father offered to forgive him if he would return home, give up his friend Hogg, and study with a private tutor. These terms appear all that any lad of Shelley's age could hope for; nevertheless he refused them, and remained in London; but, as he himself informed Hogg, his father allowed him £200 a year.

The sorrow and sympathy of his sisters were naturally awakened by this event, and they sent him loving gifts by the hand of a schoolfellow, Harriet Westbrook, a beautiful girl of sixteen, of inferior station to themselves, her father being the landlord of a tavern. In one of his visits to his sisters he heard them discuss the difficulty her father had with her; he at once enlisted himself as her champion, and declared that he would marry her. His sisters were astonished at the suddenness of this decision, as Shelley had not shown any especial liking for the young girl, but he meant what he said. He took Miss Westbrook to Scotland and married her there, as they were both under age.

Not long after he printed the "Hermit of Marlow," on occasion of the death of the Princess Charlotte. It was a mere political skit. Under the lament for the Princess he typified the death of Liberty. Not very long after he printed for private circulation a poem, begun at seventeen, "Queen Mab." We think it is a pity that this poem should still hold a place in his collected works; his second wife, Mary Shelley, believed that his mature taste would have rejected it. Nor in fact did he ever publish it; it was brought to light by a literary piracy. All that he thought worth retaining in it he reprinted in "The Demon of the World." Shelley's first marriage proved unhappy. In 1814 he abandoned his wife, child, and an infant born after this desertion; and started for Italy with Mary Godwin, the daughter of the well-known author of "Caleb

Williams" and Mary Wollstonecraft, whose opinions resembled those embraced by Shelley. It appears that, though he had abandoned Harriet, he still felt a friendly regard for her, and even wished her, we are informed, to live in the house with him and Miss Godwin as a friend ! A legal adviser showed him that this was impossible. Two years afterwards, the unhappy Harriet, who had also formed new ties, and believed herself forsaken by her lover, drowned herself. Her father had taken charge of her two poor children. Shelley would have retaken his children after Harriet's death, but Mr. Westbrook refused to yield them up. A Chancery suit ensued, and the babes were placed under other guardianship than their father's. In fact, he had never seen the boy (born after his desertion of the mother), and had never manifested any parental affection for either till he made this claim. He had an illegitimate son by Mary Godwin ; he had written a poem wholly against Christianity ;—therefore we think the law rightly adjudged the guardianship of poor Harriet's children to wiser hands than Shelley's. Before his first wife's death Shelley had published " Alastor," his first mature poem. After her death he married Miss Godwin, and lived with her in Italy. Previously, however, a friendly rivalry with Keats led to his writing " The Revolt of Islam "—the rival poem being the " Endymion."

Shelley never again revisited England. At Rome he wrote his finest poem, the " Prometheus Unbound." The awful tragedy of the " Cenci " followed, and in various parts of Italy his other poems of that date. His friend, Captain Medwin, tells us that " Julian and Maddalo " were meant to delineate himself and Lord Byron, with whom he was for some time on terms of great intimacy.

The life of this very original and gifted poet terminated at the early age of thirty. He was fond of boating, and a friend who had located near him at Venice—Captain Williams—and himself returning from Leghorn to their home near Lerici in a new boat he had built, were overtaken by a sudden storm, and it was supposed that the boat went down with them. The bodies of the friends were found eight days afterwards, cast up on the beach,

three miles apart from each other.   That of Shelley was recognised
by Mr. Trelawney (who alone saw the bodies) from the jacket
that he wore, and also from having a volume of Æschylus in
the right pocket, and Keats's "Lamia" in the left, folded back as
if put there in haste.   The state of the bodies made it necessary
to cremate them before removal, and the dead were burned with
much solemnity in the presence of Mr. Trelawney, Captain Shen-
ley, Lord Byron, and Leigh Hunt.

Shelley's remains were taken to Rome, and deposited near those
of his little son and of Keats in the Protestant cemetery.

With regard to his genius there is no longer a dissentient voice.
We may regret that he ever wrote "Queen Mab" and "The
Revolt of Islam," but "Prometheus" is unrivalled in the language;
and his minor poems have proved what perfect music English may
become in the hand of a master.

Shelley was much beloved by his friends in spite of the eccentricities and peculiarities of his character; he was, we learn, very
liberal, even generous, and full of a desire to promote (as well as
he knew how) the welfare of humanity.   His imagination pre-
ponderated over judgment and reason; and he even imagined
events to have occurred to himself, which, according to the testi-
mony of his dearest friends, had never happened.   Such a life
offers much ground for reflection and regret; but we cannot think
that Shelley lived wholly in vain when we remember that to him
his nation owes the glorious dramatic poem of "Prometheus," and
lyrics unequalled in beauty in any modern language.

The following curious ghost story respecting Shelley was related
by Byron to Captain Medwin, after his death :—

"Shortly before his fatal voyage to Leghorn, the inhabitants of
the country house at San Lorenzo were alarmed, at midnight, by
piercing shrieks.   They rushed out of their bedrooms, and found
Shelley in the saloon with his eyes wide open, and gazing on
vacancy, as though he beheld some spectre.   On waking him, he
related that he had had a vision.   He thought that a figure wrapped
in a mantle came to his bedside, and beckoned to him.   He got
up and followed it; when in the hall, the phantom lifted up the

hood of his cloak, showed Shelley the phantasm of himself—and saying, ' Siete satisfatto ? '—vanished.

"Shelley had been reading a strange drama, which is supposed to have been written by Calderon, entitled, ' El embozado, ó el encapotado.' It is so scarce, that Washington Irving told me he had sought for it without success in several of the public libraries of Spain. The story is—that a kind of Cipriano or Faust is through life thwarted in all his plans for the acquisition of wealth, or honour, or happiness, by a masked stranger, who stands in his way like some Alastor or evil spirit. He is at length in love— the day is fixed for his marriage—when the unknown contrives to sow dissension between him and his betrothed, and to break off the match. Infuriate with his wrongs, he breathes nothing but revenge, but all his attempts to discover his mysterious foe prove abortive : at length his persecutor appears of his own accord. When about to fight, the Embozado unmasks, and discovers the phantasm of himself, saying, ' Are you satisfied ? ' The hero of the play dies with horror.

"This play had worked strongly on Shelley's imagination, and accounts for the awful scene at San Lorenzo."

Long after Shelley's death, an old fisherman, dying at Spezia in 1863, confessed that he had been one of a crew who had run down Shelley's boat. They had not intended to sink her ; their purpose was robbery. They believed that Lord Byron was on board her and would have much money with him ; they knew that Shelley had taken a bag of dollars on board, and they meant to murder Byron and of course his companions, and rob the boat. But at the first touch, he said, she sank. A storm was raging at the time, and the collision must have been severe, for when Trelawney had the boat raised out of ten fathoms water, it was found that her stern-quarter was stove in. This confession came to the ears of Mr. Trelawney's daughter when in Rome in 1875, and she at once wrote to her father about it. The story was, however, contradicted in the *Athenæum* by Professor de Guberna-toris, and treated as an idle tale. Its truth, however, is not doubted by Mr. Trelawney, and the state of the boat undoubtedly attests

that the confession was a real one, and that Shelley, whose life
had been made so unhappy, thus perished by the crime of men.

On his tomb Mr. Trelawney inscribed, after the Latin inscrip-
tion, these lines from the dead poet's favourite play, "The Tempest:"—

> "Nothing of him that doth fade,
> But doth suffer a sea-change
> Into something rich and strange."

THE POETICAL WORKS

OF

PERCY BYSSHE SHELLEY.

1813.

QUEEN MAB.

THIS poem is re-printed from the edition of 1821—the first published. It was surreptitiously printed by a bookseller in the Strand (W. Clark) from one of the copies which Shelley had printed in 1813 for private distribution only. The poet sought an injunction against it. He never published "Queen Mab" himself, and his gifted wife doubted whether he would have allowed it a place in his collected poems. Probably he would not, as he had already published a portion of it (much altered) under the title of the "Demon of the World," which appeared with "Alastor" in 1816, as a Fragment. We have placed it at the end of "Queen Mab" in this edition. It will be seen that several of the alterations made in it have been inserted in the ordinary editions of the poem.

TO HARRIET * * * * *.

WHOSE is the love that, gleaming through the world,
Wards off the poisonous arrow of its scorn?
Whose is the warm and partial praise
Virtue's most sweet reward?

Beneath whose looks did my reviving soul
Riper in truth and virtuous daring grow?
Whose eyes have I gazed fondly on,
And loved mankind the more?

Harriet! on thine :—thou wert my purer mind;
Thou wert the inspiration of my song;
Thine are these early wilding flowers,
Though garlanded by me.

Then press unto thy breast this pledge of love;
And know, though time may change and years may roll,
Each floweret gathered in my heart
It consecrates to thine.

B

I.

How wonderful is Death,
  Death and his brother Sleep !
One, pale as yonder waning moon
  With lips of lurid blue ;
The other, rosy as the morn
  When throned on ocean's wave
  It blushes o'er the world :
Yet both so passing wonderful !

Hath then the gloomy Power
Whose reign is in the tainted sepulchres
  Seized on her sinless soul ?
Must then that peerless form
Which love and admiration cannot view
Without a beating heart, those azure veins
Which steal like streams along a field of snow
  That lovely outline, which is fair
    As breathing marble, perish ?
    Must putrefaction's breath
Leave nothing of this heavenly sight
  But loathsomeness and ruin ?
Spare nothing but a gloomy theme,
On which the lightest heart might moralize ?
  Or is it only a sweet slumber
    Stealing o'er sensation,
  Which the breath of roseate morning
    Chaseth into darkness ?
  Will Ianthe wake again,
And give that faithful bosom joy
Whose sleepless spirit waits to catch
Light, life, and rapture from her smile ?

Yes ! she will wake again,
Although her glowing limbs are motionless,
    And silent those sweet lips,
    Once breathing eloquence
That might have soothed a tiger's rage,
Or thawed the cold heart of a conqueror,
    Her dewy eyes are closed,
And on their lids, whose texture fine
Scarce hides the dark blue orbs beneath,
    The baby Sleep is pillowed :
    Her golden tresses shade
    The bosom's stainless pride,
Curling like tendrils of the parasite
    Around a marble column.

Hark ! whence that rushing sound ?
  'Tis like the wondrous strain
That round a lonely ruin swells,
Which, wandering on the echoing shore
  The enthusiast hears at evening :
'Tis softer than the west wind's sigh ;
'Tis wilder than the unmeasured notes
Of that strange lyre whose strings

The genii of the breezes sweep :
Those lines of rainbow light
Are like the moonbeams when they fall
Through some cathedral window, but the teints
Are such as may not find
Comparison on earth.

Behold the chariot of the Fairy Queen !
Celestial coursers paw the unyielding air ;
Their filmy pennons at her word they furl,
And stop obedient to the reins of light :
These the Queen of Spells drew in,
She spread a charm around the spot,
And leaning graceful from the ethereal car,
Long did she gaze, and silently,
Upon the slumbering maid.

Oh ! not the visioned poet in his dreams,
When silvery clouds float through the wildered brain,
When every sight of lovely, wild, and grand,
Astonishes, enraptures, elevates,
When fancy, at a glance, combines
The wondrous and the beautiful,—
So bright, so fair, so wild a shape
Hath ever yet beheld,
As that which reined the coursers of the air.
And poured the magic of her gaze
Upon the maiden's sleep.

The broad and yellow moon
Shone dimly through her form—
That form of faultless symmetry ;
The pearly and pellucid car
Moved not the moonlight's line :
'Twas not an earthly pageant :
Those who had looked upon the sight,
Passing all human glory,
Saw not the yellow moon,
Saw not the mortal scene,
Heard not the night-wind's rush,
Heard not an earthly sound,
Saw but the fairy pageant,
Heard but the heavenly strains
That filled the lonely dwelling.

The Fairy's frame was slight, yon fibrous cloud,
That catches but the palest tinge of even,
And which the straining eye can hardly seize
When melting into eastern twilight's shadow,
Were scarce so thin, so slight ; but the fair star
That gems the glittering coronet of morn,
Sheds not a light so mild, so powerful,
As that which, bursting from the Fairy's form,
Spread a purpureal halo round the scene,
Yet with an undulating motion,
Swayed to her outline gracefully.
From her celestial car
The Fairy Queen descended.

And thrice she waved her wand
Circled with wreaths of amaranth :
Her thin and misty form
Moved with the moving air,
And the clear silver tones,
As thus she spoke, were such
As are unheard by all but gifted ear.

FAIRY.

Stars ! your balmiest influence shed !
Elements ! your wrath suspend !
Sleep, Ocean, in the rocky bounds
    That circle thy domain !
Let not a breath be seen to stir
Around yon grass-grow ruin's height,
    Let even the restless gossamer
      Sleep on the moveless air !
      Soul of Ianthe ! thou,
Judged alone worthy of the envied boon,
That waits the good and the sincere ; that waits
Those who have struggled, and with resolute will
Vanquished earth's pride and meanness, burst the chains,
The icy chains of custom, and have shone
The day-stars of their age ;—Soul of Ianthe !
      Awake ! arise !

    Sudden arose
    Ianthe's Soul ; it stood
All beautiful in naked purity,
The perfect semblance of its bodily frame.
Instinct with inexpressible beauty and grace,
    Each stain of earthliness
    Had passed away, it reassumed
    Its native dignity, and stood
      Immortal amid ruin.

    Upon the couch the body lay
    Wrapt in the depth of slumber :
Its features were fixed and meaningless,
    Yet animal life was there,
And every organ yet performed
Its natural functions : 'twas a sight
Of wonder to behold the body and soul.
    The self-same lineaments, the same
    Marks of identity were there :
Yet, oh, how different ! One aspires to Heaven,
Pants for its sempiternal heritage,
And ever-changing, ever-rising still,
    Wantons in endless being.
The other, for a time the unwilling sport
Of circumstance and passion, struggles on ;
Fleets through its sad duration rapidly :
Then like an useless and worn-out machine,
    Rots, perishes, and passes.

FAIRY.

Spirit ! who hast dived so deep ;
Spirit ! who hast soared so high ;

Thou the fearless, thou the mild,
Accept the boon thy worth hath earned,
Ascend the car with me.

SPIRIT.

Do I dream ? Is this new feeling
But a visioned ghost of slumber ?
If indeed I am a soul,
A free, a disembodied soul,
Speak again to me.

FAIRY.

I am the Fairy MAB : to me 'tis given
The wonders of the human world to keep :
The secrets of the immeasurable past,
In the unfailing consciences of men,
Those stern, unflattering chroniclers, I find :
The future, from the causes which arise
In each event, I gather : not the sting
Which retributive memory implants
In the hard bosom of the selfish man ;
Nor that ecstatic and exulting throb
Which virtue's votary feels when he sums up
The thoughts and actions of a well-spent day,
Are unforeseen, unregistered by me :
And it is yet permitted me, to rend
The veil of mortal frailty, that the spirit
Clothed in its changeless purity, may know
How soonest to accomplish the great end
For which it hath its being, and may taste
That peace, which in the end all life will share.
This is the meed of virtue ; happy Soul,
Ascend the car with me !

The chains of earth's immurement
Fell from Ianthe's spirit ;
They shrank and brake like bandages of straw
Beneath a wakened giant's strength.
She knew her glorious change,
And felt in apprehension uncontrolled
New raptures opening round :
Each day-dream of her mortal life,
Each frenzied vision of the slumbers
That closed each well-spent day,
Seemed now to meet reality.

The Fairy and the Soul proceeded ;
The silver clouds disparted ;
And as the car of magic they ascended,
Again the speechless music swelled,
Again the coursers of the air
Unfurled their azure pennons, and the Queen
Shaking the beamy reins
Bade them pursue their way.

The magic car moved on.
The night was fair, and countless stars
Studded heaven's dark blue vault,—-

Just o'er the eastern wave
Peeped the first faint smile of morn :—
The magic car moved on—
From the celestial hoofs
The atmosphere in flaming sparkles flew,
And where the burning wheels
Eddied above the mountain's loftiest peak,
Was traced a line of lightning.
Now it flew far above a rock
The utmost verge of earth,
The rival of the Andes, whose dark brow
Loured o'er the silver sea.

Far, far below the chariot's path,
Calm as a slumbering babe,
Tremendous Ocean lay.
The mirror of its stillness showed
The pale and waning stars,
The chariot's fiery track,
And the grey light of morn
Tinging those fleecy clouds
That canopied the dawn.
Seemed it, that the chariot's way
Lay through the midst of an immense concave,
Radiant with million constellations, tinged
With shades of infinite colour,
And semicircled with a belt
Flashing incessant meteors.

The magic car moved on.
As they approached their goal
The coursers seemed to gather speed ;
The sea no longer was distinguished ; earth
Appeared a vast and shadowy sphere ;
The sun's unclouded orb
Rolled through the black concave ;
Its rays of rapid light
Parted around the chariot's swifter course,
And fell, like ocean's feathery spray
Dashed from the boiling surge
Before a vessel's prow.

The magic car moved on.
Earth's distant orb appeared
The smallest light that twinkles in the heaven ;
Whilst round the chariot's way
Innumerable systems rolled,
And countless spheres diffused
An ever-varying glory.
It was a sight of wonder : some
Were hornèd like the crescent moon ;
Some shed a mild and silver beam
Like Hesperus o'er the western sea ;
Some dashed athwart with trains of flame,
Like worlds to death and ruin driven ;
Some shone like suns, and as the chariot passed,
Eclipsed all other light.

Spirit of Nature ! here !
In this interminable wilderness
Of worlds, at whose immensity
Even soaring fancy staggers,
Here is thy fitting temple.
Yet not the lightest leaf
That quivers to the passing breeze
Is less instinct with thee :
Yet not the meanest worm
That lurks in graves and fattens on the dead
Less shares thy eternal breath.
Spirit of Nature ! thou !
Imperishable as this scene,
Here is thy fitting temple.

II.

If solitude hath ever led thy steps
To the wild ocean's echoing shore,
And thou hast lingered there,
Until the sun's broad orb
Seemed resting on the burnished wave,
Thou must have marked the lines
Of purple gold, that motionless
Hung o'er the sinking sphere :
Thou must have marked the billowy clouds
Edged with intolerable radiancy
Towering like rocks of jet
Crowned with a diamond wreath.
And yet there is a moment,
When the sun's highest point
Peeps like a star o'er ocean's western edge,
When those far clouds of feathery gold,
Shaded with deepest purple, gleam
Like islands on a dark blue sea ;
Then has thy fancy soared above the earth,
And furled its wearied wing
Within the Fairy's fane.

Yet not the golden islands
Gleaming in yon flood of light,
Nor the feathery curtains
Stretching o'er the sun's bright couch,
Nor the burnished ocean waves
Paving that gorgeous dome,
So fair, so wonderful a sight
As Mab's ethereal palace could afford.
Yet likest evening's vault, that faery Hall !
As Heaven, low resting on the wave, it spread
Its floors of flashing light,
Its vast and azure dome,
Its fertile golden islands
Floating on a silver sea ;
Whilst suns their mingling beamings darted
Through clouds of circumambient darkness,
And pearly battlements around
Looked o'er the immense of Heaven.
The magic car no longer moved.

The Fairy and the Spirit
Entered the Hall of Spells :
Those golden clouds
That rolled in glittering billows
Beneath the azure canopy
With the ethereal footsteps, trembled not :
The light and crimson mists,
Floating to strains of thrilling melody
Through that unearthly dwelling,
Yielded to every movement of the will.
Upon their passive swell the Spirit leaned,
And, for the varied bliss that pressed around,
Used not the glorious privilege
Of virtue and of wisdom.

Spirit ! the Fairy said,
And pointed to the gorgeous dome,
This is a wondrous sight
And mocks all human grandeur ;
But, were it virtue's only meed, to dwell
In a celestial palace, all resigned
To pleasurable impulses, immured
Within the prison of itself, the will
Of changeless nature would be unfulfilled.
Learn to make others happy. Spirit, come !
This is thine high reward :—the past shall rise ;
Thou shalt behold the present ; I will teach
The secrets of the future.

The Fairy and the Spirit
Approached the overhanging battlement.—
Below lay stretched the universe !
There, far as the remotest line
That bounds imagination's flight,
Countless and unending orbs
In mazy motion intermingled,
Yet still fulfilled immutably
Eternal nature's law.
Above, below, around
The circling systems formed
A wilderness of harmony :
Each with undeviating aim,
In eloquent silence, through the depths of space
Pursued its wondrous way.
There was a little light
That twinkled in the misty distance :
None but a spirit's eye,
Might ken that rolling orb ;
None but a spirit's eye,
And in no other place
But that celestial dwelling, might behold
Each action of this earth's inhabitants.
But matter, space, and time
In those aërial mansions cease to act ;
And all-prevailing wisdom, when it reaps
The harvest of its excellence, o'erbounds
Those obstacles, of which an earthly soul
Fears to attempt the conquest.

The Fairy pointed to the earth.
The Spirit's intellectual eye
Its kindred beings recognised.
The thronging thousands, to a passing view,
    Seemed like an anthill's citizens.
        How wonderful ! that even
The passions, prejudices, interests.
That sway the meanest being, the weak touch
        That moves the finest nerve,
        And in one human brain
Causes the faintest thought, becomes a link
        In the great chain of nature.

        Behold, the Fairy cried.
Palmyra's ruined palaces !—
        Behold ! where grandeur frowned ;
        Behold ! where pleasure smiled ;
What now remains ?—the memory
        Of senselessness and shame—
        What is immortal there ?
        Nothing—it stands to tell
        A melancholy tale to give
        An awful warning : soon
Oblivion will steal silently
        The remnant of its fame.
        Monarchs and conquerors there
Proud o'er prostrate millions trod—
The earthquakes of the human race ;
Like them, forgotten when the ruin
        That marks their shock is past.

        Beside the eternal Nile,
        The Pyramids have risen.
Nile shall pursue his changeless way :
        Those pyramids shall fall ;
Yea ! not a stone shall stand to tell
        The spot whereon they stood ;
Their very site shall be forgotten,
        As is their builder's name !

        Behold yon sterile spot ;
Where now the wandering Arab's tent
        Flaps in the desert blast.
There once old Salem's haughty fane
Reared high to heaven its thousand golden domes,
        And in the blushing face of day
        Exposed its shameful glory.
Oh ! many a widow, many an orphan cursed
The building of that fane ; and many a father,
Worn out with toil and slavery, implored
The poor man's God to sweep it from the earth,
And spare his children the detested task
Of piling stone on stone, and poisoning
        The choicest days of life,
        To soothe a dotard's vanity.
There an inhuman and uncultured race
Howled hideous praises to their Demon-God ;
They rushed to war, tore from the mother's womb

The unborn child—old age and infancy
Promiscuous perished ; their victorious arms
Left not a soul to breathe.   Oh ! they were fiends :
But what was he who taught them that the God
Of nature and benevolence had given
A special sanction to the trade of blood ?
His name and theirs are fading, and the tales
Of this barbarian nation, which imposture
Recites till terror credits, are pursuing
 Itself into forgetfulness.

 Where Athens, Rome, and Sparta stood,
 There is a moral desert now :
 The mean and miserable huts,
 The yet more wretched palaces,
 Contrasted with those ancient fanes,
 Now crumbling to oblivion ;
 The long and lonely colonnades,
 Through which the ghost of Freedom stalks,
  Seem like a well-known tune,
Which, in some dear scene we have loved to hear,
  Remembered now in sadness.
  But, oh ! how much more changed,
  How gloomier is the contrast
  Of human nature there !
Where Socrates expired, a tyrant's slave,
A coward and a fool, spreads death around—
  Then, shuddering, meets his own.
Where Cicero and Antoninus lived,
 A cowled and hypocritical monk
  Prays, curses, and deceives.

  Spirit ! ten thousand years
  Have scarcely past away,
Since, in the waste where now the savage drinks
His enemy's blood, and aping Europe's sons,
  Wakes the unholy song of war,
  Arose a stately city,
Metropolis of the western continent :
 There, now, the mossy column-stone,
Indented by time's unrelaxing grasp,
  Which once appeared to brave
  All, save its country's ruin ;
  There the wild forest scene,
Rude in the uncultivated loveliness
  Of gardens long run wild,
Seems, to the unwilling sojourner, whose steps
 Chance in that desert has delayed,
Thus to have stood since earth was what it is.
 Yet once it was the busiest haunt,
Whither, as to a common centre, flocked
 Strangers, and ships, and merchandize :
  Once peace and freedom blest
  The cultivated plain :
  But wealth, that curse of man,
Blighted the bud of its prosperity :
Virtue and wisdom, truth and liberty,
Fled, to return not, until man shall know

That they alone can give the bliss
  Worthy a soul that claims
Its kindred with eternity.

There's not one atom of yon earth
  But once was living man ;
Nor the minutest drop of rain,
That hangeth in its thinnest cloud,
    But flowed in human veins :
    And from the burning plains
    Where Libyan monsters yell,
    From the most gloomy glens
    Of Greenland's sunless clime,
    To where the golden fields
    Of fertile England spread
    Their harvest to the day,
    Thou canst not find one spot
    Whereon no city stood.

    How strange is human pride !
I tell thee that those living things,
To whom the fragile blade of grass,
    That springeth in the morn
    And perisheth ere noon,
    Is an unbounded world ;
I tell thee that those viewless beings,
Whose mansion is the smallest particle
Of the impassive atmosphere,
    Think, feel, and live like man ;
That their affections and antipathies,
    Like his, produce the laws
    Ruling their moral state ;
    And the minutest throb
    That through their frame diffuses
    The slightest, faintest motion,
    Is fixed and indispensable
    As the majestic laws
    That rule yon rolling orbs.

  The Fairy paused. The Spirit,
In ecstasy of admiration, felt
All knowledge of the past revived ; the events
    Of old and wondrous times,
Which dim tradition interruptedly
Teaches the credulous vulgar, were unfolded
  In just perspective to the view ;
Yet dim from their infinitude.
    The Spirit seemed to stand
High on an isolated pinnacle ;
The flood of ages combating below,
The depth of the unbounded universe
    Above, and all around
    Nature's unchanging harmony.

III.

  Fairy ! the Spirit said,
And on the Queen of Spells

Fixed her ethereal eyes,
I thank thee.   Thou hast given
A boon which I will not resign, and taught
A lesson not to be unlearned.   I know
The past,, and thence I will essay to glean
A warning for the future, so that man
May profit by his errors, and derive
Experience from his folly :
For, when the power of imparting joy
Is equal to the will, the human soul
Requires no other heaven.

MAB.

Turn thee, surpassing Spirit !
Much yet remains unscanned.
Thou knowest how great is man,
Thou knowest his imbecility :
Yet learn thou what he is ;
Yet learn the lofty destiny
Which restless time prepares
For every living soul.

Behold a gorgeous palace, that, amid
Yon populous city, rears its thousand towers
And seems itself a city.   Gloomy troops
Of sentinels, in stern and silent ranks,
Encompass it around : the dweller there
Cannot be free and happy ; hearest thou not
The curses of the fatherless, the groans
Of those who have no friend ?   He passes on :
The King, the wearer of a gilded chain
That binds his soul to abjectness, the fool
Whom courtiers nickname monarch, whilst a slave
Even to the basest appetites—that man
Heeds not the shriek of penury ; he smiles
At the deep curses which the destitute
Mutter in secret, and a sullen joy
Pervades his bloodless heart when thousands groan
But for those morsels which his wantonness
Wastes in unjoyous revelry, to save
All that they love from famine : when he hears
The tale of horror, to some ready-made face
Of hypocritical assent he turns,
Smothering the glow of shame, that, spite of him,
Flushes his bloated cheek.

Now to the meal
Of silence, grandeur, and excess, he drags
His palled unwilling appetite.   If gold,
Gleaming around, and numerous viands culled
From every clime, could force the loathing sense
To overcome satiety,—if wealth
The spring it draws from poisons not,—or vice,
Unfeeling, stubborn vice, converteth not
Its food to deadliest venom ; then that king
Is happy ; and the peasant who fulfils
His unforced task, when he returns at even,

And by the blazing faggot meets again
Her welcome for whom all his toil is sped,
Tastes not a sweeter meal.

                            Behold him now
Stretched on the gorgeous couch ; his fevered brain
Reels dizzily awhile : But, ah ! too soon
The slumber of intemperance subsides,
And conscience, that undying serpent, calls
Her venomous brood to their nocturnal task.
Listen ! he speaks ! oh ! mark that frenzied eye—
Oh ! mark that deadly visage.

KING.

                            No cessation !
Oh ! must this last for ever !   Awful death,
I wish, yet fear to clasp thee !—Not one moment
Of dreamless sleep !   O dear and blessèd Peace !
Why dost thou shroud thy vestal purity
In penury and dungeons ? wherefore lurkest
With danger, death, and solitude ; yet shunn'st
The palace I have built thee ?   Sacred peace !
Oh visit me but once, but pitying shed
One drop of balm upon my withered soul.

Vain man ! that palace is the virtuous heart,
And Peace defileth not her snowy robes
In such a shed as thine.   Hark ! yet he mutters ;
His slumbers are but varied agonies,
They prey like scorpions on the springs of life.
There needeth not the hell that bigots frame
To punish those who err : earth in itself
Contains at once the evil and the cure ;
And all sufficing Nature can chastise
Those who transgress her law,—she only knows
How justly to proportion to the fault
The punishment it merits.

                            Is it strange
That this poor wretch should pride him in his woe ?
Take pleasure in his abjectness, and hug
The scorpion that consumes him ?   Is it strange
That, placed on a conspicuous throne of thorns,
Grasping an iron sceptre, and immured
Within a splendid prison, whose stern bounds
Shut him from all that's good or dear on earth,
His soul asserts not its humanity ?
That man's mild nature rises not in war
Against a king's employ ?   No—'tis not strange.
He, like the vulgar, thinks, feels; acts and lives
Just as his father did ; the unconquered powers
Of precedent and custom interpose
Between a king and virtue.   Stranger yet,
To those who know not nature, nor deduce
The future from the present, it may seem,
That not one slave, who suffers from the crimes
Of this unnatural being ; not one wretch,

Whose children famish, and whose nuptial bed
Is earth's unpitying bosom, rears an arm
To dash him from his throne !

                              Those gilded flies
That, basking in the sunshine of a court,
Fatten on its corruption !—what are they ?
—The drones of the community ; they feed
On the mechanic's labour : the starved hind
For them compels the stubborn glebe to yield
Its unshared harvests ; and yon squalid form,
Leaner than fleshless misery, that wastes
A sunless life in the unwholesome mine,
Drags out in labour a protracted death,
To glut their grandeur ; many faint with to'l,
That few may know the cares and woe of sloth.

Whence, think'st thou, kings and parasites arose?
Whence that unnatural line of drones, who heap
Toil and unvanquishable penury
On those who build their palaces, and bring
Their daily bread ?—From vice, black loathsome vice ;
From rapine, madness, treachery, and wrong ;
From all that genders misery, and makes
Of earth this thorny wilderness ; from lust,
Revenge, and murder.—And when reason's voice,
Loud as the voice of nature, shall have waked
The nations ; and mankind perceive that vice
Is discord, war, and misery ; that virtue
Is peace, and happiness, and harmony ;
When man's maturer nature shall disdain
The playthings of its childhood ; kingly glare
Will lose its power to dazzle ; its authority
Will silently pass by ; the gorgeous throne
Shall stand unnoticed in the regal hall,
Fast falling to decay ; whilst falsehood's trade
Shall be as hateful and unprofitable
As that of truth is now.

                              Where is the fame
Which the vainglorious mighty of the earth
Seek to eternize ? Oh ! the faintest sound
From time's light footfall, the minutest wave
That swells the flood of ages, whelms in nothing
The unsubstantial bubble. Aye ! to-day
Stern is the tyrant's mandate, red the gaze
That flashes desolation, strong the arm
That scatters multitudes. To-morrow comes !
That mandate is a thunder-peal that died
In ages past ; that gaze, a transient flash
On which the midnight closed, and on that arm
The worm has made his meal.

                              The virtuous man,
Who, great in his humility, as kings
Are little in their grandeur ; he who leads
Invincibly a life of resolute good,

And stands amid the silent dungeon-depths
More free and fearless than the trembling judge,
Who clothed in venal power, vainly strove
To bind the impassive spirit ;—when he falls,
His mild eye beams benevolence no more :
Withered the hand outstretched but to relieve ;
Sunk reason's simple eloquence that rolled
But to appal the guilty.   Yes ! the grave
Hath quenched that eye, and death's relentless frost
Withered that arm : but the unfading fame
Which virtue hangs upon its votary's tomb ;
The deathless memory of that man, whom kings
Call to their mind and tremble ; the remembrance
With which the happy spirit contemplates
Its well-spent pilgrimage on earth,
Shall never pass away.

Nature rejects the monarch, not the man ;
The subject not the citizen : for kings
And subjects, mutual foes, for ever play
A losing game into each other's hands,
Whose stakes are vice and misery.   The man
Of virtuous soul commands not, nor obeys.
Power, like a desolating pestilence,
Pollutes whate'er it touches ; and obedience,
Bane of all genius, virtue, freedom, truth,
Makes slaves of men, and, of the human frame,
A mechanized automaton.

When Nero,
High over flaming Rome, with savage joy
Lowered like a fiend, drank with enraptured ear
The shrieks of agonizing death, beheld
The frightful desolation spread, and felt
A new created sense within his soul
Thrill to the sight, and vibrate to the sound ;
Thinkest thou his grandeur had not overcome
The force of human kindness ? and when Rome,
With one stern blow, hurled not the tyrant down,
Crushed not the arm red with her dearest blood,
Had not submissive abjectness destroyed
Nature's suggestions ?

Look on yonder earth .
The golden harvests spring : the unfailling sun
Sheds light and life ; the fruits, the flowers, the trees,
Arise in due succession ; all things speak
Peace, harmony, and love.   The universe,
In nature's silent eloquence, declares
That all fulfil the works of love and joy,—
All but the outcast Man.   He fabricates
The sword which stabs his peace ; he cherisheth
The snakes that gnaw his heart ; he raiseth up
The tyrant, whose delight is in his woe,
Whose sport is in his agony.   Yon sun,
Lights it the great alone ?   Yon silver beams,
Sleep they less sweetly on the cottage thatch,
Than on the dome of kings ?   Is mother earth

A step-dame to her numerous sons, who earn
Her unshared gifts with unremitting toil ;
A mother only to those puling babes
Who, nursed in ease and luxury, make men
The playthings of their babyhood, and mar,
In self-important childishness, that peace
Which men alone appreciate ?

Spirit of Nature ! no.
The pure diffusion of thy essence throbs
Alike in every human heart.
Thou, aye, erectest there
Thy throne of power unappealable :
Thou art the judge beneath whose nod
Man's brief and frail authority
Is powerless as the wind
That passeth idly by.
Thine the tribunal which surpasseth
The show of human justice,
As God surpasses man.

Spirit of Nature ! thou
Life of interminable multitudes ;
Soul of those mighty spheres
Whose changeless paths thro' Heaven's deep silence lie :
Soul of that smallest being,
The dwelling of whose life
Is one faint April sun-gleam ;—
Man, like these passive things,
Thy will unconsciously fulfilleth :
Like theirs, his age of endless peace,
Which time is fast maturing,
Will swiftly, surely come :
And the unbounded frame, which thou pervadest,
Will be without a flaw
Marring its perfect symmetry.

IV.

How beautiful this night ! the balmiest sigh,
Which vernal zephyrs breathe in evening's ear,
Were discord to the speaking quietude
That wraps this moveless scene.   Heaven's ebon vault,
Studded with stars unutterably bright,
Through which the moon's unclouded grandeur rolls,
Seems like a canopy which love has spread
To curtain her sleeping world.   Yon gentle hills,
Robed in a garment of untrodden snow ;
Yon darksome rocks, whence icicles depend,
So stainless, that their white and glittering spires
Tinge not the moon's pure beam ; yon castled steep,
Whose banner hangeth o'er the time-worn tower
So idly, that rapt fancy deemeth it
A metaphor of peace ; all form a scene
Where musing Solitude might love to lift
Her soul above this sphere of earthliness ;
Where Silence undisturbed might watch alone,
So cold, so bright, so still.

      The orb of day,
In southern climes, o'er ocean's waveless field
Sinks sweetly smiling : not the faintest breath
Steals o'er the unruffled deep ; the clouds of eve
Reflect unmoved the lingering beam of day ;
And vesper's image on the western main
Is beautifully still. To-morrow comes :
Cloud upon cloud, in dark and deepening mass,
Roll o'er the blackened waters ; the deep roar
Of distant thunder mutters awfully ;
Tempest unfolds its pinion o'er the gloom
That shrouds the boiling surge ; the pitiless fiend,
With all his winds and lightnings, tracks his prey ;
The torn deep yawns, the vessel finds a grave
Beneath its jagged gulf.

      Ah ! whence yon glare
That fires the arch of heaven ?—that dark red smoke
Blotting the silver moon ? The stars are quenched
In darkness, and the pure and spangling snow
Gleams faintly through the gloom that gathers round !
Hark to that roar, whose swift and deafening peals
In countless echoes through the mountains ring,
Startling pale Midnight on her starry throne !
Now swells the intermingling din ; the jar
Frequent and frightful of the bursting bomb ;
The falling beam, the shriek, the groan, the shout,
The ceaseless clangour, and the rush of men
Inebriate with rage :—loud, and more loud
The discord grows ; till pale Death shuts the scene,
And o'er the conqueror and the conquered draws
His cold and bloody shroud.—Of all the men
Whom day's departing beam saw blooming there,
In proud and vigorous health ; of all the hearts
That beat with anxious life at sunset there ;
How few survive, how few are beating now !
All is deep silence, like the fearful calm
That slumbers in the storm's portentous pause ;
Save when the frantic wail of widowed love
Comes shuddering on the blast, or the faint moan
With which some soul bursts from the frame of clay
Wrapt round its struggling powers.

      The grey morn
Dawns on the mournful scene ; the sulphurous smoke
Before the icy wind slow rolls away,
And the bright beams of frosty morning dance
Along the spangling snow. There tracks of blood
Even to the forest's depth, and scattered arms,
And lifeless warriors, whose hard lineaments
Death's self could change not, mark the dreadful path
Of the outsallying victors : far behind,
Black ashes note where their proud city stood.
Within yon forest is a gloomy glen—
Each tree which guards its darkness from the day,
Waves o'er a warrior's tomb.

     I see thee shrink,
Surpassing Spirit !—wert thou human else ?
    c

I see a shade of doubt and horror fleet
Across thy stainless features : yet fear not :
This is no unconnected misery,
Nor stands uncaused, and irretrievable.
Man's evil nature, that apology
Which kings who rule, and cowards who crouch, set up
For their unnumbered crimes, sheds not the blood
Which desolates the discord-wasted land.
From kings, and priests, and statesmen, war arose,
Whose safety is man's deep unbettered woe,
Whose grandeur his debasement.   Let the axe
Strike at the root, the poison-tree will fall ;
And where its venomed exhalations spread
Ruin, and death, and woe, where millions lay
Quenching the serpent's famine, and their bones
Bleaching unburied in the putrid blast,
A garden shall arise, in loveliness
Surpassing fabled Eden.

                                Hath Nature's soul,
That formed this world so beautiful, that spread
Earth's lap with plenty, and life's smallest chord
Strung to unchanging unison, that gave
The happy birds their dwelling in the grove,
That yielded to the wanderers of the deep
The lovely silence of the unfathomed main,
And filled the meanest worm that crawls in dust
With spirit, thought, and love ; on Man alone,
Partial in causeless malice, wantonly
Heaped ruin, vice, and slavery ; his soul
Blasted with withering curses ; placed afar
The meteor-happiness, that shuns his grasp,
But serving on the frightful gulf to glare,
Rent wide beneath his footsteps ?

                                Nature !—no !
Kings, priests and statesmen, blast the human flower
Even in its tender bud ; their influence darts
Like subtle poison through the bloodless veins
Of desolate society.   The child,
Ere he can lisp his mother's sacred name,
Swells with the unnatural pride of crime, and lifts
His baby-sword even in a hero's mood.
This infant-arm becomes the bloodiest scourge
Of devastated earth ; whilst specious names,
Learnt in soft childhood's unsuspecting hour,
Serve as the sophisms with which manhood dims
Bright reason's ray, and sanctifies the sword
Upraised to shed a brother's innocent blood.
Let priest-led slaves cease to proclaim that man
Inherits vice and misery, when force
And falsehood hang even o'er the cradled babe,
Stifling with rudest grasp all natural good.

Ah ! to the stranger-soul, when first it peeps
From its new tenement, and looks abroad
For happiness and sympathy, how stern
And desolate a tract is this wide world !

How withered all the buds of natural good !
No shade, no shelter from the sweeping storms
Of pitiless power ! On its wretched frame,
Poisoned, perchance, by the disease and woe
Heaped on the wretched parent whence it sprung
By morals, law and custom, the pure winds
Of heaven, that renovate the insect tribes,
May breathe not. The untainting light of day
May visit not its longings. It is bound
Ere it has life : yea, all the chains are forged
Long ere its being : all liberty and love
And peace is torn from its defencelessness ;
Cursed from its birth, even from its cradle doomed
To abjectness and bondage !

Throughout this varied and eternal world
Soul is the only element, the block
That for uncounted ages has remained.
The moveless pillar of a mountain's weight
Is active, living spirit. Every grain
Is sentient both in unity and part,
And the minutest atom comprehends
A world of loves and hatreds ; these beget
Evil and good : hence truth, and falsehood spring ;
Hence will, and thought, and action, all the germs
Of pain or pleasure, sympathy or hate,
That variegate the eternal universe.
Soul is not more polluted than the beams
Of heaven's pure orb, ere round their rapid lines
The taint of earth-born atmospheres arise.
Man is of soul and body, formed for deeds
Of high resolve, on fancy's boldest wing
To soar unwearied, fearlessly to turn
The keenest pangs to peacefulness, and taste
The joys which mingled sense and spirit yield.
Or he is formed for abjectness and woe,
To grovel on the dunghill of his fears,
To shrink at every sound, to quench the flame
Of natural love in sensualism, to know
That hour as blest when on his worthless days
The frozen hand of Death shall set its seal,
Yet fear the cure, though hating the disease.
The one is man that shall hereafter be :
The other, man as vice has made him now.

War is the statesman's game, the priest's delight,
The lawyer's jest, the hired assassin's trade,
And, to those royal murderers, whose mean thrones
Are bought by crimes of treachery and gore,
The bread they eat, the staff on which they lean.
Guards, garbed in blood-red livery, surround
Their palaces, participate the crimes
That force defends, and from a nation's rage
Secure the crown, which all the curses reach
That famine, frenzy, woe, and penury breathe.
These are the hired bravos who defend
The tyrant's throne—the bullies of his fear :
These are the sinks and channels of worst vice,

The refuse of society, the dregs
Of all that is most vile : their cold hearts blend
Deceit with sternness, ignorance with pride,
All that is mean and villanous, with rage
Which hopelessness of good, and self-contempt,
Alone might kindle ; they are decked in wealth,
Honour and power, then are sent abroad
To do their work.   The pestilence that stalks
In gloomy triumph through some Eastern land
Is less destroying.   They cajole with gold,
And promises of fame, the thoughtless youth
Already crushed with servitude : he knows
His wretchedness too late, and cherishes
Repentance for his ruin, when his doom
Is sealed in gold and blood.

Those too the tyrant serve, who, skilled to snare
The feet of justice in the toils of law,
Stand, ready to oppress the weaker still ;
And, right or wrong, will vindicate for gold,
Sneering at public virtue, which beneath
Their pitiless tread lies torn and trampled, where
Honour sits smiling at the sale of truth.

Then grave and hoary-headed hypocrites,
Without a hope, a passion, or a love,
Who, through a life of luxury and lies,
Have crept by flattery to the seats of power,
Support the system whence their honours flow—
They have three words :—well tyrants know their use,
Well pay them for the loan, with usury
Torn from a bleeding world !—God, Hell, and Heaven.
A vengeful, pitiless, and almighty fiend,
Whose mercy is a nickname for the rage
Of tameless tigers hungering for blood.
Hell, a red gulf of everlasting fire,
Where poisonous and undying worms prolong
Eternal misery to those hapless slaves
Whose life has been a penance for its crimes.
And Heaven, a meed for those who dare belie
Their human nature, quake, believe, and cringe
Before the mockeries of earthly power.

These tools the tyrant tempers to his work,
Wields in his wrath, and as he wills destroys,
Omnipotent in wickedness : the while
Youth springs, age moulders, manhood tamely does
His bidding, bribed by short-lived joys to lend
Force to the weakness of his trembling arm.

They rise, they fall ; one generation comes
Yielding its harvest to destruction's scythe.
It fades, another blossoms, yet behold !
Red glows the tyrant's stamp-mark on its bloom,
Withering and cankering deep its passive prime.
He has invented lying words and modes,
Empty and vain as his own coreless heart ;
Evasive meanings, nothings of much sound.

To lure the heedless victim to the toils
Spread round the valley of its paradise.

Look to thyself, priest, conqueror, or prince !
Whether thy trade is falsehood, and thy lusts
Deep wallow in the earnings of the poor,
With whom thy Master was :—or thou delightest
In numbering o'er the myriads of thy slain,
All misery weighing nothing in the scale
Against thy short-lived fame : or thou dost load
With cowardice and crime the groaning land,
A pomp-fed king.   Look to thy wretched self !
Ay, art thou not the veriest slave that e'er
Crawled on the loathing earth ?   Are not thy days
Days of unsatisfying listlessness ?
Dost thou not cry, ere night's long rack is o'er,
'' When will the morning come ?''   Is not thy youth
A vain and feverish dream of sensualism ?
Thy manhood blighted with unripe disease ?
Are not thy views of unregretted death
Drear, comfortless, and horrible ?   Thy mind
Is it not morbid as thy nerveless frame,
Incapable of judgment, hope, or love ?
And dost thou wish the errors to survive
That bar thee from all sympathies of good,
After the miserable interest
Thou hold'st in their protraction ?   When the grave
Has swallowed up thy memory and thyself,
Dost thou desire the bane that poisons earth
To twine its roots around thy coffined clay,
Spring from thy bones, and blossom on thy tomb,
That of its fruit thy babes may eat and die ?

V.

Thus do the generations of the earth
Go to the grave, and issue from the womb,
Surviving still the imperishable change
That renovates the world ; even as the leaves
Which the keen frost-wind of the waning year
Has scattered on the forest soil, and heaped
For many seasons there, though long they choke,
Loading with loathsome rottenness the land,
All germs of promise.   Yet when the tall trees
From which they fell, shorn of their lovely shapes,
Lie level with the earth to moulder there,
They fertilize the land they long deformed,
Till from the breathing lawn a forest springs
Of youth, integrity, and loveliness,
Like that which gave it life, to spring and die.
Thus suicidal selfishness, that blights
The fairest feelings of the opening heart,
Is destined to decay, whilst from the soil
Shall spring all virtue, all delight, all love,
And judgment cease to wage unnatural war
With passion's unsubduable array.

Twin-sister of religion, selfishness !
Rival in crime and falsehood, aping all

The wanton horrors of her bloody play;
Yet frozen, unimpassioned, spiritless,
Shunning the light, and owning not its name,
Compelled, by its deformity, to screen
With flimsy veil of justice and of right,
Its unattractive lineaments, that scare
All, save the brood of ignorance : at once
The cause and the effect of tyranny ;
Unblushing, hardened, sensual, and vile ;
Dead to all love but of its abjectness,
With heart impassive by more noble powers
Than unshared pleasure, sordid gain, or fame ;
Despising its own miserable being,
Which still it longs, yet fears to disenthrall,

Hence commerce springs, the venal interchange
Of all that human art or nature yield ;
Which wealth should purchase not, but want demand,
And natural kindness hasten to supply
From the full fountain of its boundless love,
For ever stifled, drained, and tainted now.
Commerce ! beneath whose poison-breathing shade
No solitary virtue dares to spring,
But poverty and wealth with equal hand
Scatter their withering curses, and unfold
The doors of premature and violent death,
To pining famine and full-fed disease,
To all that shares the lot of human life,
Which poisoned body and soul, scarce drags the chain
That lengthens as it goes and clanks behind.

Commerce has set the mark of selfishness,
The signet of its all-enslaving power
Upon a shining ore, and called it gold :
Before whose image bow the vulgar great,
The vainly rich, the miserable proud,
The mob of peasants, nobles, priests, and kings,
And with blind feelings reverence the power
That grinds them to the dust of misery.
But in the temple of their hireling hearts
Gold is a living god, and rules in scorn
All earthly things but virtue.

Since tyrants, by the sale of human life,
Heap luxuries to their sensualism, and fame
To their wide-wasting and insatiate pride,
Success has sanctioned to a credulous world
The ruin, the disgrace, the woe of war.
His hosts of blind and unresisting dupes
The despot numbers ; from his cabinet
These puppets of his schemes he moves at will,
Even as the slaves by force or famine driven,
Beneath a vulgar master, to perform
A task of cold and brutal drudgery ;—
Hardened to hope, insensible to fear,
Scarce living pulleys of a dead machine,
Mere wheels of work and articles of trade,
That grace the proud and noisy pomp of wealth !

The harmony and happiness of man
Yields to the wealth of nations ; that which lifts
His nature to the heaven of its pride,
Is bartered for the poison of his soul ;
The weight that drags to earth his towering hopes
Blighting all prospect but of selfish gain,
Withering all passion but of slavish fear,
Extinguishing all free and generous love
Of enterprise and daring, even the pulse
That fancy kindles in the beating heart
To mingle with sensation, it destroys,—
Leaves nothing but the sordid lust of self,
The grovelling hope of interest and gold,
Unqualified, unmingled, unredeemed
Even by hypocrisy.

              And statesmen boast
Of wealth ! The wordy eloquence that lives
After the ruin of their hearts, can gild
The bitter poison of a nation's woe,
Can turn the worship of the servile mob
To their corrupt and glaring idol Fame,
From virtue, trampled by its iron tread,
Although its dazzling pedestal be raised
Amid the horrors of a limb-strewn field,
With desolated dwellings smoking round.
The man of ease, who, by his warm fireside,
To deeds of charitable intercourse
And bare fulfilment of the common laws
Of decency and prejudice, confines
The struggling nature of his human heart,
Is duped by their cold sophistry ; he sheds
A passing tear perchance upon the wreck
Of earthly peace, when near his dwelling's door
The frightful waves are driven,—when his son
Is murdered by the tyrant, or religion
Drives his wife raving mad. But the poor man,
Whose life is misery, and fear, and care ;
Whom the morn wakens but to fruitless toil ;
Who ever hears his famished offspring's scream,
Whom their pale mother's uncomplaining gaze
For ever meets, and the proud rich man's eye
Flashing command, and the heart-breaking scene
Of thousands like himself ;—he little heeds
The rhetoric of tyranny ; his hate
Is quenchless as his wrongs ; he laughs to scorn
The vain and bitter mockery of words,
Feeling the horror of the tyrant's deeds,
And unrestrained, but by the arm of power,
That knows and dreads his enmity.

The iron rod of Penury still compels
Her wretched slave to bow the knee to wealth,
And poison, with unprofitable toil,
A life too void of solace to confirm
The very chains that bind him to his doom.
Nature, impartial in munificence,
Has gifted man with all-subduing will.
Matter, with all its transitory shapes,

Lies subjected and plastic at his feet,
That, weak from bondage, tremble as they tread.
How many a rustic Milton has past by,
Stifling the speechless longings of his heart,
In unremitting drudgery and care !
How many a vulgar Cato has compelled
His energies, no longer tameless then,
To mould a pin, or fabricate a nail !
How many a Newton, to whose passive ken
Those mighty spheres that gem infinity
Were only specks of tinsel, fixed in heaven
To light the midnights of his native town !

Yet every heart contains perfection's germ :
The wisest of the sages of the earth,
That ever from the stores of reason drew
Science and truth, and virtue's dreadless tone,
Were but a weak and inexperienced boy,
Proud, sensual, unimpassioned, unimbued
With pure desire and universal love,
Compared to that high being, of cloudless brain,
Untainted passion, elevated will,
Which death (who even would linger long in awe
Within his noble presence, and beneath
His changeless eyebeam) might alone subdue.
Him, every slave now dragging through the filth
Of some corrupted city his sad life,
Pining with famine, swoln with luxury,
Blunting the keenness of his spiritual sense
With narrow schemings and unworthy cares,
Or madly rushing through all violent crime,
To move the deep stagnation of his soul,—
Might imitate and equal.
                 But mean lust
Has bound its chains so tight around the earth,
That all within it but the virtuous man
Is venal : gold or fame will surely reach
The price prefixed by selfishness, to all
But him of resolute and unchanging will ;
Whom, nor the plaudits of a servile crowd,
Nor the vile joys of tainting luxury,
Can bribe to yield his elevated soul
To Tyranny or Falsehood, though they wield
With blood-red hand the sceptre of the world.

All things are sold : the very light of heaven
Is venal ; earth's unsparing gifts of love,
The smallest and most despicable things
That lurk in the abysses of the deep,
All objects of our life, even life itself,
And the poor pittance which the laws allow
Of liberty, the fellowship of man,
Those duties which his heart of human love
Should urge him to perform instinctively,
Are bought and sold as in a public mart
Of undisguising Selfishness, that sets
On each its price, the stamp-mark of her reign.
Even love is sold : the solace of all woe

Is turned to deadliest agony, old age
Shivers in selfish beauty's loathing arms,
And youth's corrupted impulses prepare
A life of horror from the blighting bane
Of commerce ; whilst the pestilence that springs
From unenjoying sensualism, has filled
All human life with hydra-headed woes.
Falsehood demands but gold to pay the pangs
Of outraged conscience ; for the slavish priest
Sets no great value on his hireling faith :
A little passing pomp, some servile souls,
Whom cowardice itself might safely chain,
Or the spare mite of avarice could bribe
To deck the triumph of their languid zeal,
Can make him minister to tyranny.
More daring crime requires a loftier meed :
Without a shudder, the slave-soldier lends
His arm to murderous deeds, and steels his heart,
When the dread eloquence of dying men,
Low mingling on the lonely field of fame,
Assails that nature, whose applause he sells
For the gross blessings of a patriot mob,
For the vile gratitude of heartless kings,
And for a cold world's good word,—viler still !

There is a nobler glory, which survives
Until our being fades, and solacing
All human care, accompanies its change;
Deserts not virtue in the dungeon's gloom,
And, in the precincts of the palace, guides
Its footsteps through that labyrinth of crime ;
Imbues his lineaments with dauntlessness,
Even when, from power's avenging hand, he takes
Its sweetest, last, and noblest title—death ;
—The consciousness of good, which neither gold,
Nor sordid fame, nor hope of heavenly bliss,
Can purchase ; but a life of resolute good,
Unalterable will, quenchless desire
Of universal happiness, the heart
That beats with it in unison, the brain
Whose ever wakeful wisdom toils to change
Reason's rich stores for its eternal weal.

This commerce of sincerest virtue needs
No mediative signs of selfishness,
No jealous intercourse of wretched gain,
No balancings of prudence, cold and long ;
In just and equal measure all is weighed,
One scale contains the sum of human weal,
And one, the good man's heart.

                     How vainly seek
The selfish for that happiness denied
To aught but virtue ! Blind and hardened, they,
Who hope for peace amid the storms of care,
Who covet power they know not how to use,
And sigh for pleasure they refuse to give,—
Madly they frustrate still their own designs ;

And, where they hope that quiet to enjoy
Which virtue pictures, bitterness of soul,
Pining regrets, and vain repentances,
Disease, disgust, and lassitude, pervade
Their valueless and miserable lives.

But hoary-headed selfishness has felt
Its death-blow, and is tottering to the grave :
A brighter morn awaits the human day,
When every transfer of earth's natural gifts
Shall be a commerce of good words and works
When poverty and wealth, the thirst of fame,
The fear of infamy, disease, and woe,
War with its million horrors, and fierce hell
Shall live but in the memory of Time,
Who, like a penitent libertine, shall start,
Look back, and shudder at his younger years.

VI.

All touch, all eye, all ear,
The Spirit felt the Fairy's burning speech.
O'er the thin texture of its frame,
The varying periods painted changing glows,
As on a summer even,
When soul-enfolding music floats around,
The stainless mirror of the lake
Re-images the eastern gloom,
Mingling convulsively its purple hues
With sunset's burnished gold.

Then thus the Spirit spoke :
It is a wild and miserable world !
Thorny, and full of care,
Which every fiend can make his prey at will.
O Fairy ! in the lapse of years,
Is there no hope in store ?
Will yon vast suns roll on
Interminably, still illuming
The night of so many wretched souls,
And see no hope for them ?
Will not the universal Spirit e'er
Revivify this withered limb of Heaven ?
The Fairy calmly smiled
In comfort, and a kindling gleam of hope
Suffused the Spirit's lineaments.
Oh ! rest thee tranquil ; chase those fearful doubts,
Which ne'er could rack an everlasting soul,
That sees the chains which bind it to its doom.
Yes ! crime and misery are in yonder earth,
Falsehood, mistake, and lust ;
But the eternal world
Contains at once the evil and the cure.
Some eminent in virtue shall start up,
Even in perversest time :
The truths of their pure lips, that never die,
Shall bind the scorpion falsehood with a wreath
Of ever-living flame,

Until the monster sting itself to death.
　How sweet a scene will earth become !
Of purest spirits, a pure dwelling-place,
Symphonious with the planetary spheres,
When man, with changeless nature coalescing,
Will undertake regeneration's work,
When its ungenial poles no longer point
　　　　To the red and baleful sun
　　　　That faintly twinkles there.

　　　　Spirit ! on yonder earth,
　Falsehood now triumphs ; deadly power
Has fixed its seal upon the lip of truth !
　　Madness and misery are there !
The happiest is most wretched ! yet confide,
Until pure health-drops from the cup of joy,
Fall like a dew of balm upon the world.
Now, to the scene I show, in silence turn,
And read the blood-stained charter of all woe,
Which Nature soon, with recreating hand,
Will blot in mercy from the book of earth.
How bold the flight of passion's wandering wing,
How swift the step of reason's firmer tread,
How calm and sweet the victories of life,
How terrorless the triumph of the grave !
How powerless were the mightiest monarch's arm,
Vain his loud threat, and impotent his frown !
How ludicrous the priest's dogmatic roar !
The weight of his exterminating curse,
How light ! and his affected charity,
To suit the pressure of the changing times,
What palpable deceit !—but for thy aid,
Religion ! but for thee, prolific fiend,
Who peoplest earth with demons, hell with men,
And heaven with slaves !

Thou taintest all thou lookest upon !—the stars,
Which on thy cradle beamed so brightly sweet,
Were gods to the distempered playfulness
Of thy untutored infancy : the trees,
The grass, the clouds, the mountains, and the sea,
All living things that walk, swim, creep or fly,
Were gods : the sun had homage, and the moon
Her worshipper.　Then thou becamest, a boy,
More daring in thy frenzies : every shape,
Monstrous or vast, or beautifully wild,
Which, from sensation's relics, fancy culls ;
The spirits of the air, the shuddering ghost,
The genii of the elements, the powers
That give a shape to nature's varied works,
Had life and place in the corrupt belief
Of thy blind heart : yet still thy youthful hands
Were pure of human blood.　Then manhood gave
Its strength and ardour to thy frenzied brain ;
Thine eager gaze scanned the stupendous scene
Whose wonders mocked the knowledge of thy pride
Their everlasting and unchanging laws
Reproached thine ignorance.　Awhile thou stoodst
Baffled and gloomy ; then thou didst sum up

The elements of all that thou didst know ;
The changing seasons, winter's leafless reign,
The budding of the heaven-breathing trees,
The eternal orbs that beautify the night,
The sun-rise, and the setting of the moon,
Earthquakes and wars, and poisons and disease,
And all their causes, to an abstract point,
Converging, thou didst bend, and called it—God !
The self-sufficing, the omnipotent,
The merciful, and the avenging God !
Who, prototype of human misrule, sits
High in heaven's realm, upon a golden throne,
Even like an earthly king ; and whose dread work,
Hell, gapes for ever for the unhappy slaves
Of fate, whom he created, in his sport,
To triumph in their torments when they fell !
Earth heard the name ; earth trembled, as the smoke
Of his revenge ascended up to heaven,
Blotting the constellations ; and the cries
Of millions, butchered in sweet confidence
And unsuspecting peace, even when the bonds
Of safety were confirmed by wordy oaths
Sworn in his dreadful name, rung through the land :
Whilst innocent babes writhed on thy stubborn spear,
And thou didst laugh to hear the mother's shriek
Of maniac gladness, as the sacred steel
Felt cold in her torn entrails !

Religion ! thou wert then in manhood's prime :
But age crept on : one God would not suffice
For senile puerility ; thou framedst
A tale to suit thy dotage, and to glut
Thy misery-thirsting soul, that the mad fiend
Thy wickedness had pictured, might afford
A plea for sating the unnatural thirst
For murder, rapine, violence, and crime,
That still consumed thy being, even when
Thou heardest the step of fate ;—that flames might light
Thy funeral scene, and the shrill horrent shrieks
Of parents dying on the pile that burned
To light their children to thy paths, the roar
Of the encircling flames, the exulting cries
Of thine apostles, loud commingling there,
        Might sate thine hungry ear
        Even on the bed of death !

But now contempt is mocking thy grey hairs ;
Thou art descending to the darksome grave,
Unhonoured and unpitied, but by those
Whose pride is passing by like thine, and sheds,
Like thine, a glare that fades before the sun
Of truth, and shines but in the dreadful night
That long has lowered above the ruined world.

Throughout these infinite orbs of mingling light,
Of which yon earth is one, is wide diffused
A spirit of activity and life,
That knows no term, cessation, or decay ;

That fades not when the lamp of earthly life,
Extinguished in the dampness of the grave,
Awhile there slumbers, more than when the babe
In the dim newness of its being feels
The impulses of sublunary things,
And all is wonder to unpractised sense :
But active, steadfast, and eternal, still
Guides the fierce whirlwind, in the tempest roars,
Cheers in the day, breathes in the balmy groves,
Strengthens in health, and poisons in disease ;
And in the storm of change, that ceaselessly
Rolls round the eternal universe, and shakes
Its undecaying battlement, presides,
Apportioning with irresistible law
The place each spring of its machine shall fill ;
So that when waves on waves tumultuous heap
Confusion to the clouds, and fiercely driven
Heaven's lightnings scorch the uprooted ocean-fords,
Whilst, to the eye of shipwrecked mariner,
Lone sitting on the bare and shuddering rock,
All seems unlinked contingency and chance :
No atom of this turbulence fulfils
A vague and unnecessitated task,
Or acts but as it must and ought to act.
Even the minutest molecule of light,
That in an April sunbeam's fleeting glow
Fulfils its destined, though invisible work,
The universal Spirit guides ; nor less,
When merciless ambition, or mad zeal,
Has led two hosts of dupes to battle-field,
That, blind, they there may dig each other's graves,
And call the sad work—glory, does it rule
All passions : not a thought, a will, an act,
No working of the tyrant's moody mind,
Nor one misgiving of the slaves who boast
Their servitude, to hide the shame they feel,
Nor the events enchaining every will,
That from the depths of unrecorded time
Have drawn all influencing virtue, pass
Unrecognised, or unforeseen by thee,
Soul of the Universe ! eternal spring
Of life and death, of happiness and woe,
Of all that chequers the phantasmal scene
That floats before our eyes in wavering light,
Which gleams but on the darkness of our prison,
  Whose chains and massy walls
  We feel, but cannot see.

Spirit of Nature ! all-sufficing Power,
Necessity ! thou mother of the world !
Unlike the God of human error, thou
Requirest no prayers or praises ; the caprice
Of man's weak will belongs no more to thee
Than do the changeful passions of his breast
To thy unvarying harmony : the slave,
Whose horrible lusts spread misery o'er the world,
And the good man, who lifts, with virtuous pride,
His being, in the sight of happiness,

That springs from his own works ; the poison-tree,
Beneath whose shade all life is withered up,
And the fair oak, whose leafy dome affords
A temple where the vows of happy love
Are registered, are equal in thy sight :
No love, no hate thou cherishest ; revenge
And favouritism, and worst desire of fame
Thou knowest not : all that the wide world contains
Are but thy passive instruments, and thou
Regardst them all with an impartial eye,
Whose joy or pain thy nature cannot feel,
   Because thou hast not human sense,
   Because thou art not human mind.

Yes ! when the sweeping storm of time
Has sung its death-dirge o'er the ruined fanes
And broken altars of the almighty fiend,
Whose name usurps thy honours, and the blood
Through centuries clotted there, has floated down
The tainted flood of ages, shalt thou live
Unchangeable ! A shrine is raised to thee
   Which, nor the tempest-breath of time,
   Nor the interminable flood,
   Over earth's slight pageant rolling,
     Availeth to destroy,—
The sensitive extension of the world.
   That wondrous and eternal fane,
Where pain and pleasure, good and evil join,
To do the will of strong necessity,
   And life, in multitudinous shapes,
Still pressing forward where no term can be,
   Like hungry and unresisting flame
Curls round the eternal columns of its strength.

VII.

SPIRIT.

I was an infant when my mother went
To see an atheist burned.   She took me there :
The dark-robed priests were met around the pile ;
The multitude was gazing silently ;
And as the culprit passed with dauntless mien,
Tempered disdain in his unaltering eye,
Mixed with a quiet smile, shone calmly forth :
The thirsty fire crept round his manly limbs ;
His resolute eyes were scorched to blindness soon ;
His death-pang rent my heart ! the insensate mob
Uttered a cry of triumph, and I wept.
Weep not, child ! cried my mother, for that man
Has said, There is no God.

FAIRY.

             There is no God !
Nature confirms the faith his death-groan sealed :
Let heaven and earth, let man's revolving race,
His ceaseless generations tell their tale ;

Let every part depending on the chain
That links it to the whole, point to the hand
That grasps its term! let every seed that falls
In silent eloquence unfold its store
Of argument : infinity within,
Infinity without, belie creation ;
The exterminable spirit it contains
Is nature's only God ; but human pride
Is skilful to invent most serious names
To hide its ignorance.

> The name of God
Has fenced about all crime with holiness,
Himself the creature of his worshippers,
Whose names, and attributes, and passions change,
Seeva, Buddh, Foh, Jehovah, God, or Lord,
Even with the human dupes who build his shrines,
Still serving o'er the war-polluted world
For desolation's watch-word ; whether hosts
Stain his death-blushing chariot-wheels, as on
Triumphantly they roll, whilst Brahmins raise
A sacred hymn to mingle with the groans ;
Or countless partners of his powers divide
His tyranny to weakness ; or the smoke
Of burning towns, the cries of female helplessness,
Unarmed old age, and youth, and infancy,
Horribly massacred, ascend to heaven
In honour of his name ; or, last and worst,
Earth groans beneath religion's iron age,
And priests dare babble of a God of peace,
Even whilst their hands are red with guiltless blood,
Murdering the while, uprooting every germ
Of truth, exterminating, spoiling all,
Making the earth a slaughter-house !

> O Spirit ! through the sense
By which thy inner nature was apprised
> Of outward shows, vague dreams have rolled,
And varied reminiscences have waked
> Tablets that never fade ;
All things have been imprinted there,
The stars, the sea, the earth, the sky,
Even the unshapeliest lineaments
> Of wild and fleeting visions
> Have left a record there
> To testify of earth.

These are my empire, for to me is given
The wonders of the human world to keep,
And fancy's thin creations to endow
With manner, being, and reality ;
Therefore a wondrous phantom, from the dreams
Of human errors dense and purblind faith,
I will evoke, to meet thy questioning.
> Ahasuerus, rise !

> A strange and woe-worn wight
> Arose beside the battlement,

And stood unmoving there.
His inessential figure cast no shade
        Upon the golden floor ;
His port and mien bore mark of many years
And chronicles of untold ancientness
Were legible within his beamless eye :
        Yet his cheek bore the mark of youth ;
Freshness and vigour knit his manly frame ;
The wisdom of old age was mingled there
        With youth's primæval dauntlessness ;
            And inexpressible woe,
Chastened by fearless resignation, gave
An awful grace to his all-speaking brow.*

SPIRIT.

Is there a God ?

AHASUERUS.

Is there a God ?—ay, an almighty God,
And vengeful as almighty !   Once his voice
Was heard on earth : earth shuddered at the sound
The fiery-visaged firmament expressed
Abhorrence, and the grave of nature yawned
To swallow all the dauntless and the good
That dared to hurl defiance at his throne,
Girt as it was with power.   None but slaves
Survived,—cold-blooded slaves, who did the work
Of tyrannous omnipotence ; whose souls
No honest indignation ever urged
To elevated daring, to one deed
Which gross and sensual self did not pollute.
These slaves built temples for the omnipotent fiend,
Gorgeous and vast : the costly altars smoked
With human blood, and hideous pæans rung
Through all the long-drawn aisles.   A murderer heard
His voice in Egypt, one whose gifts and arts
Had raised him to his eminence in power,
Accomplice of omnipotence in crime,
And confidant of the all-knowing one.
        These were Jehovah's words.

From an eternity of idleness
I, God, awoke ; in seven days' toil made earth
From nothing ; rested, and created man :
I placed him in a paradise, and there
Planted the tree of evil, so that he
Might eat and perish, and my soul procure
Wherewith to sate its malice, and to turn,

---

* The tradition of the " Wandering Jew " is, that when our Lord was wearied with the burthen of his ponderous cross, and wanted to rest before the door of Ahasuerus, the unfeeling wretch drove him away with brutality. The Saviour of mankind staggered, sinking under the heavy load, but uttered no complaint. An angel of death appeared before Ahasuerus, and exclaimed indignantly, " Barbarian ! thou hast denied rest to the Son of Man : be it denied thee also, until he comes to judge the world."

Even like a heartless conqueror of the earth,
All misery to my fame.   The race of men
Chosen to my honour, with impunity
May sate the lusts I planted in their heart.
Here I command thee hence to lead them on,
Until, with hardened feet, their conquering troops
Wade on the promised soil through woman's blood.
And make my name be dreaded through the land.
Yet ever burning flame and ceaseless woe
Shall be the doom of their eternal souls,
With every soul on this ungrateful earth,
Virtuous or vicious, weak or strong—even all
Shall perish, to fulfil the blind revenge
(Which you, to men, call justice) of their God.

> The murderer's brow
Quivered with horror.

> God omnipotent,
Is there no mercy ? must our punishment
Be endless ? will long ages roll away,
And see no term ? Oh ! wherefore hast thou made
In mockery and wrath this evil earth ?
Mercy becomes the powerful—be but just :
O God ! repent and save.

> One way remains :
I will beget a son, and he shall bear
The sins of all the world ; he shall arise
In an unnoticed corner of the earth,
And there shall die upon a cross and purge
The universal crime ; so that the few
On whom my grace descends, those who are marked
As vessels to the honour of their God,
May credit this strange sacrifice, and save
Their souls alive : millions shall live and die,
Who ne'er shall call upon their Saviour's name,
But, unredeemed, go to the gaping grave.
Thousands shall deem it an old woman's tale,
Such as the nurses frighten babes withal :
These in a gulf of anguish and of flame,
Shall curse their reprobation endlessly,
Yet tenfold pangs shall force them to avow,
Even on their beds of torment, where they howl,
My honour, and the justice of their doom.
What then avail their virtuous deeds, their thoughts
Of purity, with radiant genius bright,
Or lit with human reason's earthly ray ?
Many are called, but few will I elect.
Do thou my bidding, Moses !

> Even the murderer's cheek
Was blanched with horror, and his quivering lips
Scarce faintly uttered—O almighty one,
I tremble and obey !

O Spirit ! centuries have set their seal
On this heart of many wounds. and loaded brain,

Since the Incarnate came : humbly he came,
Veiling his horrible Godhead in the shape
Of man, scorned by the world, his name unheard,
Save by the rabble of his native town,
Even as a parish demagogue. He led
The crowd ; he taught them justice, truth, and peace
In semblance ; but he lit within their souls
The quenchless flames of zeal, and blest the sword
He brought on earth to satiate with the blood
Of truth and freedom his malignant soul.
At length his mortal frame was led to death.
I stood beside him : on the torturing cross
No pain assailed his unterrestrial sense ;
And yet he groaned.   Indignantly, I summed
The massacres and miseries which his name
Had sanctioned in my country, and I cried,
Go ! go ! in mockery.
A smile of godlike malice re-illumined
His fading lineaments.—I go, he cried,
But thou shalt wander o'er the unquiet earth
Eternally. ———The dampness of the grave
Bathed my imperishable front. I fell,
And long lay tranced upon the charmèd soil.
When I awoke hell burned within my brain,
Which staggered on its seat ; for all around
The mouldering relics of my kindred lay,
Even as the Almighty's ire arrested them,
And in their various attitudes of death
My murdered children's mute and eyeless skulls
Glared ghastily upon me.

                              But my soul,
From sight and sense of the polluting woe
Of tyranny, had long learned to prefer
Hell's freedom to the servitude of heaven.
Therefore I rose, and dauntlessly began
My lonely and unending pilgrimage,
Resolved to wage unweariable war
With my almighty tyrant, and to hurl
Defiance at his impotence to harm
Beyond the curse I bore. The very hand
That barred my passage to the peaceful grave
Has crushed the earth to misery, and given
Its empire to the chosen of his slaves.
These have I seen, even from the earliest dawn
Of weak, unstable, and precarious power ;
Then preaching peace, as now they practise war,
So, when they turned but from the massacre
Of unoffending infidels, to quench
Their thirst for ruin in the very blood
That flowed in their own veins, and pitiless zeal
Froze every human feeling, as the wife
Sheathed in her husband's heart the sacred steel,
Even whilst its hopes were dreaming of her love
And friends to friends, brothers to brothers stood
Opposed in bloodiest battle-field, and war,
Scarce satiable by fate's last death-draught waged,
Drunk from the winepress of the Almighty's wrath :

Whilst the red cross in mockery of peace,
Pointed to victory !   When the fray was done,
No remnant of the exterminated faith
Survived to tell its ruin, but the flesh,
With putrid smoke poisoning the atmosphere,
That rotted on the half-extinguished pile.

Yes ! I have seen God's worshippers unsheathe
The sword of his revenge, when grace descended,
Confirming all unnatural impulses,
To sanctify their desolating deeds ;
And frantic priests waved the ill-omened cross
O'er the unhappy earth : then shone the Sun
On showers of gore from the upflashing steel
Of safe assassination, and all crime
Made stingless by the spirits of the Lord,
And blood-red rainbows canopied the land.
Spirit ! no year of my eventful being
Has passed unstained by crime and misery,
Which flows from God's own faith. I've marked his slaves
With tongues whose lies are venomous, beguile
The insensate mob, and whilst one hand was red
With murder, feign to stretch the other out
For brotherhood and peace ; and that they now
Babble of love and mercy, whilst their deeds
Are marked with all the narrowness and crime
That freedom's young arm dare not yet chastise ;
Reason may claim our gratitude, who now
Establishing the imperishable throne
Of truth, and stubborn virtue, maketh vain
The unprevailing malice of my foe,
Whose bootless rage heaps torments for the brave,
Adds impotent eternities to pain,
Whilst keenest disappointment racks his breast
To see the smiles of peace around them play,
To frustrate, or to sanctify their doom.

Thus have I stood,—through a wild waste of years
Struggling with whirlwinds of mad agony,
Yet peaceful, and serene, and self-enshrined,
Mocking my powerless tyrant's horrible curse
With stubborn and unalterable will,
Even as a giant oak, which heaven's fierce flame
Had scathèd in the wilderness, to stand
A monument of fadeless ruin there ;
Yet peacefully and movelessly it braves
The midnight conflict of the wintry storm,
    As in the sunlight's calm it spreads
    Its worn and withered arms on high
To meet the quiet of a summer's noon.

        The Fairy waved her wand :
        Ahasuerus fled
Fast as the shapes of mingled shade and mist,
That lurk in the glens of a twilight grove,
        Flee from the morning beam :
    The matter of which dreams are made
    Not more endowed with actual life

Than this phantasmal portraiture
Of wandering human thought.

VIII.

The present and the past thou hast beheld:
It was a desolate sight.   Now, Spirit, learn
    The secrets of the future.—Time!
Unfold the brooding pinion of thy gloom,
Render thou up thy half-devourèd babes,
And from the cradles of eternity,
Where millions lie lulled to their portioned sleep
By the deep murmuring stream of passing things,
Tear thou that gloomy shroud.—Spirit, behold
        Thy glorious destiny!

        Joy to the Spirit came,
Through the wide rent in Time's eternal veil,
Hope was seen beaming through the mists of fear:
    Earth was no longer hell;
    Love, freedom, health had given
Their ripeness to the manhood of its prime,
    And all its pulses beat
Symphonious to the planetary spheres:
    Then dulcet music swelled
Concordant with the life-strings of the soul;
It throbbed in sweet and languid beatings there,
Catching new life from transitory death,—
Like the vague sighings of a wind at even,
That wakes the wavelets of the slumbering sea
And dies on the creation of its breath,
And sinks and rises, fails and swells by fits,
        Was the pure stream of feeling
        That sprung from these sweet notes,
And o'er the Spirit's human sympathies
With mild and gentle motion calmly flowed.

        Joy to the Spirit came,—
    Such joy as when a lover sees
The chosen of his soul in happiness,
        And witnesses her peace
Whose woe to him were bitterer than death,
        Sees her unfaded cheek
Glow mantling in first luxury of health,
        Thrills with her lovely eyes,
Which like two stars amid the heaving main
        Sparkle through liquid bliss.

Then in her triumph spoke the Fairy Queen
I will not call the ghost of ages gone
To unfold the frightful secrets of its lore;
        The present now is past,
And those events that desolate the earth
Have faded from the memory of Time,
Who dares not give reality to that
Whose being I annul.   To me is given
The wonders of the human world to keep,
Space, matter, time, and mind.   Futurity

Exposes now its treasure ; let the sight
Renew and strengthen all thy failing hope
O human Spirit ! spur thee to the goal
Where virtue fixes universal peace,
And midst the ebb and flow of human things,
Show somewhat stable, somewhat certain still,
A lighthouse o'er the wild of dreary waves.

The habitable earth is full of bliss ;
Those wastes of frozen billows that were hurled
By everlasting snow-storms round the poles,
Where matter dared not vegetate or live,
But ceaseless frost round the vast solitude
Bound its broad zone of stillness, are unloosed ;
And fragant zephyrs there from spicy isles
Ruffle the placid ocean-deep that rolls
Its broad, bright surges to the sloping sand,
Whose roar is wakened into echoings sweet
To murmur through the heaven-breathing groves
And melodize with man's blest nature there.

Those deserts of immeasurable sand,
Whose age-collected fervours scarce allowed
A bird to live, a blade of grass to spring,
Where the shrill chirp of the green lizard's love
Broke on the sultry silentness alone,
Now teem with countless rills and shady woods,
Corn-fields, and pastures, and white cottages ;
And where the startled wilderness beheld
A savage conqueror stained in kindred blood,
A tigress sating with the flesh of lambs,
The unnatural famine of her toothless cubs,
Whilst shouts and howlings through the desert rang ;
Sloping and smooth the daisy-spangled lawn,
Offering sweet incense to the sun-rise, smiles
To see a babe before his mother's door,
        Sharing his morning's meal
    With the green and golden basilisk
        That comes to lick his feet.

Those trackless deeps, where many a weary sail
Has seen above the illimitable plain,
Morning on night, and night on morning rise,
Whilst still no land to greet the wanderer spread
Its shadowy mountains on the sun-bright sea,
Where the loud roarings of the tempest-waves
So long have mingled with the gusty wind
In melancholy loneliness, and swept
The desert of those ocean solitudes,
But vocal to the sea-bird's harrowing shriek,
The bellowing monster, and the rushing storm ;
Now to the sweet and many mingling sounds
Of kindliest human impulses respond.
Those lonely realms bright garden-isles begem
With lightsome clouds and shining seas between,
And fertile valleys resonant with bliss,
Whilst green woods overcanopy the wave,
Which like a toil-worn labourer leaps to shore,
To meet the kisses of the flowrets there.

All things are recreated, and the flame
Of consentaneous love inspires all life :
The fertile bosom of the earth gives suck
To myriads, who still grow beneath her care,
Rewarding her with their pure perfectness :
The balmy breathings of the wind inhale
Her virtues, and diffuse them all abroad :
Health floats amid the gentle atmosphere,
Glows in the fruits, and mantles on the stream :
No storm deforms the beaming brow of heaven,
Nor scatters in the freshness of its pride
The foliage of the ever-verdant trees ;
But fruits are ever ripe, flowers ever fair,
And autumn proudly bears her matron grace,
Kindling a flush on the fair cheek of spring,
Whose virgin bloom beneath the ruddy fruit
Reflects its tint and blushes into love.

The lion now forgets to thirst for blood :
There might you see him sporting in the sun
Beside the dreadless kid ; his claws are sheathed,
His teeth are harmless, custom's force has made
His nature as the nature of a lamb.
Like passion's fruit, the nightshade's tempting bane
Poisons no more the pleasure it bestows :
All bitterness is past ; the cup of joy
Unmingled mantles to the goblet's brim,
And courts the thirsty lips it fled before.

But chief, ambiguous man ; he that can know
More misery, and dream more joy than all ;
Whose keen sensations thrill within his breast
To mingle with a loftier instinct there,
Lending their power to pleasure and to pain,
Yet raising, sharpening, and refining each ;
Who stands amid the ever-varying world,
The burthen or the glory of the earth ;
He chief perceives the change, his being notes
The gradual renovation, and defines
Each movement of its progress on his mind.

Man, where the gloom of the long polar night
Lours o'er the snow-clad rocks and frozen soil,
Where scarce the hardiest herb that braves the frost
Basks in the moonlight's ineffectual glow,
Shrank with the plants, and darkened with the night ;
His chilled and narrow energies, his heart,
Insensible to courage, truth, or love,
His stunted stature and imbecile frame,
Marked him for some abortion of the earth,
Fit compeer of the bears that roamed around,
Whose habits and enjoyments were his own :
His life a feverish dream of stagnant woe,
Whose meagre wants but scantily fulfilled,
Apprised him ever of the joyless length
Which his short being's wretchedness had reached ;
His death a pang, which famine, cold, and toil
Long on the mind, whilst yet the vital spark

Clung to the body stubbornly, had brought :
All was inflicted here that earth's revenge
Could wreak on the infringers of her law ;
One curse alone was spared—the name of God.

Nor where the tropics bound the realms of day
With a broad belt of mingling cloud and flame,
Where blue mists through the unmoving atmosphere
Scattered the seeds of pestilence, and fed
Unnatural vegetation, where the land
Teemed with all earthquake, tempest and disease,
Was man a nobler being ; slavery
Had crushed him to his country's blood-stained dust ;
Or he was bartered for the fame of power,
Which all internal impulses destroying,
Makes human will an article of trade ;
Or he was changed with Christians for their gold,
And dragged to distant isles, where to the sound
Of the flesh-mangling scourge, he does the work
Of all-polluting luxury and wealth,
Which doubly visits on the tyrants' heads
The long-protracted fulness of their woe ;
Or he was led to legal butchery,
To turn to worms beneath that burning sun,
Where kings first leagued against the rights of men,
And priests first traded with the name of God.

Even where the milder zone afforded man
A seeming shelter, yet contagion there,
Blighting his being with unnumbered ills,
Spread like a quenchless fire ; nor truth till late
Availed to arrest its progress, or create
That peace which first in bloodless victory waved
Her snowy standard o'er this favoured clime.
There man was long the train-bearer of slaves,
The mimic of surrounding misery,
The jackal of ambition's lion-rage,
The bloodhound of religion's hungry zeal.
Here now the human being stands adorning
This loveliest earth, with taintless body and mind ;
Blest from his birth with all bland impulses,
Which gently in his noble bosom wake
All kindly passions and all pure desires.
Him, still from hope to hope the bliss pursuing,
Which from the exhaustless lore of human weal
Draws on the virtuous mind, the thoughts that rise
In time-destroying infiniteness, gift
With self-enshrined eternity, that mocks
The unprevailing hoariness of age,
And man, once fleeting o'er the transient scene
Swift as an unremembered vision, stands
Immortal upon earth.   No longer now
He slays the lamb that looks him in the face,
And horribly devours his mangled flesh,
Which still avenging nature's broken law,
Kindled all putrid humours in his frame,
All evil passions, and all vain belief,
Hatred, despair, and loathing in his mind,

The germs of misery, death, disease, and crime.
No longer now the wingèd habitants,
That in the woods their sweet lives sing away,
Flee from the form of man ; but gather round,
And prune their sunny feathers on the hands
Which little children stretch in friendly sport
Towards these dreadless partners of their play.
All things are void of terror : man has lost
His terrible prerogative, and stands
An equal amidst equals.   Happiness
And science dawn though late upon the earth ;
Peace cheers the mind, health renovates the frame :
Disease and pleasure cease to mingle here,
Reason and passion cease to combat there ;
Whilst each unfettered o'er the earth extend
Their all-subduing energies, and wield
The sceptre of a vast dominion there ;
Whilst every shape and mode of matter lends
Its force to the omnipotence of mind,
Which from its dark mine drags the gem of truth
To decorate its paradise of peace.

IX.

O happy Earth ! reality of Heaven !
To which those restless souls that ceaselessly
Throng through the human universe, aspire ;
Thou consummation of all mortal hope !
Thou glorious prize of blindly-working will !
Whose rays diffused throughout all space and time,
Verge to one point and blend for ever there :
Of purest spirits thou pure dwelling-place !
Where care and sorrow, impotence and crime,
Languor, disease, and ignorance, dare not come :
O happy Earth, reality of Heaven !

Genius has seen thee in her passionate dreams,
And dim forebodings of thy loveliness
Haunting the human heart, have there entwined
Those rooted hopes of some sweet place of bliss
Where friends and lovers meet to part no more.
Thou art the end of all desire and will,
The product of all action : and the souls
That by the paths of an aspiring change
Have reached thy haven of perpetual peace,
There rest from the eternity of toil
That framed the fabric of thy perfectness.
Even Time, the conqueror, fled thee in his fear ;
That hoary giant, who, in lonely pride,
So long had ruled the world, that nations fell
Beneath his silent footstep.   Pyramids,
That for millenniums had withstood the tide
Of human things, his storm-breath drove in sand
Across that desert where their stones survived
The name of him whose pride had heaped them there.
Yon monarch, in his solitary pomp
Was but the mushroom of a summer day,
That his light-winged footstep pressed to dust :

Time was the king of earth : all things gave way
Before him, but the fixed and virtuous will,
The sacred sympathies of soul and sense,
That mocked his fury and prepared his fall.
Yet slow and gradual dawned the morn of love ;
Long lay the clouds of darkness o'er the scene,
Till from its native heaven they rolled away :
First, Crime, triumphant o'er all hope, careered
Unblushing, undisguising, bold and strong ;
Whilst Falsehood, tricked in virtue's attributes,
Long sanctified all deeds of vice and woe,
Till done by her own venomous sting to death,
She left the moral world without a law,
No longer fettering passion's fearless wing,
Nor searing reason with the brand of God.
Then steadily the happy ferment worked ;
Reason was free ; and wild though passion went
Through tangled glens and wood-embosomed meads
Gathering a garland of the strangest flowers,
Yet like the bee returning to her queen,
She bound the sweetest on her sister's brow,
Who, meek and sober, kissed the sportive child
No longer trembling at the broken rod.

Mild was the slow necessity of death :
The tranquil spirit failed beneath its grasp,
Without a groan, almost without a fear,
Calm as a voyager to some distant land,
And full of wonder, full of hope as he.
The deadly germs of languor and disease
Died in the human frame, and purity
Blessed with all gifts her earthly worshippers,
How vigorous then the athletic form of age !
How clear its open and unwrinkled brow !
Where neither avarice, cunning, pride, nor care,
Had stamped the seal of grey deformity
On all the mingling lineaments of time.
How lovely the intrepid front of youth !
Which meek-eyed courage decked with freshest grace
Courage of soul, that dreaded not a name,
And elevated will, that journeyed on
Through life's phantasmal scene in fearlessness,
With virtue, love, and pleasure, hand in hand.

Then, that sweet bondage which is freedom's self,
And rivets with sensation's softest tie
The kindred sympathies of human souls,
Needed no fetters of tyrannic law :
Those delicate and timid impulses
In nature's primal modesty arose,
And with undoubting confidence disclosed
The growing longings of its dawning love,
Unchecked by dull and selfish chastity,
That virtue of the cheaply virtuous,
Who pride themselves in senselessness and frost,
No longer prostitution's venomed bane
Poisoned the springs of happiness and life ;
Woman and man, in confidence and love,

Equal, and free, and pure, together trod
The mountain-paths of virtue, which no more
Were stained with blood from many a pilgrim's feet.

Then, where, through distant ages, long in pride
The palace of the monarch-slave had mocked
Famine's faint groan, and penury's silent tear,
A heap of crumbling ruins stood, and threw
Year after year their stones upon the field,
Wakening a lonely echo ; and the leaves
Of the old thorn, that on the topmost tower
Usurped the royal ensign's grandeur, shook
In the stern storm that swayed the topmost tower
And whispered strange tales in the whirlwind's ear.

Low through the lone cathedral's roofless aisles
The melancholy winds a death-dirge sung :
It were a sight of awfulness to see
The works of faith and slavery, so vast,
So sumptuous, yet so perishing withal !
Even as the corpse that rests beneath its wall.
A thousand mourners deck the pomp of death
To-day, the breathing marble glows above
To decorate its memory, and tongues
Are busy of its life : to-morrow worms
In silence and in darkness seize their prey.

Within the massy prison's mouldering courts,
Fearless and free the ruddy children played,
Weaving gay chaplets for their innocent brows
With the green ivy and the red wall-flower,
That mock the dungeon's unavailing gloom ;
The ponderous chains, and gratings of strong iron
There rusted amid heaps of broken stone
That mingled slowly with their native earth :
There the broad beam of day, which feebly once
Lighted the cheek of lean captivity
With a pale and sickly glare, then freely shone
On the pure smiles of infant playfulness.
No more the shuddering voice of hoarse despair
Pealed through the echoing vaults, but soothing notes
Of ivy-fingered winds and gladsome birds
And merriment were resonant around.

These ruins soon left not a wreck behind :
Their elements, wide scattered o'er the globe,
To happier shapes were moulded, and became
Ministrant to all blissful impulses :
Thus human things were perfected, and earth,
Even as a child beneath its mother's love,
Was strengthened in all excellence, and grew
Fairer and nobler with each passing year.

Now Time his dusky pennons o'er the scene
Closes in steadfast darkness, and the past
Fades from our charmèd sight.   My task is done :
Thy lore is learned.   Earth's wonders are thine own,
With all the fear and all the hope they bring.
My spells are past : the present now recurs.

Ah me ! a pathless wilderness remains
Yet unsubdued by man's reclaiming hand.

Yet, human Spirit, bravely hold thy course,
Let virtue teach thee firmly to pursue
The gradual paths of an aspiring change :
For birth, and life, and death, and that strange state
Before the naked soul has found its home,
All tend to perfect happiness, and urge
The restless wheels of being on their way,
Whose flashing spokes, instinct with infinite life,
Bicker and burn to gain their destined goal :
For birth but wakes the spirit to the sense
Of outward shows, whose unexperienced shape
New modes of passion to its frame may lend ;
Life is its state of action, and the store
Of all events is aggregated there
That variegate the eternal universe ;
Death is a gate of dreariness and gloom,
That leads to azure isles and beaming skies
And happy regions of eternal hope.
Therefore, O Spirit ! fearlessly bear on :
Though storms may break the primrose on its stalk,
Though frosts may blight the freshness of its bloom,
Yet Spring's awakening breath will woo the earth,
To feed with kindliest dews its favourite flower,
That blooms in mossy banks and darksome glens,
Lighting the greenwood with its sunny smile.

Fear not then, Spirit, death's disrobing hand,
So welcome when the tyrant is awake,
So welcome when the bigot's hell-torch burns ;
'Tis but the voyage of a darksome hour,
The transient gulf-dream of a startling sleep.
Death is no foe to virtue : Earth has seen
Love's brightest roses on the scaffold bloom,
Mingling with freedom's fadeless laurels there,
And presaging the truth of visioned bliss.
Are there not hopes within thee, which this scene
Of linked and gradual being has confirmed ?
Whose stingings bade thy heart look further still,
When to the moonlight walk by Henry led,
Sweetly and sadly thou didst talk of death ?
And wilt thou rudely tear them from thy breast,
Listening supinely to a bigot's creed,
Or tamely crouching to the tyrant's rod,
Whose iron thongs are red with human gore ?
Never : but bravely bearing on, thy will,
Is destined an eternal war to wage
With tyranny and falsehood, and uproot
The germs of misery from the human heart.
Thine is the hand whose piety would soothe
The thorny pillow of unhappy crime,
Whose impotence an easy pardon gains,
Watching its wanderings as a friend's disease :
Thine is the brow whose mildness would defy
Its fiercest rage, and brave its sternest will,
When fenced by power and master of the world.

Thou art sincere and good ; of resolute mind,
Free from heart-withering custom's cold control,
Of passion lofty, pure and unsubdued.
Earth's pride and meanness could not vanquish thee,
And therefore art thou worthy of the boon
Which thou hast now received : virtue shall keep
Thy footsteps in the path that thou hast trod,
And many days of beaming hope shall bless
Thy spotless life of sweet and sacred love.
Go, happy one, and give that bosom joy
    Whose sleepless spirit waits to catch
    Light, life, and rapture from thy smile.

    The Fairy waves her wand of charm.
Speechless with bliss the Spirit mounts the car,
    That rolled beside the battlement,
Bending her beamy eyes in thankfulness.
    Again the enchanted steeds were yoked,
    Again the burning wheels inflame
The steep descent of heaven's untrodden way.
    Fast and far the chariot flew :
    The vast and fiery globes that rolled
    Around the Fairy's palace-gate
Lessened by slow degrees, and soon appeared
Such tiny twinklers as the planet orbs
That there attendant on the solar power
With borrowed light pursued their narrower way
       Earth floated then below :
    The chariot paused a moment there ;
      The Spirit then descended :
The restless coursers pawed the ungenial soil,
Snuffed the gross air, and then, their errand done,
Unfurled their pinions to the winds of heaven.

    The Body and the Soul united then,
A gentle start convulsed Ianthe's frame
Her veiny eyelids quietly unclosed ;
Moveless awhile the dark blue orbs remained :
She looked around in wonder and beheld
Henry, who kneeled in silence by her couch,
Watching her sleep with looks of speechless love,
    And the bright beaming stars
    That through the casement shone.

1815.

THE DEMON OF THE WORLD.

A FRAGMENT.

"Nec tantum prodere vati
Quantum scire licet.   Venit ætas omnis in unam
Congeriem, miserumque premunt tot sæcula pectus."
LUCAN, *Phars.* v. 176.

How wonderful is Death,
Death and his brother Sleep !
One pale as yonder wan and hornèd moon
With lips of lurid blue ;
The other glowing like the vital morn,
When throned on ocean's wave
It breathes over the world :
Yet both so passing strange and wonderful !

Hath then the iron-sceptred Skeleton,
Whose reign is in the tainted sepulchres,
To the hell dogs that couch beneath his throne
Cast that fair prey ?   Must that divinest form,
Which love and admiration cannot view
Without a beating heart, whose azure veins
Steal like dark streams along a field of snow,
Whose outline is as fair as marble clothed
In light of some sublimest mind, decay ?
Nor putrefaction's breath
Leave aught of this pure spectacle
But loathsomeness and ruin ?—
Spare aught but a dark theme,
On which the lightest heart might moralize ?
Or is it but that downy-winged slumbers
Have charmed their nurse coy Silence near her lids
To watch their own repose ?
Will they, when morning's beam
Flows through those wells of light,
Seek far from noise and day some western cave,
Where woods and streams with soft and pausing winds
A lulling murmur weave ?—

Ianthe doth not sleep
The dreamless sleep of death :
Nor in her moonlight chamber silently
Doth Henry hear her regular pulses throb,
Or mark her delicate cheek
With interchange of hues mock the broad moon,

Outwatching weary night,
Without assured reward.
Her dewy eyes are closed :
On their translucent lids, whose texture fine
Scarce hides the dark blue orbs that burn below
With unapparent fire,
The baby Sleep is pillowed :
Her golden tresses shade
The bosom's stainless pride,
Twining like tendrils of the parasite
Around a marble column.

Hark ! whence that rushing sound ?
'Tis like a wondrous strain that sweeps
Around a lonely ruin,
When west winds sigh and evening waves respond
In whipers from the shore :
'Tis wilder than the unmeasured notes
Which from the unseen lyres of dells and groves
The genii of the breezes sweep.
Floating on waves of music and of light
The chariot of the Demon of the World
Descends in silent power :
Its shape reposed within : slight as some cloud
That catches but the palest tinge of day
When evening yields to night,
Bright as that fibrous woof when stars indue
Its transitory robe.

Four shapeless shadows bright and beautiful
Draw that strange car of glory, reins of light
Check their unearthly speed ; they stop and fold
Their wings of braided air :
The Demon leaning from the ethereal car
Gazed on the slumbering maid.
Human eye hath ne'er beheld
A shape so wild, so bright, so beautiful,
As that which o'er the maiden's charmed sleep
Waving a starry wand,
Hung like a mist of light.
Such sounds as breathed around like odorous winds
Of wakening spring arose,
Filling the chamber and the moonlight sky.

Maiden, the world's supremest spirit
Beneath the shadow of her wings
Folds all thy memory doth inherit
From ruin of divinest things,
Feelings that lure thee to betray,
And light of thoughts that pass away.

For thou hast earned a mighty boon,
The truths which wisest poets see
Dimly, thy mind may make its own,
Rewarding its own majesty,
Entranced in some diviner mood
Of self-oblivious solitude.

Custom, and Faith, and Power thou spurnest ;
    From hate and awe thy heart is free ;
Ardent and pure as day thou burnest,
    For dark and cold mortality
      A living light to cheer it long,
      The watch-fires of the world among.

Therefore from nature's inner shrine,
    Where gods and fiends in worship bend,
Majestic spirit, be it thine
    The flame to seize, the veil to rend,
      Where the vast snake Eternity
      In charmed sleep doth ever lie.

All that inspires thy voice of love,
    Or speaks in thy unclosing eyes,
Or through thy frame doth burn or move,
    Or think or feel, awake, arise !
      Spirit, leave for mine and me
      Earth's unsubstantial mimicry !

It ceased, and from the mute and moveless frame
    A radiant spirit arose,
All beautiful in naked purity.
Robed in its human hues it did ascend,
Disparting as it went the silver clouds
It moved towards the car, and took its seat
    Beside the Demon shape.

Obedient to the sweep of aëry song,
    The mighty ministers
Unfurled their prismy wings.
    The magic car moved on ;
The night was fair, innumerable stars
    Studded heaven's dark blue vault ;
    The eastern wave grew pale
    With the first smile of morn.

    The magic car moved on
    From the swift sweep of wings
The atmosphere in flaming sparkles flew
    And where the burning wheels
Eddied above the mountain's loftiest peak
    Was traced a line of lightning.
Now far above a rock the utmost verge
    Of the wide earth it flew,
The rival of the Andes, whose dark brow
    Frowned o'er the silver sea.

Far, far below the chariot's stormy path
    Calm as a slumbering babe,
    Tremendous ocean lay.
Its broad and silent mirror gave to view
    The pale and waning stars,
    The chariot's fiery track,
    And the grey light of morn
    Tinging those fleecy clouds
That cradled in their folds the infant dawn.

The chariot seemed to fly
Through the abyss of an immense concave,
Radiant with million constellations, tinged
    With shades of infinite colour,
    And semicircled with a belt
    Flashing incessant meteors.

    As they approached their goal,
The winged shadows seemed to gather speed.
The sea no longer was distinguished ; earth
Appeared a vast and shadowy sphere, suspended
    In the black concave of heaven
    With the sun's cloudless orb,
    Whose rays of rapid light
Parted around the chariot's swifter course,
And fell like ocean's feathery spray
    Dashed from the boiling surge
    Before a vessel's prow.

    The magic car moved on.
    Earth's distant orb appeared
The smallest light that twinkles in the heavens,
    Whilst round the chariot's way
Innumerable systems widely rolled,
    And countless spheres diffused
    An ever-varying glory.

It was a sight of wonder !   Some were horned,
And, like the moon's argentine crescent hung
In the dark dome of heaven, some did shed
A clear mild beam like Hesperus, while the sea
Yet glows with fading sunlight ; others dashed
Athwart the night with trains of bickering fire,
Like sphered worlds to death and ruin driven ;
Some shone like stars, and as the chariot passed
    Bedimmed all other light.

    Spirit of Nature ! here
In this interminable wilderness
Of worlds, at whose involved immensity
    Even soaring fancy staggers,
    Here is thy fitting temple.
    Yet not the lightest leaf
That quivers to the passing breeze
    Is less instinct with thee, —
    Yet not the meanest worm,
That lurks in graves and fattens on the dead,
    Less shares thy eternal breath.
    Spirit of Nature ! thou
Imperishable as this glorious scene,
    Here is thy fitting temple.

If solitude hath ever led thy steps
To the shore of the immeasurable sea,
    And thou hast lingered there
    Until the sun's broad orb
Seemed resting on the fiery line of ocean,
Thou must have marked the braided webs of gold

That without motion hang
Over the sinking sphere ;
Thou must have marked the billowy mountain clouds,
Edged with intolerable radiancy,
Towering like rocks of jet
Above the burning deep :
And yet there is a moment
When the sun's highest point
Peers like a star o'er ocean's western edge,
When those far clouds of feathery purple gleam
Like fairy lands girt by some heavenly sea ;
Then has thy rapt imagination soared
Where in the midst of all existing things
The temple of the mightiest Demon stands,
Yet not the golden islands
That gleam amid yon flood of purple light,
Nor the feathery curtains
That canopy the sun's resplendent couch,
Nor the burnished ocean waves
Paving that gorgeous dome,
So fair so wonderful a sight
As the eternal temple could afford.
The elements of all that human thought
Can frame of lovely or sublime, did join
To rear the fabric of the fane, nor aught
Of earth may image forth its majesty.
Yet likest evening's vault that faëry hall,
As heaven low resting on the wave it spread
Its floors of flashing light,
Its vast and azure dome ;
And on the verge of that obscure abyss
Where crystal battlements o'erhang the gulf
Of the dark world, ten thousand spheres diffuse
Their lustre through its adamantine gates.

The magic car no longer moved ;
The Demon and the Spirit
Entered the eternal gates.
Those clouds of aëry gold
That slept in glittering billows
Beneath the azure canopy,
With the ethereal footsteps trembled not ;
While slight and odorous mists
Floated to strains of thrilling melody
Through the vast columns and the pearly shrines.

The Demon and the Spirit
Approached the overhanging battlement.
Below lay stretched the boundless universe !
There, far as the remotest line
That limits swift imagination's flight,
Unending orbs mingled in mazy motion,
Immutably fulfilling
Eternal Nature's law.
Above, below, around,
The circling systems formed
A wilderness of harmony,
Each with undeviating aim

E

In eloquent silence through the depths of space
          Pursued its wondrous way.

Awhile the Spirit paused in ecstasy.
Yet soon she saw, as the vast spheres swept by,
Strange things within their belted orbs appear.
Like animated frenzies, dimly moved
Shadows, and skeletons, and fiendly shapes,
Thronging round human graves, and o'er the dead
Sculpturing records for each memory
In verse, such as malignant gods pronounce,
Blasting the hopes of men, when heaven and hell
Confounded burst in ruin o'er the world :
And they did build vast trophies, instruments
Of murder, human bones, barbaric gold,
Skins torn from living men, and towers of skulls
With sightless holes gazing on blinder heaven,
Mitres, and crowns, and brazen chariots stained
With blood, and scrolls of mystic wickedness,
The sanguine codes of venerable crime.
The likeness of a throned king came by,
When these had past, bearing upon his brow
A threefold crown ; his countenance was calm,
His eye severe and cold ; but his right hand
Was charged with bloody coin, and he did gnaw
By fits, with secret smiles, a human heart
Concealed beneath his robe ; and motley shapes,
A multitudinous throng, around him knelt,
With bosoms bare, and bowed heads, and false looks
Of true submission, as the sphere rolled by,
Brooking no eye to witness their foul shame,
Which human hearts must feel, while human tongues
Tremble to speak, they did rage horribly,
Breathing in self contempt fierce blasphemies
Against the Demon of the World, and high
Hurling their armed hands where the pure Spirit,
Serene and inaccessibly secure,
Stood on an isolated pinnacle,
The flood of ages combating below,
The depth of the unbounded universe
          Above, and all around
Necessity's unchanging harmony.

1815

ALASTOR;

OR,

THE SPIRIT OF SOLITUDE.

PREFACE.

THE poem entitled "Alastor," may be considered as allegorical of one of the most interesting situations of the human mind. It represents a youth of un-corrupted feelings and adventurous genius led forth by an imagination inflamed and purified through familiarity with all that is excellent and majestic, to the contemplation of the universe. He drinks deep of the fountains of knowledge, and is still insatiate. The magnificence and beauty of the external world sinks profoundly into the frame of his conceptions, and affords to their modifications a variety not to be exhausted. So long as it is possible for his desires to point towards objects thus infinite and unmeasured, he is joyous, and tranquil, and self-possessed. But the period arrives when these objects cease to suffice. His mind is at length suddenly awakened and thirsts for intercourse with an intelli-gence similar to itself. He images to himself the Being whom he loves. Con-versant with speculations of the sublimest and most perfect natures, the vision in which he embodies his own imaginations unites all of wonderful, or wise, or beautiful, which the poet, the philosopher, or the lover, could depicture. The intellectual faculties, the imagination, the functions of sense, have their respec-tive requisitions on the sympathy of corresponding powers in other human beings. The poet is represented as uniting these requisitions, and attaching them to a single image. He seeks in vain for a prototype of his conception. Blasted by his disappointment, he descends to an untimely grave.

The picture is not barren of instruction to actual men. The Poet's self-centred seclusion was avenged by the furies of an irresistible passion pursuing him to speedy ruin. But that Power which strikes the luminaries of the world with sudden darkness and extinction, by awakening them to too exquisite a perception of its influences, dooms to a slow and poisonous decay those meaner spirits that dare to abjure its dominion. Their destiny is more abject and inglorious as their delinquency is more contemptible and pernicious. They who, deluded by no generous error, instigated by no sacred thirst of doubtful know-ledge, duped by no illustrious superstition, loving nothing on this earth, and cherishing no hopes beyond, yet keep aloof from sympathies with their kind, re-joicing neither in human joy nor mourning with human grief; these, and such as they, have their apportioned curse. They languish, because none feel with them their common nature. They are morally dead. They are neither friends, nor lovers, nor fathers, nor citizens of the world, nor benefactors of their country. Among those who attempt to exist without human sympathy, the pure and tender-hearted perish through the intensity and passion of their search after its communities, when the vacancy of their spirit suddenly makes itself felt. All else, selfish, blind, and torpid, are those unforeseeing multitudes who constitute, together with their own, the lasting misery and loneliness of the world. Those who love not their fellow-beings, live unfruitful lives, and prepare for their old age a miserable grave.

> "The good die first,
> And they whose hearts are dry as summer dust,
> Burn to the socket !"

December 14, 1815.

"Nondum amabam, et amare amabam, quærebam quid amarem, amans amare."

CONFESS. St. AUGUST.

EARTH, ocean, air, beloved brotherhood !
If our great Mother has imbued my soul
With aught of natural piety to feel
Your love, and recompense the boon with mine ;
If dewy morn, and odorous noon, and even,
With sunset and its gorgeous ministers,
And solemn midnight's tingling silentness ;
If autumn's hollow sighs in the sere wood,
And winter robing with pure snow and crowns
Of starry ice the gray grass and bare boughs ;
If spring's voluptuous pantings when she breathes
Her first sweet kisses, have been dear to me ;
If no bright bird, insect, or gentle beast
I consciously have injured, but still loved
And cherished these my kindred ;—then forgive
This boast, beloved brethren, and withdraw
No portion of your wonted favour now !

Mother of this unfathomable world !
Favour my solemn song, for I have loved
Thee ever, and thee only ; I have watched
Thy shadow, and the darkness of thy steps
And my heart ever gazes on the depth
Of thy deep mysteries.   I have made my bed
In charnels and on coffins, where black death
Keeps record of the trophies won from thee,
Hoping to still these obstinate questionings
Of thee and thine, by forcing some lone ghost,
Thy messenger, to render up the tale
Of what we are.   In lone and silent hours,
When night makes a weird sound of its own stillness,
Like an inspired and desperate alchymist
Staking his very life on some dark hope,
Have I mixed awful talk and asking looks
With my most innocent love, until strange tears
Uniting with those breathless kisses, made
Such magic as compels the charmed night
To render up thy charge : . . . . and, though ne'er yet
Thou hast unveiled thy inmost sanctuary,
Enough from incommunicable dream,
And twilight phantasms and deep noonday thought
Has shone within me, that serenely now,
And moveless as a long-forgotten lyre,

Suspended in the solitary dome
Of some mysterious and deserted fane,
I wait thy breath, Great Parent, that my strain
May modulate with murmurs of the air,
And motions of the forests and the sea,
And voice of living beings, and woven hymns
Of night and day, and the deep heart of man.

    There was a Poet whose untimely tomb
No human hands with pious reverence reared,
But the charmed eddies of autumnal winds
Built o'er his mouldering bones a pyramid
Of mouldering leaves in the waste wilderness :
A lovely youth,—no mourning maiden decked
With weeping flowers, or votive cypress wreath,
The lone couch of his everlasting sleep ;
Gentle, and brave, and generous, no lorn bard
Breathed o'er his dark fate one melodious sigh :
He lived, he died, he sung, in solitude.
Strangers have wept to hear his passionate notes,
And virgins, as unknown he past, have sighed
And wasted for fond love of his wild eyes.
The fire of those soft orbs has ceased to burn,
And Silence, too enamoured of that voice,
Locks its mute music in her rugged cell.

    By solemn vision and bright silver dream,
His infancy was nurtured.   Every sight
And sound from the vast earth and ambient air,
Sent to his heart its choicest impulses.
The fountains of divine philosophy
Fled not his thirsting lips ; and all of great,
Or good, or lovely, which the sacred past
In truth or fable consecrates, he felt
And knew.   When early youth had past, he left
His cold fireside and alienated home
To seek strange truths in undiscovered lands.
Many a wide waste and tangled wilderness
Has lured his fearless steps ; and as he bought
With his sweet voice and eyes, from savage men,
His rest and food.   Nature's most secret steps
He like her shadow, has pursued, where'er
The red volcano overcanopies
Its fields of snow and pinnacles of ice
With burning smoke ; or where bitumen lakes,
On black bare pointed islets ever beat
With sluggish surge ; or where the secret caves
Rugged and dark, winding among the springs
Of fire and poison, inaccessible
To avarice or pride, their starry domes
Of diamond and of gold, expand above
Numberless and immeasurable halls,
Frequent with crystal column, and clear shrines
Of pearl, and thrones radiant with chrysolite.
Nor had that scene of ampler majesty
Than gems or gold, the varying roof of heaven
And the green earth lost in his heart its claims
To love and wonder ; he would linger long

In lonesome vales, making the wild his home,
Until the doves and squirrels would partake
From his innocuous hand his bloodless food,
Lured by the gentle meaning of his looks,
And the wild antelope, that starts whene'er
The dry leaf rustles in the brake, suspend
Her timid steps, to gaze upon a form
More graceful than her own.

                                        His wandering step,
Obedient to high thoughts, has visited
The awful ruins of the days of old :
Athens, and Tyre, and Balbec, and the waste
Where stood Jerusalem, the fallen towers
Of Babylon, the eternal pyramids,
Memphis and Thebes, and whatsoe'er of strange
Sculptured on alabaster obelisk,
Or jasper tomb, or mutilated sphinx,
Dark Ethiopia on her desert hills
Conceals.   Among the ruined temples there,
Stupendous columns, and wild images
Of more than man, where marble demons watch
The Zodiac's brazen mystery, and dead men
Hang their mute thoughts on the mute walls around,
He lingered, poring on memorials
Of the world's youth, through the long burning day
Gazed on those speechless shapes, nor, when the moon
Filled the mysterious halls with floating shades
Suspended he that task, but ever gazed
And gazed, till meaning on his vacant mind
Flashed like strong inspiration, and he saw
The thrilling secrets of the birth of time.

    Meanwhile an Arab maiden brought his food,
Her daily portion, from her father's tent,
And spread her matting for his couch, and stole
From duties and repose to tend his steps :—
Enamoured, yet not daring for deep awe
To speak her love :—and watched his nightly sleep,
Sleepless herself, to gaze upon his lips
Parted in slumber, whence the regular breath
Of innocent dreams arose : then, when red morn
Made paler the pale moon, to her cold home,
Wildered and wan and panting, she returned.

    The Poet wandering on, through Arabie
And Persia, and the wild Carmanian waste,
And o'er the aërial mountains which pour down
Indus and Oxus from their icy caves,
In joy and exultation held his way ;
Till in the vale of Cachmire, far within
Its loneliest dell, where odorous plants entwine
Beneath the hollow rocks a natural bower,
Beside a sparkling rivulet he stretched
His languid limbs.   A vision on his sleep
There came, a dream of hopes that never yet
Had flushed his cheek.   He dreamed a veiled maid
Sate near him, talking in low solemn tones.

Her voice was like the voice of his own soul
Heard in the calm of thought ; its music long,
Like woven sounds of streams and breezes, held
His inmost sense suspended in its web
Of many-coloured woof and shifting hues.
Knowledge and truth and virtue were her theme,
And lofty hopes of divine liberty,
Thoughts the most dear to him, and poesy,
Herself a poet.   Soon the solemn mood
Of her pure mind kindled through all her frame
A permeating fire : wild numbers then
She raised, with voice stifled in tremulous sobs
Subdued by its own pathos : her fair hands
Were bare alone, sweeping from some strange harp
Strange symphony, and in their branching veins
The eloquent blood told an ineffable tale.
The beating of her heart was heard to fill
The pauses of her music, and her breath
Tumultuously accorded with those fits
Of intermitted song.   Sudden she rose,
As if her heart impatiently endured
Its bursting burthen : at the sound he turned,
And saw by the warm light of their own life
Her glowing limbs beneath the sinuous veil
Of woven wind, her outspread arms now bare,
Her dark locks floating in the breath of night,
Her beamy bending eyes, her parted lips
Outstretched, and pale, and quivering eagerly.
His strong heart sunk and sickened with excess
Of love.   He reared his shuddering limbs and quelled
His gasping breath, and spread his arms to meet
Her panting bosom :—she drew back awhile,
Then, yielding to the irresistible joy,
With frantic gesture and short breathless cry
Folded his frame in her dissolving arms.
Now blackness veiled his dizzy eyes, and night
Involved and swallowed up the vision ; sleep,
Like a dark flood suspended in its course,
Rolled back its impulse on his vacant brain.

Roused by the shock, he started from his trance—
The cold white light of morning, the blue moon
Low in the west, the clear and garish hills,
The distinct valley and the vacant woods,
Spread round where he stood.—Whither have fled
The hues of heaven that canopied his bower
Of yesternight ?   The sounds that soothed his sleep,
The mystery and the majesty of earth,
The joy, the exultation ?   His wan eyes
Gaze on the empty scene as vacantly
As ocean's moon looks on the moon in heaven.
The spirit of sweet human love has sent
A vision to the sleep of him who spurned
Her choicest gifts.   He eagerly pursues
Beyond the realms of dream that fleeting shade ;
He overleaps the bounds.   Alas ! alas !
Were limbs and breath and being intertwined
Thus treacherously ?   Lost, lost, for ever lost,

In the wide pathless desert of dim sleep,
That beautiful shape ! does the dark gate of death
Conduct to thy mysterious paradise,
O Sleep ?   Does the bright arch of rainbow clouds,
And pendent mountains seen in the calm lake,
Lead only to a black and watery depth,
While death's blue vault with loathliest vapours hung,
Where every shade which the foul grave exhales
Hides its dead eye from the detested day,
Conduct, O Sleep, to thy delightful realms ?
This doubt with sudden tide flowed on his heart,
The insatiate hope which it awakened, stung
His brain even like despair.

                              While day-light held
The sky, the Poet kept mute conference
With his still soul.   At night the passion came,
Like the fierce fiend of a distempered dream,
And shook him from his rest, and led him forth
Into the darkness.—As an eagle grasped
In folds of the green serpent, feels her breast
Burn with the poison, and precipitates
Through night and day, tempest, and calm, and cloud,
Frantic with dizzying anguish, her blind flight
O'er the wide aëry wilderness : thus driven
By the bright shadow of that lovely dream,
Beneath the cold glare of the desolate night,
Through tangled swamps and deep precipitous dells,
Startling with careless step the moon light snake,
He fled.—Red morning dawned upon his flight,
Shedding the mockery of its vital hues
Upon his cheek of death.   He wandered on
Till vast Aornos seen from Petra's steep
Hung o'er the low horizon like a cloud ;
Through Balk, and where the desolated tombs
Of Parthian kings scatter to every wind
Their wasting dust, wildly he wandered on.
Day after day, a weary waste of hours,
Bearing within his life the brooding care
That ever fed on its decaying flame.
And now his limbs were lean ; his scattered hair,
Sered by the autumn of strange suffering,
Sung dirges in the wind ; his listless hand
Hung like dead bone within its withered skin ;
Life, and the lustre that consumed it, shone
As in a furnace burning secretly
From his dark eyes alone.   The cottagers,
Who ministered with human charity
His human wants, beheld with wondering awe
Their fleeting visitant.   The mountaineer,
Encountering on some dizzy precipice
That spectral form, deemed that the Spirit of wind
With lightning eyes, and eager breath, and feet
Disturbing not the drifted snow, had paused
In his career.   The infant would conceal
His troubled visage in his mother's robe
In terror at the glare of those wild eyes,
To remember their strange light in many a dream

Of after-times : but youthful maidens taught
By nature, would interpret half the woe
That wasted him, would call him with false names
Brother and friend, would press his pallid hand
At parting, and watch, dim through tears, the path
Of his departure from their father's door.

At length upon the lone Chorasmian shore
He paused, a wide and melancholy waste
Of putrid marshes—a strong impulse urged
His steps to the sea shore. A swan was there
Beside a sluggish stream among the reeds.
It rose as he approached, and with strong wings
Scaling the upward sky, bent its bright course
High over the immeasurable main.
His eyes pursued its flight.—" Thou hast a home,
Beautiful bird, thou voyagest to thine home,
Where thy sweet mate will twine her downy neck
With thine, and welcome thy return with eyes
Bright in the lustre of their own fond joy.
And what am I that I should linger here
With voice far sweeter than thy dying notes,
Spirit more vast than thine, frame more attuned
To beauty, wasting these surpassing powers
In the deaf air, to the blind earth, and heaven
That echoes not my thoughts ?" A gloomy smile
Of desperate hope wrinkled his quivering lips.
For sleep, he knew, kept most relentlessly
Its precious charge, and silent death exposed,
Faithless perhaps as sleep, a shadowy lure,
With doubtful smile mocking its own strange charms.

Startled by his own thoughts he looked around.
There was no fair fiend near him, not a sight
Or sound of awe but in his own deep mind.
A little shallop floating near the shore
Caught the impatient wandering of his gaze.
It had been long abandoned, for its sides
Gaped wide with many a rift, and its frail joints
Swayed with the undulations of the tide.
A restless impulse urged him to embark,
And meet lone Death on the drear ocean's waste ;
For well he knew that mighty Shadow loves
The slimy caverns of the populous deep.

The day was fair and sunny, sea and sky
Drank its inspiring radiance, and the wind
Swept strongly from the shore, blackening the waves.
Following his eager soul, the wanderer
Leaped in the boat, he spread his cloak aloft
On the bare mast, and took his lonely seat,
And felt the boat speed o'er the tranquil sea
Like a torn cloud before the hurricane.

As one that in a silver vision floats
Obedient to the sweep of odorous winds
Upon resplendent clouds, so rapidly
Along the dark and ruffled waters fled

The straining boat.—A whirlwind swept it on,
With fierce gusts and precipitating force,
Through the white ridges of the chafed sea.
The waves arose.   Higher and higher still
Their fierce necks writhed beneath the tempest's scourge,
Like serpents struggling in a vulture's grasp.
Calm and rejoicing in the fearful war
Of wave running on wave, and blast on blast
Descending, and black flood on whirlpool driven
With dark obliterating course, he sate :
As if their genii were the ministers
Appointed to conduct him to the light
Of those beloved eyes, the Poet sate
Holding the steady helm.   Evening came on,
The beams of sunset hung their rainbow hues
High 'mid the shifting domes of sheeted spray
That canopied his path o'er the waste deep ;
Twilight, ascending slowly from the east,
Entwined in duskier wreaths her braided locks
O'er the fair front and radiant eyes of day ;
Night followed, clad with stars.   On every side
More horribly the multitudinous streams
Of ocean's mountainous waste to mutual war
Rushed in dark tumult thundering, as to mock
The calm and spangled sky.   The little boat
Still fled before the storm ; still fled, like foam
Down the steep cataract of a wintry river ;
Now pausing on the edge of the riven wave ;
Now leaving far behind the bursting mass
That fell, convulsing ocean.   Safely fled—
As if that frail and wasted human form
Had been an elemental god.

                              At midnight
The moon arose : and lo ! the ethereal cliffs
Of Caucasus, whose icy summits shone
Among the stars like sunlight, and around
Whose caverned base the whirlpools and the waves
Bursting and eddying irresistibly
Rage and resound for ever.—Who shall save ?
The boat fled on,—the boiling torrent drove,—
The crags closed round with black and jagged arms,
The shattered mountain overhung the sea,
And faster still, beyond all human speed,
Suspended on the sweep of the smooth wave,
The little boat was driven.   A cavern there
Yawned, and amid its slant and winding depths
Ingulfed the rushing sea.   The boat fled on
With unrelaxing speed.   "Vision and Love !"
The Poet cried aloud, "I have beheld
The path of thy departure.   Sleep and death
Shall not divide us long."

                              The boat pursued
The windings of the cavern.—Daylight shone
At length upon that gloomy river's flow ;
Now, where the fiercest war among the waves
Is calm, on the unfathomable stream
The boat moved slowly.   Where the mountain riven

Exposed those black depths to the azure sky,
Ere yet the flood's enormous volume fell
Even to the base of Caucasus, with sound
That shook the everlasting rocks, the mass
Filled with one whirlpool all that ample chasm;
Stair above stair the eddying waters rose,
Circling immeasurably fast, and laved
With alternating dash the gnarled roots
Of mighty trees, that stretched their giant arms
In darkness over it. I' the midst was left,
Reflecting, yet distorting every cloud,
A pool of treacherous and tremendous calm.
Seized by the sway of the ascending stream,
With dizzy swiftness, round, and round, and round,
Ridge after ridge the straining boat arose,
Till on the verge of the extremest curve,
Where through an opening of the rocky bank,
The waters overflow, and a smooth spot
Of glassy quiet mid those battling tides
Is left, the boat paused shuddering. Shall it sink
Down the abyss? Shall the reverting stress
Of that resistless gulf embosom it?
Now shall it fall? A wandering stream of wind,
Breathed from the west, has caught the expanded sail,
And lo! with gentle motion between banks
Of mossy slope, and on a placid stream,
Beneath a woven grove, it sails, and, hark!
The ghastly torrent mingles its far roar
With the breeze murmuring in the musical woods.
Where the embowering trees recede and leave
A little space of green expanse, the cove
Is closed by meeting banks, whose yellow flowers
For ever gaze on their own drooping eyes,
Reflected in the crystal calm. The wave
Of the boat's motion marred their pensive task,
Which naught but vagrant bird, or wanton wind,
Or falling spear-grass, or their own decay
Had e'er disturbed before. The Poet longed
To deck with their bright hues his withered hair,
But on his heart its solitude returned,
And he forebore. Not the strong impulse hid
In those flushed cheeks, bent eyes, and shadowy frame,
Had yet performed its ministry : it hung
Upon his life, as lightning in a cloud
Gleams, hovering ere it vanish, ere the floods
Of night close over it.

                        The noonday sun
Now shone upon the forest, one vast mass
Of mingling shade, whose brown magnificence
A narrow vale embosoms. There, huge caves,
Scooped in the dark base of those aëry rocks
Mocking its moans, respond and roar for ever.
The meeting boughs and implicated leaves
Wove twilight o'er the Poet's path, as led
By love, or dream, or god, or mightier Death,
He sought in Nature's dearest haunt, some bank,
Her cradle, and his sepulchre. More dark

And dark the shades accumulate—the oak,
Expanding its immeasurable arms,
Embraces the light beech.   The pyramids
Of the tall cedar overarching, frame
Most solemn domes within, and far below,
Like clouds suspended in an emerald sky,
The ash and the acacia floating hang
Tremulous and pale.   Like restless serpents, clothed
In rainbow and in fire, the parasites,
Starred with ten thousand blossoms, flow around
The gray trunks, and as gamesome infants' eyes,
With gentle meanings, and most innocent wiles,
Fold their beams round the heart of those that love,
These twine their tendrils with the wedded boughs,
Uniting their close union ; the woven leaves
Make network of the dark blue light of day,
And the night's noontide clearness, mutable
As shapes in the weird clouds.   Soft mossy lawns
Beneath these canopies extend their swells,
Fragrant with perfumed herbs, and eyed with blooms
Minute yet beautiful.   One darkest glen
Sends from its woods of musk-rose, twined with jasmine,
A soul-dissolving odour, to invite
To some more lovely mystery.   Through the dell,
Silence and Twilight here, twin-sisters, keep
Their noonday watch, and sail among the shades
Like vaporous shapes half seen ; beyond, a well,
Dark, gleaming, and of most translucent wave,
Images all the woven boughs above,
And each depending leaf, and every speck
Of azure sky, darting between their chasms ;
Nor aught else in the liquid mirror laves
Its portraiture, but some inconstant star
Between one foliaged lattice twinkling fair,
Or, painted bird, sleeping beneath the moon,
Or gorgeous insect floating motionless,
Unconscious of the day, ere yet his wings
Have spread their glories to the gaze of noon.

Hither the Poet came.   His eyes beheld
Their own wan light through the reflected lines
Of his thin hair, distinct in the dark depth
Of that still fountain ; as the human heart,
Gazing in dreams over the gloomy grave,
Sees its own treacherous likeness there.   He heard
The motion of the leaves, the grass that sprung
Startled and glanced and trembled even to feel
An unaccustomed presence, and the sound
Of the sweet brook that from the secret springs
Of that dark fountain rose.   A Spirit seemed
To stand beside him—clothed in no bright robes
Of shadowy silver or enshrining light,
Borrowed from aught the visible world affords
Of grace, or majesty, or mystery ;—
But, undulating woods, and silent well,
And rippling rivulet, and evening gloom
Now deepening the dark shades, for speech assuming
Held commune with him, as if he and it

Were all that was,—only . . . when his regard
Was raised by intense pensiveness . . . two eyes,
Two starry eyes, hung in the gloom of thought,
And seemed with their serene and azure smiles
To beckon him.

    Obedient to the light
That shone within his soul, he went, pursuing
The windings of the dell.—The rivulet
Wanton and wild, through many a green ravine
Beneath the forest flowed. Sometimes it fell
Among the moss with hollow harmony
Dark and profound. Now on the polished stones
It danced ; like childhood laughing as it went :
Then through the plain in tranquil wanderings crept,
Reflecting every herb and drooping bud
That overhung its quietness.—"O stream !
Whose source is inaccessibly profound,
Whither do thy mysterious waters tend ?
Thou imagest my life. Thy darksome stillness,
Thy dazzling waves, thy loud and hollow gulfs,
Thy searchless fountain and invisible course
Have each their type in me : and the wide sky,
And measureless ocean may declare as soon
What oozy cavern or what wandering cloud
Contains thy waters, as the universe
Tell where these living thoughts reside, when stretched
Upon thy flowers my bloodless limbs shall waste
I' the passing wind !"

    Beside the glassy shore
Of the small stream he went ; he did impress
On the green moss his tremulous step, that caught
Strong shuddering from his burning limbs. As one
Roused by some joyous madness from the couch
Of fever, he did move ; yet, not like him,
Forgetful of the grave, where, when the flame
Of his frail exultation shall be spent,
He must descend. With rapid steps he went
Beneath the shade of trees, beside the flow
Of the wild babbling rivulet ; and now
The forest's solemn canopies were changed
For the uniform and lightsome evening sky.
Gray rocks did peep from the spare moss, and stemmed
The struggling brook : tall spires of windlestrae
Threw their thin shadows down the rugged slope,
And naught but gnarled roots of ancient pines,
Branchless and blasted, clenched with grasping roots
The unwilling soil. A gradual change was here,
Yet ghastly. For, as fast years flow away,
The smooth brow gathers, and the hair grows thin
And white ; and where irradiate dewy eyes
Had shone, gleam stony orbs : so from his steps
Bright flowers departed, and the beautiful shade
Of the green groves, with all their odorous winds
And musical motions. Calm, he still pursued
The stream, that with a larger volume now
Rolled through the labyrinthine dell ; and there

Fretted a path through its descending curves
With its wintry speed.   On every side now rose
Rocks, which in unimaginable forms
Lifted their black and barren pinnacles
In the light of evening, and its precipice
Obscuring the ravine, disclosed above,
'Mid toppling stones, black gulfs, and yawning caves
Whose windings gave ten thousand various tongues
To the loud stream.   Lo ! Where the pass expands
Its stony jaws, the abrupt mountain breaks,
And seems, with its accumulated crags,
To overhang the world : for wide expand
Beneath the wan stars and descending moon
Islanded seas, blue mountains, mighty streams,
Dim tracts and vast, robed in the lustrous gloom
Of leaden-coloured even, and fiery hills
Mingling their flames with twilight, on the verge
Of the remote horizon.   The near scene
In naked and severe simplicity,
Made contrast with the universe.   A pine,
Rock-rooted, stretched athwart the vacancy
Its swinging boughs, to each inconstant blast
Yielding one only response at each pause,
In most familiar cadence, with the howl
The thunder and the hiss of homeless streams
Mingling its solemn song, whilst the broad river,
Foaming and hurrying o'er its rugged path,
Fell into that immeasurable void
Scattering its waters to the passing winds.

  Yet the gray precipice, and solemn pine
And torrent, were not all ;—one silent nook
Was there.   Even on the edge of that vast mountain
Upheld by knotty roots and fallen rocks,
It overlooked in its serenity
The dark earth, and the bending vault of stars.
It was a tranquil spot, that seemed to smile
Even in the lap of horror.   Ivy clasped
The fissured stones with its entwining arms,
And did embower with leaves for ever green,
And berries dark, the smooth and even space
Of its inviolated floor ; and here
  he children of the autumnal whirlwind bore,
In wanton sport, those bright leaves, whose decay,
Red, yellow, or ethereally pale,
Rival the pride of summer.   'Tis the haunt
Of every gentle wind, whose breath can teach
The wilds to love tranquillity.   One step,
One human step alone, has ever broken
The stillness of its solitude :—one voice
Alone inspired its echoes ; even that voice
Which hither came, floating among the winds.
And led the loveliest among human forms
To make their wild haunts the depository
Of all the grace and beauty that endued
Its motions, render up its majesty,
Scatter its music on the unfeeling storm,
And to the damp leaves and blue cavern mould.

Nurses of rainbow flowers and branching moss,
Commit the colours of that varying cheek,
That snowy breast, those dark and drooping eyes.

    The dim and horned moon hung low, and poured
A sea of lustre on the horizon's verge
That overflowed its mountains. Yellow mist
Filled the unbounded atmosphere, and drank
Wan moonlight even to fulness : not a star
Shone, not a sound was heard ; the very winds,
Danger's grim playmates, on that precipice
Slept, clasped in his embrace.—O, storm of death !
Whose sightless speed divides this sullen night :
And thou, colossal Skeleton, that, still
Guiding its irresistible career
In thy devastating omnipotence,
Art king of this frail world, from the red field
Of slaughter, from the reeking hospital,
The patriot's sacred couch, the snowy bed
Of innocence, the scaffold and the throne,
A mighty voice invokes thee. Ruin calls
His brother Death. A rare and regal prey
He hath prepared, prowling around the world ;
Glutted with which thou mayst repose, and men
Go to their graves like flowers or creeping worms,
Nor ever more offer at thy dark shrine
The unheeded tribute of a broken heart.

    When on the threshold of the green recess
The wander's footsteps fell, he knew that death
Was on him. Yet a little, ere it fled
Did he resign his high and holy soul
To images of the majestic past,
That paused within his passive being now,
Like winds that bear sweet music, when they breathe
Through some dim latticed chamber. He did place
His pale lean hand upon the rugged trunk
Of the old pine. Upon an ivied stone
Reclined his languid head ; his limbs did rest,
Diffused and motionless, on the smooth brink
Of that obscurest chasm ;—and thus he lay,
Surrendering to their final impulses
The hovering powers of life. Hope and Despair,
The torturers, slept ; no mortal pain or fear
Marred his repose, the influxes of sense,
And his own being unalloyed by pain,
Yet feebler and more feeble, calmly fed
The stream of thought, till he lay breathing there
At peace, and faintly smiling :—his last sight
Was the great moon, which o'er the western line
Of the wide world her mighty horn suspended,
With whose dun beams inwoven darkness seemed
To mingle. Now upon the jagged hills
It rests, and still as the divided frame
Of the vast meteor sunk, the Poet's blood,
That ever beat in mystic sympathy
With nature's ebb and flow, grew feebler still :
And when two lessening points of light alone

Gleamed through the darkness, the alternate gasp
Of his faint respiration scarce did stir
The stagnate night :—till the minutest ray
Was quenched, the pulse yet lingered in his heart,
It paused—it fluttered. But when heaven remained
Utterly black, the murky shades involved
An image, silent, cold, and motionless,
As their own voiceless earth and vacant air.
Even as a vapour fed with golden beams
That ministered on sunlight, ere the west
Eclipses it, was now that wondrous frame—
No sense, no motion, no divinity—
A fragile lute, on whose harmonious strings
The breath of heaven did wander—a bright stream
Once fed with many-voicèd waves—a dream
Of youth, which night and time have quenched for ever
Still, dark, and dry, and unremembered now.

O, for Medea's wondrous alchymy,
Which wheresoe'er it fell made the earth gleam
With bright flowers, and the wintry boughs exhale
From vernal blooms fresh fragrance ! O, that God,
Profuse of poisons, would concede the chalice
Which but one living man has drained, who now,
Vessel of deathless wrath, a slave that feels
No proud exemption in the blighting curse
He bears, over the world wanders for ever,
Lone as incarnate death ! O, that the dream
Of dark magician in his visioned cave,
Raking the cinders of a crucible
For life and power, even when his feeble hand
Shakes in its last decay, were the true law
Of this so lovely world ! But thou art fled
Like some frail exhalation, which the dawn
Robes in its golden beams,—ah ! thou hast fled !
The brave, the gentle, and the beautiful,
The child of grace and genius. Heartless things
Are done and said i' the world, and many worms
And beasts and men live on, and mighty Earth
From sea and mountain, city and wilderness,
In vesper low or joyous orison,
Lifts still its solemn voice :—but thou art fled—
Thou canst no longer know or love the shapes
Of this phantasmal scene, who have to thee
Been purest ministers, who are, alas !
Now thou art not. Upon those pallid lips
So sweet even in their silence, on those eyes
That image sleep in death, upon that form
Yet safe from the worm's outrage, let no tear
Be shed—not even in thought. Nor, when those hues
Are gone, and those divinest lineaments,
Worn by the senseless wind, shall live alone
In the frail pauses of this simple strain,
Let not high verse, mourning the memory
Of that which is no more, or painting's woe
Or sculpture, speak in feeble imagery
Their own cold powers. Art and eloquence,
And all the shows o' the world are frail and vain

To weep a loss that turns their light to shade.
It is a woe too ' deep for tears,' when all
Is reft at once, when some surpassing Spirit,
Whose light adorned the world around it, leaves
Those who remain behind, nor sobs nor groans,
The passionate tumult of a clinging hope :
But pale despair and cold tranquillity,
Nature's vast frame, the web of human things,
Birth and the grave. that are not as they were.

THE REVOLT OF ISLAM.

Dedication.

> "There is no danger to a man, that knows
> What life and death is: there's not any law
> Exceeds his knowledge; neither is it lawful
> That he should stoop to any other law."—CHAPMAN.

TO MARY ——.*

I.

So now my summer task is ended, Mary,
And I return to thee, mine own heart's home;
As to his Queen some victor Knight of Faëry,
Earning bright spoils for her enchanted dome;
Nor thou disdain, that ere my fame become
A star among the stars of mortal night,
If it indeed may cleave its natal gloom,
Its doubtful promise thus I would unite
With thy belovèd name, thou Child of love and light.

II.

The toil which stole from thee so many an hour,
Is ended,—and the fruit is at thy feet!
No longer where the woods to frame a bower
With interlacèd branches mix and meet,
Or where with sound like many voices sweet,
Waterfalls leap among wild islands green,
Which framed for my lone boat a lone retreat
Of moss-grown trees and weeds, shall I be seen:
But beside thee, where still my heart has ever been.

III.

Thoughts of great deeds were mine, dear Friend, when first
The clouds which wrap this world from youth did pass.
I do remember well the hour which burst
My spirit's sleep: a fresh May-dawn it was,
When I walked forth upon the glittering grass,
And wept, I knew not why; until there rose
From the near schoolroom, voices, that, alas!
Were but one echo from a world of woes—
The harsh and grating strife of tyrants and of foes.

---

* Mrs. Shelley.

IV.

And then I clasped my hands and looked around—
But none was near to mock my streaming eyes,
Which poured their warm drops on the sunny ground—
So without shame, I spake :—" I will be wise,
And just, and free, and mild, if in me lies
Such power, for I grow weary to behold
The selfish and the strong still tyrannize
Without reproach or check."   I then controlled
My tears, my heart grew calm, and I was meek and bold.

V.

And from that hour did I with earnest thought
Heap knowledge from forbidden mines of lore,
Yet nothing that my tyrants knew or taught
I cared to learn, but from that secret store
Wrought linked armour for my soul, before
It might walk forth to war among mankind ;
Thus power and hope were strengthened more and more
Within me, till there came upon my mind
A sense of loneliness, a thirst with which I pined.

VI.

Alas, that love should be a blight and snare
To those who seek all sympathies in one !—
Such once I sought in vain ; then black despair,
The shadow of a starless night, was thrown
Over the world in which I moved alone :—
Yet never found I one not false to me,
Hard hearts, and cold, like weights of icy stone
Which crushed and withered mine, that could not be
Aught but a lifeless clog, until revived by thee.

VII.

Thou Friend, whose presence on my wintry heart
Fell, like bright Spring upon some herbless plain ;
How beautiful and calm and free thou wert
In thy young wisdom, when the mortal chain
Of Custom thou didst burst and rend in twain,
And walked as free as light the clouds among,
Which many an envious slave then breathed in vain
From his dim dungeon, and my spirit sprung
To meet thee from the woes which had begirt it long.

VIII.

No more alone through the world's wilderness,
Although I trod the paths of high intent,
I journeyed now : no more companionless,
Where solitude is like despair, I went.—
There is the wisdom of a stern content
When Poverty can blight the just and good,
When Infamy dares mock the innocent,
And cherished friends turn with the multitude
To trample : this was ours, and we unshaken stood !

IX.

Now has descended a serener hour,
And with inconstant fortune, friends return ;
Though suffering leaves the knowledge and the power
Which says :—Let scorn be not repaid with scorn.
And from thy side two gentle babes are born
To fill our home with smiles, and thus are we
Most fortunate beneath life's beaming morn ;
And these delights, and thou, have been to me
The parents of the Song I consecrate to thee.

X.

Is it, that now my inexperienced fingers
But strike the prelude of a loftier strain?
Or, must the lyre on which my spirit lingers
Soon pause in silence, ne'er to sound again,
Though it might shake the Anarch Custom's reign,
And charm the minds of men to Truth's own sway
Holier than was Amphion's?   I would fain
Reply in hope—but I am worn away,
And Death and Love are yet contending for their prey

XI.

And what art thou?   I know, but dare not speak :
Time may interpret to his silent years.
Yet in the paleness of thy thoughtful cheek,
And in the light thine ample forehead wears,
And in thy sweetest smiles, and in thy tears,
And in thy gentle speech, a prophecy
Is whispered, to subdue my fondest fears :
And through thine eyes, even in thy soul I see
A lamp of vestal fire burning internally.

XII.

They say that thou wert lovely from thy birth,
Of glorious parents, thou aspiring Child.
I wonder not—for One then left this earth
Whose life was like a setting planet mild.
Which clothed thee in the radiance undefiled
Of its departing glory ; still her fame
Shines on thee, through the tempests dark and wild
Which shake these latter days ; and thou canst claim
The shelter, from thy Sire, of an immortal name.

XIII.

One voice came forth from many a mighty spirit,
Which was the echo of three thousand years ;
And the tumultuous world stood mute to hear it,
As some lone man who in a desert hears
The music of his home :—unwonted fears
Fell on the pale oppressors of our race,
And Faith, and Custom, and low-thoughted cares,
Like thunder-stricken dragons, for a space
Left the torn human heart, their food and dwelling-place.

XIV.

Truth's deathless voice pauses among mankind !
If there must be no response to my cry—
If men must rise and stamp with fury blind
On his pure name who loves them,—thou and I,
Sweet friend ! can look from our tranquillity
Like lamps into the world's tempestuous night,—
Two tranquil stars, while clouds are passing by
Which wrap them from the foundering seaman's sight,
That burn from year to year with unextinguished light.

CANTO FIRST.

Οσαις δε βροτον εθνος αγλαιαις 'απτομεσθα,
Περαινει προς εσχατον
Πλοον· ναυσι δ' ουτε πεζοε ιων αν ευροις
Ες 'υπερβορεων αγωνα θαυματαν 'οδον.

PIND. *Pyth.* **x.**

I.

WHEN the last hope of trampled France had failed
Like a brief dream of unremaining glory,
From visions of despair I rose, and scaled
The peak of an aërial promontory,
Whose caverned base with the vexed surge was hoary ;
And saw the golden dawn break forth, and waken
Each cloud, and every wave :—but transitory
The calm : for sudden, the firm earth was shaken,
As if by the last wreck its frame were overtaken.

II.

So as I stood, one blast of muttering thunder
Burst in far peals along the waveless deep,
When, gathering fast, around, above and under,
Long trains of tremulous mist began to creep,
Until their complicating lines did steep
The orient sun in shadow :—not a sound
Was heard ; one horrible repose did keep
The forests and the floods, and all around.
Darkness more dread than night was poured upon the ground.

III.

Hark ! 'tis the rushing of a wind that sweeps
Earth and the ocean.   See ! the lightnings yawn
Deluging Heaven with fire, and the lashed deeps
Glitter and boil beneath : it rages on,
One mighty stream, whirlwind and waves upthrown,
Lightning, and hail, and darkness eddying by.
There is a pause—the sea-birds, that were gone
Into their caves to shriek, come forth, to spy
What calm has fallen on earth, what light is in the sky.

IV.

For, where the irresistible storm had cloven
That fearful darkness, the blue sky was seen

Fretted with many a fair cloud interwoven
Most delicately, and the ocean green,
Beneath that opening spot of blue serene,
Quivered like burning emerald : calm was spread
On all below ; but far on high, between
Earth and the upper air, the vast clouds fled,
Countless and swift as leaves on autumn's tempest shed

V.

For ever, as the war became more fierce
Between the whirlwinds and the rack on high,
That spot grew more serene ; blue light did pierce
The woof of those white clouds, which seemed to lie
Far, deep, and motionless ; while through the sky
The pallid semicircle of the moon
Past on, in slow and moving majesty ;
Its upper horn arrayed in mists, which soon
But slowly fled, like dew beneath the beams of noon.

VI.

I could not choose but gaze : a fascination
Dwelt in that moon, and sky, and clouds, which drew
My fancy thither, and in expectation
Of what I knew not, I remained :—the hue
Of the white moon, amid that heaven so blue,
Suddenly stained with shadow did appear ;
A speck, a cloud, a shape, approaching grew,
Like a great ship in the sun's sinking sphere
Beheld afar at sea, and swift it came anear.

VII.

Even like a bark, which from a chasm of mountains,
Dark, vast, and overhanging, on a river
Which there collects the strength of all its fountains,
Comes forth, whilst with the speed its frame doth quiver,
Sails, oars, and stream, tending to one endeavour ;
So, from that chasm of light a wingèd Form
On all the winds of heaven approaching ever
Floated, dilating as it came : the storm
Pursued it with fierce blasts, and lightnings swift and warm.

VIII.

A course precipitous, of dizzy speed,
Suspending thought and breath ; a monstrous sight !
For in the air do I behold indeed
An Eagle and a Serpent wreathed in fight :—
And now relaxing its impetuous flight,
Before the aërial rock on which I stood,
The Eagle, hovering, wheeled to left and right,
And hung with lingering wings over the flood,
And startled with its yells the wide air's solitude.

IX.

A shaft of light upon its wings descended,
And every golden feather gleamed therein—

Feather and scale inextricably blended.
The Serpent's mailed and many coloured skin
Shone through the plumes its coils were twined within
By many a swollen and knotted fold, and high
And far, the neck receding lithe and thin,
Sustained a crested head, which warily
Shifted and glanced before the Eagle's steadfast eye.

X.

Around, around, in ceaseless circles wheeling
With clang of wings and scream, the Eagle sailed
Incessantly—sometimes on high concealing
Its lessening orbs, sometimes as if it failed,
Drooped through the air ; and still it shrieked and wailed,
And casting back its eager head, with beak
And talon unremittingly assailed
The wreathed Serpent, who did ever seek
Upon his enemy's heart a mortal wound to wreak.

XI.

What life what power was kindled and arose
Within the sphere of that appalling fray !
For, from the encounter of those wondrous foes,
A vapour like the sea's suspended spray
Hung gathered : in the void air, far away,
Floated the shattered plumes ; bright scales did leap
Where'er the Eagle's talons made their way,
Like sparks into the darkness ; as they sweep,
Blood stains the snowy foam of the tumultuous deep.

XII.

Swift chances in that combat—many a check,
And many a change, a dark and wild turmoil ;
Sometimes the Snake around his enemy's neck
Locked in stiff rings his adamantine coil,
Until the Eagle, faint with pain and toil,
Remitted his strong flight, and near the sea
Languidly fluttered, hopeless so to foil
His adversary, who then reared on high
His red and burning crest, radiant with victory.

XIII.

Then on the white edge of the bursting surge,
Where they had sank together, would the Snake
Relax his suffocating grasp, and scourge
The wind with his wild writhings ; for to break
That chain of torment, the vast bird would shake
The strength of his unconquerable wings
As in despair, and with his sinewy neck,
Dissolve in sudden shock those linked rings,
Then soar—as swift as smoke from a volcano springs.

XIV.

Wile baffled wile, and strength encountered strength,
Thus long, but unprevailing :—the event

Of that portentous fight appeared at length :
Until the lamp of day was almost spent
It had endured, when lifeless, stark, and rent,
Hung high that mighty Serpent, and at last
Fell to the sea, while o'er the continent,
With clang of wings and scream the Eagle past,
Heavily borne away on the exhausted blast.

XV.

And with it fled the tempest, so that ocean
And earth and sky shone through the atmosphere—
Only, 'twas strange to see the red commotion
Of waves like mountains o'er the sinking sphere
Of sun-set sweep, and their fierce roar to hear
Amid the calm : down the steep path I wound
To the sea-shore—the evening was most clear
And beautiful, and there the sea I found
Calm as a cradled child in dreamless slumber bound.

XVI.

There was a Woman, beautiful as morning,
Sitting beneath the rocks, upon the sand
Of the waste sea—fair as one flower adorning
An icy wilderness—each delicate hand
Lay crossed upon her bosom, and the band
Of her dark hair had fallen, and so she sate
Looking upon the waves ; on the bare strand
Upon the sea-mark a small boat did wait,
Fair as herself, like Love by Hope left desolate.

XVII.

It seemed that this fair Shape had looked upon
That unimaginable fight, and now
That her sweet eyes were weary of the sun,
As brightly it illustrated her woe ;
For in the tears which silently to flow
Paused not, its lustre hung : she watching aye
The foam-wreathes which the faint tide wove below
Upon the spangled sands, groaned heavily,
And after every groan looked up over the sea.

XVIII.

And when she saw me wounded Serpent make
His path between the waves, her lips grew pale,
Parted, and quivered ; the tears ceased to break
From her immovable eyes ; no voice of wail
Escaped her ; but she rose, and on the gale
Loosening her star-bright robe and shadowy hair
Poured forth her voice ; the caverns of the vale
That opened to the ocean, caught it there,
And filled with silver sounds the overflowing air.

XIX.

She spake in language whose strange melody
Might not belong to earth.   I heard, alone,

What made its music more melodious be,
The pity and the love of every tone ;
But to the Snake those accents sweet were known
His native tongue and hers ; nor did he beat
The hoar spray idly then, but winding on
Through the green shadows of the waves that meet
Near to the shore, did pause beside her snowy feet.

XX.

Then on the sands the Woman sate again,
And wept and clasped her hands, and all between,
Renewed the unintelligible strain
Of her melodious voice and eloquent mien ;
And she unveiled her bosom, and the green
And glancing shadows of the sea did play
O'er its marmoreal depth :—one moment seen,
For ere the next, the Serpent did obey
Her voice, and, coiled in rest in her embrace it lay.

XXI.

Then she arose, and smiled on me with eyes
Serene yet sorrowing, like that planet fair,
While yet the daylight lingereth in the skies
Which cleaves with arrowy beams the dark-red air,
And said : To grieve is wise, but the despair
Was weak and vain which led thee here from sleep :
This shalt thou know, and more, if thou dost dare
With me and with this Serpent, o'er the deep,
A voyage divine and strange, companionship to keep.

XXII.

Her voice was like the wildest, saddest tone,
Yet sweet of some loved voice heard long ago.
I wept.   Shall this fair woman all alone,
Over the sea with that fierce Serpent go ?
His head is on her heart, and who can know
How soon he may devour his feeble prey ?—
Such were my thoughts, when the tide 'gan to flow ;
And that strange boat, like the moon's shade did sway
Amid reflected stars that in the waters lay.

XXIII.

A boat of rare device, which had no sail
But its own curvèd prow of thin moonstone,
Wrought like a web of texture fine and frail,
To catch those gentlest winds which are not known
To breathe, but by the steady speed alone
With which it cleaves the sparkling sea ; and now
We are embarked, the mountains hang and frown
Over the starry deep that gleams below
A vast and dim expanse, as o'er the waves we go.

XXIV.

And as we sailed, a strange and awful tale
That Woman told, like such mysterious dream

As makes the slumberer's cheek with wonder pale !
'Twas midnight, and around, a shoreless stream,
Wide ocean rolled, when that majestic theme
Shrined in her heart found utterance, and she bent
Her looks on mine ; those eyes a kindling beam
Of love divine into my spirit sent,
And ere her lips could move, made the air eloquent.

XXV.

Speak not to me, but hear ! much shalt thou learn,
Much must remain unthought, and more untold,
In the dark Future's ever-flowing urn :
Know then, that from the depth of ages old,
Two Powers o'er mortal things dominion hold
Ruling the world with a divided lot,
Immortal, all-pervading, manifold,
Twin Genii, equal Gods—when life and thought
Sprang forth, they burst the womb of inessential Naught.

XXVI.

The earliest dweller of the world alone,
Stood on the verge of chaos : Lo ! afar
O'er the wide wild abyss two meteors shone,
Sprung from the depth of its tempestuous jar :
A blood-red Comet and the Morning Star
Mingling their beams in combat—as he stood,
All thoughts within his mind waged mutual war,
In dreadful sympathy—when to the flood
That fair Star fell, he turned and shed his brother's blood.

XXVII.

Thus evil triumphed, and the Spirit of evil,
One Power of many shapes which none may know,
One Shape of many names ; the Fiend did revel
In victory, reigning o'er a world of woe,
For the new race of man went to and fro,
Famished and homeless, loathed and loathing, wild,
And hating good—for his immortal foe,
He changed from starry shape, beauteous and mild,
To a dire Snake, with man and beast unreconciled.

XXVIII.

The darkness lingering o'er the dawn of things,
Was Evil's breath and life : this made him strong
To soar aloft with overshadowing wings ;
And the great Spirit of Good did creep among
The nations of mankind, and every tongue
Cursed, and blasphemed him as he passed ; for none
Knew good from evil, though their names were hung
In mockery o'er the fane where many a groan,
As King, and Lord, and God, the conquering Fiend did own.

XXIX.

The fiend, whose name was Legion ; Death, Decay,
Earthquake and Blight, and Want, and Madness pale,

Wingèd and wan diseases, an array
Numerous as leaves that strew the autumnal gale ;
Poison, a snake in flowers, beneath the veil
Of food and mirth, hiding his mortal head ;
And, without whom all these might naught avail,
Fear, Hatred, Faith, and Tyranny, who spread
Those subtle nets which snare the living and the dead.

XXX.

His spirit is their power, and they his slaves
In air, and light, and thought, and language dwell ;
And keep their state from palaces to graves,
In all resorts of men—invisible,
But, when in ebon mirror, Nightmare fell
To tyrant or impostor bids them rise,
Black-wingèd demon forms—whom, from the hell,
His reign and dwelling beneath nether skies,
He loosens to their dark and blasting ministries.

XXXI.

In the world's youth his empire was as firm
As its foundations—soon the Spirit of Good,
Though in the likeness of a loathsome worm,
Sprang from the billows of the formless flood,
Which shrank and fled ; and with that fiend of blood
Renewed the doubtful war—thrones then first shook,
And earth's immense and trampled multitude,
In hope on their own powers began to look,
And Fear, the demon pale, his sanguine shrine forsook.

XXXII.

Then Greece arose, and to its bards and sages,
In dream, the golden pinioned Genii came,
Even where they slept amid the night of ages,
Steeping their hearts in the divinest flame,
Which thy breath kindled, Power of holiest name !
And oft in cycles since, when darkness gave
New weapons to thy foe, their sunlike fame
Upon the combat shone—a light to save,
Like Paradise spread forth beyond the shadowy grave.

XXXIII.

Such is this conflict—when mankind doth strive
With its oppressors in a strife of blood,
Or when free thoughts, like lightnings are alive ;
And in each bosom of the multitude
Justice and truth, with custom's hydra brood,
Wage silent war ;—when priests and kings dissemble
In smiles or frowns their fierce disquietude,
When round pure hearts, a host of hopes assemble,
The Snake and Eagle meet—the world's foundations tremble!

XXXIV.

Thou hast beheld that fight—when to thy home
Thou dost return, steep not its hearth in tears ;

Though thou may'st hear that earth is now become
The tyrant's garbage, which to his compeers,
The vile reward of their dishonoured years,
He will dividing give.—The victor Fiend
Omnipotent of yore, now quails, and fears
His triumph dearly won, which soon will lend
An impulse swift and sure to his approaching end.

XXXV.

List, stranger list, mine is an human form,
Like that thou wearest—touch me—shrink not now !
My hand thou feel'st is not a ghost's, but warm
With human blood.—'Twas many years ago,
Since first my thirsting soul aspired to know
The secrets of this wondrous world, when deep
My heart was pierced with sympathy, for woe
Which could not be mine own—and thought did keep
In dream, unnatural watch beside an infant's sleep.

XXXVI.

Woe could not be mine own, since far from men
I dwelt, a free and happy orphan child,
By the sea-shore, in a deep mountain glen ;
And near the waves, and through the forests wild
I roamed, to storm and darkness reconciled :
For I was calm while tempest shook the sky :
But when the breathless heavens in beauty smiled,
I wept, sweet tears, yet too tumultuously
For peace, and clasped my hands aloft in ecstasy.

XXXVII.

These were forebodings of my fate—before
A woman's heart beat in my virgin breast,
It had been nurtured in divinest lore :
A dying poet gave me books, and blest
With wild but holy talk the sweet unrest
In which I watched him as he died away—
A youth with hoary hair—a fleeting guest
Of our lone mountains—and this lore did sway
My spirit like a storm, contending there alway.

XXXVIII.

Thus the dark tale which history doth unfold,
I knew, but not, methinks, as others know,
For they weep not ; and Wisdom had unrolled
The clouds which hide the gulf of mortal woe :
To few can she that warning vision show,
For I loved all things with intense devotion ;
So that when Hope's deep source in fullest flow,
Like earthquake did uplift the stagnant ocean
Of human thoughts—mine shook beneath the wide emotion.

XXXIX.

When first the living blood through all these veins
Kindled a thought in sense, great France sprang forth,

And seized, as if to break, the ponderous chains
Which bind in woe the nations of the earth.
I saw, and started from my cottage hearth ;
And to the clouds and waves in tameless gladness,
Shrieked, till they caught immeasurable mirth—
And laughed in light and music : soon, sweet madness
Was poured upon my heart, a soft and thrilling sadness.

XL.

Deep slumber fell on me :—my dreams were fire,
Soft and delightful thoughts did rest and hover
Like shadows o'er my brain ; and strange desire,
The tempest of a passion, raging over
My tranquil soul, its depths with light did cover,
Which past ; and calm, and darkness, sweeter far
Came—then I loved ; but not a human lover !
For when I rose from sleep, the Morning Star
Shone through the woodbine wreaths which round my casement were.

XLI.

'Twas like an eye which seemed to smile on me.
I watched, till by the sun made pale, it sank
Under the billows of the heaving sea ;
But from its beams deep love my spirit drank,
And to my brain the boundless world now shrank
Into one thought—one image—yes, for ever !
Even like the dayspring, poured on vapours dank,
The beams of that one Star did shoot and quiver
Through my benighted mind—and were extinguished never.

XLII.

The day past thus : at night, methought in dream
A shape of speechless beauty did appear :
It stood like light on a careering stream
Of golden clouds which shook the atmosphere ;
A wingèd youth, his radiant brow did wear
The Morning Star : a wild dissolving bliss
Over my frame he breathed, approaching near,
And bent his eyes of kindling tenderness
Near mine, and on my lips impressed a lingering kiss.

XLIII.

And said : a Spirit loves thee, mortal maiden,
How wilt thou prove thy worth ? Then joy and sleep
Together fled, my soul was deeply laden,
And to the shore I went to muse and weep ;
But as I moved, over my heart did creep
A joy less soft, but more profound and strong
Than my sweet dream ; and it forbade to keep
The path of the sea-shore : that Spirit's tongue
Seemed whispering in my heart, and bore my steps along.

XLIV.

How, to that vast and peopled city led,
Which was a field of holy warfare then,

I walked among the dying and the dead,
And shared in fearless deeds with evil men.
Calm as an angel in the dragon's den—
How I braved death for liberty and truth,
And spurned at peace, and power, and fame ; and when
Those hopes had lost the glory of their youth,
How sadly I returned—might move the hearer's ruth :

XLV.

Warm tears throng fast ! the tale may not be said—
Know then, that when this grief had been subdued,
I was not left, like others, cold and dead ;
The Spirit whom I loved in solitude
Sustained his child ; the tempest-shaken wood,
The waves, the fountains, and the hush of night—
These were his voice, and well I understood
His smile divine, when the calm sea was bright
With silent stars, and Heaven was breathless with delight.

XLVI.

In lonely glens, amid the roar of rivers,
When the dim nights were moonless, have I known
Joys which no tongue can tell ; my pale lip quivers
When thought revisits them : know thou alone,
That after many wondrous years were flown,
I was awakened by a shriek of woe ;
And over me a mystic robe was thrown,
By viewless hands, and a bright Star did glow,
Before my steps—the Snake then met his mortal foe.

XLVII.

Thou fearest not then the Serpent on thy heart ?
Fear it ! she said, with brief and passionate cry,
And spake no more : that silence made me start—
I looked, and we were sailing pleasantly,
Swift as a cloud between the sea and sky,
Beneath the rising moon seen far away ;
Mountains of ice, like sapphire, piled on high
Hemming the horizon round, in silence lay
On the still waters—these we did approach alway.

XLVIII.

And swift and swifter grew the vessel's motion,
So that a dizzy trance fell on my brain—
Wild music woke me : we had past the ocean
Which girds the pole, Nature's remotest reign—
And we glode fast o'er a pellucid plain
Of waters, azure with the noon-tide day.
Ethereal mountains shone around—a Fane
Stood in the midst, girt by green isles which lay
On the blue sunny deep, resplendent far away.

XLIX.

It was a Temple, such as mortal hand
Has never built, nor ecstasy, nor dream,

Reared in the cities of enchanted land :
'Twas likest Heaven, ere yet day's purple stream
Ebbs o'er the western forest, while the gleam
Of the unrisen moon among the clouds
Is gathering—when with many a golden beam
The thronging constellations rush in crowds,
Paving with fire the sky and the marmoreal floods,

L.

Like what may be conceived of this vast dome,
When from the depths which thought can seldom pierce
Genius beholds it rise, his native home,
Girt by the deserts of the Universe.
Yet, nor in painting's light, or mightier verse,
Or sculpture's marble language can invest
That shape to mortal sense—such glooms immerse
That incommunicable sight, and rest
Upon the labouring brain and overburthened breast.

LI.

Winding among the lawny islands fair,
Whose bloomy forests starred the shadowy deep,
The wingless boat paused where an ivory stair
Its fretwork in the crystal sea did steep,
Encircling that vast Fane's aërial heap :
We disembarked, and through a portal wide
We past—whose roof of moonstone carved, did keep
A glimmering o'er the forms on every side,
Sculptures like life and thought ; immovable, deep-eyed.

LII.

We came to a vast hall, whose glorious roof
Was diamond, which had drank the lightning's sheen
In darkness, and now poured it through the woof
Of spell-inwoven clouds hung there to screen
Its blinding splendour—through such veil was seen
That work of subtlest power, divine and rare ;
Orb above orb, with starry shapes between,
And horned moons, and meteors strange and fair,
On night-black columns poised—one hollow hemisphere !

LIII.

Ten thousand columns in that quivering light
Distinct—between whose shafts wound far away
The long and labyrinthine aisles—more bright
With their own radiance than the Heaven of Day ;
And on the jasper walls around, there lay
Paintings, the poesy of mightiest thought,
Which did the Spirit's history display ;
A tale of passionate change, divinely taught,
Which, in their winged dance, unconscious Genii wrought.

LIV.

Beneath, there sate on many a sapphire throne,
The Great, who had departed from mankind,

A mighty Senate ;—some whose white hair shone
Like mountain snow, mild, beautiful, and blind.
Some, female forms, whose gestures beamed with mind ;
And ardent youths, and children bright and fair ;
And some had lyres whose strings were intertwined
With pale and clinging flames, which ever there
Waked faint yet thrilling sounds that pierced the crystal air.

LV.

One seat was vacant in the midst, a throne,
Reared on a pyramid like sculptured flame,
Distinct with circling steps which rested on
Their own deep fire—soon as the Woman came
Into that hall, she shrieked the Spirit's name
And fell ; and vanished slowly from the sight.
Darkness arose from her dissolving frame,
Which gathering, filled that dome of woven light,
Blotting its sphered stars with supernatural night.

LVI.

Then first, two glittering lights were seen to glide
In circles on the amethystine floor,
Small serpent eyes trailing from side to side,
Like meteors on a river's grassy shore,
They round each other rolled, dilating more
And more—then rose, commingling into one,
One clear and mighty planet hanging o'er
A cloud of deepest shadow, which was thrown
Athwart the glowing steps and the crystalline throne.

LVII.

The cloud which rested on that cone of flame
Was cloven ; beneath the planet sate a Form,
Fairer than tongue can speak or thought may frame,
The radiance of whose limbs rose-like and warm
Flowed forth, and did with softest light inform
The shadowy dome, the sculptures, and the state
Of those assembled shapes—with clinging charm
Sinking upon their hearts and mine—He sate
Majestic, yet most mild—calm, yet compassionate.

LVIII.

Wonder and joy a passing faintness threw
Over my brow—a hand supported me,
Whose touch was magic strength : an eye of blue
Looked into mine, like moonlight, soothingly ;
And a voice said—Thou must a listener be
This day—two mighty Spirits now return,
Like birds of calm, from the world's raging sea,
They pour fresh light from Hope's immortal urn ;
A tale of human power—despair not—list and learn !

LIX.

I looked, and lo ! one stood forth eloquently,
His eyes were dark and deep, and the clear brow

Which shadowed them was like the morning sky,
The cloudless Heaven of Spring, when in their flow
Through the bright air, the soft winds as they blow
Wake the green world—his gestures did obey
The oracular mind that made his features glow,
And where his curved lips half open lay,
Passion's divinest stream had made impetuous way.

LX.

Beneath the darkness of his outspread hair
He stood thus beautiful : but there was One
Who sate beside him like his shadow there,
And held his hand—far lovelier—she was known
To be thus fair, by the few lines alone
Which through her floating locks and gathered cloke,
Glances of soul-dissolving glory, shone :—
None else beheld her eyes—in him they woke
Memories which found a tongue, as thus he silence broke.

CANTO SECOND.

I.

The starlight smile of children, the sweet looks
Of women, the fair breast from which I fed,
The murmur of the unreposing brooks,
And the green light which shifting overhead,
Some tangled bower of vines around me shed,
The shells on the sea-sand, and the wild flowers,
The lamplight through the rafters cheerly spread,
And on the twining flax—in life's young hours
These sights and sounds did nurse my spirit's folded powers.

II.

In Argolis, beside the echoing sea,
Such impulses within my mortal frame
Arose, and they were dear to memory,
Like tokens of the dead :—but others came
Soon, in another shape : the wondrous fame
Of the past world, the vital words and deeds
Of minds whom neither time nor change can tame,
Traditions dark and old, whence evil creeds
Start forth, and whose dim shade a stream of poison feeds.

III.

I heard, as all have heard, the various story
Of human life, and wept unwilling tears.
Feeble historians of its shame and glory,
False disputants on all its hopes and fears,
Victims who worshipped ruin,—chroniclers
Of daily scorn, and slaves who loathed their state
Yet flattering power had given its ministers
A throne of judgment in the grave :—'twas fate
That among such as these my youth should seek its mate.

G

IV.

The land in which I lived, by a fell bane
Was withered up. Tyrants dwelt side by side,
And stabled in our homes,—until the chain
Stifled the captive's cry, and to abide
That blasting curse men had no shame—all vied
In evil, slave and despot ; fear with lust,
Strange fellowship through mutual hate had tied,
Like two dark serpents tangled in the dust,
Which on the paths of men their mingling poison thrust.

V.

Earth, our bright home, its mountains and its waters,
And the ethereal shapes which are suspended
Over its green expanse, and those fair daughters,
The clouds, of Sun and Ocean, who have blended
The colours of the air since first extended
It cradled the young world, none wandered forth
To see or feel : a darkness had descended
On every heart : the light which shows its worth,
Must among gentle thoughts and fearless take its birth.

VI.

This vital world, this home of happy spirits,
Was as a dungeon to my blasted kind,
All that despair from murdered hope inherits
They sought, and in their helpless misery blind,
A deeper prison and heavier chains did find,
And stronger tyrants :—a dark gulf before,
The realm of a stern Ruler, yawned : behind,
Terror and Time conflicting drove, and bore
On their tempestuous flood the shrieking wretch from shore.

VII.

Out of that Ocean's wrecks had Guilt and Woe
Framed a dark dwelling for their homeless thought,
And, starting at the ghosts which to and fro
Glide o'er its dim and gloomy strand, had brought
The worship thence which they each other taught.
Well might men loathe their life, well might they turn
Even to the ills again from which they sought
Such refuge after death !—well might they learn
To gaze on this fair world with hopeless unconcern !

VIII.

For they all pined in bondage : body and soul,
Tyrant and slave, victim and torturer, bent
Before one Power, to which supreme control
Over their will by their own weakness lent,
Made all its many names omnipotent ;
All symbols of things evil, all divine ;
And hymns of blood or mockery, which rent
The air from all its fanes, did intertwine
Imposture's impious toils round each discordant shrine.

IX.

I heard as all have heard, life's various story,
And in no careless heart transcribed the tale ;
But, from the sneers of men who have grown hoary
In shame and scorn, from groans of crowds made pale
By famine, from a mother's desolate wail
O'er her polluted child, from innocent blood
Poured on the earth, and brows anxious and pale
With the heart's warfare ; did I gather food
To feed my many thoughts : a tameless multitude !

X.

I wandered through the wrecks of days departed
Far by the desolated shore, when even
O'er the still sea and jagged islets darted
The light of moonrise ; in the northern Heaven,
Among the clouds near the horizon driven,
The mountains lay beneath one planet pale ;
Around me, broken tombs and columns riven
Looked vast in twilight, and the sorrowing gale
Waked in those ruins grey its everlasting wail !

XI.

I knew not who had framed these wonders then,
Nor, had I heard the story of their deeds ;
But dwellings of a race of mightier men,
And monuments of less ungentle creeds
Tell their own tale to him who wisely heeds
The language which they speak ; and now, to me
The moonlight making pale the blooming weeds,
The bright stars shining in the breathless sea,
Interpreted those scrolls of mortal mystery.

XII.

Such man has been, and such may yet become !
Ay, wiser, greater, gentler, even than they
Who on the fragments of yon shattered dome
Have stamped the sign of power—I felt the sway
Of the vast stream of ages bear away
My floating thoughts—my heart beat loud and fast—
Even as a storm let loose beneath the ray
Of the still moon, my spirit onward past
Beneath truth's steady beams upon its tumult cast.

XIII.

It shall be thus no more ! too long, too long,
Sons of the glorious dead, have ye lain bound
In darkness and in ruin.—Hope is strong,
Justice and Truth their winged child have found—
Awake ! arise ! until the mighty sound
Of your career shall scatter in its gust
The thrones of the oppressor, and the ground
Hide the last altar's unregarded dust,
Whose idol has so long betrayed your impious trust.

XIV.

It must be so—I will arise and waken
The multitude, and like a sulphurous hill,
Which on a sudden from its snows has shaken
The swoon of ages, it shall burst and fill
The world with cleansing fire : it must, it will—
It may not be restrained !—and who shall stand
Amid the rocking earthquake steadfast still,
But Laon ? on high Freedom's desert land
A tower whose marble walls the leaguèd storms withstand !

XV.

One summer night, in commune with the hope
Thus deeply fed, amid those ruins grey
I watched, beneath the dark sky's starry cope ;
And ever from that hour upon me lay
The burthen of this hope, and night or day,
In vision or in dream, clove to my breast :
Among mankind, or when gone far away
To the lone shores and mountains, 'twas a guest
Which followed where I fled, and watched when I did rest.

XVI.

These hopes found words through which my spirit sought
To weave a bondage of such sympathy,
As might create some response to the thought
Which ruled me now—and as the vapours lie
Bright in the outspread morning's radiancy,
So were these thoughts invested with the light
Of language : and all bosoms made reply
On which its lustre streamed, whene'er it might
Through darkness wide and deep those trancèd spirits smite.

XVII.

Yes, many an eye with dizzy tears was dim,
And oft I thought to clasp my own heart's brother,
When I could feel the listener's senses swim,
And hear his breath its own swift gaspings smother
Even as my words evoked them—and another,
And yet another, I did fondly deem,
Felt that we all were sons of one great mother ;
And the cold truth such sad reverse did seem,
As to awake in grief from some delightful dream.

XVIII.

Yes, oft beside the ruined labyrinth
Which skirts the hoary caves of the green deep,
Did Laon and his friend on one grey plinth,
Round whose worn base the wild waves hiss and leap,
Resting at eve, a lofty converse keep :
And that this friend was false, may now be said
Calmly—that he like other men could weep
Tears which are lies, and could betray and spread
Snares for that guileless heart which for his own had bled.

XIX.

Then, had no great aim recompensed my sorrow,
I must have sought dark respite from its stress
In dreamless rest, in sleep that sees no morrow—
For to tread life's dismaying wilderness
Without one smile to cheer, one voice to bless,
Amid the snares and scoffs of human kind,
Is hard—but I betrayed it not, nor less
With love that scorned return, sought to unbind
The interwoven clouds which make its wisdom blind.

XX.

With deathless minds which leave where they have past
A path of light, my soul communion knew ;
Till from that glorious intercourse, at last,
As from a mine of magic store, I drew
Words which were weapons ;—round my heart there grew
The adamantine armour of their power,
And from my fancy wings of golden hue
Sprang forth—yet not alone from wisdom's tower,
A minister of truth, these plumes young Laon bore.

XXI.

An orphan with my parents lived, whose eyes
Were loadstars of delight, which drew me home
When I might wander forth ; nor did I prize
Aught human thing beneath Heaven's mighty dome
Beyond this child : so when sad hours were come,
And baffled hope like ice still clung to me,
Since kin were cold, and friends had now become
Heartless and false, I turned from all, to be,
Cythna, the only source of tears and smiles to thee.

XXII.

What wert thou then ?   A child most infantine,
Yet wandering far beyond that innocent age
In all but its sweet looks and mien divine ;
Even then, methought, with the world's tyrant rage
A patient warfare thy young heart did wage,
When those soft eyes of scarcely conscious thought,
Some tale, or thine own fancies would engage
To overflow with tears, or converse fraught
With passion, o'er their depths its fleeting light had wrought.

XXIII.

She moved upon this earth a shape of brightness,
A power, that from its objects scarcely drew
One impulse of her being—in her lightness
Most like some radiant cloud of morning dew,
Which wanders through the waste air's pathless blue,
To nourish some far desert : she did seem
Beside me, gathering beauty as she grew,
Like the bright shade of some immortal dream
Which walks, when tempest sleeps, the wave of life's dark stream.

XXIV.

As mine own shadow was this child to me,
A second self, far dearer and more fair ;
Which clothed in undissolving radiancy,
All those steep paths which languor and despair
Of human things, had made so dark and bare,
But which I trod alone—nor, till bereft,
Of friends, and overcome by lonely care,
Knew I what solace for that loss was left,
Though by a bitter wound my trusting heart was cleft.

XXV.

Once she was dear, now she was all I had
To love in human life—this playmate sweet,
This child of twelve years old—so she was made
My sole associate, and her willing feet
Wandered with mine where earth and ocean meet,
Beyond the aërial mountains whose vast cells
The unreposing billows ever beat,
Through forests wide and old, and lawny dells,
Where boughs of incense droop over the emerald wells.

XXVI.

And warm and light I felt her clasping hand
When twined in mine : she followed where I went,
Through the lone paths of our immortal land.
It had no waste, but some memorial lent
Which strung me to my toil—some monument
Vital with mind : then, Cythna by my side,
Until the bright and beaming day were spent,
Would rest, with looks entreating to abide,
Too earnest and too sweet ever to be denied.

XXVII.

And soon I could not have refused her—thus
For ever, day and night, we two were ne'er
Parted, but when brief sleep divided us :
And when the pauses of the lulling air
Of noon beside the sea, had made a lair
For her soothed senses, in my arms she slept,
And I kept watch over her slumbers there,
While, as the shifting visions o'er her swept,
Amid her innocent rest by turns she smiled and wept.

XXVIII.

And, in the murmur of her dreams was heard
Sometimes the name of Laon :—suddenly
She would arise, and like the secret bird
Whom sunset wakens, fill the shore and sky
With her sweet accents—a wild melody !
Hymns which my soul had woven to Freedom, strong
The source of passion whence they rose, to be ;
Triumphant strains, which, like a spirit's tongue,
To the enchanted waves that child of glory sung.

XXIX.

Her white arms lifted through the shadowy stream
Of her loose hair—oh, excellently great
Seemed to me then my purpose, the vast theme
Of those impassioned songs, when Cythna sate
Amid the calm which rapture did create
After its tumult, her heart vibrating,
Her spirit o'er the ocean's floating state
From her deep eyes far wandering, on the wing
Of visions that were mine, beyond its utmost spring.

XXX.

For, before Cythna loved it, had my song
Peopled with thoughts the boundless universe,
A mighty congregation, which were strong
Where'er they trod the darkness to disperse
The cloud of that unutterable curse
Which clings upon mankind :—all things became
Slaves to my holy and heroic verse,
Earth, sea, and sky, the planets, life and fame
And fate, or whate'er else binds the world's wondrous frame.

XXXI.

And this beloved child thus felt the sway
Of my conceptions, gathering like a cloud
The very wind on which it rolls away :
Hers too were all my thoughts, ere yet endowed
With music and with light, their fountains flowed
In poesy ; and her still and earnest face,
Pallid with feelings which intensely glowed
Within, was turned on mine with speechless grace,
Watching the hopes which there her heart had learned to trace.

XXXII.

In me, communion with this purest being
Kindled intenser zeal, and made me wise
In knowledge, which in hers mine own mind seeing,
Left in the human world few mysteries :
How without fear of evil or disguise
Was Cythna !—what a spirit strong and mild,
Which death, or pain, or peril, could despise,
Yet melt in tenderness ! what genius wild
Yet mighty, was enclosed within one simple child !

XXXIII.

New lore was this—old age with its grey hair,
And wrinkled legends of unworthy things,
And icy sneers, is naught : it cannot dare
To burst the chains which life for ever flings
On the entangled soul's aspiring wings,
So is it cold and cruel, and is made
The careless slave of that dark power which brings
Evil, like blight on man, who still betrayed,
Laughs o'er the grave in which his living hopes are laid.

XXXIV.

Nor are the strong and the severe to keep
The empire of the world : thus Cythna taught
Even in the visions of her eloquent sleep,
Unconscious of the power through which she wrought
The woof of such intelligible thought,
As from the tranquil strength which cradled lay
In her smile-peopled rest, my spirit sought
Why the deceiver and the slave has sway
O'er heralds so divine of truth's arising day.

XXXV.

Within that fairest form, the female mind
Untainted by the poison clouds which rest
On the dark world, a sacred home did find :
But else, from the wide earth's maternal breast,
Victorious Evil, which had dispossest
All native power, had those fair children torn,
And made them slaves to soothe his vile unrest,
And minister to lust its joys forlorn,
Till they had learned to breathe the atmosphere of scorn.

XXXVI.

This misery, was but coldly felt, till she
Became my only friend, who had indued
My purpose with a wider sympathy ;
Thus, Cythna mourned with me the servitude
In which the half of humankind were mewed
Victims of lust and hate, the slaves of slaves,
She mourned that grace and power were thrown as food
To the hyena lust, who, among graves,
Over his loathed meal, laughing in agony, raves.

XXXVII.

And I, still gazing on that glorious child,
Even as these thoughts flushed o'er her.—"Cythna sweet,
Well with the world art thou unreconciled ;
Never will peace and human nature meet
Till free and equal man and woman greet
Domestic peace ; and ere this power can make
In human hearts its calm and holy seat ;
This slavery must be broken "—as I spake,
From Cythna's eyes a light of exultation brake.

XXXVIII.

She replied earnestly :—" It shall be mine,
This task, mine, Laon !—thou hast much to gain ;
Nor wilt thou at poor Cythna's pride repine,
If she should lead a happy female train
To meet thee over the rejoicing plain
When myriads at thy call shall throng around
The Golden City."—Then the child did strain
My arm upon her tremulous heart, and wound
Her own about my neck, till some reply she found.

XXXIX.

I smiled, and spake not—"Wherefore dost thou smile
At what I say? Laon, I am not weak,
And though my cheek might become pale the while,
With thee, if thou desirest, will I seek
Through their array of banded slaves to wreak
Ruin upon the tyrants. I had thought
It was more hard to turn my unpractised cheek
To scorn and shame, and this beloved spot
And thee, O dearest friend, to leave and murmur not.

XL.

" Whence came I what I am? thou, Laon, knowest
How a young child should thus undaunted be ;
Methinks, it is a power which thou bestowest,
Through which I seek, by most resembling thee,
So to become most good, and great and free,
Yet far beyond this Ocean's utmost roar
In towers and huts are many like to me,
Who, could they see thine eyes, or feel such lore
As I have learnt from them, like me would fear no more.

XLI.

" Think'st thou that I shall speak unskilfully,
And none will heed me ? I remember now,
How once a slave in tortures doomed to die,
Was saved, because in accents sweet and low
He sung a song his Judge loved long ago,
As he was led to death.—All shall relent
Who hear me—tears as mine have flowed, shall flow,
Hearts beat as mine now beats, with such intent
As renovates the world ; a will omnipotent !

XLII.

" Yes, I will tread Pride's golden palaces,
Through Penury's roofless huts and squalid cells
Will I descend, where'er in abjectness
Woman with some vile slave her tyrant dwells,
There with the music of thine own sweet spells
Will disenchant the captives, and will pour
For the despairing, from the crystal wells
Of thy deep spirit, reason's mighty lore,
And power shall then abound, and hope arise once more.

XLIII.

" Can man be free if woman be a slave ?
Chain one who lives, and breathes this boundless air
To the corruption of a closed grave !
Can they whose mates are beasts, condemned to bear
Scorn, heavier far than toil or anguish, dare
To trample their oppressors ? in their home
Among their babes, thou knowest a curse would wear
The shape of woman—hoary crime would come
Behind, and fraud rebuild religion's tottering dome.

XLIV.

" I am a child :—I would not yet depart.
When I go forth alone, bearing the lamp
Aloft which thou hast kindled in my heart,
Millions of slaves from many a dungeon damp
Shall leap in joy, as the benumbing cramp
Of ages leaves their limbs—no ill may harm
Thy Cythna ever—truth its radiant stamp
Has fixed, as an invulnerable charm
Upon her children's brow, dark falsehood to disarm.

XLV.

" Wait yet awhile for the appointed day—
Thou wilt depart, and I with tears shall stand
Watching thy dim sail skirt the ocean grey ;
Amid the dwellers of this lonely land
I shall remain alone—and thy command
Shall then dissolve the world's unquiet trance,
And, multitudinous as the desert sand
Borne on the storm, its millions shall advance,
Thronging round thee, the light of their deliverance.

XLVI.

" Then, like the forests of some pathless mountain,
Which from remotest glens two warring winds
Involve in fire, which not the loosened fountain
Of broadest floods might quench, shall all the kinds
Of evil, catch from our uniting minds
The spark which must consume them ;—Cythna then
Will have cast off the impotence that binds
Her childhood now, and through the paths of men
Will pass, as the charmed bird that haunts the serpent's den.

XLVII.

" We part !—O Laon, I must dare nor tremble
To meet those looks no more !—Oh, heavy stroke,
Sweet brother of my soul ! can I dissemble
The agony of this thought?"—As thus she spoke
The gathered sobs her quivering accents broke,
And in my arms she hid her beating breast.
I remained still for tears—sudden she woke
As one awakes from sleep, and wildly prest
My bosom, her whole frame impetuously possest.

XLVIII.

" We part to meet again—but yon blue waste,
Yon desert wide and deep holds no recess,
Within whose happy silence, thus embraced
We might survive all ills in one caress :
Nor doth the grave—I fear 'tis passionless—
Nor yon cold vacant Heaven :—we meet again
Within the minds of men, whose lips shall bless
Our memory, and whose hopes its light retain
When these dissevered bones are trodden in the plain."

XLIX.

I could not speak, though she had ceased, for now
The fountains of her feeling, swift and deep,
Seemed to suspend the tumult of their flow ;
So we arose, and by the starlight steep
Went homeward—neither did we speak nor weep,
But pale, were calm with passion—thus subdued
Like evening shades that o'er the mountains creep,
We moved towards our home ; where, in this mood,
Each from the other sought refuge in solitude.

CANTO THIRD.

I.

What thoughts had sway o'er Cythna's lonely slumber
That night, I know not ; but my own did seem
As if they might ten thousand years outnumber
Of waking life, the visions of a dream,
Which hid in one dim gulf the troubled stream
Of mind ; a boundless chaos wild and vast,
Whose limits yet were never memory's theme :
And I lay struggling as its whirlwinds past,
Sometimes for rapture sick, sometimes for pain aghast.

II.

Two hours, whose mighty circle did embrace
More time than might make grey the infant world,
Rolled thus, a weary and tumultuous space :
When the third came, like mist on breezes curled,
From my dim sleep a shadow was unfurled :
Methought, upon the threshold of a cave
I sate with Cythna ; drooping briony, pearled
With dew from the wild streamlet's shattered wave,
Hung, where we sate to taste the joys which Nature gave.

III.

We lived a day as we were wont to live,
But Nature had a robe of glory on,
And the bright air o'er every shape did weave
Intenser hues, so that the herbless stone,
The leafless bough among the leaves alone,
Had being clearer than its own could be,
And Cythna's pure and radiant self was shown
In this strange vision, so divine to me,
That if I loved before, now love was agony.

IV.

Morn fled, noon came, evening, then night descended,
And we prolonged calm talk beneath the sphere
Of the calm moon—when, suddenly was blended
With our repose a nameless sense of fear ;

And from the cave behind I seemed to hear
Sounds gathering upwards !—accents incomplete,
And stifled shrieks,—and now, more near and near,
A tumult and a rush of thronging feet
The cavern's secret depths beneath the earth did beat.

v.

The scene was changed ; away, away, away !
Through the air and over the sea we sped,
And Cythna in my sheltering bosom lay,
And the winds bore me—through the darkness spread
Around, the gaping earth then vomited
Legions of foul and ghastly shapes, which hung
Upon my flight ; and ever as we fled,
They plucked at Cythna—soon to me then clung
A sense of actual things those monstrous dreams among.

VI.

And I lay struggling in the impotence
Of sleep, while outward life had burst its bound,
Though, still deluded, strove the tortured sense
To its dire wanderings to adapt the sound
Which in the light of morn was poured around
Our dwelling—breathless, pale, and unaware
I rose, and all the cottage crowded found
With armed men, whose glittering swords were bare,
And whose degraded limbs the tyrant's garb did wear.

VII.

And ere with rapid lips and gathered brow
I could demand the cause—a feeble shriek
It was a feeble shriek, faint, far and low,
Arrested me—my mien grew calm and meek,
And grasping a small knife, I went to seek
That voice among the crowd—'twas Cythna's cry !
Beneath most calm resolve did agony wreak
Its whirlwind rage : so I past quietly
Till I beheld, where bound, that dearest child did lie.

VIII.

I started to behold her, for delight
And exultation, and a joyance free,
Solemn, serene, and lofty, filled the light
Of the calm smile with which she looked on me :
So that I feared some brainless ecstasy,
Wrought from that bitter woe, had wildered her—
"Farewell ! farewell !" she said, as I drew nigh.
"At first my peace was marred by this strange stir,
Now I am calm as truth—its chosen minister.

IX.

" Look not so, Laon—say farewell in hope,
These bloody men are but the slaves who bear
Their mistress to her task—it was my scope
The slavery where they drag me now, to share,

And among captives willing chains to wear
Awhile—the rest thou knowest—return, dear friend !
Let our first triumph trample the despair
Which would ensnare us now, for in the end,
In victory or in death our hopes and fears must blend."

X.

These words had fallen on my unheeding ear,
Whilst I had watched the motions of the crew
With seeming careless glance ; not many were
Around her, for their comrades just withdrew
To guard some other victim—so I drew
My knife, and with one impulse, suddenly
All unaware three of their number slew,
And grasped a fourth by the throat, and with loud cry
My countrymen invoked to death or liberty !

XI.

What followed then I know not—for a stroke
On my raised arm and naked head, came down,
Filling my eyes with blood—when I awoke,
I felt that they had bound me in my swoon,
And up a rock which overhangs the town,
By the steep path were bearing me : below,
The plain was filled with slaughter,—overthrown
The vineyards and the harvests, and the glow
Of blazing roofs shone far o'er the white Ocean's flow.

XII.

Upon that rock a mighty column stood,
Whose capital seemed sculptured in the sky,
Which to the wanderers o'er the solitude
Of distant seas, from ages long gone by,
Had made a landmark ; o'er its height to fly
Scarcely the cloud, the vulture, or the blast,
Has power—and when the shades of evening lie
On Earth and Ocean, its carved summits cast
The sunken daylight far through the aërial waste.

XIII.

They bore me to a cavern in the hill
Beneath that column, and unbound me there :
And one did strip me stark ; and one did fill
A vessel from the putrid pool ; one bare
A lighted torch, and four with friendless care
Guided my steps the cavern-paths along,
Then up a steep and dark and narrow stair
We wound, until the torches' fiery tongue
Amid the gushing day beamless and pallid hung.

XIV.

They raised me to the platform of the pile,
That column's dizzy height :—the grate of brass
Through which they thrust me, open stood the while,
As to its ponderous and suspended mass,

With chains which eat into the flesh, alas !
With brazen links, my naked limbs they bound :
The grate, as they departed to repass,
With horrid clangour fell, and the far sound
Of their retiring steps in the dense gloom were drowned.

XV.

The noon was calm and bright :—around that column
The overhanging sky and circling sea
Spread forth in silentness profound and solemn
The darkness of brief frenzy cast on me,
So that I knew not my own misery :
The islands and the mountains in the day
Like clouds reposed afar ; and I could see
The town among the woods below that lay,
And the dark rocks which bound the bright and glassy bay.

XVI.

It was so calm, that scarce the feathery weed
Sown by some eagle on the topmost stone
Swayed in the air :—so bright, that noon did breed
No shadow in the sky beside mine own—
Mine, and the shadow of my chain alone.
Below the smoke of roofs involved in flame
Rested like night, all else was clearly shown
In that broad glare, yet sound to me none came,
But of the living blood that ran within my frame.

XVII.

The peace of madness fled, and ah, too soon !
A ship was lying on the sunny main,
Its sails were flagging in the breathless noon—
Its shadow lay beyond—that sight again
Waked, with its presence, in my tranced brain
The stings of a known sorrow, keen and cold :
I knew that ship bore Cythna o'er the plain
Of waters, to her blighting slavery sold,
And watched it with such thoughts as must remain untold.

XVIII.

I watched, until the shades of evening wrapt
Earth like an exhalation—then the bark
Moved, for that calm was by the sunset snapt.
It moved a speck upon the Ocean dark :
Soon the wan stars came forth, and I could mark
Its path no more !—I sought to close mine eyes,
But like the balls, their lids were stiff and stark ;
I would have risen, but ere that I could rise,
My parched skin was split with piercing agonies.

XIX.

I gnawed my brazen chain, and sought to sever
Its adamantine links, that I might die :
O Liberty ! forgive the base endeavour,
Forgive me, if reserved for victory,

The Champion of thy faith e'er sought to fly.—
That starry night, with its clear silence, sent
Tameless resolve which laughed at misery
Into my soul—linked remembrance lent
To that such power, to me such a severe content.

XX.

To breathe, to be, to hope, or to despair
And die, I questioned not ; nor, though the Sun
Its shafts of agony kindling through the air
Moved over me, nor though in evening dun
Or when the stars their visible courses run,
Or morning, the wide universe was spread
In dreary calmness round me, did I shun
Its presence, nor seek refuge with the dead
From one faint hope whose flower a dropping poison shed.

XXI.

Two days thus past—I neither raved nor died—
Thirst raged within me, like a scorpion's nest
Built in mine entrails : I had spurned aside
The water-vessel, while despair possest
My thoughts, and now no drop remained ! the uprest
Of the third sun brought hunger—but the crust
Which had been left, was to my craving breast
Fuel, not food. I chewed the bitter dust,
And bit my bloodless arm, and licked the brazen rust.

XXII.

My brain began to fail when the fourth morn
Burst o'er the golden isles—a fearful sleep,
Which through the caverns dreary and forlorn
Of the riven soul, sent its foul dreams to sweep
With whirlwind swiftness—a fall far and deep,—
A gulf, a void, a sense of senselessness—
These things dwelt in me, even as shadows keep
Their watch in some dim charnel's loneliness,
A shoreless sea, a sky sunless and planetless !

XXIII.

The forms which peopled this terrific trance
I well remember—like a quire of devils,
Around me they involved a giddy dance ;
Legions seemed gathering from the misty levels
Of Ocean, to supply those ceaseless revels,
Foul, ceaseless shadows :—thought could not divide
The actual world from these entangling evils,
Which so bemocked themselves, that I descried
All shapes like mine own self, hideously multiplied.

XXIV.

The sense of day and night, of false and true,
Was dead within me. Yet two visions burst
That darkness—one, as since that hour I knew,
Was not a phantom of the realms accurst,

Where then my spirit dwelt—but of the first
I know not yet, was it a dream or no.
But both, though not distincter, were immersed
In hues which, when through memory's waste they flow
Make their divided streams more bright and rapid now.

XXV.

Methought that gate was lifted, and the seven
Who brought me thither, four stiff corpses bare,
And from the frieze to the four winds of Heaven
Hung them on high by the entangled hair :
Swarthy were three—the fourth was very fair :
As they retired, the golden moon upsprung,
And eagerly, out in the giddy air,
Leaning that I might eat, I stretched and clung
Over the shapeless depth in which those corpses hung.

XXVI.

A woman's shape, now lank and cold and blue,
The dwelling of the many-coloured worm
Hung there, the white and hollow cheek I drew
To my dry lips—what radiance did inform
Those horny eyes? whose was that withered form?
Alas, alas! it seemed that Cythna's ghost
Laughed in those looks, and that the flesh was warm
Within my teeth !—a whirlwind keen as frost
Then in its sinking gulfs my sickening spirit tost.

XXVII.

Then seemed it that a tameless hurricane
Arose, and bore me in its dark career
Beyond the sun, beyond the stars that wane
On the verge of formless space—it languished there,
And dying, left a silence lone and drear,
More horrible than famine :—in the deep
The shape of an old man did then appear,
Stately and beautiful, that dreadful sleep
His heavenly smiles dispersed, and I could wake and weep.

XXVIII.

And when the blinding tears had fallen, I saw
That column, and those corpses, and the moon,
And felt the poisonous tooth of hunger gnaw
My vitals, I rejoiced, as if the boon
Of senseless death would be accorded soon ;—
When from that stony gloom a voice arose,
Solemn and sweet as when low winds attune
The midnight pines ; the grate did then unclose,
And on that reverend form the moonlight did repose.

XXIX.

He struck my chains, and gently spake and smiled :
As they were loosened by that Hermit old,
Mine eyes were of their madness half beguiled,
To answer those kind looks—he did enfold

His giant arms around me, to uphold
My wretched frame, my scorched limbs he wound
In linen moist and balmy, and as cold
As dew to drooping leaves ;—the chain, with sound
Like earthquake, through the chasm of that steep stair did bound,

XXX.

As lifting me, it fell !—What next I heard,
Were billows leaping on the harbour bar,
And the shrill sea-wind, whose breath idly stirred
My hair ;—I looked abroad, and saw a star
Shining beside a sail, and distant far
That mountain and its column, the known mark
Of those who in the wide deep wandering are,
So that I feared some Spirit, fell and dark,
In trance had lain me thus within a fiendish bark.

XXXI.

For now indeed, over the salt sea billow
I sailed : yet dared not look upon the shape
Of him who ruled the helm, although the pillow
For my light head was hollowed in his lap,
And my bare limbs his mantle did enwrap,
Fearing it was a fiend : at last, he bent
O'er me his aged face, as if to snap
Those dreadful thoughts the gentle grandsire bent,
And to my inmost soul his soothing looks he sent.

XXXII.

A soft and healing potion to my lips
At intervals he raised—now looked on high,
To mark if yet the starry giant dips
His zone in the dim sea—now cheeringly,
Though he said little, did he speak to me.
" It is a friend beside thee—take good cheer,
Poor victim, thou art now at liberty !"
I joyed as those a human tone to hear,
Who in cells deep and lone have languished many a year.

XXXIII.

A dim and feeble joy, whose glimpses oft
Were quenched in a relapse of wildering dreams,
Yet still methought we sailed, until aloft
The stars of night grew pallid, and the beams
Of morn descended on the ocean streams,
And still that aged man, so grand and mild,
Tended me, even as some sick mother seems
To hang in hope over a dying child,
Till in the azure East darkness again was piled.

XXXIV.

And then the night-wind steaming from the shore,
Sent odours dying sweet across the sea,
And the swift boat the little waves which bore,
Were cut by its keen keel, though slantingly ;

H

Soon I could hear the leaves sigh, and could see
The myrtle blossoms starring the dim grove,
As past the pebbly beach the boat did flee
On sidelong wing, into a silent cove,
Where ebon pines a shade under the starlight wove.

CANTO FOURTH.

I.

The old man took the oars, and soon the bark
Smote on the beach beside a tower of stone ;
It was a crumbling heap, whose portal dark
With blooming ivy trails was overgrown ;
Upon whose floor the spangling sands were strown,
And rarest sea-shells, which the eternal flood,
Slave to the mother of the months, had thrown
Within the walls of that grey tower, which stood
A changeling of man's art, nursed amid Nature's brood

II.

When the old man his boat had anchorèd,
He wound me in his arms with tender care,
And very few, but kindly words he said,
And bore me through the tower adown a stair,
Whose smooth descent some ceaseless step to wear,
For many a year had fallen—We came at last
To a small chamber, which with mosses rare
Was tapestried, where me his soft hands placed
Upon a couch of grass and oak-leaves interlaced.

III.

The moon was darting through the lattices
Its yellow light, warm as the beams of day—
So warm, that to admit the dewy breeze,
The old man opened them ; the moonlight lay
Upon a lake whose waters wove their play
Even to the threshold of that lonely home :
Within was seen in the dim wavering ray,
The antique sculptured roof, and many a tome
Whose lore had made that sage all that he had become

IV.

The rock-built barrier of the sea was past,—
And I was on the margin of a lake,
A lonely lake, amid the forests vast
And snowy mountains :—did my spirit wake
From sleep, as many-coloured as the snake
That girds eternity ? in life and truth,
Might not my heart its cravings ever slake ?
Was Cythna then a dream, and all my youth,
And all its hopes and fears, and all its joy and truth '

V.

Thus madness came again,—a milder madness,
Which darkened naught but time's unquiet flow
With supernatural shades of clinging sadness;
That gentle Hermit, in my helpless woe,
By my sick couch was busy to and fro,
Like a strong spirit ministrant of good:
When I was healed, he led me forth to show
The wonders of his sylvan solitude,
And we together sate by that isle-fretted flood.

VI.

He knew his soothing words to weave with skill
From all my madness told; like mine own heart,
Of Cythna would he question me, until
That thrilling name had ceased to make me start,
From his familiar lips—it was not art,
Of wisdom and of justice when he spoke—
When mid soft looks of pity, there would dart
A glance as keen as is the lightning's stroke
When it doth rive the knots of some ancestral oak.

VII.

Thus slowly from my brain the darkness rolled,
My thoughts their due array did reassume
Through the enchantments of that Hermit old;
Then I bethought me of the glorious doom
Of those who sternly struggle to relume
The lamp of Hope o'er man's bewildered lot,
And, sitting by the waters, in the gloom
Of eve, to that friend's heart I told my thought—
That heart which had grown old, but had corrupted not

VIII.

That hoary man had spent his livelong age
In converse with the dead, who leave the stamp
Of ever-burning thoughts on many a page,
When they are gone into the senseless damp
Of graves;—his spirit thus became a lamp
Of splendour, like to those on which it fed,
Through peopled haunts, the City and the Camp,
Deep thirst for knowledge had his footsteps led,
And all the ways of men among mankind he read.

IX.

But custom maketh blind and obdurate
The loftiest hearts:—he had beheld the woe
In which mankind was bound, but deemed that fate
Which made them abject, would preserve them so;
And in such faith, some steadfast joy to know,
He sought this cell: but when fame went abroad,
That one in Argolis did undergo
Torture for liberty, and that the crowd
High truths from gifted lips had heard and understood;

X.

And that the multitude was gathering wide;
His spirit leaped within his aged frame,
In lonely peace he could no more abide,
But to the land on which the victor's flame
Had fed, my native land, the Hermit came :
Each heart was there a shield, and every tongue
Was as a sword of truth—young Laon's name
Rallied their secret hopes, though tyrants sung
Hymns of triumphant joy our scattered tribes among.

XI.

He came to the lone column on the rock,
And with his sweet and mighty eloquence
The hearts of those who watched it did unlock,
And made them melt in tears of penitence.
They gave him entrance free to bear me thence.
Since this, the old man said, seven years are spent,
While slowly truth on thy benighted sense
Has crept ; the hope which wildered it has lent
Meanwhile, to me the power of a sublime intent.

XII.

"Yes, from the records of my youthful state,
And from the lore of bards and sages old,
From whatsoe'er my wakened thoughts create
Out of the hopes of thine aspirings bold,
Have I collected language to unfold
Truth to my countrymen ; from shore to shore
Doctrines of human power my words have told,
They have been heard, and men aspire to more
Than they have ever gained or ever lost of yore.

XIII.

"In secret chambers parents read, and weep,
My writings to their babes, no longer blind ;
And young men gather when their tyrants sleep,
And vows of faith each to the other bind ;
And marriageable maidens, who have pined
With love, till life seemed melting through their look,
A warmer zeal, a nobler hope now find ;
And every bosom thus is rapt and shook,
Like autumn's myriad leaves in one swollen mountain brook.

XIV.

"The tyrants of the Golden City tremble
At voices which are heard about the streets,
The ministers of fraud can scarce dissemble
The lies of their own heart ; but when one meets
Another at the shrine, he inly weeps,
Though he says nothing, that the truth is known ;
Murderers are pale upon the judgment seats,
And gold grows vile even to the wealthy crone,
And laughter fills the Fane, and curses shake the Throne.

XV.

"Kind thoughts, and mighty hopes, and gentle deeds
Abound, for fearless love, and the pure law
Of mild equality and peace, succeeds
To faiths which long have held the world in awe,
Bloody and false, and cold :—as whirlpools draw
All wrecks of Ocean to their chasm, the sway
Of thy strong genius, Laon, which foresaw
This hope, compels all spirits to obey
Which round thy secret strength now throng in wild array.

XVI.

"For I have been thy passive instrument"—
(As thus the old man spake, his countenance
Gleamed on me like a spirit's)—"thou hast lent
To me, to all, the power to advance
Towards this unforeseen deliverance
From our ancestral chains—ay, thou didst rear
That lamp of hope on high, which time nor chance,
Nor change may not extinguish, and my share
Of good, was o'er the world its gathered beams to bear.

XVII.

" But I, alas ! am both unknown and old,
And though the woof of wisdom I know well
To dye in hues of language, I am cold
In seeming, and the hopes which inly dwell,
My manners note that I did long repel ;
But Laon's name to the tumultuous throng
Were like the star whose beams the waves compel
And tempests, and his soul-subduing tongue
Were as a lance to quell the mailed crest of wrong.

XVIII.

" Perchance blood need not flow, if thou at length
Wouldst rise, perchance the very slaves would spare
Their brethren and themselves ; great is the strength
Of words—for lately did a maiden fair,
Who from her childhood has been taught to bear
The tyrant's heaviest yoke, arise, and make
Her sex the law of truth and freedom hear,
And with these quiet words—' for thine own sake
I prithee spare me ;'—did with ruth so take

XIX.

" All hearts, that even the torturer who had bound
Her meek calm frame, ere it was yet impaled,
Loosened her weeping then ; nor could be found
One human hand to harm her—unassailed
Therefore she walks through the great City, veiled
In virtue's adamantine eloquence,
'Gainst scorn and death and pain thus trebly mailed,
And blending in the smiles of that defence,
The Serpent and the Dove, Wisdom and Innocence.

XX.

" The wild-eyed women throng around her path :
From their luxurious dungeons, from the dust
Of meaner thralls, from the oppressor's wrath,
Or the caresses of his sated lust
They congregate :—in her they put their trust ;
The tyrants send their armed slaves to quell
Her power ;—they, even like a thunder gust
Caught by some forest, bend beneath the spell
Of that young maiden's speech, and to their chiefs rebel.

XXI.

" Thus she doth equal laws and justice teach
To woman, outraged and polluted long ;
Gathering the sweetest fruit in human reach
For those fair hands now free, while armed wrong
Trembles before her look, though it be strong ;
Thousands thus dwell beside her, virgins bright,
And matrons with their babes, a stately throng !
Lovers renew the vows which they did plight
In early faith, and hearts long parted now unite,

XXII.

" And homeless orphans find a home near her,
And those poor victims of the proud, no less,
Fair wrecks, on whom the smiling world with stir,
Thrusts the redemption of its wickedness :—
In squalid huts, and in its   places
Sits Lust alone, while o'er the land is borne
Her voice, whose awful sweetness doth repress
All evil, and her foes relenting turn,
And cast the vote of love in hope's abandoned urn.

XXIII.

" So in the populous City, a young maiden
Has baffled havoc of the prey which he
Marks as his own, whene'er with chains o'erladen
Men make them arms to hurl down tyranny,
False arbiter between the bound and free ;
And o'er the land, in hamlets and in towns
The multitudes collect tumultuously,
And throng in arms ; but tyranny disowns
Their claim, and gathers strength around its trembling thrones

XXIV.

" Blood soon, although unwillingly to shed,
The free cannot forbear—the Queen of Slaves,
The hoodwinked Angel of the blind and dead,
Custom, with iron mace points to the graves
Where her own standard desolately waves
Over the dust of Prophets and of Kings.
Many yet stand in her array—' she paves
Her path with human hearts,' and o'er it flings
The wildering gloom of her immeasurable wings.

XXV.

There is a plain beneath the City's wall,
Bounded by misty mountains, wide and vast,
Millions there lift at Freedom's thrilling call
Ten thousand standards wide, they load the blast
Which bears one sound of many voices past,
And startles on his throne their sceptred foe :
He sits amid his idle pomp aghast,
And that his power hath past away, doth know—
Why pause the victor swords to seal his overthrow ?

XXVI.

" The tyrant's guards resistance yet maintain :
Fearless, and fierce, and hard as beasts of blood ;
They stand a speck amid the peopled plain ;
Carnage and ruin have been made their food
From infancy—ill has become their good,
And for its hateful sake their will has wove
The chains which eat their hearts—the multitude
Surrounding them, with words of human love,
Seek from their own decay their stubborn minds to move.

XXVII.

" Over the land is felt a sudden pause,
As night and day those ruthless bands around
The watch of love is kept :—a trance which awes
The thoughts of men with hope—as when the sound
Of whirlwind, whose fierce blasts the waves and clouds confound,
Dies suddenly, the mariner in fear
Feels silence sink upon his heart—thus bound
The conquerors pause, and oh ! may freemen ne'er
Clasp the relentless knees of Dread the murderer !

XXVIII.

" If blood be shed, 'tis but a change and choice
Of bonds,—from slavery to cowardice
A wretched fall !—uplift thy charmed voice,
Pour on those evil men the love that lies
Hovering within those spirit-soothing eyes—
Arise, my friend, farewell !"—As thus he spake,
From the green earth lightly I did arise,
As one out of dim dreams that doth awake,
And looked upon the depth of that reposing lake.

XXIX.

I saw my countenance reflected there ;—
And then my youth fell on me like a wind
Descending on still waters—my thin hair
Was prematurely grey, my face was lined
With channels, such as suffering leaves behind,
Not age ; my brow was pale, but in my cheek
And lips a flush of gnawing fire did find
Their food and dwelling ; though mine eyes might speak
A subtle mind and strong within a frame thus weak.

XXX.

And though their lustre now was spent and faded,
Yet in my hollow looks and withered mien
The likeness of a shape for which was braided
The brightest woof of genius, still was seen—
One who, methought, had gone from the world's scene,
And left it vacant—'twas her lover's face—
It might resemble her—it once had been
The mirror of her thoughts, and still the grace
Which her mind's shadow cast, left there a lingering trace.

XXXI.

What then was I? She slumbered with the dead.
Glory and joy and peace, had come and gone,
Doth the cloud perish when the beams are fled
Which steeped its skirts in gold? or dark and lone,
Doth it not through the paths of night unknown,
On outspread wings of its own wind upborne
Pour rain upon the earth? the stars are shown,
When the cold moon sharpens her silver horn
Under the sea, and make the wide night not forlorn.

XXXII.

Strengthened in heart, yet sad, that aged man
I left, with interchange of looks and tears,
And lingering speech, and to the Camp began
My way. O'er many a mountain chain which rears
Its hundred crests aloft, my spirit bears
My frame; o'er many a dale and many a moor,
And gaily now meseems serene earth wears
The bloomy spring's star-bright investiture,
A vision which aught sad from sadness might allure

XXXIII.

My powers revived within me, and I went
As one whom winds waft o'er the bending grass,
Through many a vale of that broad continent.
At night when I reposed, fair dreams did pass
Before my pillow;—my own Cythna was
Not like a child of death, among them ever;
When I arose from rest, a woeful mass
That gentlest sleep seemed from my life to sever,
As if the light of youth were not withdrawn for ever.

XXXIV.

Ay, as I went, that maiden who had reared
The torch of Truth afar, of whose high deeds
The Hermit in his pilgrimage had heard,
Haunted my thoughts.—Ah! Hope its sickness feeds
With whatsoe'er it finds, or flowers or weeds!
Could she be Cythna?—Was that corpse a shade
Such as self-torturing thought from madness breeds?
Why was this hope not torture? yet it made
A light around my steps which would not ever fade.

CANTO FIFTH.

I.

Over the utmost hill at length I sped,
A snowy steep :—the moon was hanging low
Over the Asian mountains, and outspread
The plain, the City, and the Camp below,
Skirted the midnight Ocean's glimmering flow,
The City's moon-lit spires and myriad lamps,
Like stars in a sublunar sky did glow,
And fires blazed far amid the scattered camps,
Like springs of flame, which burst where'er swift Earthquake
 stamps.

II.

All slept but those in watchful arms who stood,
And those who sate tending the beacon's light,
And the few sounds from that vast multitude
Made silence more profound—Oh, what a might
Of human thought was cradled in that night !
How many hearts impenetrably veiled,
Beat underneath its shade, what secret fight
Evil and good, in woven passions mailed,
Waged through that silent throng ; a war that never failed !

III.

And now the Power of Good held victory
So, through the labyrinth of many a tent,
Among the silent millions who did lie
In innocent sleep, exultingly I went ;
The moon had left Heaven desert now, but lent
From eastern morn the first faint lustre showed
An armed youth—over his spear he bent
His downward face—"A friend !" I cried aloud,
And quickly common hopes made freemen understood.

IV.

I sate beside him while the morning beam
Crept slowly over Heaven, and talked with him
Of those immortal hopes, a glorious theme !
Which led us forth, until the stars grew dim :
And all the while, methought, his voice did swim,
As if it drowned in remembrance were
Of thoughts which make the moist eyes overbrim :
At last, when daylight 'gan to fill the air,
He looked on me, and cried in wonder—"Thou art here !"

V.

Then, suddenly, I knew it was the youth
In whom its earliest hopes my spirit found ;
But envious tongues had stained his spotless truth,
And thoughtless pride his love in silence bound.

And shame and sorrow mine in toils had wound,
Whilst he was innocent, and I deluded ;
The truth now came upon me, on the ground
Tears of repenting joy, which fast intruded,
Fell fast, and o'er its peace our mingling spirits brooded.

VI.

Thus, while with rapid lips and earnest eyes
We talked, a sound of sweeping conflict spread,
As from the earth did suddenly arise ;
From every tent roused by that clamour dread,
Our bands outsprung and seized their arms—we sped
Towards the sound : our tribes were gathering far,
Those sanguine slaves amid ten thousand dead
Stabbed in their sleep, trampled in treacherous war,
The gentle hearts whose power their lives had sought to spare.

VII.

Like rabid snakes, that sting some gentle child
Who brings them food, when winter false and fair
Allures them forth with its cold smiles, so wild
They rage among the camp ;—they overbear
The patriot hosts—confusion, then despair
Descends like night—when " Laon !" one did cry :
Like a bright ghost from Heaven that shout did scare
The slaves, and widening through the vaulted sky,
Seemed sent from Earth to Heaven in sign of victory.

VIII.

In sudden panic those false murderers fled,
Like insect tribes before the northern gale :
But swifter still, our hosts encompassed
Their shattered ranks, and in a craggy vale,
Where even their fierce despair might naught avail
Hemmed them around !—and then revenge and fear
Made the high virtue of the patriots fail :
One pointed on his foe the mortal spear—
I rushed before its point, and cried, " Forbear, forbear !"

IX.

The spear transfixed my arm that was uplifted
In swift expostulation, and the blood
Gushed round its point : I smiled, and—" Oh ! thou gifted
With eloquence which shall not be withstood,
Flow thus !"—I cried in joy, "thou vital flood,
Until my heart be dry, ere thus the cause
For which thou wert aught worthy be subdued—
Ah, ye are pale,—ye weep,—your passions pause,—
'Tis well ! ye feel the truth of love's benignant laws.

X.

" Soldiers, our brethren and our friends are slain.
Ye murdered them, I think, as they did sleep !
Alas, what have ye done? the slightest pain
Which ye might suffer, there were eyes to weep ;

But ye have quenched them—there were smiles to steep
Your hearts in balm, but they are lost in woe ;
And those whom love did set his watch to keep
Around your tents truth's freedom to bestow,
Ye stabbed as they did sleep—but they forgive ye now

XI.

" O wherefore should ill ever flow from ill,
And pain still keener pain for ever breed ?
We all are brethren—even the slaves who kill
For hire, are men ; and to avenge misdeed
On the misdoer, doth but Misery feed
With her own broken heart ! O Earth, O Heaven !
And thou, dread Nature, which to every deed
And all that lives, or is, to be hath given,
Even as to thee have these done ill, and are forgiven.

XII.

" Join then your hands and hearts, and let the past
Be as a grave which gives not up its dead
To evil thoughts"—a film then overcast
My sense with dimness, for the wound, which bled
Freshly, swift shadows o'er mine eyes had shed.
When I awoke, I lay 'mid friends and foes,
And earnest countenances on me shed
The light of questioning looks, whilst one did close
My wound with balmiest herbs, and soothed me to repose !

XIII.

And one whose spear had pierced me, leaned beside
With quivering lips and humid eyes ;—and all
Seemed like some brothers on a journey wide
Gone forth, whom row strange meeting did befall
In a strange land, round one whom they might call
Their friend, their chief, their father, for assay
Of peril, which had saved them from the thrall
Of death, now suffering. Thus the vast array
Of those fraternal bands were reconciled that day.

XIV.

Lifting the thunder of their acclamation,
Towards the City then the multitude,
And I among them, went in joy—a nation
Made free by love ;—a mighty brotherhood
Linked by a jealous interchange of good ;
A glorious pageant, more magnificent
Than kingly slaves arrayed in gold and blood,
When they return from carnage, and are sent
In triumph bright beneath the populous battlement.

XV.

Afar, the city walls were thronged on high,
And myriads on each giddy turret clung,
And to each spire far lessening in the sky,
Bright pennons on the idle winds were hung ;

As we approached a shout of joyance sprung
At once from all the crowd, as if the vast
And peopled Earth its boundless skies among
The sudden clamour of delight had cast,
When from before its face some general wreck had past.

XVI.

Our armies through the City's hundred gates
Were poured, like brooks which to the rocky lair
Of some deep lake, whose silence them awaits,
Throng from the mountains when the storms are there ;
And as we past through the calm sunny air
A thousand flower-inwoven crowns were shed,
The token flowers of truth and freedom fair,
And fairest hands bound them on many a head,
Those angels of love's heaven, that over all was spread.

XVII.

I trod as one tranced in some rapturous vision :
Those bloody bands so lately reconciled,
Were, ever as they went, by the contrition
Of anger turned to love from ill beguiled,
And every one on them more gently smiled,
Because they had done evil :—the sweet awe
Of such mild looks made their own hearts grow mild,
And did with soft attraction ever draw
Their spirits to the love of freedom's equal law.

XVIII.

And they, and all, in one loud symphony
My name with Liberty commingling, lifted,
" The friend and the preserver of the free !
The parent of this joy !" and fair eyes gifted
With feelings, caught from one who had uplifted
The light of a great spirit, round me shone ;
And all the shapes of this grand scenery shifted
Like restless clouds before the steadfast sun,—
Where was that maid ? I asked, but it was known of none.

XIX.

Laone was the name her love had chosen,
For she was nameless, and her birth none knew :
Where was Laone now ?—the words were frozen
Within my lips with fear ; but to subdue
Such dreadful hope, to my great task was due,
And when at length one brought reply, that she
To-morrow would appear, I then withdrew
To judge what need for that great throng might be,
For now the stars came thick over the twilight sea.

XX.

Yet need was none for rest or food to care,
Even though that multitude was passing great,
Since each one for the other did prepare
All kindly succour—Therefore to the gate

Of the Imperial House, now desolate,
I past, and there was found aghast, alone,
The fallen Tyrant !—silently he sate
Upon the footstool of his golden throne,
Which starred with sunny gems, in its own lustre shone.

XXI.

Alone, but for one child, who led before him
A graceful dance : the only living thing
Of all the crowd, which thither to adore him
Flocked yesterday, who solace sought to bring
In his abandonment ! she knew the King
Had praised her dance of yore, and now she wove
Its circles, aye weeping and murmuring
'Mid her sad task of unregarded love,
That to no smiles it might his speechless sadness move.

XXII.

She fled to him, and wildly clasped his feet
When human steps were heard :—he moved nor spoke,
Nor changed his hue, nor raised his looks to meet
The gaze of strangers—our loud entrance woke
The echoes of the hall, which circling broke
The calm of its recesses,—like a tomb
Its sculptured walls vacantly to the stroke
Of footfalls answered, and the twilight's gloom,
Lay like a charnel's mist within the radiant dome.

XXIII.

The little child stood up when we came nigh :
Her lips and cheeks seemed very pale and wan,
But on her forehead, and within her eye
Lay beauty, which makes hearts that feed thereon
Sick with excess of sweetness ; on the throne
She leaned ;—the King with gathered brow, and lips
Wreathed by long scorn, did inly sneer and frown
With hue like that when some great painter dips
His pencil in the gloom of earthquake and eclipse.

XXIV.

She stood beside him like a rainbow braided
Within some storm, when scarce its shadows vast
From the blue paths of the swift sun have faded ;
A sweet and solemn smile, like Cythna's cast
One moment's light, which made my heart beat fast
O'er that child's parted lips—a gleam of bliss,
A shade of vanished days,—as the tears past
Which wrapt it, even as with a father's kiss
I pressed those softest eyes in trembling tenderness.

XXV.

The sceptred wretch then from that solitude
I drew, and of his change compassionate,
With words of sadness soothed his rugged mood.
But he, while pride and fear held deep debate,

With sullen guile of ill-dissembled hate
Glared on me as a toothless snake might glare !
Pity, not scorn I felt, though desolate
The desolator now, and unaware
The curses which he mocked had caught him by the hair.

XXVI.

I led him forth from that which now might seem
A gorgeous grave through portals sculptured deep
With imagery beautiful as dream
We went, and left the shades which tend on sleep
Over its unregarded gold to keep
Their silent watch.—The child trod faintingly,
And as she went, the tears which she did weep
Glanced in the starlight ; wildered seemed she,
And when I spake, for sobs she could not answer me.

XXVII.

At last the tyrant cried, "She hungers, slave,
Stab her, or give her bread !"—It was a tone
Such as sick fancies in a new made grave
Might hear.   I trembled, for the truth was known,
He with this child had thus been left alone,
And neither had gone forth for food,—but he
In mingled pride and awe cowered near his throne,
And she a nursling of captivity
Knew naught beyond those walls, nor what such change might be,

XXVIII.

And he was troubled at a charm withdrawn
Thus suddenly ; that sceptres ruled no more—
That even from gold the dreadful strength was gone,
Which once made all things subject to its power—
Such wonder seized him, as if hour by hour
The past had come again ; and the swift fall
Of one so great and terrible of yore,
To desolateness, in the hearts of all
Like wonder stirred, who saw such awful change befall.

XXIX.

A mighty crowd, such as the wide land pours
Once in a thousand years, now gathered round
The fallen tyrant ;—like the rush of showers
Of hail in spring, pattering along the ground,
Their many footsteps fell, else came no sound
From the wide multitude : that lonely man
Then knew the burthen of his change, and found,
Concealing in the dust his visage wan,
Refuge from the keen looks which through his bosom ran.

XXX.

And he was faint withal : I sate beside him
Upon the earth, and took that child so fair
From his weak arms, that ill might none betide him
Or her ;—when food was brought to them, her share

To his averted lips the child did bear,
But when she saw he had enough, she ate
And wept the while ; the lonely man's despair
Hunger then overcame, and of his state
Forgetful, on the dust as in a trance he sate.

XXXI.

Slowly the silence of the multitudes
Past, as when far is heard in some lone dell
The gathering of a wind among the woods—
And he is fallen ! they cry, he who did dwell
Like famine or the plague, or aught more fell
Among our homes, is fallen ! the murderer
Who slaked his thirsting soul as from a well
Of blood and tears with ruin ! he is here !
Sunk in a gulf of scorn from which none may him rear !

XXXII.

Then was heard—He who judged let him be brought
To judgment ! blood for blood cries from the soil
On which his crimes have deep pollution wrought !
Shall Othman only unavenged despoil?
Shall they who by the stress of grinding toil
Wrest from the unwilling earth his luxuries,
Perish for crime, while his foul blood may boil,
Or creep within his veins at will?—Arise !
And to high justice make her chosen sacrifice.

XXXIII.

"What do ye seek ? what fear ye?" then I cried,
Suddenly starting forth, " that ye should shed
The blood of Othman—if your hearts are tried
In the true love of freedom, cease to dread
This one poor lonely man—beneath Heaven spread
In purest light above us all, through earth
Maternal earth, who doth her sweet smiles shed
For all, let him go free ; until the worth
Of human nature win from these a second birth.

XXXIV.

" What call ye *justice ?* is there one who ne'er
In secret thought has wished another's ill?—
Are ye all pure? let those stand forth who hear,
And tremble not.   Shall they insult and kill,
If such they be ? their mild eyes can they fill
With the false anger of the hypocrite?
Alas, such were not pure—the chastened will
Of virtue sees that justice is the light
Of love, and not revenge, and terror and despite.'

XXXV.

The murmur of the people slowly dying,
Paused as I spake, then those who near me were,
Cast gentle looks where the lone man was lying
Shrouding his head, which now that infant fair

Clasped on her lap in silence ;—through the air
Sobs were then heard, and many kissed my feet
In pity's madness, and to the despair
Of him whom late they cursed, a solace sweet
His very victims brought—soft looks and speeches meet.

XXXVI.

Then to a home for his repose assigned,
Accompanied by the still throng he went
In silence, where to soothe his rankling mind,
Some likeness of his ancient state was lent ;
And if his heart could have been innocent
As those who pardoned him, he might have ended
His days in peace ; but his strait lips were bent,
Men said, into a smile which guile portended,
A sight with which that child like hope with fear was
   blended.

XXXVII.

'Twas midnight now, the eve of that great day
Whereon the many nations at whose call
The chains of earth like mist melted away,
Decreed to hold a sacred Festival,
A rite to attest the equality of all
Who live.   So to their homes, to dream or wake
All went.   The sleepless silence did recal
Laone to my thoughts, with hopes that make
The flood recede from which their thirst they seek to slake.

XXXVIII.

The dawn flowed forth, and from its purple fountains
I drank those hopes which make the spirit quail :
As to the plain between the misty mountains
And the great City, with a countenance pale
I went :—it was a sight which might avail
To make men weep exulting tears, for whom
Now first from human power the reverend veil
Was torn, to see Earth from her general womb
Pour forth her swarming sons to a fraternal doom :

XXXIX

To see, far glancing in the misty morning
The signs of that innumerable host,
To hear one sound of many made, the warning
Of Earth to Heaven from its free children tost,
While the eternal hills, and the sea lost
In wavering light, and, starring the blue sky
The city's myriad spires of gold, almost
With human joy made mute society,
Its witnesses with men who must hereafter be.

XL.

To see like some vast island from the Ocean,
The Altar of the Federation rear
Its pile i' the midst ; a work, which the devotion
Of millions in one night created there,

Sudden, as when the moonrise makes appear
Strange clouds in the east ; a marble pyramid
Distinct with steps : that mighty shape did wear
The light of genius ; its still shadow hid
Far ships : to know its height the morning mists forbid !

XLI.

To hear the restless multitudes forever
Around the base of that great Altar flow,
As on some mountain islet burst and shiver
Atlantic waves ; and solemnly and slow
As the wind bore that tumult to and fro,
To feel the dreamlike music, which did swim
Like beams through floating clouds on waves below
Falling in pauses, from that Altar dim
As silver-sounding tongues breathed an aërial hymn.

XLII.

To hear, to see, to live, was on that morn
Lethean joy ! so that all those assembled
Cast off their memories of the past outworn ;
Two only bosoms with their own life trembled,
And mine was one,—and we had both dissembled ;
So with a beating heart I went, and one,
Who having much, covets yet more, resembled ;
A lost and dear possession, which not won,
He walks in lonely gloom beneath the noonday sun.

XLIII.

To the great Pyramid I came : its stair
With female quires was thronged : the loveliest
Among the free, grouped with its sculptures rare ;
As I approached, the morning's golden mist,
Which now the wonder-stricken breezes kist
With their cold lips, fled, and the summit shone
Like Athos seen from Samothracia, drest
In earliest light by vintagers, and one
Sate there, a female Shape upon an ivory throne.

XLIV.

A Form most like the imagined habitant
Of silver exhalations sprung from dawn,
By winds which feed on sunrise woven, to enchant
The faiths of men : all mortal eyes were drawn,
As famished mariners through strange seas gone
Gaze on a burning watch-tower, by the light
Of those divinest lineaments—alone
With thoughts which none could share, from that fair sight
I turned in sickness, for a veil shrouded her countenance bright.

XLV.

And, neither did I hear the acclamations,
Which from brief silence bursting, filled the air
With her strange name and mine, from all the nations
Which we, they said, in strength had gathered there

I

From the sleep of bondage ; nor the vision fair
Of that bright pageantry beheld,—but blind
And silent, as a breathing corpse did fare,
Leaning upon my friend, till like a wind
To fevered cheeks, a voice flowed o'er my troubled mind.

XLVI.

Like music of some minstrel heavenly gifted,
To one whom fiends enthral, this voice to me ;
Scarce did I wish her veil to be uplifted,
I was so calm and joyous.—I could see
The platform where we stood, the statues three
Which kept their marble watch on that high shrine,
The multitudes, the mountains, and the sea ;
As when eclipse hath past, things sudden shine
To men's astonished eyes most clear and crystalline.

XLVII.

At first Laone spoke most tremulously :
But soon her voice the calmness which it shed
Gathered, and—"Thou art whom I sought to see,
And thou art our first votary here," she said :
" I had a dear friend once, but he is dead !—
And of all those on the wide earth who breathe
Thou dost resemble him alone—I spread
This veil between us two, that thou beneath
Shouldst image one who may have been long lost in death.

XLVIII.

" For this wilt thou not henceforth pardon me ?
Yes, but those joys which silence well require
Forbid reply ;—why men have chosen me
To be the Priestess of this holiest rite
I scarcely know, but that the floods of light
Which flow over the world, have borne me hither
To meet thee, long most dear ; and now unite
Thine hand with mine, and may all comfort wither
From both the hearts whose pulse in joy now beat together.

XLIX.

" If our own will as others' law we bind,
If the foul worship trampled here we fear ;
If as ourselves we cease to love our kind !"—
She paused, and pointed upwards—sculptured there
Three shapes around her ivory throne appear ;
One was a Giant, like a child asleep
On a loose rock, whose grasp crushed, as it were
In dream, sceptres and crowns ; and one did keep
Its watchful eyes in doubt whether to smile or weep ;

L.

A Woman sitting on the sculptured disk
Of the broad earth, and feeding from one breast
A human babe and a young basilisk ;
Her looks were sweet as Heaven's when loveliest

In Autumn eves.—The third Image was drest
In white wings swift as clouds in winter skies,
Beneath his feet, 'mongst ghastliest forms, represt
Lay Faith, an obscene worm, who sought to rise,
While calmly on the Sun he turned his diamond eyes.

LI.

Beside that Image then I sate, while she
Stood, 'mid the throngs which ever ebbed and flowed
Like light amid the shadows of the sea
Cast from one cloudless star, and on the crowd
That touch which none who feels forgets, bestowed ;
And whilst the sun returned the steadfast gaze
Of the great Image as o'er Heaven it glode,
That rite had place ; it ceased when sunset's blaze
Burned o'er the isles ; all stood in joy and deep amaze.
When in the silence of all spirits there
Laone's voice was felt, and through the air
Her thrilling gestures spoke most eloquently fair.

1.

" Calm art thou as yon sunset ! swift and strong
As new-fledged Eagles, beautiful and young,
That float among the blinding beams of morning ;
And underneath thy feet writhe Faith and Folly,
Custom, and Hell, and mortal Melancholy—
Hark ! the earth starts to hear the mighty warning
    Of thy voice sublime and holy ;
    Its free spirits here assembled,
    See thee, feel thee, know thee now,—
    To thy voice their hearts have trembled
    Like ten thousand clouds which flow
    With one wide wind as it flies !—
Wisdom ! thy irresistible children rise
To hail thee, and the elements they chain
And their own will to swell the glory of thy train.

2.

" O Spirit vast and deep as Night and Heaven !
Mother and soul of all to which is given
The light of life, the loveliness of being,
Lo ! thou dost reascend the human heart,
Thy throne of power, almighty as thou wert,
In dreams of Poets old grown pale by seeing
    The shade of thee :—now, millions start
    To feel thy lightnings through them burning :
    Nature, or God, or Love, or Pleasure,
    Or Sympathy the sad tears turning
    To mutual smiles, a drainless treasure,
    Descends amidst us ;—Scorn, and Hate,
Revenge and Selfishness are desolate—
A hundred nations swear that there shall be
Pity and Peace and Love among the good and free !

3.

" Eldest of things, divine Equality !
Wisdom and Love are but the slaves of thee,
The Angels of thy sway, who pour around thee
Treasures from all the cells of human thought,
And from the Stars, and from the Ocean brought,
And the last living heart whose beatings bound thee :
            The powerful and the wise had sought
            Thy coming, thou in light descending
            O'er the wide land which is thine own
            Like the spring whose breath is blending
            All blasts of fragrance into one,
            Comest upon the paths of men !—
Earth bares her general bosom to thy ken,
And all her children here in glory meet
To feed upon thy smiles, and clasp thy sacred feet.

4.

" My brethren, we are free ! the plains and mountains,
The grey sea shore, the forests and the fountains,
Are haunts of happiest dwellers ;—man and woman,
Their common bondage burst, may freely borrow
From lawless love a solace for their sorrow ;
For oft we still must weep, since we are human.
            A stormy night's serenest morrow,
            Whose showers are pity's gentle tears,
            Whose clouds are smiles of those that die
            Like infants without hopes or fears,
            And whose beams are joys that lie
            In blended hearts, now holds dominion ;
The dawn of mind, which upwards on a pinion
Borne, swift as sunrise, far illumines space,
And clasps this barren world in its own bright embrace !

5.

" My brethren, we are free ! the fruits are glowing
Beneath the stars, and the night winds are flowing
O'er the ripe corn, the birds and beasts are dreaming—
Never again may blood of bird or beast
Stain with its venomous stream a human feast,
To the pure skies in accusation steaming,
            Avenging poisons shall have ceased
            To feed disease and fear and madness,
            The dwellers of the earth and air
            Shall throng around our steps in gladness
            Seeking their food or refuge there.
Our toil from thought all glorious forms shall cull,
To make this Earth, our home, more beautiful,
And Science, and her sister Poesy,
Shall clothe in light the fields and cities of the free !

6.

" Victory, Victory to the prostrate nations !
Bear witness Night, and ye mute Constellations

Who gaze on us from your crystalline cars !
Thoughts have gone forth whose powers can sleep no more !
Victory ! Victory ! Earth's remotest shore,
Regions which groan beneath the Antarctic stars,
The green lands cradled in the roar
    Of western waves, and wildernesses
    Peopled and vast, which skirt the oceans
    Where morning dyes her golden tresses,
    Shall soon partake our high emotions :
Kings shall turn pale ! Almighty Fear
The Fiend-God, when our charmed name he hear,
Shall fade like shadow from his thousand fanes,
While Truth with Joy enthroned o'er his lost empire reigns !''

LII.

Ere she had ceased, the mists of night entwining
Their dim woof, floated o'er the infinite throng ;
She, like a spirit through the darkness shining,
In tones whose sweetness silence did prolong,
As if to lingering winds they did belong,
Poured forth her inmost soul : a passionate speech
With wild and thrilling pauses woven among,
Which whoso heard, was mute, for it could teach
To rapture like her own all listening hearts to reach.

LIII.

Her voice was as a mountain stream which sweeps
The withered leaves of Autumn to the lake,
And in some deep and narrow bay then sleeps
In the shadow of the shores ; as dead leaves wake
Under the wave, in flowers and herbs which make
Those green depths beautiful when skies are blue,
The multitude so moveless did partake
Such living change, and kindling murmurs flew
As o'er that speechless calm delight and wonder grew.

LIV.

Over the plain the throngs were scattered then
In groups around the fires, which from the sea
Even to the gorge of the first mountain glen
Blazed wide and far : the banquet of the free
Was spread beneath many a dark cypress tree,
Beneath whose spires, which swayed in the red light,
Reclining as they ate, of Liberty,
And Hope, and Justice, and Laone's name,
Earth's children did a woof of happy converse frame.

LV.

Their feast was such as Earth, the general mother,
Pours from her fairest bosom, when she smiles
In the embrace of Autumn ;—to each other
As when some parent fondly reconciles
Her warring children, she their wrath beguiles
With her own sustenance : they relenting weep :
Such was this Festival, which from their isles
And continents, and winds, and oceans deep,
All shapes might throng to share, that fly, or walk, or creep.

LVI.

Might share in peace and innocence, for gore
Or poison none this festal did pollute,
But piled on high, an overflowing store
Of pomegranates, and citrons, fairest fruit,
Melons, and dates, and figs, and many a root
Sweet and sustaining, and bright grapes ere yet
Accursed fire their mild juice could transmute
Into a mortal bane, and brown corn set
In baskets ; with pure streams their thirsting lips they wet.

LVII.

Laone had descended from the shrine,
And every deepest look and holiest mind
Fed on her form, though now those tones divine
Were silent as she past ; she did unwind
Her veil, as with the crowds of her own kind
She mixed ; some impulse made my heart refrain
From seeking her that night, so I reclined
Amidst a group, where on the utmost plain
A festal watchfire burned beside the dusky main.

LVIII.

And joyous was our feast ; pathetic talk,
And wit, and harmony of choral strains,
While far Orion o'er the waves did walk
That flow among the isles, held us in chains
Of sweet captivity, which none disdains
Who feels : but when his zone grew dim in mist
Which clothes the Ocean's bosom, o'er the plains
The multitudes went homeward to their rest,
Which that delightful day with its own shadow blest.

CANTO SIXTH.

I.

Beside the dimness of the glimmering sea,
Weaving swift language from impassioned themes,
With that dear friend I lingered, who to me
So late had been restored, beneath the gleams
Of the silver stars ; and ever in soft dreams
Of future love and peace sweet converse lapt
Our willing fancies, 'till the pallid beams
Of the last watchfire fell, and darkness wrapt
The waves, and each bright chain of floating fire was snapt

II.

And till we came even to the city's wall
And the great gate, then, none knew whence or why,
Disquiet on the multitudes did fall :
And first, one pale and breathless past us by,

And stared and spoke not ;—then with piercing cry
A troop of wild-eyed women, by the shrieks
Of their own terror driven—tumultuously
Hither and thither hurrying with pale cheeks,
Each one from fear unknown a sudden refuge seeks—

III.

Then, rallying cries of treason and of danger
Resounded : and—"They come ! to arms ! to arms !
The Tyrant is amongst us, and the stranger
Comes to enslave us in his name ! to arms !"
In vain : for Panic, the pale fiend who charms
Strength to forswear her right, those millions swept
Like waves before the tempest—these alarms
Came to me, as to know their cause I leapt
On the gate's turret, and in rage and grief and scorn I wept !

IV.

For to the North I saw the town on fire,
And its red light made morning pallid now,
Which burst over wide Asia ;—louder, higher,
The yells of victory and the screams of woe
I heard approach, and saw the throng below
Stream through the gates like foam-wrought waterfalls
Fed from a thousand storms—the fearful glow
Of bombs flares overhead—at intervals
The red artillery's bolt mangling among them falls.

V.

And now the horsemen come—and all was done
Swifter than I have spoken—I beheld
Their red swords flash in the unrisen sun.
I rushed among the rout to have repelled
That miserable flight—one moment quelled
By voice, and looks, and eloquent despair,
As if reproach from their own hearts withheld
Their steps, they stood ; but soon came pouring there
New multitudes, and did those rallied bands o'erbear.

VI.

I strove, as drifted on some cataract
By irresistible streams, some wretch might strive
Who hears its fatal roar :—the files compact
Whelmed me, and from the gate availed to drive
With quickening impulse, as each bolt did rive
Their ranks with bloodier chasm :—into the plain
Disgorged at length the dead and the alive
In one dread mass, were parted, and the stain
Of blood, from mortal steel fell o'er the fields like rain.

VII.

For now the despot's blood-hounds with their prey,
Unarmed and unaware, were gorging deep
Their gluttony of death ; the loose array
Of horsemen o'er the wide fields murdering sweep,

And with loud laughter for their tyrant reap
A harvest sown with other hopes, the while,
Far overhead, ships from Propontis keep
A killing rain of fire :—when the waves smile
As sudden earthquakes light many a volcano isle.

VIII.

Thus sudden, unexpected feast was spread
For the carrion fowls of Heaven.—I saw the sight
I moved—I lived—as o'er the heaps of dead,
Whose stony eyes glared in the morning light
I trod ;—to me there came no thought of flight,
But with loud cries of scorn which whoso heard
That dreaded death, felt in his veins the might
Of virtuous shame return, the crowd I stirred,
And desperation's hope in many hearts recurred.

IX.

A band of brothers gathering round me, made,
Although unarmed, a steadfast front, and still
Retreating, with stern looks beneath the shade
Of gathered eyebrows, did the victors fill
With doubt even in success ; deliberate will
Inspired our growing troop, not overthrown
It gained the shelter of a grassy hill,
And ever still our comrades were hewn down,
And their defenceless limbs beneath our footsteps strown.

X.

Immoveably we stood—in joy I found,
Beside me then, firm as a giant pine
Among the mountain vapours driven around,
The old man whom I loved—his eyes divine
With a mild look of courage answered mine,
And my young friend was near, and ardently
His hand grasped mine a moment—now the line
Of war extended, to our rallying cry
As myriads flocked in love and brotherhood to die.

XI.

For ever while the sun was climbing Heaven
The horseman hewed our unarmed myriads down
Safely, though when by thirst of carnage driven
Too near, those slaves were swiftly overthrown
By hundreds leaping on them :—flesh and bone
Soon made our ghastly ramparts ; then the shaft
Of the artillery from the sea was thrown
More fast and fiery, and the conquerors laughed
In pride to hear the wind our screams of torment waft.

XII.

For on one side alone the hill gave shelter,
So vast that phalanx of unconquered men,
And there the living in the blood did welter
Of the dead and dying, which, in that green glen

Like stifled torrents, made a plashy fen
Under the feet—thus was the butchery waged
While the sun clombe Heaven's eastern steep—but when
It 'gan to sink—a fiercer combat raged,
For in more doubtful strife the armies were engaged

XIII.

Within a cave upon the hill were found
A bundle of rude pikes, the instrument
Of those who war but on their native ground
For natural rights : a shout of joyance sent
Even from our hearts the wide air pierced and rent,
As those few arms the bravest and the best
Seized, and each sixth, thus armed, did now present
A line which covered and sustained the rest,
A confident phalanx, which the foes on every side invest.

XIV.

That onset turned the foes to flight almost,
But soon they saw their present strength, and knew
That coming night would to our resolute host
Bring victory, so dismounting close they drew
Their glittering files, and then the combat grew
Unequal but most horrible ;—and ever
Our myriads, whom the swift bolt overthrew,
Or the red sword, failed like a mountain river
Which rushes forth in foam to sink in sands forever.

XV.

Sorrow and shame, to see with their own kind
Our human brethren mix, like beasts of blood
To mutual ruin armed by one behind
Who sits and scoffs !—That friend so mild and good,
Who like its shadow near my youth had stood,
Was stabbed !—my old preserver's hoary hair
With the flesh clinging to its roots, was strewed
Under my feet !—I lost all sense or care,
And like the rest I grew desperate and unaware.

XVI.

The battle became ghastlier—in the midst
I paused, and saw, how ugly and how fell
O Hate ! thou art, even when thy life thou shedd'st
For love.   The ground in many a little dell
Was broken, up and down whose steeps befel
Alternate victory and defeat, and there
The combatants with rage most horrible
Strove, and their eyes started with cracking stare,
And impotent their tongues they lolled into the air,

XVII.

Flaccid and foamy, like a mad dog's hanging ;
Want, and Moon-madness, and the pest's swift Bane
When its shafts smite—while yet its bow is twanging—
Have each their mark and sign—some ghastly stain ;

And this was thine, O War ! of hate and pain
Thou loathed slave.   I saw all shapes of death
And ministered to many, o'er the plain
While carnage in the sunbeam's warmth did seethe,
Till twilight o'er the east wove her serenest wreath.

XVIII.

The few who yet survived, resolute and firm
Around me fought.   At the decline of day
Winding above the mountain's snowy term
New banners shone : they quivered in the ray
Of the sun's unseen orb—ere night the array
Of fresh troops hemmed us in—of those brave bands
I soon survived alone—and now I lay
Vanquished and faint, the grasp of bloody hands
I felt, and saw on high the glare of falling brands :

XIX.

When on my foes a sudden terror came,
And they fled, scattering—lo ! with reinless speed
A black Tartarian horse of giant frame
Comes trampling over the dead, the living bleed
Beneath the hoofs of that tremendous steed,
On which, like to an Angel, robed in white,
Sate one waving a sword ;—the hosts recede
And fly, as through their ranks with awful might,
Sweeps in the shadow of eve that Phantom swift and bright ;

XX.

And its path made a solitude.—I rose
And marked its coming : it relaxed its course
As it approached me, and the wind that flows
Through night, bore accents to mine ear whose force
Might create smiles in death—the Tartar horse
Paused, and I saw the shape its might which swayed,
And heard her musical pants, like the sweet source
Of waters in the desert, as she said,
" Mount with me, Laon, now"—I rapidly obeyed.

XXI.

Then : " Away ! away !" she cried, and stretched her sword
As 'twere a scourge over the courser's head,
And lightly shook the reins :—We spake no word
But like the vapour of the tempest fled
Over the plain ; her dark hair was dispread
Like the pine's locks upon the lingering blast ;
Over mine eyes its shadowy strings it spread
Fitfully, and the hills and streams fled fast,
As o'er their glimmering forms the steed's broad shadow past.

XXII.

And his hoofs ground the rocks to fire and dust,
His strong sides made the torrents rise in spray,
And turbulence, as of a whirlwind's gust
Surrounded us ;—and still away ! away !

Through the desert night we sped, while she alway
Gazed on a mountain which we neared, whose crest
Crowned with a marble ruin, in the ray
Of the obscure stars gleamed ;—its rugged breast
The steed strained up, and then his impulse did arrest.

XXIII.

A rocky hill which overhung the Ocean :—
From that lone ruin, when the steed that panted
Paused, might be heard the murmur of the motion
Of waters, as in spots for ever haunted
By the choicest winds of Heaven, which are enchanted
To music, by the wand of Solitude,
That wizard wild, and the far tents implanted
Upon the plain, be seen by those who stood
Thence marking the dark shore of Ocean's curved flood.

XXIV.

One moment these were heard and seen—another
Past ; and the two who stood beneath that night,
Each only heard, or saw, or felt the other ;
As from the lofty steed she did alight,
Cythna (for, from the eyes whose deepest light
Of love and sadness made my lips feel pale
With influence strange of mournfullest delight,
My own sweet Cythna looked), with joy did quail,
And felt her strength in tears of human weakness fail.

XXV.

And, for a space in my embrace she rested,
Her head on my unquiet heart reposing,
While my faint arms her languid frame invested :
At length she looked on me, and half unclosing
Her tremulous lips, said : " Friend, thy bands were losing
The battle, as I stood before the King
In bonds.—I burst them then, and swiftly choosing
The time, did seize a Tartar's sword, and spring
Upon his horse, and swift as on the whirlwind's wing,

XXVI.

" Have thou and I been borne beyond pursuer,
And we are here."—Then turning to the steed,
She pressed the white moon on his front with pure
And rose-like lips, and many a fragrant weed
From the green ruin plucked, that he might feed ;—
But I to a stone seat that Maiden led,
And kissing her fair eyes, said, " Thou hast need
Of rest," and I heaped up the courser's bed
In a green mossy nook, with mountain flowers dispread.

XXVII.

Within that ruin, where a shattered portal
Looks to the eastern stars, abandoned now
By man, to be the home of things immortal,
Memories, like awful ghosts which come and go,

And must inherit all he builds below,
When he is gone, a hall stood ; o'er whose roof
Fair clinging weeds with ivy pale did grow,
Clasping its grey rents with a verdurous woof,
A hanging dome of leaves, a canopy moon-proof.

XXVIII.

The autumnal winds, as if spell-bound, had made
A natural couch of leaves in that recess,
Which seasons none disturbed, but in the shade
Of flowering parasites, did spring love to dress
With their sweet blooms the wintry loneliness
Of those dead leaves, shedding their stars, whene'er
The wandering wind her nurslings might caress ;
Whose intertwining fingers ever there,
Made music wild and soft that filled the listening air.

XXIX.

We know not where we go, or what sweet dream
May pilot us through caverns strange and fair
Of far and pathless passion, while the stream
Of life, our bark doth on its whirlpools bear,
Spreading swift wings as sails to the dim air ;
Nor should we seek to know, so the devotion
Of love and gentle thoughts be heard still there
Louder and louder from the utmost Ocean
Of universal life, attuning its commotion.

XXX.

To the pure all things are pure !   Oblivion wrapt
Our spirits, and the fearful overthrow
Of public hope was from our being snapt,
Though linked years had bound it there ; for now
A power, a thirst, a knowledge, which below
All thoughts, like light beyond the atmosphere,
Clothing its clouds with grace, doth ever flow,
Came on us, as we sate in silence there,
Beneath the golden stars of the clear azure air.

XXXI.

In silence which doth follow talk that causes
The baffled heart to speak with sighs and tears,
When wildering passion swalloweth up the pauses
Of inexpressive speech :—the youthful years
Which we together past, their hopes and fears,
The blood itself which ran within our frames,
That likeness of the features which endears
The thoughts expressed by them, our very names,
And all the winged hours which speechless memory claims

XXXII.

Had found a voice :—and ere that voice did pass,
The night grew damp and dim, and through a rent
Of the ruin where we sate, from the morass,
A wandering Meteor by some wild wind sent,

Hung high in the green dome, to which it lent
A faint and pallid lustre ; while the song
Of blasts, in which its blue hair quivering bent,
Strewed strangest sounds the moving leaves among ;
A wondrous light, the sound as of a spirit's tongue.

XXXIII.

The Meteor showed the leaves on which we sate,
And Cythna's glowing arms, and the thick ties
Of her soft hair, which bent with gathered weight
My neck near hers, her dark and deepening eyes,
Which, as twin phantoms of one star that lies
O'er a dim well, move, though the star reposes,
Swam in our mute and liquid ecstasies,
Her marble brow, and eager lips, like roses,
With their own fragrance pale, which spring but half uncloses.

XXXIV.

The meteor to its far morass returned :
The beating of our veins one interval
Made still ; and then I felt the blood that burned
Within her frame, mingle with mine, and fall
Around my heart like fire ; and over all
A mist was spread, the sickness of a deep
And speechless swoon of joy, as might befall
Two disunited spirits when they leap
In union from this earth's obscure and fading sleep.

XXXV.

Was it one moment that confounded thus
All thought, all sense, all feeling, into one
Unutterable power, which shielded us
Even from our own cold looks, when we had gone
Into a wide and wild oblivion
Of tumult and of tenderness? or now
Had ages, such as make the moon and sun,
The seasons, and mankind their changes know,
Left fear and time unfelt by us alone below?

XXXVI.

I know not.   What are kisses whose fire clasps
The failing heart in languishment, or limb
Twined within limb? or the quick dying gasps
Of the life meeting, when the faint eyes swim
Through tears of a wide mist boundless and dim,
In one caress? What is the strong control
Which leads the heart that dizzy steep to climb,
Where far over the world those vapours roll,
Which blend two restless frames in one reposing soul?

XXXVII.

It is the shadow which doth float unseen,
But not unfelt, o'er blind mortality,
Whose divine darkness fled not, from that green
And lone recess, where lapt in peace did lie

Our linked frames ; till, from the changing sky,
That night and still another day had fled ;
And then I saw and felt.   The moon was high,
And clouds, as of a coming storm, were spread
Under its orb,—loud winds were gathering overhead.

XXXVIII.

Cythna's sweet lips seemed lurid in the moon,
Her fairest limbs with the night wind were chill,
And her dark tresses were all loosely strown
O'er her pale bosom :—all within was still,
And the sweet peace of joy did almost fill
The depth of her unfathomable look ;—
And we sate calmly, though that rocky hill,
The waves contending in its caverns strook,
For they foreknew the storm, and the grey ruin shook.

XXXIX.

There we unheeding sate, in the communion
Of interchanged vows, which, with a rite
Of faith most sweet and sacred, stamped our union.—
Few were the living hearts which could unite
Like ours, or celebrate a bridal night
With such close sympathies, for they had sprung
From linked youth, and from the gentle might
Of earliest love, delayed and cherished long,
Which common hopes and fears made, like a tempest, strong.

XL.

And such is Nature's law divine, that those
Who grow together cannot choose but love,
If faith or custom do not interpose,
Or common slavery mar what else might move
All gentlest thoughts ; as in the sacred grove
Which shades the springs of Æthiopian Nile,
That living tree, which, if the arrowy dove
Strike with her shadow, shrinks in fear awhile,
But its own kindred leaves clasps while the sunbeams smile ;

XLI.

And clings to them, when darkness may dissever
The close caresses of all duller plants
Which bloom on the wide earth—thus we for ever
Were linked, for love had nurst us in the haunts
Where knowledge, from its secret source enchants
Young hearts with the fresh music of its springing,
Ere yet its gathered flood feeds human wants,
As the great Nile feeds Egypt ; ever flinging
Light on the woven boughs which o'er its waves are swinging.

XLII.

The tones of Cythna's voice like echoes were
Of those far murmuring streams ; they rose and fell,
Mixed with mine own in the tempestuous air,—
And so we sate, until our talk befell

Of the late ruin, swift and horrible,
And how those seeds of hope might yet be sown,
Whose fruit is evil's mortal poison : well,
For us, this ruin made a watch-tower lone,
But Cythna's eyes looked faint, and now two days were gone

XLIII.

Since she had food ;—therefore I did awaken
The Tartar steed, who, from his ebon mane,
Soon as the clinging slumbers he had shaken,
Bent his thin head to seek the brazen rein.
Following me obediently ; with pain
Of heart, so deep and dread, that one caress,
When lips and heart refuse to part again,
Till they have told their fill, could scarce express
The anguish of her mute and fearful tenderness,

XLIV.

Cythna beheld me part, as I bestrode
That w"ling steed—the tempest and the night,
Which gave my path its safety as I rode
Down the ravine of rocks, did soon unite
The darkness and the tumult of their might
Borne on all winds.—For through the streaming rain
Floating at intervals the garments white
Of Cythna gleamed, and her voice once again
Came to me on the gust, and soon I reached the plain.

XLV.

I dreaded not the tempest, nor did he
Who bore me, but his eyeballs wide and red
Turned on the lightning's cleft exultingly ;
And when the earth beneath his tameless tread,
Shook with the sullen thunder, he would spread
His nostrils to the blast, and joyously
Mock the fierce peal with neighings ;—thus we sped
O'er the lit plain, and soon I could descry
Where Death and Fire had gorged the spoil of victory

XLVI.

There was a desolate village in a wood
Whose bloom-inwoven leaves now scattering fed
The hungry storm ; it was a place of blood,
A heap of hearthless walls ;—the flames were dead
Within those dwellings now—the life had fled
From all those corpses now—but the wide sky
Flooded with lightning was ribbed overhead
By the black rafters, and around did lie
Women, and babes, and men, slaughtered confusedly.

XLVII.

Beside the fountain in the market-place
Dismounting, I beheld those corpses stare
With horny eyes upon each other's face,
And on the earth and on the vacant air,

And upon me, close to the waters where
I stooped to slake my thirst ;—I shrank to taste,
For the salt bitterness of blood was there ;
But tied the steed beside, and sought in haste
If any yet survived amid that ghastly waste.

XLVIII.

No living thing was there beside one woman,
Whom I found wandering in the streets, and she
Was withered from a likeness of aught human
Into a fiend, by some strange misery :
Soon as she heard my steps she leaped on me,
And glued her burning lips to mine, and laughed
With a loud, long, and frantic laugh of glee,
And cried, " Now Mortal, thou hast deeply quaffed
The Plague's blue kisses—soon millions shall pledge the draught !

XLIX.

" My name is Pestilence—this bosom dry,
Once fed two babes—a sister and a brother—
When I came home, one in the blood did lie
Of three death-wounds—the flames had ate the other !
Since then I have no longer been a mother,
But I am Pestilence ;—hither and thither
I flit about, that I may slay and smother :—
All lips which I have kissed must surely wither,
But Death's—if thou art he, we'll go to work together !

L.

" What seek'st thou here ? the moonlight comes in flashes—
The dew is rising dankly from the dell—
'Twill moisten her ! and thou shalt see the gashes
In my sweet boy, now full of worms—but tell
First what thou seek'st."—" I seek for food."—" 'Tis well
Thou shalt have food ; Famine, my paramour,
Waits for us at the feast—cruel and fell
Is Famine, but he drives not from his door
Those whom these lips have kissed, alone.   No more, no more !"

LI.

As thus she spake, she grasped me with the strength
Of madness, and by many a ruined hearth
She led, and over many a corpse :—at length
We came to a lone hut, where on the earth
Which made its floor, she in her ghastly mirth
Gathering from all those homes now desolate,
Had piled three heaps of loaves, making a dearth
Among the dead—round which she set in state
A ring of cold, stiff babes ; silent and stark they sate.

LII.

She leaped upon a pile, and lifted high
Her mad looks to the lightning, and cried : " Eat !
Share the great feast —to-morrow we must die !"
And then she spurned the loaves with her pale feet.

Towards her bloodless guests ;—that sight to meet,
Mine eyes and my heart ached, and but that she
Who loved me, did with absent looks defeat
Despair, I might have raved in sympathy ;
But now I took the food that woman offered me ;

LIII.

And vainly having with her madness striven
If I might win her to return with me,
Departed.   In the eastern beams of Heaven
The lightning now grew pallid—rapidly,
As by the shore of the tempestuous sea
The dark steed bore me, and the mountain grey
Soon echoed to his hoofs, and I could see
Cythna among the rocks, where she alway
Had sate, with anxious eyes fixed on the lingering day.

LIV.

And joy was ours to meet : she was most pale,
Famished, and wet and weary, so I cast
My arms around her, lest my steps should fail
As to our home we went, and thus embraced,
Her full heart seemed a deeper joy to taste
Than e'er the prosperous know ; the steed behind
Trod peacefully along the mountain waste,
We reached our home ere morning could unbind
Night's latest veil, and on our bridal couch reclined.

LV.

Her chilled heart having cherished in my bosom,
And sweetest kisses past, we two did share
Our peaceful meal :—as an autumnal blossom
Which spreads its shrunk leaves in the sunny air,
After cold showers, like rainbows woven there,
Thus in her lips and cheeks the vital spirit
Mantled, and in her eyes, an atmosphere
Of health, and hope ; and sorrow languished near it,
And fear, and all that dark despondence doth inherit.

CANTO SEVENTH.

I.

So we sate joyous as the morning ray
Which fed upon the wrecks of night and storm
Now lingering on the winds ; light airs did play
Among the dewy weeds, the sun was warm,
And we sate linked in the inwoven charm
Of converse and caresses sweet and deep,
Speechless caresses, talk that might disarm
Time, though he wield the darts of death and sleep,
And those thrice mortal barbs in his own poison steep.

K

II.

I told her of my sufferings and my madness,
And how, awakened from that dreamy mood
By Liberty's uprise, the strength of gladness
Came to my spirit in my solitude ;
And all that now I was, while tears pursued
Each other down her fair and listening cheek
Fast as the thoughts which fed them, like a flood
From sunbright dales ; and when I ceased to speak,
Her accents soft and sweet the pausing air did wake.

III.

She told me a strange tale of strange endurance,
Like broken memories of many a heart
Woven into one ; to which no firm assurance,
So wild were they, could her own faith impart.
She said that not a tear did dare to start
From the swoln brain, and that her thoughts were firm
When from all mortal hope she did depart,
Borne by those slaves across the Ocean's term,
And that she reached the port without one fear infirm.

IV.

One was she among many there, the thralls
Of the cold tyrant's cruel lust : and they
Laughed mournfully in those polluted halls ;
But she was calm and sad, musing alway
On loftiest enterprise, till on a day
The tyrant heard her singing to her lute
A wild, and sad, and spirit-thrilling lay,
Like winds that die in waste—one moment mute
The evil thoughts it made, which did his breast pollute.

V.

Even when he saw her wondrous loveliness,
One moment to great Nature's sacred power
He bent, and was no longer passionless ;
But when he bade her to his secret bower
Be borne, a loveless victim, and she tore
Her locks in agony, and her words of flame
And mightier looks availed not ; then he bore
Again his load of slavery, and became
A king, a heartless beast, a pageant and a name.

VI.

She told me what a loathsome agony
Is that when selfishness mocks love's delight,
Foul as in dreams most fearful imagery
To dally with the mowing dead—that night
All torture, fear, or horror made seem light
Which the soul dreams or knows, and when the day
Shone on her awful frenzy, from the sight
Where like a Spirit in fleshly chains she lay
Struggling, aghast and pale the Tyrant fled away.

VII.

Her madness was a beam of light, a power
Which dawned through the rent soul ; and words it gave
Gestures and looks, such as in whirlwinds bore
Which might not be withstood, whence none could save
All who approached their sphere, like some calm wave
Vexed into whirlpools by the chasms beneath ;
And sympathy made each attendant slave
Fearless and free, and they began to breathe
Deep curses, like the voice of flames far underneath.

VIII.

The King felt pale upon his noonday throne :
At night two slaves he to her chamber sent,
One was a green and wrinkled eunuch, grown
From human shape into an instrument
Of all things ill—distorted, bowed and bent.
The other was a wretch from infancy
Made dumb by poison ; who naught knew or meant
But to obey : from the fire-isles came he,
A diver lean and strong, of Oman's coral sea.

IX.

They bore her to a bark, and the swift stroke
Of silent rowers clove the blue moonlight seas,
Until upon their path the morning broke ;
They anchored then, where, be there calm or breeze,
The gloomiest of the drear Symplegades
Shakes with the sleepless surge ;—the Æthiop there
Wound his long arms around her, and with knees
Like iron clasped her feet, and plunged with her
Among the closing waves out of the boundless air.

X.

" Swift as an eagle stooping from the plain
Of morning light, into some shadowy wood,
He plunged through the green silence of the main,
Through many a cavern which the eternal flood
Had scooped, as dark lairs for its monster brood ;
And among mighty shapes which fled in wonder,
And among mightier shadows which pursued
His heels, he wound : until the dark rocks under
He touched a golden chain—a sound arose like thunder.

XI.

" A stunning clang of massive bolts redoubling
Beneath the deep—a burst of waters driven
As from the roots of the sea, raging and bubbling :
And in that roof of crags a space was riven
Through which there shone the emerald beams of heaven,
Shot through the lines of many waves inwoven,
Like sunlight through acacia woods at even,
Through which, his way the diver having cloven,
Past like a spark sent up out of a burning oven.

XII.

" And then," she said, "he laid me in a cave
Above the waters, by that chasm of sea,
A fountain round and vast, in which the wave
Imprisoned, boiled and leaped perpetually,
Down which, one moment resting, he did flee,
Winning the adverse depth ; that spacious cell
Like an upaithric temple wide and high,
Whose aëry dome is inaccessible,
Was pierced with one round cleft through which the sunbeams fell.

XIII.

" Below, the fountain's brink was richly paven
With the deep's wealth, coral, and pearl, and sand
Like spangling gold, and purple shells engraven
With mystic legends by no mortal hand,
Left there, when thronging to the moon's command,
The gathering waves rent the Hesperian gate
Of mountains, and on such bright floor did stand
Columns, and shapes like statues, and the state
Of kingless thrones, which Earth did in her heart create.

XIV.

" The fiend of madness which had made its prey
Of my poor heart, was lulled to sleep awhile :
There was an interval of many a day,
And a sea-eagle brought me food the while,
Whose nest was built in that untrodden isle,
And who, to be the jailor had been taught,
Of that strange dungeon ; as a friend whose smile
Like light and rest at morn and even is sought,
That wild bird was to me, till madness misery brought.

XV.

" The misery of a madness slow and creeping,
Which made the earth seem fire, the sea seem air,
And the white clouds of noon which oft were sleeping,
In the blue heaven so beautiful and fair,
Like hosts of ghastly shadows hovering there ;
And the sea-eagle looked a fiend, who bore
Thy mangled limbs for food !—thus all things were
Transformed into the agony which I wore
Even as a poisoned robe around my bosom's core.

XVI.

" Again I knew the day and night fast fleeing,
The eagle, and the fountain, and the air ;
Another frenzy came—there seemed a being
Within me—a strange load my heart did bear,
As if some living thing had made its lair
Even in the fountains of my life :—a long
And wondrous vision wrought from my despair,
Then grew, like sweet reality among
Dim visionary woes, an unreposing throng.

XVII.

" Methought I was about to be a mother—
Month after month went by, and still I dreamed
That we should soon be all to one another,
I and my child ; and still new pulses seemed
To beat beside my heart, and still I deemed
There was a babe within—and when the rain
Of winter through the rifted cavern streamed,
Methought, after a lapse of lingering pain,
I saw that lovely shape, which near my heart had lain.

XVIII.

" It was a babe, beautiful from its birth,—
It was like thee, dear love, its eyes were thine,
Its brow, its lips, and so upon the earth
It laid its fingers, as now rest on mine
Thine own beloved :—'twas a dream divine ;
Even to remember how it fled, how swift,
How utterly, might make the heart repine,—
Though 'twas a dream."—Then Cythna did uplift
Her looks on mine, as if some doubt she sought to shift :

XIX.

A doubt which would not flee, a tenderness
Of questioning grief, a source of thronging tears ;
Which, having past, as one whom sobs oppress,
She spoke : " Yes, in the wilderness of years
Her memory, aye, like a green home appears,
She sucked her fill even at this breast, sweet love,
For many months. I had no mortal fears ;
Methought I felt her lips and breath approve,—
It was a human thing which to my bosom clove.

XX.

" I watched the dawn of her first smiles, and soon
When zenith-stars were trembling on the wave,
Or when the beams of the invisible moon,
Or sun, from many a prism within the cave
Their gem-born shadows to the water gave,
Her looks would hunt them, and with outspread hand,
From the swift lights which might that fountain pave,
She would mark one, and laugh, when that command
Slighting, it lingered there, and could not understand.

XXI.

" Methought her looks began to talk with me ;
And no articulate sounds, but something sweet
Her lips would frame,—so sweet it could not be,
That it was meaningless ; her touch would meet
Mine, and our pulses calmly flow and beat
In response while we slept : and on a day
When I was happiest in that strange retreat,
With heaps of golden shells we two did play,—
Both infants, weaving wings for time's perpetual way.

XXII.

" Ere night, methought, her waning eyes were grown
Weary with joy, and tired with our delight,
We, on the earth, like sister twins, lay down
On one fair mother's bosom :—from that night
She fled ;—like those illusions clear and bright,
Which dwell in lakes, when the red moon on high
Pause ere it wakens tempest ;—and her flight,
Though 'twas the death of brainless phantasy,
Yet smote my lonesome heart more than all misery.

XXIII.

" It seemed that in the dreary night, the diver
Who brought me thither, came again, and bore
My child away. I saw the waters quiver,
When he so swiftly sunk, as once before :
Then morning came—it shone even as of yore,
But I was changed—the very life was gone
Out of my heart—I wasted more and more,
Day after day, and sitting there alone,
Vexed the inconstant waves with my perpetual moan.

XXIV.

" I was no longer mad, and yet methought
My breasts were swoln and changed :—in every vein
The blood stood still one moment, while that thought
Was passing—with a gush of sickening pain
It ebbed even to its withered springs again :
When my wan eyes in stern resolve I turned
From that most strange delusion, which would fain
Have waked the dream for which my spirit yearned
With more than human love,—then left it unreturned.

XXV.

" So now my reason was restored to me,
I struggled with that dream, which, like a beast
Most fierce and beauteous, in my memory
Had made its lair, and on my heart did feast ;
But all that cave and all its shapes possest
By thoughts which could not fade, renewed each one
Some smile, some look, some gesture which had blest
Me heretofore : I, sitting there alone,
Vexed the inconstant waves with my perpetual moan.

XXVI.

" Time past, I know not whether months or years ;
For day, nor night, nor change of seasons made
Its note, but thoughts and unavailing tears :
And I became at last even as a shade,
A smoke, a cloud on which the winds have preyed,
Till it be thin as air ; until, one even,
A Nautilus upon the fountain played,
Spreading his azure sail where breath of Heaven
Descended not, among the waves and whirlpools driven.

XXVII.

" And when the Eagle came, that lovely thing,
Oaring with rosy feet its silver boat,
Fled near me as for shelter ; on slow wing,
The Eagle, hovering o'er its prey did float ;
But when he saw that I with fear did note
His purpose, proffering my own food to him,
The eager plumes subsided on his throat—
He came where that bright child of sea did swim,
And o'er it cast in peace his shadow broad and dim.

XXVIII.

" This wakened me, it gave me human strength
And hope, I know not whence or wherefore, rose,
But I resumed my ancient powers at length ;
My spirit felt again like one of those
Like thine, whose fate it is to make the woes
Of humankind their prey—what was this cave ?
Its deep foundation no firm purpose knows
Immutable, resistless, strong to save,
Like mind while yet it mocks the all-devouring grave.

XXIX.

" And where was Laon ? might my heart be dead,
While that far dearer heart could move and be ?
Or whilst over the earth the pall was spread,
Which I had sworn to rend ? I might be free,
Could I but win that friendly bird to me,
To bring me ropes ; and long in vain I sought
By intercourse of mutual imagery
Of objects, if such aid he could be taught ;
But fruit, and flowers, and boughs, yet never ropes he brought.

XXX.

" We live in our own world, and mine was made
From glorious phantasies of hope departed :
Ay, we are darkened with their floating shade,
Or cast a lustre on them—time imparted
Such power to me, I became fearless-hearted,
My eye and voice grew firm, calm was my mind,
And piercing, like the morn, now it has darted
Its lustre on all hidden things, behind
Yon·dim and fading clouds which load the weary wind.

XXXI.

" My mind became the book through which I grew
Wise in all human wisdom, and its cave,
Which like a mine I rifled through and through,
To me the keeping of its secrets gave—
One mind, the type of all, the moveless wave
Whose calm reflects all moving things that are,
Necessity, and love, and life, the grave,
And sympathy, fountains of hope and fear :
Justice, and truth, and time, and the world's natural sphere.

XXXII.

" And on the sand would I make signs to range
These woofs, as they were woven, of my thought ;
Clear, elemental shapes, whose smallest change
A subtler language within language wrought :
The key of truths which once were dimly taught
In old Crotona ;—and sweet melodies
Of love, in that lone solitude I caught
From mine own voice in dream, when thy dear eyes
Shone through my sleep, and did that utterance harmonize.

XXXIII.

" Thy songs were winds whereon I fled at will,
As in a winged chariot, o'er the plain
Of crystal youth ; and thou wert there to fill
My heart with joy, and there we sate again
On the grey margin of the glimmering main,
Happy as then but wiser far, for we
Smiled on the flowery grave in which were lain
Fear, Faith, and Slavery ; and mankind was free,
Equal, and pure and wise, in wisdom's prophecy.

XXXIV.

" For to my will my fancies were as slaves
To do their sweet and subtle ministries ;
And oft from that bright fountain's shadowy waves
They would make human throngs gather and rise
To combat with my overflowing eyes,
And voice made deep with passion—thus I grew
Familiar with the shock and the surprise
And war of earthly minds, from which I drew
The power which has been mine to frame their thoughts anew.

XXXV.

" And thus my prison was the populous earth—
Where I saw—even as misery dreams of morn
Before the east has given its glory birth—
Religion's pomp made desolate by the scorn
Of wisdom's faintest smile, and thrones uptorn,
And dwellings of mild people interspersed
With undivided fields of ripening corn,
And love made free—a hope which we have nurst
Even with our blood and tears—until its glory burst.

XXXVI.

" All is not lost ! there is some recompense
For hope whose fountain can be thus profound,
Even throned Evil's splendid impotence,
Girt by its hell of power, the secret sound
Of hymns to truth and freedom—the dread bound
Of life and death past fearlessly and well,
Dungeons wherein the high resolve is found,
Racks which degraded woman's greatness tell,
And what may else be good and irresistible.

XXXVII.

" Such are the thoughts which, like the fires that flare
In storm-encompassed isles, we cherish yet
In this dark ruin—such were mine even there ;
As in its sleep some odorous violet,
While yet its leaves with nightly dews are wet,
Breathes in prophetic dreams of day's uprise,
Or, as ere Scythian frost in fear has met
Spring's messengers descending from the skies,
The buds foreknow their life—this hope must ever rise.

XXXVIII.

" So years had past, when sudden earthquake rent
The depth of ocean, and the cavern crackt
With sound, as if the world's wide continent
Had fallen in universal ruin wrackt ;
And through the cleft streamed in one cataract
The stifling waters :—when I woke, the flood
Whose banded waves that crystal cave had sacked
Was ebbing round me, and my bright abode
Before me yawned—a chasm, desert, and bare, and broad.

XXXIX.

" Above me was the sky, beneath the sea :
I stood upon a point of shattered stone,
And heard loose rocks rushing tumultuously
With splash and shock into the deep—anon
All ceased, and there was silence wide and lone.
I felt that I was free ! the Ocean-spray
Quivered beneath my feet, the broad Heaven shone
Around, and in my hair the winds did play
Lingering as they pursued their unimpeded way.

XL.

" My spirit moved upon the sea like wind
Which round some thymy cape will lag and hover,
Though it can wake the still cloud, and unbind
The strength of tempest : day was almost over,
When through the fading light I could discover
A ship approaching—its white sails were fed
With the north wind—its moving shade did cover
The twilight deep ;—the mariners in dread
Cast anchor when they saw new rocks around them spread.

XLI.

" And when they saw one sitting on a crag,
They sent a boat to me ;—the sailors rowed
In awe through many a new and fearful jag
Of overhanging rock, through which there flowed
The foam of streams that cannot make abode.
They came and questioned me, but when they heard
My voice, they became silent, and they stood
And moved as men in whom new love had stirred
Deep thoughts : so to the ship we past without a word.

CANTO EIGHTH.

I.

" I sate beside the steersman then, and gazing
Upon the west, cried, 'Spread the sails ! behold !
The sinking moon is like a watch-tower blazing
Over the mountains yet ;—the City of Gold
Yon Cape alone does from the sight withhold ;
The stream is fleet—the north breathes steadily
Beneath the stars, they tremble with the cold !
Ye cannot rest upon the dreary sea !—
Haste, haste to the warm home of happier destiny !'

II.

" The Mariners obeyed—the Captain stood
Aloof, and whispering to the Pilot, said,
' Alas, alas ! I fear we are pursued
By wicked ghosts : a Phantom of the Dead,
The night before we sailed, came to my bed
In dream, like that !'—The Pilot then replied,
' It cannot be—she is a human Maid—
Her low voice makes you weep—she is some bride,
Or daughter of high birth—she can be naught beside.'

III.

" We past the islets, borne by wind and stream,
And as we sailed, the Mariners came near
And thronged around to listen ;—in the gleam
Of the pale moon I stood, as one whom fear
May not attaint, and my calm voice did rear ;
Ye all are human—yon broad moon gives light
To millions who the self-same likeness wear,
Even while I speak—beneath this very night,
Their thoughts flow on like ours, in sadness or delight.

IV.

" What dream ye ? Your own hands have built a home,
Even for yourselves on a beloved shore ;
For some, fond eyes are pining till they come,
How they will greet him when his toils are o'er,
And laughing babes rush from the well-known door !
Is this your care ? ye toil for your own good—
Ye feel and think—has some immortal power
Such purposes ? or in a human mood,
Dream ye some Power thus builds for man in solitude ?

V.

" What is that Power ? ye mock yourselves, and give
A human heart to what ye cannot know :
As if the cause of life could think and live !
'Twere as if man's own works should feel, and show
The hopes, and fears, and thoughts from which they flow,
And he be like to them. Lo ! Plague is free
To waste, Blight, Poison, Earthquake, Hail, and Snow,
Disease, and Want, and worse Necessity
Of hate and ill, and Pride, and Fear, and Tyranny.

VI.

"What is that Power. Some moon-struck sophist stood
Watching the shade from his own soul upthrown
Fill Heaven and darken Earth, and in such mood
The Form he saw and worshipped was his own,
His likeness in the world's vast mirror shown ;
And 'twere an innocent dream, but that a faith
Nursed by fear's dew of poison, grows thereon,
And that men say, that Power has chosen Death
On all who scorn its laws, to wreak immortal wrath.

VII.

"Men say that they themselves have heard and seen,
Or known from others who have known such things,
A Shade, a Form, which Earth and Heaven between
Wields an invisible rod—that Priests and Kings,
Custom, domestic sway, ay, all that brings
Man's free-born soul beneath the oppressor's heel,
Are his strong ministers, and that the stings
Of death will make the wise his vengeance feel,
Though truth and virtue arm their hearts with tenfold steel.

VIII.

"And it is said, this Power will punish wrong ;
Yes, add despair to crime, and pain to pain !
And deepest hell, and deathless snakes among,
Will bind the wretch on whom is fixed a stain,
Which, like a plague, a burthen, and a bane,
Clung to him while he lived ;—for love and hate,
Virtue and vice, they say are difference vain—
The will of strength is right—this human state
Tyrants, that they may rule, with lies thus desolate.

IX.

"Alas, what strength? opinion is more frail
Than yon dim cloud now fading on the moon
Even while we gaze, though it awhile avail
To hide the orb of truth—and every throne
Of Earth or Heaven, though shadow rests thereon,
One shape of many names :—for this ye plough
The barren waves of ocean, hence each one
Is slave or tyrant ; all betray and bow,
Command, or kill, or fear, or wreak, or suffer woe.

X.

"Its names are each a sign which maketh holy
All power—ay, the ghost, the dream, the shade,
Of power—lust, falsehood, hate, and pride, and folly ;
The pattern whence all fraud and wrong is made,
A law to which mankind has been betrayed ;
And human love, is as the name well known
Of a dear mother, whom the murderer laid
In bloody grave, and into darkness thrown,
Gathered her wildered babes around him as his own.

XI.

"O love ! who to the hearts of wandering men
Art as the calm to Ocean's weary waves !
Justice, or truth, or joy ! thou only can
From slavery and religion's labyrinth caves
Guide us, as one clear star the seaman saves.
To give to all an equal share of good,
To track the steps of freedom though through graves
She pass, to suffer all in patient mood,
To weep for crime, though stained with thy friend's dearest blood.

XII.

"To feel the peace of self-contentment's lot,
To own all sympathies, and outrage none,
And in the inmost bowers of sense and thought,
Until life's sunny day is quite gone down,
To sit and smile with Joy, or, not alone,
To kiss salt tears from the worn cheek of Woe ;
To live, as if to love and live were one—
This is not faith or law, nor those who bow
To thrones on Heaven or Earth, such destiny may know.

XIII.

"But children near their parents tremble now,
Because they must obey—one rules another,
And as one Power rules both high and low,
So man is made the captive of his brother,
And Hate is throned on high with Fear her mother,
Above the Highest—and those fountain-cells.
Whence love yet flowed when faith had choked all other,
Are darkened—Woman, as the bond-slave, dwells
Of man, a slave ; and life is poisoned in its wells.

XIV.

"Man seeks for gold in mines, that he may weave
A lasting chain for his own slavery :—
In fear and restless care that he may live
He toils for others, who must ever be
The joyless thralls of like captivity ;
He murders, for his chiefs delight in ruin ;
He builds the altar, that its idol's fee
May be his very blood ; he is pursuing,
O, blind and willing wretch ! his own obscure undoing.

XV.

"Woman !—she is his slave, she has become
A thing I weep to speak— the child of scorn,
The outcast of a desolated home,
Falsehood, and fear, and toil, like waves have worn
Channels upon her cheek, which smiles adorn,
As calm decks the false Ocean :—well ye know
What Woman is, for none of Woman born
Can choose but drain the bitter dregs of woe,
Which ever from the oppressed to the oppressors flow.

XVI.

" This need not be ; ye might arise, and will
That gold should lose its power, and thrones their glory ;
That love, which none may bind, be free to fill
The world, like light ; and evil faith, grown hoary
With crime, be quenched and die.—Yon promontory
Even now eclipses the descending moon !—
Dungeons and palaces are transitory—
High temples fade like vapour—Man alone
Remains, whose will has power when all beside is gone.

XVII.

" Let all be free and equal !—from your hearts
I feel an echo ; through my inmost frame
Like sweetest sound, seeking its mate, it darts—
Whence come ye, friends ? alas, I cannot name
All that I read of sorrow, toil, and shame,
On your worn faces ; as in legends old
Which make immortal the disastrous fame
Of conquerors and impostors false and bold,
The discord of your hearts, I in your looks behold.

XVIII.

" Whence come ye, friends? from pouring human blood
Forth on the earth ? or bring ye steel and gold,
That Kings may dupe and slay the multitude ?
Or from the famished poor, pale, weak, and cold,
Bear ye the earnings of their toil ? unfold !
Speak ! are your hands in slaughter's sanguine hue
Stained freshly? have your hearts in guile grown old ?
Know yourselves thus ! ye shall be pure as dew,
And I will be a friend and sister unto you.

XIX.

" Disguise it not—we have one human heart—
All mortal thoughts confess a common home :
Blush not for what may to thyself impart
Stains of inevitable crime : the doom
Is this, which has, or may, or must become
Thine, and all humankind's. Ye are the spoil
Which Time thus marks for the devouring tomb,
Thou and thy thoughts and they, and all the toil
Wherewith ye twine the rings of life's perpetual coil.

XX.

" Disguise it not—ye blush for what ye hate,
And Enmity is sister unto Shame ;
Look on your mind—it is the book of fate—
Ah ! it is dark with many a blazoned name
Of misery—all are mirrors of the same ;
But the dark fiend who with his iron pen
Dipped in scorn's fiery poison, makes his fame
Enduring there, would o'er the heads of men
Pass harmless, if they scorned to make their hearts his den.

XXI.

" Yes, it is Hate, that shapeless fiendly thing
Of many names, all evil, some divine,
Whom self-contempt arms with a mortal sting ;
Which, when the heart its snaky folds intwine
Is wasted quite, and when it doth repine
To gorge such bitter prey, on all beside
It turns with ninefold rage, as with its twine
When Amphisbæna some fair bird has tied,
Soon o'er the putrid mass he threats on every side.

XXII.

" Reproach not thine own soul, but know thyself,
Nor hate another's crime, nor loathe thine own.
It is the dark idolatry of self,
Which, when our thoughts and actions once are gone,
Demands that man should weep, and bleed, and groan ;
O vacant expiation ! be at rest.—
The past is Death's, the future is thine own ;
And love and joy can make the foulest breast
A paradise of flowers, where peace might build her nest.

XXIII.

" Speak thou ! whence come ye?"—A Youth made reply,
" Wearily, wearily o'er the boundless deep
We sail ;—thou readest well the misery
Told in these faded eyes, but much doth sleep
Within, which there the poor heart loves to keep,
Or dare not write on the dishonoured brow ;
Even from our childhood have we learned to steep
The bread of slavery in the tears of woe,
And never dreamed of hope or refuge until now.

XXIV.

" Yes—I must speak—my secret should have perished
Even with the heart it wasted, as a brand
Fades in the dying flame whose life it cherished,
But that no human bosom can withstand
Thee, wondrous Lady, and the mild command
Of thy keen eyes :—yes, we are wretched slaves,
Who from their wonted loves and native land
Are reft, and bear o'er the dividing waves
The unregarded prey of calm and happy graves.

XXV.

" We drag afar from pastoral vales the fairest,
Among the daughters of those mountains lone,
We drag them there, where all things best and rarest
Are stained and trampled :—years have come and gone
Since, like the ship which bears me, I have known
No thought ;—but now the eyes of one dear Maid
On mine with light of mutual love have shone—
She is my life,—I am but as the shade
Of her,—a smoke sent up from ashes, soon to fade.

XXVI.

" For she must perish in the tyrant's hall—
Alas, alas !"—He ceased, and by the sail
Sate cowering—but his sobs were heard by all,
And still before the ocean and the gale
The ship fled fast till the stars 'gan to fail,
And round me gathered with mute countenance,
The Seamen gazed, the Pilot, worn and pale
With toil, the Captain with grey locks, whose glance
Met mine in restless awe—they stood as in a trance.

XXVII.

" Recede not ! pause not now ! thou art grown old,
But Hope will make thee young, for Hope and Youth
Are children of one mother, even Love—behold !
The eternal stars gaze on us !—is the truth
Within your soul ? care for your own, or ruth
For other's sufferings ? do ye thirst to bear
A heart which not the serpent custom's tooth
May violate ?—be free ! and even here,
Swear to be firm till death ! they cried, ' We swear ! we swear !'

XXVIII.

" The very darkness shook, as with a blast
Of subterranean thunder at the cry ;
The hollow shore its thousand echoes cast
Into the night, as if the sea, and sky,
And earth, rejoiced with new-born liberty,
For in that name they swore ! Bolts were undrawn,
And on the deck, with unaccustomed eye
The captives gazing stood, and every one
Shrank as the inconstant torch upon her countenance shone.

XXIX.

" They were earth's purest children, young and fair,
With eyes the shrines of unawakened thought,
And brows as bright as spring or morning, ere
Dark time had there its evil legend wrought
In characters of cloud which wither not.—
The change was like a dream to them ; but soon
They knew the glory of their altered lot,
In the bright wisdom of youth's breathless noon,
Sweet talk, and smiles, and sighs, all bosoms did attune.

XXX.

"But one was mute, her cheeks and lips most fair,
Changing their hue like lilies newly blown,
Beneath a bright acacia's shadowy hair,
Waved by the wind amid the sunny noon,
Showed that her soul was quivering ; and full soon
That Youth arose, and breathlessly did look
On her and me, as for some speechless boon :
I smiled, and both their hands in mine I took,
And felt a soft delight from what their spirits shook.

CANTO NINTH.

I.

" That night we anchored in a woody bay,
And sleep no more around us dared to hover
Than, when all doubt and fear has past away,
It shades the couch of some unresting lover,
Whose heart is now at rest : thus night past over
In mutual joy :—around, a forest grew
Of poplars and dark oaks, whose shade did cover
The waning stars prankt in the waters blue,
And trembled in the wind which from the morning flew.

II.

" The joyous mariners, and each free maiden,
Now brought from the deep forest many a bough,
With woodland spoil most innocently laden ;
Soon wreathes of budding foliage seemed to flow
Over the mast and sails, the stern and prow
Were canopied with blooming boughs,—the while
On the slant sun's path o'er the waves we go
Rejoicing, like the dwellers of an isle
Doomed to pursue those waves that cannot cease to smile.

III.

" The many ships spotting the dark blue deep
With snowy sails, fled fast as ours came nigh,
In fear and wonder ; and on every steep
Thousands did gaze, they heard the startling cry,
Like earth's own voice lifted unconquerably
To all her children, the unbounded mirth,
The glorious joy of thy name—Liberty !
They heard !—As o'er the mountains of the earth
From peak to peak leap on the beams of morning's birth :

IV.

" So from that cry over the boundless hills,
Sudden was caught one universal sound,
Like a volcano's voice, whose thunder fills
Remotest skies,—such glorious madness found
A path through human hearts with stream which drowned
Its struggling fears and cares, dark custom's brood,
They knew not whence it came, but felt around
A wide contagion poured—they called aloud
On Liberty—that name lived on the sunny flood.

V.

" We reached the port—alas ! from many spirits
The wisdom which had waked that cry, was fled,
Like the brief glory which dark Heaven inherits
From the false dawn, which fades e'er it is spread,
Upon the night's devouring darkness shed :
Yet soon bright day will burst—even like a chasm
Of fire, to burn the shrouds outworn and dead,
Which wrap the world ; a wide enthusiasm,
To cleanse the fevered world as with an earthquake's spasm.

VI.

" I walked through the great City then, but free
From shame or fear ; those toil-worn Mariners
And happy Maidens did encompass me ;
And like a subterranean wind that stirs
Some forest among caves, the hopes and fears
From every human soul, a murmur strange
Made as I past ; and many wept, with tears
Of joy and awe, and wingèd thoughts did range,
And half-extinguished words, which prophesied of change.

VII.

" For, with strong speech I tore the veil that hid
Nature, and Truth, and Liberty, and Love,—
As one who from some mountain's pyramid,
Points to the unrisen sun !—the shades approve
His truth, and flee from every stream and grove.
Thus, gentle thoughts did many a bosom fill,—
Wisdom, the mail of tried affections wove
For many a heart, and tameless scorn of ill,
Thrice steeped in molten steel the unconquerable will.

VIII.

" Some said I was a maniac wild and lost ;
Some, that I scarce had risen from the grave
The Prophet's virgin bride, a heavenly ghost :—
Some said, I was a fiend from my weird cave,
Who had stolen human shape, and o'er the wave,
The forest, and the mountain came ;—some said
I was the child of God, sent down to save
Women from bonds and death, and on my head
The burthen of their sins would frightfully be laid.

IX.

" But soon my human words found sympathy
In human hearts : the purest and the best,
As friend with friend made common cause with me,
And they were few, but resolute ;—the rest,
Ere yet success the enterprise had blest,
Leagued with me in their hearts ;—their meals, their slumber,
Their hourly occupations were possest
By hopes which I had armed to overnumber
Those hosts of meaner cares, which life's strong wings encumber.

X.

" But chiefly women, whom my voice did waken
From their cold, careless, willing slavery,
Sought me : one truth their dreary prison has shaken,—
They looked around, and lo ! they became free !
Their many tyrants sitting desolately
In slave-deserted halls, could none restrain ;
For wrath's red fire had withered in the eye,
Whose lightning once was death,—nor fear, nor gain
Could tempt one captive now to lock another's chain.

L

XI.

" Those who were sent to bind me, wept, and felt
Their minds outsoar the bonds which clasped them round,
Even as a waxen shape may waste and melt
In the white furnace ; and a visioned swound,
A pause of hope and awe the City bound,
Which, like the silence of a tempest's birth,
When in its awful shadow it has wound
The sun, the wind, the ocean, and the earth,
Hung terrible, ere yet the lightnings have leapt forth.

XII.

" Like clouds inwoven in the silent sky,
By winds from distant regions meeting there,
In the high name of truth and liberty,
Around the City millions gathered were,
By hopes which sprang from many a hidden lair ;
Words, which the lore of truth in hues of grace
Arrayed, thine old wild songs which in the air
Like homeless odours floated, and the name
Of thee, and many a tongue which thou hadst dipped in flame.

XIII.

" The Tyrant knew his power was gone, but Fear,
The nurse of Vengeance, bade him wait the event—
That perfidy and custom, gold and prayer,
And whatsoe'er, when force is impotent,
To fraud the sceptre of the world has lent,
Might, as he judged, confirm his failing sway.
Therefore throughout the streets, the Priests he sent
To curse the rebels.—To their gods did they
For Earthquake, Plague, and Want, kneel in the public way.

XIV.

" And grave and hoary men were bribed to tell
From seats where law is made the slave of wrong,
How glorious Athens in her splendour fell,
Because her sons were free,—and that among
Mankind, the many to the few belong,
By Heaven, and Nature, and Necessity.
They said, that age was truth, and that the young
Marred with wild hopes the peace of slavery,
With which old times and men had quelled the vain and free.

XV.

" And with the falsehood of their poisonous lips
They breathed on the enduring memory
Of sages and of bards a brief eclipse ;
There was one teacher, who, necessity
Had armed, with strength and wrong against mankind,
His slave and his avenger aye to be ;
That we were weak and sinful, frail and blind,
And that the will of one was peace, and we
Should seek for naught on earth but toil and misery.

XVI.

" ' For thus we might avoid the hell hereafter.'
So spake the hypocrites, who cursed and lied ;
Alas, their sway was past, and tears and laughter
Clung to their hoary hair, withering the pride
Which in their hollow hearts dared still abide ;
And yet obscener slaves with smoother brow,
And sneers on their strait lips, thin, blue, and wide,
Said, that the rule of men was over now,
And hence, the subject world to woman's will must bow ;

XVII.

" And gold was scattered through the streets, and wine
Flowed at a hundred feasts within the wall.
In vain ! the steady towers in Heaven did shine
As they were wont, nor at the priestly call,
Left Plague her banquet in the Æthiop's hall,
Nor Famine from the rich man's portal came,
Where at her ease she ever preys on all
Who throng to kneel for food : nor fear nor shame,
Nor faith, nor discord, dimmed hope's newly kindled flame.

XVIII.

" For gold was as a god whose faith began
To fade, so that its worshippers were few,
And Faith itself, which in the heart of man
Gives shape, voice, name, to spectral Terror, knew
Its downfall, as the altars lonelier grew,
Till the Priests stood alone within the fane ;
The shafts of falsehood unpolluting flew,
And the cold sneers of calumny were vain,
The union of the free with discord's brand to stain.

XIX.

" The rest thou knowest—Lo ! we two are here—
We have survived a ruin wide and deep—
Strange thoughts are mine.—I cannot grieve or fear,
Sitting with thee upon this lonely steep
I smile, though human love should make me weep.
We have survived a joy that knows no sorrow,
And I do feel a mighty calmness creep
Over my heart, which can no longer borrow
Its hues from chance or change, dark children of to-morrow.

XX.

" We know not what will come—yet Laon, dearest,
Cythna shall be the prophetess of love,
Her lips shall rob thee of the grace thou wearest,
To hide thy heart, and clothe the shapes which rove
Within the homeless future's wintry grove ;
For I now, sitting thus beside thee, seem
Even with thy breath and blood to live and move,
And violence and wrong are as a dream
Which rolls from steadfast truth an unreturning stream.

XXI.

" The blasts of autumn drive the wingèd seeds
Over the earth,—next come the snows, and rain,
And frosts, and storms, which dreary winter leads
Out of his Scythian cave, a savage train ;
Behold ! Spring sweeps over the world again,
Shedding soft dews from her ethereal wings ;
Flowers on the mountains, fruits over the plain,
And music on the waves and woods she flings,
And love on all that lives, and calm on lifeless things.

XXII.

" O Spring, of hope, and love, and youth, and gladness
Wind-wingèd emblem ! brightest, best and fairest !
Whence comest thou, when, with dark winter's sadness
The tears that fade in sunny smiles thou sharest ;
Sister of joy, thou art the child who wearest
Thy mother's dying smile, tender and sweet ;
Thy mother Autumn, for whose grave thou bearest
Fresh flowers, and beams like flowers, with gentle feet,
Disturbing not the leaves which are her winding-sheet.

XXIII.

" Virtue, and Hope, and Love, like light and Heaven,
Surround the world.—We are their chosen slaves.
Has not the whirlwind of our spirit driven
Truth's deathless germs to thought's remotest caves ?
Lo, Winter comes !—the grief of many graves,
The frost of death, the tempest of the sword,
The flood of tyranny, whose sanguine waves
Stagnate like ice at Faith, the enchanter's word,
And bind all human hearts in its repose abhorred.

XXIV.

" The seeds are sleeping in the soil : meanwhile
The tyrant peoples dungeons with his prey,
Pale victims on the guarded scaffold smile
Because they cannot speak ; and, day by day,
The moon of wasting Science wanes away
Among her stars, and in that darkness vast
The sons of earth to their foul idols pray,
And grey Priests triumph, and like blight or blast
A shade of selfish care o'er human looks is cast.

XXV.

" This is the winter of the world ;—and here
We die, even as the winds of Autumn fade,
Expiring in the frore and foggy air.—
Behold ! Spring comes, though we must pass, who made
The promise of its birth,—even as the shade
Which from our death, as from a mountain, flings
The future, a broad sunrise ; thus arrayed
As with the plumes of overshadowing wings,
From its dark gulf of chains, Earth like an eagle springs.

XXVI.

" O dearest love ! we shall be dead and cold
Before this morn may on the world arise ;
Wouldst thou the glory of its dawn behold ?
Alas ! gaze not on me, but turn thine eyes
On thine own heart—it is a paradise
Which everlasting spring has made its own,
And while drear Winter fills the naked skies,
Sweet streams of sunny thought, and flowers fresh blown,
Are there, and weave their sounds and odours into one.

XXVII.

" In their own hearts the earnest of the hope
Which made them great, the good will ever find ;
And though some envious shade may interlope
Between the effect and it, one comes behind,
Who aye the future to the past will bind—
Necessity, whose sightless strength for ever
Evil with evil, good with good must wind
In bands of union, which no power may sever :
They must bring forth their kind, and be divided never !

XXVIII.

" The good and mighty of departed ages
Are in their graves, the innocent and free,
Heroes, and Poets, and prevailing Sages,
Who leave the vesture of their majesty
To adorn and clothe this naked world ;—and we
Are like to them—such perish, but they leave
All hope, or love, or truth, or liberty,
Whose forms their mighty spirits could conceive
To be a rule and law to ages that survive.

XXIX.

" So be the turf heaped over our remains
Even in our happy youth, and that strange lot,
Whate'er it be, when in these mingling veins
The blood is still, be ours ; let sense and thought
Pass from our being, or be numbered not
Among the things that are ; let those who come
Behind, for whom our steadfast will has bought
A calm inheritance, a glorious doom,
Insult with careless tread, our undivided tomb.

XXX.

" Our many thoughts and deeds, our life and love,
Our happiness, and all that we have been,
Immortally must live, and burn and move,
When we shall be no more ;—the world has seen
A type of peace ; and as some most serene
And lovely spot to a poor maniac's eye,
After long years, some sweet and moving scene
Of youthful hope returning suddenly,
Quells his long madness—thus man shall remember thee.

XXXI.

" And Calumny meanwhile shall feed on us,
As worms devour the dead, and near the throne
And at the altar, most accepted thus
Shall sneers and curses be ;—what we have done
None shall dare vouch, though it be truly known ;
That record shall remain, when they must pass
Who built their pride on its oblivion ;
And fame, in human hope which sculptured was,
Survive the perished scrolls of unenduring brass.

XXXII.

" The while we two, beloved, must depart,
And Sense and Reason, those enchanters fair,
Whose wand of power is hope, would bid the heart
That gazed beyond the wormy grave despair :
These eyes, these lips, this blood, seems darkly there
To fade in hideous ruin : no calm sleep
Peopling with golden dreams the stagnant air,
Seems our obscure and rotting eyes to steep
In joy ;—but senseless death—a ruin dark and deep !

XXXIII.

" These are blind fancies—reason cannot know
What sense can neither feel, nor thought conceive ;
There is delusion in the world—and woe,
And fear, and pain—we know not whence we live,
Or why, or how, or what mute Power may give
Their being to each plant, and star, and beast,
Or even these thoughts :—Come near me ! I do weave
A chain I cannot break—I am possest
With thoughts too swift and strong for one lone human breast.

XXXIV.

" Yes, yes—thy kiss is sweet, thy lips are warm—
O ! willingly belovèd, would these eyes,
Might they no more drink being from thy form,
Even as to sleep whence we again arise,
Close their faint orbs in death : I fear nor prize
Aught that can now betide, unshared by thee—
Yes, Love when wisdom fails makes Cythna wise :
Darkness and death, if death be true, must be
Dearer than life and hope, if unenjoyed with thee.

XXXV.

" Alas, our thoughts flow on with stream, whose waters
Return not to their fountain—Earth and Heaven,
The Ocean and the Sun, the clouds their daughters,
Winter, and Spring, and Morn, and Noon, and Even,
All that we are or know, is darkly driven
Towards one gulf—Lo ! what a change is come
Since I first spake—but time shall be forgiven,
Though it change all but thee !"—She ceased, night's gloom
Meanwhile had fallen on earth from the sky's sunless dome.

XXXVI.

Though she had ceased, her countenance uplifted
To Heaven, still spake, with solemn glory bright ;
Her dark deep eyes, her lips, whose motions gifted
The air they breathed with love, her locks undight ;
" Fair star of life and love," I cried, " my soul's delight,
Why lookest thou on the crystalline skies ?
O, that my spirit were yon Heaven of night,
Which gazes on thee with its thousand eyes !"
She turned to me and smiled—that smile was Paradise !

CANTO TENTH.

I.

Was there a human spirit in the steed,
That thus with his proud voice, ere night was gone,
He broke our linkèd rest ? or do indeed
All living things a common nature own,
And thought erect an universal throne,
Where many shapes one tribute ever bear ?
And Earth, their mutual mother, does she groan
To see her sons contend ? and makes she bare
Her breast, that all in peace its drainless stores may share ?

II.

I have heard friendly sounds from many a tongue,
Which was not human—the lone Nightingale
Has answered me with her most soothing song,
Out of her ivy bower, when I sate pale
With grief, and sighed beneath ; from many a dale
The Antelopes who flocked for food have spoken
With happy sounds, and motions, that avail
Like man's own speech ; and such was now the token
Of waning night, whose calm by that proud neigh was broken.

III.

Each night, that mighty steed bore me abroad,
And I returned with food to our retreat,
And dark intelligence ; the blood which flowed
Over the fields, had stained the courser's feet ;—
Soon the dust drinks that bitter dew,—then meet
The vulture, and the wild-dog, and the snake,
The wolf, and the hyena grey, and eat
The dead in horrid truce : their throngs did make
Behind the steed, a chasm like waves in a ship's wake.

IV.

For, from the utmost realms of earth, came pouring
The banded slaves whom every despot sent
At that throned traitor's summons ; like the roaring
Of fire, whose floods the wild deer circumvent

In the scorched pastures of the South ; so bent
The armies of the leagued kings around
Their files of steel and flame ;—the continent
Trembled, as with a zone of ruin bound,
Beneath their feet, the sea shook with their Navies' sound.

v.

From every nation of the earth they came,
The multitude of moving heartless things,
Whom slaves call men : obediently they came,
Like sheep whom from the fold the shepherd brings
To the stall, red with blood ; their many kings
Led them, thus erring, from their native home ;
Tartar and Frank, and millions whom the wings
Of Indian breezes lull, and many a band
The Arctic Anarch sent, and Idumea's sand,

vi.

Fertile in prodigies and lies ;—so there
Strange natures made a brotherhood of ill.
The desert savage ceased to grasp in fear
His Asian shield and bow, when, at the will
Of Europe's subtler son, the bolt would kill
Some shepherd sitting on a rock secure ;
But smiles of wondering joy his face would fill,
And savage sympathy : those slaves impure,
Each one the other thus from ill to ill did lure.

vii.

For traitorously did that foul Tyrant robe
His countenance in lies,—even at the hour
When he was snatched from death, then o'er the globe,
With secret signs from many a mountain tower,
With smoke by day, and fire by night, the power
Of kings and priests, those dark conspirators
He called :—they knew his cause their own, and swore
Like wolves, and serpents to their mutual wars
Strange truce, with many a rite which Earth and Heaven abhors.

viii.

Myriads had come—millions were on their way ;
The Tyrant past, surrounded by the steel
Of hired assassins, through the public way,
Choked with his country's dead :—his footsteps reel
On the fresh blood—he smiles, "Ay, now I feel
I am a King in truth !" he said, and took
His royal seat, and bade the torturing wheel
Be brought, and fire, and pincers, and the hook,
And scorpions ; that his soul on its revenge might look.

ix.

" But first, go slay the rebels—why return
The victor bands," he said, " millions yet live,
Of whom the weakest with one word might turn
The scales of victory yet ;—let none survive

But those within the walls—each fifth shall give
The expiation for his brethren here.
Go forth, and waste and kill!"—"O king, forgive
My speech," a soldier answered—"but we fear
The spirits of the night, and morn is drawing near;

X.

"For we were slaying still without remorse,
And now that dreadful chief beneath my hand
Defenceless lay, when, on a hell-black horse,
An Angel bright as day, waving a brand
Which flashed among the stars, past."—"Dost thou stand
Parleying with me, thou wretch?" the king replied;
"Slaves, bind him to the wheel; and of this band,
Whoso will drag that woman to his side
That scared him thus, may burn his dearest foe beside;

XI.

"And gold and glory shall be his.—Go forth!"
They rushed into the plain.—Loud was the roar
Of their career: the horsemen shook the earth;
The wheeled artillery's speed the pavement tore;
The infantry, file after file did pour
Their clouds on the utmost hills.   Five days they slew
Among the wasted fields: the sixth saw gore
Stream through the city; on the seventh, the dew
Of slaughter became stiff; and there was peace anew:

XII.

Peace in the desert fields and villages,
Between the glutted beasts and mangled dead!
Peace in the silent streets! save when the cries
Of victims to their fiery judgment led,
Made pale their voiceless lips who seemed to dread
Even in their dearest kindred, lest some tongue
Be faithless to the fear yet unbetrayed;
Peace in the Tyrant's palace, where the throng
Waste the triumphal hours in festival and song!

XIII.

Day after day the burning Sun rolled on
Over the death-polluted land—it came
Out of the east like fire, and fiercely shone
A lamp of Autumn, ripening with its flame
The few lone ears of corn;—the sky became
Stagnate with heat, so that each cloud and blast
Languished and died,—the thirsting air did claim
All moisture, and a rotting vapour past
From the unburied dead, invisible and fast.

XIV.

First Want, then Plague came on the beasts; their food
Failed, and they drew the breath of its decay.
Millions on millions, whom the scent of blood
Had lured, or who, from regions far away,

Had tracked the hosts in festival array,
From their dark deserts ; gaunt and wasting now,
Stalked like fell shades among their perished prey ;
In their green eyes a strange disease did glow,
They sank in hideous spasm, or pains severe and slow.

XV.

The fish were poisoned in the streams ; the birds
In the greenwoods perished ; the insect race
Was withered up ; the scattered flocks and herds
Who had survived the wild beasts' hungry chase
Died moaning, each upon the other's face
In helpless agony gazing ; round the City
All night, the lean hyenas their sad case
Like starving infants wailed ; a woeful ditty !
And many a mother wept, pierced with unnatural pity.

XVI.

Amid the aërial minarets on high,
The Æthiopian vultures fluttering fell
From their long line of brethren in the sky,
Startling the concourse of mankind.—Too well
These signs the coming mischief did foretell :—
Strange panic first, a deep and sickening dread
Within each heart, like ice, did sink and dwell,
A voiceless thought of evil, which did spread
With the quick glance of eyes, like withering lightnings shed.

XVII.

Day after day, when the year wanes, the frosts
Strip its green crown of leaves, till all is bare ;
So on those strange and congregated hosts
Came Famine, a swift shadow, and the air
Groaned with the burden of a new despair ;
Famine, than whom Misrule no deadlier daughter
Feeds from her thousand breasts, though sleeping there
With lidless eyes, lie Faith, and Plague, and Slaughter,
A ghastly brood ; conceived of Lethe's sullen water.

XVIII.

There was no food, the corn was trampled down,
The flocks and herds had perished : on the shore
The dead and putrid fish were ever thrown ;
The deeps were foodless, and the winds no more
Creaked with the weight of birds, but as before
Those winged things sprang forth, were void of shade ;
The vines and orchards, Autumn's golden store,
Were burned ;—so that the meanest food was weighed
With gold, and Avarice died before the god it made.

XIX.

There was no corn—in the wide market-place
All loathliest things, even human flesh, was sold ;
They weighed it in small scales—and many a face
Was fixed in eager horror then : his gold

The miser brought, the tender maid, grown bold
Through hunger, bared her scorned charms in vain ;
The mother brought her eldest born, controlled
By instinct blind as love, but turned again
And bade her infant suck, and died in silent pain.

XX.

Then fell blue Plague upon the race of man.
" O, for the sheathed steel, so late which gave
Oblivion to the dead, when the streets ran
With brothers' blood ! O, that the earthquakes grave
Would gape, or Ocean lift its stifling wave !"
Vain cries—throughout the streets, thousands pursued
Each by his fiery torture howl and rave,
Or sit, in frenzy's unimagined mood,
Upon fresh heaps of dead ; a ghastly multitude.

XXI.

It was not hunger now, but thirst.   Each well
Was choked with rotting corpses, and became
A cauldron of green mist made visible
At sunrise.   Thither still the myriads came,
Seeking to quench the agony of the flame,
Which raged like poison through their bursting veins ;
Naked they were from torture, without shame,
Spotted with nameless scars and lurid blains,
Childhood, and youth, and age, writhing in savage pains.

XXII.

It was not thirst but madness ! many saw
Their own lean image everywhere, it went
A ghastlier self beside them, till the awe
Of that dread sight to self-destruction sent
Those shrieking victims ; some, ere life was spent,
Sought, with a horrid sympathy, to shed
Contagion on the sound ; and others rent
Their matted hair, and cried aloud, " We tread
On fire ! the avenging Power his hell on earth has spread."

XXIII.

Sometimes the living by the dead were hid.
Near the great fountain in the public square,
Where corpses made a crumbling pyramid
Under the sun, was heard one stifled prayer
For life, in the hot silence of the air ;
And strange 'twas, amid that hideous heap to see
Some shrouded in their long and golden hair,
As if not dead, but slumbering quietly
Like forms which sculptors carve, then love to agony.

XXIV.

Famine had spared the palace of the king :—
He rioted in festival the while,
He and his guards and priests ; but Plague did fling
One shadow upon all.   Famine can smile

On him who brings it food, and pass, with guile
Of thankful falsehood, like a courtier grey,
The house-dog of the throne ; but many a mile
Comes Plague, a winged wolf, who loathes alway
The garbage and the scum that strangers make her prey.

XXV.

So, near the throne, amid the gorgeous feast,
Sheathed in resplendent arms, or loosely dight
To luxury, ere the mockery yet had ceased
That lingered on his lips, the warrior's might
Was loosened, and a new and ghastlier night
In dreams of frenzy lapped his eyes ; he fell
Headlong, or with stiff eyeballs sate upright
Among the guests, or raving mad, did tell
Strange truths ; a dying seer of dark oppression's hell.

XXVI.

The Princes and the Priests were pale with terror ;
That monstrous faith wherewith they ruled mankind,
Fell, like a shaft loosed by the bowman's error,
On their own hearts : they sought and they could find
No refuge—'twas the blind who led the blind !
So, through the desolate streets to the high fane,
The many-tongued and endless armies wind
In sad procession : each among the train
To his own Idol lifts his supplications vain.

XXVII.

" O God !" they cried, " we know our secret pride
Has scorned thee, and thy worship, and thy name ;
Secure in human power we have defied
Thy fearful might ; we bend in fear and shame
Before thy presence ; with the dust we claim
Kindred ; be merciful, O King of Heaven !
Most justly have we suffered for thy fame
Made dim, but be at length our sins forgiven,
Ere to despair and death thy worshippers be driven.

XXVIII.

" O King of Glory ! thou alone hast power !
Who can resist thy will? who can restrain
Thy wrath, when on the guilty thou dost shower
The shafts of thy revenge, a blistering rain ?
Greatest and best, be merciful again !
Have we not stabbed thine enemies, and made
The Earth an altar, and the Heavens a fane,
Where thou wert worshipped with their blood, and laid
Those hearts in dust which would thy searchless works have weighed ?

XXIX.

" Well didst thou loosen on this impious City
Thine angels of revenge : recall them now ;
Thy worshippers abashed, here kneel for pity,
And bind their souls by an immortal vow :

We swear by thee ! and to our oath do thou
Give sanction, from thine hell of fiends and flame,
That we will kill with fire and torments slow,
The last of those who mocked thy holy name,
And scorned the sacred laws thy prophets did proclaim."

XXX.

Thus they with trembling limbs and pallid lips
Worshipped their own hearts' image, dim and vast,
Scared by the shade wherewith they would eclipse
The light of other minds ;—troubled they past
From the great Temple ;—fiercely still and fast
The arrows of the plague among them fell,
And they on one another gazed aghast,
And through the hosts contention wild befell,
As each of his own god the wondrous works did tell.

XXXI.

And Oromaze, Joshua, and Mahomet,
Moses, and Buddh, Zerdusht, and Brahm, and Foh,
A tumult of strange names, which never met
Before, as watchwords of a single woe,
Arose ; each raging votary 'gan to throw
Aloft his armed hands, and each did howl
" Our God alone is God !" and slaughter now
Would have gone forth, when from beneath a cowl
A voice came forth, which pierced like ice through every soul.

XXXII.

'Twas an Iberian Priest from whom it came,
A zealous man, who led the legioned west
With words which faith and pride had steeped in flame,
To quell the unbelievers ; a dire guest
Even to his friends was he, for in his breast
Did hate and guile lie watchful, intertwined,
Twin serpents in one deep and winding nest ;
He loathed all faith beside his own, and pined
To wreak his fear of Heaven in vengeance on mankind.

XXXIII.

But more he loathed and hated the clear light
Of wisdom and free thought, and more did fear,
Lest, kindled once, its beams might pierce the night,
Even where his Idol stood ; for, far and near
Did many a heart in Europe leap to hear
That faith and tyranny were trampled down ;
Many a pale victim, doomed for truth to share
The murderer's cell, or see, with helpless groan,
The priests his children drag for slaves to serve their own.

XXXIV.

He dared not kill the infidels with fire
Or steel, in Europe : the slow agonies
Of legal torture mocked his keen desire :
So he made truce with those who did despise

The expiation, and the sacrifice,
That, though detested, Islam's kindred creed
Might crush for him those deadlier enemies ;
For fear of God did in his bosom breed
A jealous hate of man, an unreposing need.

XXXV.

" Peace ! Peace !" he cried, " when we are dead, the Day
Of Judgment comes, and all shall surely know
Whose God is God, each fearfully shall pay
The errors of his faith in endless woe !
But there is sent a mortal vengeance now
On earth, because an impious race had spurned
Him whom we all adore—a subtile foe,
By whom for ye this dread reward was earned,
And kingly thrones, which rest on faith, nigh overturned.

XXXVI.

" Think ye, because ye weep, and kneel, and pray,
That God will lull the pestilence ? it rose
Even from beneath his throne, where, many a day,
His mercy soothed it to a dark repose :
It walks upon the earth to judge his foes,
And what art thou and I, that he should deign
To curb his ghastly minister, or close
The gates of death, ere they receive the twain
Who shook with mortal spells his undefended reign ?

XXXVII.

" Ay, there is famine in the gulf of hell,
Its giant worms of fire for ever yawn—
Their lurid eyes are on us ! those who fell
By the swift shafts of pestilence ere dawn,
Are in their jaws ! they hunger for the spawn
Of Satan, their own brethren, who were sent
To make our souls their spoil. See ! See ! they fawn
Like dogs, and they will sleep with luxury spent,
When those detested hearts their iron fangs have rent !

XXXVIII.

" Our God may then lull Pestilence to sleep :—
Pile high the pyre of expiation now !
A forest's spoil of boughs, and on the heap
Pour venomous gums, which sullenly and slow,
When touched by flame, shall burn, and melt, and flow,
A stream of clinging fire—and fix on high
A net of iron, and spread forth below
A couch of snakes, and scorpions, and the fry
Of centipedes and worms, earth's hellish progeny !

XXXIX.

" Let Laon and Laone on that pyre,
Linked tight with burning brass, perish !—then pray
That, with this sacrifice, the withering ire
Of Heaven may be appeased." He ceased, and they

A space stood silent, as far, far away
The echoes of his voice among them died ;
And he knelt down upon the dust, alway
Muttering the curses of his speechless pride,
Whilst shame, and fear, and awe, the armies did divide.

XL.

His voice was like a blast that burst the portal
Of fabled hell ; and as he spake, each one
Saw gape beneath the chasms of fire immortal,
And Heaven above seemed cloven, where, on a throne
Girt round with storms and shadows, sate alone,
Their King and Judge—fear killed in every breast
All natural pity then, a fear unknown
Before, and with an inward fire possest,
They raged like homeless beasts whom burning woods invest.

XLI.

'Twas morn—at noon the public crier went forth,
Proclaiming through the living and the dead,
" The Monarch saith, that his great Empire's worth
Is set on Laon and Laone's head :
He who but one yet living here can lead,
Or who the life from both their hearts can wring,
Shall be the kingdom's heir, a glorious meed !
But he who both alive can hither bring,
The Princess shall espouse, and reign an equal King."

XLII.

Ere night the pyre was piled, the net of iron
Was spread above, the fearful couch below,
It overtopped the towers that did environ
That spacious square ; for Fear is never slow
To build the thrones of Hate, her mate and foe,
So, she scourged forth the maniac multitude
To rear this pyramid—tottering and slow,
Plague-stricken, foodless, like lean herds pursued
By gadflies, they have piled the heath, and gums, and wood.

XLIII.

Night came, a starless and a moonless gloom.
Until the dawn, those hosts of many a nation
Stood round that pile, as near one lover's tomb
Two gentle sisters mourn their desolation ;
And in the silence of that expectation,
Was heard on high the reptiles hiss and crawl—
It was so deep, save when the devastation
Of the swift pest with fearful interval,
Marking its path with shrieks, among the crowd would fall.

XLIV.

Morn came,—among those sleepless multitudes,
Madness, and Fear, and Plague, and Famine still
Heaped corpse on corpse, as in autumnal woods
The frosts of many a wind with dead leaves fill

Earth's cold and sullen brooks ; in silence, still
The pale survivors stood ; ere noon, the fear
Of Hell became a panic, which did kill
Like hunger or disease, with whispers drear
As " Hush ! hark ! Come they yet ? Just Heaven ! thine
    hour is near !"

XLV.

And Priests rushed through their ranks, some counterfeiting
The rage they did inspire, some mad indeed
With their own lies ; they said their god was waiting
To see his enemies writhe, and burn, and bleed,—
And that, till then, the snakes of Hell had need
Of human souls :—three hundred furnaces
Soon blazed through the wide City, where, with speed,
Men brought their infidel kindred to appease
God's wrath, and while they burned, knelt round on quivering
    knees.

XLVI.

The noontide sun was darkened with that smoke,
The winds of eve dispersed those ashes grey,
The madness which these rites had lulled, awoke
Again at sunset.—Who shall dare to say
The deeds which night and fear brought forth, or weigh
In balance just the good and evil there ?
He might man's deep and searchless heart display,
And cast a light on those dim labyrinths, where
Hope, near imagined chasms, is struggling with despair.

XLVII.

'Tis said, a mother dragged three children then,
To those fierce flames which roast the eyes in the head,
And laughed, and died ; and that unholy men,
Feasting like fiends upon the infidel dead,
Looked from their meal, and saw an Angel tread
The visible floor of Heaven, and it was she !
And, on that night, one without doubt or dread
Came to the fire, and said, " Stop, I am he !
Kill me !" they burned them both with hellish mockery.

XLVIII.

And, one by one, that night, young maidens came,
Beauteous and calm, like shapes of living stone
Clothed in the light of dreams, and by the flame
Which shrank as overgorged, they laid them down,
And sung a low sweet song, of which alone
One word was heard, and that was Liberty ;
And that some kissed their marble feet, with moan
Like love, and died, and then that they did die
With happy smiles, which sunk in white tranquillity.

CANTO ELEVENTH.

I.

She saw me not—she heard me not—alone
Upon the mountain's dizzy brink she stood ;
She spake not, breathed not, moved not—there was thrown
Over her look, the shadow of a mood
Which only clothes the heart in solitude,
A thought of voiceless depth ;—she stood alone,
Above, the Heavens were spread ;—below, the flood
Was murmuring in its caves ;—the wind had blown
Her hair apart, through which her eyes and forehead shone.

II.

A cloud was hanging o'er the western mountains ;
Before its blue and moveless depth were flying
Grey mists poured forth from the unresting fountains
Of darkness in the North :—the day was dying :—
Sudden, the sun shone forth, its beams were lying
Like boiling gold on Ocean, strange to see,
And on the shattered vapours, which defying
The power of light in vain, tossed restlessly
In the red Heaven, like wrecks in a tempestuous sea.

III.

It was a stream of living beams, whose bank
On either side by the cloud's cleft was made ;
And where its chasms that flood of glory drank,
Its waves gushed forth like fire, and as if swayed
By some mute tempest, rolled on *her ;* the shade
Of her bright image floated on the river
Of liquid light, which then did end and fade—
Her radiant shape upon its verge did shiver ;
Aloft, her flowing hair like strings of flame did quiver.

IV.

I stood beside her, but she saw me not—
She looked upon the sea, and skies, and earth ;
Rapture, and love, and admiration wrought
A passion deeper far than tears, or mirth,
Or speech, or gesture, or whate'er has birth
From common joy ; which, with the speechless feeling
That led her there united, and shot forth
From her far eyes, a light of deep revealing,
All but her dearest self from my regard concealing.

V.

Her lips were parted, and the   measured breath
Was now heard there ;—her dark and intricate eyes
Orb within orb, deeper than sleep or death,
Absorbed-the glories of the burning skies,

M

Which, mingling with her heart's deep ecstasies,
Burst from her looks and gestures ;—and a light
Of liquid tenderness like love, did rise
From her whole frame, an atmosphere which quite
Arrayed her in its beams, tremulous and soft and bright.

VI.

She would have clasped me to her glowing frame ;
Those warm and odorous lips might soon have shed
On mine the fragrance and the invisible flame
Which now the cold winds stole ;—she would have laid
Upon my languid heart her dearest head :
I might have heard her voice, tender and sweet ;
Her eyes mingling with mine, might soon have fed
My soul with their own joy.—One moment yet
I gazed—we parted then, never again to meet !

VII.

Never but once to meet on Earth again !
She heard me as I fled—her eager tone
Sunk on my heart, and almost wove a chain
Around my will to link it with her own,
So that my stern resolve was almost gone.
" I cannot reach thee ! whither dost thou fly ?
My steps are faint—Come back, thou dearest one—
Return, ah me ! return"—The wind past by
On which those accents died, faint, far, and lingeringly.

VIII.

Woe ! woe ! that moonless midnight—Want and Pest
Were horrible, but one more fell doth rear,
As in a hydra's swarming lair, its crest
Eminent among those victims—even the Fear
Of Hell : each girt by the hot atmosphere
Of his blind agony ; like a scorpion stung
By his own rage upon his burning bier
Of circling coals of fire ; but still there clung
One hope, like a keen sword on starting threads uphung ;

IX.

Not death—death was no more refuge or rest ;
Not life—it was despair to be !—not sleep,
For fiends and chasms of fire had dispossest
All natural dreams : to wake was not to weep,
But to gaze mad and pallid, at the leap
To which the Future, like a snaky scourge,
Or like some tyrant's eye, which aye doth keep
Its withering beam upon his slaves, did urge
Their steps ; they heard the roar of Hell's sulphureous surge.

X.

Each of that multitude alone, and lost
To sense of outward things, one hope yet knew ;
As on a foam-girt crag some seaman tost,
Stares at the rising tide, or like the crew

Whilst now the ship is splitting through and through ;
Each, if the tramp of a far steed was heard,
Started from sick despair, or if there flew
One murmur on the wind, or if some word
Which none can gather yet, the distant crowd has stirred.

XI.

Why became cheeks wan with the kiss of death,
Paler from hope ? they had sustained despair.
Why watched those myriads with suspended breath
Sleepless a second night ? they are not here
The victims, and hour by hour, a vision drear,
Warm corpses fall upon the clay-cold dead ;
And even in death their lips are wreathed with fear.
The crowd is mute and moveless—overhead
Silent Arcturus shines—ha ! hear'st thou not the tread

XII.

Of rushing feet ? laughter ? the shout, the scream,
Of triumph not to be contained ? see ! hark !
They come, they come, give way ! alas, ye deem
Falsely—'tis but a crowd of maniacs stark
Driven, like a troop of spectres through the dark,
From the choked well, whence a bright death-fire sprung,
A lurid earth-star, which dropped many a spark
From its blue train, and spreading widely, clung
To their wild hair, like mist the topmost pines among.

XIII.

And many from the crowd collected there,
Joined that strange dance in fearful sympathies ;
There was the silence of a long despair,
When the last echo of those terrible cries
Came from a distant street, like agonies
Stifled afar.—Before the Tyrant's throne
All night his aged Senate sate, their eyes
In stony expectation fixed ; when one
Sudden before them stood, a Stranger and alone.

XIV.

Dark Priests and haughty Warriors gazed on him
With baffled wonder, for a hermit's vest
Concealed his face ; but when he spake, his tone,
Ere yet the matter did their thoughts arrest,
Earnest, benignant, calm, as from a breast
Void of all hate or terror, made them start ;
For as with gentle accents he addressed
His speech to them, on each unwilling heart
Unusual awe did fall—a spirit-quelling dart.

XV.

" Ye Princes of the Earth, ye sit aghast
Amid the ruin which yourselves have made,
Yes, desolation heard your trumpet's blast,
And sprang from sleep !—dark Terror has obeyed

Your bidding—O, that I whom ye have made
Your foe, could set my dearest enemy free
From pain and fear ! but evil casts a shade,
Which cannot pass so soon, and Hate must be
The nurse and parent still of an ill progeny.

XVI.

" Ye turn to Heaven for aid in your distress ;
Alas, that ye, though mighty and the wise,
Who, if he dared, might not aspire to less
Than ye conceive of power, should fear the lies
Which thou, and thou, didst frame for mysteries
To blind your slaves :—consider your own thought,
An empty and a cruel sacrifice
Ye now prepare, for a vain idol wrought
Out of the fears and hate which vain desires have brought.

XVII.

" Ye seek for happiness—alas, the day !
Ye find it not in luxury nor in gold,
Nor in the fame, nor in the envied sway
For which, O willing slaves to Custom old,
Severe task mistress ! ye your hearts have sold.
Ye seek for peace, and when ye die, to dream
No evil dreams : all mortal things are cold
And senseless then ; if aught survive, I deem
It must be love and joy, for they immortal seem.

XVIII.

" Fear not the future, weep not for the past.
O, could I win your ears to dare be now
Glorious, and great, and calm ! that ye would cast
Into the dust those symbols of your woe,
Purple, and gold, and steel ! that ye would go
Proclaiming to the nations whence ye came,
That Want, and Plague, and Fear, from slavery flow;
And that mankind is free, and that the shame
Of royalty and faith is lost in freedom's fame.

XIX.

" If thus 'tis well—if not, I come to say
That Laon"—while the Stranger spoke, among
The Council sudden tumult and affray
Arose, for many of those warriors young,
Had on his eloquent accents fed and hung
Like bees on mountain flowers ; they knew the truth,
And from their thrones in vindication sprung ;
The men of faith and law then without ruth
Drew forth their secret steel, and stabbed each ardent youth.

XX.

They stabbed them in the back and sneered—a slave
Who stood behind the throne, those corpses drew
Each to its bloody, dark, and secret grave ;
And one more daring raised his steel anew

To pierce the Stranger : " What hast thou to do
With me, poor wretch ?"—Calm, solemn, and severe,
That voice unstrung his sinews, and he threw
His dagger on the ground, and pale with fear,
Sate silently—his voice then did the Stranger rear.

XXI.

" It doth avail not that I weep for ye—
Ye cannot change, since ye are old and grey,
And ye have chosen your lot—your fame must be
A book of blood, whence in a milder day
Men shall learn truth, when ye are wrapt in clay :
Now ye shall triumph. I am Laon's friend,
And him to your revenge will I betray,
So ye concede one easy boon. Attend !
For now I speak of things which ye can apprehend.

XXII.

" There is a People mighty in its youth,
A land beyond the Oceans of the West,
Where, though with rudest rites, Freedom and Truth
Are worshipped ; from a glorious Mother's breast,
Who, since high Athens fell, among the rest
Sate like the Queen of Nations, but in woe,
By inbred monsters outraged and oppressed,
Turns to her chainless child for succour now,
It draws the milk of Power in Wisdom's fullest flow.

XXIII.

" That land is like an Eagle, whose young gaze
Feeds on the noontide beam, whose golden plume
Floats moveless on the storm, and in the blaze
Of sunrise gleams when Earth is wrapt in gloom ;
An epitaph of glory for the tomb
Of murdered Europe may thy fame be made,
Great People : as the sands shalt thou become :
Thy growth is swift as morn, when night must fade ;
The multitudinous Earth shall sleep beneath thy shade.

XXIV.

" Yes, in the desert then is built a home
For Freedom. Genius is made strong to rear
The monuments of man beneath the dome
Of a new Heaven ; myriads assemble there,
Whom the proud lords of man, in rage or fear,
Drive from their wasted homes : the boon I pray
Is this,—that Cythna shall be convoyed there—
Nay, start not at the name—America !
And then to you this night Laon will I betray.

XXV.

" With me do what you will. I am your foe !"
The light of such a joy as makes the stare
Of hungry snakes like living emeralds glow,
Shone in a hundred human eyes—" Where, where

Is Laon ? haste ! fly ! drag him swiftly here !
We grant thy boon."—" I put no trust in ye,
Swear by the Power ye dread."—" We swear, we swear !"
The Stranger threw his vest back suddenly,
And smiled in gentle pride, and said, " Lo ! I am he !"

CANTO TWELFTH.

I.

The transport of a fierce and monstrous gladness
Spread through the multitudinous streets, fast flying
Upon the winds of fear ; from his dull madness
The starveling waked, and died in joy ; the dying,
Among the corpses in stark agony lying,
Just heard the happy tidings, and in hope
Closed their faint eyes ; from house to house replying
With loud acclaim, the living shook Heaven's cope,
And filled the startled Earth with echoes : morn did ope.

II.

Its pale eyes then ; and lo ! the long array
Of guards in golden arms, and priests beside,
Singing their bloody hymns, whose garbs betray
The blackness of the faith it seems to hide ;
And see, the Tyrant's gem-wrought chariot glide
Among the gloomy cowls and glittering spears—
A Shape of light is sitting by his side,
A child most beautiful.   I'the midst appears
Laon—exempt alone from mortal hopes and fears.

III.

His head and feet are bare, his hands are bound
Behind with heavy chains, yet none do wreak
Their scoffs on him, though myriads throng around ;
There are no sneers upon his lip which speak
That scorn or hate has made him bold ; his cheek
Resolve has not turned pale—his eyes are mild
And calm, and like the morn about to break,
Smile on mankind—his heart seems reconciled
To all things and itself, like a reposing child.

IV.

Tumult was in the soul of all beside,
Ill joy, or doubt, or fear ; but those who saw
Their tranquil victim pass, felt wonder glide
Into their brain, and became calm with awe.
See, the slow pageant near the pile doth draw
A thousand torches in the spacious square,
Borne by the ready slaves of ruthless law,
Await the signal round : the morning fair
Is changed to a dim night by that unnatural glare.

V.

And see! beneath a sun-bright canopy,
Upon a platform level with the pile,
The anxious Tyrant sit, enthroned on high,
Girt by the chieftains of the host; all smile
In expectation, but one child: the while
I, Laon, led by mutes, ascend my bier
Of fire, and look around; each distant isle
Is dark in the bright dawn; towers far and near,
Pierce like reposing flames the tremulous atmosphere.

VI.

There was such silence through the host, as when
An earthquake trampling on some populous town,
Has crushed ten thousand with one tread, and men
Expect the second; all were mute but one,
That fairest child, who, bold with love, alone
Stood up before the King, without avail,
Pleading for Laon's life—her stifled groan
Was heard—she trembled like an aspen pale
Among the gloomy pines of a Norwegian vale.

VII.

What were his thoughts linked in the morning sun,
Among those reptiles, stingless with delay,
Even like a tyrant's wrath!—the signal gun
Roared—hark, again! in that dread pause he lay
As in a quiet dream—the slaves obey—
A thousand torches drop—and hark, the last
Bursts on that awful silence; far away
Millions, with hearts that beat both loud and fast,
Watch for the springing flame expectant and aghast.

VIII.

They fly—the torches fall—a cry of fear
Has startled the triumphant!—they recede!
For ere the cannon's roar has died, they hear
The tramp of hoofs like earthquake, and a steed
Dark and gigantic, with the tempest's speed,
Bursts through their ranks: a woman sits thereon,
Fairer it seems than aught that earth can breed,
Calm, radiant, like the phantom of the dawn,
A spirit from the caves of daylight wandering gone.

IX.

All thought it was God's Angel come to sweep
The lingering guilty to their fiery grave;
The tyrant from his throne in dread did leap—
Her innocence his child from fear did save;
Scared by the faith they feigned, each priestly slave
Knelt for his mercy whom they served with blood,
And, like the refluence of a mighty wave
Sucked into the loud sea, the multitude
With crushing panic, fled in terror's altered mood.

x.

They pause, they blush, they gaze—a gathering shout
Bursts like one sound from the ten thousand streams
Of a tempestuous sea :—that sudden rout
One checked, who, never in his mildest dreams
Felt awe from grace or loveliness, the seams
Of his rent heart so hard and cold a creed
Had seared with blistering ice—but he misdeems
That he is wise, whose wounds do only bleed
Inly for self, thus thought the Iberian Priest indeed,

xi.

And others too, thought he was wise to see,
In pain, and fear, and hate, something divine
In love and beauty—no divinity.
Now with a bitter smile whose light did shine
Like a fiend's hope upon his lips and eyne,
He said, and the persuasion of that sneer
Rallied his trembling comrades—" Is it mine
To stand alone, when kings and soldiers fear
A woman? Heaven has sent its other victim here."

xii.

" Were it not impious," said the King, "to break
Our holy oath?"—" Impious to keep it, say !"
Shrieked the exulting Priest—" Slaves, to the stake
Bind her, and on my head the burden lay
Of her just torments :—at the Judgment Day
Will I stand up before the golden throne
Of Heaven, and cry, to thee did I betray
An Infidel ; but for me she would have known
Another moment's joy ! the glory be thine own."

xiii.

They trembled, but replied not, nor obeyed,
Pausing in breathless silence. Cythna sprung
From her gigantic steed, who, like a shade
Chased by the winds, those vacant streets among
Fled tameless, as the brazen rein she flung
Upon his neck, and kissed his mooned brow.
A piteous sight, that one so fair and young,
The clasp of such a fearful death should woo
With smiles of tender joy as beamed from Cythna now.

xiv.

The warm tears burst in spite of faith and fear,
From many a tremulous eye, but like soft dews
Which feed spring's earliest buds, hung gathered there,
Frozen by doubt,—alas, they could not choose,
But weep ; for when her faint limbs did refuse
To climb the pyre, upon the mutes she smiled ;
And with her eloquent gestures, and the hues
Of her quick lips, even as a weary child
Wins sleep from some fond nurse with its caresses mild,

XV.

She won them, though unwilling, her to bind
Near me, among the stakes. When then had fled
One soft reproach that was most thrilling kind,
She smiled on me, and nothing then we said,
But each upon the other's countenance fed
Looks of insatiate love ; the mighty veil
Which doth divide the living and the dead
Was almost rent, the world grew dim and pale,—
All light in Heaven or Earth beside our love did fail.

XVI.

Yet,—yet—one brief relapse, like the last beam
Of dying flames, the stainless air around
Hung silent and serene—a blood-red gleam
Burst upwards, hurling fiercely from the ground
The globed smoke,—I heard the mighty sound
Of its uprise, like a tempestuous ocean ;
And, through its chasms I saw, as in a swound,
The tyrant's child fall without life or motion
Before his throne, subdued by some unseen emotion.

XVII.

And is this death ? the pyre has disappeared,
The Pestilence, the Tyrant, and the throng ;
The flames grow silent—slowly there is heard
The music of a breath-suspending song,
Which, like the kiss of love when life is young,
Steeps the faint eyes in darkness sweet and deep ;
With ever changing notes it floats along,
Till on my passive soul there seemed to creep
A melody, like waves on wrinkled sands that leap.

XVIII.

The warm touch of a soft and tremulous hand
Wakened me then ; lo, Cythna sate reclined
Beside me, on the waved and golden sand
Of a clear pool, upon a bank o'ertwined
With strange and star-bright flowers, which to the wind
Breathed divine odour ; high above, was spread
The emerald heaven of trees of unknown kind,
Whose moonlike blooms and bright fruit overhead
A shadow, which was light, upon the waters shed.

XIX.

And round about sloped many a lawny mountain
With incense-bearing forests, and vast caves
Of marble radiance to that mighty fountain ;
And where the flood its own bright margin laves,
Their echoes talk with its eternal waves,
Which, from the depths whose jagged caverns breed
Their unreposing strife, it lifts and heaves,—
Till through a chasm of hills they roll, and feed
A river deep, which flies with smooth but arrowy speed.

xx.

As we sate gazing in a trance of wonder,
A boat approached, borne by the musical air
Along the waves which sung and sparkled under
Its rapid keel—a winged shape sate there,
A child with silver-shining wings, so fair,
That as her bark did through the waters glide,
The shadow of the lingering waves did wear
Light, as from starry beams ; from side to side,
While veering to the wind her plumes the bark did guide

XXI.

The boat was one curved shell of hollow pearl,
Almost translucent with the light divine
Of her within ; the prow and stern did curl
Horned on high, like the young moon supine,
When o'er dim twilight mountains dark with pine,
It floats upon the sunset's sea of beams,
Whose golden waves in many a purple line
Fade fast, till borne on sunlight's ebbing streams,
Dilating, on earth's verge the sunken meteor gleams.

XXII.

Its keel has struck the sands beside our feet ;—
Then Cythna turned to me, and from her eyes
Which swam with unshed tears, a look more sweet
Than happy love, a wild and glad surprise,
Glanced as she spake ; "Ay, this is Paradise
And not a dream, and we are all united !
Lo, that is mine own child, who in the guise
Of madness came, like day to one benighted
In lonesome woods : my heart is now too well requited !'

XXIII.

And then she wept aloud, and in her arms
Clasped that bright Shape, less marvellously fair
Than her own human hues and living charms ;
Which, as she leaned in passion's silence there,
Breathed warmth on the cold bosom of the air,
Which seemed to blush and tremble with delight ;
The glossy darkness of her streaming hair
Fell o'er that snowy child, and wrapt from sight
The fond and long embrace which did their hearts unite.

XXIV.

Then the bright child, the plumed Seraph came,
And fixed its blue and beaming eyes on mine,
And said, "I was disturbed by tremulous shame
When once we met, yet knew that I was thine
From the same hour in which thy lips divine
Kindled a clinging dream within my brain,
Which ever waked when I might sleep, to twine
Thine image with *her* memory dear, again
We meet ; exempted now from mortal fear or pain.

XXV.

" When the consuming flames had wrapt ye round,
The hope which I had cherished went away ;
I fell in agony on the senseless ground,
And hid mine eyes in dust, and far astray
My mind was gone, when bright, like dawning day,
The Spectre of the Plague before me flew,
And breathed upon my lips, and seemed to say,
' They wait for thee beloved ;'—then I knew
The death-mark on my breast, and became calm anew.

XXVI.

" It was the calm of love—for I was dying.
I saw the black and half-extinguished pyre
In its own grey and shrunken ashes lying ;
The pitchy smoke of the departed fire
Still hung in many a hollow dome and spire
Above the towers like night ; beneath whose shade
Awed by the ending of their own desire
The armies stood ; a vacancy was made
In expectation's depth, and so they stood dismayed.

XXVII.

" The frightful silence of that altered mood,
The tortures of the dying clove alone,
Till one uprose among the multitude,
And said—' The flood of time is rolling on,
We stand upon its brink, whilst *they* are gone
To glide in peace down death's mysterious stream.
Have ye done well ? They moulder flesh and bone,
Who might have made this life's envenomed dream
A sweeter draught than ye will ever taste, I deem.

XXVIII.

" ' These perish as the good and great of yore
Have perished, and their murderers will repent,
Yes, vain and barren tears shall flow before
Yon smoke has faded from the firmament
Even for this cause, that ye who must lament
The death of those that made this world so fair,
Cannot recall them now ; but then is lent
To man the wisdom of a high despair,
When such can die and he live on and linger here.

XXIX.

" ' Ay, ye may fear not now the Pestilence,
From fabled hell as by a charm withdrawn,
All power and faith must pass, since calmly hence
In pain and fire have unbelievers gone ;
And ye must sadly turn away, and moan
In secret, to his home each one returning,
And to long ages shall this hour be known ;
And slowly shall its memory, ever burning,
Fill this dark night of things with an eternal morning.

XXX.

" ' For me the world is grown too void and cold,
Since hope pursues immortal destiny
With steps thus slow—therefore shall ye behold
How those who love, yet fear not, dare to die ;
Tell to your children this !' Then suddenly
He sheathed a dagger in his heart and fell ;
My brain grew dark in death, and yet to me
There came a murmur from the crowd, to tell
Of deep and mighty change which suddenly befell.

XXXI.

" Then suddenly I stood a winged Thought
Before the immortal Senate, and the seat
Of that star-shining spirit, whence is wrought
The strength of its dominion, good and great,
The better Genius of this world's estate.
His realm around one mighty Fane is spread,
Elysian islands bright and fortunate,
Calm dwellings of the free and happy dead,
Where I am sent to lead !" These winged words she said,

XXXII.

And with the silence of her eloquent smile,
Bade us embark in her divine canoe ;
Then at the helm we took our seat, the while
Above her head those plumes of dazzling hue
Into the winds' invisible stream she threw,
Sitting beside the prow : like gossamer,
On the swift breath of morn, the vessel flew
O'er the bright whirlpools of that fountain fair,
Whose shores receded fast, while we seemed lingering there

XXXIII.

Till down that mighty stream, dark, calm, and fleet,
Between a chasm of cedarn mountains riven,
Chased by the thronging winds whose viewless feet
As swift as twinkling beams, had, under Heaven,
From woods and waves wild sounds and odours driven,
The boat fled visibly—three nights and days,
Borne like a cloud through morn, and noon, and even,
We sailed along the winding watery ways
Of the vast stream, a long and labyrinthine maze.

XXXIV.

A scene of joy and wonder to behold
That river's shapes and shadows changing ever,
Where the broad sunrise, filled with deepening gold,
Its whirlpools, where all hues did spread and quiver,
And where melodious falls did burst and shiver
Among rocks clad with flowers, the foam and spray
Sparkled like stars upon the sunny river,
Or when the moonlight poured a holier day,
One vast and glittering lake around green islands lay.

XXXV.

Morn, noon, and even, that boat of pearl outran
The streams which bore it, like the arrowy cloud
Of tempest, or the speedier thought of man,
Which flieth forth and cannot make abode,
Sometimes through forests, deep like night, we glode,
Between the walls of mighty mountains crowned
With Cyclopean piles, whose turrets proud,
The homes of the departed, dimly frowned
O'er the bright waves which girt their dark foundations round.

XXXVI.

Sometimes between the wide and flowering meadows,
Mile after mile we sailed, and 'twas delight
To see far off the sunbeams chase the shadows
Over the grass ; sometimes beneath the night
Of wide and vaulted caves, whose roofs were bright
With starry gems, we fled, whilst from their deep
And dark-green chasms, shades beautiful and white,
Amid sweet sounds across our path would sweep,
Like swift and lovely dreams that walk the waves of sleep.

XXXVII.

And ever as we sailed, our minds were full
Of love and wisdom, which would overflow
In converse wild, and sweet, and wonderful ;
And in quick smiles whose light would come and go,
Like music o'er wide waves, and in the flow
Of sudden tears, and in the mute caress—
For a deep shade was cleft, and we did know,
That virtue, though obscured on Earth, not less
Survives all mortal change in lasting loveliness.

XXXVIII.

Three days and nights we sailed, as thought and feeling
Number delightful hours—for through the sky
The sphered lamps of day and night, revealing
New changes and new glories, rolled on high,
Sun, Moon, and moonlike lamps, the progeny
Of a diviner Heaven, serene and fair :
On the fourth day, wild as a wind-wrought sea
The stream became, and fast and faster bare
The spirit-winged boat, steadily speeding there.

XXXIX.

Steady and swift, where the waves rolled like mountains
Within the vast ravine, whose rifts did pour
Tumultuous floods from their ten thousand fountains,
The thunder of whose earth-uplifting roar
Made the air sweep in whirlwinds from the shore,
Calm as a shade the boat of that fair child
Securely fled, that rapid stress before,
Amid the topmost spray, and sunbows wild,
Wreathed in the silver mist : in joy and pride we smiled.

XL.

The torrent of that wide and raging river
Is past, and our aërial speed suspended.
We look behind ; a golden mist did quiver
When its wild surges with the lake were blended :
Our bark hung there, as one line suspended
Between two heavens, that windless waveless lake ;
Which four great cataracts from four vales, attended
By mists, aye feed ; from rocks and clouds they break,
And of that azure sea a silent refuge make.

XLI.

Motionless resting on the lake awhile,
I saw its marge of snow-bright mountains rear
Their peaks aloft, I saw each radiant isle,
And in the midst, afar, even like a sphere
Hung in one hollow sky, did there appear
The Temple of the Spirit ; on the sound
Which issued thence, drawn nearer and more near,
Like the swift moon this glorious earth around,
The charmed boat approached, and there its haven found.

NOTE.

EXTRACTED FROM PREFACE TO THE FIRST EDITION OF THIS POEM.

" I trust," says Shelley, " that the reader will carefully distinguish between those opinions which have a dramatic propriety in reference to the characters which they are designed to elucidate, and such as are properly my own. The erroneous and degrading idea which men have conceived of a Supreme Being, for instance, is spoken against, but not the Supreme Being itself. The belief which some superstitious persons whom I have brought upon the stage, entertain of the Deity, as injurious to the character of his benevolence, is widely different from my own. In recommending also a great and important change in the spirit which animates the social institutions of mankind, I have avoided all flattery to those violent and malignant passions of our nature, which are ever on the watch to mingle with and to alloy the most beneficial innovations. There is no quarter given to Revenge, or Envy, or Prejudice. Love is celebrated everywhere as the sole law which should govern the moral world."

ROSALIND AND HELEN.

Rosalind, *Helen* and her *Child*.

SCENE, THE SHORE OF THE LAKE OF COMO.

HELEN.

COME hither, my sweet Rosalind.
'Tis long since thou and I have met ;
And yet methinks it were unkind
Those moments to forget.
Come sit by me. I see thee stand
By this lone lake, in this far land,
Thy loose hair in the light wind flying,
Thy sweet voice to each tone of even
United, and thine eyes replying
To the hues of yon fair heaven.
Come, gentle friend : wilt sit by me?
And be as thou wert wont to be
Ere we were disunited ?
None doth behold us now : the power
That led us forth at this lone hour
Will be but ill requited
If thou depart in scorn : oh ! come,
And talk of our abandoned home.
Remember, this is Italy,
And we are exiles. Talk with me
Of that our land, whose wilds and floods,
Barren and dark although they be,
Were dearer than these chestnut woods :
Those heathy paths, that inland stream,
And the blue mountains, shapes which seem
Like wrecks of childhood's sunny dream :
Which that we have abandoned now,
Weighs on the heart like that remorse
Which altered friendship leaves. I seek
No more our youthful intercourse.
That cannot be ! Rosalind speak,
Speak to me. Leave me not.—When morn did come,
When evening fell upon our common home,
When for one hour we parted,—do not frown
I would not chide thee, though thy faith is broken :
But turn to me. Oh ! by this cherished token,
Of woven hair, which thou wilt not disown,
Turn, as 'twere but the memory of me,
And not my scorned self who prayed to thee.

ROSALIND.

Is it a dream, or do I see
And hear frail Helen? I would flee
Thy tainting touch; but former years
Arise, and bring forbidden tears;
And my o'erburthened memory
Seeks yet its lost repose in thee.
I share thy crime. I cannot choose
But weep for thee : mine own strange grief
But seldom stoops to such relief :
Nor ever did I love thee less,
Though mourning o'er thy wickedness
Even with a sister's woe. I knew
What to the evil world is due,
And therefore sternly did refuse
To link me with the infamy
Of one so lost as Helen. Now
Bewildered by my dire despair,
Wondering I blush, and weep that thou
Shouldst love me still,—thou only !—There
Let us sit on that grey stone,
Till our mournful talk be done.

HELEN.

Alas ! not there ; I cannot bear
The murmur of this lake to hear.
A sound from thee, Rosalind dear,
Which never yet I heard elsewhere
But in our native land, recurs,
Even here where now we meet. It stirs
Too much of suffocating sorrow !
In the dell of yon dark chestnut wood
Is a stone seat, a solitude
Less like our own. The ghost of peace
Will not desert this spot. To-morrow
If thy kind feelings should not cease,
We may sit here.

ROSALIND.

                    Thou lead, my sweet,
And I will follow.

HENRY.

                    'Tis Fenici's seat.
Where are you going? This is not the way,
Mamma ; it leads behind those trees that grow
Close to the little river.

HELEN.

                              Yes : I know :
I was bewildered. Kiss me, and be gay,
Dear boy : why do you sob?

HENRY.

I do not know:
But it might break any one's heart to see
You and the lady cry so bitterly.

HELEN.

It is a gentle child, my friend.   Go home,
Henry, and play with Lilla till I come.
We only cried with joy to see each other ;
We are quite merry now : Good night.

The boy
Lifted a sudden look upon his mother,
And in the gleam of forced and hollow joy
Which lightened o'er her face, laughed with the glee
Of light and unsuspecting infancy,
And whispered in her ear, "Bring home with you
That sweet strange lady-friend."   Then off he flew,
But stopped, and beckoned with a meaning smile,
Where the road turned.   Pale Rosalind the while,
Hiding her face, stood weeping silently.

In silence then they took the way
Beneath the forest's solitude.
It was a vast and antique wood,
Through which they took their way ;
And the grey shades of evening
O'er that green wilderness did fling
Still deeper solitude.
Pursuing still the path that wound
The vast and knotted trees around
Through which slow shades were wandering,
To a deep lawny dell they came,
To a stone seat beside a spring,
O'er which the columned wood did frame
A roofless temple, like the fane
Where, ere new creeds could faith obtain,
Man's early race once knelt beneath
The overhanging deity.
O'er this fair fountain hung the sky,
Now spangled with rare stars.   The snake,
The pale snake, that with eager breath
Creeps here his noontide thirst to slake,
Is beaming with many a mingled hue,
Shed from yon dome's eternal blue,
When he floats on that dark and lucid flood
In the light of his own loveliness ;
And the birds that in the fountain dip
Their plumes, with fearless fellowship
Above and round him wheel and hover.
The fitful wind is heard to stir
One solitary leaf on high ;
The chirping of the grasshopper
Fills every pause.   There is emotion
In all that dwells at noontide here :
Then, through the intricate wild wood.
A maze of life and light and motion

N

Is woven. But there is stillness now :
Gloom, and the trance of Nature now :
The snake is in his cave asleep ;
The birds are on the branches dreaming :
Only the shadows creep :
Only the glowworm is gleaming :
Only the owls and the nightingales
Wake in this dell when daylight fails,
And grey shades gather in the woods :
And the owls have all fled far away
In a merrier glen to hoot and play,
For the moon is veiled and sleeping now.
The accustomed nightingale still broods
On her accustomed bough,
But she is mute ; for her false mate
Has fled and left her desolate.

This silent spot tradition old
Had peopled with the spectral dead.
For the roots of the speaker's hair felt cold
And stiff, as with tremulous lips he told
That a hellish shape at midnight led
The ghost of a youth with hoary hair,
And sate on the seat beside him there,
Till a naked child came wandering by,
When the fiend would change to a lady fair !
A fearful tale ! The truth was worse :
For here a sister and a brother
Had solemnized a monstrous curse,
Meeting in this fair solitude :
For beneath yon very sky,
Had they resigned to one another
Body and soul. The multitude,
Tracking them to the secret wood,
Tore limb from limb their innocent child,
And stabbed and trampled on its mother ;
But the youth, for God's most holy grace,
A priest saved to burn in the market-place.

Duly at evening Helen came
To this lone silent spot,
From the wrecks of a tale of wilder sorrow
So much of sympathy to borrow
As soothed her own dark lot.
Duly each evening from her home,
With her fair child would Helen come
To sit upon that antique seat,
While the hues of day were pale ;
And the bright boy beside her feet
Now lay, lifting at intervals
His broad blue eyes on her ;
Now, where some sudden impulse calls
Following.   He was a gentle boy,
And in all gentle sports took joy ;
Oft in a dry leaf for a boat,
With a small feather for a sail,
His fancy on that spring would float,
If some invisible breeze might stir

Its marble calm : and Helen smiled
Through tears of awe on the gay child,
To think that a boy as fair as he,
In years which never more may be,
By that same fount, in that same wood,
The like sweet fancies had pursued ;
And that a mother, lost like her,
Had mournfully sate watching him.
Then all the scene was wont to swim
Through the mist of a burning tear.

For many months had Helen known
This scene ; and now she thither turned
Her footsteps, not alone.
The friend whose falsehood she had mourned,
Sate with her on that seat of stone.
Silent they sate ; for evening,
And the power its glimpses bring
Had, with one awful shadow, quelled
The passion of their grief.   They sate
With linkèd hands, for unrepelled
Had Helen taken Rosalind's.
Like the autumn wind, when it unbinds
The tangled locks of the nightshade's hair,
Which is twined in the sultry summer air
Round the walls of an outworn sepulchre,
Did the voice of Helen, sad and sweet,
And the sound of her heart that ever beat,
As with sighs and words she breathed on her,
Unbind the knots of her friend's despair,
Till her thoughts were free to float and flow ;
And from her labouring bosom now,
Like the bursting of a prisoned flame,
The voice of a long-pent sorrow came.

ROSALIND.

I saw the dark earth fall upon
The coffin ; and I saw the stone
Laid over him whom this cold breast
Had pillowed to his nightly rest !
Thou knowest not, thou canst not know
My agony. Oh ! I could not weep :
The sources whence such blessings flow
Were not to be approached by me !
But I could smile and I could sleep,
Though with a self-accusing heart.
In morning's light, in evening's gloom,
I watched—and would not thence depart—
My husband's unlamented tomb.
My children knew their sire was gone,
But when I told them—" He is dead !"
They laughed aloud in frantic glee,
They clapped their hands and leaped about,
Answering each other's ecstasy
With many a prank and merry shout.
But I sate silent and alone,
Wrapped in the mock of mourning weed.

They laughed, for he was dead : but I
Sate with a hard and tearless eye,
And with a heart which would deny
The secret joy it could not quell,
Low muttering o'er his loathèd name ;
Till from that self-contention came
Remorse where sin was none ; a hell
Which in pure spirits should not dwell.

I'll tell thee truth. He was a man
Hard, selfish, loving only gold,
Yet full of guile : his pale eyes ran
With tears, which each some falsehood told,
And oft his smooth and bridled tongue
Would give the lie to his flushing cheek :
He was a coward to the strong :
He was a tyrant to the weak,
On whom his vengeance he would wreak :
For scorn, whose arrows search the heart,
From many a stranger's eye would dart,
And on his memory cling, and follow
His soul to its home so cold and hollow.
He was a tyrant to the weak,
And we were such, alas the day !
Oft, when my little ones at play,
Were in youth's natural lightness gay,
Or if they listened to some tale
Of travellers, or of fairy land, —
When the light from the wood-fire's dying brand
Flashed on their faces, — if they heard,
Or thought they heard, upon the stair
His footstep, the suspended word
Died on my lips : we all grew pale :
The babe at my bosom was hushed with fear
If it thought it heard its father near ;
And my two wild boys would near my knee
Cling, cowed and cowering fearfully.

I'll tell thee truth : I loved another.
His name in my ear was ever ringing,
His form to my brain was ever clinging :
Yet if some stranger breathed that name,
My lips turned white, and my heart beat fast :
My nights were once haunted by dreams of flame,
My days were dim in the shadow cast,
By the memory of the same !
Day and night, day and night,
He was my breath and life and light,
For three short years, which soon were past.
On the fourth, my gentle mother
Led me to the shrine to be
His sworn bride eternally.
And now we stood on the altar stair,
When my father came from a distant land,
And with a loud and fearful cry
Rushed between us suddenly.
I saw the stream of his thin grey hair,
I saw his lean and lifted hand,

And heard his words,—and live ! Oh, God !
Wherefore do I live?—'' Hold, hold !''
He cried,—'' I tell thee 'tis her brother !
Thy mother, boy, beneath the sod
Of yon churchyard rests in her shroud so cold :
I am now weak, and pale, and old :
We were once dear to one another,
I and that corpse ! Thou art our child!''
Then with a laugh both long and wild
The youth upon the pavement fell :
They found him dead ! All looked on me,
The spasms of my despair to see :
But I was calm. I went away :
I was clammy-cold like clay !
I did not weep : I did not speak :
But day by day, week after week,
I walked about like a corpse alive !
Alas ! sweet friend, you must believe
This heart is stone : it did not break.

My father lived a little while,
But all might see that he was dying,
He smiled with such a woful smile !
When he was in the churchyard lying
Among the worms, we grew quite poor,
So that no one would give us bread :
My mother looked at me, and said
Faint words of cheer, which only meant
That she could die and be content ;
So I went forth from the same church door
To another husband's bed.
And this was he who died at last,
When weeks and months and years had past,
Through which I firmly did fulfil
My duties, a devoted wife,
With the stern step of vanquished will,
Walking beneath the night of life,
Whose hours extinguished, like slow rain
Falling for ever, pain by pain,
The very hope of death's dear rest ;
Which, since the heart within my breast
Of natural life was dispossest,
Its strange sustainer there had been.

When flowers were dead, and grass was green
Upon my mother's grave,—that mother
Whom to outlive, and cheer, and make
My wan eyes glitter for her sake,
Was my vowed task, the single care
Which once gave life to my despair,—
When she was a thing that did not stir,
And the crawling worms were cradling her
To a sleep more deep and so more sweet
Than a baby's rocked on its nurse's knee,
I lived : a living pulse then beat
Beneath my heart that awakened me.
What was this pulse so warm and free?
Alas ! I knew it could not be

My own dull blood : 'twas like a thought
Of liquid love, that spread and wrought
Under my bosom and in my brain,
And crept with the blood through every vein
And hour by hour, day after day,
The wonder could not charm away,
But laid in sleep my wakeful pain,
Until I knew it was a child,
And then I wept.   For long, long years
These frozen eyes had shed no tears :
But now—'twas the season fair and mild
When April has wept itself to May :
I sate through the sweet sunny day
By my window bowered round with leaves,
And down my cheeks the quick tears ran
Like twinkling raindrops from the eaves,
When warm spring showers are passing o'er :
O Helen, none can ever tell
The joy it was to weep once more !

I wept to think how hard it were
To kill my babe, and take from it
The sense of light, and the warm air,
And my own fond and tender care,
And love and smiles ; ere I knew yet
That these for it might, as for me,
Be the masks of a grinning mockery.
And haply, I would dream, 'twere sweet
To feed it from my faded breast,
Or mark my own heart's restless beat
Rock it to its untroubled rest,
And watch the growing soul beneath
Dawn in faint smiles ; and hear its breath,
Half interrupted by calm sighs,
And search the depth of its fair eyes
For long departed memories !
And so I lived till that sweet load
Was lightened.   Darkly forward flowed
The stream of years, and on it bore
Two shapes of gladness to my sight ;
Two other babes, delightful more
In my lost soul's abandoned night,
Than their own country ships may be
Sailing towards wrecked mariners,
Who cling to the rock of a wintry sea.
For each, as it came, brought soothing tears
And a loosening warmth, as each one lay
Sucking the sullen milk away
About my frozen heart, did play,
And weaned it, oh how painfully !—
As they themselves were weaned each one
From that sweet food,—even from the thirst
Of death, and nothingness, and rest,
Strange inmate of a living breast !
Which all that I had undergone
Of grief and shame, since she, who first
The gates of that dark refuge closed,
Came to my sight, and almost burst

The seal of that Lethean spring;
But these fair shadows interposed:
For all delights are shadows now !
And from my brain to my dull brow
The heavy tears gather and flow :
I cannot speak : Oh let me weep !

The tears which fell from her wan eyes
Glimmered among the moonlight dew:
Her deep hard sobs and heavy sighs
Their echoes in the darkness threw.
When she grew calm, she thus did keep
The tenor of her tale :

              He died :
I know not how : he was not old,
If age be numbered by its years :
But he was bowed and bent with fears,
Pale with the quenchless thirst of gold,
Which, like fierce fever, left him weak;
And his strait lip and bloated cheek
Were warped in spasms by hollow sneers ;
And selfish cares with barren plough,
Not age, had lined his narrow brow,
And foul and cruel thoughts, which feed
Upon the withering life within,
Like vipers on some poisonous weed.
Whether his ill were death or sin
None knew, until he died indeed,
And then men owned they were the same.

Seven days within my chamber lay
That corse, and my babes made holiday :
At last I told them what is death ;
The eldest, with a kind of shame,
Came to my knees with silent breath,
And sate awe-stricken at my feet ;
And soon the others left their play,
And sate there too.   It is unmeet
To shed on the brief flower of youth
The withering knowledge of the grave ;
From me remorse then wrung that truth.

I could not bear the joy which gave
Too just a response to mine own.
In vain.   I dared not feign a groan ;
And in their artless looks I saw,
Between the mists of fear and awe,
That my own thought was theirs ; and they
Expressed it not in words, but said,
Each in its heart, how every day
Will pass in happy work and play,
Now he is dead and gone away.

After the funeral all our kin
Assembled, and the will was read.
My friend, I tell thee, even the dead
Have strength, their putrid shrouds within,

To blast and torture. Those who live
Still fear the living, but a corse
Is merciless, and power doth give
To such pale tyrants half the spoil
He rends from those who groan and toil,
Because they blush not with remorse
Among their crawling worms. Behold,
I have no child ! my tale grows old
With grief, and staggers : let it reach
The limits of my feeble speech,
And languidly at length recline
On the brink of its own grave and mine.

Thou knowest what a thing is Poverty
Among the fallen on evil days :
'Tis Crime, and Fear, and Infamy,
And houseless Want in frozen ways
Wandering ungarmented, and Pain,
And, worse than all, that inward stain,
Foul Self-contempt, which drowns in sneers
Youth's starlight smile, and makes its tears
First like hot gall, then dry for ever !
And well thou knowest a mother never
Could doom her children to this ill,
And well he knew the same. The will
Imported, that if e'er again
I sought my children to behold,
Or in my birthplace did remain
Beyond three days, whose hours were told,
They should inherit naught : and he,
To whom next came their patrimony,
A sallow lawyer, cruel and cold,
Aye watched me, as the will was read,
With eyes askance, which sought to see
The secrets of my agony ;
And with close lips and anxious brow
Stood canvassing still to and fro
The chance of my resolve, and all
The dead man's caution just did call ;
For in that killing lie 'twas said—
" She is adulterous, and doth hold
In secret that the Christian creed
Is false, and therefore is much need
That I should have a care to save
My children from eternal fire."
Friend, he was sheltered by the grave,
And therefore dared to be a liar!
In truth, the Indian on the pyre
Of her dead husband, half consumed,
As well might there be false, as I
To those abhorred embraces doomed,
Far worse than fire's brief agony.
As to the Christian creed, if true
Or false, I never questioned it :
I took it as the vulgar do :
Nor my vext soul had leisure yet
To doubt the things men say, or deem
That they are other than they seem.

All present who those crimes did hear,
In feigned or actual scorn and fear,
Men, women, children, slunk away,
Whispering with self-contented pride,
Which half suspects its own base lie.
I spoke to none, nor did abide,
But silently I went my way,
Nor noticed I where joyously
Sate my two younger babes at play,
In the courtyard through which I past;
But went with footsteps firm and fast
Till I came to the brink of the ocean green,
And there, a woman with grey hairs,
Who had my mother's servant been,
Kneeling, with many tears and prayers,
Made me accept a purse of gold,
Half of the earnings she had kept
To refuge her when weak and old.

With woe, which never sleeps or slept,
I wander now.   'Tis a vain thought—
But on yon alp, whose snowy head
'Mid the azure air is islanded
(We see it o'er the flood of cloud,
Which sunrise from its eastern caves
Drives, wrinkling into golden waves,
Hung with its precipices proud,
From that grey stone where first we met),
There, now who knows the dead feel naught ?
Should be my grave ; for he who yet
Is my soul's soul, once said : " 'Twere sweet
'Mid stars and lightnings to abide,
And winds and lulling snows, that beat
With their soft flakes the mountain wide,
When weary meteor lamps repose,
And languid storms their pinions close :
And all things strong and bright and pure,
And ever during, aye endure :
Who knows, if one were buried there,
But these things might our spirits make,
Amid the all-surrounding air,
Their own eternity partake ?"
Then 'twas a wild and playful saying
At which I laughed, or seemed to laugh:
They were his words : now heed my praying,
And let them be my epitaph.
Thy memory for a term may be
My monument.   Wilt remember me ?
I know thou wilt, and canst forgive
Whilst in this erring world to live
My soul disdained not, that I thought
Its lying forms were worthy aught,
And much less thee.

HELEN.

O speak not so,
But come to me and pour thy woe

Into this heart, full though it be,
Aye overflowing with its own:
I thought that grief had severed me
From all beside who weep and groan;
Its likeness upon earth to be,
Its express image ; but thou art
More wretched.   Sweet ! we will not part
Henceforth, if death be not division ;
If so, the dead feel no contrition.
But wilt thou hear, since last we parted
All that has left me broken hearted ?

ROSALIND.

Yes, speak.   The faintest stars are scarcely shorn
Of their thin beams by that delusive morn
Which sinks again in darkness, like the light
Of early love, soon lost in total night.

HELEN.

Alas ! Italian winds are mild,
But my bosom is cold—wintry cold—
When the warm air weaves, among the fresh leaves,
Soft music, my poor brain is wild,
And I am weak like a nursling child,
Though my soul with grief is grey and old.

ROSALIND.

Weep not at thine own words, though they must make
Me weep.   What is thy tale ?

HELEN.

                    I fear 'twill shake
Thy gentle heart with tears.   Thou well
Rememberest when we met no more,
And, though I dwelt with Lionel,
That friendless caution pierced me sore
With grief ; a wound my spirit bore
Indignantly, but when he died
With him lay dead both hope and pride.
Alas ! all hope is buried now.
But then men dreamed the aged earth
Was labouring in that mighty birth,
Which many a poet and a sage
Has aye foreseen—the happy age
When truth and love shall dwell below
Among the works and ways of men;
Which on this world not power but will
Even now is wanting to fulfil.

Among mankind what thence befell
Of strife, how vain, is known too well ;
When liberty's dear pæan fell
'Mid murderous howls.   To Lionel,

Though of great wealth and lineage high,
Yet through those dungeon walls there came
Thy thrilling light, O liberty !
And as the meteor's midnight flame
Startles the dreamer, sun-like truth
Flashed on his visionary youth,
And filled him, not with love, but faith,
And hope, and courage mute in death ;
For love and life in him were twins,
Born at one birth ; in every other
First life then love its course begins,
Though they be children of one mother;
And so through this dark world they fleet
Divided, till in death they meet :
But he loved all things ever.   Then
He past amid the strife of men,
And stood at the throne of armèd power
Pleading for a world of woe :
Secure as one on a rock-built tower
O'er the wrecks which the surge trails to and fro,
'Mid the passions wild of human kind
He stood, like a spirit calming them;
For, it was said, his words could bind
Like music the lulled crowd, and stem
That torrent of unquiet dream,
Which mortals truth and reason deem,
But is revenge and fear and pride.
Joyous he was ; and hope and peace
On all who heard him did abide,
Raining like dew from his sweet talk,
As where the evening star may walk
Along the brink of the gloomy seas,
Liquid mists of splendour quiver.
His very gestures touched to tears
The unpersuaded tyrant, never
So moved before : his presence stung
The torturers with their victim's pain,
And none knew how ; and through their ears,
The subtle witchcraft of his tongue
Unlocked the hearts of those who keep
Gold, the world's bond of slavery.
Men wondered, and some sneered to see
One sow what he could never reap :
For he is rich, they said, and young,
And might drink from the depths of luxury.
If he seeks fame, fame never crowned
The champion of a trampled creed :
If he seeks power, power is enthroned
'Mid ancient rights and wrongs, to feed
Which hungry wolves with praise and spoil,
Those who would sit near power must toil;
And such, there sitting, all may see.
What seeks he ? All that others seek
He casts away, like a vile weed
Which the sea casts unreturningly.
That poor and hungry men should break
The laws which wreak them toil and scorn,
We understand ; but Lionel

We know is rich and nobly born.
So wondered they : yet all men loved
Young Lionel, though few approved;
All but the priests, whose hatred fell
Like the unseen blight of a smiling day,
The withering honey dew, which clings
Under the bright green buds of May,
Whilst they unfold their emerald wings :
For he made verses wild and queer
On the strange creeds priests hold so dear,
Because they bring them land and gold.
Of devils and saints and all such gear,
He made tales which whoso heard or read
Would laugh till he were almost dead.
So this grew a proverb : " Don't get old
Till Lionel's ' banquet in hell' you hear,
And then you will laugh yourself young again.'
So the priests hated him, and he
Repaid their hate with cheerful glee.
Ah, smiles and joyance quickly died,
For public hope grew pale and dim
In an altered time and tide,
And in its wasting withered him,
As a summer flower that blows too soon
Droops in the smile of the waning moon,
When it scatters through an April night
The frozen dews of wrinkling blight.
None now hoped more.   Grey Power was seated
Safely on her ancestral throne ;
And Faith, the Python, undefeated,
Even to its blood-stained steps dragged on
Her foul and wounded train, and men
Were trampled and deceived again,
And words and shows again could bind
The wailing tribes of human kind
In scorn and famine.   Fire and blood
Raged round the raging multitude,
To fields remote by tyrants sent
To be the scorned instrument
With which they drag from mines of gore
The chains their slaves yet ever wore;
And in the streets men met each other,
And by old altars and in halls,
And smiled again at festivals.
But each man found in his heart's brother
Cold cheer ; for all, though half deceived,
The outworn creeds again believed,
And the same round anew began,
Which the weary world yet ever ran.

Many then wept, not tears, but gall
Within their hearts, like drops which fall
Wasting the fountain-stone away.
And in that dark and evil day
Did all desires and thoughts, that claim
Men's care—ambition, friendship, fame,
Love, hope, though hope was now despair—
Endue the colours of this change,

As from the all-surrounding air
The earth takes hues obscure and strange,
When storm and earthquake linger there.

And so, my friend, it then befell
To many, most to Lionel,
Whose hope was like the life of youth
Within him, and when dead, became
A spirit of unresting flame,
Which goaded him in his distress
Over the world's vast wilderness.
Three years he left his native land,
And on the fourth, when he returned,
None knew him : he was stricken deep
With some disease of mind, and turned
Into aught unlike Lionel.
On him, on whom, did he pause in sleep,
Serenest smiles were wont to keep,
And, did he wake, a winged band
Of bright persuasions, which had fed
On his sweet lips and liquid eyes,
Kept their swift pinions half outspread,
To do on men his least command;
On him, whom once 'twas paradise
Even to behold, now misery lay:
In his own heart 'twas merciless,
To all things else none may express
Its innocence and tenderness.
'Twas said that he had refuge sought
In love from his unquiet thought
In distant lands, and been deceived
By some strange show ; for there were found,
Blotted with tears as those relieved
By their own words are wont to do,
These mournful verses on the ground,
By all who read them blotted too.

"How am I changed ! my hopes were once like fire :
I loved, and I believed that life was love.
How am I lost ! on wings of swift desire
Among Heaven's winds my spirit once did move.
I slept, and silver dreams did aye inspire
My liquid sleep : I woke, and did approve
All nature to my heart, and thought to make
A paradise of earth for one sweet sake.

"I love, but I believe in love no more.
I feel desire, but hope not. O, from sleep
Most vainly must my weary brain implore
Its long-lost flattery now : I wake to weep,
And sit through the long day gnawing the core
Of my bitter heart, and, like a miser, keep,
Since none in what I feel take pain or pleasure,
To my own soul its self-consuming treasure."

He dwelt beside me near the sea :
And oft in the evening did we meet,
When the waves, beneath the starlight, flee
O'er the yellow sands with silver feet,
And talked : our talk was sad and sweet,

Till slowly from his mien there passed
The desolation which it spoke ;
And smiles,—as when the lightning's blast
Has parched some heaven-delighting oak,
The next spring shows leaves pale and rare,
But like flowers delicate and fair,
On its rent boughs,—again arrayed
His countenance in tender light:
His words grew subtile fire, which made
The air his hearers breathed delight :
His motions, like the winds, were free,
Which bend the bright grass gracefully,
Then fade away in circlets faint:
And winged hope, on which upborne
His soul seemed hovering in his eyes,
Like some bright spirit newly born
Floating amid the sunny skies,
Sprang forth from his rent heart anew.
Yet o'er his talk, and looks, and mien,
Tempering their loveliness too keen,
Past woe its shadow backward threw,
Till like an exhalation, spread
From flowers half drunk with evening dew,
They did become infectious : sweet
And subtile mists of sense and thought:
Which wrapt us soon, when we might meet,
Almost from our own looks and aught
The wide world holds. And so, his mind
Was healed, while mine grew sick with fear:
For ever now his health declined,
Like some frail bark which cannot bear
The impulse of an altered wind,
Though prosperous : and my heart grew full
'Mid its new joy of a new care :
For his cheek became, not pale, but fair,
As rose-o'ershadowed lilies are ;
And soon his deep and sunny hair,
In this alone less beautiful,
Like grass in tombs grew wild and rare.
The blood in his translucent veins
Beat, not like animal life, but love
Seemed now its sullen springs to move,
When life had failed, and all its pains :
And sudden sleep would seize him oft
Like death, so calm, but that a tear,
His pointed eyelashes between,
Would gather in the light serene
Of smiles, whose lustre bright and soft
Beneath lay undulating there.
His breath was like inconstant flame,
As eagerly it went and came ;
And I hung o'er him in his sleep,
Till, like an image in the lake
Which rains disturb, my tears would break
The shadow of that slumber deep :
Then he would bid me not to weep,
And say with flattery false, yet sweet,
That death and he could never meet,

If I would never part with him.
And so we loved, and did unite
All that in us was yet divided :
For when he said, that many a rite,
By men to bind but once provided,
Could not be shared by him and me,
Or they would kill him in their glee,
I shuddered, and then laughing said—
" We will have rites our faith to bind,
But our church shall be the starry night,
Our altar the grassy earth outspread,
And our priest the muttering wind."

'Twas sunset as I spoke : one star
Had scarce burst forth, when from afar
The ministers of misrule sent,
Seized upon Lionel, and bore
His chained limbs to a dreary tower,
In the midst of a city vast and wide.
For he, they said, from his mind had bent
Against their gods keen blasphemy,
For which, though his soul must roasted be
In hell's red lakes immortally,
Yet even on earth must he abide
The vengeance of their slaves : a trial,
I think, men call it. What avail
Are prayers and tears, which chase denial
From the fierce savage, nursed in hate?
What the knit soul that pleading and pale
Makes wan the quivering cheek, which late
It painted with its own delight?
We were divided. As I could,
I stilled the tingling of my blood,
And followed him in their despite,
As a widow follows, pale and wild,
The murderers and corse of her only child ;
And when we came to the prison door,
And I prayed to share his dungeon floor
With prayers which rarely have been spurned,
And when men drove me forth and I
Stared with blank frenzy on the sky,
A farewell look of love he turned,
Half calming me ; then gazed awhile,
As if through that black and massy pile,
And through the crowd around him there,
And through the dense and murky air,
And the thronged streets, he did espy
What poets know and prophesy ;
And said, with voice that made them shiver
And clung like music in my brain,
And which the mute walls spoke again
Prolonging it with deepened strain:
" Fear not, the tyrants shall rule for ever,
Or the priests of the bloody faith ;
They stand on the brink of that mighty river,
Whose waves they have tainted with death:
It is fed from the depths of a thousand dells,
Around them it foams, and rages, and swells,

And their swords and their sceptres I floating see,
Like wrecks in the surge of eternity."

I dwelt beside the prison gate,
And the strange crowd that out and in
Passed, some, no doubt, with mine own fate,
Might have fretted me with its ceaseless din,
But the fever of care was louder within.
Soon, but too late, in penitence
Or fear, his foes released him thence:
I saw his thin and languid form,
As leaning on the jailor's arm,
Whose hardened eyes grew moist the while,
To meet his mute and faded smile,
And hear his words of kind farewell,
He tottered forth from his damp cell.
Many had never wept before,
From whom fast tears then gushed and fell :
Many will relent no more,
Who sobbed like infants then : ay, all
Who thronged the prison's stony hall,
The rulers or the slaves of law,
Felt with a new surprise and awe
That they were human, till strong shame
Made them again become the same.
The prison bloodhounds, huge and grim,
From human looks the infection caught,
And fondly crouched and fawned on him ;
And men have heard the prisoners say,
Who in their rotting dungeons lay,
That from that hour, throughout one day,
The fierce despair and hate which kept
Their trampled bosoms almost slept ;
When, like twin vultures, they hung feeding
On each heart's wound, wide torn and bleeding.
Because their jailors' rule, they thought,
Grew merciful, like a parent's sway.

I know not how, but we were free :
And Lionel sate alone with me,
As the carriage drove through the streets apace ;
And we looked upon each other's face ;
And the blood in our fingers intertwined
Ran like the thoughts of a single mind,
As the swift emotions went and came
Through the veins of each united frame.
So through the long long streets we past
Of the million-peopled City vast ;
Which is that desert, where each one
Seeks his mate yet is alone,
Beloved and sought and mourned of none ;
Until the clear blue sky was seen,
And the grassy meadows bright and green,
And then I sunk in his embrace,
Enclosing there a mighty space
Of love : and so we travelled on
By woods, and fields of yellow flowers,
And towns, and villages, and towers.

Day after day of happy hours.
It was the azure time of June,
When the skies are deep in the stainless noon,
And the warm and fitful breezes shake
The fresh green leaves of the hedge-row briar,
And there were odours then to make
The very breath we did respire
A liquid element, whereon
Our spirits, like delighted things
That walk the air on subtle wings,
Floated and mingled far away,
'Mid the warm winds of the sunny day.
And when the evening star came forth
Above the curve of the new bent moon,
And light and sound ebbed from the earth,
Like the tide of the full and weary sea
To the depths of its tranquillity,
Our natures to its own repose
Did the earth's breathless sleep attune :
Like flowers, which on each other close
Their languid leaves when daylight's gone,
We lay, till new emotions came,
Which seemed to make each mortal frame
One soul of interwoven flame,
A life in life, a second birth
In worlds diviner far than earth,
Which, like two strains of harmony
That mingle in the silent sky
Then slowly disunite, past by
And left the tenderness of tears,
A soft oblivion of all fears,
A sweet sleep : so we travelled on
Till we came to the home of Lionel,
Among the mountains wild and lone,
Beside the hoary western sea,
Which near the verge of the echoing shore
The massy forest shadowed o'er.

The ancient steward, with hair all hoar,
As we alighted, wept to see
His master changed so fearfully ;
And the old man's sobs did waken me
From my dream of unremaining gladness :
The truth flashed o'er me like quick madness
When I looked, and saw that there was death
On Lionel : yet day by day
He lived, till fear grew hope and faith,
And in my soul I dared to say,
Nothing so bright can pass away :
Death is dark, and foul, and dull,
But he is—O how beautiful !
Yet day by day he grew more weak,
And his sweet voice, when he might speak,
Which ne'er was loud, became more low ;
And the light which flashed through his waxen cheek
Grew faint, as the rose-like hues which flow
From sunset o'er the Alpine snow :

O

And death seemed not like death in him,
For the spirit of life o'er every limb
Lingered, a mist of sense and thought.
When the summer wind faint odours brought
From mountain flowers, even as it passed
His cheek would change, as the noonday sea
Which the dying breeze sweeps fitfully.
If but a cloud the sky o'ercast,
You might see his colour come and go,
And the softest strain of music made
Sweet smiles, yet sad, arise and fade
Amid the dew of his tender eyes ;
And the breath, with intermitting flow,
Made his pale lips quiver and part.
You might hear the beatings of his heart,
Quick, but not strong ; and with my tresses
When oft he playfully would bind
In the bowers of mossy lonelinesses
His neck, and win me so to mingle
In the sweet depth of woven caresses,
And our faint limbs were intertwined,
Alas ! the unquiet life did tingle
From mine own heart through every vein,
Like a captive in dreams of liberty,
Who beats the walls of his stony cell.
But his, it seemed already free,
Like the shadow of fire surrounding me !
On my faint eyes and limbs did dwell
That spirit as it passed, till soon,
As a frail cloud wandering o'er the moon,
Beneath its light invisible,
Is seen when it folds its grey wings again
To alight on midnight's dusky plain,
I lived and saw, and the gathering soul
Passed from beneath that strong control,
And I fell on a life which was sick with fear
Of all the woe that now I bear.

Amid a bloomless myrtle wood,
On a green and sea-girt promontory,
Not far from where we dwelt, there stood
In record of a sweet sad story,
An altar and a temple bright
Circled by steps, and o'er the gate
Was sculptured, "To Fidelity ;"
And in the shrine an image sate
All veiled : but there was seen the light
Of smiles, which faintly could express
A mingled pain and tenderness
Through that ethereal drapery.
The left hand held the head, the right—
Beyond the veil, beneath the skin,
You might see the nerves quivering within—
Was forcing the point of a barbed dart
Into its side-convulsing heart.
An unskilled hand, yet one informed
With genius, had the marble warmed

With that pathetic life.   This tale
It told : A dog had from the sea,
When the tide was raging fearfully,
Dragged Lionel's mother, weak and pale,
Then died beside her on the sand,
And she that temple thence had planned ;
But it was Lionel's own hand
Had wrought the image.   Each new moon
That lady did, in this lone fane,
The rites of a religion sweet,
Whose god was in her heart and brain :
The season's loveliest flowers were strewn
On the marble floor beneath her feet,
And she brought crowns of sea-buds white,
Whose odour is so sweet and faint,
And weeds, like branching chrysolite,
Woven in devices fine and quaint,
And tears from her brown eyes did stain
The altar : need but look upon
That dying statue, fair and wan,
If tears should cease, to weep again :
And rare Arabian odours came,
Though the myrtle copses steaming thence
From the hissing frankincense,
Whose smoke, wool-white as ocean foam,
Hung in dense flocks beneath the dome,
That ivory dome, whose azure night
With golden stars, like heaven, was bright
O'er the split cedars pointed flame ;
And the lady's harp would kindle there
The melody of an old air,
Softer than sleep ; the villagers
Mixt their religion up with hers,
And as they listened round, shed tears.

One eve he led me to this fane :
Daylight on its last purple cloud
Was lingering grey, and soon her strain
The nightingale began ; now loud,
Climbing in circles the windless sky,
Now dying music; suddenly
'Tis scattered in a thousand notes,
And now to the hushed ear it floats
Like field smells known in infancy,
Then failing, soothes the air again.
We sate within that temple lone,
Pavilioned round with Parian stone :
His mother's harp stood near, and oft
I had awakened music soft
Amid its wires : the nightingale
Was pausing in her heaven-taught tale :
" Now drain the cup," said Lionel,
" Which the poet-bird has crowned so well
With the wine of her bright and liquid song !
Heardst thou not sweet words among
That heaven-resounding minstrelsy ?
Heardst thou not, that those who die
Awake in a world of ecstasy ?

That love, when limbs are interwoven,
And sleep, when the night of life is cloven,
And thought, to the world's dim boundaries clinging,
And music, when one beloved is singing,
Is death?   Let us drain right joyously
The cup which the sweet bird fills for me."
He paused, and to my lips he bent
His own : like spirit his words went
Through all my limbs with the speed of fire ;
And his keen eyes, glittering through mine,
Filled me with the flame divine,
Which in their orbs was burning far,
Like the light of an unmeasured star,
In the sky of midnight dark and deep ;
Yes, 'twas his soul that did inspire
Sounds, which my skill could ne'er awaken ;
And first, I felt my fingers sweep
The harp, and a long quivering cry
Burst from my lips in symphony :
The dusk and solid air was shaken,
As swift and swifter the notes came
From my touch, that wandered like quick flame,
And from my bosom, labouring
With some unutterable thing :
The awful sound of my own voice made
My faint lips tremble, in some mood
Of wordless thought Lionel stood
So pale, that even beside his cheek
The snowy column from its shade
Caught whiteness : yet his countenance
Raised upward, burned with radiance
Of spirit-piercing joy, whose light,
Like the moon struggling through the night
Of whirlwind-rifted clouds, did break
With beams that might not be confined.
I paused, but soon his gestures kindled
New power, as by the moving wind
The waves are lifted, and my song
To low soft notes now changed and dwindled,
And from the twinkling wires among,
My languid fingers drew and flung
Circles of life-dissolving sound,
Yet faint : in aery rings they bound
My Lionel, who, as every strain
Grew fainter, but more sweet, his mien
Sunk with the sound relaxedly ;
And slowly now he turned to me,
As slowly faded from his face
That awful joy : with looks serene
He was soon drawn to my embrace,
And my wild song then died away
In murmurs : words, I dare not say
We mixed, and on his lips mine fed
Till they methought felt still and cold :
" What is it with thee, love ?" I said :
No word, no look, no motion ! yes,
There was a change, but spare to guess,
Nor let that moment's hope be told.

I looked, and knew that he was dead,
And fell, as the eagle on the plain
Falls when life deserts her brain,
And the mortal lightning is veiled again.

O that I were now dead ! but such
Did they not, love, demand too much
Those dying murmurs ? He forbade.
O that I once again were mad !
And yet, dear Rosalind, not so,
For I would live to share thy woe.
Sweet boy, did I forget thee too?
Alas, we know not what we do
When we speak words.

                     No memory more
Is in my mind of that seashore.
Madness came on me, and a troop
Of misty shapes did seem to sit
Beside me, on a vessel's poop,
And the clear north wind was driving it.
Then I heard strange tongues, and saw strange flowers,
And the stars methought grew unlike ours,
And the azure sky and the stormless sea
Made me believe that I had died,
And waked in a world which was to me
Drear hell, though heaven to all beside :
Then a deep sleep fell on my mind,
Whilst animal life many long years
Had rescued from a chasm of tears ;
And when I awoke, I wept to find
That the same lady, bright and wise,
With silver locks and quick brown eyes,
The mother of my Lionel,
Had tended me in my distress,
And died some months before.   No less
Wonder, but far more peace and joy
Brought in that hour my lovely boy ;
For through that trance my soul had well
The impress of thy being kept ;
And if I waked, or if I slept,
No doubt, though memory faithless be,
Thy image ever dwelt on me ;
And thus, O Lionel, like thee
Is our sweet child.   'Tis sure most strange
I knew not of so great a change,
As that which gave him birth, who now
Is all the solace of my woe.

That Lionel great wealth had left
By will to me, and that of all
The ready lies of law bereft,
My child and me might well befall.
But let me think not of the scorn,
Which from the meanest I have borne,
When for my child's beloved sake,
I mixed with slaves, to vindicate
The very laws themselves do make :
Let me not say scorn is my fate,

Lest I be proud, suffering the same
With those who live in deathless fame.

She ceased.—" Lo, where red morning through the woods
Is burning o'er the dew," said Rosalind ;
And with these words they rose, and towards the flood
Of the blue lake, beneath the leaves now wind
With equal steps and fingers intertwined :
Thence to a lonely dwelling, where the shore
Is shadowed with steep rocks, and cypresses
Cleave with their dark green cones the silent skies,
And with their shadows the clear depths below,
And where a little terrace from its bowers,
Of blooming myrtle and faint lemon-flowers,
Scatters its sense-dissolving fragrance o'er
The liquid marble of the windless lake ;
And where the aged forest's limbs look hoar,
Under the leaves which their green garments make,
They come : 'tis Helen's home, and clean and white,
Like one which tyrants spare on our own land
In some such solitude, its casements bright
Shone through their vine-leaves in the morning sun,
And even within 'twas scarce like Italy.
And when she saw how all things there were planned,
As in an English home, dim memory
Disturbed poor Rosalind : she stood as one
Whose mind is where his body cannot be.
Till Helen led her where her child yet slept,
And said, "Observe, that brow was Lionel's,
Those lips were his, and so he ever kept
One arm in sleep, pillowing his head with it.
You cannot see his eyes, they are two wells
Of liquid love : let us not wake him yet."
But Rosalind could bear no more, and wept
A shower of burning tears, which fell upon
His face, and so his opening lashes shone
With tears unlike his own, as he did leap
In sudden wonder from his innocent sleep.

So Rosalind and Helen lived together
Thenceforth, changed in all else, yet friends again,
Such as they were, when o'er the mountain heather
They wandered in their youth, through sun and rain.
And after many years, for human things
Change even like the ocean and the wind,
Her daughter was restored to Rosalind,
And in their circle thence some visitings
Of joy 'mid their new calm would intervene ;
A lovely child she was, of looks serene,
And motions which o'er things indifferent shed
The grace and gentleness from whence they came.
And Helen's boy grew with her, and they fed
From the same flowers of thought, until each mind
Like springs which mingle in one flood became,
And in their union soon their parents saw
The shadow of the peace denied to them.
And Rosalind, for when the living stem

Is cankered in its heart, the tree must fall,
Died ere her time ; and with deep grief and awe
The pale survivors followed her remains
Beyond the region of dissolving rains,
Up the cold mountain she was wont to call
Her tomb ; and on Chiavenna's precipice
They raised a pyramid of lasting ice,
Whose polished sides, ere day had yet begun,
Caught the first glow of the unrisen sun,
The last, when it had sunk ; and through the night
The charioteers of Arctos wheeled round
Its glittering point, as seen from Helen's home,
Whose sad inhabitants each year would come,
With willing steps climbing that rugged height,
And hang long locks of hair, and garlands bound
With amaranth flowers, which, in the clime's despite,
Filled the frore air with unaccustomed light :
Such flowers, as in the wintry memory bloom
Of one friend left, adorned that frozen tomb.

Helen, whose spirit was of softer mould,
Whose sufferings too were less, death slowlier led
Into the peace of his dominion cold :
She died among her kindred, being old.
And know, that if love die not in the dead
As in the living, none of mortal kind
Are blest, as now Helen and Rosalind.

PROMETHEUS UNBOUND.

A LYRICAL DRAMA.

"Audisne hæc, Amphiarae, sub terram abdite?"

DRAMATIS PERSONÆ.

PROMETHEUS.	ASIA ⎫
DEMOGORGON.	PANTHEA ⎬ Oceanides.
JUPITER.	IONE ⎭
THE EARTH.	THE PHANTASM OF JUPITER.
OCEAN.	THE SPIRIT OF THE EARTH.
APOLLO.	SPIRITS OF THE HOURS.
MERCURY.	SPIRITS. ECHOES. FAUNS.
HERCULES.	FURIES.

PREFACE.

THE Greek tragic writers, in selecting as their subject any portion of their national history or mythology, employed in their treatment of it a certain arbitrary discretion. They by no means conceived themselves bound to adhere to the common interpretation or to imitate in story as in title their rivals and predecessors. Such a system would have amounted to a resignation of those claims to preference over their competitors which incited the composition. The Agamemnonian story was exhibited on the Athenian theatre with as many variations as dramas.

I have presumed to employ a similar licence. The "Prometheus Unbound" of Æschylus supposed the reconciliation of Jupiter with his victim as the price of the disclosure of the danger threatened to his empire by the consummation of his marriage with Thetis. Thetis, according to this view of the subject, was given in marriage to Peleus, and Prometheus, by the permission of Jupiter, delivered from his captivity by Hercules. Had I framed my story on this model, I should have done no more than have attempted to restore the lost drama of Æschylus; an ambition, which, if my preference to this mode of treating the subject had incited me to cherish, the recollection of the high comparison such an attempt would challenge might well abate. But, in truth, I was averse from a catastrophe so feeble as that of reconciling the Champion with the Oppressor of mankind. The moral interest of the fable, which is so powerfully sustained by the sufferings and endurance of Prometheus, would be annihilated if we could conceive of him as unsaying his high language and quailing before his successful and perfidious adversary. The only imaginary being resembling in any degree Prometheus, is Satan; and Prometheus is, in my judgment, a more poetical character than Satan, because, in addition to courage, and majesty, and firm and patient opposition to omnipotent force, he is susceptible of being described as exempt from the taints of ambition, envy, revenge, and a desire for personal aggrandizement, which, in the Hero of Paradise Lost, interfere with the interest. The character of Satan engenders in the mind a pernicious casuistry which leads us to weigh his faults with his wrongs, and to excuse the former because the latter exceed all measure. In the minds of those who consider that magnificent fiction with a religious feeling it engenders something worse. But Prometheus is, as it were, the type of the highest perfection of moral and intellectual nature, impelled by the purest and the truest motives, to the best and noblest ends.

This Poem was chiefly written upon the mountainous ruins of the Baths of Caracalla, among the flowery glades, and thickets of odoriferous blossoming trees, which are extended in ever winding labyrinths upon its immense platforms and dizzy arches suspended in the air. The bright blue sky of Rome, and the effect of the vigorous awakening spring in that divinest climate, and the new life with which it drenches the spirits even to intoxication, were the inspiration of this drama.

The imagery which I have employed will be found, in many instances, to have been drawn from the operations of the human mind, or from those external actions by which they are expressed. This is unusual in modern poetry, although Dante and Shakspeare are full of instances of the same kind : Dante indeed more than any other poet, and with greater success. But the Greek poets, as writers to whom no resource of awakening the sympathy of their contemporaries was unknown, were in the habitual use of this power ; and it is the study of their works (since a higher merit would probably be denied me), to which I am willing that my readers should impute this singularity.

One word is due in candour to the degree in which the study of contemporary writings may have tinged my composition, for such has been a topic of censure with regard to poems, far more popular, and indeed more deservedly popular, than mine. It is impossible that any one who inhabits the same age with such writers as those who stand in the foremost ranks of our own, can conscientiously assure himself that his language and tone of thought may not have been modified by the study of the productions of those extraordinary intellects. It is true, that, not the spirit of their genius, but the forms in which it has manifested itself, are due less to the peculiarities of their own minds than to the peculiarity of the moral and intellectual condition of the minds among which they have been produced. Thus a number of writers possess the form, whilst they want the spirit of those whom, it is alleged, they imitate ; because the former is the endowment of the age in which they live, and the latter must be the uncommunicated lightning of their own mind.

The peculiar style of intense and comprehensive imagery which distinguishes the modern literature of England, has not been, as a general power, the product of the imitation of any particular writer. The mass of capabilities remains at every period materially the same; the circumstances which awaken it to action perpetually change. If England were divided into forty republics, each equal in population and extent to Athens, there is no reason to suppose but that, under institutions not more perfect than those of Athens, each would produce philosophers and poets equal to those who (if we except Shakspeare) have never been surpassed. We owe the great writers of the golden age of our literature to that fervid awakening of the public mind which shook to dust the oldest and most oppressive form of the Christian religion. We owe Milton to the progress and development of the same spirit: the sacred Milton was, let it ever be remembered, a republican, and a bold inquirer into morals and religion. The great writers of our own age are, we have reason to suppose, the companions and forerunners of some unimagined change in our social condition or the opinions which cement it. The cloud of mind is discharging its collected lightning, and the equilibrium between institutions and opinions is now restoring, or is about to be restored.

As to imitation, poetry is a mimetic art. It creates; but it creates by combination and representation. Poetical abstractions are beautiful and new, not because the portions of which they are composed had no previous existence in the mind of man or in nature, but because the whole produced by their combination has some intelligible and beautiful analogy with those sources of emotion and thought, and with the contemporary condition of them: one great poet is a masterpiece of nature which another not only ought to study but must study. He might as wisely and as easily determine that his mind should no longer be the mirror of all that is lovely in the visible universe, as exclude from his contemplation the beautiful which exists in the writings of a great contemporary. The pretence of doing it would be a presumption in any but the greatest; the effect, even in him, would be strained, unnatural, and ineffectual. A poet is the combined product of such internal powers as modify the nature of others; and of such external influences as excite and sustain these powers; he is not one, but both. Every man's mind is, in this respect, modified by all the objects of nature and art; by every word and every suggestion which he ever admitted to act upon his consciousness; it is the mirror upon which all forms are reflected, and in which they compose one form. Poets, not otherwise than philosophers, painters, sculptors, and musicians, are, in one sense, the creators, and, in another, the creations, of their age. From this subjection the loftiest do not escape. There is a similarity between Homer and Hesiod, between Æschylus and Euripides, between Virgil and Horace, between Dante and Petrarch, between Shakspeare and Fletcher, between Dryden and Pope; each has a generic resemblance under which their specific distinctions are arranged. If this similarity be the result of imitation, I am willing to confess that I have imitated.

Let this opportunity be conceded to me of acknowledging that I have, what a Scotch philosopher characteristically terms, "a passion for reforming the world:" what passion incited him to write and publish his book, he omits to explain. For my part I had rather be damned with Plato and Lord Bacon, than go to Heaven with Paley and Malthus. But it is a mistake to suppose that I dedicate my poetical compositions solely to the direct enforcement of reform, or that I consider them in any degree as containing a reasoned system on the theory of human life. Didactic poetry is my abhorrence; nothing can be equally well expressed in prose that is not tedious and supererogatory in verse. My purpose has hitherto been simply to familiarize the highly refined imagination of the more select classes of poetical readers with beautiful idealisms of moral excellence; aware that until the mind can love, and admire, and trust, and hope, and endure, reasoned principles of moral conduct are seeds cast upon the highway of life which the unconscious passenger tramples into dust, although they would bear the harvest of his happiness. Should I live to accomplish what I purpose, that is, produce a systematical history of what appear to me to be the genuine elements of human society, let not the advocates of injustice and superstition flatter themselves that I should take Æschylus rather than Plato as my model.

The having spoken of myself with unaffected freedom will need little apology with the candid; and let the uncandid consider that they injure me less than their own hearts and minds by misrepresentation. Whatever talents a person may possess to amuse and instruct others, be they ever so inconsiderable, he is yet bound to exert them: if his attempt be ineffectual, let the punishment of an unaccomplished purpose have been sufficient; let none trouble themselves to heap the dust of oblivion upon his efforts; the pile they raise will betray his grave which might otherwise have been unknown.

ACT I.

SCENE.—*A Ravine of Icy Rocks in the Indian Caucasus.*　PROMETHEUS *is discovered bound to the Precipice.*　PANTHEA *and* IONE *are seated at his feet. Time, Night.　During the scene, Morning slowly breaks.*

Pro. Monarch of Gods and Demons, and all Spirits
But one, who throng those bright and rolling worlds
Which Thou and I alone of living things
Behold with sleepless eyes ! regard this Earth
Made multitudinous with thy slaves, whom thou
Requitest for knee-worship, prayer, and praise,
And toil, and hecatombs of broken hearts,
With fear and self-contempt and barren hope.
Whilst me, who am thy foe, eyeless in hate,
Hast thou made reign and triumph, to thy scorn,
O'er mine own misery and thy vain revenge.
Three thousand years of sleep-unsheltered hours,
And moments aye divided by keen pangs
Till they seemed years, torture and solitude,
Scorn and despair,—these are mine empire.
More glorious far than that which thou surveyest
From thine unenvied throne, O Mighty God !
Almighty, had I deigned to share the shame
Of thine ill tyranny, and hung not here
Nailed to this wall of eagle-baffling mountain,
Black, wintry, dead, unmeasured ; without herb,
Insect, or beast, or shape or sound of life.
Ah me ! alas, pain, pain ever, for ever !

No change, no pause, no hope !　Yet I endure.
I ask the Earth, have not the mountains felt ?
I ask yon Heaven, the all-beholding Sun,
Has it not seen ?　The Sea, in storm or calm,
Heaven's ever-changing Shadow, spread below,
Have its deaf waves not heard my agony ?
Ah me ! alas, pain, pain ever, for ever !

The crawling glaciers pierce me with the spears
Of their moon-freezing crystals, the bright chains
Eat with their burning cold into my bones.
Heaven's winged hound, polluting from thy lips
His beak in poison not his own, tears up
My heart ; and shapeless sights come wandering by,
The ghastly people of the realm of dream,
Mocking me : and the Earthquake-fiends are charged
To wrench the rivets from my quivering wounds
When the rocks split and close again behind :
While from their loud abysses howling throng
The genii of the storm, urging the rage
Of whirlwind, and afflict me with keen hail.
And yet to me welcome is day and night,
Whether one breaks the hoar frost of the morn,
Or starry, dim, and slow, the other climbs
The leaden-coloured east ; for then they lead
The wingless, crawling hours, one among whom—

As some dark Priest hails the reluctant victim—
Shall drag thee, cruel King, to kiss the blood
From these pale feet, which then might trample thee
If they disdained not such a prostrate slave.
Disdain ! Ah no ! I pity thee.   What ruin
Will hunt thee undefended through the wide Heaven !
How will thy soul, cloven to its depth with terror,
Gape like a hell within !   I speak in grief,
Not exultation, for I hate no more,
As then ere misery made me wise.   The curse
Once breathed on thee I would recall.   Ye Mountains,
Whose many-voicèd Echoes, through the mist
Of cataracts, flung the thunder of that spell !
Ye icy Springs, stagnant with wrinkling frost,
Which vibrated to hear me, and then crept
Shuddering through India.   Thou serenest Air,
Through which the sun walks burning without beams !
And ye swift Whirlwinds, who on poisèd wings
Hung mute and moveless o'er yon hushed abyss,
As thunder, louder than your own, made rock
The orbèd world !   If then my words had power,
Though I am changed so that aught evil wish
Is dead within ; although no memory be
Of what is hate, let them not lose it now !
What was that curse ? for ye all heard me speak.

FIRST VOICE : *From the Mountains.*

Thrice three hundred thousand years
   O'er the Earthquake's couch we stood :
Oft, as men convulsed with fears,
   We trembled in our multitude.

SECOND VOICE : *From the Springs.*

Thunderbolts had parched our water,
   We had been stained with bitter blood,
And had run mute, 'mid shrieks of slaughter,
   Through a city and a solitude.

THIRD VOICE : *From the Air.*

I had clothed, since Earth uprose,
   Its wastes in colours not their own,
And oft had my serene repose
   Been cloven by many a rending groan.

FOURTH VOICE : *From the Whirlwind.*

We had soared beneath these mountains
   Unresting ages ; nor had thunder,
Nor yon volcano's flaming fountains,
   Nor any power above or under
   Ever made us mute with wonder.

FIRST VOICE.

But never bowed our snowy crest
As at the voice of thine unrest.

SECOND VOICE.

Never such a sound before
To the Indian waves we bore.
A pilot asleep on the howling sea
Leaped up from the deck in agony,
And heard, and cried, "Ah, woe is me!"
And died as mad as the wild waves be.

THIRD VOICE.

By such dread words from Earth to Heaven
My still realm was never riven:
When its wound was closed, there stood
Darkness o'er the day like blood.

FOURTH VOICE.

And we shrank back: for dreams of ruin
To frozen caves our flight pursuing
Made us keep silence—thus—and thus—
Though silence is a hell to us.

The Earth. The tongueless Caverns of the craggy hills
Cried, "Misery!" then; the hollow Heaven replied,
"Misery!" And the Ocean's purple waves,
Climbing the land, howled to the lashing winds,
And the pale nations heard it, "Misery!"

Pro. I hear a sound of voices: not the voice
Which I gave forth. Mother, thy sons and thou
Scorn him, without whose all-enduring will
Beneath the fierce omnipotence of Jove,
Both they and thou had vanished, like thin mist
Unrolled on the morning wind. Know ye not me,
The Titan? He who made his agony
The barrier to your else all-conquering foe?
Oh, rock-embosomed lawns, and snow-fed streams,
Now seen athwart frore vapours, deep below,
Through whose o'ershadowing woods I wandered once
With Asia, drinking life from her loved eyes;
Why scorns the spirit which informs ye, now
To commune with me? me alone, who checked,
As one who checks a fiend-drawn charioteer,
The falsehood and the force of him who reigns
Supreme, and with the groans of pining slaves
Fills your dim glens and liquid wildernesses:
Why answer ye not, still? Brethren!
The Earth. They dare not.
Pro. Who dares? for I would hear that curse again.
Ha, what an awful whisper rises up!
'Tis scarce like sound: it tingles through the frame.
As lightning tingles, hovering ere it strike.
Speak, Spirit! from thine inorganic voice
I only know that thou art moving near
And love. How cursed I him?
The Earth. How canst thou hear
Who knowest not the language of the dead?
Pro. Thou art a living spirit; speak as they.

The Earth. I dare not speak like life, lest Heaven's fell King
Should hear, and link me to some wheel of pain
More torturing than the one whereon I roll.
Subtle thou art and good, and though the Gods
Hear not this voice, yet thou art more than God
Being wise and kind : earnestly hearken now.

Pro. Obscurely through my brain, like shadows dim,
Sweep awful thoughts, rapid and thick. I feel
Faint, like one mingled in entwining love ;
Yet 'tis not pleasure.

The Earth. No, thou canst not hear :
Thou art immortal, and this tongue is known
Only to those who die.

Pro. And what art thou,
O melancholy Voice ?

The Earth. I am the Earth,
Thy mother ; she within whose stony veins,
To the last fibre of the loftiest tree
Whose thin leaves trembled in the frozen air,
Joy ran, as blood within a living frame,
When thou didst from her bosom, like a cloud
Of glory, arise, a spirit of keen joy !
And at thy voice her pining sons uplifted
Their prostrate brows from the polluting dust,
And our almighty Tyrant with fierce dread
Grew pale, until his thunder chained thee here.
Then, see those million worlds which burn and roll
Around us : their inhabitants beheld
My spherèd light wane in wide Heaven ; the sea
Was lifted by strange tempest, and new fire
From earthquake-rifted mountains of bright snow
Shook its portentous hair beneath Heaven's frown ;
Lightning and Inundation vexed the plains ;
Blue thistles bloomed in cities ; foodless toads
Within voluptuous chambers panting crawled :
When Plague had fallen on man, and beast, and worm,
And famine ; and black blight on herb and tree ;
And in the corn, and vines, and meadow-grass,
Teemed ineradicable poisonous weeds
Draining their growth, for my wan breast was dry
With grief ; and the thin air, my breath, was stained
With the contagion of a mother's hate
Breathed on her child's destroyer ; ay, I heard
Thy curse, the which, if thou rememberest not,
Yet my innumerable seas and streams,
Mountains, and caves, and winds, and yon wide air,
And the inarticulate people of the dead,
Preserve, a treasured spell. We meditate
In secret joy and hope those dreadful words
But dare not speak them.

Pro. Venerable mother !
All else who live and suffer take from thee
Some comfort ; flowers, and fruits, and happy sounds,
And love, though fleeting ; these may not be mine.
But mine own words, I pray, deny me not.

The Earth. They shall be told. Ere Babylon was dust,
The Magus Zoroaster, my dead child,
Met his own image walking in the garden.

That apparition, sole of men, he saw.
For know there are two worlds of life and death :
One that which thou beholdest ; but the other
Is underneath the grave, where do inhabit
The shadows of all forms that think and live
Till death unite them and they part no more ;
Dreams and the light imaginings of men,
And all that faith creates or love desires,
Terrible, strange, sublime and beauteous shapes.
There thou art, and dost hang, a writhing shade,
'Mid whirlwind-peopled mountains ; all the gods
Are there, and all the powers of nameless worlds,
Vast, sceptred phantoms ; heroes, men, and beasts ;
And Demogorgon, a tremendous gloom ;
And he, the supreme Tyrant, on his throne
Of burning gold.   Son, one of these shall utter
The curse which all remember.   Call at will
Thine own ghost, or the ghost of Jupiter,
Hades or Typhon, or what mightier Gods
From all-prolific Evil, since thy ruin
Have sprung, and trampled on my prostrate sons.
Ask, and they must reply : so the revenge
Of the Supreme may sweep through vacant shades,
As rainy wind through the abandoned gate
Of a fallen palace.
   Pro. Mother, let not aught
Of that which may be evil, pass again
My lips, or those of aught resembling me.
Phantasm of Jupiter, arise, appear !

IONE.

My wings are folded o'er mine ears :
  My wings are crossed o'er mine eyes
Yet through their silver shade appears,
  And through their lulling plumes arise,
A Shape, a throng of sounds ;
  May it be no ill to thee
O thou of many wounds !
Near whom, for our sweet sister's sake,
Ever thus we watch and wake.

PANTHEA.

The sound is of whirlwind underground,
  Earthquake, and fire, and mountains cloven :
The shape is awful like the sound,
  Clothed in dark purple, star-inwoven.
A sceptre of pale gold
  To stay steps proud, o'er the snow cloud
His veined hand doth hold.
Cruel he looks, but calm and strong,
Like one who does, not suffers wrong.

  Phantasm of Jupiter. Why have the secret powers of this strange
    world
Driven me, a frail and empty phantom, hither
On direst storms ?   What unaccustomed sounds
Are hovering on my lips, unlike the voice

With which our pallid race hold ghastly talk
In darkness? And, proud sufferer, who art thou?
  Pro. Tremendous Image, as thou art must be
He whom thou shadowest forth. I am his foe,
The Titan. Speak the words which I would hear,
Although no thought inform thine empty voice.
  The Earth. Listen! And though your echoes must be mute,
Grey mountains, and old woods, and haunted springs,
Prophetic caves, and isle-surrounding streams,
Rejoice to hear what yet ye cannot speak.
  Phan. A spirit seizes me and speaks within:
It tears me as fire tears a thunder-cloud.
  Pan. See, how he lifts his mighty looks, the Heaven
Darkens above.
  Ione.   He speaks! O shelter me!
  Pro. I see the curse on gestures proud and cold,
And looks of firm defiance, and calm hate,
And such despair as mocks itself with smiles,
Written as on a scroll: yet speak: Oh, speak!

PHANTASM.

Fiend, I defy thee! with a calm, fixed mind,
  All that thou canst inflict I bid thee do;
Foul Tyrant both of Gods and Human-kind,
  One only being shalt thou not subdue.
Rain then thy plagues upon me here,
Ghastly disease, and frenzying fear;
And let alternate frost and fire
Eat into me, and be thine ire
Lightning, and cutting hail, and legioned forms
Of furies, driving by upon the wounding storms.

Ay, do thy worst. Thou art omnipotent.
  O'er all things but thyself I gave thee power,
And my own will. Be thy swift mischiefs sent
  To blast mankind, from yon ethereal tower.
Let thy malignant spirit move
In darkness over those I love:
On me and mine I imprecate
The utmost torture of thy hate;
And thus devote to sleepless agony
This undeclining head, while thou must reign on high.

But thou, who art the God and Lord: O, thou,
  Who fillest with thy soul this world of woe,
To whom all things of Earth and Heaven do bow
  In fear and worship: all-prevailing foe!
I curse thee! let a sufferer's curse
Clasp thee, his torturer, like remorse;
Till thy Infinity shall be
A robe of envenomed agony;
And thine Omnipotence a crown of pain,
To cling like burning gold round thy dissolving brain.

Heap on thy soul, by virtue of this Curse,
  Ill deeds, then be thou damned, beholding good;
Both infinite as is the universe,
  And thou, and thy self-torturing solitude.

An awful image of calm power
Though now thou sittest, let the hour
Come, when thou must appear to be
That which thou art internally.
And after many a false and fruitless crime
Scorn track thy lagging fall through boundless space and time.

Pro. Were these my words, O Parent?
The Earth. They were thine.
Pro. It doth repent me : words are quick and vain ;
Grief for awhile is blind, and so was mine.
I wish no living thing to suffer pain.

THE EARTH.

Misery, Oh misery to me,
That Jove at length should vanquish thee.
Wail, howl aloud, Land and Sea,
The Earth's rent heart shall answer ye.
Howl, Spirits of the living and the dead,
Your refuge, your defence lies fallen and vanquishèd.

FIRST ECHO.

Lies fallen and vanquishèd !

SECOND ECHO.

Fallen and vanquishèd !

IONE.

Fear not : 'tis but some passing spasm,
    The Titan is unvanquished still.
But see, where through the azure chasm
    Of yon forked and snowy hill
Trampling the slant winds on high
    With golden-sandalled feet, that glow
Under plumes of purple dye,
Like rose-ensanguined ivory,
    A shape comes now,
Stretching on high from his right hand
A serpent-cinctured wand.

Pan. 'Tis Jove's world-wandering herald, Mercury

IONE.

And who are those with hydra tresses
    And iron wings that climb the wind,
Whom the frowning God represses
    Like vapours steaming up behind,
Clanging loud, an endless crowd ?—

PANTHEA.

These are Jove's tempest-walking hounds
Whom he gluts with groans and blood,
When charioted on sulphurous cloud
He bursts Heaven's bounds.

P

IONE.

Are they now led, from the thin dead
On new pangs to be fed?

Pan. The Titan looks as ever, firm, not proud.
First Fury. Ha! I scent life!
Second Fury. Let me but look into his eyes!
Third Fury. The hope of torturing him smells like a heap
Of corpses, to a death-bird after battle.
First Fury. Darest thou delay, O Herald! take cheer, Hounds
Of Hell: what if the Son of Maia soon
Should make us food and sport—who can please long
The Omnipotent?

Mer. Back to your towers of iron,
And gnash beside the streams of fire and wail
Your foodless teeth. Geryon, arise! and Gorgon,
Chimæra, and thou Sphinx, subtlest of fiends
Who ministered to Thebes Heaven's poisoned wine,
Unnatural love, and more unnatural hate:
These shall perform your task.
First Fury.　　　　　　　　Oh, mercy! mercy!
We die with our desire: drive us not back!
Mer. Crouch then in silence.
　　　　　　　　　　　　Awful Sufferer
To thee unwilling, most unwillingly
I come, by the great Father's will driven down,
To execute a doom of new revenge.
Alas! I pity thee, and hate myself
That I can do no more: aye from thy sight
Returning, for a season, heaven seems hell,
So thy worn form pursues me night and day,
Smiling reproach. Wise art thou, firm and good,
But vainly wouldst stand forth alone in strife
Against the Omnipotent; as yon clear lamps
That measure and divide the weary years
From which there is no refuge, long have taught
And long must teach. Even now thy Torturer arms
With the strange might of unimagined pains
The powers who scheme slow agonies in Hell,
And my commission is to lead them here,
Or what more subtle, foul, or savage fiends
People the abyss, and leave them to their task.
Be it not so! there is a secret known
To thee, and to none else of living things,
Which may transfer the sceptre of wide Heaven,
The fear of which perplexes the Supreme:
Clothe it in words, and bid it clasp his throne
In intercession; bend thy soul in prayer,
And like a suppliant in some gorgeous fane,
Let the will kneel within thy haughty heart:
For benefits and meek submission tame
The fiercest and the mightiest.
Pro.　　　　　　　　　　Evil minds
Change good to their own nature. I gave all
He has; and in return he chains me here

Years, ages, night and day : whether the Sun
Split my parched skin, or in the moony night
The crystal-winged snow cling round my hair :
Whilst my beloved race is trampled down
By his thought-executing ministers.
Such is the tyrant's recompense : 'tis just :
He who is evil can receive no good ;
And for a world bestowed, or a friend lost,
He can feel hate, fear, shame ; not gratitude :
He but requites me for his own misdeed.
Kindness to such is keen reproach, which breaks
With bitter stings the light sleep of Revenge.
Submission, thou dost know I cannot try:
For what submission but that fatal word,
The death-seal of mankind's captivity,
Like the Sicilian's hair-suspended sword,
Which trembles o'er his crown, would he accept,
Or could I yield ?   Which yet I will not yield.
Let others flatter Crime, where it sits throned
In brief Omnipotence : secure are they :
For Justice, when triumphant, will weep down
Pity, not punishment, on her own wrongs,
Too much avenged by those who err.   I wait,
Enduring thus, the retributive hour
Which since we spake is even nearer now.
But hark, the hell-hounds clamour : fear delay :
Behold ! Heaven lours under thy Father's frown.
   Mer. Oh, that we might be spared : I to inflict
And thou to suffer !   Once more answer me :
Thou knowest not the period of Jove's power?
   Pro. I know but this, that it must come.
   Mer.   Alas !
Thou canst not count thy years to come of pain ?
   Pro. They last while Jove must reign : nor more, nor less
Do I desire or fear.
   Mer.   Yet pause, and plunge
Into Eternity, where recorded time,
Even all that we imagine, age on age,
Seems but a point, and the reluctant mind
Flags wearily in its unending flight,
Till it sink dizzy, blind, lost, shelterless ·
Perchance it has not numbered the slow years
Which thou must spend in torture, unreprieved ?
   Pro. Perchance no thought can count them, yet they pass.
   Mer. If thou might'st dwell among the Gods the while
Lapped in voluptuous joy ?
   Pro.   I would not quit
This bleak ravine, these unrepentant pains.
   Mer. Alas ! I wonder at, yet pity thee.
   Pro. Pity the self-despising slaves of Heaven,
Not me, within whose mind sits peace serene,
As light in the sun, throned : how vain is talk !
Call up the fiends.
   Ione. O, sister, look !   White fire
Has cloven to the roots yon huge snow-loaded cedar ;
How fearfully God's thunder howls behind !
   Mer. I must obey his words and thine : alas !
Most heavily remorse hangs at my heart !

Pan. See where the child of Heaven, with wingèd feet,
Runs down the slanted sunlight of the dawn.

Ione. Dear sister, close thy plumes over thine eyes
Lest thou behold and die : they come : they come
Blackening the birth of day with countless wings,
And hollow underneath, like death.

First Fury.   Prometheus !

Second Fury. Immortal Titan !

Third Fury. Champion of Heaven's slaves !

Pro. He whom some dreadful voice invokes is here,
Prometheus, the chainèd Titan.   Horrible forms,
What and who are ye ?   Never yet there came
Phantasms so foul through monster-teeming Hell
From the all-miscreative brain of Jove ;
Whilst I behold such execrable shapes,
Methinks I grow like what I contemplate,
And laugh and stare in loathsome sympathy.

First Fury. We are the ministers of pain, and fear,
And disappointment, and mistrust, and hate,
And clinging crime ; and as lean dogs pursue
Through wood and lake some struck and sobbing fawn,
We track all things that weep, and bleed, and live,
When the great King betrays them to our will.

Pro. Oh ! many fearful natures in one name,
I know ye ; and these lakes and echoes know
The darkness and the clangour of your wings.
But why more hideous than your loathed selves
Gather ye up in legions from the deep ?

Second Fury. We knew not that : Sisters, rejoice, rejoice !

Pro. Can aught exult in its deformity ?

Second Fury. The beauty of delight makes lovers glad,
Gazing on one another : so are we.
As from the rose which the pale priestess kneels
To gather for her festal crown of flowers
The aerial crimson falls, flushing her cheek,
So from our victim's destined agony
The shade which is our form invests us round,
Else we are shapeless as our mother Night.

Pro. I laugh your power, and his who sent you here,
To lowest scorn.   Pour forth the cup of pain.

First Fury. Thou thinkest we will rend thee bone from bone,
And nerve from nerve, working like fire within ?

Pro. Pain is my element, as hate is thine ;
Ye rend me now : I care not.

Second Fury. Dost imagine
We will but laugh into thy lidless eyes ?

Pro. I weigh not what ye do, but what ye suffer,
Being evil.   Cruel was the power which called
You, or aught else so wretched, into light.

Third Fury. Thou think'st we will live through thee, one by one,
Like animal life, and though we can obscure not
The soul which burns within, that we will dwell
Beside it, like a vain loud multitude
Vexing the self-content of wisest men :
That we will be dread thought beneath thy brain,
And foul desire round thine astonished heart,
And blood within thy labyrinthine veins
Crawling like agony.

Pro. Why, ye are thus now ;
Yet am I king over myself, and rule
The torturing and conflicting throngs within,
As Jove rules you when Hell grows mutinous.

Chorus of Furies.

From the ends of the earth, from the ends of the earth,
Where the night has its grave and the morning its birth,
　　Come, come, come !
Oh, ye who shake hills with the scream of your mirth,
When cities sink howling in ruin ; and ye
Who with wingless footsteps trample the sea,
And close upon Shipwreck and Famine's track,
Sit chattering with joy on the foodless wreck ;
　　　　Come, come, come !
　　Leave the bed, low, cold, and red,
　　Strewed beneath a nation dead ;
　　Leave the hatred, as in ashes
　　　Fire is left for future burning :
　　It will burst in bloodier flashes
　　　When ye stir it, soon returning :
　　Leave the self-contempt implanted
　　In young spirits, sense-enchanted,
　　Misery's yet unkindled fuel :
　　Leave Hell's secrets half unchanted
　　　To the maniac dreamer ; cruel
　　More than ye can be with hate
　　　Is he with fear.
　　　　Come, come, come !
　We are steaming up from Hell's wide gate
　　And we burden the blasts of the atmosphere,
　But vainly we toil till ye come here.
Ione. Sister, I hear the thunder of new wings.
Pan. These solid mountains quiver with the sound
Even as the tremulous air : their shadows make
The space within my plumes more black than night.

First Fury.

Your call was as a winged car
Driven on whirlwinds fast and far
It rapt us from red gulfs of war.

Second Fury.

From wide cities, famine-wasted ;

Third Fury.

Groans half heard, and blood untasted ;

Fourth Fury.

Kingly conclaves stern and cold,
Where blood with gold is bought and sold ;

Fifth Fury.

From the furnace, white and hot,
In which—

A Fury.

Speak not : whisper not :
I know all that ye would tell,
But to speak might break the spell
Which must bend the Invincible,
    The stern of thought ;
He defies the deepest power of Hell.

Fury.

Tear the veil !

Another Fury.

It is torn.

Chorus.

The pale stars of the morn
Shine on a misery, dire to be borne.
Dost thou faint, mighty Titan ?   We laugh thee to scorn.
Dost thou boast the clear knowledge thou waken'dst for man?
Then was kindled within him a thirst which outran
Those perishing waters ; a thirst for fierce fever,
Hope, love, doubt, desire, which consume him for ever.
    One came forth of gentle worth
    Smiling on the sanguine earth ;
    His words outlived him, like swift poison
        Withering up truth, peace, and pity.
    Look ! where round the wide horizon
        Many a million-peopled city
    Vomits smoke in the bright air.
    Mark that outcry of despair !
    'Tis his mild and gentle ghost
        Wailing for the faith he kindled :
    Look again, the flames almost
        To a glowworm's lamp have dwindled :
    The survivors round the embers
    Gather in dread.
        Joy, joy, joy !
Past ages crowd on thee, but each one remembers,
And the future is dark, and the present is spread
Like a pillow of thorns for thy slumberless head.

Semichorus I.

Drops of bloody agony flow
From his white and quivering brow.
Grant a little respite now :
See a disenchanted nation
Springs like day from desolation ;
To truth its state is dedicate,
And Freedom leads it forth, her mate ;
A legioned band of linked brothers
Whom Love calls children—

Semichorus II.

'Tis another's :
See how kindred murder kin :
'Tis the vintage-time for death and sin :

Blood, like new wine, bubbles within :
'Till Despair smothers
The struggling world, which slaves and tyrants win.
          [*All the* FURIES *vanish, except one.*

Ione. Hark, sister ! what a low yet dreadful groan
Quite unsuppressed is tearing up the heart
Of the good Titan, as storms tear the deep,
And beasts hear the sea moan in inland caves.
Darest thou observe how the fiends torture him?
  Pan. Alas ! I looked forth twice, but will no more.
  Ione. What didst thou see?
  Pan. A woeful sight : A youth
With patient looks nailed to a crucifix.
  Ione. What next ?
  Pan. The heaven around, the earth below
Was peopled with thick shapes of human death,
All horrible, and wrought by human hands,
And some appeared the work of human hearts,
For men were slowly killed by frowns and smiles :
And other sights too foul to speak and live
Were wandering by. Let us not tempt worse fear
By looking forth : those groans are grief enough.
  Fury. Behold an emblem : those who do endure
Deep wrongs for man, and scorn, and chains, but heap
Thousandfold torment on themselves and him.
  Pro. Remit the anguish of that lighted stare ;
Close those wan lips ; let that thorn-wounded brow
Stream not with blood ; it mingles with thy tears !
Fix, fix those tortured orbs in peace and death,
So thy sick throes shake not that crucifix,
So those pale fingers play not with thy gore.
O horrible ! Thy name I will not speak,
It hath become a curse. I see, I see
The wise, the mild, the lofty, and the just,
Whom thy slaves hate for being like to thee,
Some hunted by foul lies from their heart's home,
An early-chosen, late-lamented home ;
As hooded ounces cling to the driven hind ;
Some linked to corpses in unwholesome cells :
Some—Hear I not the multitude laugh loud ?—
Impaled in lingering fire : and mighty realms
Float by my feet, like sea-uprooted isles,
Whose sons are kneaded down in common blood
By the red light of their own burning homes.
  Fury. Blood thou canst see, and fire ; and canst hear groans :
Worse things, unheard, unseen, remain behind.
  Pro.   Worse?
  Fury. In each human heart terror survives
The ruin it has gorged : the loftiest fear
All that they would disdain to think were true :
Hypocrisy and custom make their minds
The fanes of many a worship, now outworn.
They dare not devise good for man's estate,
And yet they know not that they do not dare.
The good want power, but to weep barren tears.
The powerful goodness want : worse need for them.
The wise want love ; and those who love want wisdom ;

And all best things are thus confused to ill.
Many are strong and rich, and would be just,
But live among their suffering fellow-men
As if none felt : they know not what they do.
 Pro. Thy words are like a cloud of winged snakes;
And yet I pity those they torture not.
  Fury. Thou pitiest them ? I speak no more !

[Vanishes.

  Pro.   Ah woe !
Ah woe ! Alas ! pain, pain ever, for ever !
I close my tearless eyes, but see more clear
Thy works within my woe-illumined mind,
Thou subtle tyrant !   Peace is in the grave.
The grave hides all things beautiful and good :
I am a God and cannot find it there,
Nor would I seek it : for, though dread revenge,
This is defeat, fierce king, not victory.
The sights with which thou torturest gird my soul
With new endurance, till the hour arrives
When they shall be no types of things which are.
 Pan. Alas ! what sawest thou?
 Pro. There are two woes ;
To speak, and to behold ; thou spare me one.
Names are there, Nature's sacred watchwords, they
Were borne aloft in bright emblazonry ;
The nations thronged around, and cried aloud,
As with one voice, Truth, liberty, and love !
Suddenly fierce confusion fell from heaven
Among them : there was strife, deceit, and fear :
Tyrants rushed in, and did divide the spoil.
This was the shadow of the truth I saw.
 The Earth. I felt thy torture, son, with such mixed joy
As pain and virtue give.   To cheer thy state
I bid ascend those subtle and fair spirits,
Whose homes are the dim caves of human thought,
And who inhabit, as birds wing the wind,
Its world-surrounding ether : they behold
Beyond that twilight realm, as in a glass,
The future : may they speak comfort to thee !
 Pan. Look, sister, where a troop of spirits gather,
Like flocks of cloud in spring's delightful weather,
Thronging in the blue air!
  Ione. And see ! more come,
Like fountain-vapours when the winds are dumb,
That climb up the ravine in scattered lines.
And, hark ! is it the music of the pines ?
Is it the lake ? Is it the waterfall ?
 Pan. 'Tis something sadder, sweeter far than all.

CHORUS OF SPIRITS.

From unremembered ages we
Gentle guides and guardians be
Of heaven-oppressed mortality ;
And we breathe, and sicken not,
The atmosphere of human thought :
Be it dim, and dank, and grey,
Like a storm-extinguished day,

Travelled o'er by dying gleams ;
  Be it bright as all between
Cloudless skies and windless streams,
  Silent, liquid, and serene ;
As the birds within the wind,
  As the fish within the wave,
As the thoughts of man's own mind
  Float through all above the grave ;
We make these our liquid lair,
Voyaging cloudlike and unpent
Through the boundless element :
Thence we bear the prophecy
Which begins and ends in thee !

Ione. More yet come, one by one : the air around them
Looks radiant as the air around a star.

FIRST SPIRIT.

On a battle-trumpet's blast
I fled hither, fast, fast, fast,
'Mid the darkness upward cast.
From the dust of creeds outworn,
From the tyrant's banner torn,
Gathering 'round me, onward borne,
There was mingled many a cry—
Freedom ! Hope ! Death ! Victory !
Till they faded through the sky ;
And one sound, above, around,
One sound beneath, around, above,
Was moving ; 'twas the soul of love ;
'Twas the hope, the prophecy,
Which begins and ends in thee.

SECOND SPIRIT.

A rainbow's arch stood on the sea,
Which rocked beneath, immovably ;
And the triumphant storm did flee,
Like a conqueror, swift and proud,
Between with many a captive cloud
A shapeless, dark and rapid crowd,
Each by lightning riven in half :
I heard the thunder hoarsely laugh :
Mighty fleets were strewn like chaff
And spread beneath a hell of death
O'er the white waters.   I alit
On a great ship lightning-split,
And speeded hither on the sigh
Of one who gave an enemy
His plank, then plunged aside to die.

THIRD SPIRIT.

I sate beside a sage's bed,
And the lamp was burning red
Near the book where he had fed
When a Dream with plumes of flame,
To his pillow hovering came,
And I knew it was the same

Which had kindled long ago
Pity, eloquence, and woe;
And the world awhile below
Wore the shade, its lustre made.
It has borne me here as fleet
As Desire's lightning feet :
I must ride it back ere morrow,
Or the sage will wake in sorrow.

FOURTH SPIRIT.

On a poet's lips I slept
Dreaming like a love-adept
In the sound his breathing kept ;
Nor seeks nor finds he mortal blisses,
But feeds on the aërial kisses
Of shapes that haunt thought's wildernesses.
He will watch from dawn to gloom
The lake-reflected sun illume
The yellow bees in the ivy-bloom,
Nor heed nor see, what things they be ;
But from these create he can
Forms more real than living man,
Nurslings of immortality !
One of these awakened me,
And I sped to succour thee.

IONE.

Behold'st thou not two shapes from the east and west
Come, as two doves to one beloved nest,
Twin nurslings of the all-sustaining air
On swift still wings glide down the atmosphere ?
And, hark ! their sweet, sad·voices ! 'tis despair
Mingled with love and then dissolved in sound.

PANTHEA.

Canst thou speak, sister ? all my words are drowned.

Ione. Their beauty gives me voice. See how they float
On their sustaining wings of skiey grain,
Orange and azure deepening into gold :
Their soft smiles light the air like a star's fire.

CHORUS OF SPIRITS.

Hast thou beheld the form of Love ?

FIFTH SPIRIT.

As over wide dominions
I sped, like some swift cloud that wings the wide air's wildernesses,
That planet-crested shape swept by on lightning-braided pinions,
Scattering the liquid joy of life from his ambrosial tresses:
His footsteps paved the world with light ; but as I past 'twas fading,
And hollow Ruin yawned behind : great sages bound in madness.
And headless patriots, and pale youths who perished, unupbraiding,
Gleamed in the night. I wandered o'er, till thou, O King of sadness,
Turned by thy smile the worst I saw to recollected gladness.

SIXTH SPIRIT.

Ah, sister! Desolation is a delicate thing :
It walks not on the earth, it floats not on the air,
But treads with silent footstep, and fans with silent wing
The tender hopes which in their hearts the best and gentlest bear ;
Who, soothed to false repose by the fanning plumes above
And the music-stirring motion of its soft and busy feet,
Dream visions of aërial joy, and call the monster, Love,
And wake, and find the shadow Pain, as he whom now we greet.

CHORUS.

Though Ruin now Love's shadow be,
Following him, destroyingly,
   On Death's white and wingèd steed,
Which the fleetest cannot flee,
   Trampling down both flower and weed,
Man and beast, and foul and fair,
Like a tempest through the air ;
Thou shalt quell this horseman grim,
Woundless though in heart or limb.

Pro. Spirits, how know ye this shall be ?

CHORUS.

In the atmosphere we breathe,
As buds grow red when the snowstorms flee,
   From spring gathering up beneath,
Whose mild winds shake the elder brake,
And the wandering herdsmen know
That the white-thorn soon will blow :
Wisdom, Justice, Love, and Peace,
When they struggle to increase,
   Are to us as soft winds be
   To shepherd boys, the prophecy
Which begins and ends in thee.

Ione. Where are the Spirits fled ?

PANTHEA.

Only a sense
Remains of them, like the omnipotence
Of music, when the inspired voice and lute
Languish, ere yet the responses are mute,
Which through the deep and labyrinthine soul,
Like echoes through long caverns, wind and roll.

Pro. How fair these air-born shapes ! and yet I feel
Most vain all hope but love ; and thou art far,
Asia ! who, when my being overflowed,
Wert like a golden chalice to bright wine
Which else had sunk into the thirsty dust.
All things are still : alas ! how heavily
This quiet morning weighs upon my heart ;
Though I should dream I could even sleep with grief
If slumber were denied not. I would fain
Be what it is my destiny to be,

The saviour and the strength of suffering man,
Or sink into the original gulf of things :
There is no agony, and no solace left ;
Earth can console, Heaven can torment no more.
  Pan. Hast thou forgotten one who watches thee
The cold dark night, and never sleeps but when
The shadow of thy spirit falls on her ?
  Pro. I said all hope was vain but love : thou lovest.
  Pan. Deeply in truth ; but the eastern star looks white,
And Asia waits in that far Indian vale
The scene of her sad exile ; rugged once
And desolate and frozen, like this ravine ;
But now invested with fair flowers and herbs,
And haunted by sweet airs and sounds, which flow
Among the woods and waters, from the ether
Of her transforming presence, which would fade
If it were mingled not with thine. Farewell !

ACT II.

SCENE I.—*Morning. A lovely Vale in the Indian Caucasus.* ASIA *alone*

  Asia. From all the blasts of Heaven thou hast descended :
Yes, like a spirit, like a thought, which makes
Unwonted tears throng to the horny eyes,
And beatings haunt the desolated heart,
Which should have learnt repose : thou hast descended
Cradled in tempests ; thou dost wake, O Spring !
A child of many winds ! As suddenly
Thou comest as the memory of a dream,
Which now is sad because it hath been sweet ;
Like genius, or like joy which riseth up
As from the earth, clothing with golden clouds
The desert of our life.
This is the season, this the day, the hour ;
At sunrise thou shouldst come, sweet sister mine,
Too long desired, too long delaying, come !
How like death-worms the wingless moments crawl !
The point of one white star is quivering still
Deep in the orange light of widening morn
Beyond the purple mountains : through a chasm
Of wind-divided mist the darker lake
Reflects it : now it wanes : it gleams again
As the waves fade, and as the burning threads
Of woven cloud unravel in the pale air :
'Tis lost ! and through yon peaks of cloudlike snow
The roseate sunlight quivers : hear I not
The Æolian music of her sea-green plumes
Winnowing the crimson dawn ?

PANTHEA *enters.*

                    I feel, I see
Those eyes which burn through smiles that fade in tears,
Like stars half quenched in mists of silver dew.

Beloved and most beautiful, who wearest
The shadow of that soul by which I live,
How late thou art ! the sphered sun had climbed
The sea ; my heart was sick with hope, before
The printless air felt thy belated plumes.

Pan. Pardon, great sister ! but my wings were faint
With the delight of a remembered dream,
As are the noontide plumes of summer winds
Satiate with sweet flowers. I was wont to sleep
Peacefully, and awake refreshed and calm,
Before the sacred Titan's fall, and thy
Unhappy love, had made, through use and pity,
Both love and woe familiar to my heart
As they had grown to thine : erewhile I slept
Under the glaucous caverns of old Ocean
Within dim bowers of green and purple moss,
Our young Ione's soft and milky arms
Locked then, as now, behind my dark, moist hair,
While my shut eyes and cheek were pressed within
The folded depth of her life-breathing bosom :
But not as now, since I am made the wind
Which fails beneath the music that I bear
Of thy most wordless converse ; since dissolved
Into the sense with which love talks, my rest
Was troubled and yet sweet ; my waking hours
Too full of care and pain.

Asia.   Lift up thine eyes,
And let me read thy dream.

Pan.   As I have said,
With our sea-sister at his feet I slept.
The mountain mists, condensing at our voice
Under the moon, had spread their snowy flakes,
From the keen ice shielding our linked sleep.
Then two dreams came.   One I remember not.
But in the other his pale wound-worn limbs
Fell from Prometheus, and the azure night
Grew radiant with the glory of that form
Which lives unchanged within, and his voice fell
Like music which makes giddy the dim brain,
Faint with intoxication of keen joy :
" Sister of her whose footsteps pave the world
With loveliness—more fair than aught but her,
Whose shadow thou art—lift thine eyes on me."
I lifted them : the overpowering light
Of that immortal shape was shadowed o'er
By love ; which, from his soft and flowing limbs,
And passion-parted lips, and keen, faint eyes,
Steamed forth like vaporous fire ; an atmosphere
Which wrapt me in its all-dissolving power,
As the warm ether of the morning sun
Wraps ere it drinks some cloud of wandering dew.
I saw not, heard not, moved not, only felt
His presence flow and mingle through my blood
Till it became his life, and his grew mine,
And I was thus absorbed, until it past,
And like the vapours when the sun sinks down,
Gathering again in drops upon the pines,
And tremulous as they, in the deep night

My being was condensed; and as the rays
Of thought were slowly gathered, I could hear
His voice, whose accents lingered ere they died
Like footsteps of weak melody: thy name
Among the many sounds alone I heard
Of what might be articulate; though still
I listened through the night when sound was none.
Ione wakened then, and said to me:
" Canst thou divine what troubles me to-night?
I always knew what I desired before,
Nor ever found delight to wish in vain.
But now I cannot tell thee what I seek;
I know not; something sweet, since it is sweet
Even to desire; it is thy sport, false sister;
Thou hast discovered some enchantment old,
Whose spells have stolen my spirit as I slept
And mingled it with thine: for when just now
We kissed, I felt within thy parted lips
The sweet air that sustained me, and the warmth
Of the life-blood, for loss of which I faint,
Quivered between our intertwining arms."
I answered not, for the Eastern star grew pale,
But fled to thee.

 Asia.   Thou speakest, but thy words
Are as the air: I feel them not: O lift
Thine eyes, that I may read his written soul!

 Pan. I lift them though they droop beneath the load
Of that they would express: what canst thou see
But thine own fairest shadow imaged there?

 Asia. Thine eyes are like the deep, blue, boundless heaven
Contracted to two circles underneath
Their long, fine lashes; dark, far, measureless,
Orb within orb, and line through line inwoven.

 Pan. Why lookest thou as if a spirit past?

 Asia. There is a change: beyond their inmost depth
I see a shade, a shape: 'tis He, arrayed
In the soft light of his own smiles, which spread
Like radiance from the cloud-surrounded morn.
Prometheus, it is thine! depart not yet!
Say not those smiles that we shall meet again
Within that bright pavilion which their beams
Shall build on the waste world? The dream is told.
What shape is that between us? Its rude hair
Roughens the wind that lifts it, its regard
Is wild and quick, yet 'tis a thing of air,
For through its grey robe gleams the golden dew
Whose stars the noon has quenched not.

DREAM.

Follow! Follow!

 Pan. It is mine other dream.

 Asia. It disappears.

 Pan. It passes now into my mind. Methought
As we sate here, the flower-enfolding buds
Burst on yon lightning-blasted almond tree,
When swift from the white Scythian wilderness

A wind swept forth wrinkling the Earth with frost :
I looked, and all the blossoms were blown down ;
But on each leaf was stamped, as the bluebells
Of Hyacinth tell Apollo's written grief,
O, FOLLOW, FOLLOW!

   Asia.   As you speak, your words
Fill, pause by pause, my own forgotten sleep
With shapes.   Methought among the lawns together
We wandered, underneath the young grey dawn,
And multitudes of dense white fleecy clouds
Were wandering in thick flocks along the mountains
Shepherded by the slow, unwilling wind ;
And the white dew on the new-bladed grass,
Just piercing the dark earth, hung silently ;
And there was more which I remember not :
But on the shadows of the morning clouds,
Athwart the purple mountain slope, was written
FOLLOW, O, FOLLOW !   As they vanished by,
And on each herb, from which Heaven's dew had fallen,
The like was stamped, as with a withering fire,
A wind arose among the pines ; it shook
The clinging music from their boughs, and then
Low, sweet, faint sounds, like the farewell of ghosts,
Were heard : OH, FOLLOW, FOLLOW, FOLLOW ME !
And then I said : " Panthea, look on me."
But in the depth of those beloved eyes
Still I saw, FOLLOW, FOLLOW !

ECHO.

      Follow !   Follow !

   Pan. The crags, this clear spring morning, mock our voices
As they were spirit-tongued.

   Asia.   It is some being
Around the crags   What fine clear sounds !   O, list !

ECHOES (*unseen*).

     Echoes we : listen !
      We cannot stay :
     As dew-stars glisten
      Then fade away—
        Child of Ocean !

   Asia. Hark ! Spirits speak.   The liquid responses
Of their aërial tongues yet sound.

   Pan.   I hear.

ECHOES.

   O, follow, follow,
     As our voice recedeth
   Through the caverns hollow,
     Where the forest spreadeth ;

     (*More distant.*)

   O, follow, follow !
   Through the caverns hollow,

As the song floats thou pursue,
Where the wild bee never flew,
Through the noontide darkness deep,
By the odour-breathing sleep
Of faint night flowers, and the waves
At the fountain-lighted caves,
While our music, wild and sweet,
Mocks thy gently-falling feet,
     Child of Ocean !

Asia. Shall we pursue the sound ? It grows more faint
And distant.
     Pan.   List ! the strain floats nearer now.

ECHOES.

In the world unknown
    Sleeps a voice unspoken ;
By thy step alone
    Can its rest be broken ;
     Child of Ocean !

Asia. How the notes sink upon the ebbing wind.

ECHOES.

O, follow, follow !
Through the caverns hollow,
As the song floats thou pursue,
By the woodland noontide dew ;
By the forests, lakes, and fountains
Through the many-folded mountains ;
To the rents, and gulfs, and chasms,
Where the earth reposed from spasms,
On the day when He and thou
Parted, to commingle now ;
     Child of Ocean !

Asia. Come, sweet Panthea, link thy hand in mine,
And follow, ere the voices fade away.

SCENE II.—*A Forest, intermingled with Rocks and Caverns.* ASIA *and*
PANTHEA *pass into it. Two young Fauns are sitting on a Rock, listening.*

SEMICHORUS I. OF SPIRITS.

The path through which that lovely twain
    Have past, by cedar, pine and yew,
    And each dark tree that ever grew,
    Is curtained out from Heaven's wide blue ;
Nor sun, nor moon, nor wind, nor rain,
    Can pierce its interwoven bowers,
    Nor aught, save where some cloud of dew,
Drifted along the earth-creeping breeze,
Between the trunks of the hoar trees,
    Hangs each a pearl in the pale flowers
    Of the green laurel, blown anew ;
And bends, and then fades silently,

One frail and fair anemone :
Or when some star of many a one
That climbs and wanders through steep night,
Has found the cleft through which alone
Beams fall from high those depths upon
Ere it is borne away, away,
By the swift Heavens that cannot stay,
It scatters drops of golden light,
Like lines of rain that ne'er unite :
And the gloom divine is all around ;
And underneath is the mossy ground.

SEMICHORUS II.

There the voluptuous nightingales,
    Are awake through all the broad noonday,
When one with bliss or sadness fails,
        And through the windless ivy-boughs,
    Sick with sweet love, droops dying away
On its mate's music-panting bosom ;
Another from the swinging blossom,
        Watching to catch the languid close
    Of the last strain, then lifts on high
    The wings of the weak melody,
'Till some new strain of feeling bear
    The song, and all the woods are mute ;
When there is heard through the dim air
The rush of wings, and rising there
    Like many a lake-surrounding flute,
Sounds overflow the listener's brain
So sweet, that joy is almost pain.

SEMICHORUS I.

There those enchanted eddies play
    Of echoes, music-tongued, which draw,
    By Demogorgon's mighty law,
        With melting rapture, or sweet awe,
All spirits on that secret way ;
        As inland boats are driven to Ocean
Down streams made strong with mountain-thaw :
        And first there comes a gentle sound
        To those in talk or slumber bound,
    And wakes the destined soft emotion,
Attracts, impels them : those who saw
        Say from the breathing earth behind
        There steams a plume-uplifting wind
Which drives them on their path, while they
        Believe their own swift wings and feet
    The sweet desires within obey:
And so they float upon their way,
Until, still sweet, but loud and strong,
The storm of sound is driven along,
    Sucked up and hurrying as they fleet
    Behind, its gathering billows meet
And to the fatal mountain bear
Like clouds amid the yielding air.

First Faun. Canst thou imagine where those spirits live
Which make such delicate music in the woods ?

Q

We haunt within the least frequented caves
And closest coverts, and we know these wilds,
Yet never met them, though we hear them oft :
Where may they hide themselves ?
   Second Faun. 'Tis hard to tell:
I have heard those more skilled in spirits say,
The bubbles, which the enchantment of the sun
Sucks from the pale faint water-flowers that pave
The oozy bottom of clear lakes and pools,
Are the pavilions where such dwell and float
Under the green and golden atmosphere
Which noontide kindles through the woven leaves ;
And when these burst, and the thin fiery air,
The which they breathed within those lucent domes,
Ascends to flow like meteors through the night,
They ride on them, and rein their headlong speed,
And bow their burning crests, and glide in fire
Under the waters of the earth again.
   First Faun. If such live thus, have others other lives,
Under pink blossoms or within the bells
Of meadow flowers, or folded violets deep,
Or on their dying odours, when they die,
Or on the sunlight of the sphered dew ?
   Second Faun. Ay, many more which we may well divine.
But should we stay to speak, noontide would come,
And thwart Silenus find his goats undrawn,
And grudge to sing those wise and lovely songs
Of Fate, and Chance, and God, and Chaos old,
And love, and the chained Titan's woful dooms,
And how he shall be loosed, and make the earth
One brotherhood ; delightful strains which cheer
Our solitary twilights, and which charm
To silence the unenvying nightingales.

SCENE III.—*A Pinnacle of Rock among Mountains.* ASIA *and* PANTHE

   Pan. Hither the sound has borne us—to the realm
Of Demogorgon, and the mighty portal,
Like a volcano's meteor-breathing chasm,
Whence the oracular vapour is hurled up
Which lonely men drink wandering in their youth,
And call truth, virtue, love, genius, or joy,
That maddening wine of life, whose dregs they drain
To deep intoxication ; and uplift,
Like Mænads who cry loud, Evoe ! Evoe !
The voice which is contagion to the world.
   Asia. Fit throne for such a Power ! Magnificent !
How glorious art thou, Earth ! And if thou be
The shadow of some spirit lovelier still,
Though evil stain its work, and it should be
Like its creation, weak yet beautiful,
I could fall down and worship that and thee.
Even now my heart adoreth : Wonderful!
Look, sister, ere the vapour dim thy brain:
Beneath is a wide plain of billowy mist,
As a lake, paving in the morning sky,
With azure waves which burst in silver light,
Some Indian vale. Behold it, rolling on

Under the curdling winds, and islanding
The peak whereon we stand, midway, around,
Encinctured by the dark and blooming forests.
Dim twilight-lawns, and stream-illumined caves,
And wind-enchanted shapes of wandering mist:
And far on high the keen sky-cleaving mountains
From icy spires of sun-like radiance fling
The dawn, as lifted Ocean's dazzling spray,
From some Atlantic islet scattered up,
Spangles the wind with lamp-like water-drops.
The vale is girdled with their walls, a howl
Of cataracts from their thaw-cloven ravines
Satiates the listening wind, continuous, vast,
Awful as silence. Hark! the rushing snow!
The sun-awakened avalanche! whose mass,
Thrice sifted by the storm, had gathered there
Flake after flake, in heaven-defying minds
As thought by thought is piled, till some great truth
Is loosened, and the nations echo round,
Shaken to their roots, as do the mountains now.

    Pan. Look how the gusty sea of mist is breaking
In crimson foam, even at our feet! it rises
As Ocean at the enchantment of the moon
Round foodless men wrecked on some oozy isle.

    Asia. The fragments of the cloud are scattered up;
The wind that lifts them disentwines my hair;
Its billows now sweep o'er mine eyes; my brain
Grows dizzy; I see thin shapes within the mist.

    Pan. A countenance with beckoning smiles: there burns
An azure fire within its golden locks!
Another and another: hark! they speak!

Song of Spirits.

    To the deep, to the deep,
        Down, down!
Through the shade of sleep,
Through the cloudy strife
Of Death and of Life;
Through the veil and the bar
Of things which seem and are,
Even to the steps of the remotest throne,
        Down, down!

While the sound whirls around,
        Down, down!
As the fawn draws the hound,
As the lightning the vapour,
As a weak moth the taper;
Death, despair; love, sorrow;
Time both; to-day, to-morrow;
As steel obeys the spirit of the stone,
        Down, down!
Through the grey, void abysm,
        Down, down!
Where the air is no prism,
And the moon and stars are not,
And the cavern-crags wear not

The radiance of Heaven,
Nor the gloom to Earth given,
Where there is one pervading, one alone,
    Down, down !

In the depth of the deep
    Down, down !
Like veiled lightning asleep,
Like the spark nursed in embers,
The last look Love remembers,
Like a diamond, which shines
On the dark wealth of mines,
A spell is treasured but for thee alone.
    Down, down !

We have bound thee, we guide thee ;
    Down, down !
With the bright form beside thee ;
Resist not the weakness,
Such strength is in meekness
That the Eternal, the Immortal,
Must unloose through life's portal
The snake-like Doom coiled underneath his throne
    By that alone.

SCENE IV.—*The Cave of* DEMOGORGON.   ASIA *and* PANTHEA.

   Pan. What veilèd form sits on that ebon throne?
   Asia. The veil has fallen.
   Pan. I see a mighty darkness
Filling the seat of power, and rays of gloom
Dart round, as light from the meridian sun,
Ungazed upon and shapeless ; neither limb,
Nor form, nor outline ; yet we feel it is
A living Spirit.
   Dem. Ask what thou wouldst know.
   Asia. What canst thou tell ?
   Dem. All things thou dar'st demand.
   Asia. Who made the living world ?
   Dem. God.
   Asia. Who made all
That it contains ? thought, passion, reason, will,
Imagination ?
   Dem. God : Almighty God.
   Asia. Who made that sense which, when the winds of spring
In rarest visitation, or the voice
Of one beloved heard in youth alone,
Fills the faint eyes with falling tears which dim
The radiant looks of unbewailing flowers,
And leaves this peopled earth a solitude
When it returns no more ?
   Dem. Merciful God.
   Asia. And who made terror, madness, crime, remorse,
Which from the links of the great chain of things,
To every thought within the mind of man
Sway and drag heavily, and each one reels
Under the load towards the pit of death ;

Abandoned hope, and love that turns to hate;
And self-contempt, bitterer to drink than blood;
Pain, whose unheeded and familiar speech
Is howling, and keen shrieks, day after day ;
And Hell, or the sharp fear of Hell !
   Dem. He reigns.
   Asia. Utter his name : a world pining in pain
Asks but his name : curses shall drag him down.
   Dem. He reigns.
   Asia. I feel, I know it: who?
   Dem. He reigns.
   Asia. Who reigns ? There was the Heaven and Earth at first,
And Light and Love; then Saturn, from whose throne
Time fell, an envious shadow: such the state
Of the earth's primal spirits beneath his sway,
As the calm joy of flowers and living leaves
Before the wind or sun has withered them
And semivital worms; but he refused
The birthright of their being, knowledge, power,
The skill which wields the elements, the thought
Which pierces this dim universe like light,
Self-empire, and the majesty of love;
For thirst of which they fainted. Then Prometheus
Gave wisdom, which is strength, to Jupiter,
And with this law alone, " Let man be free,"
Clothed him with the dominion of wide Heaven.
To know nor faith, nor love, nor law; to be
Omnipotent but friendless is to reign;
And Jove now reigned; for on the race of man
First famine, and then toil, and then disease,
Strife, wounds, and ghastly death unseen before,
Fell; and the unseasonable seasons drove
With alternating shafts of frost and fire,
Their shelterless, pale tribes to mountain caves:
And in their desert hearts fierce wants he sent,
And mad disquietudes, and shadows idle
Of unreal good, which levied mutual war,
So ruining the lair wherein they raged.
Prometheus saw, and waked the legioned hopes
Which sleep within folded Elysian flowers,
Nepenthe, Moly, Amaranth, fadeless blooms,
That they might hide with thin and rainbow wings
The shape of Death; and Love he sent to bind
The disunited tendrils of that vine
Which bears the wine of life, the human heart;
And he tamed fire which, like some beast of prey,
Most terrible, but lovely, played beneath
The frown of man; and tortured to his will
Iron and gold, the slaves and signs of power,
And gems and poisons, and all subtlest forms
Hidden beneath the mountains and the waves.
He gave man speech, and speech created thought,
Which is the measure of the universe;
And Science struck the thrones of earth and heaven,
Which shook, but fell not; and the harmonious mind
Poured itself forth in all-prophetic song;
And music lifted up the listening spirit
Until it walked, exempt from mortal care,

Godlike, o'er the clear billows of sweet sound;
And human hands first mimicked and then mocked,
With moulded limbs more lovely than its own,
The human form, till marble grew divine;
And mothers, gazing, drank the love men see
Reflected in their race, behold, and perish.
He told the hidden power of herbs and springs,
And Disease drank and slept.   Death grew like sleep.
He taught the implicated orbits woven
Of the wide-wandering stars; and how the sun
Changes his lair, and by what secret spell
The pale moon is transformed, when her broad eye
Gazes not on the interlunar sea:
He taught to rule, as life directs the limbs,
The tempest-winged chariots of the Ocean,
And the Celt knew the Indian.   Cities then
Were built, and through their snowlike columns flowed
The warm winds, and the azure ether shone,
And the blue sea and shadowy hills were seen.
Such, the alleviations of his state,
Prometheus gave to man, for which he hangs
Withering in destined pain: but who rains down
Evil, the immedicable plague, which, while
Man looks on his creation like a God
And sees that it is glorious, drives him on
The wreck of his own will, the scorn of earth,
The outcast, the abandoned, the alone?
Not Jove: while yet his frown shook heaven, aye when
His adversary from adamantine chains
Cursed him, he trembled like a slave.   Declare
Who is his master?   Is he too a slave?
    Dem. All spirits are enslaved which serve things evil:
Thou knowest if Jupiter be such or no.
    Asia. Whom called'st thou God?
    Dem.   I spoke but as ye speak,
For Jove is the supreme of living things.
    Asia. Who is the master of the slave?
    Dem.   If the abysm
Could vomit forth its secrets.   But a voice
Is wanting, the deep truth is imageless;
For what would it avail to bid thee gaze
On the revolving world?   What to bid speak
Fate, Time, Occasion, Chance and Change?   To these
All things are subject but eternal Love.
    Asia. So much I asked before, and my heart gave
The response thou hast given; and of such truths
Each to itself must be the oracle.
One more demand; and do thou answer me
As my own soul would answer, did it know
That which I ask.   Prometheus shall arise
Henceforth the sun of this rejoicing world :
When shall the destined hour arrive?
    Dem.   Behold !
    Asia. The rocks are cloven, and through the purple night
I see cars drawn by rainbow-wingèd steeds
Which trample the dim winds: in each there stands
A wild-eyed charioteer urging their flight.
Some look behind, as fiends pursued them there

And yet I see no shapes but the keen stars:
Others, with burning eyes, lean forth, and drink
With eager lips the wind of their own speed,
As if the thing they loved fled on before,
And now, even now, they clasped it. Their bright locks
Stream like a comet's flashing hair: they all
Sweep onward.
    Dem.   These are the immortal Hours,
Of whom thou didst demand. One waits for thee.
    Asia. A spirit with a dreadful countenance
Checks its dark chariot by the craggy gulf.
Unlike thy brethren, ghastly charioteer,
Who art thou? Whither wouldst thou bear me? Speak!
    Spirit. I am the shadow of a destiny
More dread than is my aspect: ere yon planet
Has set, the darkness which ascends with me
Shall wrap in lasting night heaven's kingless throne.
    Asia.   What meanest thou?
    Pan.   That terrible shadow floats
Up from its throne, as may the lurid smoke
Of earthquake-ruined cities o'er the sea.
Lo! it ascends the car; the coursers fly
Terrified. watch its path among the stars
Blackening the night!
    Asia.   Thus I am answered: strange!
    Pan. See, near the verge, another chariot stays;
An ivory shell inlaid with crimson fire,
Which comes and goes within its sculptured rim
Of delicate strange tracery; the young spirit
That guides it has the dove-like eyes of hope;
How its soft smiles attract the soul! as light
Lures winged insects through the lampless air.

SPIRIT.

My coursers are fed with the lightning,
  They drink of the whirlwind's stream,
And when the red morning is bright'ning
  They bathe in the fresh sunbeam;
  They have strength for their swiftness I deem,
Then ascend with me, daughter of Ocean.

I desire: and their speed makes night kindle;
  I fear: they outstrip the Typhoon;
Ere the cloud piled on Atlas can dwindle
  We encircle the earth and the moon:
  We shall rest from long labours at noon:
Then ascend with me, daughter of Ocean.

SCENE V.—*The Car pauses within a Cloud on the Top of a snowy Mountain.*
  ASIA, PANTHEA, *and the* SPIRIT OF THE HOUR.

SPIRIT.

On the brink of the night and the morning
  My coursers are wont to respire;
But the Earth has just whispered a warning
  That their flight must be swifter than fire:
  They shall drink the hot speed of desire!

Asia. Thou breathest on their nostrils, but my breath
Would give them swifter speed.
    Spirit.   Alas! it could not.
    Pan. Oh, Spirit! pause, and tell whence is the light
Which fills the cloud? the sun is yet unrisen.
    Spirit. The sun will rise not until noon. Apollo
Is held in heaven by wonder; and the light
Which fills this vapour, as the aërial hue
Of fountain-gazing roses fills the water,
Flows from thy mighty sister.
    Pan.   Yes, I feel—
    Asia. What is it with thee, sister? Thou art pale.
    Pan. How thou art changed! I dare not look on thee;
I feel but see thee not. I scarce endure
The radiance of thy beauty. Some good change
Is working in the elements, which suffer
Thy presence thus unveiled. The Nereids tell
That on the day when the clear hyaline
Was cloven at thy uprise, and thou didst stand
Within a veined shell, which floated on
Over the calm floor of the crystal sea,
Among the Ægean isles, and by the shores
Which bear thy name; love, like the atmosphere
Of the sun's fire filling the living world,
Burst from thee, and illumined earth and heaven
And the deep ocean and the sunless caves,
And all that dwells within them: till grief cast
Eclipse upon the soul from which it came:
Such art thou now; nor is it I alone,
Thy sister, thy companion, thine own chosen one,
But the whole world which seeks thy sympathy.
Hearest thou not sounds in the air which speak the love
Of all articulate beings? Feelest thou not
The inanimate winds enamoured of thee? List!   [*Music.*
    Asia. Thy words are sweeter than aught else but his
Whose echoes they are: yet all love is sweet,
Given or returned. Common as light is love,
And its familiar voice wearies not ever.
Like the wide heaven, the all-sustaining air,
It makes the reptile equal to the God:
They who inspire it most are fortunate,
As I am now; but those who feel it most
Are happier still, after long sufferings,
As I shall soon become.
    Pan. List! Spirits speak.

Voice *in the Air, singing.*

Life of Life! thy lips enkindle
    With their love the breath between them;
And thy smiles before they dwindle
    Make the cold air fire; then screen them
In those looks, where whoso gazes
Faints, entangled in their mazes.

Child of Light! thy lips are burning
    Through the vest which seems to hide them;

As the radiant lines of morning
　　Through the clouds ere they divide them ;
And this atmosphere divinest
Shrouds thee whereso'er thou shinest.

Fair are others ; none beholds thee,
　　But thy voice sounds low and tender
Like the fairest, for it folds thee
　　From the sight, that liquid splendour,
And all feel, yet see thee never,
As I feel now, lost for ever !

Lamp of Earth ! where'er thou movest
　　Its dim shapes are clad with brightness,
And the souls of whom thou lovest
　　Walk upon the winds with lightness.
Till they fail, as I am failing,
Dizzy, lost, yet unbewailing !

ASIA.

　　My soul is an enchanted boat,
　　　Which, like a sleeping swan, doth float
Upon the silver waves of thy sweet singing ;
　　　And thine doth like an angel sit
　　　Beside the helm conducting it,
Whilst all the winds with melody are ringing.
　　　　It seems to float ever, for ever,
　　　　Upon that many-winding river,
　　　　Between mountains, woods, abysses,
　　　　A paradise of wildernesses !
Till, like one in slumber bound,
Borne to the ocean, I float down, around,
Into a sea profound, of ever-spreading sound :
　　　　Meanwhile thy spirit lifts its pinions
　　　　In music's most serene dominions ;
Catching the winds that fan that happy heaven.
　　　　And we sail on, away, afar,
　　　　Without a course, without a star,
But, by the instinct of sweet music driven ;
　　　　Till through Elysian garden islets
　　　　By thee, most beautiful of pilots,
　　　　Where never mortal pinnace glided,
　　　　The boat of my desire is guided :
Realms where the air we breathe is love,
Which in the winds on the waves doth move,
Harmonizing this earth with what we feel above.

　　　　We have passed Age's icy caves,
　　　　And Manhood's dark and tossing waves,
And Youth's smooth ocean, smiling to betray :
　　　　Beyond the glassy gulfs we flee
　　　　Of shadow-peopled Infancy,
Through Death and Birth, to a diviner day ;
　　　　A paradise of vaulted bowers,
　　　　Lit by downward-gazing flowers,
　　　　And watery paths that wind between
　　　　Wildernesses calm and green,

Peopled by shapes too bright to see,
And rest, having beheld; somewhat like thee;
Which walk upon the sea, and chant melodiously:

ACT III.

SCENE I.—*Heaven.* JUPITER *on his Throne;* THETIS *and the other Deities*
assembled.

Jup. Ye congregated powers of heaven, who share
The glory and the strength of him ye serve,
Rejoice! henceforth I am omnipotent.
All else had been subdued to me; alone
The soul of man, like an unextinguished fire,
Yet burns towards heaven with fierce reproach, and doubt,
And lamentation, and reluctant prayer,
Hurling up insurrection, which might make
Our antique empire insecure, though built
On eldest faith, and hell's coeval, fear;
And though my curses through the pendulous air,
Like snow on herbless peaks, fall flake by flake,
And cling to it; though under my wrath's might
It climbs the crags of life, step after step,
Which wound it, as ice wounds unsandalled feet,
It yet remains supreme o'er misery,
Aspiring, unrepressed, yet soon to fall:
Even now have I begotten a strange wonder,
That fatal child, the terror of the earth,
Who waits but till the distant hour arrive,
Bearing from Demogorgon's vacant throne
The dreadful might of ever-living limbs
Which clothed that awful spirit unbeheld,
To redescend and trample out the spark.

Pour forth heaven's wine, Idæan Ganymede,
And let it fill the Dædal cups like fire,
And from the flower-inwoven soil divine
Ye all-triumphant harmonies arise,
As dew from earth under   e twilight stars:
Drink! be the nectar circling through your veins
The soul of joy, ye ever-living Gods,
Till exultation burst in one wide voice
Like music from Elysian winds.
                                        And thou
Ascend beside me, veiled in the light
Of the desire which makes thee one with me,
Thetis, bright image of eternity!
When thou didst cry, "Insufferable might!
God!   Spare me! I sustain not the quick flames,
The penetrating presence; all my being,
Like him whom the Numidian seps did thaw
Into a dew with poison, is dissolved,
Sinking through its foundations:" even then
Two mighty spirits, mingling, made a third
Mightier than either, which, unbodied now,
Between us floats, felt, although unbeheld,

Waiting the incarnation, which ascends,
(Hear ye the thunder of the fiery wheels
Griding the winds?) from Demogorgon's throne.
Victory! victory! Feel'st thou not, O world,
The earthquake of his chariot thundering up
Olympus? [*The Car of the* HOUR *arrives.* DEMOGORGON *descends,
and moves towards the Throne of* JUPITER.
Awful shape, what art thou? Speak!
   Dem. Eternity. Demand no direr name.
Descend, and follow me down the abyss.
I am thy child, as thou wert Saturn's child;
Mightier than thee: and we must dwell together
Henceforth in darkness. Lift thy lightnings not.
The tyranny of heaven none may retain,
Or reassume, or hold, succeeding thee:
Yet if thou wilt, as 'tis the destiny
Of trodden worms to writhe till they are dead,
Put forth thy might.
    Jup. Detested prodigy!
Even thus beneath the deep Titanian prisons
I trample thee! thou lingerest?
                Mercy! mercy!
No pity, no release, no respite! Oh,
That thou wouldst make mine enemy my judge,
Even where he hangs, seared by my long revenge,
On Caucasus! he would not doom me thus.
Gentle and just, and dreadless, is he not
The monarch of the world? What art thou?
No refuge! no appeal!
             Sink with me then,
We two will sink on the wide waves of ruin,
Even as a vulture and a snake outspent
Drop, twisted in inextricable fight,
Into a shoreless sea. Let hell unlock
Its mounded oceans of tempestuous fire,
And whelm on them into the bottomless void
This desolated world, and thee, and me,
The conqueror and the conquered and the wreck
Of that for which they combated.
                  Ai! Ai!
The elements obey me not. I sink
Dizzily down, ever, for ever down.
And, like a cloud, mine enemy above
Darkens my fall with victory! Ai, Ai!

SCENE II.—*The Mouth of a great River in the Island Atlantis.* OCEAN *is
discovered reclining near the Shore;* APOLLO *stands beside him.*

    Ocean. He fell, thou sayest, beneath his conqueror's frown?
    Apollo. Ay, when the strife was ended which made dim
The orb I rule, and shook the solid stars,
The terrors of his eye illumined heaven
With sanguine light, through the thick ragged skirts
Of the victorious darkness, as he fell:
Like the last glare of day's red agony,
Which, from a rent among the fiery clouds,
Burns far along the tempest-wrinkled deep.

Ocean. He sunk to the abyss? To the dark void?

Apollo. An eagle so caught in some bursting cloud
On Caucasus, his thunder-baffled wings
Entangled in the whirlwind, and his eyes
Which gazed on the undazzling sun, now blinded
By the white lightning, while the ponderous hail
Beats on his struggling form, which sinks at length
Prone, and the aërial ice clings over it.

Ocean. Henceforth the fields of Heaven-reflecting sea
Which are my realm, will heave, unstained with blood,
Beneath the uplifting winds, like plains of corn
Swayed by the summer air ; my streams will flow
Round many peopled continents, and round
Fortunate isles ; and from their glassy thrones
Blue Proteus and his humid nymphs shall mark
The shadow of fair ships, as mortals see
The floating bark of the light laden moon
With that white star, its sightless pilot's crest,
Borne down the rapid sunset's ebbing sea;
Tracking their path no more by blood and groans,
And desolation, and the mingled voice
Of slavery and command; but by the light
Of wave-reflected flowers, and floating odours,
And music soft, and mild, free, gentle voices,
That sweetest music, such as spirits love.

Apollo. And I shall gaze not on the deeds which make
My mind obscure with sorrow, as eclipse
Darkens the sphere I guide; but list, I hear
The small, clear, silver lute of the young Spirit
That sits on the morning star.

Ocean. Thou must away;
Thy steeds will pause at even, till when farewell:
The loud deep calls me home even now to feed it
With azure calm out of the emerald urns
Which stand for ever full beside my throne.
Behold the Nereids under the green sea,
Their wavering limbs borne on the wind-like stream,
Their white arms lifted o'er their streaming hair
With garlands pied and starry sea-flower crowns,
Hastening to grace their mighty sister's joy.

                           [A sound of waves is heard.
It is the unpastured sea hungering for calm.
Peace, monster ; I come now.   Farewell.

Apollo.   Farewell.

SCENE III.—*Caucasus.* PROMETHEUS, HERCULES, IONE, *the* EARTH,
   SPIRITS, ASIA, *and* PANTHEA, *borne in the Car with the* SPIRIT OF THE
   HOUR. HERCULES *unbinds* PROMETHEUS, *who descends.*

Herc. Most glorious among spirits, thus doth strength
To wisdom, courage, and long-suffering love,
And thee, who art the form they animate,
Minister like a slave.

Pro.   Thy gentle words
Are sweeter even than freedom long desired
And long delayed.

               Asia, thou light of life,
Shadow of beauty unbeheld ; and ye,

Fair sister nymphs, who made long years of pain
Sweet to remember, through your love and care:
Henceforth we will not part.   There is a cave,
All overgrown with trailing odorous plants,
Which curtain out the day with leaves and flowers,
And paved with veined emerald, and a fountain
Leaps in the midst with an awakening sound.
From its curved roof the mountain's frozen tears
Like snow, or silver, or long diamond spires,
Hang downward, raining forth a doubtful light:
And there is heard the ever-moving air,
Whispering without from tree to tree, and birds,
And bees; and all around are mossy seats,
And the rough walls are clothed with long soft grass;
A simple dwelling, which shall be our own;
Where we will sit and talk of time and change,
As the world ebbs and flows, ourselves unchanged.
What can hide man from mutability ?
And if ye sigh, then I will smile ; and thou,
Ione, shall chant fragments of sea-music,
Until I weep, when ye shall smile away
The tears she brought, which yet were sweet to shed.
We will entangle buds and flowers and beams
Which twinkle on the fountain's brim, and make
Strange combinations out of common things,
Like human babes in their brief innocence;
And we will search, with looks and words of love,
For hidden thoughts, each lovelier than the last,
Our unexhausted spirits; and like lutes
Touched by the skill of the enamoured wind,
Weave harmonies divine, yet ever new,
From difference sweet where discord cannot be;
And hither come, sped on the charmed winds,
Which meet from all the points of heaven, as bees
From every flower aërial Enna feeds,
At their own island-homes in Himera,
The echoes of the human world, which tell
Of the low voice of love, almost unheard,
And dove-eyed pity's murmured pain, and music,
Itself the echo of the heart, and all
That tempers or improves man's life, now free;
And lovely apparitions, dim at first,
Then radiant, as the mind, arising bright
From the embrace of beauty, whence the forms
Of which these are the phantoms, casts on them
The gathered rays which are reality,
Shall visit us, the progeny immortal
Of Painting, Sculpture, and wrapt Poesy,
And arts, though unimagined, yet to be.
The wandering voices and the shadows these
Of all that man becomes, the mediators
Of that best worship love, by him and us
Given and returned; swift shapes and sounds, which grow
More fair and soft as man grows wise and kind,
And veil by veil, evil and error fall:
Such virtue has the cave and place around.
                              [*Turning to the* Spirit of the Hour.
For thee, fair Spirit, one toil remains.   Ione,

Give her that curved shell, which Proteus old
Made Asia's nuptial boon, breathing within it
A voice to be accomplished, and which thou
Didst hide in grass under the hollow rock.

Ione. Thou most desired Hour, more loved and lovely
Than all thy sisters, this is the mystic shell;
See the pale azure fading into silver
Lining it with a soft yet glowing light:
Looks it not like lulled music sleeping there?

Spirit. It seems in truth the fairest shell of Ocean:
Its sound must be at once both sweet and strange.

Pro. Go, borne over the cities of mankind
On whirlwind-footed coursers: once again
Outspeed the sun around the orbed world;
And as thy chariot cleaves the kindling air,
Thou breathe into the many-folded shell,
Loosening its mighty music; it shall be
As thunder mingled with clear echoes: then
Return; and thou shalt dwell beside our cave.
And thou, O Mother Earth!—

    The Earth.   I hear, I feel;
Thy lips are on me, and thy touch runs down
Even to the adamantine central gloom
Along these marble nerves; 'tis life, 'tis joy,
And through my withered, old, and icy frame
The warmth of an immortal youth shoots down
Circling.   Henceforth the many children fair
Folded in my sustaining arms; all plants,
And creeping forms, and insects rainbow-winged,
And birds, and beasts, and fish, and human shapes,
Which drew disease and pain from my wan bosom,
Draining the poison of despair, shall take
And interchange sweet nutriment; to me
Shall they become like sister-antelopes
By one fair dam, snow-white and swift as wind
Nursed among lilies near a brimming stream.
The dew-mists of my sunless sleep shall float
Under the stars like balm: night-folded flowers
Shall suck unwitting hues in their repose:
And men and beasts in happy dreams shall gather
Strength for the coming day, and all its joy:
And death shall be the last embrace of her
Who takes the life she gave, even as a mother
Folding her child, says, " Leave me not again."

Asia. Oh, mother! wherefore speak the name of death?
Cease they to love, and move, and breathe, and speak,
Who die?

    The Earth. It would avail not to reply:
Thou art immortal, and this tongue is known
But to the uncommunicating dead.
Death is the veil which those who live call life:
They sleep, and it is lifted: and meanwhile
In mild variety the seasons mild
With rainbow-skirted showers, and odorous winds,
And long blue meteors cleansing the dull night,
And the life-kindling shafts of the keen sun's
All-piercing bow, and the dew-mingled rain
Of the calm moonbeams, a soft influence mild,

Shall clothe the forests and the fields, ay, even
The crag-built deserts of the barren deep,
With ever-living leaves, and fruits, and flowers.
And thou! There is a cavern where my spirit
Was panted forth in anguish whilst thy pain
Made my heart mad, and those who did inhale it
Became mad too, and built a temple there,
And spoke, and were oracular, and lured
The erring nations round to mutual war,
And faithless faith, such as Jove kept with thee;
Which breath now rises, as amongst tall weeds
A violet's exhalation, and it fills
With a serener light and crimson air
Intense, yet soft, the rocks and woods around;
It feeds the quick growth of the serpent vine,
And the dark linked ivy tangling wild,
And budding, blown, or odour-faded blooms
Which star the winds with points of coloured light,
As they rain through them, and bright golden globes
Of fruit, suspended in their own green heaven,
And through their veined leaves and amber stems
The flowers whose purple and translucid bowls
Stand ever mantling with aërial dew,
The drink of spirits: and it circles round,
Like the soft waving wings of noonday dreams,
Inspiring calm and happy thoughts, like mine,
Now thou art thus restored. This cave is thine.
Arise! appear! [*A Spirit rises in the likeness of a winged child.*
              This is my torch-bearer;
Who let his lamp out in old time with gazing
On eyes from which he kindled it anew
With love, which is as fire, sweet daughter mine,
For such is that within thine own. Run, wayward,
And guide this company beyond the peak
Of Bacchic Nysa, Mænad-haunted mountain,
And beyond Indus and its tribute rivers,
Trampling the torrent streams and glassy lakes
With feet unwet, unwearied, undelaying,
And up the green ravine, across the vale,
Beside the windless and crystalline pool,
Where ever lies, on unerasing waves,
The image of a temple, built above,
Distinct with column, arch, and architrave,
And palm-like capital, and over-wrought,
And populous most with living imagery,
Praxitelean shapes, whose marble smiles
Fill the hushed air with everlasting love.
It is deserted now, but once it bore
Thy name, Prometheus; there the emulous youths
Bore to thy honour through the divine gloom
The lamp which was thine emblem; even as those
Who bear the untransmitted torch of hope
Into the grave, across the night of life,
As thou hast borne it most triumphantly
To this far goal of Time. Depart, farewell.
Beside that temple is the destined cave.

SCENE IV.—*A Forest. In the background a Cave.* PROMETHEUS, ASIA. PANTHEA, IONE, *and the* SPIRIT OF THE EARTH.

    Ione. Sister, it is not earthly: how it glides
Under the leaves ! how on its head there burns
A light, like a green star, whose emerald beams
Are twined with its fair hair ! how, as it moves,
The splendour drops in flakes upon the grass !
Knowest thou it ?
    Pan.   It is the delicate spirit
That guides the earth through heaven. From afar
The populous constellations call that light
The loveliest of the planets ; and sometimes
It floats along the spray of the salt sea,
Or makes its chariot of a foggy cloud,
Or walks through fields or cities while men sleep,
Or o'er the mountain tops, or down the rivers,
Or through the green waste wilderness, as now,
Wondering at all it sees. Before Jove reigned
It loved our sister Asia, and it came
Each leisure hour to drink the liquid light
Out of her eyes, for which it said it thirsted
As one bit by a dipsas, and with her
It made its childish confidence, and told her
All it had known or seen, for it saw much,
Yet idly reasoned what it saw ; and called her,
For whence it sprung it knew not, nor do I,
Mother, dear mother.

THE SPIRIT OF THE EARTH (*running to* ASIA.)

                   Mother, dearest mother ;
May I then talk with thee as I was wont ?
May I then hide my eyes in thy soft arms,
After thy looks have made them tired of joy ?
May I then play beside thee the long noons,
When work is none in the bright silent air ?
    Asia. I love thee, gentlest being, and henceforth
Can cherish thee unenvied: speak, I pray:
Thy simple talk once solaced, now delights.
    Spirit of the Earth. Mother, I am grown wiser, though a child
Cannot be wise like thee, within this day;
And happier too; happier and wiser both.
Thou knowest that toads, and snakes, and loathly worms,
And venomous and malicious beasts, and boughs
That bore ill berries in the woods, were ever
An hindrance to my walks o'er the green world:
And that, among the haunts of humankind,
Hard-featured men, or with proud, angry looks,
Or cold, staid gait, or false and hollow smiles,
Or the dull sneer of self-loved ignorance,
Or other such foul masks, with which ill thoughts
Hide that fair being whom we spirits call man;
And women too, ugliest of all things evil,
(Though fair, even in a world where thou art fair,
When good and kind, free and sincere like thee,)
When false or frowning made me sick at heart
To pass them, though they slept, and I unseen,
Well, my path lately lay through a great city

Into the woody hills surrounding it:
A sentinel was sleeping at the gate:
When there was heard a sound, so loud, it shook
The towers amid the moonlight, yet more sweet
Than any voice but thine, sweetest of all;
A long, long sound, as it would never end:
And all the inhabitants leapt suddenly
Out of their rest, and gathered in the streets,
Looking in wonder up to Heaven, while yet
The music pealed along.   I hid myself
Within a fountain in the public square,
Where I lay like the reflex of the moon
Seen in a wave under green leaves; and soon
Those ugly human shapes and visages
Of which I spoke as having wrought me pain,
Past floating through the air, and fading still
Into the winds that scattered them; and those
From whom they past seemed mild and lovely forms
After some foul disguise had fallen, and all
Were somewhat changed, and after brief surprise
And greetings of delighted wonder, all
Went to their sleep again: and when the dawn
Came, wouldst thou think that toads, and snakes, and efts,
Could e'er be beautiful? yet so they were,
And that with little change of shape or hue:
All things had put their evil nature off:
I cannot tell my joy, when o'er a lake
Upon a drooping bough with nightshade twined,
I saw two azure halcyons clinging downward
And thinning one bright bunch of amber berries,
With quick long beaks, and in the deep there lay
Those lovely forms imaged as in a sky;
So with my thoughts full of these happy changes,
We meet again, the happiest change of all.

Asia. And never will we part, till thy chaste sister
Who guides the frozen and inconstant moon
Will look on thy more warm and equal light
Till her heart thaw like flakes of April snow
And love thee.

Spirit of the Earth. What! as Asia loves Prometheus?

Asia. Peace, wanton, thou art yet not old enough.
Think ye by gazing on each other's eyes
To multiply your lovely selves, and fill
With sphered fires the interlunar air?

Spirit of the Earth. Nay, mother, while my sister trims her lamp
'Tis hard I should go darkling.

Asia. Listen! look!

The SPIRIT OF THE HOUR *enters.*

Pro. We feel what thou hast heard and seen: yet speak.

Spirit of the Hour. Soon as the sound had ceased whose thunder filled
The abysses of the sky and the wide earth,
There was a change: the impalpable thin air
And the all-circling sunlight were transformed,
As if the sense of love dissolved in them
Had folded itself round the sphered world.
My vision then grew clear, and I could see
Into the mysteries of the universe:

R

Dizzy as with delight I floated down,
Winnowing the lightsome air with languid plumes,
My coursers sought their birthplace in the sun,
Where they henceforth will live exempt from toil
Pasturing flowers of vegetable fire.
And where my moon-like car will stand within
A temple, gazed upon by Phidian forms
Of thee, and Asia, and the Earth, and me,
And you fair nymphs looking the love we feel;
In memory of the tidings it has borne;
Beneath a dome fretted with graven flowers,
Poised on twelve columns of resplendent stone,
And open to the bright and liquid sky.
Yoked to it by an amphisbenic snake
The likeness of those winged steeds will mock
The light from which they find repose. Alas,
Whither has wandered now my partial tongue
When all remains untold which ye would hear?
As I have said I floated to the earth:
It was, as it is still, the pain of bliss
To move, to breathe, to be; I wandering went
Among the haunts and dwellings of mankind,
And first was disappointed not to see
Such mighty change as I had felt within
Expressed in outward things; but soon I looked,
And behold, thrones were kingless, and men walked
One with the other even as spirits do,
None fawned, none trampled; hate, disdain, or fear,
Self-love, or self-contempt on human brows
No more inscribed, as o'er the gate of hell,
"All hope abandon ye who enter here;"
None frowned, none trembled, none with eager fear
Gazed on another's eye of cold command,
Until the subject of a tyrant's will
Became, worse fate, the abject of his own,
Which spurred him, like an outspent horse, to death.
None wrought his lips in truth-entangling lines
Which smiled the lie his tongue disdained to speak;
None, with firm sneer, trod out in his own heart
The sparks of love and hope till there remained
Those bitter ashes, a soul self-consumed,
And the wretch crept a vampire among men,
Infecting all with his own hideous ill;
None talked that common, false, cold, hollow talk
Which makes the heart deny the *yes* it breathes,
Yet question that unmeant hypocrisy
With such a self-mistrust as has no name.
And women, too, frank, beautiful, and kind
As the free heaven which rains fresh light and dew
On the wide earth, past; gentle radiant forms,
From custom's evil taint exempt and pure;
Speaking the wisdom once they could not think,
Looking emotions once they feared to feel,
And changed to all which once they dared not be,
Yet being now, made earth like heaven; nor pride,
Nor jealousy, nor envy, nor ill shame,
The bitterest of those drops of treasured gall,
Spoilt the sweet taste of the nepenthe, love.

Thrones, altars, judgment-seats, and prisons; wherein,
And beside which, by wretched men were borne
Sceptres, tiaras, swords, and chains, and tomes
Of reasoned wrong, glozed on by ignorance,
Were like those monstrous and barbaric shapes,
The ghosts of a no more remembered fame,
Which, from their unworn obelisks, look forth
In triumph o'er the palaces and tombs
Of those who were their conquerors: mouldering round
Those imaged to the pride of kings and priests,
A dark yet mighty faith, a power as wide
As is the world it wasted, and are now
But an astonishment; even so the tools
And emblems of its last captivity,
Amid the dwellings of the peopled earth,
Stand, not o'erthrown, but unregarded now.
And those foul shapes, abhorred by god and man,
Which, under many a name and many a form
Strange, savage, ghastly, dark, and execrable,
Were Jupiter, the tyrant of the world;
And which the nations, panic-stricken, served
With blood, and hearts broken by long hope, and love
Dragged to his altars soiled and garlandless,
And slain among men's unreclaiming tears,
Flattering the thing they feared, which fear was hate,
Frown, mouldering fast, o'er their abandoned shrines:
The painted veil, by those who were, called life,
Which mimicked, as with colours idly spread,
All men believed and hoped, is torn aside ;
The loathsome mask has fallen, the man remains
Sceptreless, free, uncircumscribed, but man
Equal, unclassed, tribeless, and nationless,
Exempt from awe, worship degree, the king
Over himself; just, gentle, wise: but man
Passionless; no, yet free from guilt or pain,
Which were, for his will made or suffered them,
Nor yet exempt, though ruling them like slaves,
From chance, and death, and mutability,
The clogs of that which else might oversoar
The loftiest star of unascended heaven,
Pinnacled dim in the intense inane.

ACT IV.

Scene, a Part of the Forest near the Cave of PROMETHEUS. PANTHEA *and*
IONE *are sleeping : they awaken gradually during the first Song.*

VOICE (*of unseen Spirits*).

The pale stars are gone!
For the sun, their swift shepherd,
To the folds them compelling,
In the depths of the dawn,
Hastes, in meteor-eclipsing array, and they flee
Beyond his blue dwelling,
As fawns flee the leopard.
But where are ye?

A Train of dark Forms and Shadows passes by confusedly, singing.

> Here, oh, here:
> We bear the bier
> Of the Father of many a cancelled year!
> Spectres we
> Of the dead Hours be,
> We bear Time to his tomb in eternity.
>
> Strew, oh, strew
> Hair, not yew!
> Wet the dusty pall with tears, not dew!
> Be the faded flowers
> Of Death's bare bowers
> Spread on the corpse of the King of Hours!
>
> Haste, oh, haste!
> As shades are chased,
> Trembling, by day, from heaven's blue waste.
> We melt away,
> Like dissolving spray,
> From the children of a diviner day,
> With the lullaby
> Of winds that die
> On the bosom of their own harmony!

IONE.

What dark forms were they?

PANTHEA.

> The past Hours weak and grey,
> With the spoil which their toil
> Raked together
> From the conquest but One could foil.

IONE.

Have they past?

PANTHEA.

> They have past;
> They outspeeded the blast,
> While 'tis said, they are fled:

IONE.

Whither, oh, whither?

PANTHEA.

To the dark, to the past, to the dead.

VOICE (*of unseen Spirits*).

> Bright clouds float in heaven,
> Dew-stars gleam on earth,
> Waves assemble on ocean,
> They are gathered and driven

By the storm of delight, by the panic of glee!
   They shake with emotion,
   They dance in their mirth.
      But where are ye?

   The pine boughs are singing
   Old songs with new gladness,
   The billows and fountains
   Fresh music are flinging,
Like the notes of a spirit from land and from sea;
   The storms mock the mountains
   With the thunder of gladness.
      But where are ye?

Ione. What charioteers are these?
Pan. Where are their chariots?

SEMICHORUS OF HOURS.

The voice of the Spirits of Air and of Earth
Have drawn back the figured curtain of sleep
Which covered our being and darkened our birth
In the deep.

A VOICE.

In the deep?

SEMICHORUS II.

Oh, below the deep.

SEMICHORUS I.

An hundred ages we had been kept
Cradled in visions of hate and care,
And each one who waked as his brother slept,
Found the truth—

SEMICHORUS II.

Worse than his visions were!

SEMICHORUS I.

We have heard the lute of Hope in sleep;
We have known the voice of Love in dreams,
We have felt the wand of Power, and leap—

SEMICHORUS II.

As the billows leap in the morning beams!

CHORUS.

Weave the dance on the floor of the breeze,
   Pierce with song heaven's silent light,
Enchant the day that too swiftly flees,
   To check its flight ere the cave of night.

Once the hungry Hours were hounds
   Which chased the day like a bleeding deer,
And it limped and stumbled with many wounds
   Through the nightly dells of the desert year.

But now, oh weave the mystic measure
  Of music, and dance, and shapes of light,
Let the Hours, and the spirits of might and pleasure,
  Like the clouds and sunbeams, unite.

A Voice.

Unite!

Pan. See, where the spirits of the human mind
Wrapt in sweet sounds, as in bright veils, approach.

Chorus of Spirits.

We join the throng
  Of the dance and the song,
By the whirlwind of gladness borne along;
  As the flying-fish leap
  From the Indian deep,
And mix with the sea-birds, half asleep.

Chorus of Hours.

Whence come ye, so wild and so fleet,
For sandals of lightning are on your feet,
And your wings are soft and swift as thought,
And your eyes are as love which is veiled not?

Chorus of Spirits.

We come from the mind
  Of human kind
Which was late so dusk, and obscene, and blind,
  Now 'tis an ocean
  Of clear emotion,
A heaven of serene and mighty motion.

From that deep abyss
  Of wonder and bliss,
Whose caverns are crystal palaces;
  From those skiey towers
  Where Thought's crowned powers
Sit watching your dance, ye happy Hours!

From the dim recesses
  Of woven caresses,
Where lovers catch ye by your loose tresses;
  From the azure isles,
  Where sweet Wisdom smiles,
Delaying your ships with her siren wiles;

From the temples high
  Of Man's ear and eye,
Roofed over Sculpture and Poesy;
  From the murmurings
  Of the unsealed springs
Where Science bedews his Dædal wings.

Years after years,
  Through blood, and tears,
And a thick hell of hatreds, and hopes, and fears;

We waded and flew,
And the islets were few
Where the bud-blighted flowers of happiness grew.

Our feet now, every palm,
Are sandalled with calm,
And the dew of our wings is a rain of balm;
And, beyond our eyes,
The human love lies
Which makes all it gazes on Paradise.

CHORUS OF SPIRITS AND HOURS.

Then weave the web of the mystic measure;
From the depths of the sky and the ends of the earth,
Come, swift Spirits of might and of pleasure,
Fill the dance and the music of mirth,
As the waves of a thousand streams rush by
To an ocean of splendour and harmony!

CHORUS OF SPIRITS.

Our spoil is won,
Our task is done,
We are free to dive, or soar, or run;
Beyond and around,
Or within the bound
Which clips the world with darkness round.

We'll pass the eyes
Of the starry skies
Into the hoar deep to colonize:
Death, Chaos, and Night,
From the sound of our flight,
Shall flee, like mist from a tempest's might.

And Earth, Air, and Light,
And the Spirit of Might,
Which drives round the stars in their fiery flight;
And Love, Thought, and Breath,
The powers that quell death,
Wherever we soar shall assemble beneath.

And our singing shall build
In the void's loose field
A world for the Spirit of Wisdom to wield;
We will take our plan
From the new world of man,
And our work shall be called the Promethean.

CHORUS OF HOURS.

Break the dance and scatter the song;
Let some depart and some remain.

SEMICHORUS I.

We, beyond heaven, are driven along:

SEMICHORUS II.

Us the enchantments of earth retain:

SEMICHORUS I.

Ceaseless, and rapid, and fierce, and free,
With the Spirits which build a new earth and sea,
And a heaven where yet heaven could never be.

SEMICHORUS II.

Solemn, and slow, and serene, and bright,
Leading the Day and outspeeding the Night,
With the powers of a world of perfect light.

SEMICHORUS I.

We whirl, singing loud, round the gathering sphere,
Till the trees, and the beasts, and the clouds appear
From its chaos made calm by love, not fear.

SEMICHORUS II.

We encircle the ocean and mountains of earth,
And the happy forms of its death and birth
Change to the music of our sweet mirth.

CHORUS OF HOURS AND SPIRITS.

Break the dance, and scatter the song,
    Let some depart, and some remain,
Wherever we fly we lead along
In leashes, like star-beams, soft yet strong,
    The clouds that are heavy with love's sweet rain.

Pan. Ha! they are gone!
Ione.   Yet feel you no delight
From the past sweetness?
Pan.   As the bare green hill
When some soft cloud vanishes into rain,
Laughs with a thousand drops of sunny water
To the unpavilioned sky!
Ione.   Even whilst we speak
New notes arise. What is that awful sound?
Pan. 'Tis the deep music of the rolling world
Kindling within the strings of the waved air,
Æolian modulations.
Ione.   Listen too,
How every pause is filled with under-notes,
Clear, silver, icy, keen awakening tones,
Which pierce the sense, and live within the soul,
As the sharp stars pierce winter's crystal air
And gaze upon themselves within the sea.
Pan. But see where through two openings in the forest
Which hanging branches overcanopy,
And where two runnels of a rivulet,
Between the close moss, violet-inwoven,
Have made their path of melody, like sisters
Who part with sighs that they may meet in smiles,
Turning their dear disunion to an isle

Of lovely grief, a wood of sweet sat thoughts;
Two visions of strange radiance float upon
The ocean-like enchantment of strong sound,
Which flows intenser, keener, deeper yet
Under the ground and through the windless air.

    Ione. I see a chariot like that thinnest boat,
In which the mother of the months is borne
By ebbing night into her western cave,
When she upsprings from interlunar dreams,
O'er which is curved an orblike canopy
Of gentle darkness, and the hills and woods
Distinctly seen through that dusk airy veil,
Regard like shapes in an enchanter's glass;
Its wheels are solid clouds, azure and gold,
Such as the genii of the thunder-storm
Pile on the floor of the illumined sea
When the sun rushes under it; they roll
And move and grow as with an inward wind;
Within it sits a winged infant, white
Its countenance, like the whiteness of bright snow,
Its plumes are as feathers of sunny frost,
Its limbs gleam white, through the wind-flowing folds
Of its white robe, woof of ethereal pearl.
Its hair is white, the brightness of white light
Scattered in string; yet its two eyes are heavens
Of liquid darkness, which the Deity
Within seems pouring, as a storm is poured
From jagged clouds, out of their arrowy lashes,
Tempering the cold and radiant air around,
With fire that is not brightness; in its hand
It sways a quivering moonbeam, from whose point
A guiding power directs the chariot's prow
Over its wheeled clouds, which as they roll
Over the grass, and flowers, and waves, wake sounds,
Sweet as a singing rain of silver dew.

    Pan. And from the other opening in the wood
Rushes, with loud and whirlwind harmony,
A sphere, which is as many thousand spheres,
Solid as crystal, yet through all its mass
Flow, as through empty space, music and light:
Ten thousand orbs involving and involved,
Purple and azure, white, green, and golden,
Sphere within sphere; and every space between
Peopled with unimaginable shapes,
Such as ghosts dream dwell in the lampless deep,
Yet each inter-transpicuous, and they whirl
Over each other with a thousand motions,
Upon a thousand sightless axles spinning,
And with the force of self-destroying swiftness,
Intensely, slowly, solemnly roll on,
Kindling with mingled sounds, and many tones,
Intelligible words and music wild.
With mighty whirl the multitudinous orb
Grinds the bright brook into an azure mist
Of elemental subtlety, like light;
And the wild odour of the forest flowers,
The music of the living grass and air,
The emerald light of leaf-entangled beams

Round its intense yet self-conflicting speed,
Seem kneaded into one aërial mass
Which drowns the sense. Within the orb itself,
Pillowed upon its alabaster arms,
Like to a child o'erwearied with sweet toil,
On its own folded wings, and wavy hair,
The Spirit of the Earth is laid asleep,
And you can see its little lips are moving,
Amid the changing light of their own smiles,
Like one who talks of what he loves in dream.

Ione. 'Tis only mocking the orb's harmony.

Pan. And from a star upon its forehead, shoot,
Like swords of azure fire, or golden spears
With tyrant-quelling myrtle overtwined,
Embleming heaven and earth united now,
Vast beams like spoke of some invisible wheel
Which whirl as the orb whirls, swifter than thought,
Filling the abyss with sunlike lightnings,
And perpendicular now, and now transverse,
Pierce the dark soil, and as they pierce and pass,
Make bare the secrets of the earth's deep heart;
Infinite mine of adamant and gold,
Valueless stones, and unimagined gems,
And caverns on crystalline columns poured
With vegetable silver overspread;
Wells of unfathomed fire, and water springs
Whence the great sea, even as a child is fed,
Whose vapours clothe earth's monarch mountain-tops
With kingly, ermine snow. The beams flash on
And make appear the melancholy ruins
Of cancelled cycles; anchors, beaks of ships;
Planks turned to marble; quivers, helms, and spears,
And gorgon-headed targes, and the wheels
Of scythed chariots, and the emblazonry
Of trophies, standards, and armorial beasts,
Round which death laughed, sepulchred emblems
Of dead destruction, ruin within ruin !
The wrecks beside of many a city vast,
Whose population which the earth grew over
Was mortal, but not human; see, they lie
Their monstrous works, and uncouth skeletons,
Their statues, homes and fanes; prodigious shapes
Huddled in grey annihilation, split,
Jammed in the hard, black deep; and over these,
The anatomies of unknown winged things,
And fishes which were isles of living scale,
And serpents, bony chains, twisted around
The iron crags, or within heaps of dust
To which the tortuous strength of their last pangs
Had crushed the iron crags; and over these
The jagged alligator, and the might
Of earth-convulsing behemoth, which once
Were monarch beasts, and on the slimy shores,
And weed-overgrown continents of earth,
Increased and multiplied like summer worms
On an abandoned corpse, till the blue globe
Wrapt deluge round it like a cloke, and they
Yelled, gasped, and were abolished; or some God

Whose throne was in a comet, past, and cried,
Be not! And like my words they were no more.

The Earth.

The joy, the triumph, the delight, the madness!
The boundless, overflowing, bursting gladness,
The vaporous exultation not to be confined!
    Ha! ha! the animation of delight
    Which wraps me, like an atmosphere of light,
And bears me as a cloud is borne by its own wind.

The Moon.

    Brother mine, calm wanderer,
    Happy globe of land and air,
Some Spirit is darted like a beam from thee,
    Which penetrates my frozen frame,
    And passes with the warmth of flame,
With love, and odour, and deep melody
    Through me, through me!

The Earth.

Ha! ha! the caverns of my hollow mountains,
My cloven fire-crags, sound-exulting fountains
Laugh with a vast and inextinguishable laughter.
    The oceans, and the deserts, and the abysses,
    And the deep air's unmeasured wildernesses,
Answer from all their clouds and billows, echoing after.

    They cry aloud as I do. Sceptred curse,
    Who all our green and azure universe
Threatenedst to muffle round with black destruction, sending
    A solid cloud to rain hot thunder-stones,
    And splinter and knead down my children's bones,
All I bring forth, to one void mass battering and blending.

    Until each crag-like tower, and storied column,
    Palace, and obelisk, and temple solemn,
My imperial mountains crowned with cloud, and snow, and fire;
    My sea-like forests, every blade and blossom
    Which finds a grave or cradle in my bosom,
Were stamped by thy strong hate into a lifeless mire.

    How art thou sunk, withdrawn, covered, drunk up
    By thirsty nothing, as the brackish cup
Drained by a desert-troop, a little drop for all;
    And from beneath, around, within, above,
    Filling thy void annihilation, love
Bursts in like light on caves cloven by thunder-ball.

The Moon.

    The snow upon my lifeless mountains
    Is loosened into living fountains,
My solid oceans flow, and sing, and shine:
    A spirit from my heart bursts forth,
    It clothes with unexpected birth
My cold bare bosom: Oh! it must be thine
    On mine on mine!

Gazing on thee I feel, I know
Green stalks burst forth, and bright flowers grow,
And living shapes upon my bosom move :
Music is in the sea and air,
Winged clouds soar here and there,
Dark with the rain new buds are dreaming of :
'Tis love, all love !

THE EARTH.

It interpenetrates my granite mass,
Through tangled roots and trodden clay doth pass,
Into the utmost leaves and delicatest flowers ;
Upon the winds, among the clouds 'tis spread,
It wakes a life in the forgotten dead,
They breathe a spirit up from their obscurest bowers.

And like a storm bursting its cloudy prison
With thunder, and with whirlwind, has arisen
Out of the lampless caves of unimagined being :
With earthquake shock and swiftness making shiver
Thought's stagnant chaos, unremoved for ever,
Till hate, and fear, and pain, light-vanquished shadows, fleeing,

Leave man, who was a many sided mirror,
Which could distort to many a shape of error,
This true fair world of things, a sea reflecting love ;
Which over all his kind as the sun's heaven
Gliding o'er ocean, smooth, serene, and even
Darting from starry depths radiance and light, doth move.

Leave man, even as a leprous child is left,
Who follows a sick beast to some warm cleft
Of rocks, through which the might of healing springs is poured ;
Then when it wanders home with rosy smile,
Unconscious, and its mother fears awhile
It is a spirit, then, weeps on her child restored.

Man, oh, not men ! a chain of linked thought,
Of love and might to be divided not,
Compelling the elements with adamantine stress ;
As the sun rules, even with a tyrant's gaze,
The unquiet republic of the maze
Of planets, struggling fierce towards heaven's free wilderness.

Man, one harmonious soul of many a soul,
Whose nature is its own divine control,
Where all things flow to all, as rivers to the sea ;
Familiar acts are beautiful through love ;
Labour, and pain, and grief, in life's green grove
Sport like tame beasts, none knew how gentle they could be !

His will, with all mean passions, bad delights,
And selfish cares, its trembling satellites,
A spirit ill to guide, but mighty to obey,
Is as a tempest-winged ship, whose helm
Love rules, through waves which dare not overwhelm,
Forcing life's wildest shores to own its sovereign sway

All things confess his strength.   Through the cold mass
Of marble and of colour his dreams pass;
Bright threads whence mothers weave the robes their children wear
Language is a perpetual orphic song,
Which rules with Dædal harmony a throng
Of thoughts and forms, which else senseless and shapeless were

The lightning is his slave; heaven's utmost deep
Gives up her stars, and like a flock of sheep
They pass before his eye, are numbered, and roll on!
The tempest is his steed, he strides the air;
And the abyss shouts from her depth laid bare,
Heaven, hast thou secrets? Man unveils me; I have none.

THE MOON.

The shadow of white death has past
From my path in heaven at last,
A clinging shroud of solid frost and sleep;
And through my newly-woven bowers,
Wander happy paramours,
Less mighty, but as mild as those who keep
Thy vales more deep.

THE EARTH.

As the dissolving warmth of dawn may fold
A half infrozen dew-globe, green, and gold,
And crystalline, till it becomes a winged mist,
And wanders up the vault of the blue day,
Outlives the noon, and on the sun's last ray
Hangs o'er the sea, a fleece of fire and amethyst.

THE MOON.

Thou art folded, thou art lying
In the light which is undying
Of thine own joy, and heaven's smile divine;
All suns and constellations shower
On thee a light, a life, a power
Which doth array thy sphere; thou pourest thine
On mine, on mine!

THE EARTH.

I spin beneath my pyramid of night,
Which points into the heavens dreaming delight,
Murmuring victorious joy in my enchanted sleep;
As a youth lulled in love-dreams faintly sighing,
Under the shadow of his beauty lying,
Which round his rest a watch of light and warmth doth keep

THE MOON.

As in the soft and sweet eclipse,
When soul meets soul on lovers' lips,
High hearts are calm, and brightest eyes are dull;
So when thy shadow falls on me,
Then am I mute and still, by thee
Covered; of thy love, orb most beautiful,
Full, oh, too full!

Thou art speeding round the sun
Brightest world of many a one;
Green and azure sphere which shinest
With a light which is divinest
Among all the lamps of Heaven
To whom life and light is given;
I, thy crystal paramour,
Borne beside thee by a power
Like the polar Paradise,
Magnet-like of lovers' eyes;
I, a most enamoured maiden
Whose weak brain is overladen
With the pleasure of her love,
Maniac-like around thee move
Gazing, an insatiate bride,
On thy form from every side
Like a Mænad, round the cup
Which Agave lifted up
In the weird Cadmæan forest.
Brother, wheresoe'er thou soarest
I must hurry, whirl and follow
Through the heavens wide and hollow,
Sheltered by the warm embrace
Of thy soul from hungry space,
Drinking from thy sense and sight
Beauty, majesty, and might,
As a lover or a chameleon
Grows like what it looks upon,
As a violet's gentle eye
Gazes on the azure sky
Until its hue grows like what it beholds,
As a grey and watery mist
Glows like solid amethyst
Athwart the western mountain it enfolds,
    When the sunset sleeps
        Upon its snow.

THE EARTH.

And the weak day weeps
    That it should be so.
Oh, gentle Moon, the voice of thy delight
Falls on me like thy clear and tender light
Soothing the seaman, borne the summer night,
    Through isles for ever calm:
Oh, gentle Moon, thy crystal accents pierce
The caverns of my pride's deep universe,
Charming the tiger joy, whose tramplings fierce
    Made wounds which need thy balm.

Pan. I rise as from a bath of sparkling water,
A bath of azure light, among dark rocks,
Out of the stream of sound.
Ione.   Ah me! sweet sister,
The stream of sound has ebbed away from us,
And you pretend to rise out of its wave,
Because your words fall like the clear, soft dew
Snaken from a bathing wood-nymph's limbs and hair.

Pan. Peace ! peace ! A mighty Power, which is as darkness,
Is rising out of Earth, and from the sky
Is showered like night, and from within the air
Bursts, like eclipse which had been gathered up
Into the pores of sunlight: the bright visions,
Wherein the singing spirits rode and shone,
Gleam like pale meteors through a watery night.
   Ione. There is a sense of words upon mine ear.
   Pan. An universal sound like words: Oh, list !

DEMOGORGON.

Thou, Earth, calm empire of a happy soul,
   Sphere of divinest shapes and harmonies,
Beautiful orb ! gathering as thou dost roll
   The love which paves thy path along the skies:

THE EARTH.

I hear: I am as a drop of dew that dies.

DEMOGORGON.

Thou, Moon, which gazest on the nightly Earth
   With wonder, as it gazes upon thee:
Whilst each to men, and beasts, and the swift birth
   Of birds, is beauty, love, calm, harmony:

THE MOON.

I hear: I am a leaf shaken by thee !

DEMOGORGON.

Ye kings of suns and stars, Demons and Gods,
   Ethereal Dominations, who possess
Elysian, windless, fortunate abodes
   Beyond Heaven's constellated wilderness:

A VOICE (*from above*).

Our great Republic hears, we are blest, and bless.

DEMOGORGON.

Ye happy dead, whom beams of brightest verse
   Are clouds to hide, not colours to portray,
Whether your nature is that universe
   Which once ye saw and suffered—

A VOICE (*from beneath*).

               Or as they
Whom we have left, we change and pass away.

DEMOGORGON.

Ye elemental Genii, who have homes
   From man's high mind even to the central stone
Of sullen lead; from Heaven's star-fretted domes
   To the dull weed some sea-worm battens on:

A CONFUSED VOICE.

We hear: thy words waken Oblivion.

DEMOGORGON.

Spirits, whose homes are flesh: ye beasts and birds,
　　Ye worms, and fish; ye living leaves and buds;
Lightning, and wind; and ye untameable herds,
　　Meteors and mists, which throng air's solitudes:

A VOICE.

Thy voice to us is wind among still woods.

DEMOGORGON.

Man, who wert once a despot and a slave;
　　A dupe and a deceiver; a decay;
A traveller from the cradle to the grave
　　Through the dim night of this immortal day:

ALL.

Speak: thy strong words may never pass away.

DEMOGORGON.

This is the day, which down the void abysm
At the Earth-born's spell yawns for Heaven's despotism,
　　And Conquest is dragged captive through the deep:
Love, from its awful throne of patient power
In the wise heart, from the last giddy hour
　　Of dead endurance, from the slippery, steep,
And narrow verge of crag-like agony, springs
And folds over the world its healing wings.

Gentleness, Virtue, Wisdom, and Endurance,
These are the seals of that most firm assurance
　　Which bars the pit over Destruction's strength;
And if, with infirm hand, Eternity,
Mother of many acts and hours, should free
　　The serpent that would clasp her with his length;
These are the spells by which to re-assume
An empire o'er the disentangled doom.

To suffer woes which Hope thinks infinite;
To forgive wrongs darker than death or night;
　　To defy Power, which seems omnipotent;
To love, and bear; to hope till Hope creates
From its own wreck the thing it contemplates;
　　Neither to change, nor flatter, nor repent;
This, like thy glory, Titan, is to be
Good, great and joyous, beautiful and free;
This is alone Life, Joy, Empire, and Victory.

1819.

THE CENCI.

A TRAGEDY, IN FIVE ACTS.

Dedication.

TO LEIGH HUNT, Esq.

My dear Friend,—I inscribe with your name, from a distant country, and after an absence whose months have seemed years, this the latest of my literary efforts.

Those writings which I have hitherto published, have been little else than visions which impersonate my own apprehensions of the beautiful and the just. I can also perceive in them the literary defects incidental to youth and impatience; they are dreams of what ought to be, or may be. The drama which I now present to you is a sad reality. I lay aside the presumptuous attitude of an instructor, and am content to paint, with such colours as my own heart furnishes, that which has been.

Had I known a person more highly endowed than yourself with all that it becomes a man to possess, I had solicited for this work the ornament of his name. One more gentle, honourable, innocent, and brave; one of more exalted toleration for all who do and think evil, and yet himself more free from evil; one who knows better how to receive, and how to confer a benefit, though he must ever confer far more than he can receive; one of simpler, and, in the highest sense of the word, of purer life and manners, I never knew; and I had already been fortunate in friendships when your name was added to the list.

In that patient and irreconcilable enmity with domestic and political tyranny and imposture, which the tenor of your life has illustrated, and which, had I health and talents, should illustrate mine, let us, comforting each other in our task, live and die.

All happiness attend you!

Your affectionate friend,

Percy B. Shelley.

Rome, May 29, 1819.

PREFACE.

A MANUSCRIPT was communicated to me during my travels in Italy, which was copied from the archives of the Cenci Palace at Rome, and contains a detailed account of the horrors which ended in the extinction of one of the noblest and richest families of that city, during the Pontificate of Clement VIII. in the year 1599. The story is, that an old man having spent his life in

debauchery and wickedness, conceived at length an implacable hatred towar
his children; which showed itself towards one daughter under the form of
incestuous passion, aggravated by every circumstance of cruelty and violenc
This daughter, after long and vain attempts to escape from what she consider
a perpetual contamination both of body and mind, at length plotted with h
mother-in-law and brother to murder their common tyrant. The young maide
who was urged to this tremendous deed by an impulse which overpowered
horror, was evidently a most gentle and amiable being, a creature formed
adorn and be admired, and thus violently thwarted from her nature by t
necessity of circumstance and opinion. The deed was quickly discovered, an
in spite of the most earnest prayers made to the Pope by the highest persons
Rome, the criminals were put to death. The old man had, during his li
repeatedly bought his pardon from the Pope for capital crimes of the mc
enormous and unspeakable kind, at the price of a hundred thousand crown
the death, therefore, of his victims can scarcely be accounted for by the love
justice. The Pope, among other motives for severity, probably felt that whoev
killed the Count Cenci, deprived his treasury of a certain and copious source
revenue.* Such a story, if told so as to present to the reader all the feelings
those who once acted it, their hopes and fears, their confidences and misgiving
their various interests, passions and opinions, acting upon and with each othe
yet all conspiring to one tremendous end, would be as a light to make appare
some of the most dark and secret caverns of the human heart.

On my arrival at Rome, I found that the story of the Cenci was a subject n
to be mentioned in Italian society without awakening a deep and breathle
interest; and that the feelings of the company never failed to incline to
romantic pity for the wrongs, and a passionate exculpation of the horrible dec
to which they urged her, who has been mingled two centuries with the comme
dust. All ranks of people knew the outlines of this history, and participated i
the overwhelming interest which it seems to have the magic of exciting in th
human heart. I had a copy of Guido's picture of Beatrice, which is preserve
in the Colonna Palace, and my servant instantly recognised it as the portrait o
La Cenci.

This national and universal interest which the story produces, and has pre
duced for two centuries, and among all ranks of people in a great city, when
the imagination is kept for ever active and awake, first suggested to me th
conception of its fitness for a dramatic purpose. In fact it is a tragedy whic
has already received, from its capacity of awakening and sustaining the syn
pathy of men, approbation and success. Nothing remained, as I imagine
but to clothe it to the apprehensions of my countrymen in such language an
action as would bring it home to their hearts. The deepest and the sublime
tragic compositions, King Lear, and the two plays in which the tale of Œdipu
is told, were stories which already existed in tradition, as matters of popula
belief and interest, before Shakspeare and Sophocles made them familiar to th
sympathy of all succeeding generations of mankind.

This story of the Cenci is indeed eminently fearful and monstrous: anythi
like a dry exhibition of it on the stage would be insupportable. The perso
who would treat such a subject must increase the ideal, and diminish the actu
horror of the events; so that the pleasure which arises from the poetry whic
exists in these tempestuous sufferings and crimes may mitigate the pain of th
contemplation of the moral deformity from which they spring. There mu
also be nothing attempted to make the exhibition subservient to what is vu
garly termed a moral purpose. The highest moral purpose aimed at in th

---

* The Papal Government formerly took the most extraordinary precautions again
the publicity of facts which offer so tragical a demonstration of its own wickedness ar
weakness; so that the communication of the MS. had become, until very lately, a matt
of some difficulty.

highest species of the drama, is the teaching the human heart, through its sympathies and antipathies, the knowledge of itself; in proportion to the possession of which knowledge every human being is wise, just, sincere, tolerant and kind. If dogmas can do more, it is well: but a drama is no fit place for the enforcement of them. Undoubtedly, no person can be truly dishonoured by the act of another; and the fit return to make to the most enormous injuries is kindness and forbearance, and a resolution to convert the injurer from his dark passions by peace and love. Revenge, retaliation, atonement, are pernicious mistakes. If Beatrice had thought in this manner, she would have been wiser and better; but she would never have been a tragic character: the few whom such an exhibition would have interested, could never have been sufficiently interested for a dramatic purpose, from the want of finding sympathy in their interest among the mass who surround them. It is in the restless and anatomizing casuistry with which men seek the justification of Beatrice, yet feel that she has done what needs justification; it is in the superstitious horror with which they contemplate alike her wrongs and their revenge, that the dramatic character of what she did and suffered consists.

I have endeavoured as nearly as possible to represent the characters as they probably were, and have sought to avoid the error of making them actuated by my own conceptions of right or wrong, false or true: thus, under a thin veil, converting names and actions of the sixteenth century into cold impersonations of my own mind. They are represented as Catholics, and as Catholics deeply tinged with religion. To a Protestant apprehension there will appear something unnatural in the earnest and perpetual sentiment of the relations between God and man which pervade the tragedy of the Cenci. It will especially be startled at the combination of an undoubting persuasion of the truth of the popular religion with a cool and determined perseverance in enormous guilt. But religion in Italy is not, as in Protestant countries, a cloak to be worn on particular days; or a passport which those who do not wish to be railed at carry with them to exhibit; or a gloomy passion for penetrating the impenetrable mysteries of our being, which terrifies its possessor at the darkness of the abyss to the brink of which it has conducted him. Religion coexists, as it were, in the mind of an Italian Catholic, with a faith in that of which all men have the most certain knowledge. It is interwoven with the whole fabric of life. It is adoration, faith, submission, penitence, blind admiration; not a rule for moral conduct. It has no necessary connexion with any one virtue. The most atrocious villain may be rigidly devout, and without any shock to established faith, confess himself to be so. Religion pervades intently the whole frame of society, and is, according to the temper of the mind which it inhabits, a passion, a persuasion, an excuse, a refuge; never a check. Cenci himself built a chapel in the court of his palace, and dedicated it to St. Thomas the Apostle, and established masses for the peace of his soul. Thus in the first scene of the fourth act Lucretia's design in exposing herself to the consequences of an expostulation with Cenci, after having administered the opiate, was to induce him by a feigned tale to confess himself before death; this being esteemed by Catholics as essential to salvation; and she only relinquishes her purpose when she perceives that her perseverance would expose Beatrice to new outrages.

I have avoided with great care in writing this play the introduction of what is commonly called mere poetry, and I imagine there will scarcely be found a detached simile or a single isolated description, unless Beatrice's description of the chasm appointed for her father's murder should be judged to be of that nature.*

In a dramatic composition the imagery and the passion should interpenetrate

---

* An idea in this speech was suggested by a most sublime passage in "El Purgatorio de San Patricio" of Calderon; the only plagiarism which I have intentionally committed in the whole piece.

one another, the former being reserved simply for the full development and illustration of the latter. Imagination is as the immortal God which should assume flesh for the redemption of mortal passion. It is thus that the most remote and the most familiar imagery may alike be fit for dramatic purposes when employed in the illustration of strong feeling, which raises what is low, and levels to the apprehension that which is lofty, casting over all the shadow of its own greatness. In other respects I have written more carelessly; that is, without an over-fastidious and learned choice of words. In this respect I entirely agree with those modern critics who assert that in order to move men to true sympathy we must use the familiar language of men. And that our great ancestors the ancient English poets are the writers, a study of whom might incite us to do that for our own age which they have done for theirs. But it must be the real language of men in general, and not that of any particular class to whose society the writer happens to belong. So much for what I have attempted; I need not be assured that success is a very different matter; particularly for one whose attention has but newly been awakened to the study of dramatic literature.

I endeavoured whilst at Rome to observe such monuments of this story as might be accessible to a stranger. The portrait of Beatrice at the Colonna Palace is admirable as a work of art: it was taken by Guido during her confinement in prison. But it is most interesting as a just representation of one of the loveliest specimens of the workmanship of Nature. There is a fixed and pale composure upon the features: she seems sad and stricken down in spirit, yet the despair thus expressed is lightened by the patience of gentleness. Her head is bound with folds of white drapery from which the yellow strings of her golden hair escape and fall about her neck. The moulding of her face is exquisitely delicate; the eyebrows are distinct and arched; the lips have that permanent meaning of imagination and sensibility which suffering has not repressed, and which it seems as if death scarcely could extinguish. Her forehead is large and clear; her eyes, which we are told were remarkable for their vivacity, are swollen with weeping and lustreless, but beautifully tender and serene. In the whole mien there is a simplicity and dignity which united with her exquisite loveliness and deep sorrow are inexpressibly pathetic. Beatrice Cenci appears to have been one of those rare persons in whom energy and gentleness dwell together without destroying one another: her nature was simple and profound. The crimes and miseries in which she was an actor and a sufferer are as the mask and the mantle in which circumstances clothed her for her impersonation on the scene of the world.

The Cenci Palace is of great extent; and though in part modernized, there yet remains a vast and gloomy pile of feudal architecture in the same state as during the dreadful scenes which are the subject of this tragedy. The Palace is situated in an obscure corner of Rome, near the quarter of the Jews, and from the upper windows you see the immense ruins of Mount Palatine half hidden under their profuse overgrowth of trees. There is a court in one part of the Palace (perhaps that in which Cenci built the Chapel to St. Thomas), supported by granite columns and adorned with antique friezes of fine workmanship, and built up according to the ancient Italian fashion, with balcony over balcony of open-work. One of the gates of the Palace, formed of immense stones, and leading through a passage, dark and lofty, and opening into gloomy subterranean chambers, struck me particularly. Of the Castle of Petrella, I could obtain no further information than that which is to be found in the manuscript.

DRAMATIS PERSONÆ.

COUNT FRANCESCO CENCI.
GIACOMO, } *his Sons.*
BERNARDO, }
CARDINAL CAMILLO.
ORSINO, *a Prelate.*

SAVELLA, *the Pope's Legate.*
OLIMPIO, } *Assassins.*
MARZIO, }
ANDREA, *Servant to* CENCI.
Nobles, Judges, Guards, Servants.

LUCRETIA, *Wife of* CENCI, *and Stepmother of his Children.*
BEATRICE, *his Daughter.*

*The Scene lies principally in Rome, but changes during the Fourth Act to
Petrella, a castle among the Apulian Apennines.*

TIME—*During the Pontificate of* CLEMENT VIII.

ACT I.

SCENE I.—*An Apartment in the Cenci Palace.*

Enter COUNT CENCI *and* CARDINAL CAMILLO.

Cam. That matter of the murder is hushed up
If you consent to yield his Holiness
Your fief that lies beyond the Pincian gate.
It needed all my interest in the conclave
To bend him to this point: he said that you
Bought perilous impunity with your gold;
That crimes like yours if once or twice compounded
Enriched the Church, and respited from hell
An erring soul which might repent and live;
But the glory and the interest
Of the high throne he fills, little consist
With making it a daily mart of guilt
As manifold and hideous as the deeds
Which you scarce hide from men's revolted eyes.
Cen. The third of my possessions—let it go!
Ay, I once heard the nephew of the Pope
Had sent his architect to view the ground,
Meaning to build a villa on my vines
The next time I compounded with his uncle:
I little thought he should outwit me so!
Henceforth no witness—not the lamp—shall see
That which the vassal threatened to divulge,
Whose throat is choked with dust for his reward.
The deed he saw could not have rated higher
Than his most worthless life:—it angers me!
Respited me from Hell!—So may the Devil
Respite their souls from Heaven. No doubt Pope Clement
And his most charitable nephews, pray
That the Apostle Peter and the saints
Will grant for their sake that I long enjoy
Strength, wealth, and pride, and lust, and length of days
Wherein to act the deeds which are the stewards

Of their revenue.—But much yet remains
To which they show no title.

   Cam.   Oh, Count Cenci !
So much that thou mightst honourably live
And reconcile thyself with thine own heart
And with thy God, and with the offended world.
How hideously look deeds of lust and blood
Through those snow-white and venerable hairs !
Your children should be sitting round you now,
But that you fear to read upon their looks
The shame and misery you have written there.
Where is your wife ? Where is your gentle daughter ?
Methinks her sweet looks, which make all things else
Beauteous and glad, might kill the fiend within you.
Why is she barred from all society
But her own strange and uncomplaining wrongs ?
Talk with me, Count,—you know I mean you well.
I stood beside your dark and fiery youth
Watching its bold and bad career, as men
Watch meteors, but it vanished not: I marked
Your desperate and remorseless manhood; now
Do I behold you, in dishonoured age,
Charged with a thousand unrepented crimes.
Yet I have ever hoped you would amend,
And in that hope have saved your life three times.

   Cen. For which Aldobrandino owes you now
My fief beyond the Pincian. Cardinal,
One thing, I pray you, recollect henceforth,
And so we shall converse with less restraint.
A man you knew spoke of my wife and daughter :
He was accustomed to frequent my house ;
So the next day *his* wife and daughter came
And asked if I had seen him; and I smiled :
I think they never saw him any more.

   Cam. Thou execrable man, beware !—

   Cen. Of thee ?
Nay, this is idle: we should know each other.
As to my character for what men call crime,
Seeing I please my senses as I list,
And vindicate that right with force or guile,
It is a public matter, and I care not
If I discuss it with you. I may speak
Alike to you and my own conscious heart;
For you give out that you have half reformed me,
Therefore strong vanity will keep you silent
If fear should not; both will, I do not doubt.
All men delight in sensual luxury,
All men enjoy revenge; and most exult
Over the tortures they can never feel ;
Flattering their secret peace with others' pain.
But I delight in nothing else. I love
The sight of agony, and the sense of joy,
When this shall be another's and that mine.
And I have no remorse and little fear,
Which are, I think, the checks of other men.
This mood has grown upon me, until now
Any design my captious fancy makes
The picture of its wish, and it forms none

But such as men like you would start to know,
Is as my natural food and rest debarred
Until it be accomplished.

 Cam.   Art thou not
Most miserable?

 Cen.   Why miserable?—
No. I am what you theologians call
Hardened; which they must be in impudence,
So to revile a man's peculiar taste.
True, I was happier than I am, while yet
Manhood remained to act the thing I thought;
While lust was sweeter than revenge; and now
Invention palls: ay, we must all grow old:
And but that there remains a deed to act
Whose horror might make sharp an appetite
Duller than mine—I'd do,—I know not what.
When I was young I thought of nothing else
But pleasure; and I fed on honey sweets:
Men, by St. Thomas! cannot live like bees,
And I grew tired: yet, till I killed a foe,
And heard his groans, and heard his children's groans,
Knew I not what delight was else on earth,
Which now delights me little. I the rather
Look on such pangs as terror ill conceals:
The dry, fixed eyeball; the pale, quivering lip,
Which tell me that the spirit weeps within
Tears bitterer than the bloody sweat of Christ.
I rarely kill the body, which preserves,
Like a strong prison, the soul within my power,
Wherein I feed it with the breath of fear
For hourly pain.

 Cam.   Hell's most abandoned fiend
Did never, in the drunkenness of guilt,
Speak to his heart as now you speak to me;
I thank my God that I believe you not.

    Enter ANDREA.

 Andr. My lord, a gentleman from Salamanca
Would speak with you.

 Cen. Bid him attend me in the grand saloon. [*Exit* ANDREA.

 Cam. Farewell; and I will pray
Almighty God that thy false, impious words,
Tempt not his spirit to abandon thee.   [*Exit* CAMILLO.

 Cen. The third of my possessions! I must use
Close husbandry, or gold, the old man's sword,
Falls from my withered hand. But yesterday
There came an order from the Pope to make
Fourfold provision for my cursed sons;
Whom I had sent from Rome to Salamanca,
Hoping some accident might cut them off;
And meaning if I could to starve them there.
I pray thee, God, send some quick death upon them!
Bernardo and my wife could not be worse
If dead and damned: then, as to Beatrice——
      [*Looking around him suspiciously.*
I think they cannot hear me at that door;
What if they should? And yet I need not speak,

Though the heart triumphs with itself in words,
O, thou most silent air, that shalt not hear
What now I think! Thou, pavement, which I tread
Towards her chamber,—let your echoes talk
Of my imperious step, scorning surprise,
But not of my intent! Andrea!

Enter ANDREA.

Andr. My lord!
Cen. Bid Beatrice attend me in her chamber
This evening :—no, at midnight, and alone.

[*Exeunt*

SCENE II.—*A Garden of the Cenci Palace.*

Enter BEATRICE *and* ORSINO, *as in conversation*

Beatr. Pervert not truth,
Orsino. You remember where we held
That conversation ;—nay, we see the spot
Even from this cypress ;—two long years are past
Since, on an April midnight, underneath
The moonlight ruins of Mount Palatine,
I did confess to you my secret mind.
Ors. You said you loved me then.
Beatr. You are a priest,
Speak to me not of love.
Ors. I may obtain
The dispensation of the Pope to marry.
Because I am a priest do you believe
Your image, as the hunter some struck deer,
Follows me not whether I wake or sleep?
Beatr. As I have said, speak to me not of love;
Had you a dispensation, I have not;
Nor will I leave this home of misery
Whilst my poor Bernard, and that gentle lady
To whom I owe life and these virtuous thoughts,
Must suffer what I still have strength to share.
Alas, Orsino! All the love that once
I felt for you, is turned to bitter pain.
Ours was a youthful contract, which you first
Broke, by assuming vows no Pope will loose.
And thus I love you still, but holily,
Even as a sister or a spirit might;
And so I swear a cold fidelity.
And it is well perhaps we shall not marry.
You have a sly, equivocating vein
That suits me not. Ah, wretched that I am!
Where shall I turn? Even now you look on me
As you were not my friend, and as if you
Discovered that I thought so, with false smiles
Making my true suspicion seem your wrong.
Ah! No, forgive me; sorrow makes me seem
Sterner than else my nature might have been;
I have a weight of melancholy thoughts,
And they forbode,—but what can they forbode
Worse than I now endure?
Ors. All will be well.

Is the petition yet prepared ?   You know
My zeal for all you wish, sweet Beatrice ;
Doubt not but I will use my utmost skill,
So that the Pope attend to your complaint.

 Beatr. Your zeal for all I wish ; ah me, you are cold :
Your utmost skill—speak but one word——
        [*Aside*]. Alas !
Weak and deserted creature that I am,
Here I stand bickering with my only friend ! [*To* ORSINO.
This night my father gives a sumptuous feast,
Orsino ; he has heard some happy news
From Salamanca, from my brothers there,
And with this outward show of love he mocks
His inward hate. 'Tis bold hypocrisy,
For he would gladlier celebrate their deaths,
Which I have heard him pray for on his knees :
Great God ! that such a father should be mine !
But there is mighty preparation made,
And all our kin, the Cenci, will be there,
And all the chief nobility of Rome.
And he has bidden me and my pale mother
Attire ourselves in festival array.
Poor lady ! she expects some happy change
In his dark spirit from this act ; I none.
At supper I will give you the petition :
Till when—farewell.
 Ors.   Farewell.   [*Exit* BEATRICE
          I know the Pope
Will ne'er absolve me from my priestly vow
But by absolving me from the revenue
Of many a wealthy see ; and, Beatrice,
I think to win thee at an easier rate.
Nor shall he read her eloquent petition :
He might bestow her on some poor relation
Of his sixth cousin, as he did her sister,
And I should be debarred from all access.
Then as to what she suffers from her father,
In all this there is much exaggeration :
Old men are testy and will have their way ;
A man may stab his enemy, or his vassal,
And live a free life as to wine or women,
And with a peevish temper may return
To a dull home, and rate his wife and children ;
Daughters and wives call this foul tyranny.
I shall be well content, if on my conscience
There rest no heavier sin than what they suffer
From the devices of my love—a net
From which she shall escape not. Yet I fear
Her subtle mind, her awe-inspiring gaze,
Whose beams anatomize me, nerve by nerve,
And lay me bare, and make me blush to see
My hidden thoughts.—Ah, no ! A friendless girl
Who clings to me, as to her only hope :—
I were a fool, not less than if a panther
Were panic-stricken by the antelope's eye
If she escape me.   [*Exit.*

SCENE III.—*A magnificent Hall in the Cenci Palace. A Banquet.* Enter
CENCI, LUCRETIA, BEATRICE, ORSINO, CAMILLO, NOBLES.

Cen. Welcome, my friends and kinsmen; welcome ye
Princes and Cardinals, pillars of the church,
Whose presence honours our festivity.
I have too long lived like an anchorite,
And, in my absence from your merry meetings,
An evil word is gone abroad of me:
But I do hope that you, my noble friends,
When you have shared the entertainment here,
And heard the pious cause for which 'tis given,
And we have pledged a health or two together,
Will think me flesh and blood as well as you;
Sinful indeed, for Adam made all so,
But tender-hearted, meek and pitiful.
First Guest. In truth, my Lord, you seem too light of heart,
Too sprightly and companionable a man,
To act the deeds that rumour pins on you.
                                        [*To his companion.*
I never saw such blithe and open cheer
In any eye!
Second Guest. Some most desired event,
In which we all demand a common joy,
Has brought us hither; let us hear it, Count.
Cen. It is indeed a most desired event,
If, when a parent, from a parent's heart,
Lifts from this earth to the great Father of all
A prayer, both when he lays him down to sleep
And when he rises up from dreaming it;
One supplication, one desire, one hope,
That He would grant a wish for his two sons,
Even all that he demands in their regard—
And suddenly, beyond his dearest hope,
It is accomplished, he should then rejoice,
And call his friends and kinsmen to a feast,
And task their love to grace his merriment,
Then honour me thus far—for I am he.
Beatr. [*to* LUCRETIA]. Great God! How horrible! Some dreadful ill
Must have befallen my brothers.
Lucr.   Fear not, child,
He speaks too frankly.
Beatr. Ah! my blood runs cold.
I fear that wicked laughter round his eye,
Which wrinkles up the skin even to the hair.
Cen. Here are the letters brought from Salamanca;
Beatrice, read them to your mother. God,
I thank thee! In one night didst thou perform,
By ways inscrutable, the thing I sought.
My disobedient and rebellious sons
Are dead!—Why dead!—What means this change of cheer?
You hear me not, I tell you they are dead;
And they will need no food or raiment more:
The tapers that did light them the dark way
Are their last cost. The Pope, I think, will not

Expect I should maintain them in their coffins,
Rejoice with me, my heart is wondrous glad.

   Beatr. [LUCRETIA *sinks, half fainting;* BEATRICE *supports
     her.*]   It is not true!—Dear lady, pray look up.
Had it been true, there is a God in Heaven,
He would not live to boast of such a boon.
Unnatural man, thou knowest that it is false.

   Cen. Ay, as the word of God; whom here I call
To witness that I speak the sober truth;
And whose most favouring Providence was shown
Even in the manner of their deaths. For Rocco
Was kneeling at the mass, with sixteen others,
When the church fell and crushed him to a mummy;
The rest escaped unhurt. Cristofano
Was stabbed in error by a jealous man,
Whilst she he loved was sleeping with his rival;
All in the self-same hour of the same night;
Which shows that Heaven has special care of me.
I beg those friends who love me, that they mark
The day a feast upon their calendars.
It was the twenty-seventh of December:
Ay, read the letters if you doubt my oath.

       [*The assembly appears confused; several of the guests rise.*
   First Guest. Oh, horrible! I will depart.
   Second Guest. And I.
   Third Guest. No, stay!
I do believe it is some jest; though faith,
'Tis mocking us somewhat too solemnly.
I think his son has married the Infanta,
Or found a mine of gold in Eldorado;
'Tis but to season some such news; stay, stay!
I see 'tis only raillery by his smile.

   Cen. [*Filling a bowl of wine, and lifting it up.*] Oh, thou bright
   wine, whose purple splendour leaps
And bubbles gaily in this golden bowl
Under the lamplight, as my spirits do,
To hear the death of my accursed sons!
Could I believe thou wert their mingled blood,
Then would I taste thee like a sacrament,
And pledge with thee the mighty Devil in Hell;
Who, if a father's curses, as men say,
Climb with swift wings after their children's souls,
And drag them from the very throne of Heaven,
Now triumphs in my triumph!—But thou art
Superfluous; I have drunken deep of joy,
And I will taste no other wine to-night.
Here, Andrea! Bear the bowl around.

   A Guest [*rising*]. Thou wretch!
Will none among this noble company
Check the abandoned villain?

   Cam. For God's sake
Let me dismiss the guests! You are insane,
Some ill will come of this.

   Second Guest. Seize, silence him!
   First Guest. I will!
   Third Guest. And I!

   Cen. [*Addressing those who rise with a threatening gesture*].
Who moves? Who speaks?

[*Turning to the company.*]
     'Tis nothing,
Enjoy yourselves.—Beware ! For my revenge
is as the sealed commission of a king,
That kills, and none dare name the murderer.
   [*The banquet is broken up; several of the guests are departing*
 Beatr. I do entreat you, go not, noble guests;
What, although tyranny and impious hate
Stand sheltered by a father's hoary hair ?
What, if 'tis he who clothed us in these limbs
Who tortures them, and triumphs ?   What, if we,
The desolate and the dead, were his own flesh,
His children and his wife, whom he is bound
To love and shelter?   Shall we therefore find
No refuge in this merciless wide world?
Oh, think what deep wrongs must have blotted out
First love, then reverence in a child's prone mind,
Till it thus vanquish shame and fear !   O think !
I have borne much, and kissed the sacred hand
Which crushed us to the earth, and thought its stroke
Was perhaps some paternal chastisement !
Have excused much, doubted; and when no doubt
Remained, have sought by patience, love and tears,
To soften him ; and when this could not be,
I have knelt down through the long sleepless nights,
And lifted up to God, the Father of all,
Passionate prayers: and when these were not heard
I have still borne;—until I meet you here,
Princes and kinsmen, at this hideous feast
Given at my brothers' deaths.   Two yet remain,
His wife remains and I, whom if ye save not,
Ye may soon share such merriment again
As fathers make over their children's graves.
Oh ! Prince Colonna, thou art our near kinsman;
Cardinal, thou art the Pope's chamberlain;
Camillo, thou art chief justiciary;
Take us away !
 Cen. [*He has been conversing with* CAMILLO *during the first part of*
  BEATRICE'S *speech; he hears the conclusion, and now advances*].
I hope my good friends here
Will think of their own daughters—or perhaps
Of their own throats—before they lend an ear
To this wild girl.
 Beatr. [*Not noticing the words of* CENCI].   Dare no one look on me?
None answer ?   Can one tyrant overbear
The sense of many best and wisest men ?
Or is it that I sue not in some form
Of scrupulous law, that ye deny my suit ?
Oh, God ! That I were buried with my brothers !
And that the flowers of this departed spring
Were fading on my grave !   And that my father
Were celebrating now one feast for all !
 Cam. A bitter wish for one so young and gentle;
Can we do nothing?
 Colon. Nothing that I see.
Count Cenci were a dangerous enemy:
Yet I would second any one.
 A Card. And I.

Cen. Retire to your chamber, insolent girl !

Beatr. Retire thou, impious man ! Ay, hide thyself
Where never eye can look upon thee more !
Wouldst thou have honour and obedience,
Who art a torturer? Father, never dream,
Though thou mayst overbear this company,
But ill must come of ill.—Frown not on me !
Haste, hide thyself, lest with avenging looks
My brothers' ghosts should hunt thee from thy seat !
Cover thy face from every living eye,
And start if thou but hear a human step:
Seek out some dark and silent corner, there
Bow thy white head before offended God,
And we will kneel around, and fervently
Pray that he pity both ourselves and thee.

Cen. My friends, I do lament this insane girl
Hath spoilt the mirth of our festivity.
Good night, farewell; I will not make you longer
Spectators of our dull domestic quarrels.
Another time.—   [*Exeunt all but* CENCI *and* BEATRICE
             My brain is swimming round;
Give me a bowl of wine !
    [*To* BEATRICE].   Thou painted viper !
Beast that thou art ! Fair and yet terrible !
I know a charm shall make thee meek and tame,
Now get thee from my sight !   [*Exit* BEATRICE
             Here, Andrea,
Fill up this goblet with Greek wine. I said
I would not drink this evening; but I must;
For, strange to say, I feel my spirits fail
With thinking what I have decreed to do.   [*Drinking the wine.*
Be thou the resolution of quick youth
Within my veins, and manhood's purpose stern,
And age's firm, cold, subtle villany;
As if thou wert indeed my children's blood
Which I did thirst to drink. The charm works well;
It must be done; it shall be done, I swear !   [*Exit*

ACT II.

SCENE I.—*An Apartment in the Cenci Palace.*

Enter LUCRETIA *and* BERNARDO.

Lucr. Weep not, my gentle boy; he struck but me,
Who have borne deeper wrongs. In truth, if he
Had killed me, he had done a kinder deed.
O, God Almighty, do thou look upon us,
We have no other friend but only Thee !
Yet weep not; though I love you as my own,
I am not your true mother.

Ber.   Oh more, more,
Than ever mother was to any child,
That have you been to me ! Had he not been
My father, do you think that I should weep?

Lucr. Alas ! Poor boy, what else couldst thou have done?

Enter BEATRICE.

Beatr. [*In a hurried voice*]. Did he pass this way? Have you
    seen him, brother?
Ah! No, that is his step upon the stairs;
'Tis nearer now; his hand is on the door;
Mother, if I to thee have ever been
A duteous child, now save me! Thou great God,
Whose image upon earth a father is,
Dost thou indeed abandon me? He comes;
The door is opening now; I see his face;
He frowns on others, but he smiles on me,
Even as he did after the feast last night.

Enter a Servant.

Almighty God, how merciful thou art!
'Tis but Orsino's servant.—Well, what news?
    Serv. My master bids me say, the Holy Father
Has sent back your petition thus unopened.   [*Giving a paper*
And he demands at what hour 'twere secure
To visit you again?
    Lucr. At the Ave Mary.   [*Exit* Servant
So, daughter, our last hope has failed; Ah me,
How pale you look; you tremble, and you stand
Wrapped in some fixed and fearful meditation,
As if one thought were over strong for you:
Your eyes have a chill glare; O dearest child!
Are you gone mad? If not, pray speak to me.
    Beatr. You see I am not mad; I speak to you.
    Lucr. You talked of something that your father did
After that dreadful feast? Could it be worse
Than when he smiled, and cried, My sons are dead!
And every one looked in his neighbour's face
To see if others were as white as he?
At the first word he spoke I felt the blood
Rush to my heart, and fell into a trance;
And when it past I sat all weak and wild;
Whilst you alone stood up, and with strong words
Checked his unnatural pride; and I could see
The devil was rebuked that lives in him.
Until this hour thus you have ever stood
Between us and your father's moody wrath
Like a protecting presence: your firm mind
Has been our only refuge and defence:
What can have thus subdued it? What can now
Have given you that cold melancholy look,
Succeeding to your unaccustomed fear?
    Beatr. What is it that you say? I was just thinking
'Twere better not to struggle any more.
Men, like my father, have been dark and bloody,
Yet never—O! before worse comes of it
'Twere wise to die: it ends in that at last.
    Lucr. Oh, talk not so, dear child! Tell me at once
What did your father do or say to you?
He stayed not after that accursed feast
One moment in your chamber.—Speak to me.
    Ber. Oh, sister, sister, prithee, speak to us!

Beatr. [*Speaking very slowly with a forced calmness*]. It was
   one word, mother, one little word ;
One look, one smile.
   [*Wildly*]. Oh ! He has trampled me
Under his feet, and made the blood stream down
My pallid cheeks.   And he has given us all
Ditch water, and the fever-stricken flesh
Of buffaloes, and bade us eat or starve,
And we have eaten.   He has made me look
On my beloved Bernardo, when the rust
Of heavy chains has gangrened his sweet limbs,
And I have never yet despaired—but now !
What would I say?   [*Recovering herself.*
               Ah ! No, 'tis nothing new.
The sufferings we all share have made me wild :
He only struck and cursed me as he passed ;
He said, he looked, he did ;—nothing at all
Beyond his wont, yet it disordered me.
Alas ! I am forgetful of my duty,
I should preserve my senses for your sake.
   Lucr. Nay, Beatrice ; have courage, my sweet girl.
If any one despairs it should be I,
Who loved him once, and now must live with him
Till God in pity call for him or me.
For you may, like your sister, find some husband,
And smile, years hence, with children round your knees;
Whilst I, then dead, and all this hideous coil,
Shall be remembered only as a dream.
   Beatr. Talk not to me, dear lady, of a husband.
Did you not nurse me when my mother died?
Did you not shield me and that dearest boy?
And had we any other friend but you
In infancy, with gentle words and looks,
To win our father not to murder us?
And shall I now desert you?   May the ghost
Of my dead mother plead against my soul
If I abandon her who filled the place
She left, with more, even, than a mother's love !
   Ber. And I am of my sister's mind.   Indeed
I would not leave you in this wretchedness,
Even though the Pope should make me free to live
In some blithe place, like others of my age,
With sports, and delicate food, and the fresh air.
Oh, never think that I will leave you, mother !
   Lucr. My dear, dear children !

                Enter CENCI, *suddenly.*

   Cen. What, Beatrice here !
Come hither !   [*She shrinks back, and covers her face.*
               Nay, hide not your face, 'tis fair ;
Look up !   Why, yesternight you dared to look
With disobedient insolence upon me,
Bending a stern and an inquiring brow
On what I meant; whilst I then sought to hide
That which I came to tell you—but in vain.
   Beatr. [*Wildly staggering towards the door*]. Oh, that the
   earth would gape !   Hide me, oh God?

Cen. Then it was I whose inarticulate words
Fell from my lips, and who with tottering steps
Fled from your presence, as you now from mine.
Stay, I command you: from this day and hour
Never again, I think, with fearless eye,
And brow superior, and unaltered cheek,
And that lip made for tenderness or scorn,
Shalt thou strike dumb the meanest of mankind;
Me least of all.   Now get thee to thy chamber!
Thou, too, loathed image of thy cursed mother,

                                   [*To* BERNARDO.
Thy milky, meek face makes me sick with hate!
                    [*Exeunt* BEATRICE *and* BERNARDO.
  [*Aside*]. So much has past between us as must make
Me bold, her fearful.   'Tis an awful thing
To touch such mischief as I now conceive:
So men sit shivering on the dewy bank,
And try the chill stream with their feet; once in—
How the delighted spirit pants for joy!
  Lucr. [*Advancing timidly towards him*]. Oh, husband! Pray
      forgive poor Beatrice,
She meant not any ill.
  Cen. Nor you perhaps?
Nor that young imp, whom you have taught by rote
Parricide with his alphabet?   Nor Giacomo?
Nor those two most unnatural sons, who stirred
Enmity up against me with the Pope?
Whom in one night merciful God cut off:
Innocent lambs!   They thought not any ill.
You were not here conspiring?   You said nothing
Of how I might be dungeoned as a madman;
Or be condemned to death for some offence,
And you would be the witnesses?—This failing,
How just it were to hire assassins, or
Put sudden poison in my evening drink?
Or smother me when overcome by wine?
Seeing we had no other judge but God,
And he had sentenced me, and there were none
But you to be the executioners
Of his decree enregistered in heaven?
Oh, no!   You said not this?
  Lucr. So help me God,
I never thought the things you charge me with!
  Cen. If you dare speak that wicked lie again
I'll kill you.   What! It was not by your counsel
That Beatrice disturbed the feast last night?
You did not hope to stir some enemies
Against me, and escape, and laugh to scorn
What every nerve of you now trembles at?
You judged that men were bolder than they are;
Few dare to stand between their grave and me.
  Lucr. Look not so dreadfully!   By my salvation,
I knew not aught that Beatrice designed;
Nor do I think she designed anything
Until she heard you talk of her dead brothers.
  Cen. Blaspheming liar!   You are damned for this
But I will take you where you may persuade
The stones you tread on to deliver you:

For men shall there be none but those who dare
All things; not question that which I command.
On Wednesday next I shall set out: you know
That savage rock, the Castle of Petrella:
'Tis safely walled, and moated round about:
Its dungeons under ground, and its thick towers,
Never tell tales; though they have heard and seen
What might make dumb things speak. Why do you linger?
Make speediest preparation for the journey! [*Exit* LUCRETIA.
The all-beholding sun yet shines; I hear
A busy stir of men about the streets;
I see the bright sky through the window panes:
It is a garish, broad and peering day;
Loud, light, suspicious, full of eyes and ears;
And every little corner, nook, and hole,
Is penetrated with the insolent light.
Come, darkness! Yet, what is the day to me?
And wherefore should I wish for night, who do
A deed which shall confound both night and day?
'Tis she shall grope through a bewildering mist
Of horror: if there be a sun in heaven
She shall not dare to look upon its beams,
Nor feel its warmth. Let her then wish for night;
The act I think shall soon extinguish all
For me: I bear a darker deadlier gloom
Than the earth's shade, or interlunar air
Or constellations quenched in murkiest cloud,
In which I walk secure and unbeheld
Towards my purpose.—Would that it were done! [*Exit.*

SCENE II.—*A Chamber in the Vatican.*

Enter CAMILLO *and* GIACOMO, *in conversation.*

Cam. There is an obsolete and doubtful law
By which you might obtain a bare provision
Of food and clothing—
Giac. Nothing more? Alas!
Bare must be the provision which strict law
Awards, and aged, sullen avarice pays.
Why did my father not apprentice me
To some mechanic trade? I should have then
Been trained in no high-born necessities
Which I could meet not by my daily toil.
The eldest son of a rich nobleman
Is heir to all his incapacities;
He has wide wants, and narrow powers. If you,
Cardinal Camillo, were reduced at once
From thrice-driven beds of down, and delicate food,
An hundred servants, and six palaces,
To that which nature doth indeed require?
Cam. Nay, there is reason in your plea; 'twere hard
Giac. 'Tis hard for a firm man to bear: but I
Have a dear wife, a lady of high birth,
Whose dowry in ill hour I lent my father,
Without a bond or witness to the deed:
And children, who inherit her fine senses,
The fairest creatures in this breathing world;

T

And she and they reproach me not.   Cardinal,
Do you not think the Pope would interpose,
And stretch authority beyond the law?
    Çam. Though your peculiar case is hard, I know
The Pope will not divert the course of law.
After that impious feast the other night
I spoke with him, and urged him then to check
Your father's cruel hand; he frowned and said,
" Children are disobedient, and they sting
Their fathers' hearts to madness and despair,
Requiting years of care with contumely.
I pity the Count Cenci from my heart;
His outraged love perhaps awakened hate,
And thus he is exasperated to ill.
In the great war between the old and young,
I, who have white hairs and a tottering body,
Will keep at least blameless neutrality."

Enter ORSINO.

You, my good Lord Orsino, heard those words.
    Ors. What words?
    Giac. Alas, repeat them not again!
There then is no redress for me; at least
None but that which I may achieve myself,
Since I am driven to the brink. But, say,
My innocent sister and my only brother
Are dying underneath my father's eye.
The memorable torturers of this land,
Galeaz Visconti, Borgia, Ezzelin,
Never inflicted on their meanest slave
What these endure; shall they have no protection?
    Cam. Why, if they would petition to the Pope
I see not how he could refuse it—yet
He holds it of most dangerous example
In aught to weaken the paternal power,
Being, as 'twere, the shadow of his own.
I pray you now excuse me. I have business
That will not bear delay.   [*Exit* CAMILLO.
    Giac. But you, Orsino,
Have the petition: wherefore not present it?
    Ors. I have presented it, and backed it with
My earnest prayers, and urgent interest;
It was returned unanswered. I doubt not
But that the strange and execrable deeds
Alleged in it (in truth they might well baffle
Any belief) have turned the Pope's displeasure
Upon the accusers from the criminal;
So I should guess from what Camillo said.
    Giac. My friend, that palace-walking devil, Gold,
Has whispered silence to his Holiness:
And we are left, as scorpions ringed with fire,
What should we do but strike ourselves to death?
For he who is our murderous persecutor
Is shielded by a father's holy name,
Or I would—   [*Stops abruptly.*
    Ors. What? Fear not to speak your thought.
Words are but holy as the deeds they cover:
A priest who has forsworn the God he serves;

A judge who makes truth weep at his decree;
A friend who should weave counsel, as I now,
But as the mantle of some selfish guile;
A father who is all a tyrant seems,
Were the profaner for his sacred name.

Giac. Ask me not what I think; the unwilling brain
Feigns often what it would not; and we trust
Imagination with such fantasies
As the tongue dares not fashion into words;
Which have no words, their horror makes them dim
To the mind's eye.   My heart denies itself
To think what you demand.

   Ors. But a friend's bosom
Is as the inmost cave of our own mind,
Where we sit shut from the wide gaze of day,
And from the all-communicating air.
You look what I suspected.

   Giac. Spare me now!
I am as one lost in a midnight wood,
Who dares not ask some harmless passenger
The path across the wilderness, lest he,
As my thoughts are, should be—a murderer.
I know you are my friend, and all I dare
Speak to my soul, that will I trust with thee.
But now my heart is heavy, and would take
Lone counsel from a night of sleepless care.
Pardon me, that I say farewell—farewell !
I would that to my own suspected self
I could address a word so full of peace.

   Ors. Farewell !—Be your thoughts better or more bold.
                           [*Exit* GIACOMO.

I had disposed the Cardinal Camillo
To feed his hope with cold encouragement:
It fortunately serves my close designs
That 'tis a trick of this same family
To analyse their own and other minds.
Such self-anatomy shall teach the will
Dangerous secrets: for it tempts our powers,
Knowing what must be thought, and may be done,
Into the depth of darkest purposes:
So Cenci fell into the pit; even I,
Since Beatrice unveiled me to myself,
And made me shrink from what I cannot shun,
Show a poor figure to my own esteem,
To which I grow half reconciled.   I'll do
As little mischief as I can; that thought
Shall fee the accuser conscience.   [*After a pause.*
            Now what harm
If Cenci should be murdered?—Yet, if murdered,
Wherefore by me?   And what if I could take
The profit, yet omit the sin and peril
In such an action?   Of all earthly things
I fear a man whose blows outspeed his words;
And such is Cenci: and while Cenci lives
His daughter's dowry were a secret grave,
If a priest wins her.—Oh, fair Beatrice !
Would that I loved thee not, or loving thee
Could but despise danger and gold, and all

That frowns between my wish and its effect,
Or smiles beyond it !   There is no escape:
Her bright form kneels beside me at the altar,
And follows me to the resort of men,
And fills my slumber with tumultuous dreams,
So, when I wake, my blood seems liquid fire;
And if I strike my damp and dizzy head,
My hot palm scorches it: her very name,
But spoken by a stranger, makes my heart
Sicken and pant; and thus unprofitably
I clasp the phantom of unfelt delights,
Till weak imagination half possesses
The self-created shadow.   Yet much longer
Will I not nurse this life of feverous hours:
From the unravelled hopes of Giacomo
I must work out my own dear purposes.
I see, as from a tower, the end of all:
Her father dead; her brother bound to me
By a dark secret, surer than the grave;
Her mother scared and unexpostulating
From the dread manner of her wish achieved:
And she !—Once more take courage, my faint heart;
What dares a friendless maiden matched with thee?
I have such foresight as assures success:
Some unbeheld divinity doth ever,
When dread events are near, stir up men's minds
To black suggestions; and he prospers best,
Not who becomes the instrument of ill,
But who can flatter the dark spirit, that makes
Its empire and its prey of other hearts,
Till it become his slave—as I will do.   [*Exit.*

ACT III.

SCENE I.—*An Apartment in the Cenci Palace.*

LUCRETIA, *to her enter* BEATRICE.

Beatr. [*She enters staggering, and speaks wildly*].
Reach me that handkerchief!—My brain is hurt;
My eyes are full of blood; just wipe them for me—
I see but indistinctly:—
   Lucr. My sweet child,
You have no wound; 'tis only a cold dew
That starts from your dear brow—Alas! alas!
What has befallen?
   Beatr. How comes this hair undone?
Its wandering strings must be what blind me so,
And yet I tied it fast.—O horrible!
The pavement sinks under my feet! The walls
Spin round! I see a woman weeping there,
And standing calm and motionless, whilst I
Slide giddily as the world reels—My God!
The beautiful blue heaven is flecked with blood!
The sunshine on the floor is black! The air

Is changed to vapours such as the dead breathe
In charnel pits! Pah! I am choked! There creeps
A clinging, black, contaminating mist
About me—'tis substantial, heavy, thick,
I cannot pluck it from me, for it glues
My fingers and my limbs to one another,
And eats into my sinews, and dissolves
My flesh to a pollution, poisoning
The subtle, pure, and inmost spirit of life!
My God! I never knew what the mad felt
Before; for I am mad beyond all doubt!   [*More wildly.*
No, I am dead! These putrefying limbs
Shut round and sepulchre the panting soul,
Which would burst forth into the wandering air! [*A pause.*
What hideous thought was that I had even now?
'Tis gone; and yet its burden remains here
O'er these dull eyes—upon this weary heart!
O world! O life! O day! O misery!
   Lucr. What ails thee, my poor child? She answers not!
Her spirit apprehends the sense of pain,
But not its cause; suffering has dried away
The source from which it sprung.
   Beatr. [*frantically*]. Like parricide—
Misery has killed its father: yet its father
Never like mine—O, God! What thing am I?
   Lucr. My dearest child, what has your father done?
   Beatr. [*doubtfully*]. Who art thou, questioner? I have no
      father.
   [*Aside*]. She is the mad-house nurse who tends on me,
It is a piteous office.
   [*To* LUCRETIA, *in a slow, subdued voice*]. Do you know
I thought I was that wretched Beatrice
Men speak of, whom her father sometimes hales
From hall to hall by the entangled hair;
At others, pens up naked in damp cells
Where scaly reptiles crawl, and starves her there,
Till she will eat strange flesh. This woful story
So did I overact in my sick dreams,
That I imagined—no, it cannot be!
Horrible things have been in this wild world,
Prodigious mixtures, and confusions strange
Of good and ill; and worse have been conceived
Than ever there was found a heart to do.
But never fancy imaged such a deed
As—   [*Pauses, suddenly recollecting herself.*
Who art thou? Swear to me, ere I die
With fearful expectation, that indeed
Thou art not what thou seemest—Mother!
   Lucr. Oh!
My sweet child, know you—
   Beatr. Yet speak it not:
For then if this be truth, that other too
Must be a truth, a firm enduring truth,
Linked with each lasting circumstance of life,
Never to change, never to pass away.
Why so it is. This is the Cenci Palace;
Thou art Lucretia: I am Beatrice.
I have talked some wild words, but will no more,

Mother, come near me: from this point of time,
I am—   [*Her voice dies away faintly.*
   Lucr. Alas! What has befallen thee, child?
What has thy father done?
   Beatr. What have I done?
Am I not innocent? Is it my crime
That one with white hair, and imperious brow,
Who tortured me from my forgotten years,
As parents only dare, should call himself
My father, yet should be! Oh, what am I?
What name, what place, what memory shall be mine?
What retrospects, outliving even despair?
   Lucr. He is a violent tyrant, surely, child:
We know that death alone can make us free;
His death or ours. But what can he have done
Of deadlier outrage or worse injury?
Thou art unlike thyself; thine eyes shoot forth
A wandering and strange spirit. Speak to me,
Unlock those pallid hands whose fingers twine
With one another.
   Beatr. 'Tis the restless life
Tortured within them. If I try to speak
I shall go mad. Ay, something must be done;
What, yet I know not—something which shall make
The thing that I have suffered but a shadow
In the dread lightning which avenges it;
Brief, rapid, irreversible, destroying
The consequence of what it cannot cure.
Some such thing is to be endured or done:
When I know what, I shall be still and calm,
And never anything will move me more.
But now!—Oh blood, which art my father's blood,
Circling through these contaminated veins,
If thou, poured forth on the polluted earth,
Could wash away the crime, and punishment
By which I suffer—no, that cannot be!
Many might doubt there were a God above
Who sees and permits evil, and so die:
That faith no agony shall obscure in me.
   Lucr. It must indeed have been some bitter wrong;
Yet what, I dare not guess. Oh, my lost child,
Hide not in proud impenetrable grief
Thy sufferings from my fear.
   Beatr. I hide them not.
What are the words which you would have me speak?
I, who can feign no image in my mind
Of that which has transformed me: I, whose thought
Is like a ghost shrouded and folded up
In its own formless horror: of all words,
That minister to mortal intercourse,
Which wouldst thou hear? For there is none to tell
My misery; if another ever knew
Aught like to it, she died as I will die,
And left it, as I must, without a name.
Death! Death! Our law and our religion call thee
A punishment and a reward.—Oh, which
Have I deserved?
   Lucr. The peace of innocence;

Till in your season you be called to heaven.
Whate'er you may have suffered, you have done
No evil.   Death must be the punishment
Of crime, or the reward of trampling down
The thorns which God has strewed upon the path
Which leads to immortality.
    Beatr. Ay, death—
The punishment of crime.   I pray thee, God,
Let me not be bewildered while I judge.
If I must live day after day, and keep
These limbs, the unworthy temple of thy spirit,
As a foul den from which what thou abhorrest
May mock thee, unavenged—it shall not be!
Self-murder? no, that might be no escape,
For thy decree yawns like a Hell between
Our will and it.   O! in this mortal world
There is no vindication and no law
Which can adjudge and execute the doom
Of that through which I suffer.

Enter ORSINO.

[*She approaches him solemnly*].   Welcome, friend!
I have to tell you that, since last we met,
I have endured a wrong so great and strange,
That neither life nor death can give me rest.
Ask me not what it is, for there are deeds
Which have no form, sufferings which have no tongue.
    Ors. And what is he who has thus injured you?
    Beatr. The man they call my father: a dread name.
    Ors. It cannot be—
    Beatr. What it can be, or not,
Forbear to think.   It is, and it has been;
Advise me how it shall not be again.
I thought to die, but a religious awe
Restrains me, and the dread lest death itself
Might be no refuge from the consciousness
Of what is yet unexpiated.   Oh, speak!
    Ors. Accuse him of the deed, and let the law
Avenge thee.
    Beatr. Oh, ice-hearted counsellor!
If I could find a word that might make known
The crime of my destroyer; and that done,
My tongue should, like a knife, tear out the secret
Which cankers my heart's core; ay, lay all bare,
So that my unpolluted fame should be
With vilest gossips a stale-mouthed story;
A mock, a byword, an astonishment:—
If this were done, which never shall be done,
Think of the offender's gold, his dreaded hate,
And the strange horror of the accuser's tale,
Baffling belief, and overpowering speech;
Scarce whispered, unimaginable, wrapt
In hideous hints—Oh, most assured redress!
    Ors. You will endure it then?
    Beatr. Endure!   Orsino,
It seems your counsel is small profit.   [*Turns from him, and
    speaks half to herself.*]   Ay,

All must be suddenly resolved and done.
What is this undistinguishable mist
Of thoughts, which rise, like shadow after shadow,
Darkening each other?
 Ors. Should the offender live?
Triumph in his misdeed? and make, by use,
His crime, whate'er it is, dreadful no doubt,
Thine element; until thou mayst become
Utterly lost; subdued even to the hue
Of that which thou permittest?
 Beatr. [*To herself*]. Mighty death!
Thou double-visaged shadow! Only judge!
Rightfullest arbiter!   [*She retires absorbed in thought.*
 Lucr. If the lightning
Of God has e'er descended to avenge—
 Ors. Blaspheme not! His high Providence commits
Its glory on this earth, and their own wrongs
Into the hands of men; if they neglect
To punish crime—
 Lucr. But if one, like this wretch,
Should mock, with gold, opinion, law, and power?
If there be no appeal to that which makes
The guiltiest tremble? If, because our wrongs,
For that they are unnatural, strange, and monstrous,
Exceed all measure of belief? Oh, God!
If, for the very reasons which should make
Redress most swift and sure, our injurer triumphs?
And we, the victims, bear worse punishment
Than that appointed for their torturer?
 Ors. Think not
But that there is redress where there is wrong,
So we be bold enough to seize it.
 Lucr. How?
If there were any way to make all sure,
I know not—but I think it might be good
To—
 Ors. Why, his late outrage to Beatrice;
For it is such, as I but faintly guess,
As makes remorse dishonour, and leaves her
Only one duty, how she may avenge:
You, but one refuge from ills ill endured;
Me, but one counsel—
 Lucr. For we cannot hope
That aid, or retribution, or resource,
Will arise thence, where every other one
Might find them with less need.

    [BEATRICE *advances.*]

 Ors. Then—
 Beatr. Peace, Orsino!
And, honoured lady, while I speak, I pray,
That you put off, as garments overworn,
Forbearance and respect, remorse and fear,
And all the fit restraints of daily life,
Which have been borne from childhood, but which now
Would be a mockery to my holier plea.
As I have said, I have endured a wrong,

Which, though it be expressionless, is such
As asks atonement, both for what is past,
And lest I be reserved, day after day,
To load with crimes an overburdened soul,
And be—what ye can dream not.   I have prayed
To God, and I have talked with my own heart,
And have unravelled my entangled will,
And have at length determined what is right.
Art thou my friend, Orsino?   False or true?
Pledge thy salvation ere I speak.

 Ors. I swear
To dedicate my cunning, and my strength,
My silence, and whatever else is mine,
To thy commands.

 Lucr. You think we should devise
His death?

 Beatr. And execute what is devised,
And suddenly.   We must be brief and bold.

 Ors. And yet most cautious.

 Lucr. For the jealous laws
Would punish us with death and infamy
For that which it became themselves to do.

 Beatr. Be cautious as ye may, but prompt, Orsina.
What are the means?

 Ors. I know two dull, fierce outlaws,
Who think man's spirit as a worm's, and they
Would trample out, for any slight caprice,
The meanest or the noblest life.   This mood
Is marketable here in Rome.   They sell
What we now want.

 Lucr. To-morrow, before dawn,
Cenci will take us to that lonely rock,
Petrella, in the Apulian Apennines.
If we arrive there—

 Beatr. He must not arrive.

 Ors. Will it be dark before you reach the tower?

 Lucr. The sun will scarce be set.

 Beatr. But I remember
Two miles on this side of the fort, the road
Crosses a deep ravine; 'tis rough and narrow,
And winds with short turns down the precipice;
And in its depth there is a mighty rock,
Which has, from unimaginable years,
Sustained itself with terror and with toil
Over a gulf, and with the agony
With which it clings seems slowly coming down;
Even as a wretched soul hour after hour,
Clings to the mass of life; yet clinging, leans;
And leaning, makes more dark the dread abyss
In which it fears to fall: beneath this crag,
Huge as despair, as if in weariness,
The melancholy mountain yawns; below,
You hear but see not an impetuous torrent
Raging among the caverns, and a bridge
Crosses the chasm: and high above there grow,
With intersecting trunks, from crag to crag,
Cedars, and yews, and pines; whose tangled hair
Is matted in one solid roof of shade

By the dark ivy's twine. At noonday here
'Tis twilight, and at sunset blackest night.

    Ors. Before you reach that bridge make some excuse
For spurring on your mules, or loitering
Until—

    Beatr. What sound is that?

    Lucr. Hark ! No, it cannot be a servant's step;
It must be Cenci, unexpectedly
Returned—Make some excuse for being here.

    Beatr. [*To* ORSINI, *as she goes out*]. That step we hear approa
    must never pass
The bridge of which we spoke. [*Exeunt* LUCRETIA *and* BEATRIC

    Ors. What shall I do?
Cenci must find me here, and I must bear
The imperious inquisition of his looks
As to what brought me hither: let me mask
Mine own in some inane and vacant smile.

Enter GIACOMO, *in a hurried manner.*

How ! Have you ventured hither? Know you then
That Cenci is from home ?

    Giac. I sought him here;
And now must wait till he returns.

    Ors. Great God !
Weigh you the danger of this rashness?

    Giac. Ay !
Does my destroyer know his danger? We
Are now no more, as once, parent and child,
But man to man ; the oppressor to the oppressed ;
The slanderer to the slandered ; foe to foe.
He has cast Nature off, which was his shield,
And Nature casts him off, who is her shame;
And I spurn both. Is it a father's throat
Which I will shake, and say, I ask not gold ;
I ask not happy years ; nor memories
Of tranquil childhood ; nor home-sheltered love ;
Though all these hast thou torn from me, and more ;
But only my fair fame ; only one hoard
Of peace, which I thought hidden from thy hate,
Under the penury heaped on me by thee ;
Or I will—God can understand and pardon,
Why should I speak with man ?

    Ors. Be calm, dear friend.

    Giac. Well, I will calmly tell you what he did.
This old Francesco Cenci, as you know,
Borrowed the dowry of my wife from me,
And then denied the loan ; and left me so
In poverty, the which I sought to mend
By holding a poor office in the state.
It had been promised to me, and already
I bought new clothing for my ragged babes,
And my wife smiled ; and my heart knew repose ;
When Cenci's intercession, as I found,
Conferred this office on a wretch, whom thus
He paid for vilest service. I returned
With this ill news, and we sate sad together
Solacing our despondency with tears
Of such affection and unbroken faith

As temper life's worst bitterness ; when he,
As he is wont, came to upbraid and curse,
Mocking our poverty, and telling us
Such was God's scourge for disobedient sons.
And then, that I might strike him dumb with shame,
I spoke of my wife's dowry ; but he coined
A brief yet specious tale, how I had wasted
The sum in secret riot ; and he saw
My wife was touched, and he went smiling forth.
And when I knew the impression he had made,
And felt my wife insult with silent scorn
My ardent truth, and look averse and cold,
I went forth too ; but soon returned again ;
Yet not so soon but that my wife had taught
My children her harsh thoughts, and they all cried,
" Give us clothes, father ! Give us better food !
What you in one night squander were enough
For months !" I looked, and saw that home was hell ;
And to that hell will I return no more
Until mine enemy has rendered up
Atonement, or, as he gave life to me
I will, reversing nature's law—
    Ors. Trust me,
The compensation which thou seekest here
Will be denied.
    Giac. Then—Are you not my friend ?
Did you not hint at the alternative,
Upon the brink of which you see I stand,
The other day when we conversed together ?
My wrongs were then less. That word parricide,
Although I am resolved, haunts me like fear.
    Ors. It must be fear itself, for the bare word
Is hollow mockery. Mark, how wisest God
Draws to one point the threads of a just doom,
So sanctifying it : what you devise
Is, as it were, accomplished.
    Giac. Is he dead ?
    Ors. His grave is ready. Know that since we met
Cenci has done an outrage to his daughter.
    Giac. What outrage ?
    Ors. That she speaks not, but you may
Conceive such half conjectures as I do,
From her fixed paleness, and the lofty grief
Of her stern brow, bent on the idle air,
And her severe unmodulated voice,
Drowning both tenderness and dread ; and last
From this—that whilst her stepmother and I,
Bewildered in our horror, talked together
With obscure hints ; both self-misunderstood,
And darkly guessing, stumbling, in our talk,
Over the truth, and yet to its revenge,
She interrupted us, and with a look
Which told before she spoke it, he must die :—
    Giac. It is enough. My doubts are well appeased ;
There is a higher reason for the act
Than mine ; there is a holier judge than me,
A more unblamed avenger. Beatrice,
Who in the gentleness of thy sweet youth

Hast never trodden on a worm, or bruised
A living flower, but thou hast pitied it
With needless tears ! Fair sister, thou in whom
Men wondered how such loveliness and wisdom
Did not destroy each other ! Is there made
Ravage of thee ? O, heart, I ask no more
Justification ! Shall I wait, Orsino,
Till he return, and stab him at the door ?

   Ors. Not so ; some accident might interpose
To rescue him from what is now most sure ;
And you are unprovided where to fly,
How to excuse or to conceal. Nay, listen :
All is contrived ; success is so assured
That—

             Enter BEATRICE.

   Beatr. 'Tis my brother's voice ! You know me not ?
   Giac. My sister, my lost sister !
   Beatr. Lost indeed !
I see Orsino has talked with you, and
That you conjecture things too horrible
To speak, yet far less than the truth. Now, stay not,
He might return: yet kiss me ; I shall know
That then thou hast consented to his death.
Farewell, farewell ! Let piety to God,
Brotherly love, justice, and clemency,
And all things that make tender hardest hearts,
Make thine hard, brother. Answer not: farewell. [*Exeunt several*

SCENE II.— *A mean Apartment in Giacomo's House.* GIACOMO *alone.*

   Giac. 'Tis midnight, and Orsino comes not yet.
              [*Thunder, and the sound of a storm.*
What ! can the everlasting elements
Feel with a worm like man ? If so, the shaft
Of mercy-winged lightning would not fall
On stones and trees.   My wife and children sleep:
They are now living in unmeaning dreams :
But I must wake, still doubting if that deed
Be just, which was most necessary.   O,
Thou unreplenished lamp ! whose narrow fire
Is shaken by the wind, and on whose edge
Devouring darkness hovers !   Thou small flame,
Which, as a dying pulse rises and falls,
Still flickerest up and down, how very soon,
Did I not feed thee, wouldst thou fail, and be
As thou hadst never been ! So wastes and sinks
Even now, perhaps, the life that kindled mine :
But that no power can fill with vital oil,
That broken lamp of flesh. Ha! 'tis the blood
Which fed these veins, that ebbs till all is cold :
It is the form that moulded mine, that sinks
Into the white and yellow spasms of death:
It is the soul by which mine was arrayed
In God's immortal likeness, which now stands
Naked before Heaven's judgment seat ! [*A bell strikes.*
           One ! Two !

'The hours crawl on; and, when my hairs are white,
My son will then perhaps be waiting thus,
Tortured between just hate and vain remorse;
Chiding the tardy messenger of news
Like those which I expect. I almost wish
He be not dead, although my wrongs are great;
Yet—'tis Orsino's step—

Enter ORSINO.

Speak!

Ors. I am come
To say he has escaped.
    Giac. Escaped!
    Ors. And safe
Within Petrella. He past by the spot
Appointed for the deed an hour too soon.
    Giac. Are we the fools of such contingences?
And do we waste in blind misgivings thus
The hours when we should act? Then wind and thunder,
Which seemed to howl his knell, is the loud laughter
With which Heaven mocks our weakness! I henceforth
Will ne'er repent of aught, designed or done,
But my repentance.
    Ors. See, the lamp is out.
    Giac. If no remorse is ours when the dim air
Has drank this innocent flame, why should we quail
When Cenci's life, that light by which ill spirits
See the worst deeds they prompt, shall sink for ever?
No, I am hardened.
    Ors. Why, what need of this?
Who feared the pale intrusion of remorse
In a just deed? Although our first plan failed,
Doubt not but he will soon be laid to rest.
But light the lamp; let us not talk i' the dark.
    Giac. [*Lighting the lamp*]. And yet once quenched,
I can not thus relume
My father's life: do you not think his ghost
Might plead that argument with God?
    Ors. Once gone,
You cannot now recall your sister's peace;
Your own extinguished years of youth and hope;
Nor your wife's bitter words; nor all the taunts
Which, from the prosperous, weak misfortune takes;
Nor your dead mother; nor—
    Giac. O, speak no more!
I am resolved, although this very hand
Must quench the life that animated it.
    Ors. There is no need of that. Listen: you know
Olimpio, the castellan of Petrella
In old Colonna's time; him whom your father
Degraded from his post? And Marzio,
That desperate wretch, whom he deprived last year
Of a reward of blood, well earned and due?
    Giac. I knew Olimpio; and they say he hated
Old Cenci so, that in his silent rage
His lips grew white only to see him pass.
Of Marzio I know nothing.
    Ors. Marzio's hate

Matches Olimpio's. I have sent these men,
But in your name, and as at your request,
To talk with Beatrice and Lucretia.

   Giac. Only to talk?

   Ors. The moments which even now
Pass onward to to-morrow's midnight hour
May memorize their flight with death: ere then
They must have talked, and may perhaps have done,
And made an end—

   Giac. Listen! What sound is that?

   Ors. The house-dog moans, and the beams crack: naught else

   Giac. It is my wife complaining in her sleep:
I doubt not she is saying bitter things
Of me; and all my children round her dreaming
That I deny them sustenance.

   Ors. Whilst he
Who truly took it from them, and who fills
Their hungry rest with bitterness, now sleeps
Lapped in bad pleasures, and triumphantly
Mocks thee in visions of successful hate
Too like the truth of day.

   Giac. If e'er he wakes
Again, I will not trust to hireling hands—

   Ors. Why, that were well. I must be gone; good night:
When next we meet may all be done!

   Giac. And all
Forgotten: Oh, that I had never been!   [*Exeunt.*

ACT IV.

SCENE I.—*An Apartment in the Castle of Petrella.*

Enter CENCI.

   Cen. She comes not; yet I left her even now
Vanquished and faint. She knows the penalty
Of her delay: yet what if threats are vain?
Am I not now within Petrella's moat?
Or fear I still the eyes and ears of Rome?
Might I not drag her by the golden hair?
Stamp on her? Keep her sleepless till her brain
Be overworn? Tame her with chains and famine?
Less would suffice. Yet so to leave undone
What I most seek! No, 'tis her stubborn will,
Which, by its own consent, shall stoop as low
As that which drags it down.

Enter LUCRETIA.

               Thou loathed wretch!
Hide thee from my abhorrence; fly, begone!
Yet stay! Bid Beatrice come hither.

   Lucr. Oh,
Husband! I pray, for thine own wretched sake,
Heed what thou dost. A man who walks like thee
Through crimes, and through the danger of his crimes,
Each hour may stumble o'er a sudden grave.

And thou art old; thy hairs are hoary grey;
As thou wouldst save thyself from death and hell,
Pity thy daughter; give her to some friend
In marriage: so that she may tempt thee not
To hatred, or worse thoughts, if worse there be.

Cen. What! like her sister who has found a home
To mock my hate from with prosperity?
Strange ruin shall destroy both her and thee
And all that yet remain. My death may be
Rapid, her destiny outspeeds it. Go,
Bid her come hither, and before my mood
Be changed, lest I should drag her by the hair.

Lucr. She sent me to thee, husband. At thy presence
She fell, as thou dost know, into a trance;
And in that trance she heard a voice which said,
"Cenci must die! Let him confess himself!
Even now the accusing angel waits to hear
If God, to punish his enormous crimes,
Harden his dying heart!"

Cen. Why—such things are:
No doubt divine revealings may be made.
'Tis plain I have been favoured from above,
For when I cursed my sons they died—Ay—so—
As to the right or wrong that's talk—repentance—
Repentance is an easy moment's work,
And more depends on God than me. Well—well—
I must give up the greater point, which was
To poison and corrupt her soul. [*A pause;* LUCRETIA *approaches
anxiously, and then shrinks back as he speaks.*]

                     One, two;
Ay—Rocco and Cristofano my curse
Strangled: and Giacomo, I think, will find
Life a worse Hell than that beyond the grave:
Beatrice shall, if there be skill in hate,
Die in despair, blaspheming: to Bernardo,
He is so innocent, I will bequeath
The memory of these deeds, and make his youth
The sepulchre of hope, where evil thoughts
Shall grow like weeds on a neglected tomb.
When all is done, out in the wide Campagna
I will pile up my silver and my gold;
My costly robes, paintings, and tapestries;
My parchments and all records of my wealth;
And make a bonfire in my joy, and leave
Of my possessions nothing but my name;
Which shall be an inheritance to strip
Its wearer bare as infamy. That done,
My soul, which is a scourge, will I resign
Into the hands of Him who wielded it;
Be it for its own punishment or theirs,
He will not ask it of me till the lash
Be broken in its last and deepest wound;
Until its hate be all inflicted. Yet,
Lest death outspeed my purpose, let me make
Short work and sure—   [*Going.*

Lucr. [*Stops him*]. Oh, stay! It was a feint:
She had no vision, and she heard no voice.
I said it but to awe thee.

Cen. That is well.
Vile palterer with the sacred truth of God,
Be thy soul choked with that blaspheming lie !
For Beatrice worse terrors are in store,
To bend her to my will.
    Lucr. Oh ! to what will ?
What cruel sufferings, more than she has known,
Canst thou inflict ?
    Cen. Andrea ! Go call my daughter,
And if she comes not tell her that I come.
What sufferings ? I will drag her, step by step,
Through infamies unheard of among men :
She shall stand shelterless in the broad noon
Of public scorn, for acts blazoned abroad,
One among which shall be—What ? Canst thou guess ?
She shall become (for what she most abhors
Shall have a fascination to entrap
Her loathing will) to her own conscious self
All she appears to others ; and when dead,
As she shall die unshrived and unforgiven,
A rebel to her father and her God,
Her corpse shall be abandoned to the hounds ;
Her name shall be the terror of the earth ;
Her spirit shall approach the throne of God
Plague-spotted with my curses. I will make
Body and soul a monstrous lump of ruin.

Enter ANDREA.

    Andr. The lady Beatrice—
    Cen. Speak, pale slave ! What
Said she ?
    Andr. My Lord, 'twas what she looked ; she said,
"Go tell my father that I see the gulf
Of Hell between us two, which he may pass :
I will not."   [*Exit* ANDREA
    Cen. Go thou quick, Lucretia,
Tell her to come ; yet let her understand
Her coming is consent ; and say, moreover,
That if she come not I will curse her.   [*Exit* LUCRETIA
                         Ha !
With what but with a father's curse doth God
Panic-strike armed victory, and make pale
Cities in their prosperity ? The world's Father
Must grant a parent's prayer against his child,
Be he who asks even what men call me.
Will not the deaths of her rebellious brothers
Awe her before I speak ? For I on them
Did imprecate quick ruin, and it came.

Enter LUCRETIA.

Well ! what ? Speak, wretch !
    Lucr. She said, "I cannot come ;
Go tell my father that I see a torrent
Of his own blood raging between us."
    Cen. [*Kneeling*]. God !
Hear me ! If this most specious mass of flesh,
Which thou hast made my daughter ; this my blood,
This particle of my divided being ;

Or rather, this my bane and my disease,
Whose sight infects and poisons me; this devil
Which sprung from me as from a hell, was meant
To aught good use; if her bright loveliness
Was kindled to illumine this dark world;
If nursed by thy selectest dew of love
Such virtues blossom in her as should make
The peace of life, I pray thee, for my sake,
As thou the common God and Father art
Of her, and me, and all; reverse that doom !
Earth, in the name of God, let her food be
Poison, until she be encrusted round
With leprous stains ! Heaven, rain upon her head
The blistering drops of the Maremma's dew,
Till she be speckled like a toad; parch up
Those love-enkindled lips; warp those fine limbs
To loathed lameness ! All beholding sun,
Strike in thine envy those life-darting eyes
With thine own blinding beams !
 Lucr. Peace ! Peace !
For thine own sake unsay those dreadful words.
When high God grants, he punishes such prayers.
 Cen. [*Leaping up, and throwing his right hand towards Heaven*]
He does his will, I mine ! This in addition,
That if she have a child—
 Lucr. Horrible thought !
 Cen. That if she ever have a child ; and thou,
Quick Nature ! I adjure thee by thy God,
That thou be fruitful in her, and increase
And multiply, fulfilling his command,
And my deep imprecation ! May it be
A hideous likeness of herself; that, as
From a distorting mirror, she may see
Her image mixed with what she most abhors,
Smiling upon her from her nursing breast.
And that the child may from its infancy
Grow, day by day, more wicked and deformed,
Turning her mother's love to misery:
And that both she and it may live, until
It shall repay her care and pain with hate,
Or what may else be more unnatural.
So he may hunt her through the clamorous scoffs
Of the loud world to a dishonoured grave.
Shall I revoke this curse? Go, bid her come,
Before my words are chronicled in heaven.

       [*Exit* LUCRETIA.

I do not feel as if I were a man,
But like a fiend appointed to chastise
The offences of some unremembered world.
My blood is running up and down my veins;
A fearful pleasure makes it prick and tingle:
I feel a giddy sickness of strange awe;
My heart is beating with an expectation
Of horrid joy.

   Enter LUCRETIA.

     What ? Speak !
 Lucr. She bids thee curse;
     U

And if thy curses, as they cannot do,
Could kill her soul—
 Cen. She would not come. 'Tis well,
I can do both: first take what I demand,
And then extort concession. To thy chamber!
Fly ere I spurn thee: and beware this night
That thou cross not my footsteps. It were safer
To come between the tiger and his prey.

          [Exit LUCRETIA.

It must be late; mine eyes grow weary dim
With unaccustomed heaviness of sleep.
Conscience! Oh, thou most insolent of lies!
They say that sleep, that healing dew of heaven,
Steeps not in balm the foldings of the brain
Which thinks thee an impostor. I will go,
First to belie thee with an hour of rest,
Which will be deep and calm, I feel: and then—
O, multitudinous Hell, the fiends will shake
Thine arches with the laughter of their joy!
There shall be lamentation heard in Heaven
As o'er an angel fallen; and upon Earth
All good shall droop and sicken, and ill things
Shall, with a spirit of unnatural life,
Stir and be quickened; even as I am now.

             [Exit.

SCENE II.—*Before the Castle of Petrella.*

Enter BEATRICE *and* LUCRETIA *above on the Ramparts.*

 Beatr. They come not yet.
 Lucr. 'Tis scarce midnight.
 Beatr. How slow
Behind the course of thought, even sick with speed.
Lags leaden-footed time!
 Lucr. The minutes pass—
If he should wake before the deed is done?
 Beatr. O mother! he must never wake again.
What thou hast said persuades me that our act
Will but dislodge a spirit of deep hell
Out of a human form.
 Lucr. 'Tis true he spoke
Of death and judgment with strange confidence
For one so wicked; as a man believing
In God, yet recking not of good or ill.
And yet to die without confession!
 Beatr. Oh!
Believe that Heaven is merciful and just,
And will not add our dread necessity
To the amount of his offences.

Enter OLIMPIO *and* MARZIO *below.*

 Lucr. See,
They come.
 Beatr. All mortal things must hasten thus
To their dark end. Let us go down.

     [Exeunt LUCRETIA *and* BEATRICE *from above.*
 Olim. How feel you to this work?
 Mar. As one who thinks

A thousand crowns excellent market price
For an old murderer's life.   Your cheeks are pale.
  Olim. It is the white reflection of your own,
Which you call pale.
  Mar. Is that their natural hue?
  Olim. Or 'tis my hate, and the deferred desire
To wreak it, which extinguishes their blood.
  Mar. You are inclined then to this business?
  Olim. Ay,
If one should bribe me with a thousand crowns
To kill a serpent which had stung my child,
I could not be more willing.

     Enter BEATRICE *and* LUCRETIA *below.*

Noble ladies!
  Beatr. Are ye resolved?
  Olim. Is he asleep?
  Mar. Is all
Quiet?
  Lucr. I mixed an opiate with his drink:
He sleeps so soundly—
  Beatr. That his death will be
But as a change of sin-chastising dreams,
A dark continuance of the Hell within him,
Which God extinguish!   But ye are resolved?
Ye know it is a high and holy deed?
  Olim. We are resolved.
  Mar. As to how this act
Be warranted, it rests with you.
  Beatr. Well, follow!
  Olim. Hush! Hark! What noise is that?
  Mar. Ha! some one comes!
  Beatr. Ye conscience-stricken cravens, rock to rest
Your baby hearts.   It is the iron gate,
Which ye left open, swinging to the wind,
That enters whistling as in scorn.   Come, follow!
And be your steps like mine, light, quick, and bold.   [*Exeunt.*

SCENE III.—*An Apartment in the Castle.   Enter* BEATRICE *and*
        LUCRETIA.

  Lucr. They are about it now.
  Beatr. Nay, it is done.
  Lucr. I have not heard him groan.
  Beatr. He will not groan.
  Lucr. What sound is that?
  Beatr. List! 'tis the tread of feet
About his bed.
  Lucr. My God!
If he be now a cold stiff corpse.
  Beatr. O, fear not
What may be done, but what is left undone:
The act seals all.

     Enter OLIMPIO *and* MARZIO.

        Is it accomplished?
  Mar. What?

Olim. Did you not call?
Beatr. When?
Olim. Now.
Beatr. I ask if all is over?
Olim. We dare not kill an old and sleeping man;
His thin grey hair, his stern and reverent brow,
His veined hands crossed on his heaving breast,
And the calm innocent sleep in which he lay,
Quelled me.   Indeed, indeed, I cannot do it.
Mar. But I was bolder; for I chid Olimpio,
And bade him bear his wrongs to his own grave
And leave me the reward.   And now my knife
Touched the loose wrinkled throat, when the old man
Stirred in his sleep, and said, "God! hear, O hear
A father's curse!   What, art thou not our Father?"
And then he laughed.   I knew it was the ghost
Of my dead father speaking through his lips,
And could not kill him.
Beatr. Miserable slaves!
Where, if ye dare not kill a sleeping man,
Found ye the boldness to return to me
With such a deed undone?   Base palterers!
Cowards and traitors!   Why, the very conscience
Which ye would sell for gold and for revenge
Is an equivocation: it sleeps over
A thousand daily acts disgracing men;
And when a deed where mercy insults heaven—
Why do I talk?
        [*Snatching a dagger from one of them and raising it.*]
                Hadst thou a tongue to say,
She murdered her own father, I must do it!
But never dream ye shall outlive him long!
Olim. Stop, for God's sake!
Mar. I will go back and kill him.
Olim. Give me the weapon, we must do thy will.
Beatr. Take it! Depart! Return!
                              [*Exeunt* OLIMPIO *and* MARZIO.
                How pale thou art!
We do but that which 'twere a deadly crime
To leave undone.
Lucr. Would it were done!
Beatr. Even whilst
That doubt is passing through your mind, the world
Is conscious of a change.   Darkness and hell
Have swallowed up the vapour they sent forth
To blacken the sweet light of life.   My breath
Comes, methinks, lighter, and the jellied blood
Runs freely through my veins.   Hark!

Enter OLIMPIO *and* MARZIO.

                He is—
Olim. Dead!
Mar. We strangled him that there might be no blood;
And then we threw his heavy corpse i' the garden
Under the balcony; 'twill seem it fell.
Beatr. [*Giving them a bag of coin*]. Here, take this gold,
    and hasten to your homes.
And, Marzio, because thou wast only awed

By that which made me tremble, wear thou this !
[*Clothes him in a rich mantle.*
It was the mantle which my grandfather
Wore in his high prosperity, and men
Envied his state : so may they envy thine.
Thou wert a weapon in the hand of God
To a just use. Live long and thrive ! And, mark,
If thou hast crimes, repent : this deed is none. [*A horn is sounded.*
   Lucr. Hark ! 'tis the castle horn ; my God, it sounds
Like the last trump.
   Beatr. Some tedious guest is coming.
   Lucr. The drawbridge is let down; there is a tramp
Of horses in the court ; fly, hide yourselves !
[*Exeunt* OLIMPIO *and* MARZIO.
   Beatr. Let us retire to counterfeit deep rest ;
I scarcely need to counterfeit it now :
The spirit which doth reign within these limbs
Seems strangely undisturbed. I could even sleep
Fearless and calm : all ill is surely past. [*Exeunt.*

SCENE IV.—*Another Apartment in the Castle.*

Enter on one side the Legate SAVELLA, *introduced by a* Servant, *and on
the other* LUCRETIA *and* BERNARDO.

   Sav. Lady, my duty to his Holiness
Be my excuse that thus unseasonably
I break upon your rest. I must speak with
Count Cenci ; doth he sleep?
   Lucr. [*In a hurried and confused manner*]. I think he sleeps ;
Yet, wake him not, I pray, spare me awhile,
He is a wicked and a wrathful man ;
Should he be roused out of his sleep to-night,
Which is, I know, a hell of angry dreams,
It were not well ; indeed it were not well.
Wait till daybreak—
           [*Aside*]. O, I am deadly sick !
   Sav. I grieve thus to distress you, but the Count
Must answer charges of the gravest import,
And suddenly; such my commission is.
   Lucr. [*With increased agitation*]. I dare not rouse him : I know
   none who dare :
'Twere perilous ;—you might as safely waken
A serpent ; or a corpse in which some fiend
Were laid to sleep.
   Sav. Lady, my moments here
Are counted. I must rouse him from his sleep,
Since none else dare.
   Lucr. [*Aside*]. O, terror ! O, despair !

[*To* BERNARDO].

Bernardo, conduct you the Lord Legate to
Your father's chamber. [*Exeunt* SAVELLA *and* BERNARDO.

Enter BEATRICE.

   Beatr. 'Tis a messenger
Come to arrest the culprit who now stands
Before the throne of unappealable God.

Both Earth and Heaven, consenting arbiters,
Acquit our deed.
    Lucr. Oh, agony of fear !
Would that he yet might live ! Even now I heard
The Legate's followers whisper, as they passed,
They had a warrant for his instant death.
All was prepared by unforbidden means,
Which we must pay so dearly, having done.
Even now they search the tower, and find the body;
Now they suspect the truth ; now they consult
Before they come to tax us with the fact :
O, horrible, 'tis all discovered !
    Beatr. Mother,
What is done wisely, is done well. Be bold
As thou art just. 'Tis like a truant child
To fear that others know what thou hast done,
Even from thine own strong consciousness, and thus
Write on unsteady eyes and altered cheeks
All thou wouldst hide. Be faithful to thyself,
And fear no other witness but thy fear.
For if, as cannot be, some circumstance
Should rise in accusation, we can blind
Suspicion with such cheap astonishment,
Or overbear it with such guiltless pride,
As murderers cannot feign. The deed is done,
And what may follow now regards not me.
I am as universal as the light ;
Free as the earth-surrounding air ; as firm
As the world's centre. Consequence, to me,
Is as the wind which strikes the solid rock
But shakes it not.   [*A cry within, and tumult.*
    Voices. Murder ! murder ! murder !

      Enter BERNARDO *and* SAVELLA.

    Sav. [*To his followers*]. Go, search the castle round; sound
    the alarm ;
Look to the gates that none escape !
    Beatr. What now ?
    Ber. I know not what to say : my father's dead !
    Beatr. How ? dead ? he only sleeps : you mistake, brother.
His sleep is very calm, very like death :
'Tis wonderful how well a tyrant sleeps.
He is not *dead ?*
    Ber. Dead ! murdered !
    Lucr. [*With extreme agitation*]. Oh, no, no,
He is not murdered, though he may be dead ;
I have alone the keys of those apartments.
    Sav. Ha ! Is it so?
    Beatr. My lord, I pray excuse us ;
We will retire ; my mother is not well :
She seems quite overcome with this strange horror.
        [*Exeunt* LUCRETIA *and* BEATRICE.
    Sav. Can you suspect who may have murdered him ?
    Ber. I know not what to think.
    Sav. Can you name any
Who had an interest in his death ?
    Ber. Alas !
I can name none who had not ; and those most

Who most lament that such a deed is done;
My mother, and my sister, and myself.
 Sav. 'Tis strange! There were clear marks of violence.
I found the old man's body in the moonlight
Hanging beneath the window of his chamber,
Among the branches of a pine: he could not
Have fallen there, for all his limbs lay heaped
And effortless; 'tis true there was no blood.
Favour me, sir, (it much imports your house
That all should be made clear), to tell the ladies
That I request their presence.   [*Exit* BERNARDO.

   Enter Guards, *bringing in* MARZIO.

 Guard. We have one.
 Officer. My lord, we found this ruffian and another
Lurking among the rocks; there is no doubt
But that they are the murderers of Count Cenci:
Each had a bag of coin; this fellow wore
A gold-inwoven robe, which, shining bright
Under the dark rocks to the glimmering moon,
Betrayed them to our notice: the other fell
Desperately fighting.
 Sav. What does he confess?
 Officer. He keeps firm silence; but these lines found on him
May speak.
 Sav. Their language is at least sincere.   [*Reads.*

    " TO THE LADY BEATRICE.

 " That the atonement of what my nature sickens to conjecture
may **soon** arrive, I send thee, at thy brother's desire, those who
will speak and do more than I dare write—
      " Thy devoted servant,
           " ORSINO."

   Enter LUCRETIA, BEATRICE, *and* BERNARDO.

Knowest thou this writing, lady?
 Beatr. No.
 Sav. Nor thou?
 Lucr. [*Her conduct throughout the scene is marked by extreme
agitation*]. Where was it found? What is it? It should be
Orsini's hand! It speaks of that strange horror
Which never yet found utterance, but which made
Between that hapless child and her dead father
A gulf of obscure hatred.
 Sav.   Is it so?
Is it true, lady, that thy father did
Such outrages as to awaken in thee
Unfilial hate?
 Beatr. Not hate, 'twas more than hate:
This is most true, yet wherefore question me?
 Sav. There is a deed demanding question done;
Thou hast a secret which will answer not.
 Beatr. What sayest? My lord, your words are bold and rash.
 Sav. I do arrest all present in the name
Of the Pope's Holiness. You must to Rome.
 Lucr. O, not to Rome! Indeed we are not guilty.
 Beatr. Guilty! Who dares talk of guilt? My lord,

I am more innocent of parricide
Than is a child born fatherless. Dear mother,
Your gentleness and patience are no shield
For this keen-judging world, this two-edged lie,
Which seems, but is not. What! will human laws
Rather will ye who are their ministers,
Bar all access to retribution first,
And then, when heaven doth interpose to do
What ye neglect, arming familiar things
To the redress of an unwonted crime,
Make ye the victims who demanded it
Culprits? 'Tis ye are culprits! That poor wretch
Who stands so pale, and trembling, and amazed,
If it be true he murdered Cenci, was
A sword in the right hand of justest God.
Wherefore should I have wielded it? Unless
The crimes which mortal tongue dare never name
God therefore scruples to avenge.

    Sav.   You own
That you desired his death?

    Beatr. It would have been
A crime no less than his, if for one moment,
That fierce desire had faded in my heart.
'Tis true I did believe, and hope, and pray,
Ay, I even knew—for God is wise and just,
That some strange sudden death hung over him.
'Tis true that this did happen, and most true
There was no other rest for me on earth,
No other hope in Heaven: now what of this?

    Sav. Strange thoughts beget strange deeds; and here are both
I judge thee not.

    Beatr. And yet if you arrest me,
You are the judge and executioner
Of that which is the life of life: the breath
Of accusation kills an innocent name,
And leaves for lame acquittal the poor life
Which is a mask without it. 'Tis most false
That I am guilty of foul parricide;
Although I must rejoice, for justest cause,
That other hands have sent my father's soul
To ask the mercy he denied to me.
Now leave us free: stain not a noble house
With vague surmises of rejected crime;
Add to our sufferings and your own neglect
No heavier sum; let them have been enough;
Leave us the wreck we have.

    Sav. I dare not, lady.
I pray that you prepare yourselves for Rome:
There the Pope's further pleasure will be known.

    Lucr. O, not to Rome! O, take us not to Rome!

    Beatr. Why not to Rome, dear mother? There as here
Our innocence is as an armed heel
To trample accusation. God is there
As here, and with his shadow ever clothes
The innocent, the injured, and the weak;
And such are we. Cheer up, dear lady, lean
On me; collect your wandering thoughts. My lord,
As soon as you have taken some refreshment,

And had all such examinations made
Upon the spot, as may be necessary
To the full understanding of this matter,
We shall be ready.   Mother, will you come?
   Lucr. Ha! they will bind us to the rack, and wrest
Self-accusation from our agony!
Will Giacomo be there? Orsino? Marzio?
All present; all confronted; all demanding
Each from the others' countenance the thing
Which is in every heart! O, misery! [*She faints and is borne out.*
   Sav. She faints: an ill appearance this.
   Beatr. My Lord,
She knows not yet the uses of the world.
She fears that power is as a beast which grasps
And loosens not: a snake, whose look transmutes
All things to guilt which is its nutriment;
She cannot know how well the supine slaves
Of blind authority read the truth of things
When written on a brow of guilelessness:
She sees not yet triumphant Innocence
Stand at the judgment-seat of mortal man,
A judge and an accuser of the wrong
Which drags it there.   Prepare yourself, my Lord;
Our suite will join yours in the court below.   [*Exeunt.*

ACT V.

SCENE I.—*An Apartment in Orsino's Palace.*

Enter ORSINO *and* GIACOMO.

   Giac. Do evil deeds thus quickly come to end?
O, that the vain remorse which must chastise
Crimes done, had but as loud a voice to warn
As its keen sting is mortal to avenge!
O, that the hour when present had cast off
The mantle of its mystery, and shown
The ghastly form with which it now returns
When its scared game is roused, cheering the hounds
Of conscience to their prey! Alas! Alas!
It was a wicked thought, a piteous deed,
To kill an old and hoary-headed father.
   Ors. It has turned out unluckily, in truth.
   Giac. To violate the sacred doors of sleep;
To cheat kind nature of the placid death
Which she prepares for over-wearied age;
To drag from Heaven an unrepentant soul
Which might have quenched in reconciling prayers
A life of burning crimes—
   Ors.   You cannot say
I urged you to the deed.
   Giac.   O, had I never
Found in thy smooth and ready countenance
The mirror of my darkest thoughts; hadst thou
Never with hints and questions made me look
Upon the monster of my thought, until
It grew familiar to desire—

Ors.   'Tis thus
Men cast the blame of their unprosperous acts
Upon the abettors of their own resolve:
Or anything but their weak, guilty selves.
And yet, confess the truth, it is the peril
In which you stand that gives you this pale sickness
Of penitence; confess 'tis fear disguised
From its own shame that takes the mantle now
Of thin remorse.   What if we yet were safe?
  Giac. How can that be?   Already Beatrice,
Lucretia, and the murderer, are in prison.
I doubt not officers are, whilst we speak,
Sent to arrest us.
  Ors.   I have all prepared
For instant flight.   We can escape even now,
So we take fleet occasion by the hair.
  Giac. Rather expire in tortures, as I may.
What! will you cast by self-accusing flight
Assured conviction upon Beatrice?
She, who alone in this unnatural work,
Stands like God's angel ministered upon
By fiends; avenging such a nameless wrong
As turns black parricide to piety;
Whilst we for basest ends—I fear, Orsino,
While I consider all your words and looks,
Comparing them with your proposal now,
That you must be a villain.   For what end
Could you engage in such a perilous crime,
Training me on with hints, and signs, and smiles,
Even to this gulf? Thou art no liar? No,
Thou art a lie! Traitor and murderer!
Coward and slave! But, no, defend thyself;   [*Drawing.*
Let the sword speak what the indignant tongue
Disdains to brand thee with.
  Ors. Put up your weapon.
Is it the desperation of your fear
Makes you thus rash and sudden with a friend,
Now ruined for your sake? If honest anger
Have moved you, know, that what I just proposed
Was but to try you.   As for me, I think
Thankless affection led me to this point,
From which, if my firm temper could repent,
I cannot now recede.   Even whilst we speak
The ministers of justice wait below:
They grant me these brief moments.   Now if you
Have any word of melancholy comfort
To speak to your pale wife, 'twere best to pass
Out at the postern, and avoid them so.
  Giac. O, generous friend! how canst thou pardon me?
Would that my life could purchase thine!
  Ors. That wish
Now comes a day too late.   Haste; fare thee well!
Hear'st thou not steps along the corridor?   [*Exit* GIACOMO.
I'm sorry for it; but the guards are waiting
At his own gate, and such was my contrivance
That I might rid me both of him and them.
I thought to act a solemn comedy
Upon the painted scene of this new world,

And to attain my own peculiar ends
By some such plot of mingled good and ill
As others weave; but there arose a Power
Which grasped and snapped the threads of my device
And turned it to a net of ruin—Ha!   [*A shout is heard.*
Is that my name I hear proclaimed abroad?
But I will pass, wrapt in a vile disguise;
Rags on my back, and a false innocence
Upon my face, through the misdeeming crow
Which judges by what seems.   'Tis easy then
For a new name and for a country new,
And a new life, fashioned on old desires,
To change the honours of abandoned Rome.
And these must be the masks of that within,
Which must remain unaltered.   Oh, I fear
That what is past will never let me rest!
Why, when none else is conscious but myself
Of my misdeeds, should my own heart's contempt
Trouble me? Have I not the power to fly
My own reproaches? Shall I be the slave
Of—what? A word? which those of this false world
Employ against each other, not themselves;
As men wear daggers not for self-offence.
But if I am mistaken, where shall I
Find the disguise to hide me from myself,
As now I skulk from every other eye?   [*Exit.*

SCENE II.—*A Hall of Justice.* CAMILLO, JUDGES, *&c., are discovered
seated.* MARZIO *is led in.*

 First Judge. Accused, do you persist in your denial?
I ask you, are you innocent, or guilty?
I demand who were the participators
In your offence? Speak truth and the whole truth.
 Mar. My God! I did not kill him; I know nothing;
Olimpio sold the robe to me from which
You would infer my guilt.
 Second Judge. Away with him!
 First Judge. Dare you, with lips yet white from the rack's kiss,
Speak false? Is it so soft a questioner,
That you would bandy lover's talk with it
Till it wind out your life and soul? Away!
 Mar. Spare me! O, spare! I will confess.
 First Judge. Then speak.
 Mar. I strangled him in his sleep.
 First Judge. Who urged you to it?
 Mar. His own son Giacomo, and the young prelate
Orsino sent me to Petrella; there
The ladies Beatrice and Lucretia
Tempted me with a thousand crowns, and I
And my companion forthwith murdered him.
Now let me die.
 First Judge. This sounds as bad as truth. Guards, there,
Lead forth the prisoners.

  Enter LUCRETIA, BEATRICE, *and* GIACOMO, *guarded.*

   Look upon this man;
When did you see him last?

Beatr. We never saw him.

Mar. You know me too well, Lady Beatrice.

Beatr. I know thee ! How ? where ? when ?

Mar. You know 'twas I
Whom you did urge with menaces and bribes
To kill your father. When the thing was done
You clothed me in a robe of woven gold
And bade me thrive: how I have thriven, you see.
You, my Lord Giacomo, Lady Lucretia,
You know that what I speak is true.

[BEATRICE *advances towards him ; he covers his face, and
　　shrinks back*].　　　　　　　　O, dart
The terrible resentment of those eyes
On the dead earth ! Turn them away from me !
They wound: 'twas torture forced the truth. My Lords,
Having said this, let me be led to death.

Beatr. Poor wretch, I pity thee: yet stay awhile.

Cam. Guards, lead him not away.

Beatr. Cardinal Camillo,
You have a good repute for gentleness
And wisdom: can it be that you sit here
To countenance a wicked farce like this ?
When some obscure and trembling slave is dragged
From sufferings which might shake the sternest heart,
And bade to answer, not as he believes,
But as those may suspect or do desire,
Whose questions thence suggest their own reply;
And that in peril of such hideous torments
As merciful God spares even the damned. Speak now
The thing you surely know, which is, that you
If your fine frame were stretched upon that wheel,
And you were told: "Confess that you did poison
Your little nephew; that fair blue-eyed child
Who was the loadstar of your life:"—and though
All see, since his most swift and piteous death,
That day and night, and heaven and earth, and time,
And all the things hoped for or done therein
Are changed to you, through your exceeding grief,
Yet you would say, " I confess anything:"
And beg from your tormentors, like that slave,
The refuge of dishonourable death.
I pray thee, Cardinal, that thou assert
My innocence.

Cam. [*Much moved*]. What shall we think, my Lords!
Shame on these tears ! I thought the heart was frozen
Which is their fountain. I would pledge my soul
That she is guiltless.

Judge. Yet she must be tortured.

Cam I would as soon have tortured mine own nephew:
(If he now lived he would be just her age;
His hair, too, was her colour, and his eyes,
Like her's in shape, but blue and not so deep)
As that most perfect image of God's love
That ever came sorrowing upon the earth.
She is as pure as speechless infancy !

Judge. Well, be her purity on your head, my Lord,
If you forbid the rack. His Holiness
Enjoined us to pursue this monstrous crime

By the severest forms of law; nay, even
To stretch a point against the criminals.
The prisoners stand accused of parricide
Upon such evidence as justifies
Torture.

    Beatr. What evidence? This man's?

    Judge. Even so.

    Beatr. [*To* MARZIO]. Come near. And who art thou thus chosen forth
Out of the multitude of living men
To kill the innocent?

    Mar.   I am Marzio,
Thy father's vassal.

    Beatr. Fix thine eyes on mine;
Answer to what I ask.   [*Turning to the* JUDGES].
                I prithee mark
His countenance: unlike bold calumny
Which sometimes dares not speak the thing it looks,
He dares not look the thing he speaks, but bends
His gaze on the blind earth.   [*To* MARZIO].
            What! wilt thou say
That I did murder my own father?

    Mar. Oh!
Spare me! My brain swims round—I cannot speak—
It was that horrid torture forced the truth.
Take me away! Let her not look on me!
I am a guilty, miserable wretch;
I have said all I know; now, let me die!

    Beatr. My Lords, if by my nature I had been
So stern as to have planned the crime alleged,
Which your suspicions dictate to this slave,
And the rack makes him utter, do you think
I should have left this two-edged instrument
Of my misdeed; this man, this bloody knife
With my own name engraven on the heft
Lying unsheathed amid a world of foes,
For my own death? That with such horrible need
For deepest silence, I should have neglected
So trivial a precaution, as the making
His tomb the keeper of a secret written
On a thief's memory? What is his poor life?
What are a thousand lives? A parricide
Has trampled them like dust; and see, he lives! [*Turning to* MARZIO].
And thou—

    Mar. Oh, spare me! Speak to me no more!
That stern yet piteous look, those solemn tones,
Wound worse than torture.   [*To the* JUDGES].
             I have told it all;
For pity's sake lead me away to death.

    Cam. Guards, lead him nearer the Lady Beatrice,
He shrinks from her regard like autumn's leaf
From the keen breath of the serenest north.

    Beatr. Oh, thou who tremblest on the giddy verge
Of life and death, pause ere thou answerest me;
So mayst thou answer God with less dismay:
What evil have we done thee? I, alas!
Have lived but on this earth a few sad years
And so my lot was ordered, that a father
First turned the moments of awakening life

To drops, each poisoning youth's sweet hope ; and then
Stabbed with one blow my everlasting soul;
And my untainted fame; and even that peace
Which sleeps within the core of the heart's heart.
But the wound was not mortal; so my hate
Became the only worship I could lift
To our great Father, who in pity and love,
Armed thee, as thou dost say, to cut him off;
And thus his wrong becomes my accusation;
And art thou the accuser ? If thou hopest
Mercy in heaven, show justice upon earth:
Worse than a bloody hand is a hard heart.
If thou hast done murders, made thy life's path
Over the trampled laws of God and man,
Rush not before thy Judge, and say: "My Maker,
I have done this and more ; for there was one
Who was most pure and innocent on earth ;
And because she endured what never any
Guilty or innocent, endured before ;
Because her wrongs could not be told, not thought ;
Because Thy hand at length did rescue her ;
I with my words killed her and all her kin."
Think, I adjure you, what it is to slay
The reverence living in the minds of men
Towards our ancient house, and stainless fame !
Think what it is to strangle infant pity,
Cradled in the belief of guileless looks,
Till it become a crime to suffer.   Think
What 'tis to blot with infamy and blood
All that which shows like innocence, and is,
Hear me, great God ! I swear, most innocent,
So that the world lose all discrimination
Between the sly, fierce, wild regard of guilt,
And that which now compels thee to reply
To what I ask : Am I, or am I not
A parricide ?
   Mar. Thou art not !
   Judge. What is this?
   Mar. I here declare those whom I did accuse
Are innocent.   'Tis I alone am guilty.
   Judge. Drag him away to torments; let them be
Subtle and long drawn out, to tear the folds
Of the heart's inmost cell.   Unbind him not
Till he confess.
   Mar. Torture me as ye will:
A keener pang has wrung a higher truth
From my last breath.   She is most innocent !
Bloodhounds, not men, glut yourselves well with me ;
I will not give you that fine piece of nature
To rend and ruin.   [*Exit* MARZIO, *guarded.*
   Cam. What say ye now, my Lords ?
   Judge. Let tortures strain the truth till it be white
As snow thrice sifted by the frozen wind.
   Cam. Yet stained with blood.
   Judge [*To* BEATRICE]. Know you this paper, lady?
   Beatr. Entrap me not with questions.   Who stands here
As my accuser ?   Ha ! wilt thou be he,
Who art my judge ?   Accuser, witness, judge,

What, all in one ? Here is Orsino's name ;
Where is Orsino ? Let his eye meet mine.
What means this scrawl ? Alas ! Ye know not what,
And therefore on the chance that it may be
Some evil, will ye kill us ?

Enter an Officer.

Officer. Marzio's dead.
Judge. What did he say ?
Officer. Nothing. As soon as we
Had bound him on the wheel, he smiled on us,
As one who baffles a deep adversary;
And holding his breath, died.
Judge. There remains nothing
But to apply the question to those prisoners,
Who yet remain stubborn.
Cam. I overrule
Further proceedings, and in the behalf
Of these most innocent and noble persons
Will use my interest with the Holy Father.
Judge. Let the Pope's pleasure then be done. Meanwhile
Conduct these culprits each to separate cells ;
And be the engines ready: for this night,
If the Pope's resolution be as grave,
Pious, and just as once, I'll wring the truth
Out of those nerves and sinews, groan by groan. [*Exeunt.*

SCENE III.—*The Cell of a Prison.*

BEATRICE *is discovered asleep on a Couch. Enter* BERNARDO.

Ber. How gently slumber rests upon her face,
Like the last thoughts of some day sweetly spent
Closing in night and dreams, and so prolonged.
After such torments as she bore last night,
How light and soft her breathing comes. Ay me !
Methinks that I shall never sleep again.
But I must shake the heavenly dew of rest
From this sweet folded flower, thus—wake ! awake !
What, sister, canst thou sleep ?
Beatr. [*Awaking*]. I was just dreaming
That we were all in Paradise. Thou knowest
This cell seems like a kind of Paradise
After our father's presence.
Ber. Dear, dear sister,
Would that thy dream were not a dream. Oh, God !
How shall I tell ?
Beatr. What wouldst thou tell, sweet brother ?
Ber. Look not so calm and happy, or even whilst
I stand considering what I have to say
My heart will break.
Beatr. See now, thou mak'st me weep :
How very friendless thou wouldst be, dear child,
If I were dead. Say what thou hast to say.
Ber. They have confessed; they could endure no more
The tortures—
Beatr. Ha ! What was there to confess ?
They must have told some weak and wicked lie
To flatter their tormentors. Have they said

That they were guilty? O, white innocence,
That thou shouldst wear the mask of guilt to hide
Thine awful and serenest countenance
From those who know thee not!

Enter JUDGE, *with* LUCRETIA *and* GIACOMO, *guarded.*

               Ignoble hearts!
For some brief spasms of pain, which are at least
As mortal as the limbs through which they pass,
Are centuries of high splendour laid in dust?
And that eternal honour which should live
Sun-like, above the reek of mortal fame,
Changed to a mockery and a by-word? What!
Will you give up these bodies to be dragged
At horses' heels, so that our hair should sweep
The footsteps of the vain and senseless crowd,
Who, that they may make our calamity
Their worship and their spectacle, will leave
The churches and the theatres as void
As their own hearts? Shall the light multitude
Fling, at their choice, curses or faded pity,
Sad funeral flowers to deck a living corpse,
Upon us as we pass to pass away,
And leave—what memory of our having been?
Infamy, blood, terror, despair? O thou,
Who wert a mother to the parentless,
Kill not thy child! Let not her wrongs kill thee!
Brother, lie down with me upon the rack,
And let us each be silent as a corpse;
It soon will be as soft as any grave.
'Tis but the falsehood it can wring from fear
Makes the rack cruel.
    Giac. They will tear the truth
Even from thee at last, those cruel pains:
For pity's sake say thou art guilty now.
    Lucr. O, speak the truth! Let us all quickly die;
And after death, God is our judge, not they;
He will have mercy on us.
    Ber. If indeed
It can be true, say so, dear sister mine;
And then the Pope will surely pardon you,
And all be well.
    Judge. Confess, or I will warp
Your limbs with such keen tortures—
    Beatr. Tortures! Turn
The rack henceforth into a spinning wheel!
Torture your dog, that he may tell when last
He lapped the blood his master shed—not me!
My pangs are of the mind, and of the heart,
And of the soul; ay, of the inmost soul,
Which weeps within tears as of burning gall
To see, in this ill world where none are true,
My kindred false to their deserted selves.
And with considering all the wretched life
Which I have lived, and its now wretched end,
And the small justice shown by Heaven and Earth
To me or mine; and what a tyrant thou art,
And what slaves these; and what a world we make,

The oppressor and the oppressed—such pangs compel
My answer. What is it thou wouldst with me?
  Judge. Art thou not guilty of thy father's death?
  Beatr. Or wilt thou rather tax thy judging God
That he permitted such an act as that
Which I have suffered, and which he beheld;
Made it unutterable, and took from it
All refuge, all revenge, all consequence,
But that which thou hast called my father's death?
Which is or is not what men call a crime,
Which either I have done, or have not done;
Say what ye will. I shall deny no more.
If ye desire it thus, thus let it be.
And so an end of all. Now do your will;
No other pains shall force another word.
  Judge. She is convicted, but has not confessed.
Be it enough. Until their final sentence
Let none have converse with them. You, young lord,
Linger not here!
  Beatr. O, tear him not away!
  Judge. Guards do your duty.
  Ber. [*Embracing* BEATRICE]. Oh! would ye divide body from soul?
  Officer. That is the headsman's business.
      [*Exeunt all but* LUCRETIA, BEATRICE, *and* GIACOMO.
  Giac. Have I confessed? Is it all over now?
No hope! No refuge! O weak, wicked tongue,
Which hast destroyed me, would that thou hadst been
Cut out and thrown to dogs first? To have killed
My father first, and then betrayed my sister;
Ay, thee! the one thing innocent and pure
In this black guilty world, to that which I
So well deserve! My wife! my little ones!
Destitute, helpless, and I—Father! God!
Canst thou forgive even the unforgiving,
When their full hearts break thus, thus!
      [*Covers his face, and weeps.*

  Lucr. O, my child!
To what a dreadful end are we all come!
Why did I yield? Why did I not sustain
Those torments? Oh, that I were all dissolved
Into these fast and unavailing tears,
Which flow and feel not!
  Beatr. What 'twas weak to do,
'Tis weaker to lament, once being done;
Take cheer! The God who knew my wrong, and made
Our speedy act the angel of his wrath,
Seems, and but seems to have abandoned us.
Let us not think that we shall die for this.
Brother, sit near me; give me your firm hand,
You had a manly heart. Bear up! Bear up!
O, dearest lady, put your gentle head
Upon my lap, and try to sleep awhile:
Your eyes look pale, hollow, and overworn,
With heaviness of watching and slow grief.
Come, I will sing you some low, sleepy tune,
Not cheerful, nor yet sad; some dull old thing,
Some outworn and unused monotony,
Such as our country gossips sing and spin.

Till they almost forget they live: lie down!
So, that will do.   Have I forgot the words?
Faith! They are sadder than I thought they were.

SONG.

False friend, wilt thou smile or weep
When my life is laid asleep?
Little cares for a smile or a tear,
The clay-cold corpse upon the bier!
  Farewell! Heigho!
   What is this whispers low?
There is a snake in thy smile, my dear;
And bitter poison within thy tear.

Sweet sleep, were death like to thee,
Or if thou couldst mortal be,
I would close these eyes of pain;
When to wake? Never again.
  O world! Farewell!
   Listen to the passing bell!
It says, thou and I must part,
With a light and a heavy heart.   [*The scene closes.*

SCENE IV.—*A Hall of the Prison.*

Enter CAMILLO *and* BERNARDO.

 Cam. The Pope is stern; not to be moved or bent.
He looked as calm and keen as is the engine
Which tortures and which kills, exempt itself
From aught that it inflicts; a marble form,
A rite, a law, a custom: not a man.
He frowned, as if to frown had been the trick
Of his machinery, on the advocates
Presenting the defence; which he tore
And threw behind, muttering with hoarse, harsh voice:
"Which among ye defended their old father,
Killed in his sleep?"   Then to another: "Thou
Dost this in virtue of thy place; 'tis well."
He turned to me then, looking deprecation,
And said these three words, coldly: "They must die."
 Ber. And yet you left him not?
 Cam. I urged him still;
Pleading, as I could guess, the devilish wrong
Which prompted your unnatural parent's death.
And he replied: "Paolo Santa Croce
Murdered his mother yester evening,
And he is fled.   Parricide grows so rife,
That soon, for some just cause, no doubt, the young
Will strangle us all, dozing in our chairs.
Authority, and power, and hoary hair,
Are grown crimes capital.   You are my nephew,
You come to ask their pardon; stay a moment;
Here is their sentence; never see me more
Till, to the letter, it be all fulfilled."
 Ber. O God, not so! I did believe indeed
That all you said was but sad preparation

For happy news.   O, there are words and looks
To bend the sternest purpose!   Once I knew them,
Now I forget them at my dearest need.
What think you if I seek him out, and bathe
His feet and robe with hot and bitter tears?
Importune him with prayers, vexing his brain
With my perpetual cries, until in rage
He strike me with his pastoral cross, and trample
Upon my prostrate head, so that my blood
May stain the senseless dust on which he treads,
And remorse waken mercy?   I will do it!
O, wait till I return!   [*Rushes out.*
      Cam. Alas! poor boy!
A wreck-devoted seaman thus might pray
To the deaf sea.

Enter LUCRETIA, BEATRICE, *and* GIACOMO, *guarded.*

      Beatr. I hardly dare to fear
That thou bring'st other news than a just pardon.
      Cam. May God in heaven be less inexorable
To the Pope's prayers, than he has been to mine.
Here is the sentence and the warrant.
      Beatr. [*Wildly*]. Oh,
My God! can it be possible I have
To die so suddenly?   So young to go
Under the obscure, cold, rotting, wormy ground!
To be nailed down into a narrow place;
To see no more sweet sunshine; hear no more
Blithe voice of living thing; muse not again
Upon familiar thoughts, sad, yet thus lost—
How fearful!   To be nothing!   Or to be—
What?   O, where am I?   Let me not go mad!
Sweet Heaven, forgive weak thoughts!   If there should be
No God, no Heaven, no Earth in the void world;
The wide, grey, lampless, deep, unpeopled world!
If all things then should be—my father's spirit,
His eye, his voice, his touch, surrounding me;
The atmosphere and breath of my dead life!
If sometimes, as a shape more like himself,
Even the form which tortured me on earth,
Masked in grey hairs and wrinkles, he should come
And wind me in his hellish arms, and fix
His eyes on mine, and drag me down, down, down
For was he not alone omnipotent
On earth and ever present?   Even though dead,
Does not his spirit live in all that breathe,
And work for me and mine still the same ruin,
Scorn, pain, despair?   Who ever yet returned
To teach the laws of death's untrodden realm?
Unjust perhaps as those which drive us now,
O, whither, whither?
      Lucr. Trust in God's sweet love,
The tender promises of Christ: ere night
Think we shall be in Paradise.
      Beatr. 'Tis past!
Whatever comes, my heart shall sink no more.
And yet, I know not why, your words strike chill:
How tedious, false, and cold seem all things.   I

Have met with much injustice in this world ;
No difference has been made by God or man,
Or any power moulding my wretched lot,
'Twixt good or evil, as regarded me.
I am cut off from the only world I know,
From light, and life, and love, in youth's sweet prime.
You do well telling me to trust in God:
I hope I do trust in him. In whom else
Can any trust ? And yet my heart is cold.

> [*During the latter speeches* GIACOMO *has retired conversing
> with* CAMILLO, *who now goes out.* GIACOMO *advances*].

   Giac. Know you not, mother—sister, know you not ?
Bernardo even now is gone to implore
The Pope to grant our pardon.
   Lucr. Child, perhaps
It will be granted. We may all then live
To make these woes a tale for distant years :
O, what a thought ! It gushes to my heart
Like the warm blood.
   Beatr. Yet both will soon be cold.
O, trample out that thought ! Worse than despair,
Worse than the bitterness of death, is hope :
It is the only ill which can find place
Upon the giddy, sharp and narrow hour
Tottering beneath us. Plead with the swift frost
That it should spare the eldest flower of spring :
Plead with awakening earthquake, o'er whose couch
Even now a city stands, strong, fair and free ;
Now stench and blackness yawn, like death. O, plead
With famine, or wind-walking pestilence,
Blind lightning, or the deaf sea, not with man !
Cruel, cold, formal man ! righteous in words,
In deeds a Cain. No, mother, we must die :
Since such is the reward of innocent lives ;
Such the alleviation of worst wrongs.
And whilst our murderers live, and hard, cold men,
Smiling and slow, walk through a world of tears
To death as to life's sleep ; 'twere just the grave
Were some strange joy for us. Come, obscure Death,
And wind me in thine all-embracing arms !
Like a fond mother hide me in thy bosom,
And rock me to the sleep from which none wake.
Live ye, who live, subject to one another
As we were once, who now—

BERNARDO rushes in.

   Ber.   Oh, horrible !
That tears, that looks, that hope poured forth in prayer,
Even till the heart is vacant and despairs,
Should all be vain ! The ministers of death
Are waiting round the doors. I thought I saw
Blood on the face of one—what if 'twere fancy ?
Soon the heart's blood of all I love on earth
Will sprinkle him, and he will wipe it off
As if 'twere only rain. O life ! O world !
Cover me ! let me be no more ! To see
That perfect mirror of pure innocence
Wherein I gazed, and grew happy and good,

Shivered to dust ! To see thee, Beatrice,
Who made all lovely thou didst look upon—
Thee, light of life—dead, dark ! while I say, sister,
To hear I have no sister ; and thou, mother,
Whose love was a bond to all our loves—
Dead ! The sweet bond broken !

Enter CAMILLO *and* Guards.

    They come ! Let me
Kiss those warm lips before their crimson leaves
Are blighted—white—cold. Say farewell, before
Death chokes that gentle voice ! O, let me hear
You speak !
 Beatr. Farewell, my tender brother. Think
Of our sad fate with gentleness, as now :
And let mild pitying thoughts lighten for thee
Thy sorrow's load. Err not in harsh despair,
But tears and patience. One thing more, my child,
For thine own sake be constant to the love
Thou bearest us ; and to the faith that I,
Though wrapt in a strange cloud of crime and shame,
Lived ever holy and unstained. And though
Ill tongues shall wound me, and our common name
Be as a mark stamped on thine innocent brow
For men to point at as they pass, do thou
Forbear, and never think a thought unkind
Of those, who perhaps love thee in their graves.
So mayest thou die as I do ; fear and pain
Being subdued. Farewell ! farewell ! farewell !
 Ber. I cannot say, farewell !
 Cam. O, Lady Beatrice !
 Beatr. Give yourself no unnecessary pain,
My dear Lord Cardinal. Here, mother, tie
My girdle for me, and bind up this hair
In any simple knot ; ay, that does well.
And yours I see is coming down. How often
Have we done this for one another ! now
We shall not do it any more. My lord,
We are quite ready. Well, 'tis very well.

1821.

EPIPSYCHIDION:

VERSES ADDRESSED TO THE NOBLE AND UNFORTUNATE LADY,

EMILIA V——.

NOW IMPRISONED IN THE CONVENT OF ———.

"L'anima amante si slancia fuori del creato, e si crea nel infinito un Mondo tutto per essa, diverso assai da questo oscuro e pauroso baratro."—HER OWN WORDS.

ADVERTISEMENT.

THE Writer of the following Lines died at Florence, as he was preparing for a voyage to one of the wildest of the Sporades, which he had bought, and where he had fitted up the ruins of an old building, and where it was his hope to have realized a scheme of life, suited, perhaps, to that happier and better world of which he is now an inhabitant, but hardly practicable in this. His life was singular; less on account of the romantic vicissitudes which diversified it, than the ideal tinge which it received from his own character and feelings. The present poem, like the "Vita Nuova" of Dante, is sufficiently intelligible to a certain class of readers without a matter-of-fact history of the circumstances to which it relates; and to a certain other class it must ever remain incomprehensible from a defect of a common organ of perception for the ideas of which it treats. Not but that, *gran vergogna sarebbe a colui, che rimasse cosa sotto veste di figura, o di colore rettorico: e domandato non sapesse denudare le sue parole da cotal veste, in guisa che avessero verace intendimento.*

The present poem appears to have been intended by the Writer as the dedication to some longer one. The stanza on the following page is almost a literal translation from Dante's famous Canzone—

"*Voi, ch' intendendo, il terzo ciel movete, &c.*"

The presumptuous application of the concluding lines to his own composition will raise a smile at the expense of my unfortunate friend: be it a smile not of contempt, but pity.   S.

> MY Song, I fear that thou wilt find but few
> Who fitly shall conceive thy reasoning,
> Of such hard matter dost thou entertain;
> Whence, if by misadventure, chance should bring

Thee to base company (as chance may do),
Quite unaware of what thou dost contain,
I prithee, comfort thy sweet self again,
My last delight! tell them that they are dull,
And bid them own that thou art beautiful.

———

Sweet Spirit! Sister of that orphan one,
Whose empire is the name thou weepest on,
In my heart's temple I suspend to thee
These votive wreaths of withered memory.

Poor captive bird! who, from thy narrow cage,
Pourest such music, that it might assuage
The rugged hearts of those who prisoned thee,
Were they not deaf to all sweet melody:
This song shall be thy rose: its petals pale
Are dead, indeed, my adored Nightingale!
But soft and fragrant is the faded blossom,
And it has no thorn left to wound thy bosom.

High, spirit-winged Heart! who dost for ever
Beat thine unfeeling bars with vain endeavour,
Till those bright plumes of thought, in which arrayed
It over-soared this low and worldly shade,
Lie shattered; and thy panting, wounded breast
Stains with dear blood its unmaternal nest!
I weep vain tears: blood would less bitter be,
Yet poured forth gladlier, could it profit thee.

Seraph of Heaven! too gentle to be human,
Veiling beneath that radiant form of Woman
All that is insupportable in thee
Of light, and love, and immortality!
Sweet Benediction in the Eternal Curse!
Veiled Glory of this lampless Universe!
Thou Moon beyond the clouds! Thou living Form
Among the Dead! Thou Star above the Storm!
Thou Wonder, and thou Beauty, and thou Terror!
Thou Harmony of Nature's art! Thou Mirror
In whom, as in the splendour of the Sun,
All shapes look glorious which thou gazest on!
Ay, even the dim words which obscure thee now
Flash, lightning-like, with unaccustomed glow;
I pray thee that thou blot from this sad song
All of its much mortality and wrong,
With those clear drops, which start like sacred dew
From the twin lights thy sweet soul darkens through,
Weeping, till sorrow becomes ecstasy:
Then smile on it, so that it may not die.

I never thought before my death to see
Youth's vision thus made perfect. Emily,
I love thee; though the world by no thin name
Will hide that love, from its unvalued shame.
Would we two had been twins of the same mother!
Or, that the name my heart lent to another
Could be a sister's bond for her and thee,
Blending two beams of one eternity!

Yet were one lawful and the other true,
These names, though dear, could paint not, as is due,
How beyond refuge I am thine.   Ah me!
I am not thine: I am a part of *thee.*

   Sweet Lamp! my moth-like Muse has burnt its wings,
Or, like a dying swan who soars and sings,
Young Love should teach Time, in his own grey style,
All that thou art.   Art thou not void of guile,
A lovely soul formed to be blest and bless?
A well of sealed and secret happiness,
Whose waters like blithe light and music are,
Vanquishing dissonance and gloom?   A Star
Which moves not in the moving Heavens, alone?
A smile amid dark frowns? a gentle tone
Amid rude voices? a beloved light?
A Solitude, a Refuge, a Delight?
A Lute, which those who love has taught to play
Make music on, to soothe the roughest day
And lull fond grief asleep? a buried treasure?
A cradle of young thoughts of wingless pleasure?
A violet-shrouded grave of Woe?—I measure
The world of fancies, seeking one like thee,
And find—alas! mine own infirmity.

   She met me, Stranger, upon life's rough way,
And lured me towards sweet Death; as Night by Day,
Winter by Spring, or Sorrow by swift Hope,
Led into light, life, peace.   An antelope,
In the suspended impulse of its lightness,
Were less ethereally light: the brightness
Of her divinest presence trembles through
Her limbs, as underneath a cloud of dew
Embodied in the windless Heaven of June,
Amid the splendour-winged stars, the Moon
Burns, inextinguishably beautiful:
And from her lips, as from a hyacinth full
Of honey-dew, a liquid murmur drops,
Killing the sense with passion; sweet as stops
Of planetary music heard in trance.
In her mild lights the starry spirits dance,
The sunbeams of those wells which ever leap
Under the lightnings of the soul—too deep
For the brief fathom-line of thought or sense.
The glory of her being, issuing thence,
Stains the dead, blank, cold air with a warm shade
Of unentangled intermixture made
By Love, of light and motion: one intense
Diffusion, one serene Omnipresence,
Whose flowing outlines mingle in their flowing
Around her cheeks and utmost fingers glowing
With the unintermitted blood, which there
Quivers (as in a fleece of snow-like air
The crimson pulse of living morning quiver),
Continuously prolonged, and ending never,
Till they are lost, and in that Beauty furled
Which penetrates and clasps and fills the world;

Scarce visible from extreme loveliness.
Warm fragrance seems to fall from her light dress,
And her loose hair; and where some heavy tress
The air of her own speed has disentwined,
The sweetest seems to satiate the faint wind;
And in the soul a wild odour is felt,
Beyond the sense, like fiery dews that melt
Into the bosom of a frozen bud.
See where she stands! a mortal shape endued
With love and life, and light and deity,
And motion which may change but cannot die;
An image of some bright Eternity;
A shadow of some golden dream; a Splendour
Leaving the third sphere pilotless; a tender
Reflection of the eternal Moon of Love
Under whose motions life's dull billows move;
A Metaphor of Spring and Youth and Morning;
A Vision like incarnate April, warning,
With smiles and tears, Frost the Anatomy
Into his summer grave.

            Ah! woe is me!
What have I dared? where am I lifted? how
Shall I descend, and perish not? I know
That Love makes all things equal: I have heard
By mine own heart this joyous truth averred:
The spirit of the worm beneath the sod
In love and worship, blends itself with God.

    Spouse! Sister! Angel! Pilot of the Fate
Whose course has been so starless! O too late
Beloved! O too soon adored, by me!
For in the fields of immortality
My spirit should at first have worshipped thine,
A divine presence in a place divine;
Or should have moved beside it on this earth,
A shadow of that substance, from its birth;
But not as now:—I love thee; yes, I feel
That on the fountain of my heart a seal
Is set, to keep its waters pure and bright
For thee, since in those *tears* thou hast delight.
We—are we not formed, as notes of music are,
For one another, though dissimilar;
Such differences without discord, as can make
Those sweetest sounds, in which all spirits shake
As trembling leaves in a continuous air?

    Thy wisdom speaks in me, and bids me dare
Beacon the rocks on which high hearts are wrecked.
I never was attached to that great sect,
Whose doctrine is, that each one should select
Out of the crowd a mistress or a friend,
And all the rest, though fair and wise, commend
To cold oblivion, though it is in the code
Of modern morals, and the beaten road
Which those poor slaves with weary footsteps tread,
Who travel to their home among the dead

By the broad highway of the world, and so,
With one chained friend, perhaps a jealous foe,
The dreariest and the longest journey go.

True love in this differs from gold and clay,
That to divide is not to take away.
Love is like understanding, that grows bright
Gazing on many truths; 'tis like thy light,
Imagination ! which, from earth and sky,
And from the depths of human fantasy,
As from a thousand prisms and mirrors, fills
The Universe with glorious beams, and kills
Error, the worm, with many a sun-like arrow
Of its reverberated lightning.   Narrow
The heart that loves, the brain that contemplates,
The life that wears, the spirit that creates
One object, and one form, and builds thereby
A sepulchre for its eternity.

Mind from its object differs most in this:
Evil from good; misery from happiness;
The baser from the nobler; the impure
And frail, from what is clear and must endure.
If you divide suffering and dross, you may
Diminish till it is consumed away;
If you divide pleasure and love and thought,
Each part exceeds the whole; and we know not
How much, while any yet remains unshared,
Of pleasure may be gained, of sorrow spared :
This truth is that deep well, whence sages draw
The unenvied light of hope; the eternal law
By which those live, to whom this world of life
Is as a garden ravaged, and whose strife
Tills for the promise of a later birth
The wilderness of this Elysian earth.

There was a Being whom my spirit oft
Met on its visioned wanderings, far aloft,
In the clear golden prime of my youth's dawn,
Upon the fairy isles of sunny lawn,
Amid the enchanted mountains, and the caves
Of divine sleep, and on the air-like waves
Of wonder-level dream, whose tremulous floor
Paved her light steps;—on an imagined shore,
Under the grey beak of some promontory
She met me, robed in such exceeding glory,
That I beheld her not.   In solitudes
Her voice came to me through the whispering woods,
And from the fountains and the odours deep
Of flowers, which, like lips murmuring in their sleep
Of the sweet kisses which had lulled them there.
Breathed but of *her* to the enamoured air;
And from the breezes whether low or loud,
And from the rain of every passing cloud,
And from the singing of the summer birds,
And from all sounds, all silence.   In the words
Of antique verse and high romance,—in form,
Sound, colour—in whatever checks that Storm

Which with the shattered present chokes the past
And in that best philosophy, whose taste
Makes this cold common hell, our life, a doom
As glorious as a fiery martyrdom;
Her Spirit was the harmony of truth.

Then from the caverns of my dreary youth
I sprang, as one sandalled with plumes of fire,
And towards the loadstar of my one desire,
I flitted, like a dizzy moth, whose flight
Is as a dead leaf's in the owlet light,
When it would seek in Hesper's setting sphere
A radiant death, a fiery sepulchre,
As if it were a lamp of earthly flame.
But She, whom prayers or tears could not tame,
Past, like a God throned on a winged planet,
Whose burning plumes to tenfold swiftness fan it,
Into the dreary cone of our life's shade;
And as a man with mighty loss dismayed,
I would have followed, though the grave between
Yawned like a gulf whose spectres are unseen:
When a voice said:—" O Thou of hearts the weakest,
The phantom is beside thee whom thou seekest."
Then I—"Where?" the world's echo answered "Where!"
And in that silence, and in my despair,
I questioned every tongueless wind that flew
Over my tower of mourning, if it knew
Whither 'twas fled, this soul out of my soul;
And murmured names and spells which have control
Over the sightless tyrants of our fate;
But neither prayer nor verse could dissipate
The night which closed on her; nor uncreate
That world within this Chaos, mine and me,
Of which she was the veiled Divinity,
The world I say of thoughts that worshipped her:
And therefore I went forth, with hope and fear
And every gentle passion sick to death,
Feeding my course with expectation's breath,
Into the wintry forest of our life;
And struggling through its error with vain strife,
And stumbling in my weakness and my haste,
And half bewildered by new forms, I past
Seeking among those untaught foresters
If I could find one form resembling hers,
In which she might have masked herself from me.
There,—One, whose voice was venomed melody
Sate by a well, under blue nightshade bowers;
The breath of her false mouth was like faint flowers,
Her touch was as electric poison,—flame
Out of her looks into my vitals came,
And from her living cheeks and bosom flew
A killing air, which pierced like honey-dew
Into the core of my green heart, and lay
Upon its leaves ; until, as hair grown grey
O'er a young brow, they hid its unblown prime
With ruins of unseasonable time.

In many mortal forms I rashly sought
The shadow of that idol of my thought.

And some were fair—but beauty dies away :
Others were wise—but honied words betray ;
And One was true—oh ! why not true to me ?
Then, as a hunted deer that could not flee,
I turned upon my thoughts, and stood at bay,
Wounded and weak and panting ; the cold day
Trembled, for pity of my strife and pain.
When, like a noonday dawn, there shone again
Deliverance. One stood on my path who seemed
As like the glorious shape which I had dreamed,
As is the Moon, whose changes ever run
Into themselves, to the eternal Sun ;
The cold chaste Moon, the Queen of Heaven's bright isles,
Who makes all beautiful on which she smiles.
That wandering shrine of soft yet icy flame
Which ever is transformed, yet still the same,
And warms not but illumes. Young and fair
As the descended Spirit of that sphere,
She hid me, as the Moon may hide the night
From its own darkness, until all was bright
Between the Heaven and Earth of my calm mind.
And as a cloud charioted by the wind,
She led me to a cave in that wild place,
And sate beside me, with her downward face
Illumining my slumbers, like the Moon
Waxing and waning o'er Endymion.
And I was laid asleep, spirit and limb,
And all my being became bright or dim
As the Moon's image in the summer sea,
According as she smiled or frowned on me ;
And there I lay, within a chaste cold bed :
Alas, I then was nor alive nor dead :
For at her silver voice came Death and Life,
Unmindful each of their accustomed strife,
Masked like twin babes, a sister and a brother,
The wandering hopes of one abandoned mother,
And through the cavern without wings they flew,
And cried, " Away, he is not of our crew."
I wept, and though it be a dream, I weep.

What storms then shook the ocean of my sleep,
Blotting that Moon, whose pale and waning lips
Then shrank as in the sickness of eclipse ;
And how my soul was as a lampless sea,
And who was then its Tempest ; and when She,
The Planet of that hour, was quenched, what frost
Crept o'er those waters, till from coast to coast
The moving billows of my being fell
Into a death of ice, immovable ;
And then—what earthquakes made it gape and split,
The white Moon smiling all the while on it,
These words conceal :—If not, each word would be
The key of staunchless tears. Weep not for me !

At length, into the obscure Forest came
The Vision I had sought through grief and shame.
Athwart that wintry wilderness of thorns
Flashed from her motion splendour like the Morn's,

And from her presence life was radiated
Through the grey earth and branches bare and dead,
So that her way was paved, and roofed above
With flowers as soft as thoughts of budding love ;
And music from her respiration spread
Like light,—all other sounds were penetrated
By the small, still, sweet spirit of that sound,
So that the savage winds hung mute around,
And odours warm and fresh fell from her hair
Dissolving the dull cold in the frore air :
Soft as an Incarnation of the Sun,
When light is changed to love, this glorious One
Floated into the cavern where I lay,
And called my Spirit, and the dreaming clay
Was lifted by the thing that dreamed below
As smoke by fire, and in her beauty's glow
I stood, and felt the dawn of my long night
Was penetrating me with living light :
I knew it was the Vision veiled from me
So many years—that it was Emily.

Twin Spheres of light who rule this passive Earth,
This world of love, this *me ;* and into birth
Awaken all its fruits and flowers, and dart
Magnetic might into its central heart ;
And lift its billows and its mists, and guide
By everlasting laws, each wind and tide
To its fit cloud, and its appointed cave,
And lull its storms, each in the craggy grave
Which was its cradle, luring to faint bowers
The armies of the rainbow-wingèd showers ;
And, as those married lights, which from the towers
Of Heaven look forth and fold the wandering globe
In liquid sleep and splendour, as a robe ;
And all their many-mingled influence blend,
If equal, yet unlike, to one sweet end ;
So ye, bright regents, with alternate sway
Govern my sphere of being, night and day !
Thou, not disdaining even a borrowed might ;
Thou, not eclipsing a remoter light ;
And, through the shadow of the seasons three,
From Spring to Autumn's sere maturity,
Light it into the Winter of the tomb,
Where it may ripen to a brighter bloom.
Thou, too, O Comet, beautiful and fierce,
Who drew the heart of this frail Universe
Towards thine own ; till, wrecked in that convulsion,
Alternating attraction and repulsion,
Thine went astray and that was rent in twain ;
Oh, float into our azure heaven again !
Be there love's folding-star at thy return :
The living Sun will feed thee from its urn
Of golden fire ; the Moon will veil her horn
In thy last smiles ; adoring Even and Morn
Will worship thee with incense of calm breath
And lights and shadows ; as the star of Death
And Birth is worshipped by those sisters wild

Called Hope and Fear—upon the heart are piled
Their offerings,—of this sacrifice divine
A World shall be the altar.

Lady mine,
Scorn not these flowers of thought, the fading birth
Which from its heart of hearts that plant put forth
Whose fruit made perfect by thy sunny eyes,
Will be as of the trees of Paradise.

The day is come, and thou wilt fly with me.
To whatsoe'er of dull mortality
Is mine, remain a vestal sister still;
To the intense, the deep, the imperishable,
Not mine but me, henceforth be thou united
Even as a bride, delighting and delighted.
Thine hour is come:—the destined Star has risen
Which shall descend upon a vacant prison.
The walls are high, the gates are strong, thick set
The sentinels—but true love never yet
Was thus constrained: it overleaps all fence:
Like lightning, with invisible violence
Piercing its continents; like Heaven's free breath,
Which he who grasps can hold not; liker Death,
Who rides upon a thought, and makes his way
Through temple, tower, and palace, and the array
Of arms: more strength has Love than he or they ·
For it can burst his charnel, and make free
The limbs in chains, the heart in agony,
The soul in dust and chaos.

Emily,
A ship is floating in the harbour now,
A wind is hovering o'er the mountain's brow;
There is a path on the sea's azure floor,
No keel has ever ploughed that path before;
The halcyons brood around the foamless isles;
The treacherous Ocean has forsworn its wiles;
The merry mariners are bold and free:
Say, my heart's sister, wilt thou sail with me?
Our bark is as an albatross, whose nest
Is a far Eden of the purple East;
And we between her wings will sit, while Night
And Day, and Storm, and Calm, pursue their flight.
Our ministers, along the boundless Sea,
Treading each other's heels, unheededly.
It is an isle under Ionian skies,
Beautiful as a wreck of Paradise,
And, for the harbours are not safe and good,
This land would have remained a solitude
But for some pastoral people native there,
Who from the Elysian, clear, and golden air
Draw the last spirit of the age of gold,
Simple and spirited; innocent and bold
The blue Ægean girds this chosen home,
With ever-changing sound and light and foam,
Kissing the sifted sands, and caverns hoar;
And all the winds wandering along the shore

Undulate with the undulating tide:
There are thick woods where sylvan forms abide;
And many a fountain, rivulet, and pond,
As clear as elemental diamond,
Or serene morning air; and far beyond,
The mossy tracks made by the goats and deer
(Which the rough shepherd treads but once a year),
Pierce into glades, caverns, and bowers, and halls
Built round with ivy, which the waterfalls
Illumining, with sound that never fails
Accompany the noonday nightingales;
And all the place is peopled with sweet airs;
The light clear element which the isle wears
Is heavy with the scent of lemon-flowers,
Which floats like mist laden with unseen showers,
And falls upon the eyelids like faint sleep;
And from the moss violets and jonquils peep,
And dart their arrowy odour through the brain
Till you might faint with that delicious pain.
And every motion, odour, beam and tone,
With that deep music is in unison;
Which is a soul within the soul—they seem
Like echoes of an antenatal dream.
It is an isle 'twixt Heaven, Air, Earth, and Sea,
Cradled, and hung in clear tranquillity;
Bright as that wandering Eden Lucifer,
Washed by the soft blue Oceans of young air.
It is a favoured place. Famine or Blight,
Pestilence, War, and Earthquake, never light
Upon its mountain peaks; blind vultures, they
Sail onward far upon their fatal way:
The winged storms, chanting their thunder-psalm
To other lands, leave azure chasms of calm
Over this isle, or weep themselves in dew,
From which its fields and woods ever renew
Their green and golden immortality.
And from the sea there rise, and from the sky
There fall, clear exhalations, soft and bright,
Veil after veil, each hiding some delight,
Which Sun or Moon or zephyr draw aside,
Till the isle's beauty, like a naked bride
Glowing at once with love and loveliness,
Blushes and trembles at its own excess:
Yet, like a buried lamp, a Soul no less
Burns in the heart of this delicious isle,
An atom of the Eternal, whose own smile
Unfolds itself, and may be felt not seen
O'er the grey rocks, blue waves, and forests green,
Filling their bare and void interstices.
But the chief marvel of the wilderness
Is a lone dwelling, built by whom or how
None of the rustic island-people know:
'Tis not a tower of strength, though with its height
it overtops the woods; but, for delight,
Some wise and tender Ocean-King, ere crime
Had been invented, in the world's young prime,
Reared it, a wonder of that simple time,
An envy of the isles, a pleasure-house

Made sacred to his sister and his spouse.
It scarce seems now a wreck of human art,
But, as it were Titanic; in the heart
Of Earth having assumed its form, then grown
Out of the mountains, from the living stone,
Lifting itself in caverns light and high:
For all the antique and learned imagery
Has been erased, and in the place of it
The ivy and the wild-vine interknit
The volumes of their many-twining stems;
Parasite flowers illumine with dewy gems
The lampless halls, and when they fade, the sky
Peeps through their winter-woof of tracery
With moonlight patches, or star atoms keen,
Or fragments of the day's intense serene;
Working mosaic on their Parian floors,
And, day and night, aloof, from the high towers
And terraces, the Earth and Ocean seem
To sleep in one another's arms, and dream
Of waves, flowers, clouds, woods, rocks, and all that we
Read in their smiles, and call reality.

This isle and house are mine, and I have vowed
Thee to be lady of the solitude.
And I have fitted up some chambers there
Looking towards the golden Eastern air,
And level with the living winds, which flow
Like waves above the living waves below.
I have sent books and music there, and all
Those instruments with which high spirits call
The future from its cradle, and the past
Out of its grave, and make the present last
In thoughts and joys which sleep, but cannot die,
Folded within their own eternity.
Our simple life wants little, and true taste
Hires not the pale drudge Luxury, to waste
The scene it would adorn, and therefore still,
Nature, with all her children, haunts the hill.
The ringdove, in the embowering ivy, yet
Keeps up her love-lament, and the owls flit
Round the evening tower, and the young stars glance
Between the quick bats in their twilight dance;
The spotted deer bask in the fresh moonlight
Before our gate, and the slow, silent night
Is measured by the pants of their calm sleep.
Be this our home in life, and when years heap
Their withered hours, like leaves, on our decay,
Let us become the overhanging day, .
The living soul of this Elysian isle,
Conscious, inseparable, one.   Meanwhile
We two will rise, and sit, and walk together,
Under the roof of blue Ionian weather,
And wander in the meadows, or ascend
The mossy mountains, where the blue heavens bend
With lightest winds, to touch their paramour;
Or linger, where the pebble-paven shore,
Under the quick, faint kisses of the sea
Trembles and sparkles as with ecstasy,—

Possessing and possessed by all that is
Within that calm circumference of bliss,
And by each other, till to love and live
Be one :—or, at the noontide hour, arrive
Where some old cavern hoar seems yet to keep
The moonlight of the expired night asleep,
Through which the awakened day can never peep;
A veil for our seclusion, close as Night's,
Where secure sleep may kill thine innocent lights;
Sleep, the fresh dew of languid love, the rain
Whose drops quench kisses till they burn again.
And we will talk, until thought's melody
Become too sweet for utterance, and it die
In words, to live again in looks, which dart
With thrilling tone into the voiceless heart,
Harmonizing silence without a sound.
Our breath shall intermix, our bosoms bound,
And our veins beat together ; and our lips,
With other eloquence than words, eclipse
The soul that burns between them, and the wells
Which boil under our being's inmost cells,
The fountains of our deepest life shall be
Confused in passion's golden purity,
As mountain-springs under the morning Sun.
We shall become the same, we shall be one
Spirit within two frames, oh ! wherefore two?
One passion in twin-hearts, which grows and grew,
Till, like two meteors of expanding flame,
Those spheres instinct with it become the same,
Touch, mingle, are transfigured ; ever still
Burning, yet ever inconsumable :
In one another's substance finding food,
Like flames too pure and light and unimbued
To nourish their bright lives with baser prey,
Which point to Heaven and cannot pass away :
One hope within two wills, one will beneath
Two overshadowing minds, one life, one death,
One Heaven, one Hell, one immortality,
And one annihilation.   Woe is me !
The winged words on which my soul would pierce
Into the height of love's rare Universe,
Are chains of lead around its flight of fire.
I pant, I sink, I tremble, I expire !

———

Weak Verses go, kneel at your Sovereign's feet,
And say :—" We are the masters of thy slave ;
What wouldest thou with us and ours and thine ?"
Then call your sisters from Oblivion's cave,
All singing loud : " Love's very pain is sweet,
But its reward is in the world divine,
Which, if not here, it builds beyond the grave."
So shall ye live when I am there.   Then haste
Over the hearts of men, until ye meet
Marina, Vanna, Primus, and the rest,
And bid them love each other and be blest :
And leave the troop which errs, and which reproves
And come and be my guest,—for I am Love's.

Y

1821.

ADONAIS.

AN ELEGY ON THE DEATH OF JOHN KEATS.

PREFACE.

" Φάρμακον ἦλθε, βίων, ποτὶ σόν στόμα, φάρμακον εἶδες,
Πῶς τευ τοῖς χείλεσσι ποτέδραμε, κοὐκ ἐγλυκανθη ;
Τίς δὲ βροτὸς τοσσοῦτον ἀνάμερος. ἢ κεράσαι τοι,
Η δοῦναι λαλέοντι τὸ φάρμακον; ἔκφυγεν ὠδάν."

MOSCHUS, *Epitaph. Bion.*

IT is my intention to subjoin to the London edition of this poem, a criticis
upon the claims of its lamented object to be classed among the writers of t
highest genius who have adorned our age. My known repugnance to t
narrow principles of taste on which several of his earlier compositions we
modelled, prove, at least, that I am an impartial judge. I consider the fra
ment of "Hyperion" as second to nothing that was ever produced by a writ
of the same years.

John Keats died at Rome of a consumption, in his twenty-fourth year, on t
23rd of February, 1821; and was buried in the romantic and lonely cemetery
the Protestants in that city, under the pyramid which is the tomb of Cesti
and the massy walls and towers, now mouldering and desolate, which form
the circuit of ancient Rome. The cemetery is an open space among the ruir
covered in winter with violets and daisies. It might make one in love wi
death, to think that one should be buried in so sweet a place.

The genius of the lamented person to whose memory I have dedicated the
unworthy verses, was not less delicate and fragile than it was beautiful; a
where canker-worms abound, what wonder if its young flower was blighted
the bud? The savage criticism on his "Endymion," which appeared in t
Quarterly Review, produced the most violent effect on his susceptible min
the agitation thus originated ended in the rupture of a bloodvessel in the lung
a rapid consumption ensued, and the succeeding acknowledgments from mc
candid critics, of the true greatness of his powers, were ineffectual to heal t
wound thus wantonly inflicted.

It may be well said that these wretched men know not what they do. Th
scatter their insults and their slanders without heed as to whether the poison
shaft lights on a heart made callous by many blows, or one, like Keats's, coi
posed of more penetrable stuff. One of their associates is, to my knowledge,
most base and unprincipled calumniator. As to "Endymion," was it a poe
whatever may be its defects, to be treated contemptuously by those who h
celebrated with various degrees of complacency and panegyric, "Paris," a
"Woman," and a "Syrian Tale," and Mrs. Lefanu, and Mr. Barrett, and M
Howard Payne, and a long list of the illustrious obscure? Are these the m
who, in their venal goodnature, presumed to draw a parallel between the Re

322

Mr. Milman and Lord Byron? What gnat did they strain at here, after having swallowed all those camels? Against what woman taken in adultery, dares the foremost of these literary prostitutes to cast his opprobrious stone? Miserable man! you, one of the meanest, have wantonly defaced one of the noblest specimens of the workmanship of God. Nor shall it be your excuse, that, murderer as you are, you have spoken daggers, but used none.

The circumstances of the closing scene of poor Keats's life were not made known to me until the Elegy was ready for the press. I am given to understand that the wound which his sensitive spirit had received from the criticism of "Endymion," was exasperated by the bitter sense of unrequited benefits; the poor fellow seems to have been hooted from the stage of life, no less by those on whom he had wasted the promise of his genius, than those on whom he had lavished his fortune and his care. He was accompanied to Rome, and attended in his last illness by Mr. Severn, a young artist of the highest promise, who, I have been informed, "almost risked his own life, and sacrificed every prospect to unwearied attendance upon his dying friend." Had I known these circumstances before the completion of my poem, I should have been tempted to add my feeble tribute of applause to the more solid recompense which the virtuous man finds in the recollection of his own motives. Mr. Severn can dispense with a reward from "such stuff as dreams are made of." His conduct is a golden augury of the success of his future career—may the unextinguished Spirit of his illustrious friend animate the creations of his pencil, and plead against Oblivion for his name!

" Ἀστὴρ πρὶν μὲν ἔλαμπες ἐνὶ ζώοισιν ἑῷος.
Νῦν δὲ θανὼν λάμπεις ἕσπερος ἐν φθιμένοις."—PLATO.

I.

I WEEP for Adonais—he is dead!
Oh! weep for Adonais, though our tears
Thaw not the frost which binds so dear a head!
And thou, sad Hour, selected from all years
To mourn our loss, rouse thy obscure compeers,
And teach them thine own sorrow! Say: "With me
Died Adonais! Till the future dares
Forget the past, his fate and fame shall be
An echo and a light unto eternity."

II.

Where wert thou, mighty Mother, when he lay,
When thy Son lay, pierced by the shaft which flies
In darkness? Where was lorn Urania
When Adonais died? With veilèd eyes,
'Mid listening Echoes, in her Paradise
She sate, while one, with soft enamoured breath,
Rekindled all the fading melodies
With which, like flowers that mock the corse beneath,
He had adorned and hid the coming bulk of Death.

III.

O, weep for Adonais—he is dead!
Wake, melancholy Mother, wake and weep!
Yet wherefore? Quench within their burning bed
Thy fiery tears, and let thy loud heart keep

Like his, a mute and uncomplaining sleep;
For he is gone, where all things wise and fair
Descend :—oh, dream not that the amorous Deep
Will yet restore him to the vital air;
Death feeds on his mute voice, and laughs at our despair.

IV.

Most musical of mourners, weep again !
Lament anew, Urania !—He died,
Who was the Sire of an immortal strain,
Blind, old, and lonely, when his country's pride,
The priest, the slave, and the liberticide,
Trampled and mocked with many a loathèd rite
Of lust and blood ; he went, unterrified,
Into the gulf of death : but his clear Sprite
Yet reigns o'er earth ; the third among the sons of light.

V.

Most musical of mourners, weep anew {
Not all to that bright station dared to climb ;
And happier they their happiness who knew,
Whose tapers yet burn through that night of time
In which suns perished ; others more sublime,
Struck by the envious wrath of man or God,
Have sunk, extinct in their refulgent prime ;
And some yet live, treading the thorny road,
Which leads, through toil and hate, to Fame's serene abode

VI.

But now thy youngest, dearest one, has perished,
The nursling of thy widowhood, who grew,
Like a pale flower by some sad maiden cherished.
And fed with true love tears, instead of dew ;
Most musical of mourners, weep anew !
Thy extreme hope, the loveliest and the last,
The bloom, whose petals nipt before they blew
Died on the promise of the fruit, is waste ;
The broken lily lies—the storm is overpast.

VII.

To that high Capital, where kingly Death
Keeps his pale court in beauty and decay,
He came ; and bought, with price of purest breath,
A grave among the eternal.—Come away !
Haste, while the vault of blue Italian day
Is yet his fitting charnel-roof ! while still
He lies, as if in dewy sleep he lay ;
Awake him not ! surely he takes his fill
Of deep and liquid rest, forgetful of all ill.

VIII.

He will awake no more, oh, never more !
Within the twilight chamber spreads apace
The shadow of white Death, and at the door
Invisible Corruption waits to trace,

His extreme way to her dim dwelling-place ;
The eternal Hunger sits, but pity and awe
Soothe her pale rage, nor dares she to deface
So fair a prey, till darkness, and the law
Of change shall o'er his sleep the mortal curtain draw.*

IX.

O, weep for Adonais !—The quick Dreams,
The passion-winged Ministers of thought,
Who were his flocks, whom near the living streams
Of his young spirit he fed, and whom he taught
The love which was its music, wander not,—
Wander no more, from kindling brain to brain,
But droop there, whence they sprung ; and mourn their lot
Round the cold heart, where, after their sweet pain,
They ne'er will gather strength, nor find a home again.

X.

And one with trembling hands clasps his cold head,
And fans him with her moonlight wings, and cries :
"Our love, our hope, our sorrow, is not dead :
See, on the silken fringe of his faint eyes,
Like dew upon a sleeping flower, there lies
A tear some Dream has loosened from his brain."
Lost Angel of a ruined Paradise !
She knew not 'twas her own ; as with no stain
She faded, like a cloud which had outwept its rain.

XI.

One from a lucid urn of starry dew
Washed his light limbs as if embalming them ;
Another clipt her profuse locks, and threw
The wreath upon him, like an anadem,
Which frozen tears instead of pearls begem ;
Another in her wilful grief would break
Her bow and winged reed, as if to stem
A greater loss with one which was more weak ;
And dull the barbed fire against his frozen cheek.

XII.

Another Splendour on his mouth alit,
That mouth, whence it was wont to draw the breath
Which gave it strength to pierce the guarded wit,
And pass into the panting heart beneath
With lightning and with music : the damp death
Quenched its caress upon his icy lips ;
And, as a dying meteor stains a wreath
Of moonlight vapour, which the cold night clips,
It flushed through his pale limbs, and passed to its eclipse.

XIII.

And others came . . . Desires and Adorations,
Wingèd Persuasions and veiled Destinies,

---

* In the original edition the last line ran thus :—
    Of mortal change shall fill the grave which is her maw.

Splendours, and Glooms, and glimmering Incarnations
Of hopes and fears, and twilight Fantasies ;
And Sorrow, with her family of Sighs,
And Pleasure, blind with tears, led by the gleam
Of her own dying smile instead of eyes,
 Came in slow pomp ;—the moving pomp might seem
Like pageantry of mist on an autumnal stream.

XIV.

All he had loved, and moulded into thought,
From shape, and hue, and odour, and sweet sound,
Lamented Adonais.   Morning sought
Her eastern watch-tower, and her hair unbound,
Wet with the tears which should adorn the ground,
Dimmed the aërial eyes that kindle day ;
Afar the melancholy thunder moaned,
Pale Ocean in unquiet slumber lay,
And the wild winds flew round, sobbing in their dismay.

XV.

Lost Echo sits amid the voiceless mountains,
And feeds her grief with his remembered lay,
And will no more reply to winds or fountains,
Or amorous birds perched on the young green spray,
Or herdsman's horn, or bell at closing day;
Since she can mimic not his lips, more dear
Than those for whose disdain she pined away
Into a shadow of all sounds:—a drear
Murmur, between their songs, is all the woodmen hear.

XVI.

Grief made the young Spring wild, and she threw down
Her kindling buds, as if she Autumn were,
Or they dead leaves; since her delight is flown,
For whom should she have waked the sullen year?
To Phœbus was not Hyacinth so dear,
Not to himself Narcissus, as to both
Thou Adonais: wan they stand and sere
Amid the faint companions of their youth,
With dew all turned to tears; odour, to sighing ruth.

XVII.

Thy spirit's sister, the lorn nightingale
Mourns not her mate with such melodious pain;
Not so the eagle, who like thee could scale
Heaven, and could nourish in the sun's domain
Her mighty youth with morning, doth complain,
Soaring and screaming round her empty nest,
As Albion wails for thee: the curse of Cain
Light on his head who pierced thy innocent breast,
And scared the angel soul that was its earthly guest !

XVIII.

Ah woe is me !   Winter is come and gone,
But grief returns with the revolving year;

The airs and streams renew their joyous tone;
The ants, the bees, the swallows, reappear;
Fresh leaves and flowers deck the dead Season's bier;
The amorous birds now pair in every brake,
And build their mossy homes in field and brere;
And the green lizard, and the golden snake,
Like unimprisoned flames, out of their trance awake.

XIX.

Through wood and stream and field and hill and Ocean
A quickening life from the Earth's heart has burst
As it has ever done, with change and motion,
From the great morning of the world when first
God dawned on Chaos; in its steam immersed,
The lamps of Heaven flash with a softer light;
All baser things pant with life's sacred thirst;
Diffuse themselves; and spend in love's delight,
The beauty and the joy of their renewèd might.

XX.

The leprous corpse touched by this spirit tender
Exhales itself in flowers of gentle breath;
Like incarnations of the stars, when splendour
Is changed to fragrance, they illumine death
And mock the merry worm that wakes beneath;
Naught we know, dies. Shall that alone which knows
Be as a sword consumed before the sheath
By sightless lightning?—the intense atom glows
A moment, then is quenched in a most cold repose.

XXI.

Alas! that all we loved of him should be,
But for our grief, as if it had not been,
And grief itself be mortal! Woe is me!
Whence are we, and why are we? of what scene
The actors or spectators? Great and mean
Meet massed in death, who lends what life must borrow.
As long as skies are blue, and fields are green,
Evening must usher night, night urge the morrow,
Month follow month with woe, and year wake year to sorrow.

XXII.

He will awake no more, oh, never more!
"Wake thou," cried Misery, "childless Mother, rise
Out of thy sleep, and slake, in thy heart's core,
A wound more fierce than his with tears and sighs."
And all the Dreams that watched Urania's eyes,
And all the Echoes whom their sister's song
Had held in holy silence, cried: "Arise!"
Swift as a thought by the snake Memory stung,
From her ambrosial rest the fading Splendour sprung.

XXIII.

She rose like an Autumnal Night, that springs
Out of the East, and follows wild and drear

The golden Day, which, on eternal wings,
Even as a ghost abandoning a bier,
Had left the Earth a corpse.   Sorrow and fear
So struck, so roused, so rapt Urania,
So saddened round her like an atmosphere
Of stormy mist; so swept her on her way
Even to the mournful place where Adonais lay.

XXIV.

Out of her secret Paradise she sped,
Through camps and cities rough with stone, and steel,
And human hearts, which to her aery tread
Yielding not, wounded the invisible
Palms of her tender feet where'er they fell:
And barbed tongues, and thoughts more sharp than they
Rent the soft Form they never could repel,
Whose sacred blood, like the young tears of May,
Paved with eternal flowers that undeserving way.

XXV.

In the death-chamber for a moment Death
Shamed by the presence of that living Might
Blushed to annihilation, and the breath
Revisited those lips, and life's pale light
Flashed through those limbs, so late her dear delight.
" Leave me not wild and drear and comfortless,
As silent lightning leaves the starless night !
Leave me not !" cried Urania: her distress
Roused Death: Death rose and smiled, and met her vain caress

XXVI.

"Stay yet awhile ! speak to me once again;
Kiss me, so long but as a kiss may live;
And in my heartless breast and burning brain
That word, that kiss shall all thoughts else survive,
With food of saddest memory kept alive,
Now thou art dead, as if it were a part
Of thee, my Adonais !   I would give
All that I am to be as thou now art !
But I am chained to Time, and cannot thence depart!

XXVII.

"Oh gentle child, beautiful as thou wert,
Why didst thou leave the trodden paths of men
Too soon, and with weak hands though mighty heart
Dare the unpastured dragon in his den ?
Defenceless as thou wert, oh where was then
Wisdom the mirrored shield, or Scorn the spear?
Or hadst thou waited the full cycle, when
Thy spirit should have filled its crescent sphere,
The monsters of life's waste had fled from thee like deer.

XXVIII.

" The herded wolves, bold only to pursue ;
The obscene ravens, clamorous o'er the dead ;

The vultures to the conqueror's banner true,
Who feed where Desolation first has fed,
And whose wings rain contagion;—how they fled,
When like Apollo, from his golden bow,
The Pythian of the age one arrow sped
And smiled!—The spoilers tempt no second blow,
They fawn on the proud feet that spurn them as they go.

XXIX.

" The sun comes forth, and many reptiles spawn;
He sets, and each ephemeral insect then
Is gathered into death without a dawn,
And the immortal stars awake again;
So is it in the world of living men:
A godlike mind soars forth, in its delight
Making earth bare and veiling heaven, and when
It sinks, the swarms that dimmed or shared its light
Leave to its kindred lamps the spirit's awful night."

XXX.

Thus ceased she: and the mountain shepherds came,
Their garlands sere, their magic mantles rent;
The Pilgrim of Eternity, whose fame
Over his living head like Heaven is bent,
An early but enduring monument,
Came, veiling all the lightnings of his song
In sorrow; from her wilds Ierne sent
The sweetest lyrist of her saddest wrong,
And love taught grief to fall like music from his tongue.

XXXI.

'Midst others of less note, came one frail Form,
A phantom among men; companionless
As the last cloud of an expiring storm
Whose thunder is its knell; he, as I guess,
Had gazed on Nature's naked loveliness,
Actæon-like, and now he fled astray
With feeble steps o'er the world's wilderness,
And his own thoughts, along that rugged way,
Pursued, like raging hounds, their father and their prey.

XXXII.

A pard-like Spirit beautiful and swift—
A Love in desolation masked;—a Power
Girt round with weakness;—it can scarce uplift
The weight of the superincumbent hour;
It is a dying lamp, a falling shower,
A breaking billow;—even whilst we speak
Is it not broken? On the withering flower
The killing sun smiles brightly: on a cheek
The life can burn in blood, even while the heart may break.

XXXIII.

His head was bound with pansies over-blown,
And faded violets, white, and pied, and blue;

And a light spear topped with a cypress cone,
Round whose rude shaft dark ivy-tresses grew,
Yet dripping with the forest's noonday dew,
Vibrated, as the ever-beating heart
Shook the weak hand that grasped it; of that crew
He came the last, neglected and apart:
A herd-abandoned deer, struck by the hunter's dart.

XXXIV.

All stood aloof, and at his partial moan
Smiled through their tears ; well knew that gentle band
Who in another's fate now wept his own;
As in the accents of an unknown land
He sung new sorrow; sad Urania scanned
The Stranger's mien, and murmured: "Who art thou?"
He answered not, but with a sudden hand
Made bare his branded and ensanguined brow,
Which was like Cain's or Christ's.—Oh ! that it should be so !

XXXV.

What softer voice is hushed over the dead ?
Athwart what brow is that dark mantle thrown ?
What form leans sadly o'er the white deathbed,
In mockery of monumental stone,
The heavy heart heaving without a moan ?
If it be He, who, gentlest of the wise,
Taught, soothed, loved, honoured the departed one;
Let me not vex, with inharmonious sighs,
The silence of that heart's accepted sacrifice.

XXXVI.

Our Adonais has drunk poison—oh,
What deaf and viperous murderer could crown
Life's early cup with such a draught of woe?
The nameless worm would now itself disown:
It felt, yet could escape the magic tone
Whose prelude held all envy, hate, and wrong,
But what was howling in one breast alone,
Silent with expectation of the song,
Whose master's hand is cold, whose silver lyre unstrung.

XXXVII.

Live thou, whose infamy is not thy fame !
Live ! fear no heavier chastisement from me,
Thou noteless blot on a remembered name !
But to thyself, and know thyself to be !
And ever at thy season be thou free
To spill the venom, when thy fangs o'erflow;
Remorse and Self-contempt shall cling to thee;
Hot Shame shall burn upon thy secret brow,
And like a beaten hound tremble thou shalt—as now.

XXXVIII.

Nor let us weep that our delight is fled
Far from these carrion kites that scream below;

He wakes or sleeps with the enduring dead:
Thou canst not soar where he is sitting now.
Dust to the dust! but the pure spirit shall flow
Back to the burning fountain whence it came,
A portion of the Eternal, which must glow
Through time and change, unquenchably the same,
Whilst thy cold embers choke the sordid hearth of shame

XXXIX.

Peace, peace! he is not dead, he doth not sleep—
He hath awakened from the dream of life—
'Tis we, who, lost in stormy visions, keep
With phantoms an unprofitable strife,
And in mad trance strike with our spirit's knife
Invulnerable nothings.—*We* decay
Like corpses in a charnel; fear and grief
Convulse us and consume us day by day,
And cold hopes swarm like worms within our living clay.

XL.

He has outsoared the shadow of our night;
Envy and calumny, and hate and pain,
And that unrest which men miscall delight,
Can touch him not and torture not again;
From the contagion of the world's slow stain
He is secure, and now can never mourn
A heart grown cold, a head grown grey in vain;
Nor, when the spirit's self has ceased to burn,
With sparkless ashes load an unlamented urn.

XLI.

He lives, he wakes—'tis Death is dead, not he;
Mourn not for Adonais.—Thou, young Dawn,
Turn all thy dew to splendour, for from thee
The spirit thou lamentest is not gone;
Ye caverns and ye forests, cease to moan!
Cease ye faint flowers and fountains, and thou Air,
Which like a mourning veil thy scarf hadst thrown
O'er the abandoned Earth, now leave it bare
Even to the joyous stars which smile on its despair.

XLII.

He is made one with Nature: there is heard
His voice in all her music, from the moan
Of thunder, to the song of night's sweet bird;
He is a presence to be felt and known
In darkness and in light, from herb and stone,
Spreading itself where'er that Power may move
Which has withdrawn his being to its own;
Which wields the world with never-wearied love,
Sustains it from beneath, and kindles it above.

XLIII.

He is a portion of the loveliness
Which once he made more lovely: he doth bear

His part, while the one Spirit's plastic stress
Sweeps through the dull dense world, compelling there
All new successions to the forms they wear;
Torturing the unwilling dross that checks its flight
To its own likeness, as each mass they bear;
And bursting in its beauty and its might
From trees and beasts and men into the Heaven's light.

XLIV.

The splendours of the firmament of time
May be eclipsed, but are extinguished not;
Like stars to their appointed height they climb,
And death is a low mist which cannot blot
The brightness it may veil.   When lofty thought
Lifts a young heart above its mortal lair,
And love and life contend in it, for what
Shall be its earthly doom, the dead live there
And move like winds of light on dark and stormy air.

XLV.

The inheritors of unfulfilled renown
Rose from their thrones, built beyond mortal thought,
Far in the Unapparent.   Chatterton
Rose pale, his solemn agony had not
Yet faded from him; Sidney as he fought
And as he fell, and as he lived and loved,
Sublimely mild, a spirit without spot,
Arose; and Lucan, by his death approved:
Oblivion as they rose shrank like a thing reproved.

XLVI.

And many more, whose names on earth are dark,
But whose transmitted effluence cannot die
So long as fire outlives the parent spark,
Rose, robed in dazzling immortality.
"Thou art become as one of us," they cry;
"It was for thee yon kingless sphere has long
Swung blind in unascended majesty,
Silent alone amid an Heaven of Song.
Assume thy wingèd throne, thou Vesper of our throng!"

XLVII.

Who mourns for Adonais? oh come forth,
Fond wretch! and know thyself and him aright.
Clasp with thy panting soul the pendulous Earth
As from a centre, dart thy spirit's light
Beyond all worlds, until its spacious might
Satiate the void circumference: then shrink
Even to a point within our day and night;
And keep thy heart light, lest it make thee sink
When hope has kindled hope, and lured thee to the brink.

XLVIII.

Or go to Rome, which is the sepulchre,
O, not of him, but of our joy: 'tis nought

That ages, empires, and religions there
Lie buried in the ravage they have wrought;
For such as he can lend,—they borrow not
Glory from those who made the world their prey;
And he is gathered to the kings of thought
Who waged contention with their time's decay,
And of the past are all that cannot pass away.

XLIX.

Go thou to Rome,—at once the Paradise,
The grave, the city, and the wilderness;
And where its wrecks like shattered mountains rise,
And flowering weeds, and fragrant copses dress
The bones of Desolation's nakedness,
Pass, till the Spirit of the spot shall lead
Thy footsteps to a slope of green access,
Where, like an infant's smile, over the dead
A light of laughing flowers along the grass is spread.

L.

And grey walls moulder round, on which dull Time
Feeds, like slow fire upon a hoary brand;
And one keen pyramid with wedge sublime,
Pavilioning the dust of him who planned
This refuge for his memory, doth stand
Like flame transformed to marble; and beneath
A field is spread, on which a newer band
Have pitched in Heaven's smile their camp of death,
Welcoming him we lose with scarce extinguished breath.

LI.

Here, pause: these graves are all too young as yet
To have outgrown the sorrow which consigned
Its charge to each; and if the seal is set,
Here, on one fountain of a mourning mind,
Break it not thou! too surely shalt thou find
Thine own well full, if thou returnest home,
Of tears and gall. From the world's bitter wind
Seek shelter in the shadow of the tomb.
What Adonais is, why fear we to become?

LII.

The One remains, the many change and pass;
Heaven's light for ever shines, Earth's shadows fly;
Life, like a dome of many-coloured glass,
Stains the white radiance of Eternity,
Until Death tramples it to fragments.—Die,
If thou wouldst be with that which thou dost seek!
Follow where all is fled!—Rome's azure sky,
Flowers, ruins, statues, music, words, are weak
The glory they transfuse with fitting truth to speak.

LIII.

Why linger, why turn back, why shrink, my Heart?
Thy hopes are gone before: from all things here

They have departed; thou shouldst now depart!
A light is passed from the revolving year,
And man, and woman; and what still is dear
Attracts to crush, repels to make thee wither.
The soft sky smiles, the low wind whispers near:
'Tis Adonais calls! oh, hasten thither,
No more let Life divide what Death can join together.

LIV.

That Light whose smile kindles the Universe,
That Beauty in which all things work and move,
That Benediction which the eclipsing Curse
Of birth can quench not, that sustaining Love
Which through the web of being blindly wove
By man and beast and earth and air and sea,
Burns bright or dim, as each are mirrors of
The fire for which all thirst; now beams on me
Consuming the last clouds of cold mortality.

LV.

The breath whose might I have invoked in song
Descends on me; my spirit's bark is driven
Far from the shore, far from the trembling throng
Whose sails were never to the tempest given;
The massy earth and sphered skies are riven!
I am borne darkly, fearfully, afar;
Whilst burning through the inmost veil of Heaven,
The soul of Adonais, like a star,
Beacons from the abode where the Eternal are.

1821.

HELLAS.

A LYRICAL DRAMA.

"Μάντις εἰμ' ἐσθλῶν ἀγώνων."—ŒDIP. COLON.

TO HIS EXCELLENCY

PRINCE ALEXANDER MAVROCORDATO,

LATE SECRETARY FOR FOREIGN AFFAIRS TO THE HOSPODAR OF WALLACHIA,

THE DRAMA OF HELLAS IS INSCRIBED,

AS AN IMPERFECT TOKEN OF THE ADMIRATION, SYMPATHY,
AND FRIENDSHIP, OF THE AUTHOR.

Pisa, November 1, 1821.

PREFACE.

THE poem of "Hellas," written at the suggestion of the events of the moment, is a mere improvise, and derives its interest (should it be found to possess any) solely from the intense sympathy which the author feels with the cause he would celebrate.

The subject, in its present state, is insusceptible of being treated otherwise than lyrically: and, if I have called this poem a drama from the circumstance of its being composed in dialogue, the licence is not greater than that which has been assumed by other poets who have called their productions epics only because they have been divided into twelve or twenty-four books.

The "Persæ" of Æschylus afforded me the first model of my conception, although the decision of the glorious contest now waging in Greece being yet suspended forbids a catastrophe parallel to the return of Xerxes and the desolation of the Persians. I have therefore contented myself with exhibiting a series of lyric pictures, and with having wrought upon the curtain of futurity, which falls upon the unfinished scene, such figures of indistinct and visionary delineation as suggest the final triumph of the Greek cause, as a portion of the cause of civilization and social improvement.

The drama (if drama it must be called) is, however, so inartificial that I doubt whether, if recited on the Thespian waggon to an Athenian village at the Dionysiaca, it would have obtained the prize of the goat. I shall bear with equanimity any punishment greater than the loss of such a reward, which the Aristarchi of the hour may think fit to inflict.

The only *goat-song* which I have yet attempted has, I confess, in spite of the

335

unfavourable nature of the subject, received a greater and a more valuable portion of applause than I expected, or than it deserved.

Common fame is the only authority which I can allege for the details which form the basis of the poem, and I must trespass upon the forgiveness of my readers for the display of newspaper erudition to which I have been reduced. Undoubtedly, until the conclusion of the war, it will be impossible to obtain an account of it sufficiently authentic for historical materials; but poets have their privilege, and it is unquestionable that actions of the most exalted courage have been performed by the Greeks—that they have gained more than one naval victory—and that their defeat in Wallachia was signalized by circumstances of heroism more glorious even than victory.

The apathy of the rulers of the civilized world to the astonishing circumstance of the descendants of that nation to which they owe their civilization rising as it were from the ashes of their ruin is something perfectly inexplicable to a mere spectator of the shows of this mortal scene. We are all Greeks. Our laws, our literature, our religion, our arts, have their root in Greece. But for Greece—Rome, the instructor, the conqueror, or the metropolis, of our ancestors, would have spread no illumination with her arms, and we might still have been savages and idolaters; or, what is worse, might have arrived at such a stagnant and miserable state of social institutions as China and Japan possess.

The human form and the human mind attained to a perfection in Greece which has impressed its image on those faultless productions whose very fragments are the despair of modern art; and has propagated impulses which cannot cease, through a thousand channels of manifest or imperceptible operation, to ennoble and delight mankind until the extinction of the race.

The modern Greek is the descendant of those glorious beings whom the imagination almost refuses to figure to itself as belonging to our kind; and he inherits much of their sensibility, their rapidity of conception, their enthusiasm, and their courage. If in many instances he is degraded by moral and political slavery to the practice of the basest vices it engenders, and that below the level of ordinary degradation; let us reflect that the corruption of the best produces the worst, and that habits which subsist only in relation to a peculiar state of social institution may be expected to cease as soon as that relation is dissolved. In fact, the Greeks, since the admirable novel of "Anastatius" could have been a faithful picture of their manners, have undergone most important changes; the flower of their youth, returning to their country from the universities of Italy, Germany, and France, have communicated to their fellow-citizens the latest results of that social perfection of which their ancestors were the original source. The university of Chios contained, before the breaking out of the revolution, eight hundred students, and among them several Germans and Americans. The munificence and energy of many of the Greek princes and merchants, directed to the renovation of their country with a spirit and a wisdom which have few examples, are above all praise.

The English permit their own oppressors to act according to their natural sympathy with the Turkish tyrant, and to brand upon their name the indelible blot of an alliance with the enemies of domestic happiness, of Christianity, and civilization.

Russia desires to possess, not to liberate, Greece; and is contented to see the Turks, its natural enemies, and the Greeks, its intended slaves, enfeeble each other, until one or both fall into its net. The wise and generous policy of England would have consisted in establishing the independence of Greece, and in maintaining it both against Russia and the Turk;—but when was the oppressor generous or just?

The Spanish peninsula is already free. France is tranquil in the enjoyment of a partial exemption from the abuses which its unnatural and feeble government is vainly attempting to revive. The seed of blood and misery has been sown in Italy, and a more vigorous race is arising to go forth to the harvest. The world waits only the news of a revolution of Germany, to see the tyrants who have pinnacled themselves on its supineness precipitated into the ruin from which they shall never arise. Well do these destroyers of mankind know their enemy, when they impute the insurrection in Greece to the same spirit before which they tremble throughout the rest of Europe; and that enemy well knows the power and the cunning of its opponents, and watches the moment of their approaching weakness and inevitable division, to wrest the bloody sceptres from their grasp.

DRAMATIS PERSONÆ.

MAHMUD.	DAOOD.
HASSAN.	AHASUERUS.
CHORUS of Greek Captive Women.	The Phantom of Mahomet the Second.

Messengers, Slaves, and Attendants.

SCENE—*Constantinople.* TIME—*Sunset.*

SCENE.—*A Terrace on the Seraglio.*

MAHMUD, *sleeping; an Indian Slave sitting beside his Couch.*

CHORUS OF GREEK CAPTIVE WOMEN.

WE strew these opiate flowers
 On thy restless pillow,—
They were stripped from orient bowers,
 By the Indian billow.
  Be thy sleep
  Calm and deep,
Like theirs who fell—not ours who weep!

INDIAN.

Away, unlovely dreams!
 Away, false shapes of sleep!
Be his, as heaven seems,
 Clear and bright and deep,
Soft as love, and calm as death,
Sweet as a summer night without a breath.

CHORUS.

Sleep, sleep! Our song is laden
 With the soul of slumber;
It was sung by a Samian maiden
 Whose lover was of the number
  Who now keep
  That calm sleep
Whence none may wake, where none shall weep.

INDIAN.

I touch thy temples pale,
 I breathe my soul on thee!
And, could my prayers avail,
 All my joy should be
Dead, and I would live to weep,
So thou mightst win one hour of quiet sleep.

z

Chorus.

Breathe low, low,
The spell of the mighty Mistress now!
When Conscience lulls her sated snake,
And tyrants sleep, let Freedom wake.
Breathe low, low,
The words which, like secret fire, shall flow
Through the veins of the frozen earth—low, low.

Semichorus I.

Life may change, but it may fly not:
Hope may vanish, but can die not;
Truth be veiled, but still it burneth;
Love repulsed,—but it returneth.

Semichorus II.

Yet were life a charnel where
Hope lay coffined with Despair;
Yet were truth a sacred lie;
Love were lust—

Semichorus I.

If Liberty
Lent not life its soul of light,
Hope its iris of delight,
Truth its prophet's robe to wear,
Love its power to give and bear.

Chorus.

In the great morning of the world,
The Spirit of God with might unfurled
The flag of Freedom over chaos,
    And all its banded anarchs fled,
Like vultures frighted from Imaus
    Before an earthquake's tread.
So from Time's tempestuous dawn
Freedom's splendour burst and shone:
Thermopylæ and Marathon
Caught, like mountains beacon-lighted,
    The springing fire.   The wingèd glory
On Philippi half alighted,
    Like an eagle on a promontory.
Its unwearied wings could fan
The quenchless ashes of Milan.
From age to age, from man to man,
It lived; and lit from land to land
Florence, Albion, Switzerland.
Then night fell; and, as from night,
Re-assuming fiery flight,
From the west swift Freedom came,
    Against the course of heaven and doom,
A second sun arrayed in flame,
    To burn, to kindle, to illume.
From far Atlantis its young beams
Chased the shadows and the dreams.
France, with all her sanguine steams,

Hid, but quenched it not; again
Through clouds its shafts of glory rain
From utmost Germany to Spain.
As an eagle fed with morning
Scorns the embattled tempest's warning
When she seeks her aerie hanging
In the mountain-cedar's hair,
And her brood expect the clanging
  Of her wings through the wild air,
Sick with famine;—Freedom so
To what of Greece remaineth now
Returns; her hoary ruins glow
Like orient mountains lost in day;
  Beneath the safety of her wings
Her renovated nurslings play,
  And in the naked lightnings
Of truth they purge their dazzled eyes.
Let Freedom leave,—where'er she flies,
A desert, or a paradise;
Let the beautiful and the brave
Share her glory, or a grave !

SEMICHORUS I.

With the gifts of gladness
Greece did thy cradle strew.

SEMICHORUS II.

With the tears of sadness
Greece did thy shroud bedew.

SEMICHORUS I.

With an orphan's affection
She followed thy bier through **Time:**

SEMICHORUS II.

And at thy resurrection
Reappeareth, like thou, sublime.

SEMICHORUS I.

If heaven should resume thee,
To heaven shall her spirit ascend.

SEMICHORUS II.

If hell should entomb thee,
To hell shall her high hearts bend.

SEMICHORUS I.

If annihilation—

SEMICHORUS II.

Dust let her glories be;
  And a name and a nation
Be forgotten, Freedom, with thee ;

INDIAN.

His brow grows darker—Breathe not—move not ;
He starts—he shudders.   Ye, that love not,
With your panting loud and fast
Have awakened him at last.

Mahmud [*Starting from his sleep*]. Man the Seraglio-guard !
   make fast the gate !
What ! from a cannonade of three short hours ?
'Tis false ! that breach towards the Bosphorus
Cannot be practicable yet—Who stirs ?
Stand to the match; that, when the foe prevails,
One spark may mix in reconciling ruin
The conqueror and the conquered !   Heave the tower
Into the gap—wrench off the roof !

Enter HASSAN.

              Ha ! what !
The truth of day lightens upon my dream,
And I am Mahmud still.
   Hassan.   Your Sublime Highness
Is strangely moved.
   Mahmud.   The times do cast strange shadows
Lest they, being first in peril as in glory,
Be whelmed in the fierce ebb:—and these are of them.
Thrice has a gloomy vision hunted me
As thus from sleep into the troubled day ;
It shakes me as the tempest shakes the sea,
Leaving no figure upon memory's glass.
Would that . . . no matter. Thou didst say thou knewest
A Jew whose spirit is a chronicle
Of strange and secret and forgotten things.
I bade thee summon him:—'tis said his tribe
Dream, and are wise interpreters of dreams.
   Hassan. The Jew of whom I spake is old—so old
He seems to have outlived a world's decay;
The hoary mountains and the wrinkled ocean
Seem younger still than he: his hair and beard
Are whiter than the tempest-sifted snow;
His cold pale limbs and pulseless arteries
Are like the fibres of a cloud instinct
With light, and, to the soul that quickens them,
Are as the atoms of the mountain-drift
To the winter wind: but from his eye looks forth
A life of unconsumèd thought which pierces
The present, and the past, and the to-come.
Some say that this is he whom the great prophet
Jesus, the son of Joseph, for his mockery,
Mocked with the curse of immortality.
Some feign that he is Enoch: others dream
He was pre-Adamite, and has survived
Cycles of generation and of ruin.
The sage, in truth, by dreadful abstinence,
And conquering penance of the mutinous flesh,
Deep contemplation and unwearied study,
In years outstretched beyond the date of man,
May have attained to sovereignty and science

Over those strong and secret things and thoughts
Which others fear and know not.
    Mahmud.   I would talk
With this old Jew.
    Hassan.   Thy will is even now
Made known to him where he dwells in a sea-cavern
'Mid the Demonesi, less accessible
Than thou or God !   He who would question him
Must sail alone at sunset where the stream
Of ocean sleeps around those foamless isles,
When the young moon is westering as now,
And evening airs wander upon the wave;
And, when the pines of that bee-pasturing isle,
Green Erebinthus, quench the fiery shadow
Of his gilt prow within the sapphire water,
Then must the lonely helmsman cry aloud
" Ahasuerus !" and the caverns round
Will answer "Ahasuerus !" If his prayer
Be granted, a faint meteor will arise,
Lighting him over Marmora; and a wind
Will rush out of the sighing pine-forest,
And with the wind a storm of harmony
Unutterably sweet, and pilot him
Through the soft twilight to the Bosphorus:
Thence, at the hour and place and circumstance
Fit for the matter of their conference,
The Jew appears.   Few dare, and few who dare
Win the desired communion . . . But that shout
Bodes—   [*A shout within.*
    Mahmud. Evil, doubtless; like all human sounds,
Let me converse with spirits.
    Hassan.   That shout again . . .
    Mahmud. This Jew whom thou hast summoned—
    Hassan.   Will be here—
    Mahmud. When the omnipotent hour to which are yoked
He, I, and all things, shall compel—enough.
Silence those mutineers—that drunken crew
That crowd about the pilot in the storm.
Ay, strike the foremost shorter by a head.
They weary me, and I have need of rest.
Kings are like stars—they rise and set, they have
The worship of the world, but no repose. [*Exeunt severally.*

CHORUS.

Worlds on worlds are rolling ever
    From creation to decay,
Like the bubbles on a river,
    Sparkling, bursting, borne away.
        But they are still immortal
    Who, through birth's orient portal
And death's dark chasm hurrying to and fro,
        Clothe their unceasing flight
        In the brief dust and light
Gathered around their chariots as they go;
        New shapes they still may weave,
        New gods, new laws, receive:
Bright or dim are they, as the robes they last
    On Death's bare ribs had cast.

A Power from the unknown God,
A Promethean Conqueror, came;
Like a triumphal path he trod
The thorns of death and shame.
A mortal shape to him
Was like the vapour dim
Which the orient planet animates with light.
Hell, sin, and slavery, came,
Like bloodhounds mild and tame,
Nor preyed until their Lord had taken flight.
The moon of Mahomet
Arose, and it shall set:
While, blazoned as on heaven's immortal noon,
The Cross leads generations on.

Swift as the radiant shapes of sleep
From one whose dreams are Paradise
Fly, when the fond wretch wakes to weep,
And day peers forth with her blank eyes;
So fleet, so faint, so fair,
The Powers of Earth and Air
Fled from the folding-star of Bethlehem:
Apollo, Pan, and Love,
And even Olympian Jove,
Grew weak, for killing Truth had glared on them.
Our hills and seas and streams,
Dispeopled of their dreams,
Their waters turned to blood, their dew to tears,
Wailed for the golden years.

Enter MAHMUD, HASSAN, DAOOD, *and others.*

Mahmud. More gold? Our ancestors bought gold with victory
And shall I sell it for defeat?
Daood.   The Janizars
Clamour for pay.
Mahmud.   Go bid them pay themselves
With Christian blood! Are there no Grecian virgins
Whose shrieks and spasms and tears they may enjoy?
No infidel children to impale on spears?
No hoary priests after that Patriarch
Who bent the curse against his country's heart,
Which clove his own at last? Go bid them kill:
Blood is the seed of gold.
Daood.   It has been sown,
And yet the harvest to the sicklemen
Is as a grain to each.
Mahmud.   Then take this signet:
Unlock the seventh chamber, in which lie
The treasures of victorious Solyman.
An empire's spoils stored for a day of ruin;
O spirit of my sires! is it not come?
The prey-birds and the wolves are gorged and sleep;
But these, who spread their feast on the red earth,
Hunger for gold, which fills not.—See them fed,
Then lead them to the rivers of fresh death.   [*Exit* DAOOD.
O! miserable dawn, after a night
More glorious than the day which it usurped!
O faith in God! O power on earth! O word

Of the great Prophet, whose o'ershadowing wings
Darkened the thrones and idols of the West,
Now bright!—for thy sake cursèd be the hour,
Even as a father by an evil child,
When the orient moon of Islam rolled in triumph
From Caucasus to white Ceraunia!
Ruin above, and anarchy below;
Terror without, and treachery within;
The chalice of destruction full, and all
Thirsting to drink; and who among us dares
To dash it from his lips? and where is Hope?
    Hassan. The lamp of our dominion still rides high;
One God is God—Mahomet is his Prophet.
Four hundred thousand Moslems, from the limits
Of utmost Asia, irresistibly
Throng, like full clouds at the sirocco's cry,
But not, like them, to weep their strength in tears;
They bear destroying lightning, and their step
Wakes earthquake, to consume and overwhelm,
And reign in ruin.   Phrygian Olympus,
Timolus, and Latmos, and Mycale, roughen
With horrent arms; and lofty ships even now,
Like vapours anchored to a mountain's edge,
Freighted with fire and whirlwind, wait at Scala
The convoy of the ever-veering wind.
Samos is drunk with blood;—the Greek has paid
Brief victory with swift loss and long despair.
The false Moldavian serfs fled fast and far
When the fierce shout of "Allah-illa-Allah!"
Rose like the warcry of the northern wind
Which kills the sluggish clouds, and leaves a flock
Of wild swans struggling with the naked storm;
So were the lost Greeks on the Danube's day!
If night is mute, yet the returning sun
Kindles the voices of the morning birds;
Nor at thy bidding less exultingly
Than birds rejoicing in the golden day
The Anarchies of Africa unleash
Their tempest-wingèd eities of the sea,
To speak in thunder to the rebel world.
Like sulphurous clouds half-shattered by the storm,
They sweep the pale Ægean; while the Queen
Of Ocean, bound upon her island throne
Far in the West, sits mourning that her sons,
Who frown on freedom, spare a smile for thee:
Russia still hovers, as an eagle might
Within a cloud near which a kite and crane
Hang tangled in inextricable fight,
To stoop upon the victor;—for she fears
The name of Freedom, even as she hates thine.
But recreant Austria loves thee as the grave
Loves pestilence, and her slow dogs of war,
Fleshed with the chase, come up from Italy,
And howl upon their limits: for they see
The panther, Freedom, fled to her old cover
Amid seas and mountains, and a mightier brood
Crouch round.   What anarch wears a crown or mitre,
Or bears the sword, or grasps the key of gold,

Whose friends are not thy friends, whose foes thy foes?
Our arsenals and our armouries are full;
Our forts defy assault; ten thousand cannon
Lie ranged upon the beach, and hour by hour
Their earth-convulsing wheels affright the city;
The galloping of fiery steeds makes pale
The Christian merchant; and the yellow Jew
Hides his hoard deeper in the faithless earth.
Like clouds, and like the shadows of the clouds,
Over the hills of Anatolia,
Swift in wide troops the Tartar chivalry
Sweep;—the far-flashing of their starry lances
Reverberates the dying light of day.
We have one God, one king, one hope, one law;
But many-headed Insurrection stands
Divided in itself, and soon must fall.

  Mahmud. Proud words, when deeds come short, are
   seasonable:
Look, Hassan, on yon crescent moon, emblazoned
Upon that shattered flag of fiery cloud
Which leads the rear of the departing day;
Wan emblem of an empire fading now!
See how it trembles in the blood-red air,
And, like a mighty lamp whose oil is spent
Shrinks on the horizon's edge, while, from above,
One star with insolent and victorious light
Hovers above its fall, and with keen beams,
Like arrows through a fainting antelope,
Strikes its weak form to death.

  Hassan.   Even as that moon
Renews itself—

  Mahmud.   Shall we be not renewed!
Far other bark than ours were needed now
To stem the torrent of descending time:
The spirit that lifts the slave before his lord
Stalks through the capitals of armèd kings,
And spreads his ensign in the wilderness;
Exults in chains; and, when the rebel falls,
Cries like the blood of Abel from the dust;
And the inheritors of earth, like beasts
When earthquake is unleashed, with idiot fear
Cower in their kingly dens—as I do now.
What were defeat, when victory must appal!
Or danger, when security looks pale!
How said the messenger who, from the fort
Islanded in the Danube, saw the battle
Of Bucharest?—that—

  Hassan.   Ibrahim's scimitar
Drew with its gleam swift victory from heaven,
To burn before him in the night of battle—
A light and a destruction.

  Mahmud.   Ay, the day
Was ours; but how?

  Hassan.   The light Wallachians,
The Arnaut, Servian, and Albanian allies,
Fled from the glance of our artillery
Almost before the thunderstone alit;
One half the Grecian army made a bridge

Or safe and slow retreat, with Moslem dead:
The other—
  Mahmud. Speak—tremble not—
  Hassan.   Islanded
By victor myriads, formed in hollow square
With rough and steadfast front, and thrice flung back
The deluge of our foaming cavalry;
Thrice their keen wedge of battle pierced our lines.
Our baffled army trembled like one man
Before a host, and gave them space; but soon
From the surrounding hills the batteries blazed,
Kneading them down with fire and iron rain;
Yet none approached; till, like a field of corn
Under the hook of the swart sickleman,
The band, entrenched in mounds of Turkish dead,
Grew weak and few. Then said the Pacha, "Slaves,
Render yourselves—they have abandoned you—
What hope of refuge or retreat or aid?
We grant your lives,"—"Grant that which is thine own,'
Cried one, and fell upon his sword, and died!
Another—"God, and man, and hope, abandon me;
But I to them and to myself remain
Constant;" he bowed his head, and his heart burst.
A third exclaimed: "There is a refuge, tyrant,
Where thou dar'st not pursue, and canst not harm
Shouldst thou pursue; there we shall meet again."
Then held his breath, and after a brief spasm
The indignant spirit cast its mortal garment
Among the slain—dead earth upon the earth!
So these survivors, each by different ways,
Some strange, all sudden, none dishonourable,
Met in triumphant death; and, when our army
Closed in, while yet wonder and awe and shame
Held back the base hyenas of the battle
That feed upon the dead, and fly the living,
One rose out of the chaos of the slain:
And if it were a corpse which some dread spirit
Of the old saviours of the land we rule
Had lifted in its anger, wandering by;
Or if there burned within the dying man
Unquenchable disdain of death, and faith
Creating what it feigned;—I cannot tell—
But he cried, "Phantoms of the free, we come!
Armies of the eternal, ye who strike
To dust the citadels of sanguine kings,
And shake the souls throned on their stony hearts,
And thaw their frostwork diadems like dew;
O ye who float around this clime, and weave
The garment of the glory which it wears;
Whose fame, though earth betray the dust it clasped,
Lies sepulchred in monumental thought;
Progenitors of all that yet is great,
Ascribe to your bright senate, oh accept
In your high ministrations, us your sons—
Us first, and the more glorious yet to come!
And ye, weak conquerors! giants who look pale
When the crushed worm rebels beneath your tread,
The vultures and the dogs, your pensioners tame,

Are overgorged ; but, like oppressors, still
They crave the relic of Destruction's feast.
The exhalations and the thirsty winds
Are sick with blood; the dew is foul with death;
Heaven's light is quenched in slaughter; thus where'er
Upon your camps, cities, or towers, or fleets,
The obscene birds the reeking remnants cast
Of these dead limbs,—upon your streams and mountains,
Upon your fields, your gardens, and your housetops,
Where'er the winds shall creep, or the clouds fly,
Or the dews fall, or the angry sun look down
With poisoned light—Famine and Pestilence
And Panic shall wage war upon our side !
Nature from all her boundaries is moved
Against ye : Time has found ye light as foam.
The Earth rebels; and Good and Evil stake
Their empire o'er the unborn world of men
On this one cast; but, ere the die be thrown,
The renovated genius of our race,
Proud umpire of the impious game, descends,
A seraph-wingèd Victory bestriding
The tempest of the Omnipotence of God,
Which sweeps all things to their appointed doom,
And you to oblivion !"—More he would have said,
But—

    Mahmud. Died—as thou shouldst ere thy lips had painted
Their ruin in the hues of our success.
A rebel's crime, gilt with a rebel's tongue !
Thy heart is Greek, Hassan.

    Hassan.   It may be so:
A spirit not my own wrenched me within,
And I have spoken words I fear and hate;
Yet would I die for—

    Mahmud.   Live ! O live ! outlive
Me and this sinking empire.—But the fleet—

    Hassan. Alas !

    Mahmud.   The fleet which, like a flock of clouds
Chased by the wind, flies the insurgent banner,
Our wingèd castles from their merchant ships !
Our myriads before their pirate bands !
Our arms before their chains ! our years of empire
Before their centuries of servile fear !
Death is awake ! Repulsèd on the waters
They own no more the thunder-bearing banner
Of Mahmud; but, like hounds of a base breed,
Gorge from a stranger's hand, and rend their master.

    Hassan. Latmos and Ampelos and Phanae saw
The wreck—

    Mahmud. The caves of the Icarian isles
Told each to the other in loud mockery,
And with the tongue as of a thousand echoes,
First of the sea-convulsing fight—and then——
Thou darest to speak :—senseless are the mountains;
Interpret thou their voice.

    Hassan.   My presence bore
A part in that day's shame. The Grecian fleet
Bore down at daybreak from the north, and hung
As multitudinous on the ocean line

As cranes upon the cloudless Thracian wind.
Our squadron, convoying ten thousand men,
Was stretching towards Nauplia when the battle
Was kindled.—
First through the hail of our artillery
The agile Hydriote barks with press of sail
Dashed:—ship to ship, cannon to cannon, man
To man, were grappled in the embrace of war,
Inextricable but by death or victory.
The tempest of the raging fight convulsed
To its crystalline depths that stainless sea,
And shook heaven's roof of golden morning clouds
Poised on a hundred azure mountain-isles.
In the brief trances of the artillery,
One cry from the destroyed and the destroyer
Rose, and a cloud of desolation wrapped
The unforeseen event, till the north wind
Sprung from the sea, lifting the heavy veil
Of battle-smoke—then "victory—victory!"
For, as we thought, three frigates from Algiers
Bore down from Naxos to our aid, but soon
The abhorrèd Cross glimmered behind, before,
Among, around us: and that fatal sign
Dried with its beams the strength of Moslem hearts,
As the sun drinks the dew.—What more? We fled!
Our noonday path over the sanguine foam
Was beaconed—and the glare struck the sun pale—
By our consuming transports; the fierce light
Made all the shadows of our sails blood-red,
And every countenance blank. Some ships lay feeding
The ravening fire even to the water's level;
Some were blown up; some, settling heavily,
Sunk; and the shrieks of our companions died
Upon the wind that bore us fast and far,
Even after they were dead. Nine thousand perished!
We met the vultures, legioned in the air,
Stemming the torrent of the tainted wind:
They, screaming from their cloudy mountain peaks,
Stooped through the sulphurous battle-smoke, and perched
Each on the weltering carcass that we loved,
Like its ill angel or its damnèd soul
Riding upon the bosom of the sea.
We saw the dogfish hastening to their feast.
Joy waked the voiceless people of the sea,'
And ravening Famine left his ocean-cave
To dwell with war, with us, and with despair.
We met night three hours to the west of Patmos,
And, with night, tempest—
   Mahmud.   Cease!

Enter a MESSENGER.

   Messenger.   Your Sublime Highness,
That Christian hound the Muscovite Ambassador
Has left the city. If the rebel fleet
Had anchored in the port, had victory
Crowned the Greek legions in the Hippodrome,
Panic were tamer. Obedience and Mutiny,
Like giants in contention planet-struck,

Stand gazing on each other.—There is peace
In Stamboul.

    Mahmud. Is the grave not calmer still?
Its ruins shall be mine!

    Hassan.   Fear not the Russian;
The tiger leagues not with the stag at bay
Against the hunter. Cunning, base, and cruel
He crouches, watching till the spoil be won;
And must be paid for his reserve, in blood.
After the war is fought, yield the sleek Russian
That which thou canst not keep, his deserved portion
Of blood, which shall not flow through streets and fields,
Rivers and seas, like that which we may win,
But stagnate in the veins of Christian slaves!

Enter SECOND MESSENGER.

    Second Messenger. Nauplia, Tripolizza, Mothon, Athens,
Navarin, Artas, Monembasia,
Corinth, and Thebes, are carried by assault,
And every Islamite who made his dogs
Fat with the flesh of Galilean slaves
Passed at the edge of the sword: the lust of blood,
Which made our warriors drunk, is quenched in death;
But like a fiery plague breaks out anew
In deeds which make the Christian cause look pale
In its own light. The garrison of Patras
Has store but for ten days, nor is there hope
But from the Briton; at once slave and tyrant,
His wishes still are weaker than his fears,
Or he would sell what faith may yet remain
From the oaths broke in Genoa and in Norway;
And, if you buy him not, your treasury
Is empty even of promises—his own coin!
The freedman of a western poet-chief
Holds Attica with seven thousand rebels,
And has beat back the pacha of Negropont.
The aged Ali sits in Yanina,
A crownless metaphor of empire;
His name, that shadow of his withered might,
Holds our besieging army, like a spell,
In prey to famine, pest, and mutiny:
He, bastioned in his citadel, looks forth
Joyless upon the sapphire lake that mirrors
The ruins of the city where he reigned,
Childless and sceptreless. The Greek has reaped
The costly harvest his own blood matured,
Not the sower, Ali,—who has bought a truce
From Ypsilanti, with ten camel-loads
Of Indian gold.

Enter a THIRD MESSENGER.

    Mahmud.   What more?
    Third Messenger.   The Christian tribes
Of Lebanon and the Syrian wilderness
Are in revolt;—Damascus, Hems, Aleppo,
Tremble; the Arab menaces Medina;
The Æthiop has entrenched himself in Sennaar,
And keeps the Egyptian rebel well employed,

Who denies homage, claims investiture
As price of tardy aid.   Persia demands
The cities on the Tigris, and the Georgians
Refuse their living tribute.   Crete and Cyprus,
Like mountain-twins that from each other's veins
Catch the volcano-fire and earthquake spasm,
Shake in the general fever.   Through the city,
Like birds before a storm, the Santons shriek,
And prophecyings horrible and new
Are heard among the crowd; that sea of men
Sleeps on the wrecks it made, breathless and still.
A Dervise learnèd in the Koran preaches
That it is written how the sins of Islam
Must raise up a destroyer even now.
The Greeks expect a Saviour from the west;
Who shall not come, men say, in clouds and glory,
But in the omnipresence of that Spirit
In which all live and are.   Ominous signs
Are blazoned broadly on the noonday sky;
One saw a red cross stamped upon the sun:
It has rained blood; and monstrous births declare
The secret wrath of Nature and her Lord.
The army encamped upon the Cydaris,
Was roused last night by the alarm of battle,
And saw two hosts conflicting in the air,
The shadows doubtless of the unborn time
Cast on the mirror of the night.   While yet
The fight hung balanced, there arose a storm
Which swept the phantoms from among the stars.
At the third watch, the Spirit of the Plague
Was heard abroad flapping among the tents:
Those who relieved watch found the sentinels dead.
The last news from the camp is that a thousand
Have sickened, and—

Enter a FOURTH MESSENGER.

   Mahmud.   And thou, pale ghost, dim shadow
Of some untimely rumour, speak !
   Fourth Messenger.   One comes
Fainting with toil, covered with foam and blood.
He stood, he says, upon Clelonites'
Promontory, which o'erlooks the isles that groan
Under the Briton's frown, and all their waters
Then trembling in the splendour of the moon,
When, as the wandering clouds unveiled or hid
Her boundless light, he saw two adverse fleets
Stalk through the night in the horizon's glimmer,
Mingling fierce thunders and sulphureous gleams,
And smoke which strangled every infant wind
That soothed the silver clouds through the deep air.
At length the battle slept.   But the Sirocco
Awoke, and drove his flock of thunder-clouds
Over the sea-horizon, blotting out
All objects—save that in the faint moon-glimpse
He saw, or dreamed he saw, the Turkish admiral,
And two the loftiest of our ships of war,
With the bright image of that Queen of Heaven,

Who hid perhaps her face for grief, reversed;
And the abhorred Cross—

Enter an ATTENDANT.

 Attendant.   Your Sublime Highness,
The Jew who——
 Mahmud.   Could not come more seasonably:
Bid him attend. I'll hear no more ! Too long
We gaze on danger through the mist of fear,
And multiply upon our shattered hopes
The images of ruin. Come what will !
To-morrow and to-morrow are as lamps
Set in our path to light us to the edge
Through rough and smooth; nor can we suffer aught
Which he inflicts not in whose hand we are. *[Exeunt.*

SEMICHORUS I.

Would I were the wingèd cloud
Of a tempest swift and loud !
  I would scorn
  The smile of morn,
And the wave where the moonrise is born !
  I would leave
  The Spirits of Eve
A shroud for the corpse of the Day to weave
  From other threads than mine !
Bask in the blue noon divine
  Who would ? Not I.

SEMICHORUS II.

Whither to fly ?

SEMICHOROUS I.

Where the rocks that gird the Ægean
Echo to the battle pæan
  Of the free,
  I would flee
A tempestuous herald of victory !
  My golden rain
  For the Grecian slain
Should mingle in tears with the bloody main
  And my solemn thunder-knell
Should ring to the world the passing-bell
  Of tyranny !

SEMICHORUS II.

Ah king ! wilt thou chain
  The rack and the rain?
Wilt thou fetter the lightning and hurricane?
  The storms are free;
   But we—

CHORUS.

O Slavery ! thou frost of the world's prime,
 Killing its flowers and leaving its thorns bare !

Thy touch has stamped these limbs with crime,
These brows thy branding garland bear;
But the free heart, the impassive soul,
Scorn thy control!

SEMICHORUS I.

" Let there be light!" said Liberty;
And, like sunrise from the sea,
Athens arose!—Around her born,
Shone, like mountains in the morn,
Glorious states;—and are they now
Ashes, wrecks, oblivion?

SEMICHORUS II.

Go
Where Thermæ and Asopus swallowed
Persia, as the sand does foam.
Deluge upon deluge followed,
Discord, Macedon, and Rome:
And lastly thou!

SEMICHORUS I.

Temples and towers,
Citadels and marts, and they
Who live and die there, have been ours,
And may be thine, and must decay;
But Greece and her foundations are
Built below the tide of war,
Based on the crystalline sea
Of thought and its eternity;
Her citizens, imperial spirits,
Rule the present from the past;
On all this world of men inherits
Their seal is set.

SEMICHORUS II.

Hear ye the blast
Whose Orphic thunder thrilling calls
From ruin her Titanian walls?
Whose spirit shakes the sapless bones
Of Slavery? Argos, Corinth, Crete,
Hear, and from their mountain thrones
The demons and the nymphs repeat
The harmony.

SEMICHORUS I.

I hear! I hear!

SEMICHORUS II.

The world's eyeless charioteer,
Destiny, is hurrying by!
What faith is crushed, what empire bleeds,
Beneath her earthquake-footed steeds?
What eagle-wingèd Victory sits
At her right hand? What shadow flits

Before? what splendour rolls behind?
Ruin and Renovation cry,
" Who but we?"

SEMICHORUS I.

I hear! I hear!
The hiss as of a rushing wind,
The roar as of an ocean foaming,
The thunder as of earthquake coming.
I hear! I hear!
The crash as of an empire falling,
The shrieks as of a people calling
" Mercy! Mercy!"—how they thrill!
Then a shout of " Kill! kill! kill!"
And then a small still voice, thus—

SEMICHORUS II.

For
Revenge, and Wrong, bring forth their kind:
The foul cubs like their parents are;
Their den is in the guilty mind,
And Conscience feeds them with despair.

SEMICHORUS I.

In sacred Athens, near the fane
Of Wisdom, Pity's altar stood;
Serve not the unknown God in vain;
But pay *that* broken shrine again
Love for hate, and tears for blood.

Enter MAHMUD *and* AHASUERUS.

Mahmud. Thou art a man, thou sayest, even as we—
Ahasuerus. No more.
Mahmud. But raised above thy fellow-men
By thought, as I by power.
Ahasuerus. Thou sayest so.
Mahmud. Thou art an adept in the difficult lore
Of Greek and Frank philosophy; thou numberest
The flowers, and thou measurest the stars;
Thou severest element from element;
Thy spirit is present in the past, and sees
The birth of this old world through all its cycles
Of desolation and of loveliness,
And when man was not, and how man became
The monarch and the slave of this low sphere,
And all its narrow circles—it is much—
I honour thee, and would be what thou art
Were I not what I am; but the unborn hour,
Cradled in fear and hope, conflicting storms,
Who shall unveil? Nor thou, nor I, nor any
Mighty or wise. I apprehended not
What thou hast taught me, but I now perceive
That thou art no interpreter of dreams;
Thou dost not own that art, device, or God,
Can make the future present—let it come!
Moreover thou disdainest us and ours.
Thou art as God, whom thou contemplatest.

Ahasuerus. Disdain thee?—not the worm beneath my feet!
The Fathomless has care for meaner things
Than thou canst dream, and has made pride for those
Who would be what they may not, or would seem
That which they are not. Sultan! talk no more
Of thee and me, the future and the past;
But look on that which cannot change—the One,
The unborn and the undying. Earth and ocean,
Space, and the isles of life or light that gem
The sapphire floods of interstellar air,
This firmament pavilioned upon chaos,
With all its cressets of immortal fire,
Whose outwall, bastionèd impregnably
Against the escape of boldest thoughts, repels them
As Calpe the Atlantic clouds—this Whole
Of suns and worlds and men and beasts and flowers,
With all the silent or tempestuous workings
By which they have been, are, or cease to be,
Is but a vision;—all that it inherits
Are motes of a sick eye, bubbles and dreams:
Thought is its cradle and its grave; nor less
The future and the past are idle shadows
Of thought's eternal flight—they have no being;
Nought is but that which feels itself to be.
  Mahmud. What meanest thou? thy words stream like a tempest
Of dazzling mist within my brain—they shake
The earth on which I stand, and hang like night
On heaven above me. What can they avail?
They cast on all things surest, brightest, best,
Doubt, insecurity, astonishment.
  Ahasuerus. Mistake me not! All is contained in each.
Dodona's forest to an acorn's cup
Is that which has been, or will be, to that
Which is—the absent to the present. Thought
Alone, and its quick elements, Will, Passion,
Reason, Imagination, cannot die;
They are what that which they regard appears,
The stuff whence mutability can weave
All that it hath dominion o'er,—worlds, worms,
Empires, and superstitions. What has thought
To do with time or place or circumstance?
Wouldst thou behold the future? Ask and have!
Knock, and it shall be opened—look, and lo!
The coming age is shadowed on the past,
As on a glass.
  Mahmud. Wild, wilder thoughts convulse
My spirit!—Did not Mahomet the Second
Win Stamboul?
  Ahasuerus. Thou wouldst ask that giant spirit
The written fortunes of thy house and faith.
Thou wouldst cite one out of the grave to tell
How what was born in blood must die.
  Mahmud.   Thy words
Have power on me! I see——
  Ahasuerus.   What hearest thou?
  Mahmud. A far whisper——
Terrible silence.
  Ahasuerus.   What succeeds?

Mahmud.　　　　　　　　　　The sound
As of the assault of an imperial city;
The hiss of inextinguishable fire,
The roar of giant cannon; the earthquaking
Fall of vast bastions and precipitous towers,
The shock of crags shot from strange engineery;
The clash of wheels, and clang of armèd hoofs
And crash of brazen mail, as of the wreck
Of adamantine mountains;—the mad blast
Of trumpets, and the neigh of raging steeds,
And shrieks of women whose thrill jars the blood;
And one sweet laugh, most horrible to hear,
As of a joyous infant waked, and playing
With its dead mother's breast, and now more loud
The mingled battle-cry—ha! hear I not
"Ἐν τούτῳ νίκη!"—"Allah-illa-Allah?"

　　Ahasuerus. The sulphurous mist is raised—thou seest—
　　Mahmud.　　　　　　　　　　A chasm,
As of two mountains, in the wall of Stamboul;
And in that ghastly breach the Islamites,
Like giants on the ruins of a world,
Stand in the light of sunrise. In the dust
Glimmers a kingless diadem, and one
Of regal port has cast himself beneath
The stream of war. Another, proudly clad
In golden arms, spurs a Tartarian barb
Into the gap, and with his iron mace
Directs the torrent of that tide of men, —
And seems—he *is*—Mahomet!

　　Ahasuerus.　　　　　　　　What thou seest
Is but the ghost of thy forgotten dream.
A dream itself, yet less, perhaps, than that
Thou call'st reality. Thou mayst behold
How cities on which Empire sleeps enthroned
Bow their towered crests to mutability.
Poised by the flood, e'en on the height thou holdest,
Thou mayst now learn how the full tide of power
Ebbs to its depths.—Inheritor of glory,
Conceived in darkness, born in blood, and nourished
With tears and toil, thou seest the mortal throes
Of that whose birth was but the same. The past
Now stands before thee like an Incarnation
Of the To-come; yet, wouldst thou commune with
That portion of thyself which was ere thou
Didst start for this brief race whose crown is death,
Dissolve, with that strong faith and fervent passion
Which called it from the uncreated deep,
Yon cloud of war with its tempestuous phantoms
Of raging death; and draw with mighty will
The Imperial Shade hither.　　　　　[*Exit* AHASUERUS.

THE PHANTOM OF MAHOMET THE SECOND *appears.*

　　Mahmud.　　　　　　　　Approach!
　　Phantom.　　　　　　　　　　I come
Thence whither thou must go. The grave is fitter
To take the living than give up the dead;
Yet has thy faith prevailed, and I am here.
The heavy fragments of the power which fell

When I arose, like shapeless crags and clouds,
Hang round my throne on the abyss, and voices
Of strange lament soothe my supreme repose,
Wailing for glory never to return.
A later Empire nods in its decay;
The autumn of a greener faith is come;
And wolfish change, like winter, howls to strip
The foliage in which Fame, the eagle, built
Her aerie, while Dominion whelped below.
The storm is in its branches, and the frost
Is on its leaves, and the blank deep expects
Oblivion on oblivion, spoil on spoil,
Ruin on ruin: thou art slow, my son;
The anarchs of the world of darkness keep
A throne for thee, round which thine empire lies
Boundless and mute; and, for thy subjects, thou,
Like us, shalt rule the ghosts of murdered life,
The phantoms of the powers who rule thee now--
Mutinous passions, and conflicting fears,
And hopes that sate themselves on dust, and die!
Stripped of their mortal strength, as thou of thine.
Islam must fall; but we will reign together
Over its ruins in the world of death:
And if the trunk be dry, yet shall the seed
Unfold itself even in the shape of that
Which gathers birth in its decay.   Woe! woe!
To the weak people tangled in the grasp
Of its last spasms.
  Mahmud.   Spirit, woe to all!
Woe to the wronged and the avenger! woe
To the destroyer, woe to the destroyed!
Woe to the dupe, and woe to the deceiver!
Woe to the oppressed, and woe to the oppressor!
Woe both to those that suffer and inflict;
Those who are born, and those who die!   But say,
Imperial shadow of the thing I am,
When, how, by whom, Destruction must accomplish
Her consummation!
  Phantom.   Ask the cold pale Hour,
Rich in reversion of impending death,
When he shall fall upon whose ripe grey hairs
Sit care and sorrow and infirmity—
The weight which Crime, whose wings are plumed with years,
Leaves in his flight from ravaged heart to heart
Over the heads of men, under which burden
They bow themselves unto the gravè: fond wretch!
He leans upon his crutch, and talks of years
To come, and how in hours of youth renewed
He will renew lost joys, and——
  Voice without.   Victory! victory!   [THE PHANTOM *vanishes*
  Mahmud.   What sound of the importunate earth has broken
My mighty trance?
  Voice without.   Victory! victory!
  Mahmud.   Weak lightning before darkness! poor faint smile
Of dying Islam! voice which art the response
Of hollow weakness!--Do I wake and live?
Were there such things, or may the unquiet brain,
Vexed by the wise mad talk of the old Jew,

Have shaped itself these shadows of its fear?
It matters not!—for nought we see or dream,
Possess, or lose, or grasp at, can be worth
More than it gives or teaches. Come what may,
The future must become the past; and I,
As they were to whom once this present hour,
This gloomy crag of time to which I cling,
Seemed an Elysian isle of peace and joy
Never to be attained.—I must rebuke
This drunkenness of triumph ere it die,
And, dying, bring despair.—Victory!—Poor slaves!

[*Exit* MAHMUD.

Voice without. Shout in the jubilee of death! The Greeks
Are as a brood of lions in the net,
Round which the kingly hunters of the earth
Stand smiling. Anarchs, ye whose daily food
Are curses, groans, and gold, the fruit of death,
From Thule to the girdle of the world,
Come, feast! The board groans with the flesh of men;
The cup is foaming with a nation's blood—
Famine and Thirst await: eat, drink, and die!

SEMICHORUS I.

Victorious Wrong with vulture scream
Salutes the risen sun, pursues the flying day!
I saw her, ghastly as a tyrant's dream,
Perch on the trembling pyramid of night,
Beneath which earth and all her realms pavilioned lay
In visions of the dawning undelight.
Who shall impede her flight?
Who rob her of her prey?

Voice without. Victory! victory! Russia's famished eagles
Dare not to prey beneath the crescent's light!
Impale the remnant of the Greeks! despoil!
Violate! make their flesh cheaper than dust!

SEMICHORUS II.

Thou voice which art
The herald of the ill in splendour hid!
Thou echo of the hollow heart
Of Monarchy, bear me to thine abode
When desolation flashes o'er a world destroyed.
Oh bear me to those isles of jagged cloud
Which float like mountains on the earthquakes 'mid
The momentary oceans of the lightning,
Or to some toppling promontory proud
Of solid tempest, whose black pyramid,
Riven, overhangs the founts intensely brightening
Of those dawn-tinted deluges of fire,
Before their waves expire,
When heaven and earth are light, and only light
In the thunder-night!

Voice without. Victory! victory! Austria, Russia, England,
And that tame serpent, that poor shadow, France,
Cry peace; and that means death when monarchs speak.
Ho there! bring torches, sharpen those red stakes;

These chains are light, fitter for slaves and poisoners
Than Greeks!—Kill! plunder! burn! let none remain!

SEMICHORUS I.

Alas for Liberty,
If numbers, wealth, or unfulfilling years,
Or fate, can quell the free!
Alas for Virtue, when
Torments, or contumely, or the sneers
Of erring-judging men,
Can break the heart where it abides.
Alas! if Love, whose smile makes this obscure world splendid,
Can change, with all its false times and tides,
Like hope and terror—
Alas for Love!
And Truth, who wanderest lone and unbefriended,
If thou canst veil thy lie-consuming mirror
Before the dazzled eyes of Error,
Alas for thee! Image of the Above!

SEMICHORUS II.

Repulse, with plumes from Conquest torn,
Led the Ten-thousand from the limits of the morn
Through many a hostile anarchy:
At length they wept aloud and cried "The sea! the sea!"
Through exile, persecution, and despair,
Rome was, and young Atlantis shall become,
The wonder, or the terror, or the tomb,
Of all whose step wakes Power lulled in her savage lair.
But Greece was as a hermit child
Whose fairest thoughts and limbs were built
To woman's growth by dreams so mild
She knew not pain or guilt.
And now . . . O Victory, blush! and Empire, tremble!
When ye desert the free—
If Greece must be
A wreck, yet shall its fragments re-assemble,
And build themselves again impregnably
In a diviner clime,
To Amphionic music, on some cape sublime
Which frowns above the idle foam of time.

SEMICHORUS I.

Let the tyrants rule the desert they have made;
Let the free possess the paradise they claim;
Be the fortune of our fierce oppressors weighed
With our ruin, our resistance, and our name!

SEMICHORUS II.

Our dead shall be the seed of their decay,
Our survivors be the shadows of their pride;
Our adversity a dream to pass away—
Their dishonour a remembrance to abide.

Voice without. Victory! victory! The bought Briton sends
The keys of ocean to the Islamite.

Now shall the blazon of the Cross be veiled,
And British skill directing Othman might
Thunder-strike rebel victory.   Oh keep holy
This jubilee of unrevengèd blood !
Kill ! crush ! despoil !   Let not a Greek escape !

SEMICHORUS I.

Darkness has dawned in the east
    On the noon of time:
The death-birds descend to their feast
    From the hungry clime.
Let Freedom and Peace flee far
    To a sunnier strand,
And follow Love's folding-star
    To the evening land.

SEMICHORUS II.

The young moon has fed
    Her exhausted horn
        With the sunset's fire;
The weak day is dead,
    But the night is not born;
And, like loveliness panting with wild desire
    While it trembles with fear and delight,
Hesperus flies from awakening night,
And pants in its beauty and speed with light
    Fast-flashing, soft, and bright.
Thou beacon of love ! thou lamp of the free !
    Guide us far far away
To climes where now veiled by the ardour of day,
    Thou art hidden
From waves on which weary noon
    Faints in her summer swoon,
Between kingless continents sinless as Eden,
Around mountains and islands inviolably
    Pranked on the sapphire sea.

SEMICHORUS I.

Through the sunset of hope,
    Like the shapes of a dream,
What paradise islands of glory gleam !
    Beneath heaven's cope,
    Their shadows more clear float by—
The sound of their oceans, the light of their sky
The music and fragrance their solitudes breathe,
Burst like morning on dream, or like heaven on death,
    Through the walls of our prison;
And Greece, which was dead, is arisen !

CHORUS.

The world's great age begins anew,
    The golden years return,
The earth doth like a snake renew
    Her winter weeds outworn:
Heaven smiles, and faiths and empires gleam
Like wrecks of a dissolving dream.

A brighter Hellas rears its mountains
  From waves serener far;
A new Peneus rolls his fountains
  Against the morning star;
Where fairer Tempes bloom, there sleep
Young Cyclads on a sunnier deep.

A loftier Argo cleaves the main,
  Fraught with a later prize;
Another Orpheus sings again,
  And loves, and weeps, and dies;
A new Ulysses leaves once more
Calypso for his native shore.

Oh! write no more the Tale of Troy,
  If earth Death's scroll must be!
Nor mix with Laian rage the joy
  Which dawns upon the free,
Although a subtler Sphinx renew
Riddles of death Thebes never knew.

Another Athens shall arise,
  And to remoter time
Bequeath, like sunset to the skies,
  The splendour of its prime;
And leave, if naught so bright may live,
All earth can take or heaven can give.

Saturn and Love their long repose
  Shall burst more bright and good*
Than all who fell, than one who rose,
  Than many unsubdued:
Not gold, not blood, their altar dowers,
But votive tears and symbol flowers.

Oh cease! must hate and death return?
  Cease! must men kill and die?
Cease! drain not to its dregs the urn
  Of bitter prophecy.
The world is weary of the past,
Oh might it die or rest at last!

* From Mrs. Shelley's edition: there was a hiatus in the first edition.

1824

THE WITCH OF ATLAS.

I.

BEFORE those cruel Twins, whom at one birth
  Incestuous Change bore to her father Time,
Error and Truth, had hunted from the earth
  All those bright natures which adorned its prime,
And left us nothing to believe in, worth
  The pains of putting into learned rhyme,
A lady-witch there lived on Atlas' mountain
Within a cavern by a secret fountain.

II.

Her mother was one of the Atlantides :
  The all-beholding Sun had ne'er beholden
In his wide voyage o'er continents and seas
  So fair a creature, as she lay enfolden
In the warm shadow of her loveliness ;
  He kissed her with his beams, and made all golden
The chamber of grey rock in which she lay—
She, in that dream of joy, dissolved away.

III.

'Tis said, she was first changed into a vapour,
  And then into a cloud, such clouds as flit,
Like splendour-winged moths about a taper,
  Round the red west when the sun dies in it :
And then into a meteor, such as caper
  On hill-tops when the moon is in a fit ;
Then, into one of those mysterious stars
Which hide themselves between the Earth and Mars.

IV.

Ten times the Mother of the Months had bent
  Her bow beside the folding-star, and bidden
With that bright sign the billows to indent
  The sea-deserted sand : like children chidden,
At her command they ever came and went :
  Since in that cave a dewy splendour hidden,
Took shape and motion : with the living form
Of this embodied Power, the cave grew warm.

V.

A lovely lady garmented in light
  From her own beauty—deep her eyes, as are

360

Two openings of unfathomable night
   Seen through a tempest's cloven roof—her hair
Dark—the dim brain whirls dizzy with delight,
   Picturing her form ; her soft smiles shone afar,
And her low voice was heard like love, and drew
All living things towards this wonder new.

VI.

And first the spotted cameleopard came,
   And then the wise and fearless elephant ;
Then the sly serpent, in the golden flame
   Of his own volumes intervolved ;—all gaunt
And sanguine beasts her gentle looks made tame.
   They drank before her at her sacred fount ;
And every beast of beating heart grew bold,
Such gentleness and power even to behold.

VII.

The brinded lioness led forth her young,
   That she might teach them how they should forego
Their inborn thirst of death ; the pard unstrung
   His sinews at her feet, and sought to know
With looks whose motions spoke without a tongue
   How he might be as gentle as the doe.
The magic circle of her voice and eyes
All savage natures did imparadise.

VIII.

And old Silenus, shaking a green stick
   Of lilies, and the wood-gods in a crew
Came, blithe, as in the olive copses thick
   Cicadæ are, drunk with the noonday dew:
And Driope and Faunus followed quick,
   Teasing the God to sing them something new,
Till in this cave they found the lady lone,
Sitting upon a seat of emerald stone.

IX.

And Universal Pan, 'tis said, was there,
   And though none saw him,—through the adamant
Of the deep mountains, through the trackless air,
   And through those living spirits, like a want
He past out of his everlasting lair
   Where the quick heart of the great world doth pant,
And felt that wondrous lady all alone,—
And she felt him, upon her emerald throne.

X.

And every nymph of stream and spreading tree,
   And every shepherdess of Ocean's flocks,
Who drives her white waves over the green sea;
   And Ocean, with the brine on his grey locks,
And quaint Priapus with his company
   All came, much wondering how the enwombed rocks
Could have brought forth so beautiful a birth ;
Her love subdued their wonder and their mirth.

XI.

The herdsmen and the mountain maidens came,
　　And the rude kings of pastoral Garamant—
Their spirits shook within them, as a flame
　　Stirred by the air under a cavern gaunt:
Pigmies, and Polyphemes, by many a name,
　　Centaurs and Satyrs, and such shapes as haunt
Wet clefts,—and lumps neither alive nor dead,
Dog-headed, bosom-eyed, and bird-footed.

XII.

For she was beautiful: her beauty made
　　The bright world dim, and everything beside
Seemed like the fleeting image of a shade:
　　No thought of living spirit could abide,
Which to her looks had ever been betrayed,
　　On any object in the world so wide,
On any hope within the circling skies,
But on her form, and in her inmost eyes.

XIII.

Which when the lady knew, she took her spindle
　　And twined three threads of fleecy mist, and three
Long lines of light, such as the dawn may kindle
　　The clouds and waves and mountains with, and she
As many star-beams, ere their lamps could dwindle
　　In the belated moon, wound skilfully;
And with these threads a subtle veil she wove—
A shadow for the splendour of her love.

XIV.

The deep recesses of her odorous dwelling
　　Were stored with magic treasures—sounds of air,
Which had the power all spirits of compelling,
　　Folded in cells of crystal silence there;
Such as we hear in youth, and think the feeling
　　Will never die—yet ere we are aware,
The feeling and the sound are fled and gone,
And the regret they leave remains alone.

XV.

And there lay Visions swift, and sweet, and quaint,
　　Each in its thin sheath like a chrysalis;
Some eager to burst forth, some weak and faint
　　With the soft burden of intensest bliss;
It is its work to bear to many a saint
　　Whose heart adores the shrine which holiest is,
Even Love's—and others white, green, grey and black,
And of all shapes—and each was at her beck.

XVI.

And odours in a kind of aviary
　　Of ever-blooming Eden-trees she kept,
Clipt in a floating net, a love-sick Fairy
　　Had woven from dew-beams while the moon yet slept;

As bats at the wired window of a dairy,
  They beat their vans; and each was an adept,
When loosed and missioned, making wings of winds,
To stir sweet thoughts or sad in destined minds.

XVII.

And liquors clear and sweet, whose healthful might
  Could medicine the sick soul to happy sleep,
And change eternal death into a night
  Of glorious dreams—or if eyes needs must weep,
Could make their tears all wonder and delight,
  She in her crystal vials did closely keep:
If men could drink of those clear vials, 'tis said
The living were not envied of the dead.

XVIII.

Her cave was stored with scrolls of strange device,
  The works of some Saturnian Archimage,
Which taught the expiations at whose price
  Men from the Gods might win that happy age
Too lightly lost, redeeming native vice;
  And which might quench the earth-consuming rage
Of gold and blood—till men should live and move
Harmonious as the sacred stars above.

XIX.

And how all things that seem untameable,
  Not to be checked and not to be confined,
Obey the spells of wisdom's wizard skill;
  Time, Earth and Fire—the Ocean and the Wind,
And all their shapes—and man's imperial will;
  And other scrolls whose writings did unbind
The inmost lore of Love—let the profane
Tremble to ask what secrets they contain.

XX.

And wondrous works of substances unknown,
  To which the enchantment of her father's power
Had changed those ragged blocks of savage stone,
  Were heaped in the recesses of her bower;
Carved lamps and chalices, and phials which shone
  In their own golden beams—each like a flower,
Out of whose depth a firefly shakes his light
Under a cypress in a starless night.

XXI.

At first she lived alone in this wild home,
  And her own thoughts were each a minister,
Clothing themselves or with the ocean-foam,
  Or with the wind, or with the speed of fire,
To work whatever purposes might come
  Into her mind; such power her mighty Sire
Had girt them with, whether to fly or run,
Through all the regions which he shines upon.

XXII.

The Ocean-nymphs and Hamadryades,
  Oreads and Naiads with long weedy locks,
Offered to do her bidding through the seas,
  Under the earth, and in the hollow rocks,
And far beneath the matted roots of trees,
  And in the gnarled heart of stubborn oaks,
So they might live for ever in the light
Of her sweet presence—each a satellite.

XXIII.

"This may not be," the wizard maid replied;
  "The fountains where the Naiades bedew
Their shining hair, at length are drained and dried;
  The solid oaks forget their strength, and strew
Their latest leaf upon the mountains wide;
  The boundless ocean, like a drop of dew
Will be consumed—the stubborn centre must
Be scattered, like a cloud of summer dust.

XXIV.

"And ye with them will perish one by one:
  If I must sigh to think that this shall be,
If I must weep when the surviving Sun
  Shall smile on your decay—Oh, ask not me
To love you till your little race is run;
  I cannot die as ye must—over me
Your leaves shall glance—the streams in which ye dwell
Shall be my paths henceforth, and so, farewell!"

XXV.

She spoke and wept: the dark and azure well
  Sparkled beneath the shower of her bright tears,
And every little circlet where they fell,
  Flung to the cavern-roof inconstant spheres
And intertangled lines of light:—a knell
  Of sobbing voices came upon her ears
From those departing Forms, o'er the serene
Of the white streams and of the forest green.

XXVI.

All day the wizard lady sat aloof
  Spelling out scrolls of dread antiquity
Under the cavern's fountain-lighted roof;
  Or broidering the pictured poesy
Of some high tale upon her growing woof,
  Which the sweet splendour of her smiles could dye
In hues outshining heaven—and ever she
Added some grace to the wrought poesy.

XXVII.

While on her hearth lay blazing many a piece
  Of sandal wood, rare gums and cinnamon;
Men scarcely know how beautiful fire is,
  Each flame of it is as a precious stone

Dissolved in ever moving light, and this
　Belongs to each and all who gaze upon.
The Witch beheld it not, for in her hand
She held a woof that dimmed the burning brand.

XXVIII.

This lady never slept, but lay in trance
　All night within the fountain—as in sleep.
Its emerald crags glowed in her beauty's glance:
　Through the green splendour of the water deep
She saw the constellations reel and dance
　Like fireflies—and withal did ever keep
The tenour of her contemplations calm,
With open eyes, closed feet and folded palm.

XXIX.

And when the whirlwinds and the clouds descended
　From the white pinnacles of that cold hill,
She past at dewfall to a space extended,
　Where in a lawn of flowering asphodel
Amid a wood of pines and cedars blended,
　There yawned an inextinguishable well
Of crimson fire, full even to the brim
And overflowing all the margin trim.

XXX.

Within the which she lay when the fierce war
　Of wintry winds shook that innocuous liquor
In many a mimic moon and bearded star
　O'er woods and lawns—the serpent heard it flicker
In sleep, and dreaming still, he crept afar—
　And when the windless snow descended thicker
Than autumn leaves, she watched it as it came
Melt on the surface of the level flame.

XXXI.

She had a Boat which some say Vulcan wrought
　For Venus, as the chariot of her star;
But it was found too feeble to be fraught
　With all the ardours in that sphere which are,
And so she sold it, and Apollo bought,
　And gave it to this daughter: from a car
Changed to the fairest and the lightest boat
Which ever upon mortal stream did float.

XXXII.

And others say, that when but three hours old,
　The first-born Love out of his cradle leapt,
And clove dun Chaos with his wings of gold,
　And like an horticultural adept,
Stole a strange seed, and wrapt it up in mould,
　And sowed it in his mother's star, and kept
Watering it all the summer with sweet dew,
And with his wings fanning it as it grew.

XXXIII.

The plant grew strong and green—the snowy flower
    Fell, and the long and gourd-like fruit began
To turn the light and dew by inward power
    To its own substance; woven tracery ran
Of light firm texture, ribbed and branching, o'er
    The solid rind, like a leaf's veined fan,
Of which Love scooped this boat, and with soft motion
Piloted it round the circumfluous ocean.

XXXIV.

This boat she moored upon her fount, and lit
    A living spirit within all its frame,
Breathing the soul of swiftness into it.
    Couched on the fountain like a panther tame,
One of the train at Evan's feet that sit;
    Or as on Vesta's sceptre a swift flame,
Or on blind Homer's heart a winged thought,—
In joyous expectation lay the boat.

XXXV.

Then by strange art she kneaded fire and snow
    Together, tempering the repugnant mass
With liquid love—all things together grow
    Through which the harmony of love can pass;
And a fair Shape out of her hands did flow
    A living Image, which did far surpass
In beauty that bright shape of vital stone
Which drew the heart out of Pygmalion.

XXXVI.

A sexless thing it was, and in its growth
    It seemed to have developed no defect
Of either sex, yet all the grace of both,—
    In gentleness and strength its limbs were decked;
The bosom swelled lightly with its full youth,
    The countenance was such as might select
Some artist that his skill should never die,
Imaging forth such perfect purity.

XXXVII.

From its smooth shoulders hung two rapid wings,
    Fit to have borne it to the seventh sphere,
Tipt with the speed of liquid lightnings,
    Dyed in the ardours of the atmosphere:
She led her creature to the boiling springs
    Where the light boat was moored—and said, "Sit here!"
And pointed to the prow, and took *her* seat
Beside the rudder with opposing feet.

XXXVIII.

And down the streams which clove those mountains vast
    Around their inland islets, and amid
The panther-peopled forests, whose shade cast
    Darkness and odours, and a pleasure hid

In melancholy gloom, the pinnace past;
  By many a star-surrounded pyramid
Of icy crag cleaving the purple sky,
And caverns yawning round unfathomably.

XXXIX.

The silver noon into that winding dell,
  With slanted gleam athwart the forest tops,
Tempered like golden evening, feebly fell;
  A green and glowing light, like that which drops
From folded lilies in which glowworms dwell,
  When earth over her face night's mantle wraps;
Between the severed mountains lay on high
Over the stream, a narrow rift of sky.

XL.

And ever as she went, the Image lay
  With folded wings and unawakened eyes;
And o'er its gentle countenance did lay
  The busy dreams, as thick as summer flies,
Chasing the rapid smiles that would not stay,
  And drinking the warm tears, and the sweet sighs
Inhaling, which, with busy murmur vain,
They had aroused from that full heart and brain.

XLI.

And ever down the proud vale, like a cloud
  Upon a stream of wind, the pinnace went:
Now lingering on the pools, in which abode
  The calm and darkness of the deep content
In which they paused; now o'er the shallow road
  Of white and dancing waters all besprent
With sand and polished pebbles:—mortal boat
In such a shallow rapid could not float.

XLII.

And down the earthquaking cataracts which shiver
  Their snow-like waters into golden air,
Or under chasms unfathomable ever
  Sepulchre them, till in their rage they tear
A subterranean portal for the river,
  It fled—the circling sunbows did upbear
Its fall down the hoar precipice of spray,
Lighting it far upon its lampless way.

XLIII.

And when the wizard lady would ascend
  The labyrinths of some many winding vale,
Which to the inmost mountain upward tend—
  She called " Hermaphroditus!" and the pale
And heavy hue which slumber could extend
  Over its lips and eyes, as on the gale
A rapid shadow from a slope of grass,
Into the darkness of the stream did pass

XLIV.

And it unfurled its heaven-coloured pinions,
  With stars of fire spotting the stream below;
And from above into the Sun's dominions
  Flinging a glory, like the golden glow
In which spring clothes her emerald-winged minions.
  All interwoven with fine feathery snow
And moonlight splendour of intensest rime,
With which frost paints the pines in winter time.

XLV.

And then it winnowed the Elysian air
  Which ever hung about that lady bright,
With its ethereal vans—and speeding there,
  Like a star up the torrent of the night,
Or a swift eagle in the morning glare
  Breasting the whirlwind with impetuous flight;
The pinnace, oared by those enchanted wings,
Clove the fierce streams towards their upper springs.

XLVI.

The water flashed like sunlight, by the prow
  Of a noon-wandering meteor flung to Heaven;
The still air seemed as if its waves did flow
  In tempest down the mountains,—loosely driven
The lady's radiant hair streamed to and fro:
  Beneath, the billows having vainly striven
Indignant and impetuous, roared to feel
The swift and steady motion of the keel.

XLVII.

Or, when the weary moon was in the wane,
  Or in the noon of interlunar night,
The lady-witch in visions could not chain
  Her spirit; but sailed forth under the light
Of shooting stars, and bade extend amain
  His storm-outspeeding wings, the Hermaphrodite;
She to the Austral waters took her way,
Beyond the fabulous Thamondocona.

XLVIII.

Where, like a meadow which no scythe has shaven,
  Which rain could never bend, or whirl-blast shake,
With the Antarctic constellations paven,
  Canopus and his crew, lay th' Austral lake—
There she would build herself a windless haven
  Out of the clouds whose moving turrets make
The bastions of the storm, when through the sky
The spirits of the tempest thundered by.

XLIX.

A haven, beneath whose translucent floor
  The tremulous stars sparkled unfathomably,
And around which, the solid vapours hoar,
  Based on the level waters, to the sky

Lifted their dreadful crags; and like a shore
  Of wintry mountains, inaccessibly
Hemmed in with rifts and precipices grey,
  And hanging crags, many a cove and bay.

L.

And whilst the outer lake beneath the lash
  Of the winds' scourge, foamed like a wounded thing;
And the incessant hail with stony clash
  Ploughed up the waters, and the flagging wing
Of the roused cormorant in the lightning flash
  Looked like the wreck of some wind-wandering
Fragment of inky thundersmoke—this haven
Was as a gem to copy Heaven engraven.

LI.

On which that lady played her many pranks,
  Circling the image of a shooting star,
Even as a tiger on Hydaspes' banks
  Outspeeds the Antelopes which speediest are,
In her light boat; and many quips and cranks
  She played upon the water: till the car
Of the late moon, like a sick matron wan,
To journey from the misty east began.

LII.

And then she called out of the hollow turrets
  Of those high clouds, white, golden and vermilion.
The armies of her ministering spirits—
  In mighty legions million after million
They came, each troop emblazoning its merits
  On meteor flags; and many a proud pavilion,
Of the intertexture of the atmosphere,
They pitched upon the plain of the calm mere.

LIII.

They framed the imperial tent of their great Queen
  Of woven exhalations, underlaid
With lambent lightning-fire, as may be seen
  A dome of thin and open ivory inlaid
With crimson silk—cressets from the serene
  Hung there, and on the water for her tread,
A tapestry of fleece-like mist was strewn,
Dyed in the beams of the ascending moon.

LIV.

And on a throne o'erlaid with starlight, caught
  Upon those wandering isles of aery dew,
Which highest shoals of mountain shipwreck not,
  She sate, and heard all that had happened new
Between the earth and moon since they had brought
  The last intelligence—and now she grew
Pale as that moon, lost in the watery night—
And now she wept, and now she laughed outright.

B B

LV.

These were tame pleasures.—She would often climb
　The steepest ladder of the crudded rack
Up to some beaked cape of cloud sublime,
　And like Arion on the dolphin's back
Ride singing through the shoreless air.　Oft-time
　Following the serpent lightning's winding track,
She ran upon the platforms of the wind,
And laughed to hear the fireballs roar behind.

LVI.

And sometimes to those streams of upper air,
　Which whirl the earth in its diurnal round,
She would ascend, and win the spirits there
　To let her join their chorus.　Mortals found
That on those days the sky was calm and fair,
　And mystic snatches of harmonious sound
Wandered upon the earth where'er she past,
And happy thoughts of hope, too sweet to last.

LVII.

But her choice sport was, in the hours of sleep,
　To glide adown old Nilus, when he threads
Egypt and Æthiopia, from the steep
　Of utmost Axumè, until he spreads,
Like a calm flock of silver-fleeced sheep,
　His waters on the plain: and crested heads
Of cities and proud temples gleam amid
And many a vapour-belted pyramid.

LVIII.

By Mœris and the Mareotid lakes,
　Strewn with faint blooms like bridal chamber floors;
Where naked boys bridling tame water-snakes,
　Or charioteering ghastly alligators,
Had left on the sweet waters mighty wakes
　Of those huge forms:—within the brazen doors
Of the great Labyrinth slept both boy and beast,
Tired with the pomp of their Osirian feast.

LIX.

And where within the surface of the river
　The shadows of the massy temples lie,
And never are erased—but tremble ever
　Like things which every cloud can doom to die,
Through lotus-pav'n canals, and wheresoever
　The works of man pierced that serenest sky
With tombs, and towers, and fanes, 'twas her delight
To wander in the shadow of the night.

LX.

With motion like the spirit of that wind
　Whose soft step deepens slumber, her light feet
Passed through the peopled haunts of human kind,
　Scattering sweet visions from her presence sweet,

Through fane and palace-court and labyrinth mined
  With many a dark and subterranean street
Under the Nile ; through chambers high and deep
She passed, observing mortals in their sleep.

LXI.

A pleasure sweet doubtless it was to see
  Mortals subdued in all the shapes of sleep.
Here lay two sister-twins in infancy ;
  There, a lone youth who in his dreams did weep ;
Within, two lovers linked innocently
  In their loose locks which over both did creep
Like ivy from one stem ;—and there lay calm,
Old age with snow-bright hair and folded palm.

LXII.

But other troubled forms of sleep she saw,
  Not to be mirrored in a holy song,
Distortions foul of supernatural awe,
  And pale imaginings of visioned wrong,
And all the code of custom's lawless law
  Written upon the brows of old and young :
"This," said the wizard maiden, "is the strife,
Which stirs the liquid surface of man's life."

LXIII.

And little did the sight disturb her soul—
  We, the weak mariners of that wide lake
Where'er its shores extend or billows roll,
  Our course unpiloted and starless make
O'er its wild surface to an unknown goal—
  But she in the calm depths her way could take,
Where in bright bowers immortal forms abide,
Beneath the weltering of the restless tide.

LXIV.

And she saw princes couched under the glow
  Of sunlike gems ; and round each temple-court
In dormitories ranged, row after row,
  She saw the priests asleep,—all of one sort,
For all were educated to be so.
  The peasants in their huts, and in the port
The sailors she saw cradled on the waves,
And the dead lulled within their dreamless graves.

LXV.

And all the forms in which those spirits lay,
  Were to her sight like the diaphanous
Veils, in which those sweet ladies oft array
  Their delicate limbs, who would conceal from us
Only their scorn of all concealment : they
  Move in the light of their own beauty thus.
But these, and all now lay with sleep upon them,
And little thought a Witch was looking on them.

LXVI.

She all those human figures breathing there
　　Beheld as living spirits—to her eyes
The naked beauty of the soul lay bare,
　　And often through a rude and worn disguise
She saw the inner form most bright and fair—
　　And then,—she had a charm of strange device,
Which murmured on mute lips with tender tone,
Could make that spirit mingle with her own.

LXVII.

Alas, Aurora ! what wouldst thou have given
　　For such a charm, when Tithon became grey ?
Or how much, Venus, of thy silver Heaven
　　Wouldst thou have yielded, ere Proserpina
Had half (oh ! why not all ?) the debt forgiven
　　Which dear Adonis had been doomed to pay,
To any witch who would have taught you it ?
The Heliad doth not know its value yet.

LXVIII.

'Tis said in after times her spirit free
　　Knew what love was, and felt itself alone—
But holy Dian could not chaster be
　　Before she stooped to kiss Endymion,
Than now this lady—like a sexless bee
　　Tasting all blossoms, and confined to none—
Among those mortal forms, the wizard maiden
Passed with an eye serene and heart unladen.

LXIX.

To those she saw most beautiful, she gave
　　Strange panacea in a crystal bowl.
They drank in their deep sleep of that sweet wave,
　　And lived thenceforth as if some control
Mightier than life, were in them ; and the grave
　　Of such, when death oppressed the weary soul,
Was as a green and overarching bower
Lit by the gems of many a starry flower.

LXX.

For on the night that they were buried, she
　　Restored the embalmers ruining, and shook
The light out of the funeral lamps, to be
　　A mimic day within that deathy nook ;
And she unwound the woven imagery
　　Of second childhood's swaddling bands, and took
The coffin, its last cradle, from its niche,
And threw it with contempt into a ditch.

LXXI.

And there the body lay, age after age,
　　Mute, breathing, beating, warm, and undecaying
Like one asleep in a green hermitage,
　　With gentle sleep about its eyelids playing,

And living in its dreams beyond the rage
    Of death or life ; while they were still arraying
In liveries ever new, the rapid, blind
And fleeting generations of mankind.

LXXII.

And she would write strange dreams upon the brain
    Of those who were less beautiful, and make
All harsh and crooked purposes more vain
    Than in the desert is the serpent's wake
Which the sand covers,—all his evil gain
    The miser in such dreams would rise and shade
Into a beggar's lap ;—the lying scribe
Would his own lies betray without a bribe.

LXXIII.

The priests would write an explanation full,
    Translating hieroglyphics into Greek,
How the God Apis, really was a bull,
    And nothing more ; and bid the herald stick
The same against the temple doors, and pull
    The old cant down ; they licensed all to speak
Whate'er they thought of hawks, and cats, and geese,
By pastoral letters to each diocese.

LXXIV.

The king would dress an ape up in his crown
    And robes, and seat him on his glorious seat,
And on the right hand of the sunlike throne
    Would place a gaudy mock-bird to repeat
The chatterings of the monkey.—Every one
    Of the prone courtiers crawled to kiss the feet
Of their great Emperor when the morning came ;
And kissed—alas, how many kiss the same !

LXXV.

The soldiers dreamed that they were blacksmiths, and
    Walked out of quarters in somnambulism,
Round the red anvils you might see them stand
    Like Cyclopses in Vulcan's sooty abysm,
Beating their swords to ploughshares ;—in a band
    The jailors sent those of the liberal schism
Free through the streets of Memphis ; much, I wis,
To the annoyance of King Amasis.

LXXVI.

And timid lovers who had been so coy,
    They hardly knew whether they loved or not,
Would rise out of their rest and take sweet joy,
    To the fulfilment of their inmost thought ;
And when next day the maiden and the boy
    Met one another, both, like sinners caught,
Blushed at the thing which each believed was done
Only in fancy—till the tenth moon shone ;

LXXVII.

And then the Witch would let them take no ill:
　Of many thousand schemes which lovers find
The Witch found one,—and so they took their fill
　Of happiness in marriage warm and kind.
Friends who by practice of some envious skill,
　Were torn apart, a wide wound, mind from mind!
She did unite again with visions clear
Of deep affection and of truth sincere.

LXXVIII.

These were the pranks she played among the cities
　Of mortal men, and what she did to sprites
And Gods, entangling them in her sweet ditties
　To do her will, and show their subtle slights,
I will declare another time; for it is
　A tale more fit for the weird winter nights—
Than for these garish summer days, when we
Scarcely believe much more than we can see.

1819.

JULIAN AND MADDALO:

A CONVERSATION.

> " The meadows with fresh streams, the bees with thyme,
> The goats with the green leaves of budding spring,
> Are saturated not—nor Love with tears."—VIRGIL'S *Gallus*.

COUNT MADDALO is a Venetian nobleman of ancient family and of great fortune, who, without mixing much in the society of his countrymen, resides chiefly at his magnificent palace in that city. He is a person of the most consummate genius; and capable, if he would direct his energies to such an end, of becoming the redeemer of his degraded country. But it is his weakness to be proud: he derives, from a comparison of his own extraordinary mind with the dwarfish intellects that surround him, an intense apprehension of the nothingness of human life. His passions and his powers are incomparably greater than those of other men, and instead of the latter having been employed in curbing the former, they have mutually lent each other strength. His ambition preys upon itself, for want of objects which it can consider worthy of exertion. I say that Maddalo is proud, because I can find no other word to express the concentered and impatient feelings which consume him; but it is on his own hopes and affections only that he seems to trample, for in social life no human being can be more gentle, patient, and unassuming than Maddalo. He is cheerful, frank, and witty. His more serious conversation is a sort of intoxication; men are held by it as by a spell. He has travelled much; and there is an inexpressible charm in his relation of his adventures in different countries.

Julian is an Englishman of good family, passionately attached to those philosophical notions which assert the power of man over his own mind, and the immense improvements of which, by the extinction of certain moral superstitions, human society may be yet susceptible. Without concealing the evil in the world, he is for ever speculating how good may be made superior. He is a complete infidel, and a scoffer at all things reputed holy; and Maddalo takes a wicked pleasure in drawing out his taunts against religion. What Maddalo thinks on these matters is not exactly known. Julian, in spite of his heterodox opinions, is conjectured by his friends to possess some good qualities. How far this is possible, the pious reader will determine. Julian is rather serious.

Of the Maniac I can give no information. He seems by his own account to have been disappointed in love. He was evidently a very cultivated and amiable person when in his right senses. His story, told at length, might be like many other stories of the same kind: the unconnected exclamations of his agony will perhaps be found a sufficient comment for the text of every heart.

I RODE one evening with Count Maddalo
Upon the bank of land which breaks the flow
Of Adria towards Venice: a bare strand
Of hillocks, heaped from ever-shifting sand,
Matted with thistles and amphibious weeds,
Such as from earth's embrace the salt ooze breeds,
Is this; an uninhabited seaside,
Which the lone fisher, when his nets are dried,
Abandons; and no other object breaks
The waste, but one dwarf tree and some few stakes
Broken and unrepaired, and the tide makes
A narrow space of level sand thereon,
Where 'twas our wont to ride while day went down.
This ride was my delight. I love all waste
And solitary places; where we taste
The pleasure of believing what we see
Is boundless, as we wish our souls to be:
And such was this wide ocean, and this shore
More barren than its billows; and yet more
Than all, with a remembered friend I love
To ride as I then rode;—for the winds drove
The living spray along the sunny air
Into our faces; the blue heavens were bare,
Stripped to their depths by the awakening north;
And, from the waves, sound like delight broke forth
Harmonizing with solitude, and sent
Into our hearts aërial merriment.
So, as we rode, we talked; and the swift thought,
Winging itself with laughter, lingered not,
But flew from brain to brain,—such glee was ours,
Charged with light memories of remembered hours,
None slow enough for sadness: till we came
Homeward, which always makes the spirit tame.
This day had been cheerful but cold, and now
The sun was sinking, and the wind also.
Our talk grew somewhat serious, as may be
Talk interrupted with such raillery
As mocks itself, because it cannot scorn
The thoughts it would extinguish:—'twas forlorn,
Yet pleasing; such as once, so poets tell,
The devils held within the dales of hell,
Concerning God, freewill, and destiny.
Of all that Earth has been, or yet may be;
All that vain men imagine or believe,
Or hope can paint, or suffering can achieve,
We descanted; and I (for ever still
Is it not wise to make the best of ill?)
Argued against despondency; but pride
Made my companion take the darker side.
The sense that he was greater than his kind
Had struck, methinks, his eagle spirit blind
By gazing on its own exceeding light.
Meanwhile the sun paused ere it should alight
Over the horizon of the mountains—Oh !
How beautiful is sunset, when the glow
Of heaven descends upon a land like thee,
Thou paradise of exiles, Italy !

Thy mountains, seas, and vineyards, and the towers
Of cities they encircle !—It was ours
To stand on thee, beholding it: and then,
Just where we had dismounted, the Count's men
Were waiting for us with the gondola.
As those who pause on some delightful way,
Though bent on pleasant pilgrimage, we stood,
Looking upon the evening and the flood,
Which lay between the city and the shore,
Paved with the image of the sky: the hoar
And aery Alps, towards the north, appeared,
Through mist, an heaven-sustaining bulwark, reared
Between the east and west; and half the sky
Was roofed with clouds of rich emblazonry,
Dark purple at the zenith, which still grew
Down the steep west into a wondrous hue
Brighter than burning gold, even to the rent
Where the swift sun yet paused in his descent
Among the many folded hills—they were
Those famous Euganean hills, which bear,
As seen from Lido, through the harbour piles,
The likeness of a clump of peaked isles—
And then, as if the earth and sea had been
Dissolved into one lake of fire, were seen
Those mountains towering, as from waves of flame,
Around the vaporous sun, from which there came
The inmost purple spirit of light, and made
Their very peaks transparent. "Ere it fade,"
Said my companion, "I will show you soon
A better station." So, o'er the lagune
We glided; and from that funereal bark
I leaned, and saw the city, and could mark
How from their many isles, in evening's gleam,
Its temples and its palaces did seem
Like fabrics of enchantment piled to heaven.
I was about to speak, when—"We are even
Now at the point I meant," said Maddalo,
And bade the gondolieri cease to row.
"Look, Julian, on the west, and listen well
If you hear not a deep and heavy bell."
I looked, and saw between us and the sun
A building on an island, such an one
As age to age might add, for uses vile,—
A windowless, deformed and dreary pile;
And on the top an open tower, where hung
A bell, which in the radiance swayed and swung,
We could just hear its hoarse and iron tongue:
The broad sun sank behind it, and it tolled
In strong and black relief. "What we behold
Shall be the madhouse and its belfry tower,"
Said Maddalo; "and even at this hour,
Those who may cross the water hear that bell,
Which calls the maniacs, each one from his cell,
To vespers."—"As much skill as need to pray,
In thanks or hope for their dark lot have they,
To their stern Maker," I replied.—"Oh, ho !
You talk as in years past," said Maddalo.
"'Tis strange men change not. You were ever still

Among Christ's flock a perilous infidel,
A wolf for the meek lambs: if you can't swim,
Beware of Providence." I looked on him,
But the gay smile had faded from his eye.
"And such," he cried, "is our mortality;
And this must be the emblem and the sign
Of what should be eternal and divine;
And like that black and dreary bell the soul,
Hung in an heaven-illumined tower, must toll
Our thoughts and our desires to meet below
Round the rent heart, and pray—as madmen do;
For what? they know not, till the night of death,
As sunset that strange vision, severeth
Our memory from itself, and us from all
We sought, and yet were baffled." I recall
The sense of what he said, although I mar
The force of his expressions. The broad star
Of day meanwhile had sunk behind the hill;
And the black bell became invisible;
And the red tower looked grey; and all between,
The churches, ships, and palaces, were seen
Huddled in gloom: into the purple sea
The orange hues of heaven sunk silently.
We hardly spoke, and soon the gondola
Conveyed me to my lodging by the way.

The following morn was rainy, cold, and dim:
Ere Maddalo arose I called on him,
And whilst I waited, with his child I played;
A lovelier toy sweet Nature never made;
A serious, subtle, wild, yet gentle being;
Graceful without design, and unforeseeing;
With eyes—Oh! speak not of her eyes! which seem
Twin mirrors of Italian Heaven, yet gleam
With such deep meaning as we never see
But in the human countenance. With me
She was a special favourite: I had nursed
Her fine and feeble limbs, when she came first
To this bleak world; and she yet seemed to know
On second sight, her ancient playfellow,
Less changed than she was by six months or so.
For, after her first shyness was worn out,
We sate there, rolling billiard balls about,
When the Count entered. Salutations past:
"The words you spoke last night might well have cast
A darkness on my spirit:—if man be
The passive thing you say, I should not see
Much harm in the religions and old saws,
(Though *I* may never own such leaden laws),
Which break a teachless nature to the yoke:
Mine is another faith."—Thus much I spoke,
And, noting he replied not, added—"See
This lovely child; blithe, innocent and free;
She spends a happy time, with little care;
While we to such sick thoughts subjected are,
As came on you last night. It is our will
Which thus enchains us to permitted ill.
We might be otherwise; we might be all

We dream of, happy, high, majestical.
Where is the love, beauty, and truth we seek,
But in our minds? And if we were not weak,
Should we be less in deed than in desire?"—
"Ay, if we were not weak,—and we aspire,
How vainly! to be strong," said Maddalo:
"You talk Utopia"—

                "It remains to know,"
I then rejoined, "and those who try, may find
How strong the chains are which our spirit bind:
Brittle perchance as straw. We are assured
Much may be conquered, much may be endured,
Of what degrades and crushes us. We know
That we have power over ourselves to do
And suffer—*what*, we know not till we try;
But something nobler than to live and die:
So taught the kings of old philosophy,
Who reigned before religion made men blind;
And those who suffer with their suffering kind,
Yet feel this faith, religion."

                    "My dear friend,"
Said Maddalo, "my judgment will not bend
To your opinion, though I think you might
Make such a system refutation-tight,
As far as words go. I knew one like you,
Who to this city came some months ago,
With whom I argued in this sort—and he
Is now gone mad—and so he answered me,
Poor fellow!—But if you would like to go,
We'll visit him, and his wild talk will show
How vain are such aspiring theories."

"I hope to prove the induction otherwise,
And that a want of that true theory still,
Which seeks a soul of goodness in things ill,
Or in himself or others, has thus bowed
His being:—there are some by nature proud,
Who, patient in all else, demand but this—
To love and be beloved with gentleness:
And being scorned, what wonder if they die
Some living death? This is not destiny,
But man's own wilful ill."

                As thus I spoke,
Servants announced the gondola, and we
Through the fast-falling rain and high-wrought sea
Sailed to the island where the madhouse stands.
We disembarked. The clap of tortured hands,
Fierce yells, and howlings, and lamentings keen,
And laughter where complaint had merrier been,
Accosted us. We climbed the oozy stairs
Into an old courtyard. I heard on high,
Then, fragments of most touching melody,
But looking up saw not the singer there.
Through the black bars in the tempestuous air
I saw, like weeds on a wrecked palace growing,
Long tangled locks flung wildly forth and flowing,
Of those who on a sudden were beguiled
Into strange silence, and looked forth and smiled,

Hearing sweet sounds.   Then I:—

"Methinks there were
A cure of these with patience and kind care,
If music can thus move.   But what is he,
Whom we seek here?"

"Of his sad history
I know but this," said Maddalo: "he came
To Venice a dejected man, and fame
Said he was wealthy, or he had been so.
Some thought the loss of fortune wrought him woe;
But he was ever talking in such sort
As you do—but more sadly; he seemed hurt,
Even as a man with his peculiar wrong,
To hear but of the oppression of the strong,
Or those absurd deceits (I think with you
In some respects, you know) which carry through
The excellent impostors of this earth
When they outface detection.   He had worth,
Poor fellow! but a humorist in his way."

"Alas, what drove him mad!"

"I cannot say:
A lady came with him from France, and when
She left him and returned, he wandered then
About yon lonely isles of desert sand,
Till he grew wild.   He had no cash or land
Remaining:—the police had brought him here—
Some fancy took him, and he would not bear
Removal, so I fitted up for him
Those rooms beside the sea, to please his whim;
And sent him busts, and books, and urns for flowers,
Which had adorned his life in happier hours,
And instruments of music.   You may guess
A stranger could do little more or less
For one so gentle and unfortunate—
And those are his sweet strains which charm the weight
From madmen's chains, and make this hell appear
A heaven of sacred silence, hushed to hear."

"Nay, this was kind of you—he had no claim,
As the world says."

"None but the very same
Which I on all mankind, were I, as he,
Fallen to such deep reverse.   His melody
Is interrupted now; we hear the din
Of madmen, shriek on shriek, again begin:
Let us now visit him: after this strain,
He ever communes with himself again,
And sees and hears not any."

Having said
These words, we called the keeper, and he led
To an apartment opening on the sea.
There the poor wretch was sitting mournfully
Near a piano, his pale fingers twined
One with the other; and the ooze and wind

Rushed through an open casement, and did sway
His hair, and starred it with the brackish spray;
His head was leaning on a music-book,
And he was muttering; and his lean limbs shook;
His lips were pressed against a folded leaf
In hue too beautiful for health, and grief
Smiled in their motions as they lay apart,
As one who wrought from his own fervid heart
The eloquence of passion: soon he raised
His sad meek face and eyes lustrous and glazed,
And spoke—sometimes as one who wrote, and thought
His words might move some heart that heeded not,
If sent to distant lands;—and then as one
Reproaching deeds never to be undone,
With wondering self-compassion;—then his speech
Was lost in grief, and then his words came each
Unmodulated and expressionless,—
But that from one jarred accent you might guess
It was despair made them so uniform:
And all the while the loud and gusty storm
Hissed through the window, and we stood behind,
Stealing his accents from the envious wind,
Unseen. I yet remember what he said
Distinctly, such impression his words made.

   " Month after month," he cried, " to bear this load,
And, as a jade urged by the whip and goad,
To drag life on—which like a heavy chain
Lengthens behind with many a link of pain,
And not to speak my grief— O, not to dare
To give a human voice to my despair;
But live, and move, and, wretched thing ! smile on,
As if I never went aside to groan,
And wear this mask of falsehood even to those
Who are most dear—not for my own repose—
Alas ! no scorn, or pain, or hate, could be
So heavy as that falsehood is to me—
But that I cannot bear more altered faces
Than needs must be, more changed and cold embraces,
More misery, disappointment, and mistrust
To own me for their father. Would the dust
Were covered in upon my body now !
That the life ceased to toil within my brow !
And then these thoughts would at the last be fled:
Let us not fear such pain can vex the dead.

   " What Power delights to torture us ? I know
That to myself I do not wholly owe
What now I suffer, though in part I may.
Alas ! none strewed fresh flowers upon the way
Where, wandering heedlessly, I met pale Pain,
My shadow, which will leave me not again.
If I have erred, there was no joy in error,
But pain, and insult, and unrest, and terror;
I have not, as some do, bought penitence
With pleasure, and a dark yet sweet offence;
For then if love, and tenderness, and truth
Had overlived Hope's momentary youth,

My creed should have redeemed me from repenting;
But loathed scorn and outrage unrelenting
Met love excited by far other seeming
Until the end was gained:—as one from dreaming
Of sweetest peace, I woke; and found my state
Such as it is.

        "O, thou, my spirit's mate !
Who, for thou art compassionate and wise,
Wouldst pity me from thy most gentle eyes
If this sad writing thou shouldst ever see,
My secret groans must be unheard by thee;
Thou wouldst weep tears, bitter as blood, to know
Thy lost friend's incommunicable woe.
Ye few by whom my nature has been weighed
In friendship, let me not that name degrade,
By placing on your hearts the secret load
Which crushes mine to dust.   There is one road
To peace, and that is truth, which follow ye !
Love sometimes leads astray to misery.
Yet think not, though subdued (and I may well
Say that I am subdued)—that the full hell
Within me would infect the untainted breast
Of sacred nature with its own unrest;
As some perverted beings think to find
In scorn or hate a medicine for the mind
Which scorn or hate hath wounded.—O, how vain !
The dagger heals not, but may rend again.
Believe that I am ever still the same
In creed as in resolve; and what may tame
My heart, must leave the understanding free,
Or all would sink under this agony.
Nor dream that I will join the vulgar eye,
Or with my silence sanction tyranny,
Or seek a moment's shelter from my pain
In any madness which the world calls gain;
Ambition, or revenge, or thoughts as stern
As those which make me what I am, or turn
To avarice or misanthropy or lust.
Heap on me soon, O grave, thy welcome dust !
Till then the dungeon may demand its prey;
And Poverty and Shame may meet and say,
Halting beside me in the public way,—
'That love-devoted youth is ours: let's sit
Beside him: he may live some six months yet.'
Or the red scaffold, as our country bends,
May ask some willing victim; or ye, friends !
May fall under some sorrow, which this heart
Or hand may share, or vanquish, or avert;
I am prepared, in truth, with no proud joy,
To do or suffer aught, as when a boy
I did devote to justice, and to love,
My nature, worthless now.

        "I must remove
A veil from my pent mind.   'Tis torn aside !
O ! pallid as Death's dedicated bride,
Thou mockery which art sitting by my side

Am I not wan like thee? At the grave's call
I haste, invited to thy wedding-ball,
To meet the ghastly paramour, for whom
Thou hast deserted me,—and made the tomb
Thy bridal bed. But I beside thy feet
Will lie, and watch ye from my winding-sheet
Thus—wide awake though dead——Yet stay, O stay!
Go not so soon—I know not what I say—
Hear but my reasons—I am mad, I fear,
My fancy is o'erwrought—thou art not here.
Pale art thou, 'tis most true—but thou art gone—
Thy work is finished; I am left alone.

    *   *   *   *

" Nay, was it I who wooed thee to this breast,
Which like a serpent thou envenomest
As in repayment of the warmth it lent?
Didst thou not seek me for thine own content?
Did not thy love awaken mine? I thought
That thou wert she who said 'You kiss me not
Ever; I fear you do not love me now.'
In truth I loved even to my overthrow
Her, who would fain forget these words; but they
Cling to her mind, and cannot pass away.

    *   *   *   *

" You say that I am proud; that when I speak,
My lip is tortured with the wrongs, which break
The spirit it expresses.—Never one
Humbled himself before, as I have done!
Even the instinctive worm on which we tread
Turns, though it wound not—then, with prostrate head,
Sinks in the dust, and writhes like me—and dies:
——No:—wears a living death of agonies!
As the slow shadows of the pointed grass
Mark the eternal periods, its pangs pass,
Slow, ever-moving, making moments be
As mine seem,—each an immortality!

    *   *   *   *

" That you had never seen me! never heard
My voice! and, more than all, had ne'er endured
The deep pollution of my loathed embrace!
That your eyes ne'er had lied love in my face!
That, like some maniac monk, I had torn out
The nerves of manhood by their bleeding root
With mine own quivering fingers! so that ne'er
Our hearts had for a moment mingled there,
To disunite in horror! These were not
With thee like some suppressed and hideous thought,
Which flits athwart our musings, but can find
No rest within a pure and gentle mind—
Thou sealed'st them with many a bare broad word,
And seared'st my memory o'er them,—for I heard
And can forget not—they were ministered,
One after one, those curses. Mix them up
Like self-destroying poisons in one cup;
And they will make one blessing, which thou ne'er
Didst imprecate for on me——death!

                       " It were
A cruel punishment for one most cruel,
If such can love, to make that love the fuel
Of the mind's hell—hate, scorn, remorse, despair:
But *me*, whose heart a stranger's tear might wear,
As water-drops the sandy fountain stone;
Who loved and pitied all things, and could moan
For woes which others hear not, and could see
The absent with the glass of fantasy,
And near the poor and trampled sit and weep,
Following the captive to his dungeon deep;
Me, who am as a nerve o'er which do creep
The else-unfelt oppressions of this earth,
And was to thee the flame upon thy hearth,
When all beside was cold:—that thou on me
Shouldst rain these plagues of blistering agony—
Such curses are from lips once eloquent
With love's too partial praise !   Let none relent
Who intend deeds too dreadful for a name
Henceforth, if an example for the same
They seek:—for thou on me lookedst so and so,
And didst speak thus and thus.   I live to show
How much men bear and die not.

         *   *   *   *

                       " Thou wilt tell,
With the grimace of hate, how horrible
It was to meet my love when thine grew less;
Thou wilt admire how I could e'er address
Such features to love's work. . . . This taunt, though true
(For indeed nature nor in form nor hue
Bestowed on me her choicest workmanship)
Shall not be thy defence : for since thy life
Met mine first, years long past,—since thine eye kindled
With soft fire under mine,—I have not dwindled,
Nor changed in mind, or body, or in aught
But as love changes what it loveth not
After long years and many trials.

         *   *   *   *

                       " How vain
Are words !   I thought never to speak again,
Not even in secret, not to my own heart—
But from my lips the unwilling accents start,
And from my pen the words flow as I write,
Dazzling my eyes with scalding tears—my sight
Is dim to see that charactered in vain,
On this unfeeling leaf, which burns the brain
And eats into it, blotting all things fair,
And wise and good, which time had written there.
Those who inflict must suffer, for they see
The work of their own hearts, and that must be
Our chastisement or recompense.—O, child !
I would that thine were like to be more mild
For both our wretched sakes,—for thine the most,
Who feel'st already all that thou hast lost,
Without the power to wish it thine again.
And, as slow years pass, a funereal train,

Each with the ghost of some lost hope or friend
Following it like its shadow, wilt thou bend
No thought on my dead memory?

*   *   *   *

       " Alas, love !
Fear me not : against thee I'd not move
A finger in despite.   Do I not live
That thou mayst have less bitter cause to grieve ?
I give thee tears for scorn, and love for hate;
And, that thy lot may be less desolate
Than his on whom thou tramplest, I refrain
From that sweet sleep which medicines all pain.
Then—when thou speakest of me—never say,
' He could forgive not'—Here I cast away
All human passions, all revenge, all pride;
I think, speak, act no ill; I do but hide
Under these words, like embers, every spark
Of that which has consumed me.   Quick and dark
The grave is yawning:—as its roof shall cover
My limbs with dust and worms, under and over;
So let oblivion hide this grief—The air
Closes upon my accents, as despair
Upon my heart—let death upon despair !"

  He ceased, and overcome, leant back awhile;
Then rising, with a melancholy smile,
Went to a sofa, and lay down, and slept
A heavy sleep, and in his dreams he wept,
And muttered some familiar name, and we
Wept without shame in his society.
I think I never was impressed so much;
The man who were not, must have lacked a touch
Of human nature.—Then we lingered not,
Although our argument was quite forgot;
But, calling the attendants, went to dine
At Maddalo's:—yet neither cheer nor wine
Could give us spirits, for we talked of him,
And nothing else, till daylight made stars dim.
And we agreed it was some dreadful ill
Wrought on him boldly, yet unspeakable,
By a dear friend; some deadly change in love
Of one vowed deeply which he dreamed not of;
For whose sake he, it seemed, had fixed a blot
Of falsehood in his mind, which flourished not
But in the light of all-beholding truth;
And having stamped this canker on his youth,
She had abandoned him:—and how much more
Might be his woe, we guessed not:—he had store
Of friends and fortune once, as we could guess
From his nice habits and his gentleness;
These now were lost—it were a grief indeed
If he had changed one unsustaining reed
For all that such a man might else adorn.
The colours of his mind seemed yet unworn;
For the wild language of his grief was high—
Such as in measure were called poetry.
And I remember one remark, which then
Maddalo made: he said—" Most wretched men

Are cradled into poetry by wrong:
They learn in suffering what they teach in song."

If I had been an unconnected man,
I, from this moment, should have formed some plan
Never to leave sweet Venice: for to me
It was delight to ride by the lone sea:
And then the town is silent—one may write,
Or read in gondolas by day or night,
Having the little brazen lamp alight,
Unseen, uninterrupted:—books are there,
Pictures, and casts from all those statues fair
Which were twin-born with poetry;—and all
We seek in towns, with little to recal
Regret for the green country:—I might sit
In Maddalo's great palace, and his wit
And subtle talk would cheer the winter night,
And make me know myself:—and the firelight
Would flash upon our faces, till the day
Might dawn, and make me wonder at my stay.
But I had friends in London too.   The chief
Attraction here was that I sought relief
From the deep tenderness that maniac wrought
Within me—'twas perhaps an idle thought,
But I imagined that if, day by day,
I watched him, and seldom went away,
And studied all the beatings of his heart
With zeal, as men study some stubborn art
For their own good, and could by patience find
An entrance to the caverns of his mind,
I might reclaim him from his dark estate.
In friendships I had been most fortunate,
Yet never saw I one whom I would call
More willingly my friend;—and this was all
Accomplished not;—such dreams of baseless good
Oft come and go, in crowds or solitude,
And leave no trace !—but what I now designed,
Made, for long years, impression on my mind.
—The following morning, urged by my affairs,
I left bright Venice.—

                              After many years,
And many changes, I returned; the name
Of Venice, and its aspect, was the same;
But Maddalo was travelling, far away,
Among the mountains of Armenia.
His dog was dead: his child had now become
A woman, such as it has been my doom
To meet with few; a wonder of this earth,
Where there is little of transcendent worth,—
Like one of Shakspeare's women.   Kindly she,
And with a manner beyond courtesy,
Received her father's friend; and, when I asked
Of the lorn maniac, she her memory tasked,
And told, as she had heard, the mournful tale:
" That the poor sufferer's health began to fail,
Two years from my departure; but that then
The lady, who had left him, came again.

Her mien had been imperious, but she now
Looked meek; perhaps remorse had brought her low.
Her coming made him better; and they stayed
Together at my father's,—for I played,
As I remember, with the lady's shawl;
I might be six years old:—But, after all,
She left him."—

           " Why, her heart must have been tough;
How did it end?"

               " And was not this enough ?
They met, they parted."

                   " Child, is there no more?"

"Something within that interval, which bore
The stamp of *why* they parted, *how* they met;
Yet if thine aged eyes disdain to wet
Those wrinkled cheeks with youth's remembered tears,
Ask me no more; but let the silent years
Be closed and cered over their memory,
As yon mute marble where their corpses lie."
I urged and questioned still: she told me how
All happened—but the cold world shall not know.

Rome, May, 1819.

Satires.

1819.

PETER BELL THE THIRD.

BY MICHING MALLECHO, ESQ.

> " Is it a party in a parlour,
>   Crammed just as they on earth were crammed,
>   Some sipping punch—some sipping tea,
>   But, as you by their faces see,
>   All silent, and all—damned ?"
>   *Peter Bell*, by W. WORDSWORTH.

> " *Ophelia.* What means this, my lord ?
>   *Hamlet.* Marry, this is Miching Mallecho ; it means mischief."
>   SHAKSPEARE.

Dedication.

TO THOMAS BROWN, ESQ., THE YOUNGER, H.F.

DEAR TOM,—Allow me to request you to introduce Mr. Peter Bell to the respectable family of the Fudges. Although he may fall short of those very considerable personages in the more active properties which characterize the Rat and the Apostate, I suspect that even you, their historian, will confess that he surpasses them in the more peculiarly legitimate qualification of intolerable dulness.

You know Mr. Examiner Hunt ; well—it was he who presented me to two of the Mr. Bells. My intimacy with the younger Mr. Bell naturally sprung from this introduction to his brothers. And, in presenting him to you, I have the satisfaction of being able to assure you that he is considerably the dullest of the three.

There is this particular advantage in an acquaintance with any one of the Peter Bells—that, if you know one Peter Bell, you know three Peter Bells ; they are not one, but three ; not three, but one. An awful mystery, which, after having caused torrents of blood, and having been hymned by groans enough to deafen the music of the spheres, is at length illustrated, to the satisfaction of all parties in the theological world, by the nature of Mr. Peter Bell.

Peter is a polyhedric Peter, or a Peter with many sides. He changes colours like a chameleon, and his coat like a snake. He is a Proteus of a Peter. He was at first sublime, pathetic, impressive, profound ; then dull ; then prosy and dull ; and now dull—oh, so very dull ! it is an ultra-legitimate dulness.

You will perceive that it is not necessary to consider Hell and the Devil as supernatural machinery. The whole scene of my epic is in "this world which is"—so Peter informed us before his conversion to *White Obi*——

> "The world of all of us, *and where*
> *We find our happiness, or not at all.*"

Let me observe that I have spent six or seven days in composing this sublime piece ; the orb of my moonlight genius has made the fourth part of its revolution round the dull earth which you inhabit, driving you mad, while it has retained its calmness and its splendour, and I have been fitting this its last phase "to occupy a permanent station in the literature of my country."

Your works, indeed, dear Tom, sell better ; but mine are far superior. The public is no judge ; posterity sets all to rights.

Allow me to observe that so much has been written of Peter Bell that the present history can be considered only, like the "Iliad," as a continuation of that series of cyclic poems which have already been candidates for bestowing immortality upon, at the same time that they receive it from, his character and adventures. In this point of view, I have violated no rule of syntax in beginning my composition with a conjunction : the full stop which closes the poem continued by me being, like the full stops at the end of the "Iliad" and "Odyssey," a full stop of a very qualified import.

Hoping that the immortality which you have given to the Fudges you will receive from them ; and in the firm expectation that, when London shall be an habitation of bitterns ; when St. Paul's and Westminster Abbey shall stand, shapeless and nameless ruins, in the midst of an unpeopled marsh ; when the piers of Waterloo Bridge shall become the nuclei of islets of reeds and osiers, and cast the jagged shadows of their broken arches on the solitary stream ; some transatlantic commentator will be weighing, in the scales of some new and now unimagined system of criticism, the respective merits of the Bells and the Fudges, and their historians,

I remain, dear Tom,
Yours sincerely,
MICHING MALLECHO.

December 1, 1819.

P.S.—Pray excuse the date of place ; so soon as the profits of the publication come in, I mean to hire lodgings in a more respectable street.

PROLOGUE.

PETER BELLS, one, two, and three,
O'er the wide world wandering be.—
First, the antenatal Peter,
Wrapped in weeds of the same metre,
The so long predestined raiment,
Clothed in which to walk his way meant
The second Peter ; whose ambition
Is to link the proposition
As the mean of two extremes—
(This was learnt from Aldrich's themes)—
Shielding from the guilt of schism
The orthodox syllogism ;
The first Peter—he who was
Like the shadow in the glass
Of the second, yet unripe,
His substantial antitype.—

Then came Peter Bell the Second
Who henceforward must be reckoned
The body of a double soul,
And that portion of the whole
Without which the rest would seem
Ends of a disjointed dream.—
And the Third is he who has
O'er the grave been forced to pass
To the other side, which is—
Go and try else—just like this.

Peter Bell the First was Peter
Smugger, milder, softer, neater,
Like the soul before it is
Born from that world into this.
The next Peter Bell was he
Predevote, like you and me,
To good or evil as may come ;
His was the severer doom,—
For he was an evil cotter,
And a polygamic Potter.
And the last is Peter Bell
Damned since our first parents feil,
Damned eternally to Hell—
Surely he deserves it well !

———

PART I.—DEATH.

I.

AND Peter Bell, when he had been
    With fresh-imported hell-fire warmed,
Grew serious—from his dress and mien
'Twas very plainly to be seen
    Peter was quite reformed.

II.

His eyes turned up, his mouth turned down ;
    His accent caught a nasal twang ;
He oiled his hair ; there might be heard
The grace of God in every word
    Which Peter said or sang.

III.

But Peter now grew old, and had
    An ill no doctor could unravel ;
His torments almost drove him mad ;
Some said it was a fever bad,
    Some swore it was the gravel.

IV.

His holy friends then came about,
    And with long preaching and persuasion
Convinced the patient that, without
The smallest shadow of a doubt,
    He was predestined to damnation.

V.

They said : " Thy name is Peter *Bell*,
  Thy skin is of a brimstone *hue ;*
Alive or dead—ay, sick or well—
The one God made to rhyme with *hell ;*
  The other, I think, rhymes with *you*."

VI.

Then Peter set up such a yell
  The nurse who with some water gruel
Was climbing up the stairs as well
As her old legs could climb them, fell,
  And broke them both—the fall was cruel.

VII.

The parson from the casement leapt
  Into the lake of Windermere :
And many an eel—though no adept
In God's right reason for it—kept
  Gnawing his kidneys half a year.

VIII.

And all the rest rushed through the door,
  And tumbled over one another,
And broke their skulls.—Upon the floor
Meanwhile sat Peter Bell, and swore,
  And cursed his father and his mother.

IX.

And raved of God and sin and death,
  Blaspheming like an infidel;
And said that with his clenched teeth
He'd seize the earth from underneath,
  And drag it with him down to hell.

X.

As he was speaking, came a spasm,
  And wrenched his gnashing teeth asunder.
Like one who sees a strange phantasm
He lay,—there was a silent chasm
  Betwixt his upper jaw and under.

XI.

And yellow death lay on his face;
  And a fixed smile that was not human
Told, as I understand the case,
That he was gone to the wrong place:—
  I heard all this from the old woman.

XII.

Then there came down from Langdale Pike
  A cloud, with lightning, wind, and hail;
It swept over the mountains like
An ocean, and I heard it strike
  The woods and crags of Grasmere Vale.

XIII.

And I saw the black storm come
   Nearer, minute after minute;
Its thunder made the cataracts dumb;
With hiss and clash and hollow hum,
   It neared as if the Devil was in it.

XIV.

The Devil *was* in it:—he had bought
   Peter for half-a-crown. And, when
The storm which bore him vanished, nought
That in the house that storm had caught
   Was ever seen again.

XV.

The gaping neighbours came next day—
   They found all vanished from the shore.
The bible whence he used to pray
Half scorched under a hen-coop lay;
   Smashed glass—and nothing more.

PART II.—THE DEVIL.

I.

The Devil, I safely can aver,
   Has neither hoof nor tail, nor sting;
Nor is he, as some sages swear,
A spirit neither here nor there,—
   In nothing, yet in everything.

II.

He is—what we are: for sometimes
   The Devil is a gentleman;
At others a bard bartering rhymes
For sack; a statesman spinning crimes;
   A swindler living as he can;

III.

A thief who cometh in the night,
   With whole boots and net pantaloons,
Like some one whom it were not right
To mention; or the luckless wight
   From whom he steals nine silver spoons.

IV.

But in this case he did appear
   Like a slop-merchant from Wapping,
And with smug face and eye severe
On every side did perk and peer
   Till he saw Peter dead or napping.

V.

He had on an upper Benjamin
   (For he was of the driving schism)

In the which he wrapped his skin
From the storm he travelled in,
 For fear of rheumatism.

VI.

He called the ghost out of the corse.
 It was exceedingly like Peter,—
Only its voice was hollow and hoarse:
It had a queerish look of course:
 Its dress too was a little neater.

VII.

The Devil knew not his name and lot,
 Peter knew not that he was Bell:
Each had an upper stream of thought
Which made all seem as it was not,
 Fitting itself to all things well.

VIII.

Peter thought he had parents dear,
 Brothers, sisters, cousins, cronies,
In the fens of Lincolnshire.
He perhaps had found them there,
 Had he gone and boldly shown his

IX.

Solemn phiz in his own village;
 Where he thought oft when a boy
He'd clomb the orchard walls to pillage
The produce of his neighbour's tillage,
 With marvellous pride and joy.

X.

And the Devil thought he had,
 'Mid the misery and confusion
Of an unjust war, just made
A fortune by the gainful trade
 Of giving soldiers rations bad—
  (The world is full of strange delusion);

XI.

That he had a mansion planned
 In a square like Grosvenor Square;
That he was aping fashion, and
That he now came to Westmoreland
 To see what was romantic there.

XII.

And all this, though quite ideal—
 Ready at a breath to vanish—
Was a state not more unreal
Than the peace he could not feel,
 Or the care he could not banish.

XIII.

After a little conversation,
   The Devil told Peter, if he chose,
He'd bring him to the world of fashion
By giving him a situation
   In his own service—and new clothes.

XIV.

And Peter bowed, quite pleased and proud;
   And, after waiting some few days
For a new livery—dirty yellow
Turned up with black,—the wretched fellow
   Was bowled to Hell in the Devil's chaise.

PART III.—HELL.

I.

Hell is a city much like London—
   A populous and a smoky city;
There are all sorts of people undone,
And there is little or no fun done;
   Small justice shown and still less pity.

II.

There is a Castles, and a Canning,
   A Cobbett, and a Castlereagh;
All sorts of caitiff corpses planning
All sorts of cozening, for trepanning
   Corpses less corrupt than they.

III.

There is a * * *, who has lost
   His wits, or sold them, none knows which;
He walks about a double ghost,
And, though as thin as Fraud almost,
   Ever grows more grim and rich.

IV.

There is a Chancery Court; a King;
   A manufacturing mob; a set
Of thieves who by themselves are sent
Similar thieves to represent;
   An army; and a public debt;—

V.

Which last is a scheme of paper-money,
   And means, being interpreted—
" Bees, keep your wax—give us the honey;
And we will plant, while skies are sunny,
   Flowers, which in winter serve instead."

VI.

There is great talk of revolution,
    And a great chance of despotism;
German soldiers—camps—confusion—
Tumults—lotteries—rage—delusion—
    Gin—suicide—and Methodism;—

VII.

Taxes too on wine and bread,
    And meat and beer and tea and cheese;
From which those patriots pure are fed
Who gorge, before they reel to bed,
    The tenfold essence of all these.

VIII

There are mincing women, mewing
    (Like cats, who *amant miserè*)
Of their own virtue, and pursuing
Their gentler sisters to that ruin
    Without which—what were chastity?

X.

Lawyers, judges, old hobnobbers,
    Are there,—bailiffs—Chancellors—
Bishops—great and little robbers—
Rhymsters—pamphleteers—stock-jobbers—
    Men of glory in the wars,—

X.

Things whose trade is over ladies
    To lean, and flirt and stare and simper,
Till all that is divine in woman
Grows cruel, courteous, smooth, inhuman,
    Crucified 'twixt a smile and whimper.

XI.

Thrusting, toiling, wailing, moiling,
    Frowning, preaching—such a riot!
Each with never-ceasing labour,
Whilst he thinks he cheats his neighbour,
    Cheating his own heart of quiet.

XII.

And all these meet at levees,—
    Dinners convivial and political—
Suppers of epic poets—teas
Where small-talk dies in agonies—
    Breakfasts professional and critical;—

XIII.

Lunches and snacks so aldermanic
    That one would furnish forth ten dinners
Where reigns a Cretan tonguèd panic.
Lest news—Russ, Dutch, or Alemanic—
    Should make some losers, and some winners;—

XIV.

At conversazioni, balls,
    Conventicles, and drawing-rooms;
Courts of law, committees, calls
Of a morning, clubs, book-stalls,
    Churches, masquerades, and tombs.

XV.

And this is Hell: and in this smother
    All are damnable and damned;
Each one, damning, damns the other;
They are damned by one another,—
    By none other are they damned.

XVI.

'Tis a lie to say "God damns."
    Where was Heaven's Attorney General
When they first gave out such flams?
Let there be an end of shams:
    They are mines of poisonous mineral.

XVII.

Statesmen damn themselves to be
    Cursed; and lawyers damn their souls
To the auction of a fee;
Churchmen damn themselves to see
    God's sweet love in burning coals:—

XVIII.

The rich are damned, beyond all cure,
    To taunt and starve and trample on
The weak and wretched; and the poor
Damn their broken hearts to endure
    Stripe on stripe with groan on groan:—

XIX.

Sometimes the poor are damned indeed
    To take—not means for being blessed—
But Cobbett's snuff, revenge; that weed
From which the worms that it doth feed
    Squeeze less than they before possessed:—

XX.

And some few, like we know who,
    Damned—but God alone knows why—
To believe their minds are given
To make this ugly Hell a Heaven;
    In which faith they live and die.

XXI.

Thus,—as, in a town plague-stricken,
    Each man (be he sound or no)
Must indifferently sicken;
As, when day begins to thicken
    None knows a pigeon from a crow,—

XXII.

So good and bad, sane and mad;
    The oppressor and the oppressed;
Those who weep to see what others
Smile to inflict upon their brothers;
    Lovers, haters, worst and best:

XXIII.

All are damned—They breathe an air,
    Thick, infected, joy-dispelling;
Each pursues what seems most fair,
Mining like moles through mind, and there
Scoop palace-caverns vast, where Care
    In thronèd state is ever dwelling.

PART IV.—SIN.

I.

Lo, Peter in Hell's Grosvenor Square,
    A footman in the Devil's service !
And the misjudging world would swear
That every man in service there
    To virtue would prefer vice.

II.

But Peter, though now damned, was not
    What Peter was before damnation.
Men oftentimes prepare a lot
Which, ere it finds them, is not what
    Suits with their genuine station.

III.

All things that Peter saw and felt
    Had a peculiar aspect to him;
And, when they came within the belt
Of his own nature, seemed to melt,
    Like cloud to cloud, into him.

IV.

And so, the outward world uniting,
    To that within him, he became
Considerably uninviting
To those who, meditation slighting,
    Were moulded in a different frame.

V.

And he scorned them, and they scorned him:
    And he scorned all they did; and they
Did all that men of their own trim
Are wont to do to please their whim,
    Drinking, lying, swearing, play.

VI.

Such were his fellow-servants; thus
   His virtue, like our own, was built
Too much on that indignant fuss
Hypocrite Pride stirs up in us
   To bully one another's guilt.

VII.

He had a mind which was somehow
   At once circumference and centre
Of all he might or feel or know;
Nothing went ever out, although
   Something did ever enter.

VIII.

He had as much imagination
   As a pint-pot;—he never could
Fancy another situation,
From which to dart his contemplation,
   Than that wherein he stood.

IX.

Yet his was individual mind,
   And new-created all he saw
In a new manner, and refined
Those new creations, and combined
   Them by a master-spirit's law.

X.

Thus—although unimaginative—
   An apprehension clear, intense,
Of his mind's work, had made alive
The things it wrought on; I believe
   Wakening a sort of thought in sense.

XI.

But from the first 'twas Peter's drift
   To be a kind of moral eunuch:
He touched the hem of Nature's shift,—
Felt faint,—and never dared uplift
   The closest all-concealing tunic.

XII.

She laughed the while with an arch smile,
   And kissed him with a sister's kiss,
And said: " My best Diogenes,
I love you well—but, if you please,
   Tempt not again my deepest bliss.

XIII.

" 'Tis you are cold; for I, not coy,
   Yield love for love, frank, warm, and true;
And Burns, a Scottish peasant boy—
His errors prove it—knew my joy
   More, learned friend, than you.

XIV.

" *Bocca baciata non perde ventura,*
   Anzi rinnuova come fa la luna :—
So thought Boccaccio, whose sweet words might cure a
Male prude, like you, from what you now endure, a
   Low-tide in soul, like a stagnant laguna."

XV.

Then Peter rubbed his eyes severe,
   And smoothed his spacious forehead down
With his broad palm;—'twixt love and fear,
He looked, as he no doubt felt, queer.
   And in his dream sate down.

XVI.

The Devil was no uncommon creature;
   A leaden-witted thief—just huddled
Out of the dross and scum of nature;
A toad-like lump of limb and feature,
   With mind and heart and fancy muddled.

XVII.

He was that heavy dull cold thing
   The Spirit of Evil well may be:
A drone too base to have a sting;
Who gluts, and grimes his lazy wing,
   And calls lust " luxury."

XVIII.

Now he was quite the kind of wight
   Round whom collect, at a fixed era,
Venison, turtle, hock, and claret—
Good cheer, and those who come to share it-
   And best East Indian madeira.

XIX.

It was his fancy to invite
   Men of science, wit, and learning,
Who came to lend each other light;
He proudly thought that his gold's might
   Had set those spirits burning.

XX.

And men of learning, science, wit,
   Considered him as you and I
Think of some rotten tree, and sit
Lounging and dining under it,
   Exposed to the wide sky.

XXI.

And all the while, with loose fat smile,
   The willing wretch sat winking there;
Believing 'twas his power that made
That jovial scene, and that all paid
   Homage to his unnoticed chair.

XXII.

Though to be sure this place was Hell;
　　He was the Devil; and all they—
What though the claret circled well,
And wit, like ocean, rose and fell?—
　　Were damned eternally.

PART V.—GRACE.

I.

Among the guests who often stayed
　　Till the Devil's petits-soupers,
A man there came, fair as a maid;
And Peter noted what he said,
　　　　Standing behind his master's chair.

II.

He was a mighty poet and
　　A subtle-souled psychologist;
All things he seemed to understand
Of old or new, of sea or land—
　　　　But his own mind, which was a mist.

III.

This was a man who might have turned
　　Hell into Heaven—and so in gladness
A Heaven unto himself have earned:
But he in shadows undiscerned
　　　　Trusted, and damned himself to madness.

IV.

He spoke of poetry, and how
　　Divine it was—"a light—a love—
A spirit which like wind doth blow
As it listeth, to and fro;
　　　　A dew rained down from God above;

V.

"A power which comes and goes like dream,
　　And which none can ever trace—
Heaven's light on earth—Truth's brightest beam."
And when he ceased there lay the gleam
　　　　Of those words upon his face.

VI.

Now Peter, when he heard such talk,
　　Would, heedless of a broken pate,
Stand like a man asleep, or baulk
Some wishing guest of knife or fork,
　　　　Or drop and break his master's plate.

VII.

At night he oft would start and wake
　　Like a lover, and began

In a wild measure songs to make
On moor and glen and rocky lake,
    And on the heart of man;

VIII.

And on the universal sky—
    And the wide earth's bosom green,—
And the sweet strange mystery
Of what beyond these things may lie,
    And yet remain unseen.

IX.

For in his thought he visited
    The spots in which, ere dead and damned,
He his wayward life had led;
Yet knew not whence the thoughts were fed
    Which thus his fancy crammed.

X.

And these obscure remembrances
    Stirred such harmony in Peter
That, whensoever he should please,
He could speak of rocks and trees
    In poetic metre.

XI.

For, though it was without a sense
    Of memory, yet he remembered well
Many a ditch and quickset fence;
Of lakes he had intelligence;
    He knew something of heath and fell.

XII.

He had also dim recollections
    Of pedlars tramping on their rounds;
Milk-pans and pails; and odd collections
Of saws and proverbs; and reflections
    Old parsons make in burying-grounds.

XIII.

But Peter's verse was clear, and came
    Announcing, from the frozen hearth
Of a cold age, that none might tame
The soul of that diviner flame
    It augured to the earth:—

XIV.

Like gentle rains on the dry plains,
    Making that green which late was grey,
Or like the sudden moon that stains
Some gloomy chamber's window-panes
    With a broad light like day.

XV.

For language was in Peter's hand
    Like clay while he was yet a potter:
And he made songs for all the land
Sweet both to feel and understand,
    As pipkins late to mountain cotter.

XVI.

And Mr.—— the bookseller
　　Gave twenty pounds for some.　Then, scorning
A footman's yellow coat to wear,
Peter (too proud of heart, I fear)
　　Instantly gave the Devil warning.

XVII.

Whereat the Devil took offence,
　　And swore in his soul a great oath then,
That for his damned impertinence
He'd bring them to a proper sense
　　Of what was due to gentlemen !

PART VI.—DAMNATION.

I.

"Oh that mine enemy had written
　　A book !" cried Job :—a fearful curse,
If to the Arab, as the Briton,
'Twas galling to be critic-bitten :—
　　The Devil to Peter wished no worse.

II.

When Peter's next new book found vent,
　　The Devil to all the first Reviews
A copy of it slily sent
With five pound note as compliment,
　　And this short notice—"Pray abuse."

III.

Then *seriatim*, month and quarter,
　　Appeared such mad tirades !—One said :
"Peter seduced Mrs. Foy's daughter ;
Then drowned the mother in Ullswater,
　　The last thing as he went to bed."

IV.

Another : "Let him shave his head.
　　Where's Dr. Willis ?—Or is he joking ?
What does the rascal mean or hope,
No longer imitating Pope,
　　In that barbarian Shakspeare poking ?

V.

One more : "Is incest not enough
　　And must there be adultery too?
Grace after meat ?　Miscreant and liar ?
Thief ! blackguard ! scoundrel ! fool !　Hell fire
　　Is twenty times too good for you.

VI.

"By that last book of yours WE think
　　You've double-damned yourself to scorn ;

We warned you whilst yet on the brink
You stood.   From your black name will shrink
     The babe that is unborn."

VII.

All these Reviews the Devil made
     Up in a parcel, which he had
Safely to Peter's house conveyed.
For carriage, tenpence Peter paid—
     Untied them—read them—went half mad.

VIII.

"What!" cried he, "this is my reward
     For nights of thought, and days of toil?
Do poets, but to be abhorred
By men of whom they never heard,
     Consume their spirits' oil?

IX.

"What have I done to them?—and who
     Is Mrs. Foy? 'Tis very cruel
To speak of me and Emma so!
Adultery! God defend me! Oh!
     I've half a mind to fight a duel."

X.

"Or," cried he, a grave look collecting,
     "Is it my genius, like the moon,
Sets those who stand her face inspecting
That face within their brain reflecting,
     Like a crazed bell-chime, out of tune?"

XI.

For Peter did not know the town;
     But thought, as country readers do,
For half a guinea or a crown
He bought oblivion or renown
     From God's own voice in a review.

XII.

All Peter did on this occasion
     Was writing some sad stuff in prose.
It is a dangerous invasion
When poets criticise; their station
     Is to delight, not pose.

XIII.

The Devil then sent to Leipsic fair
     For Born's translation of Kant's book;
A world of words, tail foremost, where
Right, wrong—false, true—and foul and fair—
     As in a lottery-wheel are shook.

XIV.

Five thousand crammed octavo pages
     Of German psychologics,—he

Who his *furor verborum* assuages
Thereon deserves just seven months' wages
    More than will e'er be due to me.

XV.

I looked on them nine several days,
    And then I saw that they were bad;
A friend, too, spoke in their dispraise,—
He never read them; with amaze
    I found Sir William Drummond had.

XVI.

When the book came, the Devil sent
    It to P. Verbovale, Esquire,
With a brief note of compliment,
By that night's Carlisle mail.   It went,
    And set his soul on fire :—

XVII.

Fire which *ex luce præbens fumum*
    Made him beyond the bottom see
Of truth's clear well.   When I and you, Ma'am,
Go, as we shall do, *subter humum*,
    We may know more than he.

XVIII.

Now Peter ran to seed in soul
    Into a walking paradox
(For he was neither part nor whole,
Nor good nor bad, nor knave nor fool)
    Among the woods and rocks.

XIX.

Furious he rode where late he ran,
    Lashing and spurring his tame hobby;
Turned to a formal puritan,
A solemn and unsexual man—
    He half believed *White Obi.*

XX.

This steed in vision he would ride,
    High trotting over nine-inch bridges,
With Flibbertigibbet, imp of pride,
Mocking and mowing by his side—
A mad-brained goblin for a guide—
    Over cornfields, gates, and hedges.

XXI.

After these ghastly rides, he came
    Home to his heart, and found from thence
Much stolen of its accustomed flame;
His thoughts grew weak, drowsy, and lame
    Of their intelligence.

XXII.

To Peter's view, all seemed one hue;
　He was no whig, he was no tory;
No deist and no Christian he;
He got so subtle that to be
　　Nothing was all his glory.

XXIII.

One single point in his belief
　From his organization sprung,—
The heart-enrooted faith, the chief
Ear in his doctrines' blighted sheaf,
　　That "happiness is wrong."

XXIV.

So thought Calvin and Dominic ;
　So think their fierce successors, who
Even now would neither stint nor stick
Our flesh from off our bones to pick,
　　If they might "do their do."

XXV.

His morals thus were undermined:—
　The old Peter Bell, the hard old potter,
Was born anew within his mind;
He grew dull, harsh, sly, unrefined,
　　As when he tramped beside the Otter.

XXVI.

In the death hues of agony
　Lambently flashing from a fish,
Now Peter felt amused to see
Shades like a rainbow's rise and flee,
　　Mixed with a certain hungry wish.

XXVII.

So in his Country's dying face
　He looked—and, lovely as she lay,
Seeking in vain his last embrace,
Wailing her own abandoned case,
　　With hardened sneer he turned away:

XXVIII.

And coolly to his own Soul said:
　" Do you not think that we might make
A poem on her when she's dead ?—
Or no ! a thought is in my head !
　　Her shroud for a new sheet I'll take.

XXIX.

" My wife wants one.　Let who will bury
　This mangled corpse !　And I and you,
My dearest Soul, will then make merry,
As the Prince Regent did with Sherry,—
　　Ay, and at last desert me too."

XXX.

And so his soul would not be gay,
    But moaned within him; like a fawn
Moaning within a cave, it lay
Wounded and wasting, day by day,
    Till all its life of life was gone.

XXXI.

As troubled skies stain waters clear,
    The storm in Peter's heart and mind
Now made his verses dark and queer;
They were the ghosts of what they were,
    Shaking dim graveclothes in the wind:—

XXXII.

For he now raved enormous folly,
    Of baptisms; Sunday-schools, and graves.
'Twould make George Colman melancholy
To have heard him, like a male Molly,
    Chanting those stupid staves.

XXXIII.

Yet the Reviews, who heaped abuse
    On Peter while he wrote for freedom,
So soon as in his song they spy
The folly which soothes tyranny,
    Praise him, for those who feed 'em.

XXXIV.

He was a man too great to scan;
    A planet lost in truth's keen rays;
His virtue, awful and prodigious;
He was the most sublime, religious,
    Pure-minded poet of these days.

XXXV.

As soon as he read that, cried Peter,
    "Eureka! I have found the way
To make a better thing of metre
Than e'er was made by living creature
    Up to this blessed day."

XXXVI.

Then Peter wrote odes to the Devil;—
    In one of which he meekly said:
        "May Carnage and Slaughter,
        Thy niece and thy daughter,
        May Rapine and Famine,
        Thy gorge ever cramming,
    Glut thee with living and dead!

XXXVII.

        "May Death and Damnation
        And Consternation

Flit up from Hell with pure intent !
　　Slash them at Manchester,
　　Glasgow, Leeds, and Chester;
Drench all with blood from Avon to Trent !

XXXVIII.

　"Let thy body-guard yeomen
　　Hew down babes and women;
And laugh with bold triumph till heaven be rent !
　　When Moloch in Jewry
　　Munched children with fury,
It was thou, Devil, dining with pure intent."

PART VII.—DOUBLE DAMNATION.

I.

The Devil now knew his proper cue.
　　Soon as he read the ode, he drove
To his friend Lord Mac Murderchouse's,
A man of interest in both houses,
　　And said:—" For money or for love,

II.

" Pray find some cure or sinecure,
　　To feed him from the superfluous taxes
A friend of ours—a poet: fewer
Have fluttered tamer to the lure
　　Than he." His lordship stands and racks his

III.

Stupid brains, while one might count
　　As many beads as he had boroughs,—
At length replies (from his mean front,
Like one who rubs out an account,
　　Smoothing away the unmeaning furrows):

IV.

" It happens, fortunately, dear sir,
　　I can. I hope I need require
No pledge from you that he will stir
In our affairs; like Oliver,
　　That he'll be worthy of his hire."

V.

These words exchanged, the news sent off
　　To Peter, home the Devil hied,—
Took to his bed. He had no cough,
No doctor,—meat and drink enough,
　　Yet that same night he died.

VI.

The Devil's corpse was leaded down;
　　His decent heirs enjoyed his pelf,
Mourning-coaches many a one
Followed his hearse along the town:—
　　Where was the Devil himself?

VII.

When Peter heard of his promotion,
  His eyes grew like two stars for bliss.
There was a bow of sleek devotion
Engendering in his back; each motion
  Seemed a Lord's shoe to kiss.

VIII.

He hired a house, bought plate, and made
  A genteel drive up to his door,
With sifted gravel neatly laid,—
As if defying all who said
  Peter was ever poor.

IX.

But a disease soon struck into
  The very life and soul of Peter.
He walked about—slept—had the hue
Of health upon his cheeks—and few
  Dug better—none a heartier eater:—

X.

And yet a strange and horrid curse
  Clung upon Peter, night and day.
Month after month the thing grew worse,
And deadlier than in this my verse
  I can find strength to say.

XI.

Peter was dull—(he was at first
  Dull)—oh so dull, so very dull!
Whether he talked, wrote, or rehearsed,
Still with his dulness was he cursed—
  Dull, beyond all conception dull.

XII.

No one could read his books—no mortal,
  But a few natural friends, would hear him;
The parson came not near his portal;
His state was like that of the immortal
  Described by Swift—no man could bear him.

XIII.

His sister, wife, and children yawned,
  With a long, slow, and drear ennui
All human patience far beyond;
Their hopes of heaven each would have pawned
  Anywhere else to be.

XIV.

But in his verse and in his prose
  The essence of his dulness was
Concentred and compressed so close
'Twould have made Guatimozin doze
  On his red gridiron of brass,

XV.

A printer's boy, folding those pages,
  Fell slumbrously upon one side,
Like those famed Seven who slept three ages.
To wakeful frenzy's vigil rages,
    As opiates, were the same applied.

XVI.

Even the Reviewers who were hired
  To do the work of his reviewing,
With adamantine nerves, grew tired;—
Gaping and torpid they retired,
    To dream of what they should be doing.

XVII.

And worse and worse the drowsy curse
  Yawned in him till it grew a pest;
A wide contagious atmosphere
Creeping like cold through all things near;
    A power to infect and to infest.

XVIII.

His servant-maids and dogs grew dull;
  His kitten, late a sportive elf;
The woods and lakes so beautiful
Of dim stupidity were full;
    All grew dull as Peter's self.

XIX.

The earth under his feet, the springs
  Which lived within it a quick life—
The air, the winds of many wings
That fan it with new murmurings—
    Were dead to their harmonious strife.

XX.

The birds and beasts within the wood,
  The insects and each creeping thing,
Were now a silent multitude;
Love's work was left unwrought—no brood
    Near Peter's house took wing.

XXI.

And every neighbouring cottager
  Stupidly yawned upon the other;
No jackass brayed, no little cur
Cocked up his ears; no man would stir
    To save a dying mother.

XXII.

Yet from all that charmed district went
  But some half-idiot and half-knave,
Who, rather than pay any rent,
Would live with marvellous content
    Over his father's grave.

XXIII.

No bailiff dared within that space,
  For fear of the dull charm, to enter;
A man would bear upon his face,
For fifteen months, in any case,
  The yawn of such a venture.

XXIV.

Seven miles above—below—around—
  This pest of dulness holds its sway,
A ghastly life without a sound.
To Peter's soul the spell is bound—
  How should it ever pass away?

1820.

ŒDIPUS TYRANNUS;

OR,

SWELLFOOT THE TYRANT.

A TRAGEDY, IN TWO ACTS. TRANSLATED FROM THE ORIGINAL DORIC.

> " Choose Reform or civil war,
> When through thy streets, instead of hare with dogs,
> A CONSORT-QUEEN shall hunt a KING with hogs,
> Riding on the IONIAN MINOTAUR."

ADVERTISEMENT.

THIS Tragedy is one of a triad, or system of three Plays (an arrangement according to which the Greeks were accustomed to connect their Dramatic representations), elucidating the wonderful and appalling fortunes of the SWELLFOOT dynasty. It was evidently written by some *learned Theban ;* and, from its characteristic dulness, apparently before the duties on the importation of *Attic salt* had been repealed by the Bœotarchs. The tenderness with which he treats the Pigs proves him to have been a *sus Bœotiæ ;* possibly *Epicuri de grege porcus ;* for, as the poet observes,

> " A fellow feeling makes us wondrous kind."

No liberty has been taken with the translation of this remarkable piece of antiquity, except the suppressing a seditious and blasphemous Chorus of the Pigs and Bulls at the last act. The word Hoydipouse (or more properly Œdipus), has been rendered literally SWELLFOOT, without its having been conceived necessary to determine whether a swelling of the hind or the fore feet of the Swinish Monarch is particularly indicated.

Should the remaining portions of this Tragedy be found, entitled "Swellfoot in Angaria" and "Charité," the Translator might be tempted to give them to the reading Public.

DRAMATIS PERSONÆ.

TYRANT SWELLFOOT, *King of Thebes.*	THE GADFLY.
	THE LEECH.
IONA TAURINA, *his Queen.*	THE RAT.
MAMMON, *Arch-Priest of Famine.*	THE MINOTAUR.
PURGANAX ⎫ *Wizards, Ministers of*	MOSES, *the Sow-gelder.*
DAKRY ⎬ SWELLFOOT.	SOLOMON, *the Porkman.*
LAOCTONOS ⎭	ZEPHANIAH, *Pig-butcher.*

CHORUS *of the Swinish Multitude.*
Guards, Attendants, Priests, &c. &c.
SCENE—*Thebes.*

ACT I.

SCENE I.—*A magnificent Temple, built of thigh-bones and death's-heads, and tiled with scalps. Over the Altar the statue of Famine, veiled; a number of boars, sows, and sucking-pigs, crowned with thistle, shamrock, and oak, sitting on the steps, and clinging round the altar of the Temple. Enter* SWELLFOOT *in his royal robes, without perceiving the pigs.*

> *Swellfoot.* Thou supreme Goddess! by whose power divine
> These graceful limbs are clothed in proud array
>   [*He contemplates himself with satisfaction.*
> Of gold and purple, and this kingly paunch
> Swells like a sail before a favouring breeze,
> And these most sacred nether promontories
> Lie satisfied with layers of fat; and these
> Bœotian cheeks, like Egypt's pyramid
> (Nor with less toil were their foundations laid),
> Sustain the cone of my untroubled brain,
> That point, the emblem of a pointless nothing!
> Thou to whom Kings and laurelled Emperors,
> Radical butchers, Paper-money-millers,
> Bishops and deacons, and the entire army
> Of those fat martyrs to the persecution
> Of stifling turtle-soup, and brandy-devils,
> Offer their secret vows! Thou plenteous Ceres
> Of their Eleusis, hail!
>
>   *The Swine.* Eigh! eigh! eigh! eigh!
>   *Swellf.* Ha! what are ye,
> Who, crowned with leaves devoted to the Furies
> Cling round this sacred shrine?
>   *Swine.* Aigh! aigh! aigh!
>   *Swellf.* What! ye that are
> The very beasts that offered at her altar
> With blood and groans, salt-cake, and fat, and inwards
> Ever propitiate her reluctant will
> When taxes are withheld?
>   *Swine.* Ugh! ugh! ugh!
>   *Swellf.*   What! ye who grub
> With filthy snouts my red potatoes up
> In Allan's rushy bog? who eat the oats
> Up, from my cavalry in the Hebrides?
> Who swill the hog-wash soup my cooks digest
> From bones, and rags, and scraps of shoe-leather,
> Which should be given to cleaner Pigs than you?

The Swine.—Semichorus I.

The same, alas! the same;
Though only now the name
Of pig remains to me.

Semichorus II.

If 'twere your kingly will
Us wretched swine to kill,
What should we yield to thee?

Swellf. Why, skin and bones, and some few hairs for mortar.

Chorus of Swine.

I have heard your Laureate sing
That pity was a royal thing;
Under your mighty ancestors, we pigs
Were blessed as nightingales on myrtle sprigs,
Or grasshoppers that live on noonday dew,
And sung, old annals tell, as sweetly too,
But now our styes are fallen in, we catch
The murrain and the mange, the scab and itch;
Sometimes your royal dogs tear down our thatch,
And then we seek the shelter of a ditch;
Hog-wash or grains, or ruta baga, none
Has yet been ours since your reign begun.

First Sow.

My pigs, 'tis in vain to tug.

Second Sow.

I could almost eat my litter.

First Pig.

I suck, but no milk will come from the dug.

Second Pig.

Our skin and our bones would be bitter.

The Boars.

We fight for this rag of greasy rug,
Though a trough of wash would be fitter.

Semichorus.

Happier swine were they than we,
Drowned in the Gadarean sea,—
I wish that pity would drive out the devils,
Which in your royal bosom hold their revels.
And sink us in the waves of thy compassion!
Alas! the Pigs are an unhappy nation!
Now if your Majesty would have our bristles
To bind your mortar with, or fill our colons
With rich blood, or make brawn out of our gristles,
In policy—ask else your royal Solons—

You ought to give us hog-wash and clean straw,
And styes well thatched ; besides it is the law !
   Swellf. This is sedition and rank blasphemy !
Ho ! there, my guards !

Enter a GUARD.

   Guard.   Your sacred Majesty.
   Swellf. Call in the Jews, Solomon the court porkman,
Moses the sow-gelder, and Zephaniah the hog-butcher.
   Guard. They are in waiting, Sire.

Enter SOLOMON, MOSES, *and* ZEPHANIAH.

   Swellf. Out with your knife, old Moses, and spay those sows
                         [*The Pigs run about in consternation.*
That load the earth with pigs ; cut close and deep,
Moral restraint, I see, has no effect,
Nor prostitution, nor our own example,
Starvation, typhus fever, war, nor prison—
This was the art which the arch-priest of Famine
Hinted at in his charge to the Theban clergy—
Cut close and deep, good Moses.
   Moses.   Let your Majesty.
Keep the boars quiet, else——
   Swellf.   Zephaniah, cut
That fat hog's throat ; the brute seems overfed ;
Seditious hunks ! to whine for want of grains.
   Zeph. Your sacred Majesty, he has the dropsy ;
We shall find pints of hydatids in's liver.
He has not half an inch of wholesome fat
Upon his carious ribs—
   Swellf.   'Tis all the same ;
He'll serve instead of riot-money, when
Our murmuring troops bivouac in Thebes' streets ;
And January winds, after a day
Of butchering, will make them relish carrion.
Now, Solomon, I'll sell you in a lump
The whole kit of them.
   Sol.   Why, your Majesty,
I could not give——
   Swellf.   Kill them out of the way ;
That shall be price enough, and let me hear
Their everlasting grunts and whines no more !
                   [*Exeunt, driving in the Swine.*

Enter MAMMON, *the Arch-Priest ; and* PURGANAX, *Chief of the Council of Wizards.*

   Pur. The future looks as black as death, a cloud,
Dark as the frown of Hell, hangs over it.
The troops grow mutinous—the revenue fails—
There's something rotten in us—for the level
Of the State slopes, its very bases topple,
The boldest turn their backs upon themselves !
   Mam. Why, what's the matter, my dear fellow, now ?
Do the troops mutiny ?—decimate some regiments ;
Does money fail?—come to my mint—coin paper,
Till gold be at a discount, and, ashamed

To show his bilious face, go purge himself,
In emulation of her vestal whiteness.
 Pur. Oh, would that this were all ! The oracle !
 Mam. Why, it was I who spoke that oracle,
And whether I was dead-drunk or inspired,
I cannot well remember ; nor, in truth,
The oracle itself !
 Pur.   The words went thus :—
" Bœotia, choose reform or civil war !
When through the streets, instead of hare with dogs,
A Consort Queen shall hunt a King with hogs,
Riding on the Ionian Minotaur."
 Mam. Now, if the oracle had ne'er foretold
This sad alternative, it must arrive,
Or not, and so it must now that it has,
And whether I was urged by grace divine
Or Lesbian liquor to declare these words,
Which must, as all words must, be false or true ;
It matters not : for the same power made all,
Oracle, wine, and me, and you—or none—
'Tis the same thing. If you knew as much
Of oracles as I do——
 Pur.   You arch-priests
Believe in nothing ; if you were to dream
Of a particular number in the lottery,
You would not buy the ticket ?
 Mam.   Yet our tickets
Are seldom blanks. But what steps have you taken ?
For prophecies when once they get abroad,
Like liars who tell the truth to serve their ends,
Or hypocrites who, from assuming virtue,
Do the same actions that the virtuous do,
Contrive their own fulfilment. This Iona—
Well—you know what the chaste Pasiphae did,
Wife to that most religious King of Crete,
And still how popular the tale is here;
And these dull swine of Thebes boast their descent
From the free Minotaur. You know they still
Call themselves Bulls, though thus degenerate,
And everything relating to a bull
Is popular and respectable in Thebes.
Their arms are seven bulls in a field gules,
They think their strength consists in eating beef,—
Now there were danger in the precedent,
If Queen Iona——
 Purg.   I have taken good care
That shall not be. I struck the crust o' the earth
With this enchanted rod, and Hell lay bare !
And from a cavern full of ugly shapes,
I chose a LEECH, a GADFLY, and a RAT.
The gadfly was the same which Juno sent
To agitate Io,* and which Ezechiel† mentions
That the Lord whistled for out of the mountains
Of utmost Ethiopia, to torment

---

* The *Prometheus Bound* of Æschylus.
† " And the Lord whistled for the gadfly out of Æthiopia, and for the bee of E ypt.
&c.—*Ezechiel.*

Mesopotamian Babylon.   The beast
Has a loud trumpet like the Scarabee,
His crooked tail is barbed with many stings,
Each able to make a thousand wounds, and each
Immedicable; from his convex eyes
He sees fair things in many hideous shapes,
And trumpets all his falsehood to the world.
Like other beetles, he is fed on dung—
He has eleven feet with which he crawls,
Trailing a blistering slime, and this foul beast
Has tracked Iona from the Theban limits,
From isle to isle, from city unto city,
Urging her flight from the far Chersonese
To fabulous Solyma, and the Ætnean Isle,
Ortygia, Melite, and Calypso's Rock,
And the swart tribes of Garamant and Fez,
Æolia and Elysium, and thy shores,
Parthenope, which now, alas! are free!
And through the fortunate Saturnian land,
Into the darkness of the West.
　　Mam.   But if
This Gadfly should drive Iona hither?
　　Purg. Gods! what an *if!* but there is my grey RAT;
So thin with want, he can crawl in and out
Of any narrow chink and filthy hole,
And he shall creep into her dressing-room,
And—
　　Mam. My dear friend, where are your wits! as if
She does not always toast a piece of cheese,
And bait the trap? and rats, when lean enough
To crawl through *such* chinks——
　　Purg.   But my LEECH—a leech
Fit to suck blood, with lubricous round rings,
Capaciously expatiative, which make
His little body like a red balloon,
As full of blood as that of hydrogene,
Sucked from men's hearts; insatiably he sucks
And clings, and pulls—a horse-leech, whose deep maw
The plethoric King Swellfoot could not fill,
And who, till full, will cling for ever.
　　Mam.   This
For Queen Iona might suffice, and less;
But 'tis the swinish multitude I fear,
And in that fear I have——
　　Purg.   Done what?
　　Mam.   Disinherited
My eldest son Chrysaor, because he
Attended public meetings, and would always
Stand prating there of commerce, public faith,
Economy, and unadulterate coin,
And other topics, ultra-radical;
And have entailed my estate, called the Fool's Paradise,
And funds in fairy-money, bonds, and bills,
Upon my accomplished daughter Banknotina,
And married her to the gallows.*

---

* "If one should marry a gallows, and beget young gibbets, I never saw one s
prone."--*Cymbeline.*

Purg.   A good match!
Mam. A high connexion, Purganax. The bridegroom
Is of a very ancient family,
Of Hounslow Heath, Tyburn, and the New Drop,
And has great influence in both Houses;—Oh!
He makes the fondest husband; nay, *too* fond,—
New-married people should not kiss in public;
But the poor souls love one another so!
And then my little grandchildren, the gibbets,
Promising children as you ever saw,—
The young playing at hanging, the elder learning
How to hold radicals. They are well taught too,
For every gibbet says its catechism
And reads a select chapter in the Bible
Before it goes to play. [*A most tremendous humming is heard.*
Purg.   Ha! what do I hear?

Enter the GADFLY.

Mam. Your Gadfly, as it seems, is tired of gadding.

Gadfly. Hum! hum! hum!
From the lakes of the Alps, and the cold grey scalps
  Of the mountains, I come,
  Hum! hum! hum!
From Morocco and Fez, and the high palaces
  Of golden Byzantium;
From the temples divine of old Palestine,
  From Athens and Rome,
  With a ha! and a hum!
  I come! I come!

  All inn-doors and windows
   Were open to me:
  I saw all that sin does,
   Which lamps hardly see
That burn in the night by the curtained bed,—
The impudent lamps! for they blushed not red,
  Dinging and singing,
  From slumber I rung her,
Loud as the clank of an ironmonger;
  Hum! hum! hum!

  Far, far, far!
With the trump of my lips, and the sting at my hips,
  I drove her—afar!
  Far, far, far!
From city to city, abandoned of pity,
  A ship without needle or star;—
Homeless she passed, like a cloud on the blast,
  Seeking peace, finding war;
  She is here in her car,
  From afar and afar;
  Hum! hum!
I have stung her and wrung her,
  The venom is working;
And if you had hung her
  With canting and quirking,

E E

She could not be deader than she will be soon;
I have driven her close to you, under the moon,
    Night and day, hum! hum! ha!
   I have hummed her and drummed her
From place to place, till at last I have dumbed her,
    Hum! hum! hum!

Leech.   I will suck
       Blood or muck!
The disease of the state is a plethory,
Who so to fit to reduce it as I?
Rat.   I'll slyly seize and
    Let blood from her weasand,—
Creeping through crevice, and chink, and cranny,
With my snakey tail, and my sides so scranny.
Purg. Aroint ye! thou unprofitable worm!   [*To the* LEECH.
And thou, dull beetle, get thee back to hell!   [*To the* GADFLY.
To sting the ghosts of Babylonian kings,
And the ox-headed Io—
Swine [*within*]. Ugh, ugh, ugh!
    Hail! Iona the divine,
    We will be no longer swine,
    But bulls with horns and dewlaps.
    Rat.   For,
    You know, my lord, the Minotaur——
Purg. [*fiercely*]. Be silent! get to hell! or I will call
The cat out of the kitchen.
           Well, Lord Mammon,
This is a pretty business.   [*Exit the* RAT.
    Mam.   I will go
And spell some scheme to make it ugly then.   [*Exit.*

Enter SWELLFOOT.

Swellfoot. She is returned! Taurina is in Thebes
When Swellfoot wishes that she were in hell!
Oh Hymen, clothed in yellow jealousy,
And waving o'er the couch of wedded kings
The torch of discord with its fiery hair;
This is thy work, thou patron saint of queens!
Swellfoot is wived! though parted by the sea,
The very name of wife had conjugal rights;
Her cursed image ate, drank, slept with me,
And in the arms of Adiposa oft
Her memory has received a husband's——
    [*A loud tumult, and cries of* "Iona for ever!—No Swellfoot!"
    Swellf.   Hark!
How the swine cry Iona Taurina;
I suffer the real presence; Purganax,
Off with her head!
    Purg.   But I must first impanel
A jury of the pigs.
    Swellf.   Pack them then.
Purg. Or fattening some few in two separate styes,
And giving them clean straw, tying some bits
Of ribbon round their legs—giving their sows
Some tawdry lace, and bits of lustre glass,
And their young boars white and red rags, and tails

Of cows, and jay feathers, and sticking cauliflowers
Between the ears of the old ones; and, when
They are persuaded, that by the inherent virtue
Of these things, they are all imperial pigs,
Good Lord! they'd rip each other's bellies up,
Not to say help us in destroying *her.*

   Swellf. This plan might be tried too;—where's General
Laoctonos?

            Enter LAOCTONOS *and* DAKRY.

                It is my royal pleasure
That you, Lord General, bring the head and body,
If separate, it would please me better, hither
Of Queen Iona.

   Laoc. That pleasure I well knew,
And made a charge with those battalions bold,
Called, from their dress and grin, the royal apes,
Upon the swine, who in a hollow square
Enclosed her, and received the first attack
Like so many rhinoceroses, and then
Retreating in good order, with bare tusks
And wrinkled snouts presented to the foe,
Bore her in triumph to the public stye.
What is still worse, some sows upon the ground
Have given the ape-guards apples, nuts, and gin,
And they all whisk their tails aloft, and cry,
"Long live Iona! down with Swellfoot!"

   Purg.   Hark!

   The Swine [*without*]. Long live Iona! down with Swellfoot!

   Dakry.   I
Went to the garret of the swineherd's tower
Which overlooks the stye, and made a long
Harangue (all words) to the assembled swine,
Of delicacy, mercy, judgment, law,
Morals, and precedents, and purity,
Adultery, destitution, and divorce,
Piety, faith, and state necessity,
And how I loved the Queen!—and then I wept
With the pathos of my own eloquence,
And every tear turned to a millstone, which
Brained many a gaping pig, and there was made
A slough of blood and brains upon the place,
Greased with the pounded bacon; round and round
The millstones rolled, ploughing the pavement up,
And hurling sucking pigs into the air,
With dust and stones.

              Enter MAMMON.

   Mam.   I wonder that grey wizards
Like you should be so beardless in their schemes;
It had been but a point of policy
To keep Iona and the swine apart.
Divide and rule! but ye have made a junction
Between two parties who will govern you
But for my art.—Behold this BAG! it is
The poison BAG of that Green Spider huge,

On which our spies skulked in ovation through
The streets of Thebes, when they were paved with dead:
A bane so much the deadlier fills it now,
As calumny is worse than death,—for here
The Gadfly's venom, fifty times distilled,
Is mingled with the vomit of the Leech,
In due proportion, and black ratsbane, which
That very Rat, who, like the Pontic tyrant,
Nurtures himself on poison, dare not touch;
All is sealed up with the broad seal of Fraud,
Who is the Devil's Lord High Chancellor,
And over it the Primate of all Hell
Murmured this pious baptism:—" Be thou called
The GREEN BAG; and this power and grace be thine:
That thy contents, on whomsoever poured,
Turn innocence to guilt, and gentlest looks
To savage, foul, and fierce deformity.
Let all baptized by thy infernal dew
Be called adulterer, drunkard, liar, wretch !
No name left out which orthodoxy loves,
Court Journal or legitimate Review !—
Be they called tyrant, beast, fool, glutton, lover
Of other wives and husbands than their own—
The heaviest sin on this side of the Alps !
Wither they to a ghastly caricature
Of what was human ! let not man or beast
Behold their face with unaverted eyes !
Or hear their names with ears that tingle not
With blood of indignation, rage, and shame !"
This is a perilous liquor;—good my Lords,

     [SWELLFOOT *approaches to touch the* GREEN BAG.

Beware ! for God's sake, beware !—if you should break
The seal, and touch the fatal liquor——

    Purg.   There !
Give it to me: I have been used to handle
All sorts of poisons. His dread Majesty
Only desires to see the colour of it.

    Mam. Now, with a little common sense, my Lords,
Only undoing all that has been done
(Yet so as it may seem we but confirm it),
Our victory is assured. We must entice
Her Majesty from the stye, and make the pigs
Believe that the contents of the GREEN BAG
Are the true test of guilt or innocence.
And that, if she be guilty, 'twill transform her
To manifest deformity like guilt.
If innocent, she will become transfigured
Into an angel, such as they say she is;
And they will see her flying through the air,
So bright that she will dim the noonday sun;
Showering down blessings in the shape of comfits.
This, trust a priest, is just the sort of thing
Swine will believe. I'll wager you will see them
Climbing upon the thatch of their low styes,
With pieces of smoked glass, to watch her sail
Among the clouds, and some will hold the flaps
Of one another's ears between their teeth,
To catch the coming hail of comfits in.

You, Purganax, who have the gift of the gab,
Make them a solemn speech to this effect:
I go to put in readiness the feast
Kept to the honour of our goddess Famine,
Where, for more glory, let the ceremony
Take place of the uglification of the Queen.

Dakry [*To* SWELLFOOT]. I, as the keeper of your sacred conscience,
Humbly remind your Majesty that the care
Of your high office, as man-milliner
To red Bellona, should not be deferred.

Purg. All part, in happier plight to meet again.   [*Exeunt.*

ACT II.

SCENE I.—*The Public Stye.   The* BOARS *in full Assembly.*

Enter PURGANAX.

Purg. Grant me your patience, Gentlemen and Boars,
Ye, by whose patience under public burdens
The glorious constitution of these styes
Subsists, and shall subsist.   The lean-pig rates
Grow with the growing populace of swine,
The taxes, that true source of piggishness,
(How can I find a more appropriate term
To include religion, morals, peace, and plenty,
And all that fit Bœotia as a nation
To teach the other nations how to live?)
Increase with piggishness itself; and still
Does the revenue, that great spring of all
The patronage, and pensions, and by-payments,
Which free-born pigs regard with jealous eyes,
Diminish, till at length, by glorious steps,
All the land's produce will be merged in taxes,
And the revenue will amount to—nothing!
The failure of a foreign market for
Sausages, bristles, and blood puddings,
And such home manufactures, is but partial;
And, that the population of the pigs,
Instead of hog-wash, has been fed on straw
And water, is a fact which is—you know—
That is—it is a state-necessity—
Temporary, of course.   Those impious pigs,
Who, by frequent squeaks, have dared to impugn
The settled Swellfoot system, or to make
Irreverent mockery of the genuflexions
Inculcated by the arch-priest, have been whipt
Into a loyal and an orthodox whine.
Things being in this happy state, the Queen
Iona—

A loud cry from the Pigs. She is innocent! most innocent!

Purg. That is the very thing that I was saying,
Gentlemen Swine; the Queen Iona being
Most innocent, no doubt, returns to Thebes,
And the lean sows and boars collect about her,
Wishing to make her think that WE believe
(I mean those more substantial pigs who swill

Rich hog-wash, while the others mouth damp straw),
That she is guilty; thus, the lean-pig faction
Seeks to obtain that hog-wash, which has been
Your immemorial right, and which I will
Maintain you in to the last drop of—

   A Boar [_interrupting him_].   What
Does any one accuse her of?

   Purg.   Why, no one
Makes _any_ positive accusation;—but
There were hints dropt, and so the privy wizards
Conceived that it became them to advise
His Majesty to investigate their truth;
Not for his own sake; he could be content
To let his wife play any pranks she pleased,
If by that sufferance, _he_ could please the pigs;
But then he fears the morals of the swine,
The sows especially, and what effect
It might produce upon the purity and
Religion of the rising generation
Of sucking pigs, if it could be suspected
That Queen Iona—   [_A pause._

   First Boar.   Well, go on; we long
To hear what she can possibly have done.

   Purg. Why, it is hinted, that a certain bull—
Thus much is _known;_—the milk-white bulls that feed
Beside Clitumnus and the crystal lakes
Of the Cisalpine mountains, in fresh dews
Of lotos-grass and blossoming asphodel,
Sleeking their silken hair, and with sweet breath
Loading the morning winds until they faint
With living fragrance, are so beautiful !—
Well, _I_ say nothing;—but Europa rode
On such a one from Asia into Crete,
And the enamoured sea grew calm beneath
His gliding beauty. And Pasiphae,
Iona's grandmother,—but _she_ is innocent !
And that both you and I, and all assert.

   First Boar. Most innocent !

   Purg.   Behold this BAG; a bag—

   Second Boar. Oh ! no Green BAGS ! ! Jealousy's eyes are green,
Scorpions are green, and water-snakes, and efts,
And verdigris, and—

   Purg.   Honourable swine,
In piggish souls can prepossessions reign ?
Allow me to remind you, grass is green—
All flesh is grass;—no bacon but is flesh—
Ye are but bacon. This divining BAG
(Which is not green, but only bacon colour)
Is filled with liquor, which if sprinkled o'er
A woman guilty of—we all know what—
Makes her so hideous, till she finds one blind
She never can commit the like again.
If innocent, she will turn into an angel,
And rain down blessings in the shape of comfits
As she flies up to heaven. Now, my proposal
Is to convert her sacred Majesty
Into an angel (as I am sure we shall do),
By pouring on her head this mystic water.   [_Showing the bag._

I know that she is innocent; I wish
Only to prove her so to all the world.

   First Boar. Excellent, just, and noble Purganax!

   Second Boar. How glorious it will be to see her Majesty
Flying above our heads, her petticoats
Streaming like—like—like—

   Third Boar.   Anything.

   Purg.   Oh, no!
But like a standard of an admiral's ship,
Or like the banner of a conquering host,
Or like a cloud dyed in the dying day,
Unravelled on the blast from a white mountain;
Or like a meteor, or a war steed's mane,
Or waterfall from a dizzy precipice
Scattered upon the wind.

   First Boar.   Or a cow's tail,—

   Second Boar. Or *anything,* as the learned Boar observed.

   Purg. Gentlemen Boars, I move a resolution,
That her most sacred Majesty should be
Invited to attend the feast of Famine,
And to receive upon her chaste white body
Dews of Apotheosis from this BAG.

   [*A great confusion is heard of the* PIGS OUT OF DOORS, *which
     communicates itself to those within. During the first
     Strophe, the doors of the Stye are staved in, and a number
     of exceedingly lean Pigs and Sows and Boars rush in.*

SEMICHORUS I.

No! Yes!

SEMICHORUS II.

Yes! No!

SEMICHORUS I.

A law!

SEMICHORUS II.

A flaw!

SEMICHORUS I.

Porkers, we shall lose our wash,
    Or must share it with the lean pigs!

   First Boar. Order! order! be not rash!
Was there ever such a scene, Pigs!

   An Old Sow [*rushing in*]. I never saw so fine a dash
Since I first began to wean pigs.

   Second Boar [*solemnly*]. The Queen will be an angel time enough.
I vote, in form of an amendment, that
Purganax rub a little of that stuff
Upon his face—

   Purg. [*His heart is seen to beat through his waistcoat*]. Gods!
    What would ye be at?

SEMICHORUS I.

Purganax has plainly shown a
    Cloven foot and jackdaw feather.

SEMICHORUS II.

I vote Swellfoot and Iona
Try the magic test together;
Whenever royal spouses bicker,
Both should try the magic liquor.

An Old Boar [aside]. A miserable state is that of pigs,
For if their drivers would tear caps and wigs,
    The swine must bite each other's ear therefore.
An Old Sow [aside]. A wretched lot Jove has assigned to swine;
Squabbling makes pig-herds hungry, and they dine
    On bacon, and whip sucking-pigs the more.

CHORUS.

Hog-wash has been ta'en away:
    If the Bull-Queen is divested,
We shall be in every way
    Hunted, stript, exposed, molested;
Let us do whate'er we may
    That she shall not be arrested.
QUEEN, we entrench you with walls of brawn,
    And palisades of tusks, sharp as a bayonet;
Place your most sacred person here.   We pawn
    Our lives that none a finger dare to lay on it.
        Those who wrong you, wrong us;
            Those who hate you, hate us;
        Those who sting you, sting us;
            Those who bait you, bait us:
The *oracle* is now about to be
Fulfilled by circumvolving destiny;
Which says: "Thebes, choose *reform* or *civil war*,
    When through your streets instead of hare with dogs,
    A CONSORT QUEEN shall hunt a KING with Hogs,
Riding upon the IONIAN MINOTAUR."

Enter IONA TAURINA.

Iona Taurina [coming forward]. Gentlemen swine, and gentle
    lady-pigs,
The tender heart of every boar acquits
Their QUEEN of any act incongruous
With native piggishness, and she reposing
With confidence upon the grunting nation,
Has thrown herself, her cause, her life, her all,
Her innocence, into their hoggish arms;
Nor has the expectation been deceived
Of finding shelter there.   Yet know, great boars
(For such who ever lives among you finds you,
And so do I), the innocent are proud !
I have accepted your protection only
In compliment of your kind love and care,
Not for necessity.   The innocent
Are safest there where trials and dangers wait;
Innocent Queens o'er white-hot ploughshares tread,
Unsinged, and ladies, Erin's laureate sings it,*

---

* " Rich and rare were the gems she wore."—See MOORE's *Irish Melodies.*

Decked with rare gems, and beauty rarer still,
Walked from Killarney to the Giant's Causeway,
Through rebels, smugglers, troops of yeomanry,
White boys and orange boys and constables,
Tithe-proctors, and excise people, uninjured !
Thus I—
Lord PURGANAX, I do commit myself
Into your custody, and am prepared
To stand the test, whatever it may be !

   Purg. This magnanimity in your sacred Majesty
Must please the pigs.   You cannot fail of being
A heavenly angel.   Smoke your bits of glass,
Ye loyal swine, or her transfiguration
Will blind your wondering eyes.

   An Old Boar [*aside*].   Take care, my Lord,
They do not smoke you first.

   Purg.   At the approaching feast
Of Famine, let the expiation be.

   Swine. Content ! content !

   Iona Taurina [*aside*].   I, most content of all,
Know that my foes even thus prepare their fall !   [*Exeunt omnes.*

SCENE II.—*The interior of the Temple of* FAMINE.   *The statue of the Goddess, a skeleton clothed in party-coloured rags, seated upon a heap of skulls and loaves intermingled.   A number of exceedingly fat Priests in black garments arrayed on each side, with marrow-bones and cleavers in their hands.   A flourish of trumpets.   Enter* MAMMON *as Arch-priest,* SWELLFOOT, DAKRY, PURGANAX, LAOCTONOS, *followed by* IONA TAURINA *guarded.   On the other side enter the Swine.*

CHORUS OF PRIESTS,

Accompanied by the Court Porkman on marrow-bones and cleavers.

Goddess bare, and gaunt, and pale,
Empress of the world, all hail !
What though Cretans old called thee
City-crested Cybele ?
      We call thee FAMINE !
Goddess of fasts and feasts, starving and cramming ;
Through thee, for emperors, kings, and priests, and lords,
Who rule by viziers, sceptres, bank-notes, words,
   The earth pours forth its plenteous fruits,
   Corn, wool, linen, flesh, and roots—
Those who consume these fruits through thee grow fat,
   Those who produce these fruits through thee grow lean,
Whatever change takes place, oh, stick to that !
   And let things be as they have ever been ;
     At least while we remain thy priests,
     And proclaim thy fasts and feasts !
Through thee the sacred SWELLFOOT dynasty
Is based upon a rock amid that sea
Whose waves are swine—so let it ever be !

   [SWELLFOOT, &c., *seat themselves at a table, magnificently covered at the upper end of the Temple.   Attendants pass over the stage with hog-wash in pails.   A number of pigs, exceedingly lean, follow them licking up the wash.*

Mam. I fear your sacred Majesty has lost
The appetite which you were used to have.
Allow me now to recommend this dish—
A simple kickshaw by your Persian cook,
Such as is served at the great King's second table.
The price and pains which its ingredients cost,
Might have maintained some dozen families
A winter or two—not more—so plain a dish
Could scarcely disagree.—

 Swellfoot.   After the trial,
And these fastidious pigs are gone, perhaps
I may recover my lost appetite.
I feel the gout flying about my stomach—
Give me a glass of Maraschino punch.

 Purg. [*filling his glass and standing up*]. The glorious con-
    stitution of the Pigs !

 All. A toast ! a toast ! stand up and three times three !

 Dakry. No heel-taps—darken daylights !

 Laoc.   Claret, somehow,
Puts me in mind of blood, and blood of claret !

 Swellf. Laoctonos is fishing for a compliment,
But 'tis his due. Yes, you have drunk more wine,
And shed more blood than any man in Thebes.
[*To* PURGANAX]. For God's sake stop the grunting of those pigs!

 Purg. We dare not, Sire, 'tis Famine's privilege.

CHORUS OF SWINE.

Hail to thee, hail to thee, Famine !
 Thy throne is on blood, and thy robe is of rags ;
  Thou devil which livest on damning ;
Saint of new churches, and cant, and GREEN BAGS,
  Till in pity and terror thou risest,
 Confounding the schemes of the wisest,
 When thou liftest thy skeleton form,
  When the loaves and the skulls roll about,
We will greet thee—the voice of a storm
  Would be lost in our terrible shout !

Then hail to thee, hail to thee, Famine !
Hail to thee, Empress of Earth !
  When thou risest, dividing possessions ;
  When thou risest, uprooting oppressions ;
In the pride of thy ghastly mirth,
Over palaces, temples, and graves,
We will rush as thy minister-slaves,
 Trampling behind in thy train,
 Till all be made level again !

 Mam. I hear a crackling of the giant bones
Of the dread image, and in the black pits
Which once were eyes I see two livid flames.
These prodigies are oracular, and show
The presence of the unseen Deity.
Mighty events are hastening to their doom !

 Swellf. I only hear the lean and mutinous swine
Grunting about the temple.

 Dakry.   In a crisis
Of such exceeding delicacy, I think

We ought to put her Majesty the QUEEN
Upon her trial without delay.
 Mam.   The BAG
Is here.
 Purg. I have rehearsed the entire scene,
With an ox-bladder and some ditch-water,
On Lady P.—it cannot fail.   [*Taking up the bag.*
   [*To* SWELLFOOT]. Your Majesty
In such a filthy business had better
Stand on one side, lest it should sprinkle you,
A spot or two on me would do no harm,
Nay, it might hide the blood, which the sad genius
Of the Green Isle has fixed, as by a spell,
Upon my brow—which would stain all its seas,
But which those seas could never wash away!
 Iona Taurina. My lord, I am ready—nay, I am impatient—
To undergo the test.

> [*A graceful figure in a semi-transparent veil passes unnoticed
> through the Temple; the word* LIBERTY *is seen through the
> veil, as if it were written in fire upon its forehead. Its
> words are almost drowned in the furious grunting of the
> Pigs, and the business of the trial. She kneels on the steps
> of the Altar, and speaks in tones at first faint and low, but
> which ever become louder and louder.*

  Mighty Empress! Death's white wife!
  Ghastly mother-in-law of life!
   By the God who made thee such,
   By the magic of thy touch,
   By the starving and the cramming,
Of fasts and feasts!—by thy dread self, O Famine!
I charge thee! when thou wake the multitude,
Thou lead them not upon the paths of blood.
   The earth did never mean her foison
   For those who crown life's cup with poison
Of fanatic rage and meaningless revenge—
   But for those radiant spirits, who are still
The standard-bearers in the van of Change.
   Be they th' appointed stewards, to fill
   The lap of Pain, and Toil, and Age!
   Remit, O Queen! thy accustomed rage!
Be what thou art not! In voice faint and low
FREEDOM calls *Famine*, her eternal foe,
To brief alliance, hollow truce.—Rise now!

> [*Whilst the veiled Figure has been chanting this strophe,* MAM-
> MON, DAKRY, LAOCTONOS, *and* SWELLFOOT *have sur-
> rounded* IONA TAURINA, *who, with her hands folded on
> her breast, and her eyes lifted to Heaven, stands, as with
> saint-like resignation, to wait the issue of the business, in
> perfect confidence of her innocence.*

> [PURGANAX, *after unsealing the* GREEN BAG, *is gravely about
> to pour the liquor upon her head, when suddenly the whole
> expression of her figure and countenance changes; she snatches
> it from his hand with a loud laugh of triumph, and empties
> it over* SWELLFOOT *and his whole Court, who are instantly
> changed into a number of filthy and ugly animals, and rush
> out of the Temple. The image of* FAMINE *then arises with*

a tremendous sound, the Pigs *begin scrambling for the loaves,
and are tripped up by the skulls; all those who eat the loaves
are turned into* Bulls, *and arrange themselves quietly behind
the Altar. The image of* FAMINE *sinks through a chasm in
the earth, and a* MINOTAUR *rises.*

Mino. I am the Ionian Minotaur, the mightiest
Of all Europa's taurine progeny—
I am the old traditional man-bull;
And from my ancestors having been Ionian,
I am called Ion, which by interpretation
Is JOHN; in plain Theban, that is to say—
My name's JOHN BULL. I am a famous hunter,
And can leap any gate in all Bœotia,
Even the palings of the royal park,
Or double ditch about the new enclosures;
And, if your Majesty will deign to mount me,
At least till you have hunted down your game,
I will not throw you.

IONA TAURINA.

[*During this speech she has been putting on boots and spurs,
and a hunting-cap, buckishly cocked on one side, and,
tucking up her hair, she leaps nimbly on his back.*

Hoa! hoa! tallyho! tallyho! ho! ho!
Come, let us hunt these ugly badgers down,
These stinking foxes, these devouring otters,
These hares, these wolves, these anything but men.
Hey for a whipper-in! my loyal pigs,
Now let your noses be as keen as beagles,
Your steps as swift as greyhounds, and your cries
More dulcet and symphonious than the bells
Of village-towers, on sunshine-holiday;
Wake all the dewy woods with jangling music.
Give them no law (are they not beasts of blood?)
But such as they gave you. Tallyho! ho!
Through forest, furze, and bog, and den, and desert,
Pursue the ugly beasts! tallyho! ho!

FULL CHORUS OF IONA AND THE SWINE.

Tallyho! tallyho!
Through rain, hail, and snow,
    Through brake, gorse, and briar,
    Through fen, flood, and mire,
We go! we go!

Tallyho! tallyho!
Through pond, ditch, and slough,
    Wind them, and find them,
    Like the Devil behind them,
Tallyho! tallyho!

[*Exeunt in full cry;* IONA *driving on the* SWINE, *with the
empty* GREEN BAG.

1832.

THE MASQUE OF ANARCHY.*

I.

As I lay asleep in Italy,
There came a voice from over the sea,
And with great power it forth led me
To walk in the visions of Poesy.

II.

I met Murder on the way—
He had a mask like Castlereagh—
Very smooth he looked, yet grim;
Seven bloodhounds followed him:

III.

All were fat; and well they might
Be in admirable plight,
For one by one, and two by two,
He tossed them human hearts to chew,
Which from his wide cloak he drew.

IV.

Next came Fraud, and he had on,
Like Lord E——, an ermined gown;
His big tears, for he wept well,
Turned to mill-stones as they fell;

V.

And the little children, who
Round his feet played to and fro,
Thinking every tear a gem,
Had their brains knocked out by them.

VI.

Clothed with the * * as with light,
And the shadows of the night,
Like * * * next, Hypocrisy,
On a crocodile rode by.

VII.

And many more Destructions played
In this ghastly masquerade,
All disguised, even to the eyes,
Like bishops, lawyers, peers, or spies.

VIII.

Last came Anarchy; he rode
On a white horse, splashed with blood;
He was pale even to the lips,
Like Death in the Apocalypse.

IX.

And he wore a kingly crown;
And in his grasp a sceptre shone;
And on his brow this mark I saw—
" I am God, and King, and Law !"

X.

With a pace stately and fast,
Over English land he past,
Trampling to a mire of blood
The adoring multitude.

XI.

And a mighty troop around,
With their trampling shook the ground,
Waving each a bloody sword,
For the service of their Lord.

XII.

And with glorious triumph, they
Rode through England proud and gay,
Drunk as with intoxication
Of the wine of desolation.

XIII.

O'er fields and towns, from sea to sea,
Passed the pageant swift and free,
Tearing up, and trampling down,
Till they came to London town.

XIV.

And each dweller, panic-stricken,
Felt his heart with terror sicken,
Hearing the tempestuous cry
Of the triumph of Anarchy.

* Written on hearing of the bloodshed at Manchester in 1819, and published by
Leigh Hunt in 1832

XV.

For with pomp to meet him came,
Clothed in arms like blood and flame,
The hired murderers who did sing,
"Thou art God, and Law, and King.

XVI.

"We have waited, weak and lone,
For thy coming, Mighty One!
Our purses are empty, our swords are
cold,
Give us glory, and blood, and gold."

XVII.

Lawyers and priests, a motley crowd,
To the earth their pale brows bowed;
Like a bad prayer not over loud,
Whispering—"Thou art Law and
God."

XVIII.

Then all cried with one accord,
"Thou art King, and God, and Lord;
Anarchy, to thee we bow,
Be thy name made holy now!"

XIX.

And Anarchy, the skeleton,
Bowed and grinned to every one,
As well as if his education,
Had cost ten millions to the nation.

XX.

For he knew the palaces
Of our kings were nightly his;
His the sceptre, crown, and globe,
And the gold-inwoven robe.

XXI.

So he sent his slaves before
To seize upon the Bank and Tower,
And was proceeding with intent
To meet his pensioned parliament,

XXII.

When one fled past, a maniac maid,
And her name was Hope, she said:
But she looked more like Despair;
And she cried out in the air;

XXIII.

"My father, Time, is weak and grey
With waiting for a better day;
See how idiot-like he stands,
Fumbling with his palsied hands!

XXIV.

"He has had child after child,
And the dust of death is piled
Over every one but me—
Misery! oh, Misery!"

XXV.

Then she lay down in the street,
Right before the horses' feet,
Expecting with a patient eye,
Murder, Fraud, and Anarchy.

XXVI.

When between her and her foes
A mist, a light, an image rose,
Small at first, and weak and frail
Like the vapour of the vale:

XXVII.

Till, as clouds grow on the blast,
Like tower-crowned giants striding
fast,
And glare with lightnings as they fly,
And speak in thunder to the sky,

XXVIII.

It grew—a shape arrayed in mail
Brighter than the viper's scale.
And upborne on wings whose grain
Was as the light of sunny rain.

XXIX.

On its helm, seen far away,
A planet, like the morning's, lay;
And those plumes it light rained
through,
Like a shower of crimson dew.

XXX.

With step as soft as wind it passed
O'er the heads of men—so fast
That they knew the presence there,
And looked—and all was empty air.

XXXI.

As flowers beneath the footstep waken,
As stars from night's loose hair are
shaken,
As waves arise when loud winds call,
Thoughts sprung where'er that step
did fall.

XXXII.

And the prostrate multitude
Looked—and ankle deep in blood,
Hope, that maiden most serene,
Was walking with a quiet mien:

XXXIII.

And Anarchy, the ghastly birth,
Lay dead earth upon the earth;
The Horse of Death, tameless as wind,
Fled, and with his hoofs did grind
To dust the murderers thronged
    behind.

XXXIV.

A rushing light of clouds and splendour,
A sense, awakening and yet tender,
Was heard and felt—and at its close
These words of joy and fear arose;

XXXV.

(As if their own indignant earth,
Which gave the sons of England birth,
Had felt their blood upon her brow,
And shuddering with a mother's throe,

XXXVI.

Had turned every drop of blood,
By which her face had been bedewed,
To an accent unwithstood,
As if her heart had cried aloud:)

XXXVII.

" Men of England, Heirs of Glory,
Heroes of unwritten story,
Nurslings of one mighty mother,
Hopes of her, and one another,

XXXVIII.

" Rise, like lions after slumber,
In unvanquishable number,
Shake your chains to earth like dew,
Which in sleep had fall'n on you.

XXXIX.

" What is Freedom ? Ye can tell
That which Slavery is too well.
For its very name has grown
To an echo of your own.

XL.

" 'Tis to work, and have such pay
As just keeps life from day to day
In your limbs, as in a cell
For the tyrants' use to dwell:

XLI.

" So that ye for them are made,
Loom, and plough, and sword, and
    spade,
With or without your own will, bent
To their defence and nourishment.

XLII.

" 'Tis to see your children weak
With their mothers pine and peak,
When the winter winds are bleak:—
They are dying whilst I speak.

XLIII.

" 'Tis to hunger for such diet,
As the rich man in his riot
Casts to the fat dogs that lie
Surfeiting beneath his eye.

XLIV.

" 'Tis to let the Ghost of Gold
Take from toil a thousandfold,
More than e'er its substance could
In the tyrannies of old:

XLV.

" Paper coin—that forgery
Of the title deeds, which ye
Hold to something of the worth
Of the inheritance of Earth.

XLVI.

" 'Tis to be a slave in soul,
And to hold no strong control
Over your own wills, but be
All that others make of ye.

XLVII.

" And at length when ye complain,
With a murmur weak and vain,
'Tis to see the tyrant's crew
Ride over your wives and you:—
Blood is on the grass like dew.

XLVIII.

" Then it is to feel revenge,
Fiercely thirsting to exchange
Blood for blood—and wrong for wrong:
DO NOT THUS, WHEN YE ARE STRONG.

XLIX.

" Birds find rest in narrow nest,
When weary of the winged quest;
Beasts find fare in woody lair,
When storm and snow are in the air.

L.

" Asses, swine have litter spread,
And with fitting food are fed;
All things have a home but one,
Thou, oh Englishman, hast none !

LI.

" This is Slavery—savage men,
Or wild beasts within a den,
Would endure not as ye do:
But such ills they never knew.

LII.

" What art thou, Freedom?   Oh !
    could Slaves
Answer from their living graves
This demand, tyrants would flee
Like a dream's dim imagery.

LIII.

" Thou art not, as impostors say,
A shadow soon to pass away,
A superstition, and a name
Echoing from the caves of Fame.

LIV.

" For the labourer thou art bread,
And a comely table spread,
From his daily labour come,
In a neat and happy home.

LV.

" Thou art clothes, and fire, and food
For the trampled multitude:
No—in countries that are free
Such starvation cannot be,
As in England now we see.

LVI.

" To the rich thou art a check,
When his foot is on the neck
Of his victim; thou dost make
That he treads upon a snake.

LVII.

" Thou art Justice—ne'er for gold
May thy righteous laws be sold,
As laws are in England:—thou
Shield'st alike the high and low.

LVIII.

" Thou art Wisdom—Freedom never
Dreams that God will damn for ever
All who think those things untrue,
Of which priests made such ado.

LIX.

" Thou art Peace—never by thee
Would blood and treasure wasted be,
As tyrants wasted them, when all
Leagued to quench thy flame in Gaul.

LX.

" What if English toil and blood
Was poured forth, even as a flood !
It availed,—oh Liberty !
To dim—but not extinguish thee.

LXI.

" Thou art Love—the rich have kist
Thy feet, and like him following Christ,
Give their substance to the free,
And through the rough world follow
    thee.

LXII.

" Oh turn their wealth to arms, and
    make
War for thy beloved sake,
On wealth *and* war and fraud: whence
    they
Drew the power which is their prey.

LXIII.

" Science, and Poetry, and Thought,
Are thy lamps; they make the lot
Of the dwellers in a cot
So serene, they curse it not.

LXIV.

" Spirit, Patience, Gentleness,
All that can adorn and bless,
Art thou: let deeds, not words, express,
Thine exceeding loveliness.

LXV.

" Let a great assembly be
Of the fearless, of the free,
On some spot of English ground,
Where the plains stretch wide around.

LXVI.

" Let the blue sky overhead,
The green earth, on which ye tread,
All that must eternal be,
Witness the solemnity.

LXVII.

" From the corners uttermost
Of the bounds of English coast;
From every hut, village, and town,
Where those who live and suffer, moan
For others' misery and their own:

LXVIII.

" From the workhouse and the prison,
Where pale as corpses newly risen,
Women, children, young, and old,
Groan for pain and weep for cold;

LXIX.

'From the haunts of daily life,
Where is waged the daily strife
With common wants and common
cares,
Which sow the human heart with
tares;

LXX.

'' Lastly, from the palaces,
Where the murmur of distress
Echoes, like the distant sound
Of a wind alive around;

LXXI.

'Those prison-halls of wealth and
fashion,
Where some few feel such compassion
For those who groan, and toil, and
wail,
As must make their brethren pale;

LXXII.

''Ye who suffer woes untold,
Or to feel, or to behold
Your lost country bought and sold
With a price of blood and gold;

LXXIII.

''Let a vast assembly be,
And with a great solemnity
Declare with measured words, that ye
Are, as God has made ye, free !

LXXIV.

'Be your strong and simple words
Keen to wound as sharpened swords,
And wide as targes let them be;
With their shade to cover ye.

LXXV.

'Let the tyrants pour around
With a quick and startling sound,
Like the loosening of a sea,
Troops of armed emblazonry.

LXXVI.

'Let the charged artillery drive,
Till the dead air seems alive
With the clash of clanging wheels,
And the tramp of horses' heels.

LXXVII.

'Let the fixed bayonet
Gleam with sharp desire to wet
Its bright point in English blood,
Looking keen as one for food.

LXXVIII.

" Let the horsemen's scimitars
Wheel and flash, like sphereless stars,
Thirsting to eclipse their burning
In a sea of death and mourning.

LXXIX.

'' Stand ye calm and resolute,
Like a forest close and mute;
With folded arms, and looks which are
Weapons of an unvanquished war.

LXXX.

'' And let Panic, who outspeeds
The career of armed steeds,
Pass, a disregarded shade,
Through your phalanx undismayed.

LXXXI.

''Let the laws of your own land,
Good or ill, between ye stand,
Hand to hand, and foot to foot,
Arbiters of the dispute.

LXXXII.

'' The old laws of England—they
Whose reverend heads with age are
grey,
Children of a wiser day;
And whose solemn voice must be
Thine own echo—Liberty !

LXXXIII.

'' On those who first should violate
Such sacred heralds in their state,
Rest the blood that must ensue,
And it will not rest on you.

LXXXIV.

'' And if then the tyrants dare,
Let them ride among you thére;
Slash, and stab, and maim, and hew
What they like, that let them do.

LXXXV.

'' With folded arms and steady eyes,
And little fear and less surprise,
Look upon them as they stay
Till their rage has died away:

LXXXVI.

'' Then they will return with shame,
To the place from which they came,
And the blood thus shed will speak
In hot blushes on their cheek:

LXXXVII.

"Every woman in the land
Will point at them, as they stand—
They will hardly dare to greet
Their acquaintance in the street:

LXXXVIII.

"And the bold, true warriors,
Who have hugged Danger in wars,
Will turn to those who would be free
Ashamed of such base company:

LXXXIX.

"And that slaughter to the nation
Shall steam up like inspiration,

Eloquent, oracular,
A volcano heard afar:

XC.

"And these words shall then become
Like Oppression's thundered doom,
Ringing through each heart and brain,
Heard again—again—again.

XCI.

"Rise like lions after slumber
In unvanquishable NUMBER!
Shake your chains to earth, like dew
Which in sleep had fall'n on you:
YE ARE MANY—THEY ARE FEW."

LINES TO A CRITIC.

HONEY from silkworms who can gather,
    Or silk from the yellow bee?
The grass may grow in winter weather,
    As soon as hate in me.

Hate men who cant, and men who pray,
    And men who rail like thee;
An equal passion to repay,—
    They are not coy like me.

Or seek some slave of power and gold,
    To be thy dear heart's mate,
Thy love will move that bigot cold,
    Sooner than me, thy hate.

A passion like the one I prove
    Cannot divided be;
I hate thy want of truth and love,
    How should I then hate thee?

LINES

WRITTEN DURING THE CASTLEREAGH ADMINISTRATION.

I.

CORPSES are cold in the tomb;
Stones on the pavement are dumb;
Abortions are dead in the womb,
And their mothers look pale—like the white shore
    Of Albion, free no more.

II.

Her sons are as stones in the way—
They are masses of senseless clay—
They are trodden, and move not away;
The abortion with which *she* travaileth
    Is Liberty, smitten to death.

III.

Then trample and dance, thou oppressor,
For thy victim is no redressor !
Thou art sole lord and possessor
Of her corpses and clods and abortions—they pave
    Thy path to the grave.

IV.

Hear'st thou the festival din
Of Death and Destruction and Sin
And Wealth crying '' Havoc !'' within ?
'Tis the bacchanal triumph which makes Truth dumb,
    Thine epithalamium.

V.

Ay, marry thy ghastly Wife !
Let Fear and Disquiet and Strife
Spread thy couch in the chamber of Life !
Marry Ruin, thou tyrant ! and God be thy guide
    To the bed of the bride !

SONG—TO THE MEN OF ENGLAND.

I.

MEN of England, wherefore plough
For the lords who lay ye low ?
Wherefore weave with toil and care
The rich robes your tyrants wear ?

II.

Wherefore feed and clothe and save,
From the cradle to the grave,
Those ungrateful drones who would
Drain your sweat—nay, drink your blood ?

III.

Wherefore, Bees of England, forge
Many a weapon, chain, and scourge,
That these stingless drones may spoil
The forced produce of your toil ?

IV.

Have ye leisure, comfort, calm,
Shelter, food, love's gentle balm ?
Or what is it ye buy so dear
With your pain and with your fear ?

V.

The seed ye sow another reaps;
The wealth ye find another keeps;
The robes ye weave another wears;
The arms ye forge another bears.

VI.

Sow seed,—but let no tyrant reap;
Find wealth,—let no impostor heap;
Weave robes,—let not the idle wear;
Forge arms, in your defence to bear.

VII.

Shrink to your cellars, holes, and cells;
In halls ye deck another dwells.
Why shake the chains ye wrought ? Ye see
The steel ye tempered glance on ye.

VIII.

With plough and spade and hoe and loom,
Trace your grave, and build your tomb,
And weave your winding-sheet, till fair
England be your sepulchre !

SIMILES FOR TWO POLITICAL CHARACTERS OF 1819.

I.

As from an ancestral oak
  Two empty ravens sound their clarion,
Yell by yell and croak by croak,
When they scent the noonday smoke
  Of fresh human carrion:

II.

As two gibbering night-birds flit
  From their bowers of deadly hue
Through the night to frighten it,
When the moon is in a fit,
  And the stars are none or few:

III.

As a shark and dogfish wait
  Under an Atlantic isle
For the negro-ship whose freight
Is the theme of their debate,
  Wrinkling their red gills the while—

IV.

Are ye, two vultures sick for battle,
  Two scorpions under one wet stone,
Two bloodless wolves whose dry throats rattle,
Two crows perched on the murrained cattle,
  Two vipers tangled into one.

ENGLAND IN 1819.

An old, mad, blind, despised, and dying king,—
  Princes, the dregs of their dull race, who flow
Through public scorn, mud from a muddy spring,—
  Rulers who neither see nor feel nor know,
But leech-like to their fainting country cling,
  Till they drop, blind in blood, without a blow,—
A people starved and stabbed in the untilled field,—
  An army which liberticide and prey
Make as a two-edged sword to all who wield,—
  Golden and sanguine laws which tempt and slay,—
Religion Christless, Godless, a book sealed,—
A Senate—time's worst statute unrepealed,—
  Are graves from which a glorious Phantom may
  Burst to illumine our tempestuous day.

GOD SAVE THE QUEEN.

1819.

I.

GOD prosper, speed, and save,
God raise from England's grave,
       Her murdered Queen !
Pave with swift victory
The steps of Liberty,
Whom Britons own to be
       Immortal Queen !

II.

See, she comes throned on high
On swift Eternity !
       God save the Queen !
Millions on millions wait,
Firm, rapid, and elate,
On her majestic state—
       God save the Queen !

III.

She is Thine own pure soul
Moulding the mighty whole.
       God save the Queen !
She is Thine own deep love
Rained down from heaven above.
Wherever she rest or move,
       God save our Queen !

IV.

'Wilder her enemies
In their own dark disguise !
       God save our Queen !
All earthly things that dare
Her sacred name to bear,
Strip them, as kings are, bare;
       God save the Queen !

V.

Be her eternal throne
Built in our hearts alone—
       God save the Queen !
Let the oppressor hold
Canopied seats of gold;
She sits enthroned of old
       O'er our hearts Queen.

VI.

Lips touched by seraphim
Breathe out the choral hymn,
       "God save the Queen !"
Sweet as if angels sang,
Loud as that trumpet's clang
Wakening the world's dead gang,—
       God save the Queen !

Early Poems.

ΔΑΚΡΥΣΙ ΔΙΟΙΣΩ ΠΟΤΜΟΝ ΑΠΟΤΜΟΝ.*

O THERE are spirits in the air,
  And genii of the evening breeze,
And gentle ghosts, with eyes as fair
  As star-beams among twilight trees:
Such lovely ministers to meet
Oft hast thou turned from men thy lonely feet.

With mountain winds, and babbling springs,
  And moonlight seas, that are the voice
Of these inexplicable things
  Thou didst hold commune, and rejoice
When they did answer thee; but they
Cast, like a worthless boon, thy love away.

And thou hast sought in starry eyes
  Beams that were never meant for thine,
Another's wealth:—tame sacrifice
  To a fond faith! still dost thou pine?
Still dost thou hope that greeting hands,
Voice, looks, or lips, may answer thy demands?

Ah! wherefore didst thou build thine hope
  On the false earth's inconstancy?
Did thine own mind afford no scope
  Of love, or moving thoughts to thee?
That natural scenes or human smiles
Could steal the power to wind thee in their wiles.

Yes, all the faithless smiles are fled
  Whose falsehood left thee broken-hearted;
The glory of the moon is dead;
  Night's ghosts and dreams have now departed;
Thine own soul still is true to thee,
But changed to a foul fiend through misery.

This fiend, whose ghastly presence ever
  Beside thee like thy shadow hangs,
Dream not to chase;—the mad endeavour
  Would scourge thee to severer pangs.
Be as thou art. Thy settled fate,
Dark as it is, all change would aggravate.

---

* This poem was addressed to Coleridge.

STANZAS.—APRIL, 1814.

AWAY ! the moor is dark beneath the moon,
  Rapid clouds have drank the last pale beam of even:
Away ! the gathering winds will call the darkness soon,
  And profoundest midnight shroud the serene lights of heaven.

Pause not ! The time is past ! Every voice cries, Away !
  Tempt not with one last tear thy friend's ungentle mood:
Thy lover's eye, so glazed and cold, dares not entreat thy stay:
  Duty and dereliction guide thee back to solitude.

Away, away ! to thy sad and silent home;
  Pour bitter tears on its desolated hearth;
Watch the dim shades as like ghosts they go and come,
  And complicate strange webs of melancholy mirth.

The leaves of wasted autumn woods shall float around thine head:
  The blooms of dewy spring shall gleam beneath thy feet:
But thy soul or this world must fade in the frost that binds the dead,
  Ere midnight's frown and morning's smile, ere thou and peace may meet

The cloud shadows of midnight possess their own repose,
  For the weary winds are silent, or the moon is in the deep:
Some respite to its turbulence unresting ocean knows:
  Whatever moves, or toils, or grieves, hath its appointed sleep.

Thou in the grave shalt rest—yet till the phantoms flee
  Which that house and heath and garden made dear to thee erewhile,
Thy remembrance, and repentance, and deep musings are not free
  From the music of two voices and the light of one sweet smile.

MUTABILITY.

WE are as clouds that veil the midnight moon;
  How restlessly they speed, and gleam, and quiver,
Streaking the darkness radiantly !—yet soon
  Night closes round, and they are lost for ever:

Or like forgotten lyres, whose dissonant strings
  Give various response to each varying blast,
To whose frail frame no second motion brings
  One mood or modulation like the last.

We rest.—A dream has power to poison sleep;
  We rise.—One wandering thought pollutes the day
We feel, conceive or reason, laugh or weep;
  Embrace fond woe, or cast our cares away:

It is the same !—For, be it joy or sorrow,
  The path of its departure still is free:
Man's yesterday may ne'er be like his morrow;
  Nought may endure but Mutability.

DEATH.

"There is no work, nor device, nor knowledge, nor wisdom, in the grave, whither thou goest."—ECCLESIASTES

THE pale, the cold, and the moony smile
   Which the meteor-beam of a starless night
Sheds on a lonely and sea-girt isle,
   Ere the dawning of morn's undoubted light,
Is the flame of life so fickle and wan
That flits round our steps till their strength is gone.

O man! hold thee on in courage of soul
   Through the stormy shades of thy worldly way,
And the billows of cloud that around thee roll
   Shall sleep in the light of a wondrous day,
Where hell and heaven shall leave thee free
To the universe of destiny.

This world is the nurse of all we know,
   This world is the mother of all we feel,
And the coming of death is a fearful blow
   To a brain unencompassed with nerves of steel;
When all that we know, or feel, or see,
Shall pass like an unreal mystery.

The secret things of the grave are there,
   Where all but this frame must surely be,
Though the fine-wrought eye and the wondrous ear
   No longer will live to hear or to see
All that is great and all that is strange
In the boundless realm of unending change.

Who telleth a tale of unspeaking death?
   Who lifteth the veil of what is to come?
Who painteth the shadows that are beneath
   The wide-winding caves of the peopled tomb?
Or uniteth the hopes of what shall be
With the fears and the love for that which we see?

A SUMMER-EVENING CHURCHYARD, LECHLADE, GLOUCESTERSHIRE.

THE wind has swept from the wide atmosphere
Each vapour that obscured the sunset's ray;
And pallid evening twines its beaming hair
In duskier braids around the languid eyes of day;
Silence and twilight, unbeloved of men,
Creep hand in hand from yon obscurest glen.

They breathe their spells towards the departing day,
Encompassing the earth, air, stars, and sea;
Light, sound, and motion own the potent sway,
Responding to the charm with its own mystery.
The winds are still, or the dry church-tower grass
Knows not their gentle motions as they pass.

Thou too, aërial Pile ! whose pinnacles
Point from one shrine like pyramids of fire,
Obeyst in silence their sweet solemn spells,
Clothing in hues of heaven thy dim and distant spire,
Around whose lessening and invisible height
Gather among the stars the clouds of night.

The dead are sleeping in their sepulchres ;
And, mouldering as they sleep, a thrilling sound,
Half sense, half thought, among the darkness stirs,
Breathed from their wormy beds all living things around,
And mingling with the still night and mute sky
Its awful hush is felt inaudibly.

Thus solemnized and softened, death is mild
And terrorless as this serenest night :
Here could I hope, like some inquiring child
Sporting on graves, that death did hide from human sight
Sweet secrets, or beside its breathless sleep
That loveliest dreams perpetual watch did keep.

TO WORDSWORTH.

POET of Nature, thou hast wept to know
   That things depart which never may return :
Childhood and youth, friendship, and love's first glow,
   Have fled like sweet dreams, leaving thee to mourn.
These common woes I feel.   One loss is mine,
   Which thou too feel'st, yet I alone deplore.
Thou wert as a lone star whose light did shine
   On some frail bark in winter's midnight roar :
Thou hast like to a rock-built refuge stood
Above the blind and battling multitude :
In honoured poverty thy voice did weave
   Songs consecrate to truth and liberty.
Deserting these, thou leavest me to grieve,
   Thus, having been, that thou shouldst cease to be.

Miscellaneous Poems.

THE SENSITIVE PLANT.

PART FIRST.

A SENSITIVE PLANT in a garden grew,
And the young winds fed it with silver dew,
**And it opened its fan-like leaves to the light,
And closed them beneath the kisses of night.**

And the Spring arose on the garden fair,
Like the Spirit of Love felt everywhere ;
And each flower and herb on Earth's dark breast
Rose from the dreams of its wintry rest.

But none ever trembled and panted with bliss
In the garden, the field, and the wilderness,
Like a doe in the noontide with love's sweet want,
As the companionless Sensitive Plant.

The snowdrop, and then the violet,
Arose from the ground with warm rain wet,
And their breath was mixed with fresh odour, sent
From the turf, like the voice and the instrument.

Then the pied windflowers and the tulip tall,
And narcissi, the fairest among them all,
Who gaze on their eyes in the stream's recess,
Till they die of their own dear loveliness ;

And the Naiad-like lily of the vale,
Whom youth makes so fair and passion so pale,
That the light of its tremulous bells is seen
Through their pavilions of tender green ;

And the hyacinth purple, and white, and blue,
Which flung from its bells a sweet peal anew
Of music so delicate, soft, and intense,
It was felt like an odour within the sense ;

And the rose like a nymph to the bath addrest,
Which unveiled the depth of her glowing breast,
Till, fold after fold, to the fainting air
The soul of her beauty and love lay bare ;

And the wand-like lily, which lifted up,
As a Mænad, its moonlight-coloured cup,
Till the fiery star, which is its eye,
Gazed through clear dew on the tender sky ;

And the jessamine faint, and the sweet tuberose,
The sweetest flower for scent that blows ;
And all rare blossoms from every clime
Grew in that garden in perfect prime.

And on the stream whose inconstant bosom
Was prankt under boughs of embowering blossom,
With golden and green light, slanting through
Their heaven of many a tangled hue,

Broad water-lilies lay tremulously,
And starry river-buds glimmered by,
And around them the soft stream did glide and dance
With a motion of sweet sound and radiance.

And the sinuous paths of lawn and moss,
Which led through the garden along and across,
Some open at once to the sun and the breeze,
Some lost among bowers of blossoming trees,

Were all paved with daisies and delicate bells
As fair as the fabulous asphodels,
And flowrets which drooping as day drooped too
Fell into pavilions, white, purple, and blue,
To roof the glowworm from the evening dew.

And from this undefiled Paradise
The flowers (as an infant's awakening eyes
Smile on its mother, whose singing sweet
Can first lull, and at last must awaken it),

When Heaven's blithe winds had unfolded them,
As mine-lamps enkindle a hidden gem,
Shone smiling to Heaven, and every one
Shared joy in the light of the gentle sun ;

For each one was interpenetrated
With the light and the odour its neighbour shed,
Like young lovers whom youth and love make dear
Wrapped and filled by their mutual atmosphere.

But the Sensitive Plant which could give small fruit
Of the love which it felt from the leaf to the root,
Received more than all, it loved more than ever,
Where none wanted but it, could belong to the giver,

For the Sensitive Plant has no bright flower;
Radiance and odour are not its dower;
It loves, even like Love, its deep heart is full,
It desires what it has not, the Beautiful !

The light winds which from unsustaining wings
Shed the music of many murmurings;
The beams which dart from many a star
Of the flowers whose hues they bear afar;

The plumed insects swift and free,
Like golden boats on a sunny sea,
Laden with light and odour, which pass
Over the gleam of the living grass:

The unseen clouds of the dew, which lie
Like fire in the flowers till the sun rides high,
Then wander like spirits among the spheres,
Each cloud faint with the fragrance it bears;

The quivering vapours of dim noontide,
Which like a sea o'er the warm earth glide,
In which every sound, and odour, and beam,
Move, as reeds in a single stream;

Each and all like ministering angels were
For the Sensitive Plant sweet joy to bear,
Whilst the lagging hours of the day went by
Like windless clouds o'er a tender sky.

And when evening descended from Heaven above,
And the Earth was all rest, and the air was all love,
And delight, though less bright, was far more deep,
And the day's veil fell from the world of sleep,

And the beasts, and the birds, and the insects were drowned
In an ocean of dreams without a sound;
Whose waves never mark, though they ever impress
The light sand which paves it, consciousness;

(Only over head the sweet nightingale
Ever sang more sweet as the day might fail,
And snatches of its Elysian chant
Were mixed with the dreams of the Sensitive Plant).

The Sensitive Plant was the earliest
Up-gathered into the bosom of rest;
A sweet child weary of its delight,
The feeblest and yet the favourite,
Cradled within the embrace of night.

PART SECOND.

There was a Power in this sweet place,
An Eve in this Eden; a ruling grace
Which to the flowers did they waken or dream,
Was as God is to the starry scheme.

A Lady, the wonder of her kind,
Whose form was upborne by a lovely mind
Which, dilating, had moulded her mien and motion
Like a sea-flower unfolded beneath the ocean,

Tended the garden from morn to even:
And the meteors of that sublunar heaven,
Like the lamps of the air when night walks forth,
Laughed round her footsteps up from the Earth!

She had no companion of mortal race,
But her tremulous breath and her flushing face
Told, whilst the moon kissed the sleep from her eyes,
That her dreams were less slumber than Paradise:

As if some bright Spirit for her sweet sake
Had deserted heaven while the stars were awake,
As if yet around her he lingering were,
Though the veil of daylight concealed him from her.

Her step seemed to pity the grass it prest;
You might hear by the heaving of her breast,
That the coming and going of the wind
Brought pleasure there and left passion behind.

And wherever her airy footstep trod,
Her trailing hair from the grassy sod
Erased its light vestige, with shadowy sweep,
Like a sunny storm o'er the dark green deep.

I doubt not the flowers of that garden sweet
Rejoiced in the sound of her gentle feet;
I doubt not they felt the spirit that came
From her glowing fingers through all their frame.

She sprinkled bright water from the stream
On those that were faint with the sunny beam;
And out of the cups of the heavy flowers
She emptied the rain of the thunder showers.

She lifted their heads with her tender hands,
And sustained them with rods and osier bands;
If the flowers had been her own infants she
Could never have nursed them more tenderly.

And all killing insects and gnawing worms,
And things of obscene and unlovely forms,
She bore in a basket of Indian woof,
Into the rough woods far aloof,

In a basket, of grasses and wild flowers full,
The freshest her gentle hands could pull
For the poor banished insects, whose intent,
Although they did ill, was innocent.

But the bee and the beamlike ephemeris
Whose path is the lightning's, and soft moths that kiss
The sweet lips of the flowers, and harm not, did she
Make her attendant angels be.

And many an antenatal tomb,
Where butterflies dream of the life to come,
She left clinging round the smooth and dark
Edge of the odorous cedar bark.

This fairest creature from earliest spring
Thus moved through the garden ministering
All the sweet season of summer tide,
And ere the first leaf looked brown—she died !

PART THIRD.

Three days the flowers of the garden fair,
Like stars when the moon is awakened, were,
Or the waves of Baiæ, ere luminous
She floats up through the smoke of Vesuvius.

And on the fourth, the Sensitive Plant
Felt the sound of the funeral chant,
And the steps of the bearers, heavy and slow,
And the sobs of the mourners deep and low;

The weary sound and the heavy breath,
And the silent motions of passing death,
And the smell, cold, oppressive, and dank,
Sent through the pores of the coffin plank;

The dark grass, and the flowers among the grass,
Were bright with tears as the crowd did pass;
From their sighs the wind caught a mournful tone,
And sate in the pines, and gave groan for groan.

The garden, once fair, became cold and foul,
Like the corpse of her who had been its soul,
Which at first was lovely as if in sleep,
Then slowly changed, till it grew a heap
To make men tremble who never weep.

Swift summer into the autumn flowed,
And frost in the mist of the morning rode,
Though the noonday sun looked clear and bright,
Mocking the spoil of the secret night.

The rose leaves, like flakes of crimson snow,
Paved the turf and the moss below.
The lilies were drooping, and white, and wan,
Like the head and the skin of a dying man.

And Indian plants, of scent and hue
The sweetest that ever were fed on dew,
Leaf after leaf, day after day,
Were massed into the common clay.

And the leaves, brown, yellow, and grey, and red,
And white with the whiteness of what is dead,
Like troops of ghosts on the dry wind past;
Their whistling noise made the birds aghast.

And the gusty winds waked the winged seeds,
Out of their birthplace of ugly weeds,
Till they clung round many a sweet flower's stem,
Which rotted into the earth with them.

The water-blooms under the rivulet
Fell from the stalks on which they were set;
And the eddies drove them here and there,
As the winds did those of the upper air.

Then the rain came down, and the broken stalks,
Were bent and tangled across the walks;
And the leafless network of parasite bowers
Massed into ruin; and all sweet flowers.

Between the time of the wind and the snow,
All loathliest weeds began to grow,
Whose coarse leaves were splashed with many a speck,
Like the water-snake's belly and the toad's back.

And thistles, and nettles, and darnels rank,
And the dock, and henbane, and hemlock dank,
Stretched out its long and hollow shank,
And stifled the air till the dead wind stank.

And plants, at whose names the verse feels loath,
Filled the place with a monstrous undergrowth,
Prickly, and pulpous, and blistering, and blue,
Livid, and starred with a lurid dew.

And agarics and fungi, with mildew and mould
Started like mist from the wet ground cold;
Pale, fleshy, as if the decaying dead
With a spirit of growth had been animated!

Their moss rotted off them, flake by flake,
Till the thick stalk stuck like a murderer's stake,
Where rags of loose flesh yet tremble on high,
Infecting the winds that wander by.

Spawn, weeds, and filth, a leprous scum,
Made the running rivulet thick and dumb,
And at its outlet flags huge as stakes
Dammed it up with roots knotted like water-snakes.

And hour by hour, when the air was still,
The vapours arose which have strength to kill:
At morn they were seen, at noon they were felt,
At night they were darkness no star could melt.

And unctuous meteors from spray to spray
Crept and flitted in broad noonday
Unseen; every branch on which they alit
By a venomous blight was burned and bit.

The Sensitive Plant like one forbid
Wept, and the tears within each lid
Of its folded leaves which together grew
Were changed to a blight of frozen glue.

For the leaves soon fell, and the branches soon
By the heavy axe of the blast were hewn;
The sap shrank to the root through every pore
As blood to a heart that will beat no more.

For Winter came: the wind was his whip:
One choppy finger was on his lip:
He had torn the cataracts from the hills
And they clanked at his girdle like manacles;

His breath was a chain which without a sound
The earth, and the air, and the water bound;
He came, fiercely driven, in his chariot-throne
By the tenfold blasts of the arctic zone.

Then the weeds which were forms of living death
Fled from the frost to the earth beneath.
Their decay and sudden flight from frost
Was but like the vanishing of a ghost!

And under the roots of the Sensitive Plant
The moles and the dormice died for want:
The birds dropped stiff from the frozen air
And were caught in the branches naked and bare.

First there came down a thawing rain
And its dull drops froze on the boughs again,
Then there steamed up a freezing dew
Which to the drops of the thaw-rain grew;

And a northern whirlwind, wandering about
Like a wolf that had smelt a dead child out,
Shook the boughs thus laden, and heavy and stiff,
And snapped them off with his rigid griff.

When winter had gone and spring came back
The Sensitive Plant was a leafless wreck;
But the mandrakes, and toadstools, and docks, and darnels
Rose like the dead from their ruined charnels.

CONCLUSION.

Whether the Sensitive Plant, or that
Which within its boughs like a spirit sat
Ere its outward form had known decay,
Now felt this change, I cannot say.

Whether that lady's gentle mind,
No longer with the form combined
Which scattered love, as stars do light,
Found sadness, where it left delight,

I dare not guess; but in this life
Of error, ignorance, and strife,
Where nothing is, but all things seem,
And we the shadows of the dream,

It is a modest creed, and yet
Pleasant if one considers it,
To own that death itself must be,
Like all the rest, a mockery.

That garden sweet, that lady fair,
And all sweet shapes and odours there,
In truth have never passed away:
Tis we, 'tis ours, are changed; not they.

For love, and beauty, and delight,
There is no death nor change: their might
Exceeds our organs, which endure
No light, being themselves obscure.

A VISION OF THE SEA.

Tis the terror of tempest. The rags of the sail
Are flickering in ribbons within the fierce gale:
From the stark night of vapours the dim rain is driven,
And when lightning is loosed, like a deluge from heaven,
She sees the black trunks of the water-spouts spin,
And bend, as if heaven was ruining in,
Which they seemed to sustain with their terrible mass
As if ocean had sunk from beneath them: they pass

To their graves in the deep with an earthquake of sound,
And the waves and the thunders made silent around
Leave the wind to its echo.   The vessel, now tossed
Through the low-trailing rack of the tempest, is lost
In the skirts of the thunder-cloud: now down the sweep
Of the wind-cloven wave to the chasm of the deep
It sinks, and the walls of the watery vale
Whose depths of dread calm are unmoved by the gale,
Dim mirrors of ruin hang gleaming about;
While the surf, like a chaos of stars, like a rout
Of death-flames, like whirlpools of fire-flowing iron
With splendour and terror the black ship environ,
Or like sulphur-flakes hurled from a mine of pale fire
In fountains spout o'er it.   In many a spire
The pyramid-billows with white points of brine
In the cope of the lightning inconstantly shine,
As piercing the sky from the floor of the sea.
The great ship seems splitting ! it cracks as a tree,
While an earthquake is splintering its root, ere the blast
Of the whirlwind that stripped it of branches has past.
The intense thunder-balls which are raining from heaven
Have shattered its mast, and it stands black and riven.
The chinks suck destruction.   The heavy dead hulk
On the living sea rolls an inanimate bulk,
Like a corpse on the clay which is hungering to fold
Its corruption around it.   Meanwhile, from the hold,
One deck is burst up from the waters below,
And it splits like the ice when the thaw-breezes blow
O'er the lakes of the desert !   Who sit on the other ?
Is that all the crew that lie burying each other,
Like the dead in a breach, round the foremast ?   Are those
Twin tigers, who burst, when the waters arose,
In the agony of terror, their chains in the hold
(What now makes them tame, is what then made them bold);
Who crouch, side by side, and have driven, like a crank,
The deep grip of their claws through the vibrating plank.
Are these all ?   Nine weeks the tall vessel had lain
On the windless expanse of the watery plain,
Where the death-darting sun cast no shadow at noon,
And there seemed to be fire in the beams of the moon,
Till a lead-coloured fog gathered up from the deep
Whose breath was quick pestilence; then, the cold sleep
Crept, like blight through the ears of a thick field of corn,
O'er the populous vessel.   And even and morn,
With their hammocks for coffins the seamen aghast
Like dead men the dead limbs of their comrades cast
Down the deep, which closed on them above and around,
And the sharks and the dogfish their grave-clothes unbound,
And were glutted like Jews with this manna rained down
From God on their wilderness.   One after one
The mariners died ; on the eve of this day,
When the tempest was gathering in cloudy array,
But seven remained.   Six the thunder has smitten,
And they lie black as mummies on which Time has written
His scorn of the embalmer ; the seventh from the deck
An oak-splinter pierced through his breast and his back,
And hung out to the tempest, a wreck on the wreck.
No more ?   At the helm sits a woman more fair

G G

Than heaven, when, unbinding its star-braided hair,
It sinks with the sun on the earth and the sea.
She clasps a bright child on her upgathered knee,
It laughs at the lightning, it mocks the mixed thunder
Of the air and the sea, with desire and with wonder
It is beckoning the tigers to rise and come near.
It would play with those eyes where the radiance of fear
Is outshining the meteors ; its bosom beats high,
The heart-fire of pleasure has kindled its eye ;
Whilst its mother's is lustreless.   " Smile not, my child,
But sleep deeply and sweetly, and so be beguiled
Of the pang that awaits us, whatever that be,
So dreadful since thou must divide it with me !
Dream, sleep !   This pale bosom, thy cradle and bed,
Will it rock thee not, infant ? 'Tis beating with dread !
Alas ! what is life, what is death, what are we,
That when the ship sinks we no longer may be ?
What ! to see thee no more, and to feel thee no more ?
Not to be after life what we have been before ?
Not to touch those sweet hands ? Not to look on those eyes,
Those lips, and that hair, all that smiling disguise
Thou yet wearest, sweet spirit, which I, day by day,
Have so long called my child, but which now fades away
Like a rainbow, and I the fallen shower ?"   Lo ! the ship
Is settling, it topples, the leeward ports dip ;
The tigers leap up when they feel the slow brine
Crawling inch by inch on them, hair, ears, limbs, and eyne,
Stand rigid with horror : a loud, long, hoarse cry
Bursts at once from their vitals tremendously,
And 'tis borne down the mountainous vale of the wave,
Rebounding, like thunder, from crag to cave,
Mixed with the clash of the lashing rain,
Hurried on by the might of the hurricane :
The hurricane came from the west, and passed on
By the path of the gate of the eastern sun,
Transversely dividing the stream of the storm ;
As an arrowy serpent, pursuing the form
Of an elephant, bursts through the brakes of the waste.
Black as a cormorant the screaming blast,
Between ocean and heaven, like an ocean, past,
Till it came to the clouds on the verge of the world
Which, based on the sea and to heaven upcurled,
Like columns and walls did surround and sustain
The dome of the tempest : it rent them in twain,
As a flood rends its barriers of mountainous crag :
And the dense clouds in many a ruin and rag,
Like the stones of a temple ere earthquake has past,
Like the dust of its fall, on the whirlwind are cast ;
They are scattered like foam on the torrent ; and where
The wind has burst out from the chasm, from the air
Of clear morning, the beams of the sunrise flow in,
Unimpeded, keen, golden, and crystalline,
Banded armies of light and of air ; at one gate
They encounter, but interpenetrate.
And that breach in the tempest is widening away,
And the caverns of clouds are torn up by the day,
And the fierce winds are sinking with weary wings
Lulled by the motion and murmurings.

And the long glassy heave of the rocking sea,
And overhead glorious, but dreadful to see
The wrecks of the tempest, like vapours of gold,
Are consuming in sunrise. The heaped waves behold
The deep calm of blue heaven dilating above,
And, like passions made still by the presence of Love,
Beneath the clear surface reflecting it slide
Tremulous with soft influence ; extending its tide
From the Andes to Atlas, round mountain and isle,
Round sea-birds and wrecks, paved with heaven's azure smile.
The wide world of waters is vibrating. Where
Is the ship ? On the verge of the wave where it lay
One tiger is mingled in ghastly affray
With a sea-snake. The foam and the smoke of the battle
Stain the clear air with sunbows ; the jar, and the rattle
Of solid bones crushed by the infinite stress
Of the snake's adamantine voluminousness ;
And the hum of the hot blood that spouts and rains
Where the grip of the tiger has wounded the veins,
Swollen with rage, strength, and effort ; the whirl and the splash
As of some hideous engine whose brazen teeth smash
The thin winds and soft waves into thunder ; the screams
And hissings crawl fast o'er the smooth ocean streams,
Each sound like a centipede. Near this commotion,
A blue shark is hanging within the blue ocean,
The fin-winged tomb of the victor. The other
Is winning his way from the fate of his brother
To his own with the speed of despair. Lo ! a boat
Advances; twelve rowers with the impulse of thought
Urge on the keen keel, the brine foams. At the stern
Three marksmen stand levelling. Hot bullets burn
In the breast of the tiger, which yet bears him on
To his refuge and ruin. One fragment alone,
'Tis dwindling and sinking, 'tis now almost gone,
Of the wreck of the vessel peers out of the sea.
With her left hand she grasps it impetuously,
With her right she sustains her fair infant. Death, Fear,
Love, Beauty, are mixed in the atmosphere;
Which trembles and burns with the fervour of dread
Around her wild eyes, her bright hand, and her head,
Like a meteor of light o'er the waters ! her child
Is yet smiling, and playing, and murmuring; so smiled
The false deep ere the storm. Like a sister and brother
The child and the ocean still smile on each other,
Whilst———

ODES.

ODE TO HEAVEN.

Chorus of Spirits.

First Spirit.

PALACE-ROOF of cloudless nights !
Paradise of golden lights !
  Deep, immeasurable, vast,
Which art now and which wert then !

Of the present and the past,
Of the eternal where and when,
    Presence-chamber, temple, home,
    Ever-canopying dome,
        Of acts and ages yet to come!

Glorious shapes have life in thee,
Earth, and all earth's company;
    Living globes which ever throng
Thy deep chasms and wildernesses;
    And green worlds that glide along;
And swift stars with flashing tresses;
    And icy moons most cold and bright,
    And mighty suns beyond the night,
        Atoms of intensest light.

Even thy name is as a god,
Heaven! for thou art the abode
    Of that power which is the glass
Wherein man his nature sees.
    Generations as they pass
Worship thee with bended knees.
    Their unremaining gods and they
    Like a river roll away:
        Thou remainest such alway.

SECOND SPIRIT.

Thou art but the mind's first chamber,
Round which its young fancies clamber,
    Like weak insects in a cave,
Lighted up by stalactites;
    But the portal of the grave,
Where a world of new delights
    Will make thy best glories seem
    But a dim and noonday gleam
        From the shadow of a dream!

THIRD SPIRIT.

Peace! the abyss is wreathed with scorn
At your presumption, atom-born!
    What is heaven? and what are ye
Who its brief expanse inherit?
    What are suns and spheres which flee
With the instinct of that spirit
    Of which ye are but a part?
    Drops which Nature's mighty heart
        Drives through thinnest veins.   Depart!

What is heaven? a globe of dew,
Filling in the morning new
    Some eyed flower whose young leaves waken
On an unimagined world:
    Constellated suns unshaken,
Orbits measureless, are furled
    In that frail and fading sphere.
    With ten millions gathered there,
        To tremble, gleam, and disappear.

ODE TO THE WEST WIND.*

I.

O, WILD West Wind, thou breath of Autumn's being,
Thou, from whose unseen presence the leaves dead
Are driven, like ghosts from an enchanter fleeing,

Yellow, and black, and pale, and hectic red,
Pestilence-stricken multitudes: O, thou,
Who chariotest to their dark wintry bed

The winged seeds, where they lie cold and low,
Each like a corpse within its grave, until
Thine azure sister of the spring shall blow

Her clarion o'er the dreaming earth, and fill
(Driving sweet buds like flocks to feed in air)
With living hues and odours plain and hill:

Wild Spirit, which art moving everywhere;
Destroyer and preserver; hear, O hear!

II.

Thou on whose stream, 'mid the steep sky's commotion,
Loose clouds like earth's decaying leaves are shed,
Shook from the tangled boughs of Heaven and Ocean,

Angels of rain and lightning: there are spread
On the blue surface of thine airy surge,
Like the bright hair uplifted from the head

Of some fierce Mænad, even from the dim verge
Of the horizon to the zenith's height
The locks of the approaching storm.   Thou dirge

Of the dying year, to which this closing night
Will be the dome of a vast sepulchre,
Vaulted with all thy congregated might

Of vapours, from whose solid atmosphere
Black rain, and fire, and hail will burst; O hear!

III.

Thou who didst waken from his summer dreams
The blue Mediterranean, where he lay,
Lulled by the coil of his crystalline streams,

Beside a pumice isle in Baiæ's bay,
And saw in sleep old palaces and towers
Quivering within the wave's intenser day,

---

* This poem was conceived and chiefly written in a wood that skirts the Arno, near Florence, and on a day when that tempestuous wind, whose temperature is at once mild and animating, was collecting the vapours which pour down the autumnal rains. They began, as I foresaw, at sunset with a violent tempest of hail and rain, attended by that magnificent thunder and lightning peculiar to the Cisalpine regions.

The phenomenon alluded to at the conclusion of the third stanza is well known to naturalists. The vegetation at the bottom of the sea, of rivers, and of lakes, sympathizes with that of the land in the change of seasons, and is consequently influenced by the winds which announce it.

All overgrown with azure moss and flowers
So sweet, the sense faints picturing them ! Thou
For whose path the Atlantic's level powers

Cleave themselves into chasms, while far below
The sea-blooms and the oozy woods which wear
The sapless foliage of the ocean, know

Thy voice, and suddenly grow grey with fear,
And tremble and despoil themselves: O hear !

IV.

If I were a dead leaf thou mightest hear;
If I were a swift cloud to fly with thee;
A wave to pant beneath thy power, and share

The impulse of thy strength, only less free
Than thou, O, uncontrollable ! If even
I were as in my boyhood, and could be

The comrade of thy wanderings over heaven,
As then, when to outstrip thy skyey speed
Scarce seemed a vision; I would ne'er have striven

As thus with thee in prayer in my sore need.
Oh ! lift me as a wave, a leaf, a cloud !
I fall upon the thorns of life ! I bleed !

A heavy weight of hours has chained and bowed
One too like thee: tameless, and swift, and proud.

V.

Make me thy lyre, even as the forest is:
What if my leaves are falling like its own !
The tumult of thy mighty harmonies

Will take from both a deep, autumnal tone,
Sweet though in sadness.   Be thou, spirit fierce,
My spirit ! Be thou me, impetuous one !

Drive my dead thoughts over the universe
Like withered leaves to quicken a new birth !
And, by the incantation of this verse,

Scatter, as from an unextinguished hearth
Ashes and sparks, my words among mankind !
Be through my lips to unawakened earth

The trumpet of a prophecy ! O, wind,
If Winter comes, can Spring be far behind?

AN ODE.

[WRITTEN, OCTOBER, 1819, BEFORE THE SPANIARDS HAD RECOVERED
THEIR LIBERTY].

ARISE, arise, arise !
There is blood on the earth that denies ye bread;
Be your wounds like eyes
To weep for the dead, the dead, the dead.

What other grief were it just to pay?
Your sons, your wives, your brethren, were they;
Who said they were slain on the battle day?

Awaken, awaken, awaken!
The slave and the tyrant are twin-born foes;
Be the cold chains shaken
To the dust where your kindred repose, repose:
Their bones in the grave will start and move,
When they hear the voices of those they love,
Most loud in the holy combat above.

Wave, wave high the banner!
When freedom is riding to conquest by:
Though the slaves that fan her
Be famine and toil, giving sigh for sigh.
And ye who attend her imperial car,
Lift not your hands in the banded war,
But in her defence whose children ye are.

Glory, glory, glory,
To those who have greatly suffered and done!
Never name in story
Was greater than that which ye shall have won,
Conquerors have conquered their foes alone,
Whose revenge, pride, and power they have overthrown:
Ride ye, more victorious, over your own.

Bind, bind every brow
With crownals of violet, ivy, and pine:
Hide the blood-stains now
With hues which sweet nature has made divine:
Green strength, azure hope, and eternity.
But let not the pansy among them be;
Ye were injured, and that means memory.

ODE TO LIBERTY.

" Yet, Freedom, yet thy banner torn but flying,
Streams like a thunder-storm against the wind."—Byron.

I.

A GLORIOUS people vibrated again
The lightning of the nations: Liberty
From heart to heart, from tower to tower, o'er Spain,
Scattering contagious fire into the sky,
Gleamed. My soul spurned the chains of its dismay,
And, in the rapid plumes of song,
Clothed itself, sublime and strong;
As a young eagle soars the morning clouds among,
Hovering in verse o'er its accustomed prey;
Till from its station in the heaven of fame
The Spirit's whirlwind rapt it, and the ray
Of the remotest sphere of living flame
Which paves the void was from behind it flung,
As foam from a ship's swiftness, when there came
A voice out of the deep: I will record the same.

II.

The Sun and the serenest Moon sprang forth:
  The burning stars of the abyss were hurled
Into the depths of heaven. The dædal earth,
  That island in the ocean of the world,
Hung in its cloud of all-sustaining air:
      But this divinest universe
      Was yet a chaos and a curse,
For thou wert not: but power from worst producing worse,
  The spirit of the beasts was kindled there,
    And of the birds, and of the watery forms,
  And there was war among them, and despair
    Within them, raging without truce or terms:
The bosom of their violated nurse
  Groaned, for beasts warred on beasts, and worms on worms,
  And men on men; each heart was as a hell of storms.

III.

Man, the imperial shape, then multiplied
  His generations under the pavilion
Of the Sun's throne: palace and pyramid,
  Temple and prison, to many a swarming million,
Were, as to mountain-wolves their ragged caves.
      This human living multitude
      Was savage, cunning, blind, and rude,
For thou wert not; but o'er the populous solitude,
  Like one fierce cloud over a waste of waves
    Hung tyranny; beneath, sate deified
  The sister-pest, congregator of slaves
    Into the shadow of her pinions wide;
Anarchs and priests who feed on gold and blood,
  Till with the stain their inmost souls are dyed,
  Drove the astonished herds of men from every side.

IV.

The nodding promontories, and blue isles,
  And cloud-like mountains, and dividuous waves
Of Greece, basked glorious in the open smiles
  Of favouring heaven: from their enchanted caves
Prophetic echoes flung dim melody.
      On the unapprehensive wild
      The vine, the corn, the olive mild,
Grew savage yet, to human use unreconciled;
  And, like unfolded flowers beneath the sea,
    Like the man's thought dark in the infant's brain,
  Like aught that is which wraps what is to be,
    Art's deathless dreams lay veiled by many a vein
Of Parian stone ; and yet a speechless child,
  Verse murmured, and Philosophy did strain
  Her lidless eyes for thee: when o'er the Ægean main

V.

Athens arose: a city such as vision
  Builds from the purple crags and silver towers
Of battlemented cloud, as in derision
  Of kingliest masonry: the ocean-floors

Pave it; the evening sky pavilions it;
    Its portals are inhabited
    By thunder-zoned winds, each head
Within its cloudy wings with sunfire garlanded,
    A divine work! Athens diviner yet
    Gleamed with its crest of columns, on the will
Of man, as on a mount of diamond, set;
    For thou wert, and thine all-creative skill
Peopled with forms that mock the eternal dead
    In marble immortality, that hill
    Which was thine earliest throne and latest oracle.

VI.

Within the surface of Time's fleeting river
    Its wrinkled image lies, as then it lay
Immovably unquiet, and for ever
    It trembles, but it cannot pass away!
The voices of thy bards and sages thunder
      With an earth-awakening blast
      Through the caverns of the past;
Religion veils her eyes; Oppression shrinks aghast:
    A winged sound of joy, and love, and wonder,
    Which soars where Expectation never flew,
    Rending the veil of space and time asunder!
    One ocean feeds the clouds, and streams, and dew;
One sun illumines heaven; one spirit vast
    With life and love makes chaos ever new,
    As Athens doth the world with thy delight renew.

VII.

Then Rome was, and from thy deep bosom fairest,
    Like a wolf-cub from a Cadmæan Mænad,*
She drew the milk of greatness, though thy dearest
    From that Elysian food was yet unweaned;
And many a deed of terrible uprightness
      By thy sweet love was sanctified;
      And in thy smile, and by thy side,
Saintly Camillus lived, and firm Atilius died.
    But when tears stained thy robe of vestal whiteness,
    And gold profaned thy capitolian throne,
    Thou didst desert, with spirit-winged lightness,
      The senate of the tyrants: they sunk prone
Slaves of one tyrant: Palatinus sighed
    Faint echoes of Ionian song: that tone
    Thou didst delay to hear, lamenting to disown.

VIII.

From what Hyrcanian glen or frozen hill,
    Or piny promontory of the Arctic main,
Or utmost islet inaccessible
    Didst thou lament the ruin of thy reign,
Teaching the woods and waves, and desert rocks,
      And every Naiad's ice-cold urn,
      To talk in echoes sad and stern,
Of that sublimest love which man had dared unlearn

---

* See the Bacchæ of Euripides.

For neither didst thou watch the wizard flocks
  Of the Scald's dreams, nor haunt the Druid's sleep.
What if the tears rained through thy shattered locks
  Were quickly dried? for thou didst groan, not weep,
When from its sea of death to kill and burn,
  The Galilean serpent forth did creep,
And made thy world an undistinguishable heap.

IX.

A thousand years the Earth cried, Where art thou?
  And then the shadow of thy coming fell
On Saxon Alfred's olive-cinctured brow:
  And many a warrior-peopled citadel,
Like rocks which fire lifts out of the flat deep,
    Arose in sacred Italy,
    Frowning o'er the tempestuous sea
Of kings, and priests, and slaves, in tower-crowned majesty,
  That multitudinous anarchy did sweep,
    And burst around their walls, like idle foam,
Whilst from the human spirit's deepest deep
    Strange melody with love and awe struck dumb
Dissonant arms; and Art, which cannot die,
  With divine wand traced on our earthly home
Fit imagery to pave heaven's everlasting dome.

X.

Thou huntress swifter than the Moon! thou terror
  Of the world's wolves! thou bearer of the quiver,
Whose sunlike shafts pierce tempest-winged Error,
  As light may pierce the clouds when they dissever
In the calm regions of the orient day!
    Luther caught thy wakening glance,
    Like lightning, from his leaden lance
Reflected, it dissolved the visions of the trance
  In which, as in a tomb, the nations lay;
    And England's prophets hailed thee as their queen,
In songs whose music cannot pass away,
    Though it must flow for ever: not unseen
Before the spirit-sighted countenance
  Of Milton didst thou pass, from the sad scene
Beyond whose night he saw, with a dejected mien.

XI.

The eager hours and unreluctant years
  As on a dawn-illumined mountain stood,
Trampling to silence their loud hopes and fears,
  Darkening each other with their multitude,
And cried aloud, Liberty! Indignation
    Answered Pity from her cave;
    Death grew pale within the grave,
And Desolation howled to the destroyer, Save!
  When like heaven's sun girt by the exhalation
    Of its own glorious light, thou didst arise,
Chasing thy foes from nation unto nation
    Like shadows: as if day had cloven the skies
At dreaming midnight o'er the western wave,
  Men started, staggering with a glad surprise,
Under the lightnings of thine unfamiliar eyes.

XII.

Thou heaven of earth ! what spells could pall thee then,
    In ominous eclipse ? a thousand years
Bred from the slime of deep oppression's den,
    Dyed all thy liquid light with blood and tears,
Till thy sweet stars could weep the stain away;
        How like Bacchanals of blood
        Round France, the ghastly vintage, stood
Destruction's sceptred slaves, and Folly's mitred brood !
    When one, like them, but mightier far than they,
        The Anarch of thine own bewildered powers
    Rose : armies mingled in obscure array,
        Like clouds with clouds, darkening the sacred bowers
Of serene heaven. He, by the past pursued,
    Rests with those dead, but unforgotten hours,
    Whose ghosts scare victor kings in their ancestral towers.

XIII.

England yet sleeps: was she not called of old ?
    Spain calls her now, as with its thrilling thunder
Vesuvius wakens Ætna, and the cold
    Snow-crags by its reply are cloven in sunder:
O'er the lit waves every Æolian isle
        From Pithecusa to Pelorus
        Howls, and leaps, and glares in chorus :
They cry, Be dim! ye lamps of heaven suspended o'er us.
    Her chains are threads of gold, she need but smile
        And they dissolve ; but Spain's were links of steel,
Till bit to dust by virtue's keenest file.
        Twins of a single destiny ! appeal
To the eternal years enthroned before us,
    In the dim West, impress us from a seal,
All ye have thought and done ! Time cannot dare conceal.

XIV.

Tomb of Arminius ! render up thy dead,
    Till, like a standard from a watch-tower's staff,
His soul may stream over the tyrant's head;
    Thy victory shall be his epitaph,
Wild Bacchanal of truth's mysterious wine,
        King-deluded Germany,
        His dead spirit lives in thee.
Why do we fear or hope? thou art already free !
    And thou, lost Paradise of this divine
        And glorious world ! thou flowery wilderness !
Thou island of eternity ! thou shrine
        Where desolation clothed with loveliness,
Worships the thing thou wert ! O Italy,
    Gather thy blood into thy heart; repress
   The beasts who make their dens thy sacred palaces

XV.

O, that the free would stamp the impious name
    Of * * * * into the dust ! or write it there,
So that this blot upon the page of fame
    Were as a serpent's path, which the light air

Erases, and the flat sands close behind !
    Ye the oracle have heard:
      Lift the victory-flashing sword,
And cut the snaky knots of this foul gordian word,
    Which weak itself as stubble, yet can bind
      Into a mass, irrefragably firm,
    The axes and the rods which awe mankind;
    The sound has poison in it, 'tis the sperm
Of what makes life foul, cankerous, and abhorred;
    Disdain not thou, at thine appointed term,
    To set thine armed heel on this reluctant worm.

XVI.

O, that the wise from their bright minds would kindle
    Such lamps within the dome of this dim world,
That the pale name of PRIEST might shrink and dwindle
    Into the hell from which it first was hurled,
    A scoff of impious pride from fiends impure;
      Till human thoughts might kneel alone
      Each before the judgment-throne
Of its own aweless soul, or of the power unknown !
    O, that the words which make the thoughts obscure
      From which they spring, as clouds of glimmering dew
    From a white lake blot heaven's blue portraiture,
      Were stript of their thin masks and various hue
And frowns and smiles and splendours not their own,
    Till in the nakedness of false and true
    They stand before their Lord, each to receive its due.

XVII.

He who taught man to vanquish whatsoever
    Can be between the cradle and the grave
Crowned him the King of Life.   O vain endeavour !
    If on his own high will a willing slave,
He has enthroned the oppression and the oppressor.
      What if earth can clothe and feed
      Amplest millions at their need,
And power in thought be as the tree within the seed ?
    O, what if Art, an ardent intercessor,
      Driving on fiery wings to Nature's throne,
    Checks the great mother stooping to caress her,
      And cries: Give me, thy child, dominion
Over all height and depth ? if Life can breed
    New wants, and wealth from those who toil and groan
    Rend of thy gifts and hers a thousand fold for one.

XVIII.

Come Thou, but lead out of the inmost cave
    Of man's deep spirit, as the morning-star
Beckons the Sun from the Eoan wave,
    Wisdom.   I hear the pennons of her car
Self-moving, like cloud charioted by flame;
      Comes she not, and come ye not,
      Rulers of eternal thought,
To judge, with solemn truth, life's ill-apportioned lot ?
    Blind Love, and equal Justice, and the Fame

Of what has been, the Hope of what will be?
O, Liberty! if such could be thy name
   Wert thou disjoined from these, or they from thee:
If thine or theirs were treasures to be bought
   By blood or tears, have not the wise and free
   Wept tears, and blood like tears? The solemn harmony

XIX.

Paused, and the spirit of that mighty singing
   To its abyss was suddenly withdrawn;
Then, as a wild swan, when sublimely winging
   Its path athwart the thunder-smoke of dawn,
Sinks headlong through the aërial golden light
     On the heavy sounding plain
     When the bolt has pierced its brain;
As summer clouds dissolve, unburthened of their rain;
   As a far taper fades with fading night,
     As a brief insect dies with dying day,
   My song, its pinions disarrayed of might,
     Drooped; o'er it closed the echoes far away
Of the great voice which did its flight sustain,
   As waves which lately paved his watery way
   Hiss round a drowner's head in their tempestuous play.

ODE TO NAPLES.*

EPODE I. α.

I STOOD within the city disinterred;†
   And heard the autumnal leaves like light footfalls
Of spirits passing through the streets; and heard
   The mountain's slumberous voice at intervals
     Thrill through those roofless halls;
The oracular thunder penetrating shook
   The listening soul in my suspended blood;
I felt that Earth out of her deep heart spoke—
   I felt, but heard not:—through white columns glowed
     The isle-sustaining Ocean-flood,
A plane of light between two Heavens of azure:
   Around me gleamed many a bright sepulchre
Of whose pure beauty, Time, as if his pleasure
   Were to spare Death, had never made erasure;
     But every living lineament was clear
     As in the sculptor's thought; and there
The wreathes of stony myrtle, ivy and pine,
   Like winter leaves o'ergrown by moulded snow,
   Seemed only not to move and grow
Because the crystal silence of the air
     Weighed on their life, even as the Power divine
     Which then lulled all things, brooded upon mine.

---

* The Author has connected many recollections of his visit to Pompeii and Baiæ with the enthusiasm excited by the intelligence of the proclamation of a Constitutional Government at Naples. This has given a tinge of picturesque and descriptive imagery to the introductory Epodes which depicture these scenes, and some of the majestic feelings permanently connected with the scene of this animating event.—*Author's Note.*

   † Pompeii.

EPODE II. *a.*

Then gentle winds arose
With many a mingled close
Of wild Æolian sound and mountain odour keen;
And where the Baian ocean
Welters with airlike motion
Within, above, around its bowers of starry green,
Moving the sea flowers in those purple caves
Even as the ever stormless atmosphere
Floats o'er the Elysian realm,
It bore me like an Angel, o'er the waves
Of sunlight, whose swift pinnace of dewy air
No storm can overwhelm;
I sailed, where ever flows
Under the calm Serene
A spirit of deep emotion
From the unknown graves
Of the dead kings of Melody.*
Shadowy Aornos darkened o'er the helm
The horizontal ether; heaven stript bare
Its depths over Elysium, where the prow
Made the invisible water white as snow;
From that Typhæan mount, Inarime
There streamed a sunlike vapour, like the standard
Of some ethereal host;
Whilst from all the coast,
Louder and louder, gathering round, there wandered
Over the oracular woods and divine sea
Prophesyings which grew articulate—
They seize me—I must speak them—be they fate!

STROPHE *a.* I.

Naples! thou Heart of men which ever pantest
Naked, beneath the lidless eye of heaven!
Elysian City which to calm enchantest
The mutinous air and sea: they round thee, even
As sleep round Love, are driven!
Metropolis of a ruined Paradise
Long lost, late won, and yet but half regained!
Bright Altar of the bloodless sacrifice,
Which armed Victory offers up unstained
To Love, the flower-enchained!
Thou which wert once, and then didst cease to be,
Now art, and henceforth ever shalt be, free,
If Hope, and Truth, and Justice can avail,
Hail, hail, all hail!

STROPHE *β,* 2.

Thou youngest giant birth
Which from the groaning earth
Leap'st, clothed in armour of impenetrable scale!
Last, of the Intercessors!
Who 'gainst the Crowned Transgressors
Pleadest before God's love! Arrayed in Wisdom's mail,

---

* Homer and Virgil.

Wave thy lightning lance in mirth
Nor let thy high heart fail,
Though from their hundred gates the leagued Oppressors,
With hurried legions move!
Hail, hail, all hail!

ANTISTROPHE α.

What though Cimmerian Anarchs dare blaspheme
Freedom and thee? thy shield is as a mirror
To make their blind slaves see, and with fierce gleam
To turn his hungry sword upon the wearer,
A new Acteon's error
Shall theirs have been—devoured by their own hounds!
Be thou like the imperial Basilisk
Killing thy foe with unapparent wounds!
Gaze on oppression, till at that dread risk
Aghast she pass from the Earth's disk,
Fear not, but gaze—for freemen mightier grow,
And slaves more feeble, gazing on their foe;
If Hope and Truth and Justice may avail,
Thou shalt be great—all hail!

ANTISTROPHE β. 2.

From Freedom's form divine,
From Nature's inmost shrine,
Strip every impious gawd, rend Error veil by veil:
O'er Ruin desolate,
O'er Falsehood's fallen state
Sit thou sublime, unawed; be the Destroyer pale!
And equal laws be thine,
And winged words let sail,
Freighted with truth even from the throne of God:
That wealth, surviving fate,
Be thine.—All hail!

ANTISTROPHE α. γ.

Didst thou not start to hear Spain's thrilling pæan
From land to land re-echoed solemnly,
Till silence became music?   From the Ææan*
To the cold Alps, eternal Italy
Starts to hear thine!   The Sea
Which paves the desert streets of Venice laughs
In light and music; widowed Genoa wan
By moonlight spells ancestral epitaphs,
Murmuring, where is Doria? fair Milan,
Within whose veins long ran
The viper's† palsying venom, lifts her heel
To bruise his head.   The signal and the seal
(If Hope and Truth and Justice can avail)
Art Thou of all these hopes.—O hail!

ANTISTROPHE β. γ.

Florence! beneath the sun,
Of cities fairest one,

---

* Ææa, the island of Circe.
† The viper was the armorial device of the Visconti, tyrants of Milan.

Blushes within her bower for Freedom's expectation:
    From eyes of quenchless hope
     Rome tears the priestly cope,
As ruling once by power, so now by admiration,
     An athlete strip to run
     From a remoter station
For the high prize lost on Philippi's shore:—
    As then Hope, Truth, and Justice did avail,
    So now may Fraud and Wrong!   O hail!

EPODE I. β.

Hear ye the march as of the Earth-born Forms
    Arrayed against the everliving Gods?
The crash and darkness of a thousand storms
    Bursting their inaccessible abodes
     Of crags and thunder-clouds?
See ye the banners blazoned to the day,
    Inwrought with emblems of barbaric pride?
Dissonant threats kill Silence far away,
    The serene Heaven which wraps our Eden wide
     With iron light is dyed,
The Anarchs of the North lead forth their legions
    Like Chaos o'er creation, uncreating;
An hundred tribes nourished on strange religions
    And lawless slaveries,—down the aërial regions
     Of the white Alps, desolating,
     Famished wolves that bide no waiting,
Blotting the glowing footsteps of old glory,
Trampling our columned cities into dust,
     Their dull and savage lust
On Beauty's corse to sickness satiating—
They come!   The fields they tread look black and hoary
With fire—from their red feet the streams run gory!

EPODE II. β.

    Great Spirit, deepest Love!
    Which rulest and dost move
All things which live and are, within the Italian shore;
    Who spreadest heaven around it,
    Whose woods, rocks, waves, surround it;
Who sittest in thy star, o'er Ocean's western floor,
    Spirit of beauty! at whose soft command
    The sunbeams and the showers distil its foison
     From the Earth's bosom chill;
O bid those beams be each a blinding brand
Of lightning! bid those showers be dews of poison!
     Bid the Earth's plenty kill!
     Bid thy bright Heaven above,
     Whilst light and darkness bound it,
     Be their tomb who planned
     To make it ours and thine!
Or, with thine harmonizing ardours fill
And raise thy sons, as o'er the prone horizon
Thy lamp feeds every twilight wave with fire
Be man's high hope and unextinct desire,
The instrument to work thy will divine!
Then clouds from sunbeams, antelopes from leopards,

And frowns and fears from Thee,
  Would not more swiftly flee
Than Celtic wolves from the Ausonian shepherds.
  Whatever, Spirit, from thy starry shrine
  Thou yieldest or withholdest, Oh let be
  This city of thy worship ever free !

September, 1820.

PRINCE ATHANASE:

A FRAGMENT.

THERE was a youth, who, as with toil and travel,
Had grown quite weak and grey before his time;
Nor any could the restless griefs unravel

Which burned within him, withering up his prime
And goading him, like fiends, from land to land.
Not his the load of any secret crime,

For nought of ill his heart could understand,
But pity and wild sorrow for the same;—
Not his the thirst for glory or command,

Baffled with blast of hope-consuming shame;
Nor evil joys which fire the vulgar breast
And quench in speedy smoke its feeble flame,

Had left within his soul their dark unrest:
Nor what religion fables of the grave
Feared he,—Philosophy's accepted guest.

For none than he a purer heart could have,
Or that loved good more for itself alone;
Of nought in heaven or earth was he the slave.

What sorrow deep, and shadowy, and unknown,
Sent him, a hopeless wanderer, through mankind ;
If with a human sadness he did groan,

He had a gentle yet aspiring mind;
Just, innocent, with varied learning fed,
And such a glorious consolation find

In others' joy, when all their own is dead:
He loved, and laboured for his kind in grief,
And yet, unlike all others, it is said,

That from such toil he never found relief;
Although a child of fortune and of power,
Of an ancestral name the orphan chief.

His soul had wedded wisdom, and her dower
Is love and justice, clothed in which he sate
Apart from men, as in a lonely tower,

Pitying the tumult of their dark estate—
Yet even in youth did he not e'er abuse
The strength of wealth or thought, to consecrate

H H

Those false opinions which the harsh rich use
To blind the world they famish for their pride;
Nor did he hold from any man his dues,

But like a steward in honest dealings tried,
With those who toiled and wept, the poor and wise
His riches and his cares he did divide.

Fearless he was, and scorning all disguise,
What he dared do or think, though men might start,
He spoke with mild, yet unaverted eyes ;

Liberal he was of soul, and frank of heart,
And to his many friends—all loved him well—
Whate'er he knew or felt he would impart,

If words he found those inmost thoughts to tell ;
If not, he smiled or wept ; and his weak foes
He neither spurned nor hated, though with fell

And mortal hate their thousand voices rose,
They passed like aimless arrows from his ear—
Nor did his heart or mind its portal close

To those, or them, or any whom life's sphere
May comprehend within its wide array.
What sadness made that vernal spirit sere?

He knew not.   Though his life, day after day,
Was failing like an unreplenished stream,
Though in his eyes a cloud and burthen lay,

Through which his soul, like Vesper's serene beam
Piercing the chasms of ever-rising clouds,
Shone, softly burning ; though his lips did seem

Like reeds which quiver in impetuous floods ;
And through his sleep, and o'er each waking hour,
Thoughts after thoughts, unresting multitudes,

Were driven within him, by some secret power,
Which bade them blaze, and live, and roll afar,
Like lights and sounds, from haunted tower to tower

O'er castled mountains borne, when tempest's war
Is levied by the night-contending winds,
And the pale dalesman watch with eager ear ;—

Though such were in his spirit, as the fiends
Which wake and feed on everliving woe,—
What was this grief, which ne'er in other minds

A mirror found,—he knew not—none could know ;
But on whoe'er might question him he turned
The light of his frank eyes, as if to show,

He knew not of the grief within that burned,
But asked forbearance with a mournful look ;
Or spoke in words from which none ever learned

The cause of his disquietude ; or shook
With spasms of silent passion ; or turned pale :
So that his friends soon rarely undertook

To stir his secret pain without avail ;—
For all who knew and loved him then perceived
That there was drawn an adamantine veil

Between his heart and mind,—both unrelieved
Wrought in his brain and bosom separate strife.
Some said that he was mad, others believed

That memories of an antenatal life
Made this, where now he dwelt, a penal hell ;
And others said that such mysterious grief

From God's displeasure, like a darkness, fell
On souls like his which owned no higher law
Than love ; love calm, steadfast, invincible

By mortal fear or supernatural awe ;
And others,—" 'Tis the shadow of a dream
Which the veiled eye of memory never saw

" But through the soul's abyss, like some dark stream
Through shattered mines and caverns underground
Rolls, shaking its foundations ; and no beam

" Of joy may rise, but it is quenched and drowned
In the dim whirlpools of this dream obscure,
Soon its exhausted waters will have found

" A lair of rest beneath thy spirit pure,
O Athanase !—in one so good and great,
Evil or tumult cannot long endure."

So spake they : idly of another's state
Babbling vain words and fond philosophy ;
This was their consolation ; such debate

Men held with one another ; nor did he
Like one who labours with a human woe
Decline this talk ; as if its theme might be

Another, not himself, he to and fro
Questioned and canvassed it with subtlest wit,
And none but those who loved him best could know

That which he knew not, how it galled and bit
His weary mind, this converse vain and cold ;
For like an eyeless nightmare grief did sit

Upon his being ; a snake which fold by fold
Pressed out the life of life, a clinging fiend
Which clenched him if he stirred with deadlier hold ;—
And so his grief remained—let it remain—untold.*

December, 1817.

* The Author was pursuing a fuller development of the ideal character of Athanase,
when it struck him that in an attempt at extreme refinement and analysis, his conceptions
might be betrayed into the assuming a morbid character. The reader will judge whether
he is a loser or gainer by this difference.—*Author's Note.*

PART II.

FRAGMENT I.

PRINCE Athanase had one beloved friend,
An old, old man, with hair of silver white,
And lips where heavenly smiles would hang and blend

With his wise words; and eyes whose arrowy light
Shone like the reflex of a thousand minds.
He was the last whom superstition's blight

Had spared in Greece—the blight that cramps and blinds,—
And in his olive bower at Œnoe
Had sate from earliest youth.   Like one who finds

A fertile island in the barren sea,
One mariner who has survived his mates
Many a drear month in a great ship—so he

With soul-sustaining songs, and sweet debates
Of ancient lore, there fed his lonely being:—
"The mind becomes that which it contemplates,"—

And thus Zonoras, by for ever seeing
Their bright creations, grew like wisest men;
And when he heard the crash of nations fleeing

A bloodier power than ruled thy ruins then,
O sacred Hellas ! many weary years
He wandered, till the path of Laian's glen

Was grass-grown—and the unremembered tears
Were dry in Laian for their honoured chief,
Who fell in Byzant, pierced by Moslem spears:—

And as the lady looked with faithful grief
From her high lattice o'er the rugged path,
Where she once saw that horseman toil, with brief

And blighting hope, who with the news of death
Struck body and soul as with a mortal blight,
She saw beneath the chestnuts, far beneath,

An old man toiling up, a weary wight;
And soon within her hospitable hall
She saw his white hairs glittering in the light

Of the wood fire, and round his shoulders fall ;
And his wan visage and his withered mien
Yet calm and [   ] and majestical.

And Athanase, her child, who must have been
Then three years old, sate opposite and gazed.

FRAGMENT II.

Such was Zonoras; and as daylight finds
An amaranth glittering on the path of frost,
When autumn nights have nipt all weaker kinds,

Thus had his age, dark, cold, and tempest-tost,
Shone truth upon Zonoras; and he filled
From fountains pure, nigh overgrown and lost,

The spirit of Prince Athanase, a child,
With soul-sustaining songs of ancient lore
And philosophic wisdom, clear and mild.

And sweet and subtle talk they evermore,
The pupil and master shared ; until,
Sharing the undiminishable store,

The youth, as shadows on a grassy hill
Outrun the winds that chase them, soon outran
His teacher, and did teach with native skill

Strange truths and new to that experienced man;
Still they were friends, as few have ever been
Who mark the extremes of life's discordant span.

And in the caverns of the forest green,
Or by the rocks of echoing ocean hoar,
Zonoras and Prince Athanase were seen

By summer woodmen; and when winter's roar
Sounded o'er earth and sea its blast of war,
The Balearic fisher, driven from shore,

Hanging upon the peaked wave afar,
Then saw their lamp from Laian's turret gleam,
Piercing the stormy darkness like a star,

Which pours beyond the sea one steadfast beam,
Whilst all the constellations of the sky
Seemed wrecked.   They did but seem—

For, lo ! the wintry clouds are all gone by,
And bright Arcturus through yon pines is glowing,
And far o'er southern waves, immovably

Belted Orion hangs—warm light is flowing
From the young moon into the sunset's chasm.—
" O, summer night ! with power divine, bestowing

" On thine own bird the sweet enthusiasm
Which overflows in notes of liquid gladness,
Filling the sky like light !   How many a spasm

" Of fevered brains, oppressed with grief and madness,
Were lulled by thee, delightful nightingale !
And these soft waves, murmuring a gentle sadness,

" And the far sighings of yon piny dale
Made vocal by some wind, we feel not here,—
I bear alone what nothing may avail

" To lighten—a strange load !"—No human ear
Heard this lament; but o'er the visage wan
Of Athanase, a ruffling atmosphere

Of dark emotion, a swift shadow ran,
Like wind upon some forest-bosomed lake,
Glassy and dark.—And that divine old man

Beheld his mystic friend's whole being shake,
Even where its inmost depths were gloomiest—
And with a calm and measured voice he spake,

And with a soft and equal pressure, prest
That cold lean hand:—"Dost thou remember yet
When the curved moon then lingering in the west

"Paused in yon waves her mighty horns to wet,
How in those beams we walked, half resting on the sea?
'Tis just one year—sure thou dost not forget

"Then Plato's words of light in thee and me
Lingered like moonlight in the moonless east,
For we had just then read—thy memory

"Is faithful now—the story of the feast;
And Agathon and Diotima seemed
From death and [   ] released."

FRAGMENT III.

'Twas at the season when the Earth upsprings
From slumber, as a sphered angel's child,
Shadowing its eyes with green and golden wings,

Stands up before its mother bright and mild,
Of whose soft voice the air expectant seems—
So stood before the sun, which shone and smiled

To see it rise thus joyous from its dreams,
The fresh and radiant Earth.   The hoary grove
Waxed green—and flowers burst forth like starry beams;—

The grass in the warm sun did start and move,
And sea-buds burst under the waves serene:—
How many a one, though none be near to love,

Loves then the shade of his own soul, half seen
In any mirror—or the spring's young minions,
The winged leaves amid the copses green;—

How many a spirit then puts on the pinions
Of fancy, and outstrips the lagging blast,
And his own steps—and over wide dominions

Sweeps in his dream-drawn chariot, far and fast,
More fleet than storms—the wide world shrinks below,
When winter and despondency are past.

'Twas at this season that Prince Athanase
Past the white Alps—those eagle-baffling mountains
Slept in their shrouds of snow;—beside the ways

The waterfalls were voiceless—for their fountains
Were changed to mines of sunless crystal now,
Or by the curdling winds—like brazen wings

Which clanged alone the mountain's marble brow,
Warped into adamantine fretwork, hung
And filled with frozen light the chasm below.

FRAGMENT IV.

Thou art the wine whose drunkenness is all
We can desire, O Love! and happy souls,
Ere from thy vine the leaves of autumn fall,

Catch thee, and feed from their o'erflowing bowls
Thousands who thirst for thy ambrosial dew;—
Thou art the radiance which where ocean rolls

Invests it; and when heavens are blue
Thou fillest them; and when the earth is fair
The shadow of thy moving wings imbue

Its deserts and its mountains, till they wear
Beauty like some bright robe;—thou ever soarest
Among the towers of men, and as soft air

In spring, which moves the unawakened forest,
Clothing with leaves its branches bare and bleak,
Thou floatest among men: and aye implorest

That which from thee they should implore:—the weak
Alone kneel to thee, offering up the hearts
The strong have broken—yet where shall any seek

A garment whom thou clothest not?

Marlow, 1817.

———◆———

TO A SKYLARK.

HAIL to thee, blithe spirit!
    Bird thou never wert,
That from heaven, or near it,
    Pourest thy full heart
In profuse strains of unpremeditated
    art.

Higher still and higher
    From the earth thou springest
Like a cloud of fire;
    The blue deep thou wingest,
And singing still dost soar, and soaring
    ever singest.

In the golden lightning
    Of the sunken sun,
O'er which clouds are brightning,
    Thou dost float and run;
Like an unbodied joy whose race is
    just begun.

The pale purple even
    Melts around thy flight;
Like a star of heaven,
    In the broad daylight
Thou art unseen, but yet I hear thy
    shrill delight,

Keen as are the arrows
    Of that silver sphere,
Whose intense lamp narrows
    In the white dawn clear,
Until we hardly see, we feel that it is
    there.

All the earth and air
    With thy voice is loud,
As, when night is bare,
    From one lonely cloud
The moon rains out her beams, and
    heaven is overflowed.

What thou art we know not;
    What is most like thee?
From rainbow clouds there flow not
    Drops so bright to see,
As from thy presence showers a rain of
    melody.

Like a poet hidden
    In the light of thought,
Singing hymns unbidden,
    Till the world is wrought
To sympathy with hopes and fears it
    heeded not:

Like a high-born maiden
    In a palace tower,
Soothing her love-laden
    Soul in secret hour
With music sweet as love, which over-
    flows her bower:

Like a glow-worm golden
    In a dell of dew,
Scattering unbeholden
    Its aërial hue
Among the flowers and grass, which
    screen it from the view:

Like a rose embowered
    In its own green leaves,
By warm winds deflowered,
    Till the scent it gives
Makes faint with two much sweet these
    heavy-winged thieves:

Sound of vernal showers
    On the twinkling grass,
Rain-awakened flowers,
    All that ever was
Joyous, and clear, and fresh, thy music
    doth surpass:

Teach us, sprite or bird,
    What sweet thoughts are thine:
I have never heard,
    Praise of love or wine
That panted forth a flood of rapture
    so divine.

Chorus Hymenæal,
    Or triumphal chaunt,
Matched with thine would be all

But an empty vaunt,
A thing wherein we feel there is some
    hidden want.

What objects are the fountains
    Of thy happy strain?
What fields, or waves, or mountains?
    What shapes of sky or plain?
What love of thine own kind? what
    ignorance of pain?

With thy clear keen joyance
    Languor cannot be:
Shadow of annoyance
    Never came near thee:
Thou lovest; but ne'er knew love's sad
    satiety.

Waking or asleep,
    Thou of death must deem
Things more true and deep
    Than we mortals dream,
Or how could thy notes flow in such a
    crystal stream?

We look before and after,
    And pine for what is not:
Our sincerest laughter
    With some pain is fraught;
Our sweetest songs are those that tell
    of saddest thought.

Yet if we could scorn
    Hate, and pride, and fear;
If we were things born
    Not to shed a tear,
I know not how thy joy we ever should
    come near.

Better than all measures
    Of delightful sound,
Better than all treasures
    That in books are found,
Thy skill to poet were, thou scorner
    of the ground!

Teach me half the gladness
    That thy brain must know,
Such harmonious madness
    From my lips would flow,
The world should listen then, as I am
    listening now.

LETTER TO MARIA GISBORNE.

Leghorn, July 1, 1820.

THE spider spreads her webs, whether she be
In poet's tower, cellar, or barn, or tree;
The silkworm in the dark green mulberry leaves
His winding sheet and cradle ever weaves;
So I, a thing whom moralists call worm,
Sit spinning still round this decaying form,
From the fine threads of rare and subtle thought—
No net of words in garish colours wrought
To catch the idle buzzers of the day—
But a soft cell, where when that fades away,
Memory may clothe in wings my living name
And feed it with the asphodels of fame,
Which in those hearts which most remember me
Grow, making love an immortality.

Whoever should behold me now, I wist,
Would think I were a mighty mechanist,
Bent with sublime Archimedean art
To breathe a soul into the iron heart
Of some machine portentous, or strange gin,
Which by the force of figured spells might win
Its way over the sea, and sport therein;
For round the walls are hung dread engines, such
As Vulcan never wrought for Jove to clutch
Ixion or the Titan:—or the quick
Wit of that man of God, St. Dominic,
To convince Atheist, Turk, or Heretic;
Or those in philosophic councils met,
Who thought to pay some interest for the debt
They owed   *   *   *   *
By giving a faint foretaste of damnation
To Shakspeare, Sidney, Spenser and the rest
Who made our land an island of the blest,
When lamp-like Spain, who now relumes her fire
On Freedom's hearth, grew dim with Empire:—
With thumbscrews, wheels, with tooth and spike and jag,
Which fishes found under the utmost crag
Of Cornwall and the storm-encompassed isles,
Where to the sky the rude sea seldom smiles
Unless in treacherous wrath, as on the morn
When the exulting elements in scorn
Satiated with destroyed destruction, lay
Sleeping in beauty on their mangled prey,
As panthers sleep:—and other strange and dread
Magical forms the brick floor overspread——
Proteus transformed to metal did not make
More figures, or more strange; nor did he take
Such shapes of unintelligible brass,
Or heap himself in such a horrid mass
Of tin and iron not to be understood,
And forms of unimaginable wood,
To puzzle Tubal Cain and all his brood:

Great screws, and cones, and wheels, and grooved blocks,
The elements of what will stand the shocks
Of wave and wind and time.—Upon the table
More knacks and quips there be than I am able
To catalogize in this verse of mine:—
A pretty bowl of wood—not full of wine,
But quicksilver; that dew which the gnomes drink
When at their subterranean toil they swink,
Pledging the demons of the earthquake, who
Reply to them in lava-cry, halloo!
And call out to the cities o'er their head,—
Roofs, towns and shrines,—the dying and the dead
Crash through the chinks of earth—and then all quaff
Another rouse, and hold their sides and laugh.
This quicksilver no gnome has drunk—within
The walnut bowl it lies, veined and thin,
In colour like the wake of light that stains
The Tuscan deep, when from the moist moon rains
The inmost shower of its white fire—the breeze
Is still—blue heaven smiles over the pale seas.
And in this bowl of quicksilver—for I
Yield to the impulse of an infancy
Outlasting manhood—I have made to float
A rude idealism of a paper boat—
A hollow screw with cogs—Henry will know
The thing I mean and laugh at me,—if so
He fears not I should do more mischief.—Next
Lie bills and calculations much perplext,
With steam-boats, frigates, and machinery quaint
Traced over them in blue and yellow paint.
Then comes a range of mathematical
Instruments, for plans nautical and statical,
A heap of rosin, a green broken glass
With ink in it;—a china cup that was
What it will never be again, I think,
A thing from which sweet lips were wont to drink
The liquor doctors rail at—and which I
Will quaff in spite of them—and when we die
We'll toss up who died first of drinking tea,
And cry out,—heads or tails? where'er we be.
Near that a dusty paint box, some old hooks,
A half-burnt match, an ivory block, three books,
Where conic sections, spherics, logarithms,
To great Lap lace, from Saunderson and Sims
Lie heaped in their harmonious disarray
Of figures,—disentangle them who may.
Baron de Tott's memoirs beside them lie,
And some odd volumes of old chemistry.
Near them a most inexplicable thing,
With least in the middle—I'm conjecturing
How to make Henry understand;—but—no,
I'll leave, as Spenser says, with many mo,
This secret in the pregnant womb of time,
Too vast a matter for so weak a rhyme.

And here like some weird Archimage sit I,
Plotting dark spells, and devilish enginery,

The self-impelling steam-wheels of the mind
Which pump up oaths from clergymen, and grind
The gentle spirit of our meek reviews
Into a powdery foam of salt abuse,
Ruffling the ocean of their self-content;—
I sit—and smile or sigh as is my bent,
But not for them—Libeccio rushes round
With an inconstant and an idle sound,
I heed him more than them—the thunder-smoke
Is gathering on the mountains, like a cloak
Folded athwart their shoulders broad and bare;
The ripe corn under the undulating air
Undulates like an ocean;—and the vines
Are trembling wide in all their trellised lines—
The murmur of the awakening sea doth fill
The empty pauses of the blast;—the hill
Looks hoary through the white electric rain,
And from the glens beyond, in sullen strain
The interrupted thunder howls; above
One chasm of heaven smiles, like the age of love
On the unquiet world;—while such things are,
How could one worth your friendship heed the war
Of worms? The shriek of the world's carrion jays,
Their censure, or their wonder, or their praise?

You are not here! the quaint witch Memory sees
In vacant chairs, your absent images,
And points where once you sat, and now should be
But are not.—I demand if ever we
Shall meet as then we met;—and she replies,
Veiling in awe her second-sighted eyes:
" I know the past alone—but summon home
My sister Hope, she speaks of all to come."
But I, an old diviner, who know well
Every false verse of that sweet oracle,
Turned to the sad enchantress once again,
And sought a respite from my gentle pain,
In acting every passage o'er and o'er
Of our communion.—How on the sea shore
We watched the ocean and the sky together,
Under the roof of blue Italian weather;
How I ran home through last year's thunder-storm,
And felt the transverse lightning linger warm
Upon my cheek:—and how we often made
Treats for each other, where good will outweighed
The frugal luxury of our country cheer,
As it well might, were it less firm and clear
Than ours must ever be;—and how we spun
A shroud of talk to hide us from the sun
Of this familiar life, which seems to be
But is not,—or is but quaint mockery
Of all we would believe; or sadly blame
The jarring and inexplicable frame
Of this wrong world:—and then anatomize
The purposes and thoughts of men whose eyes
Were closed in distant years;—or widely guess
The issue of the earth's great business,

When we shall be as we no longer are;
Like babbling gossips safe, who hear the war
Of winds, and sigh, but tremble not; or how
You listened to some interrupted flow
Of visionary rhyme;—in joy and pain
Struck from the inmost fountains of my brain,
With little skill perhaps;—or how we sought
Those deepest wells of passion or of thought
Wrought by wise poets in the waste of years.
Staining the sacred waters with our tears;
Quenching a thirst ever to be renewed !
Or how I, wisest lady ! then indued
The language of a land which now is free,
And winged with thoughts of truth and majesty,
Flits round the tyrant's sceptre like a cloud,
And bursts the peopled prisons, and cries aloud,
" My name is Legion !"—that majestic tongue
Which Calderon over the desert flung
Of ages and of nations; and which found
An echo in our hearts, and with the sound
Startled oblivion;—thou wert then to me
As is a nurse—when inarticulately
A child would talk as its grown parents do.
If living winds the rapid clouds pursue,
If hawks chase doves through the aërial way,
Huntsmen the innocent deer, and beasts their prey,
Why should not we rouse with the spirit's blast
Out of the forest of the pathless past
These recollected pleasures ?

                        You are now
In London, that great sea, whose ebb and flow
At once is deaf and loud, and on the shore
Vomits its wrecks, and still howls on for more.
Yet in its depth what treasures !   You will see

    *   *   *   *   *

You will see Coleridge; he who sits obscure
In the exceeding lustre and the pure
Intense irradiation of a mind,
Which, with its own internal lustre blind,
Flags wearily through darkness and despair—
A cloud-encircled meteor of the air,
A hooded eagle among blinking owls.
You will see Hunt; one of those happy souls
Which are the salt of the earth, and without whom
This world would smell like what it is—a tomb;
Who is, what others seem;—his room no doubt
Is still adorned by many a cast from Shout,
With graceful flowers, tastefully placed about;
And coronals of bay from ribbons hung,
And brighter wreaths in neat disorder flung,
The gifts of the most learned among some dozens
Of female friends, sisters-in-law, and cousins.
And there is he with his eternal puns,
Which beat the dullest brain for smiles, like duns
Thundering for money at a poet's door;
Alas ! it is no use to say, " I'm poor !"

Or oft in graver mood, when he will look
Things wiser than were ever said in book,
Except in Shakspeare's wisest tenderness.
You will see Hogg, and I cannot express
His virtues, though I know that they are great,
Because he locks, then barricades, the gate
Within which they inhabit;—of his wit
And wisdom, you'll cry out when you are bit.
He is a pearl within an oyster shell,
One of the richest of the deep. And there
Is English Peacock with his mountain Fair
Turned into a Flamingo,—that shy bird
That gleams i' the Indian air. Have you not heard
When a man marries, dies, or turns Hindoo,
His best friends hear no more of him? but you
Will see him and will like him too, I hope,
With the milk-white Snowdonian Antelope
Matched with this cameleopard; his fine wit
Makes such a wound, the knife is lost in it;
A strain too learned for a shallow age,
Too wise for selfish bigots;—let his page
Which charms the chosen spirits of the age,
Fold itself up for a serener clime
Of years to come, and find its recompense
In that just expectation. Wit and sense,
Virtue and human knowledge, all that might
Make this dull world a business of delight,
Are all combined in Horace Smith.—And these,
With some exceptions, which I need not tease
Your patience by descanting on, are all
You and I know in London.

                 I recal
My thoughts and bid you look upon the night.
As water does a sponge, so the moonlight
Fills the void, hollow, universal air.
What see you?—Unpavilioned heaven is fair,
Whether the moon into her chamber gone,
Leaves midnight to the golden stars, or wan
Climbs with diminished beams the azure steep;
Or whether clouds sail o'er the inverse deep,
Piloted by the many wandering blast,
And the rare stars rush through them, dim and fast.
All this is beautiful in every land.
But what see you beside? A shabby stand
Of hackney-coaches—a brick house or wall,
Fencing some lonely court, white with the scrawl
Of our unhappy politics;—or worse—
A wretched woman reeling by, whose curse
Mixed with the watchman's, partner of her trade,
You must accept in place of serenade—

I see a chaos of green leaves and fruit
Built round dark caverns, even to the root
Of the living stems who feed them; in whose bowers
There sleep in their dark dew the folded flowers;
Beyond, the surface of the unsickled corn
Trembles not in the slumbering air, and borne

In circles quaint, and ever-changing dance,
Like winged stars the fireflies flash and glance
Pale in the open moonshine ; but each one
Under the dark trees seems a little sun,
A meteor tamed ; a fixed star gone astray
From the silver regions of the milky way.
Afar the Contadino's song is heard,
Rude, but made sweet by distance ;—and a bird
Which cannot be a nightingale, and yet
I know none else that sings so sweet as it
At this late hour ;—and then all is still :—
Now Italy or London, which you will !

Next winter you must pass with me ; I'll have
My house by that time turned into a grave
Of dead despondence and low-thoughted care,
And all the dreams which our tormentors are.
Oh that Hunt, Hogg, Peacock, and Smith were there,
With everything belonging to them fair !—
We will have books ; Spanish, Italian, Greek,

*   *   *   *   *   *   *

*   *   *   *   *   *   *

Though we eat little flesh and drink no wine,
Yet let's be merry : we'll have tea and toast ;
Custards for supper, and an endless host
Of syllabubs and jellies and mince-pies,
And other such ladylike luxuries,—
Feasting on which we will philosophize.
And we'll have fires out of the Grand Duke's wood,
To thaw the six weeks' winter in our blood.
And then we'll talk ;—what shall we talk about ?
Oh ! there are themes enough for many a bout
Of thought-entangled descant ;—as to nerves
With cones and parallelograms and curves,
I've sworn to strangle them if once they dare
To bother me,—when you are with me there.
And they shall never more sip laudanum
From Helicon or Himeros ;*—we'll come
And in despite of * * * and of the devil,
Will make our friendly philosophic revel
Outlast the leafless time ;—till buds and flowers
Warn the obscure, inevitable hours
Sweet meeting by sad parting to renew ;—
" To-morrow to fresh woods and pastures new."

THE TRIUMPH OF LIFE.

SWIFT as a spirit hastening to his task
Of glory and of good, the Sun sprang forth
Rejoicing in his splendour, and the mask

Of darkness fell from the awakened Earth—
The smokeless altars of the mountain-snows
Flamed above crimson clouds, and at the birth

---

* Ἵμερος, from which the river Himera was named, is, with some slight shade of difference, a synonyme of Love.

Of light, the Ocean's orison arose,
To which the birds tempered their matin lay.
All flowers in field or forest which unclose

Their trembling eyelids to the kiss of day,
Swinging their censers in the element,
With orient incense lit by the new ray

Burned slow and inconsumably, and sent
Their odorous sighs up to the smiling air ;
And, in succession due, did continent,

Isle, ocean, and all things that in them wear
The form and character of mortal mould,
Rise as the sun their father rose, to bear

Their portion of the toil, which he of old
Took as his own and then imposed on them :
But I, whom thoughts which must remain untold

Had kept as wakeful as the stars that gem
The cone of night, now they were laid asleep
Stretched my faint limbs beneath the hoary stem

Which an old chestnut flung athwart the steep
Of a green Apennine : before me fled
The night ; behind me rose the day ; the deep

Was at my feet, and Heaven above my head,
When a strange trance over my fancy grew
Which was not slumber, for the shade it spread

Was so transparent, that the scene came through
As clear as when a veil of light is drawn
O'er evening hills they glimmer ; and I knew

That I had felt the freshness of that dawn,
Bathed in the same cold dew my brow and hair,
And sate as thus upon that slope of lawn

Under the selfsame bough, and heard as there
The birds, the fountains and the ocean hold
Sweet talk in music through the enamoured air,
And then a vision on my brain was rolled.

———

As in that trance of wondrous thought I lay,
This was the tenour of my waking dream :—
Methought I sate beside a public way

Thick strewn with summer dust, and a great stream
Of people there was hurrying to and fro,
Numerous as gnats upon the evening gleam,

All hastening onward, yet none seemed to know
Whither he went, or whence he came, or why
He made one of the multitude, and so

Was borne amid the crowd, as through the sky
One of the million leaves of summer's bier;
Old age and youth, manhood and infancy

Mixed in one mighty torrent did appear,
Some flying from the thing they feared, and some
Seeking the object of another's fear;

And others as with steps towards the tomb,
Pored on the trodden worms that crawled beneath,
And others mournfully within the gloom

Of their own shadow walked and called it death;
And some fled from it as it were a ghost,
Half fainting in the affliction of vain breath:

But more with motions, which each other crost,
Pursued or spurned the shadows the clouds threw,
Or birds within the noon-day ether lost,

Upon that path where flowers never grew,
And weary with vain toil and faint for thirst,
Heard not the fountains, whose melodious dew

Out of their mossy cells for ever burst;
Nor felt the breeze which from the forest told
Of grassy paths and wood, lawn-interspersed,

With over-arching elms and caverns cold,
And violet banks where sweet dreams brood, but they
Pursued their serious folly as of old.

And as I gazed, methought that in the way
The throng grew wilder, as the woods of June
When the south wind shakes the extinguished day,

And a cold glare, intenser than the noon,
But icy cold, obscured with [blinding] light
The sun, as he the stars.   Like the young moon

When on the sunlit limits of the night
Her white shell trembles amid crimson air,
And whilst the sleeping tempest gathers might,

Doth, as the herald of its coming, bear
The ghost of its dead mother, whose dim frown
Bends in dark ether from her infant's chair,

So came a chariot on the silent storm
Of its own rushing splendour, and a Shape
So sate within, as one whom years deform,

Beneath a dusky hood and double cape,
Crouching within the shadow of a tomb,
And o'er what seemed the head a cloud-like crape

Was bent, a dun and faint ethereal gloom
Tempering the light upon the chariot beam;
A Janus-visaged shadow did assume

The guidance of that wonder-winged team;
The shapes which drew it in thick lightnings
Were lost;—I heard alone on the air's soft stream

The music of their ever-moving wings.
All the four faces of that charioteer
Had their eyes banded; little profit brings

Speed in the van and blindness in the rear,
Nor then avail the beams that quench the sun
Or that with banded eyes could pierce the sphere

Of all that is, has been or will be done;
So ill was the car guided—but it past
With solemn speed majestically on.

The crowd gave way, and I rose aghast,
Or seemed to rise, so mighty was the trance,
And saw, like clouds upon the thunders blast,

The million with fierce song and maniac dance
Raging around—such seemed the jubilee
As when to meet some conqueror's advance

Imperial Rome poured forth her living sea
From senate house, and forum, and theatre,
When [   ] upon the free

Had bound a yoke, which soon they stooped to bear.
Nor wanted here the just similitude
Of a triumphal pageant, for where'er

The chariot rolled, a captive multitude
Was driven;—all those who had grown old in power
Or misery,—all who had their age subdued

By action or by suffering, and whose hour
Was drained to its last sand in weal or woe,
So that the trunk survived both fruit and flower;

All those whose fame or infamy must grow
Till the great winter lay the form and name
Of this green earth with them for ever low;—

All but the sacred few who could not tame
Their spirits to the conquerors—but as soon
As they had touched the world with living flame,

Fled back like eagles to their native noon,
Or those who put aside the diadem
Of earthly thrones or gems [   ]

Were there, of Athens or Jerusalem,
Were neither mid the mighty captives seen,
Nor mid the ribald crowd that followed them,

Nor those who went before fierce and obscene.
The wild dance maddens in the van, and those
Who lead it—fleet as shadows on the green,

Outspeed the chariot, and without repose
Mix with each other in tempestuous measure
To savage music, wilder as it grows,

They, tortured by their agonizing pleasure,
Convulsed and on the rapid whirlwinds spun
Of that fierce spirit, whose unholy leisure

Was soothed by mischief since the world begun,
Throw back their heads and loose their streaming hair;
And in their dance round her who dims the sun,

Maidens and youths fling their wild arms in air
As their feet twinkle; they recede, and now
Bending within each other's atmosphere

Kindle invisibly—and as they glow,
Like moths by light attracted and repelled,
Oft to their bright destruction come and go,

Till like two clouds into one vale impelled
That shake the mountains when their lightnings mingle
And die in rain—the fiery band which held

Their natures, snaps—the shock still may tingle;
One falls and then another in the path
Senseless—nor is the desolation single,

Yet ere I can say *where*—the chariot hath
Past over them—nor other trace I find
But as of foam after the ocean's wrath

Is spent upon the desert shore;—behind,
Old men and women foully disarrayed,
Shake their grey hairs in the insulting wind,

To seek, to [   ], to strain with limbs decayed,
Limping to reach the light which leaves them still
Farther behind and deeper in the shade.

But not the less with impotence of will
They wheel, though ghastly shadows interpose
Round them and round each other, and fulfil

Their work, and in the dust from whence they rose
Sink, and corruption veils them as they lie,
And past in these performs what [   ] in those.

Struck to the heart by this sad pageantry,
Half to myself I said—And what is this?
Whose shape is that within the car?   And why—

I would have added—is all here amiss?
But a voice answered—" Life !"—I turned, and knew
(Oh Heaven, have mercy on such wretchedness !)

That what I thought was an old root which grew
To strange distortion out of the hill side,
Was indeed one of those deluded crew,

And that the grass, which methought hung so wide
And white, was but his thin discoloured hair,
And that the holes it vainly sought to hide,

Were or had been eyes:—"If thou canst, forbear
To join the dance, which I had well foreborne!"
Said the grim Feature; of my thought aware,

" I will unfold that which to this deep scorn
Led me and my companions, and relate
The progress of the pageant since the morn;

"If thirst of knowledge shall not then abate,
Follow it thou even to the night, but I
Am weary."—Then like one who with the weight

Of his own words is staggered, wearily
He paused; and ere he could resume, I cried:
" First, who art thou?"—" Before thy memory,

" I feared, loved, hated, suffered, did and died,
And if the spark with which Heaven lit my spirit
Had been with purer sentiment supplied,

"Corruption would not now thus much inherit
Of what was once Rousseau,—nor this disguise
Stained that which ought to have disdained to wear it;

" If I have been extinguished, yet there rise
A thousand beacons from the spark I bore"—
"And who are those chained to the car?"—" The wise,

"The great, the unforgotten,—they who wore
Mitres and helms and crowns, or wreaths of light,
Signs of thought's empire over thought—their lore

" Taught them not this, to know themselves; their might
Could not repress the mystery within,
And for the morn of truth they feigned, deep night

" Caught them ere evening."—" Who is he with chin
Upon his breast, and hands crost on his chain?"—
" The Child of a fierce hour; he sought to win

"The world, and lost all that it did contain
Of greatness, in its hope destroyed; and more
Of fame and peace than virtue's self can gain

" Without the opportunity which bore
Him on its eagle pinions to the peak
From which a thousand climbers have before

" Fall'n, as Napoleon fell."—I felt my cheek
Alter, to see the shadow pass away
Whose grasp had left the giant world so weak,

That every pigmy kicked it as it lay;
And much I grieved to think how power and will
In opposition rule our mortal day,

And why God made irreconcilable
Good and the means of good; and for despair
I half disdained mine eyes' desire to fill

With the spent vision of the times that were
And scarce have ceased to be.—"Dost thou behold,"
Said my guide, "those spoilers spoiled, Voltaire,

" Frederic, and Paul, Catherine, and Leopold,
And hoary anarchs, demagogues, and sage—
——— names the world thinks always old,

" For in the battle, life and they did wage,
She remained conqueror.   I was overcome
By my own heart alone, which neither age,

" Nor tears, nor infamy, nor now the tomb
Could temper to its object."—"Let them pass,"
I cried, " the world and its mysterious doom

" Is not so much more glorious than it was,
That I desire to worship those who drew
New figures on its false and fragile glass

" As the old faded."—" Figures ever new
Rise on the bubble, paint them as you may;
We have but thrown, as those before us threw,

" Our shadows on it as it past away.
But mark how chained to the triumphal chair
The mighty phantoms of an elder day;

" All that is mortal of great Plato there
Expiates the joy and woe his master knew not;
The star that ruled his doom was far too fair,

"And life, where long that flower of Heaven grew not,
Conquered that heart by love, which gold, or pain,
Or age, or sloth, or slavery could subdue not.

"And near walk the [   ] twain,
The tutor and his pupil, whom Dominion
Followed as tame as vulture in a chain.

"The world was darkened beneath either pinion
Of him whom from the flock of conquerors
Fame singled out for her thunder-bearing minion;

" The other long outlived both woes and wars,
Throned in the thoughts of men, and still had kept
The jealous key of truth's eternal doors,

" If Bacon's eagle spirit had not leapt
Like lightning out of darkness—he compelled
The Proteus shape of Nature as it slept

" To wake, and lead him to the caves that held
The treasure of the secrets of its reign.
See the great bards of elder time, who quelled

" The passions which they sung, as by their strain
May well be known: their living melody
Tempers its own contagion to the vein

"Of those who are infected with it—I
Have suffered what I wrote, or viler pain !
And so my words have seeds of misery"——

*　　　*　　　*　　　*　　　*　　　*
　　*　　　*　　　*　　　*　　　*　　　*
*　　　*　　　*　　　*　　　*　　　*

[There is a chasm here in the MS. which it is impossible to
　　fill up.　It appears from the context, that other shapes
　　pass, and that Rousseau still stood beside the dreamer,
　　as]—

—— he pointed to a company,
Midst whom I quickly recognised the heirs
Of Cæsar's crime, from him to Constantine;
The anarch chiefs, whose force and murderous snares

Had founded many a sceptre-bearing line,
And spread the plague of gold and blood abroad:
And Gregory and John, and men divine,

Who rose like shadows between man and God;
Till that eclipse, still hanging over heaven,
Was worshipped by the world o'er which they strode,

For the true sun it quenched—" "Their power was given
But to destroy," replied the leader: " I
Am one of those who have created, even

" If it be but a world of agony."—
" Whence comest thou ? and whither goest thou ?
How did thy course begin ?" I said, " and why ?

" Mine eyes are sick of this perpetual flow
Of people, and my heart sick of one sad thought—
Speak !"—" Whence I am, I partly seem to know,

" And how and by what paths I have been brought
To this dread pass, methinks even thou mayst guess;
Why this should be, my mind can compass not;

" Whither the conqueror hurries me, still less;
But follow thou, and from spectator turn
Actor or victim in this wretchedess,

" And what thou wouldst be taught I then may learn
From thee.　Now listen:—In the April prime,
When all the forest tips began to burn

" With kindling green, touched by the azure clime
Of the young year's dawn, I was laid asleep
Under a mountain, which from unknown time

" Had yawned into a cavern, high and deep;
And from it came a gentle rivulet,
Whose water, like clear air, in its calm sweep

" Bent the soft grass, and kept for ever wet
The stems of the sweet flowers, and filled the grove
With sounds, which whoso hears must needs forget

" All pleasure and all pain, all hate and love,
Which they had known before that hour of rest;
A sleeping mother then would dream not of

" Her only child who died upon her breast
At eventide—a king would mourn no more
The crown of which his brows were dispossest

" When the sun lingered o'er his ocean floor,
To gild his rival's new prosperity.
Thou wouldst forget thus vainly to deplore

" Ills, which if ills can find no cure from thee,
The thought of which no other sleep will quell,
Nor other music blot from memory,

" So sweet and deep is the oblivious spell;
And whether life had been before that sleep
The heaven which I imagine, or a hell

" Like this harsh world in which I wake to weep,
I know not.   I arose, and for a space
The scene of woods and waters seemed to keep,

" 'Though it was now broad day, a gentle trace
Of light diviner than the common sun
Sheds on the common earth, and all the place

" Was filled with magic sounds woven into one
Oblivious melody, confusing sense
Amid the gliding waves and shadows dun;

" And, as I looked, the bright omnipresence
Of morning through the orient cavern flowed,
And the sun's image radiantly intense

" Burned on the waters of the well that glowed
Like gold, and threaded all the forest's maze
With winding paths of emerald fire; there stood

" Amid the sun, as he amid the blaze
Of his own glory, on the vibrating
Floor of the fountain, paved with flashing rays,

" A Shape all light, which with one hand did fling
Dew on the earth, as if she were the dawn,
And the invisible rain did ever sing

" A silver music on the mossy lawn;
And still before me on the dusky grass,
Iris her many-coloured scarf had drawn:

" In her right hand she bore a crystal glass,
Mantling with bright Nepenthe; the fierce splendour
Fell from her as she moved under the mass

" Out of the deep cavern, with palms so tender,
Their tread broke not the mirror of its billow;
She glided along the river, and did bend her

" Head under the dark boughs, till like a willow,
Her fair hair swept the bosom of the stream
That whispered with delight to be its pillow.

" As one enamoured is upborne in dream
O'er lily-paven lakes mid silver mist,
To wondrous music, so this shape might seem

" Partly to tread the waves with feet which kissed
The dancing foam; partly to glide along
The air which roughened the moist amethyst,

" Or the faint morning beams that fell among
The trees, or the soft shadows of the trees;
And her feet, ever to the ceaseless song

" Of leaves, and winds, and waves, and birds, and bees,
And falling drops, moved to a measure new
Yet sweet, as on the summer evening breeze,

" Up from the lake a shape of golden dew
Between two rocks, athwart the rising moon.
Dances i' the wind, where never eagle flew,

" And still her feet, no less than the sweet tune
To which they moved, seemed as they moved, to blot
The thoughts of him who gazed on them; and soon

" All that was, seemed as if it had been not;
And all the gazer's mind was strewn beneath
Her feet like embers; and she, thought by thought,

" Trampled its sparks into the dust of death;
As day upon the threshold of the east
Treads out the lamps of night, until the breath

" Of darkness re-illumine even the least
Of heaven's living eyes—like day she came,
Making the night a dream; and ere she ceased

" To move, as one between desire and shame
Suspended, I said—If, as it doth seem,
Thou comest from the realm without a name,

" Into this valley of perpetual dream,
Show whence I came, and where I am, and why—
Pass not away upon the passing stream.

" Arise and quench thy thirst, was her reply.
And as a shut lily, stricken by the wand
Of dewy morning's vital alchemy,

" I rose; and, bending at her sweet command,
Touched with faint lips the cup she raised,
And suddenly my brain became as sand

" Where the first wave had more than half erased
The track of deer on desert Labrador;
Whilst the wolf, from which they fled amazed,

"Leaves his stamp visibly upon the shore,
Until the second bursts; so on my sight
Burst a new vision, never seen before,

"And the fair shape waned in the coming light,
As veil by veil the silent splendour drops
From Lucifer, amid the chrysolite

"Of sunrise, ere it tinge the mountain tops;
And as the presence of that fairest planet,
Although unseen, is felt by one who hopes

"That his day's path may end as he began it,
In that star's smile, whose light is like the scent
Of a jonquil when evening breezes fan it,

"Or the soft note in which his dear lament
The Brescian shepherd breathes, or the caress
That turned his weary slumber to content;*

"So knew I in that light's severe excess
The presence of that shape which on the stream
Moved, as I moved along the wilderness,

"More dimly than a day-appearing dream,
The ghost of a forgotten form of sleep;
A light of heaven, whose half-extinguished beam

"Through the sick day in which we wake to weep,
Glimmers, for ever sought, for ever lost;
So did that shape its obscure tenour keep

"Beside my path, as silent as a ghost;
But the new Vision, and the cold bright car,
With solemn speed and stunning music, crost

"The forest, and as if from some dread war
Triumphantly returning, the loud million
Fiercely extolled the fortune of her star.

"A moving arch of victory, the vermilion
And green and azure plumes of Iris had
Built high over her wind-winged pavilion,

"And underneath ethereal glory clad
The wilderness, and far before her flew
The tempest of the splendour, which forbade

"Shadow to fall from leaf and stone; the crew
Seemed in that light, like atomies to dance
Within a sunbeam;—some upon the new

"Embroidery of flowers, that did enhance
The grassy vesture of the desert, played,
Forgetful of the chariot's swift advance;

---

* The favourite song, "Stanco di pascolar le peccorelle," is a Brescian national air.

" Others stood gazing, till within the shade
Of the great mountain its light left them dim;
Others outspeeded it; and others made

" Circles around it, like the clouds that swim
Round the high moon in a bright sea of air;
And more did follow, with exulting hymn,

" The chariot and the captives fettered there:
But all like bubbles on an eddying flood
Fled into the same track at last, and were

" Borne onward.—I among the multitude
Was swept—me, sweetest flowers delayed not long,
Me, not the shadow nor the solitude;

" Me, not that falling stream's Lethean song;
Me, not the phantom of that early form,
Which moved upon its motion—but among

" The thickest billows of that living storm
I plunged, and bared my bosom to the clime
Of that cold light, whose airs too soon deform.

" Before the chariot had begun to climb
The opposing steep of that mysterious dell,
Behold a wonder worthy of the rhyme

" Of him who from the lowest depths of hell,
Through every paradise and through all glory,
Love led serene, and who returned to tell

" The words of hate and care; the wondrous story
How all things are transfigured except Love;
For deaf as is a sea, which wrath makes hoary,

" The world can hear not the sweet notes that move
The sphere whose light is melody to lovers—
A wonder worthy of his rhyme—the grove

" Grew dense with shadows to its inmost covers,
The earth was grey with phantoms, and the air
Was peopled with dim forms, as when there hovers

" A flock of vampire-bats before the glare
Of the tropic sun, bringing, ere evening,
Strange night upon some Indian vale ;—thus were

" Phantoms diffused around ; and some did fling
Shadows of shadows, yet unlike themselves,
Behind them ; some like eaglets on the wing

" Were lost in the white day ; others like elves
Danced in a thousand unimagined shapes
Upon the sunny streams and grassy shelves ;

" And others sate chattering like restless apes
On vulgar hands,   *   *   *   *
Some made a cradle of the ermined capes

" Of kingly mantles ; some across the tire
Of pontiffs rode, like demons ; others played
Under the crown which girt with empire

" A baby's or an idiot's brow, and made
Their nests in it.   The old anatomies
Sate hatching their bare broods under the shade

" Of demon wings, and laughed from their dead eyes
To reassume the delegated power,
Arrayed in which those worms did monarchize,

" Who make this earth their charnel.   Others more
Humble, like falcons, sate upon the fist
Of common men, and round their heads did soar ;

" Or like small gnats and flies, as thick as mist
On evening marshes, thronged about the brow
Of lawyers, statesmen, priest and theorist ;

" And others, like discoloured flakes of snow
On fairest bosoms and the sunniest hair,
Fell, and were melted by the youthful glow

" Which they extinguished ; and, like tears, they were
A veil to those from whose faint lids they rained
In drops of sorrow.   I became aware

" Of whence those forms proceeded which thus stained
The track in which we moved.   After brief space,
From every form the beauty slowly waned ;

" From every firmest limb and fairest face
The strength and freshness fell like dust, and left
The action and the shape without the grace

" Of life.   The marble brow of youth was cleft
With care ; and in those eyes where once hope shone,
Desire, like a lioness bereft

" Of her last cub, glared ere it died ; each one
Of that great crowd sent forth incessantly
These shadows, numerous as the dead leaves blown

" In autumn evening from a poplar tree.
Each like himself and like each other were
At first ; but some distorted seemed to be

" Obscure clouds, moulded by the casual air ;
And of this stuff the car's creative ray
Wrapt all the busy phantoms that were there,

" As the sun shapes the clouds ; thus on the way
Mask after mask fell from the countenance
And form of all ; and long before the day

" Was old, the joy which waked like heaven's glance
The sleepers in the oblivious valley, died ;
And some grew weary of the ghastly dance,

" And fell, as I have fallen, by the way side;
Those soonest from whose forms most shadows past,
And least of strength and beauty did abide.

" Then, what is life ? I cried."—

FRAGMENTS

FROM AN UNFINISHED DRAMA.

HE came like a dream in the dawn of life,
  He fled like a shadow before its noon ;
He is gone, and my peace is turned to strife,
  And I wander and wane like the weary moon.
      O sweet Echo wake,
      And for my sake
Make answer the while my heart shall break !

But my heart has a music which Echo's lips,
  Though tender and true, yet can answer not,
And the shadow that moves in the soul's eclipse
  Can return not the kiss by his now forgot ;
      Sweet lips ! he who hath
      On my desolate path
Cast the darkness of absence worse than death !

Indian. And if my grief should still be dearer to me
Than all the pleasure in the world beside,
Why would you lighten it ?—
  Lady.   I offer only
That which I seek, some human sympathy
In this mysterious island.
  Indian. Oh ! my friend,
My sister, my beloved ! What do I say ?
My brain is dizzy and I scarce know whether
I speak to thee or her. Peace, perturbed heart !
I am to thee only as thou to mine,
The passing wind which heals the brow at noon,
And may strike cold into the breast at night,
Yet cannot linger where it soothes the most,
Or long soothe could it linger. But you said
You also loved ?
  Lady.   Loved ! Oh, I love. Methinks
This word of love is fit for all the world,
And that for gentle hearts another name
Would speak of gentler thoughts than the world owns.
I have loved.
  Indian.   And thou lovest not ? if so
Young as thou art thou canst afford to weep.
  Lady. Oh ! would that I could claim exemption
From all the bitterness of that sweet name.
I loved, I love, and when I love no more
Let joys and grief perish, and leave despair
To ring the knell of youth. He stood beside me,
The embodied vision of the brightest dream,
Which like a dawn heralds the day of life ;

The shadow of his presence made my world
A paradise. All familiar things he touched,
All common words he spoke, became to me
Like forms and sounds of a diviner world.
He was as is the sun in his fierce youth,
As terrible and lovely as a tempest;
He came, and went, and left me what I am.
Alas ! Why must I think how oft we two
Have sate together near the river springs,
Under the green pavilion which the willow
Spreads on the floor of the unbroken fountain,
Strewn by the nurslings that linger there,
Over that islet paved with flowers and moss,
While the musk-rose leaves, like flakes of crimson snow,
Showered on us, and the dove mourned in the pine,
Sad prophetess of sorrows not our own.
    Indian. Your breath is like soft music, your words are
The echoes of a voice which on my heart
Sleeps like a melody of early days.
But as you said—
    Lady.   He was so awful, yet
So beautiful in mystery and terror,
Calming me as the loveliness of heaven
Smooths the unquiet sea:—and yet not so,
For he seemed stormy, and would often seem
A quenchless sun masked in portentous clouds;
For such his thoughts, and even his actions were;
But he was not of them, nor they of him,
But as they hid his splendour from the earth.
Some said he was a man of blood and peril,
And steeped in bitter infamy to the lips.
More need was there I should be innocent,
More need that I should be most true and kind,
And much more need that there should be found one
To share remorse, and scorn and solitude,
And all the ills that wait on those who do
The tasks of ruin in the world of life.
He fled and I have followed him.

February, 1822.

ON THE MEDUSA OF LEONARDO DA VINCI,

IN THE FLORENTINE GALLERY.

It lieth, gazing on the midnight sky,
    Upon the cloudy mountain peak supine;
Below, far lands are seen tremblingly;
    Its horror and its beauty are divine.
Upon its lips and eyelids seem to lie
    Loveliness like a shadow, from which shrine,
Fiery and lurid, struggling underneath,
The agonies of anguish and of death.

Yet it is less the horror than the grace
    Which turns the gazer's spirit into stone;
Whereon the lineaments of that dead face
    Are graven, till the characters be grown

Into itself, and thought no more can trace;
   'Tis the melodious hue of beauty thrown
Athwart the darkness and the glare of pain,
   Which humanize and harmonize the strain.

And from its head as from one body grow,
   As [   ] grass out of a watery rock,
Hairs which are vipers, and they curl and flow
   And their long tangles in each other lock,
And with unending involutions show
   Their mailed radiance, as it were to mock
The torture and the death within, and saw
The solid air with many a ragged jaw.

And from a stone beside a poisonous eft
   Peeps idly into those Gorgonian eyes;
Whilst in the air a ghastly bat, bereft
   Of sense, has flitted with a mad surprise
Out of the cave this hideous light had cleft,
   And he comes hastening like a moth that hies
After a taper; and the midnight sky
Flares, a light more dread than obscurity.

'Tis the tempestuous loveliness of terror;
   For from the serpents gleams a brazen glare
Kindled by that inextricable error,
   Which makes a thrilling vapour of the air
Become a [   ] and evershifting mirror
   Of all the beauty and the terror there—
A woman's countenance, with serpent locks,
Gazing in death on heaven from those wet rocks

Florence, 1819.

SONG.

RARELY, rarely, comest thou,
   Spirit of Delight !
Wherefore hast thou left me now
   Many a day and night ?
Many a weary night and day
'Tis since thou art fled away.

How shall ever one like me
   Win thee back again ?
With the joyous and the free
   Thou wilt scoff at pain.
Spirit false ! thou hast forgot
All but those who need thee not.

As a lizard with the shade
   Of a trembling leaf,
Thou with sorrow art dismayed;
   Even the sighs of grief
Reproach thee, that thou art not near,
And reproach thou wilt not hear.

Let me set my mournful ditty
   To a merry measure,
Thou wilt never come for pity,
   Thou wilt come for pleasure,
Pity then will cut away
Those cruel wings, and thou wilt stay.

I love all that thou lovest,
   Spirit of Delight !
The fresh Earth in new leaves drest,
   And the starry night;
Autumn evening, and the morn
When the golden mists are born

I love snow, and all the forms
   Of the radiant frost:
I love waves, and winds, and storms,
   Everything almost
Which is Nature's, and may be
Untainted by man's misery.

I love tranquil solitude,
  And such society
As is quiet, wise and good;
  Between thee and me
What difference? but thou dost possess
The things I seek, not love them less.

I love Love—though he has wings,
  And like light can flee,
But above all other things,
  Spirit, I love thee—
Thou art love and life! O come,
Make once more my heart thy home.

TO CONSTANTIA,

SINGING.

THUS to be lost and thus to sink and die,
    Perchance were death indeed!—Constantia, turn!
In thy dark eyes a power like light doth lie,
    Even though the sounds which were thy voice, which burn
Between thy lips, are laid to sleep;
    Within thy breath, and on thy hair, like odour it is yet,
And from thy touch like fire doth leap.
    Even while I write, my burning cheeks are wet,
    Alas, that the torn heart can bleed, but not forget!

A breathless awe, like the swift change
    Unseen, but felt in youthful slumbers,
Wild, sweet, but uncommunicably strange,
    Thou breathest now in fast ascending numbers.
The cope of heaven seems rent and cloven
    By the enchantment of thy strain,
And on my shoulders wings are woven,
    To follow its sublime career,
Beyond the mighty moons that wane
    Upon the verge of nature's utmost sphere,
    Till the world's shadowy walls are past and disappear.

Her voice is hovering o'er my soul—it lingers
    O'ershadowing it with soft and lulling wings,
The blood and life within those snowy fingers
    Teach witchcraft to the instrumental strings.
My brain is wild, my breath comes quick—
    The blood is listening in my frame,
And thronging shadows, fast and thick,
    Fall on my overflowing eyes;
My heart is quivering like a flame;
    As morning dew, that in the sunbeam dies,
    I am dissolved in these consuming ecstasies.

I have no life, Constantia, now, but thee,
    Whilst, like the world-surrounding air, thy song
Flows on, and fills all things with melody.
    Now is thy voice a tempest swift and strong,
On which, like one in trance upborne,
    Secure o'er rocks and waves I sweep,
Rejoicing like a cloud of morn.
    Now 'tis the breath of summer night,
Which when the starry waters sleep,
    Round western isles, with incense-blossoms bright,
    Lingering, suspends my soul in its voluptuous flight.

THE FUGITIVES.

I.

THE waters are flashing,
The white hail is dashing,
The lightnings are glancing,
The hoar-spray is dancing
    Away !

The whirlwind is rolling,
The thunder is tolling,
The forest is swinging,
The minster bells ringing—
    Come away !

The Earth is like Ocean,
Wreck-strewn and in motion:
Bird, beast, man and worm
Have crept out of the storm—
    Come away !

II.

" Our boat has one sail,
And the helmsman is pale;
A bold pilot I trow,
Who should follow us now,"—
    Shouted He—

And she cried: " Ply the oar !
Put off gaily from shore !"
As she spoke, bolts of death
Mixed with hail, specked their path
    O'er the sea.

And from isle, tower and rock,
The blue beacon cloud broke,
And though dumb in the blast,
The red cannon flashed fast
    From the lee.

III.

" And, fear'st thou, and fear'st thou ?
And, seest thou, and hear'st thou ?
And, drive we not free
O'er the terrible sea,
    I and thou ?"

One boat-cloak did cover
The loved and the lover—
Their blood beats one measure,
They murmur proud pleasure
    Soft and low;

While around the lashed Ocean,
Like mountains in motion,
Is withdrawn and uplifted,
Sunk, shattered and shifted
    To and fro.

IV.

In the court of the fortress
Beside the pale portress,
Like a bloodhound well beaten,
The bridegroom stands, eaten
    By shame;

On the topmost watch-turret,
As a death-boding spirit,
Stands the grey tyrant father,
To his voice the mad weather
    Seems tame;

And with curses as wild
As ere clung to child,
He devotes to the blast
The best, loveliest and last
    Of his name !

A LAMENT.

SWIFTER far than summer's flight,
Swifter far than youth's delight,
Swifter far than happy night,
    Art thou come and gone:
As the earth when leaves are dead,
As the night when sleep is sped,
As the heart when joy is fled,
    I am left lone, alone.

The swallow Summer comes again,
The owlet Night resumes her reign,
But the wild swan Youth is fain
    To fly with thee, false as thou.

My heart each day desires the morrow,
Sleep itself is turned to sorrow,
Vainly would my winter borrow
    Sunny leaves from any bough.

Lilies for a bridal bed,
Roses for a matron's head,
Violets for a maiden dead,
    Pansies let my flowers be:
On the living grave I bear,
Scatter them without a tear,
Let no friend, however dear,
    Waste one hope, one fear for me.

THE PINE FOREST

OF THE CASCINE, NEAR PISA.

DEAREST, best and brightest,
 Come away,
To the woods and to the fields !
Dearer than this fairest day,
Which like thee to those in sorrow,
Comes to bid a sweet good-morrow
To the rough year just awake
In its cradle in the brake.

The eldest of the hours of spring,
Into the winter wandering,
Looked upon the leafless wood ;
And the banks all bare and rude
Found it seems this halcyon morn,
In February's bosom born,
Bending from heaven, in azure mirth,
Kissed the cold forehead of the earth,
And smiled upon the silent sea,
And bade the frozen streams be free;
And waked to music all the fountains,
And breathed upon the rigid mountains,
And made the wintry world appear
Like one on whom thou smilest, dear.

Radiant Sister of the Day,
Awake ! arise ! and come away !
To the wild woods and the plains,
To the pools where winter rains
Image all the roof of leaves,
Where the Pine its garland weaves,
Sapless, grey, and ivy dun
Round stones that never kiss the sun,
To the sandhills of the sea,
Where the earliest violets be.

Now the last day of many days,
All beautiful and bright as thou,
The loveliest and the last, is dead,
Rise Memory, and write its praise,
And do thy wonted work and trace
The epitaph of glory fled:
For the Earth hath changed its face,
A frown is on the Heaven's brow.

We wandered to the Pine Forest
 That skirts the Ocean's foam,
The lightest wind was in its nest,
 The tempest in its home.

The whispering waves were half asleep,
 The clouds were gone to play,
And on the woods, and on the deep,
 The smile of Heaven lay.

It seemed as if the day were one
 Sent from beyond the skies,
Which shed to earth above the sun
 A light of Paradise.

We paused amid the Pines that stood
 The giants of the waste,
Tortured by storms to shapes as rude,
 As serpents interlaced.

How calm it was—the silence there
 By such a chain was bound,
That even the busy woodpecker
 Made stiller by her sound

The inviolable quietness;
 The breath of peace we drew,
With its soft motion made not less
 The calm that round us grew.

It seemed that from the remotest seat
 Of the white mountain's waste,
To the bright flower beneath our feet,
 A magic circle traced ;

A spirit interfused around,
 A thinking silent life,
To momentary peace it bound
 Our mortal Nature's strife.

For still it seemed the centre of
 The magic circle there,
Was one whose being filled with love
 The breathless atmosphere.

Were not the crocuses that grew
 Under that ilex tree,
As beautiful in scent and hue
 As ever fed the bee ?

We stood beside the pools that lie
 Under the forest bough,
And each seemed like unto a sky
 Gulfed in a world below;

A purple firmament of light,
 Which in the dark earth lay,
More boundless than the depth of
 night,
 And clearer than the day—

In which the massy forests grew,
 As in the upper air,
More perfect both in shape and hue
 Than any waving there.

Like one beloved, the scene had lent
  To the dark water's breast
Its every leaf and lineament
  With that clear truth expressed.

There lay far glades and neighbouring
    lawn,
  And through the dark green crowd
The white sun twinkling like the dawn
  Under a speckled cloud.

Sweet views, which in our world above
  Can never well be seen,
Were imaged by the water's love
  Of that fair forest green.

And all was interfused beneath
  With an Elysium air,
An atmosphere without a breath,
  A silence sleeping there.

Until a wandering wind crept by,
  Like an unwelcome thought,
Which from my mind's too faithful eye
  Blots thy bright image out.

For thou art good and dear and kind,
  The forest ever green,
But less of peace in S——'s mind,
  Than calm in waters seen.

  2nd February, 1822.

TO NIGHT.

SWIFTLY walk over the western wave,
        Spirit of Night !
Out of the misty eastern cave,
Where, all the long and lone daylight,
Thou wovest dreams of joy and fear,
Which make thee terrible and dear,—
        Swift be thy flight !

Wrap thy form in a mantle grey,
        Star-inwrought !
Blind with thine hair the eyes of day,
Kiss her until she be wearied out,
Then wander o'er city, and sea, and land,
Touching all with thine opiate wand—
        Come, long sought !

When I arose and saw the dawn,
        I sighed for thee ;
When light rode high, and the dew was gone,
And noon lay heavy on flower and tree,
And the weary Day turned to his rest,
Lingering like an unloved guest,
        I sighed for thee.

Thy brother Death came, and cried,
        Wouldst thou me ?
Thy sweet child Sleep, the filmy-eyed,
        Murmured like a noontide bee,
Shall I nestle near thy side ?
Wouldst thou me ?—And I replied,
        No, not thee !

Death will come when thou art dead,
        Soon, too soon—
Sleep will come when thou art fled ;
Of neither would I ask the boon
I ask of thee, beloved Night—
Swift be thine approaching flight,
        Come soon, soon !

K K

EVENING.

PONTE A MARE, PISA.

THE sun is set; the swallows are asleep;
　　The bats are flitting fast in the grey air;
The slow soft toads out of damp corners creep,
　　And evening's breath, wandering here and there
Over the quivering surface of the stream,
Wakes not one ripple from its silent dream.

There is no dew on the dry grass to-night,
　　Nor damp within the shadow of the trees;
The wind is intermitting, dry, and light;
　　And in the inconstant motion of the breeze
The dust and straws are driven up and down,
And whirled about the pavement of the town.

Within the surface of the fleeting river
　　The wrinkled image of the city lay,
Immovably unquiet, and for ever
　　It trembles, but it never fades away;
Go to the [　　　　　　　　　　　]
You, being changed, will find it then as now.

The chasm in which the sun has sunk is shut
　　By darkest barriers of enormous cloud,
Like mountain over mountain huddled—but
　　Growing and moving upwards in a crowd,
And over it a space of watery blue,
Which the keen evening star is shining through

THE BOAT ON THE SERCHIO.

OUR boat is asleep in Serchio's stream,
Its sails are folded like thoughts in a dream,
The helm sways idly, hither and thither;
Dominic, the boatman, has brought the mast,
And the oars and the sails; but 'tis sleeping fast,
Like a beast, unconscious of its tether.

The stars burnt out in the pale blue air,
And the thin white moon lay withering there,
To tower, and cavern, and rift and tree,
The owl and the bat fled drowsily.
Day had kindled the dewy woods,
And the rocks above and the stream below,
And the vapours in their multitudes,
And the Apennine's shroud of summer snow,
And clothed with light of aery gold
The mists in their eastern caves uprolled.

Day had awakened all things that be,
The lark and the thrush and the swallow free,
And the milkmaid's song and the mower's scythe.
And the matin-bell and the mountan bee:

Fireflies were quenched on the dewy corn,
Glowworms went out on the river's brim,
Like lamps which a student forgets to trim :
The beetle forgot to wind his horn,
The crickets were still in the meadow and hill :
Like a flock of rooks at a farmer's gun
Night's dreams and terrors, every one,
Fled from the brains which are their prey,
From the lamp's death to the morning ray :

All rose to do the task He set to each,
Who shaped us to His ends and not our own ;
The million rose to learn, and one to teach
What none yet ever knew or can be known ;

              And many rose
Whose woe was such that fear became desire ;
Melchior and Lionel were not among those ;
They from the throng of men had stepped aside,
And made their home under the green hill side.
It was that hill, whose intervening brow
Screens Lucca from the Pisan's envious eye,
Which the circumfluous plain waving below,
Like a wide lake of green fertility,
With streams and fields and marshes bare,
Divides from the far Apennines—which lie
Islanded in the immeasurable air.

" What think you, as she lies in her green cove,
Our little sleeping boat is dreaming of?
If morning dreams are true, why I should guess
That she was dreaming of our idleness,
And of the miles of watery way
We should have led her by this time of day?"—

            ——" Never mind," said Lionel,
" Give care to the winds, they can bear it well
About yon poplar tops; and see
The white clouds are driving merrily,
And the stars we miss this morn will light
More willingly our return to-night.
List, my dear fellow, the breeze blows fair;
How it scatters Dominic's long black hair,
Singing of us, and our lazy motions,
If I can guess a boat's emotions."

The chain is loosed, the sails are spread,
The living breath is fresh behind,
As with dews and sunrise fed,
Comes the laughing morning wind;
The sails are full, the boat makes head
Against the Serchio's torrent fierce,
Then flags with intermitting course,
And hangs upon the wave, [   ]
Which fervid from its mountain source
Shallow, smooth and strong doth come,—
Swift as fire, tempestuously
It sweeps into the affrighted sea;

In morning's smile its eddies coil,
Its billows sparkle, toss and boil,
Torturing all its quiet light
Into columns fierce and bright.

     The Serchio, twisting forth
Between the marble barriers which it clove
At Ripafratta, leads through the dread chasm
The wave that died the death which lovers love,
Living in what it sought; as if this spasm
Had not yet past, the toppling mountains cling,
But the clear stream in full enthusiasm
Pours itself on the plain, until wandering,
Down one clear path of effluence crystalline
Sends its clear waves, that they may fling
At Arno's feet tribute of corn and wine,
Then, through the pestilential deserts wild
Of tangled marsh and woods of stunted fir,
It rushes to the Ocean.

July, 1821.

———◆———

THE ZUCCA.*

I.

SUMMER was dead and Autumn was expiring,
   And infant Winter laughed upon the land
All cloudlessly and cold; when I, desiring
   More in this world than any understand,
Wept o'er the beauty, which like sea retiring,
   Had left the earth bare as the wave-worn sand
Of my poor heart, and o'er the grass and flowers
Pale for the falsehood of the flattering hours.

II.

Summer was dead, but I yet lived to weep
   The instability of all but weeping;
And on the earth lulled in her winter sleep
   I woke, and envied her as she was sleeping.
Too happy Earth! over thy face shall creep
   The wakening vernal airs, until thou, leaping
From unremembered dreams, shalt [   ] see
No death divide thy immortality.

III.

I loved—O no, I mean not one of ye,
   Or any earthly one, though ye are dear
As human heart to human heart may be;
   I loved, I know not what—but this low sphere
And all that it contains, contains not thee,
   Thou, whom seen nowhere, I feel everywhere,
Dim object of my soul's idolatry.
Veiled art thou like—

—————————————

* Pumpkin.

IV.

By Heaven and Earth, from all whose shapes thou flowest,
  Neither to be contained, delayed, or hidden,
Making divine the loftiest and the lowest,
  When for a moment thou art not forbidden
To live within the life which thou bestowest;
  And leaving noblest things vacant and chidden,
Cold as a corpse after the spirit's flight,
Blank as the sun after the birth of night.

V.

In winds, and trees, and streams, and all things common,
  In music and the sweet unconscious tone
Of animals, and voices which are human,
  Meant to express some feelings of their own;
In the soft motions and rare smile of woman,
  In flowers and leaves, and in the fresh grass shown,
Or dying in the autumn, I the most
Adore thee present or lament thee lost.

VI.

And thus I went, lamenting when I saw
  A plant upon the river's margin lie,
Like one who loved beyond his Nature's law,
  And in despair had cast him down to die;
Its leaves which had outlived the frost, the thaw
  Had blighted as a heart which hatred's eye
Can blast not, but which pity kills; the dew
Lay on its spotted leaves like tears too true.

VII.

The Heavens had wept upon it, but the Earth
  Had crushed it on her unmaternal breast.

*   *   *   *   *

VIII.

I bore it to my chamber, and I planted
  It in a vase full of the lightest mould;
The winter beams which out of Heaven slanted
  Fell through the window panes, disrobed of cold
Upon its leaves and flowers; the star which panted
  In evening for the Day, whose car has rolled
Over the horizon's wave, with looks of light
Smiled on it from the threshold of the night.

IX.

The mitigated influences of air
  And light revived the plant, and from it grew
Strong leaves and tendrils, and its flowers fair,
  Full as a cup with the vine's burning dew,
O'erflowed with golden colours; an atmosphere
  Of vital warmth enfolded it anew,
And every impulse sent to every part
The unbeheld pulsations of its heart.

X.

Well might the plant grow beautiful and strong,
　　Even if the sun and air had smiled not on it;
For one wept o'er it all the winter long
　　Tears pure as Heaven's rain, which fell upon it
Hour after hour; for sounds of softest song
　　Mixed with the stringed melodies that won it
To leave the gentle lips on which it slept,
Had loosed the heart of him who sat and wept.

XI.

Had loosed his heart, and shook the leaves and flowers
　　On which he wept, the while the savage storm
Waked by the darkest of December's hours
　　Was raving round the chamber hushed and warm;
The birds were shivering in their leafless bowers,
　　The fish were frozen in the pools, the form
Of every summer plant was dead [　　　]
Whilst this　　　*　　　*　　　*　　　*

January, 1822.

———◆———

DEATH.

THEY die—the dead return not—Misery
　　Sits near an open grave and calls them over,
A Youth with hoary hair and haggard eye—
　　They are the names of kindred, friend, and lover,
Which he so feebly called—they all are gone!
Fond wretch, all dead, those vacant names alone,
　　This most familiar scene, my pain—
　　These tombs alone remain.

Misery, my sweetest friend—oh! weep no more!
　　Thou wilt not be consoled—I wonder not!
For I have seen thee from thy dwelling's door
　　Watch the calm sunset with them, and this spot
Was even as bright and calm, but transitory,
And now thy hopes are gone, thy hair is hoary;
　　This most familiar scene, my pain—
　　These tombs alone remain.

———◆———

A LAMENT.

OH, world! oh, life! oh, time!
On whose last steps I climb
　　Trembling at that where I had stood
　　before;
When will return the glory of your
　　prime?
　　　No more—O, never more!

Out of the day and night
A joy has taken flight;
　　Fresh spring, and summer, and
　　winter hoar,
Move my faint heart with grief, but
　　with delight
　　　No more—O, never more!

LOVE'S PHILOSOPHY.

THE fountains mingle with the river,
  And the rivers with the ocean,
The winds of heaven mix for ever
  With a sweet emotion;
Nothing in the world is single;
  All things by a law divine
In one another's being mingle—
  Why not I with thine?

See the mountains kiss high heaven,
  And the waves clasp one another;
No sister flower would be forgiven
  If it disdained its brother:
And the sunlight clasps the earth,
  And the moonbeams kiss the sea,
What are all these kissings worth,
  If thou kiss not me?

January, 1820.

TO EMELIA VIVIANI.

MADONNA, wherefore hast thou sent to me
    Sweet basil and mignonette?
Embleming love and health, which never yet
In the same wreath might be.
    Alas, and they are wet!
Is it with thy kisses or thy tears?
    For never rain or dew
    Such fragrance drew
From plant or flower—the very doubt endears
    My sadness ever new,
The sighs I breathe, the tears I shed for thee.

March, 1821.

TO ——

I FEAR thy kisses, gentle maiden,
  Thou needest not fear mine;
My spirit is too deeply laden
  Ever to burden thine.

I fear thy mien, thy tones, thy motion,
  Thou needest not fear mine;
Innocent is the heart's devotion
  With which I worship thine.

LINES.

WHEN the lamp is shattered
The light in the dust lies dead—
  When the cloud is scattered
The rainbow's glory is shed.

When the lute is broken,
Sweet tones are remembered not;
  When the lips have spoken,
Loved accents are soon forgot.

  As music and splendour
Survive not the lamp and the lute,
  The heart's echoes render
No song when the spirit is mute:
No song but sad dirges,
Like the wind through a ruined cell,
  Or the mournful surges
That ring the dead seaman's knell.

  When hearts have once mingled
Love first leaves the well-built nest,
  The weak one is singled
To endure what it once possest.
  O Love! who bewailest
The frailty of all things here,
  Why choose you the frailest
For your cradle, your home and your bier?

  Its passions will rock thee
As the storms rock the ravens on high:
  Bright reason will mock thee,
Like the sun from a wintry sky.
  From thy nest every rafter
Will rot, and thine eagle home
  Leave the naked to laughter,
When leaves fall and cold winds come.

TO WILLIAM SHELLEY.

(With what truth I may say—
    Roma! Roma! Roma!
Non è più come era prima!)

MY lost William, thou in whom
  Some bright spirit lived, and did
That decaying robe consume
  Which its lustre faintly hid,
Here its ashes find a tomb,
  But beneath this pyramid
Thou art not—if a thing divine
Like thee can die, thy funeral shrine
Is thy mother's grief and mine.

Where art thou, my gentle child?
  Let me think thy spirit feeds,
Within its life intense and mild,
  The love of living leaves and weeds,
Among these tombs and ruins wild;
  Let me think that through low seeds
Of the sweet flowers and sunny grass,
Into their hues and scents may pass
A portion—

  June, 1819.

AN ALLEGORY.

A PORTAL as of shadowy adamant
    Stands yawning on the highway of
      the life
Which we all tread, a cavern huge and
    gaunt ;
    Around it rages an unceasing strife
Of shadows, like the restless clouds
    that haunt
The gap of some cleft mountain, lifted
    high
Into the whirlwinds of the upper sky.

And many passed it by with careless
    tread,
    Not knowing that a shadowy [   ]
Tracks every traveller even to where
    the dead
    Wait peacefully for their companion
    new;
But others, by more curious humour
    led,
    Pause to examine,—these are very
    few,
And they learn little there, except to
    know
That shadows follow them where'er
    they go.

MUTABILITY.

THE flower that smiles to-day
    To-morrow dies ;
All that we wish to stay,
    Tempts and then flies ;
What is this world's delight ?
Lightning that mocks the night,
Brief even as bright.

Virtue, how frail it is !
    Friendship too rare !
Love, how it sells poor bliss
    For proud despair !
But we, though soon they fall,
Survive their joy and all
Which ours we call.

Whilst skies are blue and bright,
    Whilst flowers are gay,
Whilst eyes that change ere night
    Make glad the day ;
Whilst yet the calm hours creep,
Dream thou—and from thy sleep
Then wake to weep.

FROM THE ARABIC.

AN IMITATION.

MY faint spirit was sitting in the light
    Of thy looks, my love ;
It panted for thee like the hind at noon
    For the brooks, my love.
Thy barb whose hoofs outspeed the
    tempest's flight
    Bore thee far from me ;
My heart, for my weak feet were weary
    soon,
    Did companion thee.

Ah ! fleeter far than fleetest storm or
    steed,
    Or the death they bear,
The heart which tender thought
    clothes like a dove
    With the wings of care ;
In the battle, in the darkness, in the
    need,
    Shall mine cling to thee,
Nor claim one smile for all the com-
    fort, love,
    It may bring to thee.

TO ——

ONE word is too often profaned
    For me to profane it,
One feeling too falsely disdained
    For thee to disdain it.
One hope is too like despair
    For prudence to smother,
And Pity from thee more dear,
    Than that from another.

I can give not what men call love,
    But wilt thou accept not
The worship the heart lifts above
    And the Heavens reject not,
The desire of the moth for the star,
    Of the night for the morrow,
The devotion to something afar
    From the sphere of our sorrow ?

MUSIC.

I PANT for the music which is divine,
    My heart in its thirst is a dying
    flower ;
Pour forth the sound like enchanted
    wine,
    Loosen the notes in a silver shower;
Like a herbless plain, for the gentle
    rain,
I gasp, I faint, till they wake again.

Let me drink of the spirit of that sweet
    sound,
    More, O more,—I am thirsting yet,
It loosens the serpent which care has
    bound
Upon my heart to stifle it;
The dissolving strain, through every
    vein,
Passes into my heart and brain.

As the scent of a violet withered up,
    Which grew by the brink of a silver
        lake;
When the hot noon has drained its
        dewy cup,
    And mist there was none its thirst
        to slake—
And the violet lay dead while the
        odour flew
On the wings of the wind o'er the
        waters blue—

As one who drinks from a charmed cup
    Of foaming, and sparkling and mur-
        muring wine
Whom, a mighty Enchantress filling up,
    Invites to love with her kiss divine.

    *   *   *   *
    *   *   *   *

LINES.

THE cold earth slept below;
    Above the cold sky shone;
        And all around,
        With a chilling sound,
From caves of ice and fields of snow,
The breath of night like death did flow
    Beneath the sinking moon.

The wintry hedge was black,
    The green grass was not seen,
        The birds did rest
        On the bare thorn's breast,
Whose roots, beside the pathway track,
Had bound their folds o'er many a
        crack
    Which the frost had made between.

Thine eyes glowed in the glare
    Of the moon's dying light;
        As a fen-fire's beam,
        On a sluggish stream,
Gleams dimly—so the moon shone
        there,
And it yellowed the strings of thy
        tangled hair
    That shook in the wind of night.

The moon made thy lips pale, beloved;
    The wind made thy bosom chill;
        The night did shed
        On thy dear head
Its frozen dew, and thou didst lie
Where the bitter breath of the naked sky
    Might visit thee at will.

November, 1815.

DEATH.

DEATH is here and death is there,
Death is busy everywhere,
All around, within, beneath,
Above is death—and we are death.

Death has set his mark and seal
On all we are and all we feel,
On all we know and all we fear,

    *   *   *   *

First our pleasures die—and then
Our hopes, and then our fears—and
    when
These are dead, the debt is due,
Dust claims dust—and we die too.

All things that we love and cherish,
Like ourselves must fade and perish,
Such is our rude mortal lot,
Love itself would, did they not.

TO ——

WHEN passion's trance is overpast,
If tenderness and truth could last
Or live, whilst all wild feelings keep
Some mortal slumber, dark and deep,
I should not weep, I should not weep!

It were enough to feel, to see
Thy soft eyes gazing tenderly,
And dream the rest—and burn and be
The secret food of fires unseen,
Couldst thou but be as thou hast been.

After the slumber of the year
The woodland violets reappear,
All things revive in field or grove,
And sky and sea, but two, which move,
And for all others, life and love.

PASSAGE OF THE APENNINES.

LISTEN, listen, Mary mine,
To the whisper of the Apennine,
It bursts on the roof like the thunder's
    roar,
Or like the sea on a northern shore,

Heard in its raging ebb and flow
By the captives pent in the cave below.
The Apennine in the light of day
Is a mighty mountain dim and grey,
Which between the earth and sky doth
    lay;
But when night comes, a chaos dread
On the dim starlight then is spread,
And the Apennine walks abroad with
    the storm.

May 4th, 1818.

TO MARY SHELLEY.

Oh! Mary dear, that you were here
With your brown eyes bright and clear,
And your sweet voice, like a bird
Singing love to its lone mate
In the ivy bower disconsolate;
Voice the sweetest ever heard!
And your brow more   *   *
Than the   *   *   *   sky
Of this azure Italy.
Mary dear, come to me soon,
I am not well whilst thou art far;
As sunset to the sphered moon,
As twilight to the western star,
Thou, beloved, art to me.

Oh! Mary dear, that you were here;
The Castle echo whispers "Here!"

    Este, September, 1818.

THE PAST.

Wilt thou forget the happy hours
Which we buried in Love's sweet
    bowers,
Heaping over their corpses cold
Blossoms and leaves, instead of mould?
Blossoms which were the joys that fell,
And leaves, the hopes that yet remain.

Forget the dead, the past? O yet
There are ghosts that may take re-
    venge for it,
Memories that make the heart a tomb,
Regrets which glide through the
    spirit's gloom,
And with ghastly whispers tell
That joy, once lost, is pain.

SONG OF A SPIRIT.

Within the silent centre of the earth
My mansion is; where I lived ensphered
From the beginning, and around my
    sleep

Have woven all the wondrous imagery
Of this dim spot, which mortals call
    the world;
Infinite depths of unknown elements
Massed into one impenetrable mask;
Sheets of immeasurable fire, and veins
Of gold and stone, and adamantine
    iron.
And as a veil in which I walk through
    Heaven
I have wrought mountains, seas, and
    waves, and clouds,
And lastly light, whose interfusion
    dawns
In the dark space of interstellar air.

LIBERTY.

The fiery mountains answer each
    other;
Their thunderings are echoed from
    zone to zone;
The tempestuous oceans awake one
    another,
And the ice-rocks are shaken round
    winter's zone
        When the clarion of the Ty-
        phoon is blown.

From a single cloud the lightning
    flashes,
Whilst a thousand isles are illumined
    around,
Earthquake is trampling one city to
    ashes,
An hundred are shuddering and totter-
    ing; the sound
        Is bellowing underground.

But keener thy gaze than the light-
    ning's glare,
And swifter thy step than the earth-
    quake's tramp;
Thou deafenest the rage of the ocean;
    thy stare
Makes blind the volcanoes; the sun's
    bright lamp
        To thine is a fen-fire damp.

From billow and mountain and ex-
    halation
The sunlight is darted through vapour
    and blast;
From spirit to spirit, from nation to
    nation,
From city to hamlet thy dawning is
    cast—
And tyrants and slaves are like
    shadows of night
        In the van of the morning light.

TO ——

MINE eyes were dim with tears unshed;
  Yes, I was firm—thus wert not thou;
My baffled looks did fear yet dread
  To meet thy looks—I could not know
How anxiously they sought to shine
With soothing pity upon mine.

To sit and curb the soul's mute rage
  Which preys upon itself alone;
To curse the life which is the cage
  Of fettered grief that dares not groan,
Hiding from many a careless eye
The scorned load of agony.

Whilst thou alone, then not regarded,
  The [   ] thou alone should be,
To spend years thus, and be rewarded,
  As thou, sweet love, requited me
When none were near—Oh! I did wake
From torture for that moment's sake.

Upon my heart thy accents sweet
  Of peace and pity, fell like dew
On flowers half dead;—thy lips did meet
  Mine tremblingly; thy dark eyes threw
Thy soft persuasion on my brain,
Charming away its dream of pain.

We are not happy, sweet; our state
  Is strange and full of doubt and fear;
More need of words that ills abate;
  Reserve or censure come not near
Our sacred friendship, lest there be
No solace left for thou and me.

Gentle and good and mild thou art,
  Nor I can live if thou appear
Aught but thyself, or turn thine heart
  Away from me, or stoop to wear
The mask of scorn, although it be
To hide the love thou feel'st for me.

* * *

THE ISLE.

THERE was a little lawny islet
By anemone and violet,
  Like mosaic, paven:
And its roof was flowers and leaves
Which the summer's breath enweaves,
Where nor sun nor showers nor breeze
Pierce the pines and tallest trees,
  Each a gem engraven.
Girt by many an azure wave
With which the clouds and mountains pave
  A lake's blue chasm.

TO ——

MUSIC, when soft voices die,
Vibrates in the memory—
Odours, when sweet violets sicken,
Live within the sense they quicken.

Rose leaves, when the rose is dead,
Are heaped for the beloved's bed;
And so thy thoughts, when thou art gone,
Love itself shall slumber on.

* * *

TIME.

UNFATHOMABLE Sea! whose waves are years,
  Ocean of Time, whose waters of deep woe
Are brackish with the salt of human tears!
  Thou shoreless flood, which in thy ebb and flow
Claspest the limits of mortality!
And sick of prey, yet howling on for more,
Vomitest thy wrecks on its inhospitable shore,
Treacherous in calm, and terrible in storm,
  Who shall put forth on thee,
  Unfathomable Sea?

* * *

LINES.

THAT time is dead for ever, child,
Drowned, frozen, dead for ever!
  We look on the past
  And stare aghast
At the spectres wailing, pale and ghast,
Of hopes which thou and I beguiled
  To death on life's dark river.

The stream we gazed on then, rolled by;
Its waves are unreturning;
  But we yet stand
  In a lone land,
Like tombs to mark the memory
Of hopes and fears, which fade and flee
In the light of life's dim morning.

November 5th, 1817.

* * *

A SONG.

A WIDOW bird sate mourning for her love
  Upon a wintry bough;
The frozen wind crept on above,
  The freezing stream below.

There was no leaf upon the forest bare,
  No flower upon the ground,
And little motion in the air
    Except the mill-wheel's sound.

THE WORLD'S WANDERERS.

TELL me, thou star, whose wings of
    light
Speed thee in thy fiery flight,
In what cavern of the night
    Will thy pinions close now?

Tell me, moon, thou pale and grey
Pilgrim of heaven's homeless way,
In what depth of night or day
    Seekest thou repose now?

Weary wind, who wanderest
Like the world's rejected guest,
Hast thou still some secret nest
    On the tree or billow?

A DIRGE.

ROUGH wind, that moanest loud
    Grief too sad for song;
Wild wind, when sullen cloud
    Knells all the night long;
Sad storm, whose tears are vain,
Bare woods, whose branches stain,
Deep caves and dreary main,
    Wail for the world's wrong!

LINES.

FAR, far away, O ye
    Halcyons of memory,
Seek some far calmer nest
Than this abandoned breast;

No news of your false spring
To my heart's winter bring,
Once having gone, in vain
    Ye come again.

Vultures, who build your bowers
High in the Future's towers,
Withered hopes on hopes are spread,
Dying joys choked by the dead,
Will serve your beaks for prey
    Many a day.

DIRGE FOR THE YEAR.

ORPHAN hours, the year is dead,
    Come and sigh, come and weep!
Merry hours, smile instead,
    For the year is but asleep.
See, it smiles as it is sleeping,
Mocking your untimely weeping.

As an earthquake rocks a corse
    In its coffin in the clay,
So White Winter, that rough nurse,
    Rocks the death-cold year to-day;
Solemn hours! wait aloud
For your mother in her shroud.

As the wild air stirs and sways
    The tree-swung cradle of a child,
So the breath of these rude days
    Rocks the year:—be calm and mild,
Trembling hours, she will arise
With new love within her eyes.

January grey is here,
    Like a sexton by her grave:
February bears the bier,
    March with grief doth howl and rave,
And April weeps—but, O ye hours,
Follow with May's fairest flowers.

        January 1st, 1821.

MONT BLANC.

LINES WRITTEN IN THE VALE OF CHAMOUNI.

I.

THE everlasting universe of things
Flows through the mind, and rolls its rapid waves,
Now dark—now glittering—now reflecting gloom—
Now lending splendour, where from secret springs
The source of human thought its tribute brings
Of waters,—with a sound but half its own,
Such as a feeble brook will oft assume
In the wild woods, among the mountains lone,
Where waterfalls around it leap for ever,
Where woods and winds contend, and a vast river
Over its rocks ceaselessly bursts and raves.

II.

Thus thou, Ravine of Arve—dark, deep Ravine—
Thou many-coloured, many-voiced vale,
Over whose pines and crags and caverns sail
Fast cloud, shadows, and sunbeams: awful scene,
Where Power in likeness of the Arve comes down
From the ice gulfs that gird his secret throne,
Bursting through these dark mountains like the flame
Of lightning through the tempest;—thou dost lie,
Thy giant brood of pines around thee clinging,
Children of elder time, in whose devotion
The chainless winds still come and ever came
To drink their odours, and their mighty swinging
To hear—an old and solemn harmony:
Thine earthly rainbows stretched across the sweep
Of the ethereal waterfall, whose veil
Robes some unsculptured image; the strange sleep
Which, when the voices of the desert fail,
Wraps all in its own deep eternity;
Thy caverns echoing to the Arve's commotion
A loud, lone sound, no other sound can tame;
Thou art pervaded with that ceaseless motion,
Thou art the path of that unresting sound—
Dizzy Ravine! and when I gaze on thee
I seem as in a trance sublime and strange
To muse on my own separate fantasy,
My own, my human mind, which passively
Now renders and receives fast influencings,
Holding an unremitting interchange
With the clear universe of things around:
One legion of wild thoughts, whose wandering wings
Now float above thy darkness, and now rest
Where that or thou art no unbidden guest,
In the still cave of the witch Poesy,
Seeking among the shadows that pass by
Ghosts of all things that are, some shade of thee,
Some phantom, some faint image; till the breast
From which they fled recalls them, thou art there!

III.

Some say that gleams of a remoter world
Visit the soul in sleep,—that death is slumber,
And that its shapes the busy thoughts outnumber
Of those who wake and live.—I look on high;
Has some unknown omnipotence unfurled
The veil of life and death? or do I lie
In dream, and does the mightier world of sleep
Spread far around and inaccessibly
Its circles? For the very spirit fails,
Driven like a homeless cloud from steep to steep
That vanishes along the viewless gales!
Far, far above, piercing the infinite sky,
Mont Blanc appears,—still, snowy, and serene—
Its subject mountains their unearthly forms
Pile around it, ice and rock; broad vales between
Of frozen floods, unfathomable deeps,
Blue as the overhanging heaven, that spread
And wind among the accumulated steeps:

A desert peopled by the storms alone,
Save when the eagle brings some hunter's bone,
And the wolf tracks her there—how hideously
Its shapes are heaped around ! rude, bare, and high,
Ghastly, and scarred, and riven.—Is this the scene
Where the old Earthquake-demon taught her young
Ruin ? Were these their toys ? or did a sea
Of fire envelope once this silent snow ?
None can reply—all seems eternal now.
The wilderness has a mysterious tongue
Which teaches awful doubt, or faith so mild,
So solemn, so serene, that man may be
But for such faith with nature reconciled ;
Thou hast a voice, great Mountain, to repeal
Large codes of fraud and woe ; not understood
By all, but which the wise, and great, and good
Interpret, or make felt, or deeply feel.

IV.

The fields, the lakes, the forests, and the streams,
Ocean, and all the living things that dwell
Within the dædal earth ; lightning and rain,
Earthquake, and fiery flood, and hurricane,
The torpor of the year when feeble dreams
Visit the hidden buds, or dreamless sleep
Holds every future leaf and flower ;—the bound
With which from that detested trance they leap ;
The works and ways of man, their death and birth,
And that of him and all that his may be ;
All things that move and breathe with toil and sound
Are born and die, revolve, subside and swell.
Power dwells apart in its tranquillity
Remote, serene, and inaccessible :
And *this*, the naked countenance of earth,
On which I gaze, even these primeval mountains,
Teach the adverting mind.   The glaciers creep
Like snakes that watch their prey, from their far fountains,
Slow rolling on ; there, many a precipice
Frost and the Sun in scorn of mortal power
Have piled—dome, pyramid, and pinnacle,
A city of death, distinct with many a tower
And wall impregnable of beaming ice.
Yet not a city, but a flood of ruin
Is there, that from the boundaries of the sky
Rolls its perpetual stream; vast pines are strewing
Its destined path, or in the mangled soil
Branchless and shattered stand; the rocks, drawn down
From yon remotest waste, have overthrown
The limits of the dead and living world,
Never to be reclaimed.   The dwelling-place
Of insects, beasts, and birds becomes its spoil;
Their food and their retreat for ever gone,
So much of life and joy is lost.   The race
Of man flies far in dread; his work and dwelling
Vanish, like smoke before the tempest's stream,
And their place is not known.   Below, vast caves
Shine in the rushing torrent's restless gleam,
Which from those secret chasms in tumult welling

Meet in the vale, and one majestic River,
The breath and blood of distant lands, for ever
Rolls its loud waters to the ocean waves,
Breathes its swift vapours to the circling air.

v.

Mont Blanc yet gleams on high:—the power is there,
The still and solemn power of many sights
And many sounds, and much of life and death.
In the calm darkness of the moonless nights,
In the lone glare of day, the snows descend
Upon that Mountain; none beholds them there,
Nor when the flakes burn in the sinking sun,
Or the star-beams dart through them:—Winds contend
Silently there, and heap the snow with breath
Rapid and strong, but silently ! Its home
The voiceless lightning in these solitudes
Keeps innocently, and like vapour broods
Over the snow. The secret strength of things
Which governs thought, and to the infinite dome
Of heaven is as a law, inhabits thee !
And what were thou, and earth, and stars, and sea
If to the human mind's imaginings
Silence and solitude were vacancy ?

Switzerland, June 23, 1816.

THE SUNSET.

THERE late was One within whose subtle being
As light and wind within some delicate cloud,
That fades amid the blue noon's burning sky,
Genius and death contended. None may know
The sweetness of the joy which made his breath
Fail, like the trances of the summer air,
When, with the Lady of his love, who then
First knew the unreserve of mingled being,
He walked along the pathway of a field
Which to the east a hoar wood shadowed o'er,
But to the west was open to the sky.
There now the sun had sunk, but lines of gold
Hung on the ashen clouds, and on the points
Of the far level grass and nodding flowers
And the old dandelion's hoary beard,
And, mingled with the shades of twilight, lay
On the brown massy woods—and in the east
The broad and burning moon lingeringly rose
Between the black trunks of the crowded trees,
While the faint stars were gathering overhead.
" Is it not strange, Isabel," said the youth,
" I never saw the sun ? We will walk here
To-morrow; thou shalt look on it with me."

That night the youth and lady mingled lay
In love and sleep—but when the morning came
The lady found her lover dead and cold.
Let none believe that God in mercy gave

That stroke. The lady died not, nor grew wild,
But year by year lived on—in truth I think
Her gentleness and patience and sad smiles,
And that she did not die, but lived to tend
Her aged father, were a kind of madness,
If madness 'tis to be unlike the world.
For but to see her were to read the tale
Woven by some subtlest bard, to make hard hearts
Dissolve away in wisdom-working grief;
Her eyelashes were worn away with tears,
Her lips and cheeks were like things dead—so pale;
Her hands were thin, and through their wandering veins
And weak articulations might be seen
Day's ruddy light. The tomb of thy dead self
Which one vexed ghost inhabits, night and day,
Is all, lost child, that now remains of thee !

    "Inheritor of more than earth can give,
Passionless calm and silence unreproved
Whether the dead find, oh, not sleep ! but rest,
And are the uncomplaining things they seem,
Or live, or drop in the deep sea of Love;
Oh, that like thine, mine epitaph were—Peace !"
    This was the only moan she ever made
1816.

MARIANNE'S DREAM.

A PALE dream came to a Lady fair,
    And said, a boon, a boon, I pray !
I know the secrets of the air,
    And things are lost in the glare of day,
Which I can make the sleeping see,
If they will put their trust in me.

And thou shalt know of things unknown,
    If thou wilt let me rest between
The veiny lids, whose fringe is thrown
    Over thine eyes so dark and sheen:
And half in hope, and half in fright,
The Lady closed her eyes so bright.

At first all deadly shapes were driven
    Tumultuously across her sleep,
And o'er the vast cope of bending heaven
    All ghastly visaged clouds did sweep;
And the Lady ever looked to spy
If the gold sun shone forth on high.

And as towards the east she turned,
    She saw aloft in the morning air,
Which now with hues of sunrise burned
    A great black Anchor rising there;
And wherever the Lady turned her eyes
It hung before her in the skies.

The sky was blue as the summer sea,
    The depths were cloudless overhead

The air was calm as it could be,
　There was no sight or sound of dread,
But that black Anchor floating still
Over the piny eastern hill.

The Lady grew sick with a weight of fear
　To see that Anchor ever hanging,
And veiled her eyes; she then did hear
　The sound as of a dim low clanging,
And looked abroad if she might know
Was it aught else, or but the flow
Of the blood in her own veins, to and fro.

There was a mist in the sunless air,
　Which shook as it were with an earthquake's shock,
But the very weeds that blossomed there
　Were moveless, and each mighty rock
Stood on its basis steadfastly;
The Anchor was seen no more on high.

But piled around, with summits hid
　In lines of cloud at intervals,
Stood many a mountain pyramid
　Among whose everlasting walls
Two mighty cities shone, and ever
Through the red mist their domes did quiver.

On two dread mountains, from whose crest,
　Might seem, the eagle, for her brood,
Would ne'er have hung her dizzy nest,
　Those tower-encircled cities stood,
A vision strange such towers to see,
Sculptured and wrought so gorgeously,
Where human art could never be.

And columns framed of marble white,
　And giant fanes, dome over dome
Piled and triumphant gates, all bright
　With workmanship that could not come
From touch of mortal instrument,
Shot o'er the vales, or lustre lent
From its own shapes magnificent.

But still the Lady heard that clang
　Filling the wide air far away;
And still the mist whose light did hang
　Among the mountains shook alway,
So that the Lady's heart beat fast,
As half in joy, and half aghast,
On those high domes her look she cast.

Sudden, from out that city sprung
　A light that made the earth grow red;
Two flames that each with quivering tongue
　Licked its high domes, and overhead
Among those mighty towers and fanes
Dropped fire, as a volcano rains
Its sulphurous ruin on the plains.

L L

And hark ! a rush as if the deep
   Had burst its bonds ; she looked behind
And saw over the western steep
   A raging flood descend, and wind
Through that wide vale ; she felt no fear,
But said within herself, 'tis clear
These towers are Nature's own, and she
To save them has sent forth the sea.

And now those raging billows came
   Where that fair Lady sate, and she
Was borne towards the showering flame
   By the wild waves heaped tumultuously,
And on a little plank, the flow
Of the whirlpool bore her to and fro.

The waves were fiercely vomited
   From every tower and every dome,
And dreary light did widely shed
   O'er that vast flood's suspended foam,
Beneath the smoke which hung its night
On the stained cope of heaven's light.

The plank whereon that Lady sate
   Was driven through the chasms, about and about,
Between the peaks so desolate
   Of the drowning mountain, in and out,
As the thistle-beard on a whirlwind sails—
While the flood was filling those hollow vales.

At last her plank an eddy crost,
   And bore her to the city's wall,
Which now the flood had reached almost ;
   It might the stoutest heart appal
To hear the fire roar and hiss
Through the domes of those mighty palaces.

The eddy whirled her round and round
   Before a gorgeous gate, which stood
Piercing the clouds of smoke which bound
   Its aery arch with light like blood ;
She looked on that gate of marble clear,
With wonder that extinguished fear.

For it was filled with sculptures rarest,
   Of forms most beautiful and strange,
Like nothing human, but the fairest
   Of winged shapes, whose legions range
Throughout the sleep of those that are,
Like this same Lady, good and fair.

And as she looked, still lovelier grew
   Those marble forms ;—the sculptor sure
Was a strong spirit, and the hue
   Of his own mind did there endure
After the touch, whose power had braided
Such grace, was in some sad change faded.

She looked, the flames were dim, the flood
  Grew tranquil as a woodland river
Winding through hills in solitude ;
  Those marble shapes then seemed to quiver,
And their fair limbs to float in motion,
Like weeds unfolding in the ocean.

And their lips moved ; one seemed to speak,
  When suddenly the mountain crackt,
And through the chasm the flood did break
  With an earth-uplifting cataract :
The statues gave a joyous scream,
And on its wings the pale thin dream
Lifted the Lady from the stream.

The dizzy flight of that phantom pale
  Waked the fair Lady from her sleep,
And she arose, while from the veil
  Of her dark eyes the dream did creep,
And she walked about as one who knew
That sleep has sights as clear and true
As any waking eyes can view.

Marlow, 1817.

LINES TO AN INDIAN AIR.

I ARISE from dreams of thee
In the first sweet sleep of night,
When the winds are breathing low,
And the stars are shining bright :
I arise from dreams of thee,
And a spirit in my feet
Has led me—who knows how ?
To thy chamber window, sweet !

The wandering airs they faint
On the dark, the silent stream—
The champak odours fail
Like sweet thoughts in a dream ;
The nightingale's complaint,
It dies upon her heart,
As I must die on thine,
Beloved as thou art !

O lift me from the grass !
I die, I faint, I fail !
Let thy love in kisses rain
On my lips and eyelids pale.
My cheek is cold and white, alas !
My heart beats loud and fast,
Oh ! press it close to thine again,
Where it will break at last.

STANZAS.

THE sun is warm, the sky is clear,
  The waves are dancing fast and bright,
Blue isles and snowy mountains wear

The purple noon's transparent light :
The breath of the moist earth is light
    Around its unexpanded buds ;
Like many a voice of one delight,
    The winds, the birds, the ocean floods,
The City's voice itself is soft, like Solitude's.

I see the Deep's untrampled floor
    With green and purple seaweeds strown ;
I see the waves upon the shore,
    Like light dissolved in star-showers, thrown :
I sit upon the sands alone,
    The lightning of the noontide ocean
Is flashing round me, and a tone
    Arises from its measured motion,
How sweet ! did any heart now share in my emotion.

Alas ! I have nor hope nor health,
    Nor peace within nor calm around,
Nor that content surpassing wealth
    The sage in meditation found,
And walked with inward glory crowned—
    Nor fame, nor power, nor love, nor leisure.
Others I see whom these surround—
    Smiling they live and call life pleasure;
To me that cup has been dealt in another measure.

Yet now despair itself is mild,
    Even as the winds and waters are ;
I could lie down like a tired child,
    And weep away the life of care
Which I have borne and yet must bear,
    Till death like sleep might steal on me,
And I might feel in the warm air
    My cheek grow cold, and hear the sea
Breathe o'er my dying brain its last monotony.

Some might lament that I were cold,
    As I, when this sweet day is gone,
Which my lost heart, too soon grown old,
    Insults with this untimely moan ;
They might lament—for I am one
    Whom men love not,—and yet regret,
Unlike this day, which, when the sun
    Shall on its stainless glory set,
Will linger, though enjoyed, like joy in memory yet.

December, 1818.

AUTUMN:

A DIRGE.

THE warm sun is failing, the bleak wind is wailing,
The bare boughs are sighing, the pale flowers are dying,
            And the year
On the earth her deathbed, in a shroud of leaves dead,
            Is lying.

Come, months, come away,
From November to May,
In your saddest array ;
Follow the bier
Of the dead cold year,
And like dim shadows watch by her sepulchre.

The chill rain is falling, the nipt worm is crawling,
The rivers are swelling, the thunder is knelling
For the year ;
The blithe swallows are flown, and the lizards each gone
To his dwelling ;
Come, months, come away;
Put on white, black, and grey,
Let your light sisters play—
Ye, follow the bier
Of the dead cold year,
And make her grave green with tear on tear.

THE CLOUD.

I BRING fresh showers for the thirsting flowers,
From the seas and the streams ;
I bear light shade for the leaves when laid
In their noonday dreams.
From my wings are shaken the dews that waken
The sweet birds every one,
When rocked to rest on their mother's breast,
As she dances about the sun.
I wield the flail of the lashing hail,
And whiten the green plains under,
And then again I dissolve it in rain,
And laugh as I pass in thunder.

I sift the snow on the mountains below,
And their great pines groan aghast ;
And all the night 'tis my pillow white,
While I sleep in the arms of the blast.
Sublime on the towers of my skiey bowers,
Lightning my pilot sits,
In a cavern under is fettered the thunder,
It struggles and howls at fits ;
Over earth and ocean, with gentle motion,
This pilot is guiding me,
Lured by the love of the genii that move
In the depths of the purple sea ;
Over the rills, and the crags, and the hills,
Over the lakes and the plains,
Wherever he dream, under mountain or stream,
The Spirit he loves remains ;
And I all the while bask in heaven's blue smile,
Whilst he is dissolving in rains.

The sanguine sunrise, with his meteor eyes,
And his burning plumes outspread,
Leaps on the back of my sailing rack,
When the morning star shines dead.

As on the jag of a mountain crag,
　　Which an earthquake rocks and swings,
An eagle alit one moment may sit
　　In the light of its golden wings.
And when sunset may breathe, from the lit sea beneath,
　　Its ardours of rest and of love,
And the crimson pall of eve may fall
　　From the depth of heaven above,
With wings folded I rest, on mine airy nest,
　　As still as a brooding dove.

That orbèd maiden with white fire laden,
　　Whom mortals call the moon,
Glides glimmering o'er my fleece-like floor,
　　By the midnight breezes strewn ;
And wherever the heat of her unseen feet,
　　Which only the angels hear,
May have broken the woof of my tent's thin roof,
　　The stars peep behind her and peer ;
And I laugh to see them whirl and flee,
　　Like a swarm of golden bees,
When I widen the rent in my wind-built tent,
　　Till the calm rivers, lakes, and seas,
Like strips of the sky fallen through me on high,
　　Are each paved with the moon and these.

I bind the sun's throne with a burning zone,
　　And the moon's with a girdle of pearl;
The volcanoes are dim, and the stars reel and swim,
　　When the whirlwinds my banner unfurl.
From cape to cape, with a bridge-like shape,
　　Over a torrent sea,
Sunbeam-proof, I hang like a roof,
　　The mountains its columns be.
The triumphal arch through which I march
　　With hurricane, fire, and snow,
When the powers of the air are chained to my chair,
　　Is the million-coloured bow;
The sphere-fire above its soft colours wove,
　　While the moist earth was laughing below.

I am the daughter of earth and water,
　　And the nursling of the sky;
I pass through the pores of the ocean and shores ;
　　I change, but I cannot die.
For after the rain when with never a stain,
　　The pavilion of heaven is bare,
And the winds and sunbeams with their convex gleams,
　　Build up the blue dome of air,
I silently laugh at my own cenotaph,
　　And out of the caverns of rain,
Like a child from the womb, like a ghost from the tomb,
　　I arise and unbuild it again.

AN EXHORTATION.

CHAMELEONS feed on light and air;
   Poets' food is love and fame.
If in this wide world of care
   Poets could but find the same
With as little toil as they,
    Would they ever change their hue
   As the light chameleons do,
Suiting it to every ray
    Twenty times a-day?

Poets are on this cold earth
   As chameleons might be
Hidden from their early birth
   In a cave beneath the sea.
Where light is, chameleons change;
    Where love is not, poets do.
   Fame is love disguised: if few
Find either, never think it strange
    That poets range.

Yet dare not stain with wealth or power
   A poet's free and heavenly mind.
If bright chameleons should devour
   Any food but beams and wind,
They would grow as earthly soon
    As their brother lizards are.
   Children of a sunnier star,
Spirits from beyond the moon,
    Oh! refuse the boon!

LINES WRITTEN AMONG THE EUGANEAN HILLS,

OCTOBER, 1818.

MANY a green isle needs must be
In the deep wide sea of misery,
Or the mariner, worn and wan,
Never thus could voyage on
Day and night, and night and day,
Drifting on his dreary way,
With the solid darkness black
Closing round his vessel's track;
Whilst above the sunless sky,
Big with clouds, hangs heavily,
And behind the tempest fleet
Hurries on with lightning feet,
Riving sail, and cord, and plank,
Till the ship has almost drank
Death from the o'er-brimming deep;
And sinks down, down, like that sleep
When the dreamer seems to be
Weltering through eternity;
And the dim low line before
Of a dark and a distant shore
Still recedes, as ever still
Longing with divided will,

But no power to seek or shun,
He is ever drifted on
O'er the unreposing wave
To the haven of the grave.
What, if there no friends will greet;
What, if there no heart will meet
His with love's impatient beat;
Wander wheresoe'er he may,
Can he dream before that day
To find refuge from distress
In friendship's smile, in love's caress?
Then 'twill wreak him little woe
Whether such there be or no:
Senseless is the breast, and cold,
Which relenting love would fold;
Bloodless are the veins and chill
Which the pulse of pain did fill;
Every little living nerve
That from bitter words did swerve
Round the tortured lips and brow,
Are like sapless leaflets now
Frozen upon December's bough.

On the beach of a northern sea
Which tempests shake eternally,
As once the wretch there lay to sleep,
Lies a solitary heap,
One white skull and seven dry bones,
On the margin of the stones,
Where a few grey rushes stand,
Boundaries of the sea and land:
Nor is heard one voice of wail
But the seamews, as they sail
O'er the billows of the gale;
Or the whirlwind up and down
Howling, like a slaughtered town,
When a king in glory rides
Through the pomp of fratricides:
Those unburied bones around
There is many a mournful sound;
There is no lament for him,
Like a sunless vapour, dim,
Who once clothed with life and thought
What now moves nor murmurs not.

Ay, many flowering islands lie
In the waters of wide Agony:
To such a one this morn was led,
My bark by soft winds piloted:
'Mid the mountains Euganean
I stood listening to the pæan,
With which the legioned rooks did hail
The sun's uprise majestical;
Gathering round with wings all hoar,
Through the dewy mist they soar
Like grey shades, till the eastern heaven
Bursts, and then, as clouds of even,
Flecked with fire and azure, lie
In the unfathomable sky,
So their plumes of purple grain,
Starred with drops of golden rain,
Gleam above the sunlight woods,
As in silent multitudes
On the morning's fitful gale
Through the broken mist they sail,
And the vapours cloven and gleaming
Follow down the dark steep streaming,
Till all is bright, and clear, and still,
Round the solitary hill.

Beneath is spread like a green sea
The waveless plain of Lombardy,
Bounded by the vaporous air,
Islanded by cities fair;
Underneath day's azure eyes
Ocean's nursling, Venice lies,
A peopled labyrinth of walls,
Amphitrite's destined halls,
Which her hoary sire now paves
With his blue and beaming waves.
Lo! the sun upsprings behind,
Broad, red, radiant, half reclined

On the level quivering line
Of the waters crystalline;
And before that chasm of light,
As within a furnace bright,
Column, tower, and dome, and spire,
Shine like obelisks of fire,
Pointing with inconstant motion
From the altar of dark ocean
To the sapphire-tinted skies;
As the flames of sacrifice
From the marble shrines did rise,
As to pierce the dome of gold
Where Apollo spoke of old.

Sun-girt City, thou hast been
Ocean's child, and then his queen·
Now is come a darker day,
And thou soon must be his prey,
If the power that raised thee here
Hallow so thy watery bier.
A less drear ruin then than now,
With thy conquest-branded brow
Stooping to the slave of slaves
From thy throne, among the waves
Wilt thou be, when the seamew
Flies, as once before it flew,
O'er thine isles depopulate,
And all is in its ancient state,
Save where many a palace gate
With green sea-flowers overgrown
Like a rock of ocean's own,
Topples o'er the abandoned sea
As the tides change sullenly.
The fisher on his watery way,
Wandering at the close of day,
Will spread his sail and seize his oar
Till he pass the gloomy shore,
Lest thy dead should, from their sleep
Bursting o'er the starlight deep,
Lead a rapid masque of death
O'er the waters of his path.

Those who alone thy towers behold
Quivering through aërial gold,
As I now behold them here,
Would imagine not they were
Sepulchres, where human forms,
Like pollution-nourished worms
To the corpse of greatness cling,
Murdered, and now mouldering:
But if Freedom should awake
In her omnipotence, and shake
From the Celtic Anarch's hold
All the keys of dungeons cold,
Where a hundred cities lie
Chained like thee, ingloriously,
Thou and all thy sister band
Might adorn this sunny land,

Twining memories of old time
With new virtues more sublime;
If not, perish thou and they,
Clouds which stain truth's rising day
By her sun consumed away,
Earth can spare ye: while like flowers,
In the waste of years and hours,
From your dust new nations spring
With more kindly blossoming.
Perish ! let there only be
Floating o'er thy hearthless sea,
As the garment of thy sky
Clothes the world immortally,
One remembrance, more sublime
Than the tattered pall of time,
Which scarce hides thy visage wan;
That a tempest-cleaving swan
Of the songs of Albion,
Driven from his ancestral streams
By the might of evil dreams,
Found a nest in thee; and Ocean
Welcomed him with such emotion
That its joy grew his, and sprung
From his lips like music flung
O'er a mighty thunder-fit,
Chastening terror: what though yet
Poesy's unfailing river,
Which through Albion winds for ever,
Lashing with melodious wave
Many a sacred poet's grave,
Mourn its latest nursling fled !
What though thou with all thy dead
Scarce can for this fame repay
Aught thine own,—oh, rather say,
Though thy sins and slaveries foul
Overcloud a sunlike soul !
As the ghost of Homer clings
Round Scamander's wasting springs;
As divinest Shakspeare's might
Fills Avon and the world with light
Like omniscient power, which he
Imaged 'mid mortality;
As the love from Petrarch's urn,
Yet amid yon hills doth burn,
A quenchless lamp, by which the heart
Sees things unearthly; so thou art,
Mighty spirit: so shall be
The city that did refuge thee.

Lo, the sun floats up the sky
Like thought-wingèd Liberty,
Till the universal light
Seems to level plain and height;
From the sea a mist has spread,
And the beams of morn lie dead
On the towers of Venice now.
Like its glory long ago.

By the skirts of that grey cloud
Many-domed Padua proud
Stands, a peopled solitude,
'Mid the harvest shining plain,
Where the peasant heaps his grain
In the garner of his foe,
And the milk-white oxen slow
With the purple vintage strain,
Heaped upon the creaking wain,
That the brutal Celt may swill
Drunken sleep with savage will ;
And the sickle to the sword
Lies unchanged, though many a lord,
Like a weed whose shade is poison,
Overgrows this region's foison,
Sheaves of whom are ripe to come
To destruction's harvest home:
Men must reap the things they sow,
Force from force must ever flow,
Or worse; but 'tis a bitter woe
That love or reason cannot change
The despot's rage, the slave's revenge.

Padua, thou within whose walls
Those mute guests at festivals,
Son and Mother, Death and Sin,
Played at dice for Ezzelin,
Till Death cried, " I win, I win !"
And Sin cursed to lose the wager,
But Death promised, to assuage her,
That he would petition for
Her to be made Vice-Emperor,
When the destined years were o'er,
Over all between the Po
And the eastern Alpine snow,
Under the mighty Austrian.
Sin smiled so as Sin only can,
And since that time, ay, long before,
Both have ruled from shore to shore,
That incestuous pair, who follow
Tyrants as the sun the swallow,
As Repentance follows Crime,
And as changes follow Time.

In thine halls the lamp of learning,
Padua, now no more is burning;
Like a meteor, whose wild way
Is lost over the grave of day,
It gleams betrayed and to betray :
Once remotest nations came
To adore that sacred flame,
When it lit not many a hearth
On this cold and gloomy earth :
Now new fires from antique light
Spring beneath the wide world's might;
But their spark lies dead in thee,
Trampled out by tyranny.
As the Norway woodman quells,
In the depth of piny dells,

One light flame among the brakes,
While the boundless forest shakes,
And its mighty trunks are torn
By the fire thus lowly born :
The spark beneath his feet is dead,
He starts to see the flames it fed
Howling through the darkened sky
With a myriad tongues victoriously,
And sinks down in fear : so thou,
O tyranny, beholdest now
Light around thee, and thou hearest
The loud flames ascend, and fearest :
Grovel on the earth : ay, hide
In the dust thy purple pride !

Noon descends around me now :
'Tis the noon of autumn's glow,
When a soft and purple mist
Like a vaporous amethyst,
Or an air-dissolvèd star
Mingling light and fragrance, far
From the curved horizon's bound
To the point of heaven's profound,
Fills the overflowing sky ;
And the plains that silent lie
Underneath, the leaves unsodden
Where the infant frost has trodden
With his morning-wingèd feet,
Whose bright print is gleaming yet ;
And the red and golden vines,
Piercing with their trellised lines
The rough, dark-skirted wilderness ;
The dun and bladed grass no less,
Pointing from this hoary tower
In the windless air ; the flower
Glimmering at my feet ; the line
Of the olive-sandalled Apennine
In the south dimly islanded ;
And the Alps, whose snows are spread
High between the clouds and sun ;
And of living things each one ;
And my spirit which so long
Darkened this swift stream of song,
Interpenetrated lie
By the glory of the sky :
Be it love, light, harmony,
Odour, or the soul of all
Which from heaven like dew doth fall,
Or the mind which feeds this verse
Peopling the lone universe.

Noon descends, and after noon
Autumn's evening meets me soon,
Leading the infantine moon,

And that one star, which to her
Almost seems to minister
Half the crimson light she brings
From the sunset's radiant springs :
And the soft dreams of the morn
(Which like wingèd winds had borne
To that silent isle, which lies
'Mid remembered agonies,
The frail bark of this lone being),
Pass, to other sufferers fleeing,
And its ancient pilot, Pain,
Sits beside the helm again.

Other flowering isles must be
In the sea of life and agony :
Other spirits float and flee
O'er that gulf : even now, perhaps,
On some rock the wild wave wraps,
With folded wings they waiting sit
For my bark, to pilot it
To some calm and blooming cove,
Where for me, and those I love,
May a windless bower be built,
Far from passion, pain, and guilt,
In a dell 'mid lawny hills,
Which the wild sea-murmur fills,
And soft sunshine, and the sound
Of old forests echoing round,
And the light and smell divine
Of all flowers that breathe and shine :
We may live so happy there,
That the spirits of the air,
Envying us, may even entice
To our healing paradise
The polluting multitude ;
But their rage would be subdued
By that clime divine and calm,
And the winds whose wings rain balm
On the uplifted soul, and leaves
Under which the bright sea heaves ;
While each breathless interval
In their whisperings musical
The inspired soul supplies
With its own deep melodies,
And the love which heals all strife
Circling, like the breath of life,
All things in that sweet abode
With its own mild brotherhood :
They, not it would change ; and soon
Every sprite beneath the moon
Would repent its envy vain,
And the earth grow young again.

HYMN TO INTELLECTUAL BEAUTY.

THE awful shadow of some unseen Power
Floats though unseen among us ; visiting
    This various world with as inconstant wing
As summer winds that creep from flower to flower ;
Like moonbeams that behind some piny mountain shower,
      It visits with inconstant glance
      Each human heart and countenance ;
Like hues and harmonies of evening,
      Like clouds in starlight widely spread,
      Like memory of music fled,
      Like aught that for its grace may be
Dear, and yet dearer for its mystery.

Spirit of BEAUTY, that dost consecrate
      With thine own hues all thou dost shine upon
      Of human thought or form, where art thou gone ?
Why dost thou pass away and leave our state,
This dim vast vale of tears, vacant and desolate ?
      Ask why the sunlight not for ever
      Weaves rainbows o'er yon mountain river ;
Why aught should fail and fade that once is shown ;
      Why fear and dream and death and birth
      Cast on the daylight of this earth
      Such gloom, why man has such a scope
For love and hate, despondency and hope ?

No voice from some sublimer world hath ever
      To sage or poet these responses given :
      Therefore the names of Demon, Ghost, and Heaven,
Remain the records of their vain endeavour :
Frail spells, whose uttered charm might not avail to sever,
      From all we hear and all we see,
      Doubt, chance, and mutability.
Thy light alone, like mist o'er mountains driven,
      Or music by the night wind sent
      Through strings of some still instrument,
      Or moonlight on a midnight stream,
Gives grace and truth to life's unquiet dream.

Love, Hope, and Self-esteem, like clouds, depart
      And come, for some uncertain moments lent.
      Man were immortal, and omnipotent,
Didst thou, unknown and awful as thou art,
Keep with thy glorious train firm state within his heart.
      Thou messenger of sympathies
      That wax and wane in lover's eyes;
Thou, that to human thought art nourishment,
      Like darkness to a dying flame !
      Depart not as thy shadow came:
      Depart not, lest the grave should be,
Like life and fear, a dark reality.

While yet a boy I sought for ghosts, and sped
      Through many a listening chamber, cave and ruin,
      And starlight wood, with fearful steps pursuing
Hopes of high talk with the departed dead.
I called on poisonous names with which our youth is fed:

I was not heard: I saw them not:
　　When musing deeply on the lot
　　　Of life, at that sweet time when winds are wooing
　　　All vital things that wake to bring
　　　News of birds and blossoming,
　　Sudden thy shadow fell on me:
I shrieked, and clasped my hands in ecstasy!

I vowed that I would dedicate my powers
　　To thee and thine: have I not kept the vow?
　　　With beating heart and streaming eyes, even now
　　I call the phantoms of a thousand hours
Each from his voiceless grave: they have in visioned bowers
　　Of studious zeal or love's delight
　　Outwatched with me the envious night:
They know that never joy illumed my brow,
　　Unlinked with hope that thou wouldst free
　　This world from its dark slavery,
　　That thou, O awful LOVELINESS,
Wouldst give whate'er these words cannot express.

The day becomes more solemn and serene
　　When noon is past: there is a harmony
　　　In autumn, and a lustre in its sky,
　　Which through the summer is not heard or seen,
As if it could not be, as if it had not been!
　　Thus let thy power, which like the truth
　　Of nature on my passive youth
Descended, to my outward life supply
　　Its calm, to one who worships thee,
　　And every form containing thee,
　　Whom, SPIRIT fair, thy spells did bind
To fear himself, and love all human kind.

ARETHUSA.

ARETHUSA arose
　　From her couch of snows
In the Acroceraunian mountains,—
　　From cloud and from crag,
　　With many a jag,
Shepherding her bright fountains.
　　She leapt down the rocks
　　With her rainbow locks
Streaming among the streams;
　　Her steps paved with green
　　The downward ravine
Which slopes to the western gleams:
　　And gliding and springing,
　　She went, ever singing,
In murmurs as soft as sleep;
　　The Earth seemed to love her,
　　And Heaven smiled above her,
As she lingered towards the deep.

　　Then Alpheus bold,
　　On his glacier cold,
With his trident the mountains strook;

And opened a chasm
　　In the rocks;—with the spasm
All Erymanthus shook.
　　And the black south wind
　　It concealed behind
The urns of the silent snow,
　　And earthquake and thunder
　　Did rend in sunder
The bars of the springs below:
　　The beard and the hair
　　Of the river God were
Seen through the torrent's sweep,
　　As he followed the light
　　Of the fleet nymph's flight
To the brink of the Dorian deep.

　　"Oh, save me! Oh, guide me!
　　And bid the deep hide me.
For he grasps me now by the hair!"
　　The loud Ocean heard,
　　To its blue depth stirred,
And divided at her prayer;

And under the water
  The Earth's white daughter
Fled like a sunny beam,
  Behind her descended,
  Her billows unblended
With the brackish Dorian stream:
  Like a gloomy stain
  On the emerald main
Alpheus rushed behind,—
  As an eagle pursuing
  A dove to its ruin
Down the streams of the cloudy wind.

  Under the bowers
  Where the Ocean Powers
Sit on their pearlèd thrones,
  Through the coral woods
  Of the weltering floods,
Over heaps of unvalued stones :
  Through the dim beams
  Which amid the streams
Weave a network of coloured light ;
  And under the caves,
  Where the shadowy waves
Are as green as the forest's night :
  Outspeeding the shark,
  And the swordfish dark,

Under the ocean foam,
  And up through the rifts
  Of the mountain clifts
They passed to their Dorian home.

  And now from their fountains
  In Enna's mountains,
Down one vale where the morning basks,
  Like friends once parted
  Grown single-hearted,
They ply their watery tasks.
  At sunrise they leap
  From their cradles steep
In the cave of the shelving hill;
  At noontide they flow
  Through the woods below
And the meadows of Asphodel;
  And at night they sleep
  In the rocking deep
Beneath the Ortygian shore ;
  Like spirits that lie
  In the azure sky
When they love but live no more.

  Pisa, 1820.

THE QUESTION.

I DREAMED that, as I wandered by the way,
  Bare winter suddenly was changed to spring,
And gentle odours led my steps astray,
  Mixed with a sound of waters murmuring
Along a shelving bank of turf, which lay
  Under a copse, and hardly dared to fling
Its green arms round the bosom of the stream,
But kissed it and then fled, as thou mightest in dream.

There grew pied wind-flowers and violets,
  Daisies, those pearled Arcturi of the earth,
The constellated flower that never sets;
  Faint oxlips; tender bluebells, at whose birth
The sod scarce heaved; and that tall flower that wets
  Its mother's face with heaven-collected tears,
When the low wind, its playmate's voice, it hears.

And in the warm hedge grew lush eglantine,
  Green cowbind and the moonlight-coloured May,
And cherry blossoms, and white cups, whose wine
  Was the bright dew yet drained not by the day;
And wild roses, and ivy serpentine,
  With its dark buds and leaves, wandering astray;
And flowers azure, black and streaked with gold,
Fairer than any wakened eyes behold.

And nearer to the river's trembling edge
  There grew broad flag flowers, purple prankt with white.

And starry river buds among the sedge,
  And floating water-lilies, broad and bright,
Which lit the oak that overhung the hedge
  With moonlight beams of their own watery light;
And bulrushes, and reeds of such deep green
As soothed the dazzled eye with sober sheen.

Methought that of these visionary flowers
  I made a nosegay, bound in such a way
That the same hues, which in their natural bowers
  Were mingled or opposed, the like array
Kept these imprisoned children of the Hours
  Within my hand,—and then, elate and gay,
I hastened to the spot whence I had come,
That I might there present it!—Oh! to whom?

HYMN OF APOLLO.

The sleepless Hours who watch me as I lie,
  Curtained with star-enwoven tapestries,
From the broad moonlight of the sky,
  Fanning the busy dreams from my dim eyes,—
Waken me when their Mother, the grey Dawn,
Tells them that dreams and that the moon is gone.

Then I arise, and climbing Heaven's blue dome,
  I walk over the mountains and the waves,
Leaving my robe upon the ocean foam;
  My footsteps pave the clouds with fire; the caves
Are filled with my bright presence, and the air
Leaves the green earth to my embraces bare.

The sunbeams are my shafts, with which I kill
  Deceit, that loves the night and fears the day;
All men who do or even imagine ill
  Fly me, and from the glory of my ray
Good minds and open actions take new might,
Until diminished by the reign of night.

I feed the clouds, the rainbows and the flowers
  With their ethereal colours; the Moon's globe
And the pure stars in their eternal bowers
  Are cinctured with my power as with a robe;
Whatever lamps on Earth or Heaven may shine,
Are portions of one power, which is mine.

I stand at noon upon the peak of Heaven,
  Then with unwilling steps I wander down
Into the clouds of the Atlantic even;
  For grief that I depart they weep and frown:
What look is more delightful than the smile
With which I soothe them from the western isle?

I am the eye with which the Universe
  Beholds itself and knows itself divine;
All harmony of instrument or verse,
  All prophecy, all medicine are mine,
All light of art or nature;—to my song,
Victory and praise in their own right belong.

HYMN OF PAN.

FROM the forests and highlands
 We come, we come ;
From the river-girt islands,
 Where loud waves are dumb
  Listening to my sweet pipings.
The wind in the reeds and the rushes,
 The bees on the bells of thyme,
The birds on the myrtle bushes,
 The cicale above in the lime,
And the lizards below in the grass,
Were as silent as ever old Tmolus* was,
  Listening to my sweet pipings.

Liquid Peneus was flowing,
 And all dark Tempe lay
In Pelion's shadow, outgrowing
 The light of the dying day,
  Speeded by my sweet pipings.
The Sileni, and Sylvans, and Fauns,
 And the Nymphs of the woods and waves,
To the edge of the moist river-lawns,
 And the brink of the dewy caves,
And all that did then attend and follow
Were silent with love, as you now, Apollo,
  With envy of my sweet pipings.

I sang of the dancing stars,
 I sang of the dædal Earth,
And of Heaven—and the giant wars,
 And Love, and Death, and Birth,—
  And then I changed my pipings,—
Singing how down the vale of Menalus
 I pursued a maiden and clasped a reed :
Gods and men, we are all deluded thus !
 It breaks in our bosom and then we bleed :
All wept, as I think both ye now would,
If envy or age had not frozen your blood,
  At the sorrow of my sweet pipings.

THE TWO SPIRITS:

AN ALLEGORY.

FIRST SPIRIT.

OH thou, who plumed with strong desire
 Would float above the earth, beware !
A Shadow tracks thy flight of fire—
  Night is coming !
Bright are the regions of the air,
 And among the winds and beams
It were delight to wander there—
  Night is coming !

------

* This and the former poem were written at the request of a friend, to be inserted in a drama on the subject of Midas. Apollo and Pan contended before Tmolus for the prize in music.

SECOND SPIRIT.

The deathless stars are bright above;
　　If I would cross the shade of night,
Within my heart is the lamp of love,
　　　　　And that is day!
And the moon will smile with gentle light
　　On my golden plumes where'er they move;
The meteors will linger round my flight
　　　　　And make night day.

FIRST SPIRIT.

But if the whirlwinds of darkness waken
　　Hail and lightning and stormy rain;
See the bounds of the air are shaken—
　　　　　Night is coming!
The red swift clouds of the hurricane
　　Yon declining sun have overtaken,
The clash of the hail sweeps over the plain—
　　　　　Night is coming!

SECOND SPIRIT.

I see the light, and I hear the sound;
　　I'll sail on the flood of the tempest dark
With the calm within and the light around
　　　　　Which makes night day:
And thou, when the gloom is deep and stark,
　　Look from thy dull earth, slumber-bound,
My moon-like flight thou then mayst mark
　　　　　On high, far away.

Some say, there is a precipice
　　Where one vast pine is frozen to ruin
O'er piles of snow and chasms of ice
　　　　　'Mid Alpine mountains;
And that the languid storm pursuing
　　That winged shape for ever flies
Round those hoar branches, aye renewing
　　　　　Its aery fountains.

Some say, when nights are dry and clear,
　　And the death dews sleep on the morass,
Sweet whispers are heard by the traveller
　　　　　Which make night day:
And a silver shape like his early love doth pass
　　Upborne by her wild and glittering hair,
And when he awakes on the fragrant grass,
　　　　　He finds night day.

A FRAGMENT.

THEY were two cousins, almost like to twins,
Except that from the catalogue of sins
Nature had razed their love—which could not be
But by dissevering their nativity.
And so they grew together, like two flowers
Upon one stem, which the same beams and showers

Lull or awaken in their purple prime,
Which the same hand will gather—the same clime
Shake with decay.   This fair day smiles to see
All those who love,—and who ever loved like thee,
Fiordispina?   Scarcely Cosimo,
Within whose bosom and whose brain now glow
The ardours of a vision which obscure
The very idol of its portraiture ;
He faints, dissolved into a sense of love ;
But thou art as a planet sphered above,
But thou art Love itself—ruling the motion
Of his subjected spirit—such emotion
Must end in sin or sorrow, if sweet May
Had not brought forth this morn—your wedding day.

A BRIDAL SONG.

THE golden gates of sleep unbar
  Where strength and beauty met to-
    gether,
Kindle their image like a star
  In a sea of glassy weather.
Night, with all thy stars look down,—
  Darkness, weep thy holiest dew,—
Never smiled the inconstant moon
    On a pair so true.
Let eyes not see their own delight ;
Haste, swift Hour, and thy flight
    Oft renew.

Fairies, sprites, and angels keep her !
  Holy stars, permit no wrong !
And return to wake the sleeper,
    Dawn,—ere it be long.
Oh joy ! oh fear ! what will be done
In the absence of the sun !
    Come along !

SONG, ON A FADED VIOLET.

THE odour from the flower is gone,
  Which like thy kisses breathed on
    me ;
The colour from the flower is flown,
  Which glowed of thee, and only thee !

A shrivelled, lifeless, vacant form,
  It lies on my abandoned breast,
And mocks the heart which yet is warm
  With cold and silent rest.

I weep—my tears revive it not !
  I sigh—it breathes no more on me ;
Its mute and uncomplaining lot
  Is such as mine should be.

GOOD NIGHT.

GOOD night ? ah ! no ; the hour is ill
  Which severs those it should unite ;
Let us remain together still,
  Then it will be *good* night.

How can I call the lone night good,
  Though thy sweet wishes wing its
    flight ?
Be it not said, thought, understood,
  Then it will be *good* night.

To hearts which near each other move
  From evening close to morning light,
The night is good ; because, my love,
  They never *say* good night.

TO-MORROW.

WHERE art thou, beloved To-morrow ?
  Whom young and old and strong
    and weak,
Rich and poor, through joy and sorrow,
  Thy sweet smiles we ever seek,—
In thy place—ah ! well-a-day !
We find the thing we fled—To-day.

MAZENGHI.*

OH ! foster-nurse of man's abandoned
    glory,
Since Athens, its great mother, sunk
    in splendour ;

* This fragment refers to an event, told
in Sismondi's " Histoire des Républiques
Italiennes," which occurred during the war
when Florence finally subdued Pisa, and
reduced it to a province.   The opening
stanzas are addressed to the conquering
city.

Thou shadowest forth that mighty shape in story,
As ocean its wrecked fanes, severe yet tender :
The light-invested angel Poesy
Was drawn from the dim world to welcome thee.

And thou in painting didst transcribe all taught
By loftiest meditations ; marble knew
The sculptor's fearless soul—and as he wrought,
The grace of his own power and freedom grew.

And more than all, heroic, just, sublime
Thou wert among the false—was this thy crime ?

Yes ; and on Pisa's marble walls the twine
Of direst weeds hangs garlanded—the snake
Inhabits its wrecked palaces ;—in thine
A beast of subtler venom now doth make
Its lair, and sits amid their glories overthrown,
And thus thy victim's fate is as thine own.

The sweetest flowers are ever frail and rare,
And love and freedom blossoms but to wither ;
And good and ill like vines entangled are,
So that their grapes may oft be plucked together ;
Divide the vintage ere thou drink, then make
Thy heart rejoice for dead Mazenghi's sake.

No record of his crime remains in story,
But if the morning bright as evening shone,
It was some high and holy deed, by glory
Pursued into forgetfulness, which won
From the blind crowd he made secure and free
The patriot's meed, toil, death, and infamy.

For when by sound of trumpet was declared
A price upon his life, and there was set
A penalty of blood on all who shared
So much of water with him as might wet
His lips, which speech divided not— he went
Alone, as you may guess, to banishment.

Amid the mountains, like a hunted beast,
He hid himself, and hunger, cold, and toil,
Month after month endured ; it was a feast
Whene'er he found those globes of deep red gold
Which in the woods the strawberry-tree doth bear,
Suspended in their emerald atmosphere.

And in the roofless huts of vast morasses,
Deserted by the fever-stricken serf,
All overgrown with reeds and long rank grasses,
And hillocks heaped of moss-inwoven turf,
And where the huge and speckled aloe made,
Rooted in stones, a broad and pointed shade,

He housed himself.   There is a point of strand
Near Veda's tower and town ; and on one side
The treacherous marsh divides it from the land,
Shadowed by pine and ilex forests wide,
And on the other creeps eternally,
Through muddy weeds, the shallow, sullen sea.

Naples, 1818.

THE WOODMAN AND THE NIGHTINGALE.

A WOODMAN whose rough heart was out of tune
(I think such hearts yet never came to good)
Hated to hear, under the stars or moon

One nightingale in an interfluous wood
Satiate the hungry dark with melody ;
And as a vale is watered by a flood.

Or as the moonlight fills the open sky
Struggling with darkness—as a tuberose
Peoples some Indian dell with scents
which lie

Like clouds above the flower from
which they rose,
The singing of that happy nightingale
In this sweet forest, from the golden
close

Of evening, till the star of dawn may
fail,
Was interfused upon the silentness ;
The folded roses and the violets pale

Heard her within their slumbers, the
abyss
Of heaven with all its planets ; the dull
ear
Of the night-cradled earth ; the loneliness

Of the circumfluous waters,—every
sphere
And every flower and beam and cloud
and wave,
And every wind of the mute atmosphere,

And every beast stretched in its rugged
cave,
And every bird lulled on its mossy
bough,
And every silver moth fresh from the
grave,

Which is its cradle—ever from below
Aspiring like one who loves too fair,
too far,
To be consumed within the purest glow

Of one serene and unapproachèd star,
As if it were a lamp of earthly light,
Unconscious, as some human lovers
are,

Itself how low, how high beyond all
height
The heaven where it would perish !—
and every form
That worshipped in the temple of the
night

Was awed into delight, and by the
charm
Girt as with an interminable zone,
Whilst that sweet bird, whose music
was a storm

Of sound, shook forth the dull oblivion
Out of their dreams ; harmony became
love
In every soul but one   *   *   *

———

And so this man returned with axe and
saw
At evening close from killing the tall
treen,
The soul of whom by nature's gentle
law

Was each a wood-nymph, and kept
ever green
The pavement and the roof of the wild
copse,
Chequering the sunlight of the blue
serene

With jagged leaves,—and from the
forest tops
Singing the winds to sleep—or weeping oft
Fast showers of aërial water drops

Into their mother's bosom, sweet and
soft,
Nature's pure tears which have no bitterness ;
Around the cradles of the birds aloft

They spread themselves into the loveliness
Of fan-like leaves, and over pallid
flowers
Hang like moist clouds :—or, where
high branches kiss,

Make a green space among the silent
bowers,
Like a vast fane in a metropolis,
Surrounded by the columns and the
towers

All overwrought with branch-like tra-
ceries
In which there is religion—and the
mute
Persuasion of unkindled melodies,

Odours and gleams and murmurs,
which the lute
Of the blind pilot-spirit of the blast
Stirs as it sails, now grave and now
acute,

Wakening the leaves and waves ere it
has past
To such brief unison as on the brain
One tone, which never can recur, has
cast,

One accent never to return again.

WRITTEN ON HEARING THE NEWS OF THE DEATH OF NAPOLEON.

WHAT ! alive and so bold, oh earth ?
Art thou not over bold ?
What ! leapest thou forth as of old
In the light of thy morning mirth,
The last of the flock of the starry fold ?
Ha ! leapest thou forth as of old ?
Are not the limbs still when the ghost is fled,
And canst thou move, Napoleon being dead ?

How ! is not thy quick heart cold ?
What spark is alive on thy hearth ?
How ! is not *his* death-knell knolled,
And livest *thou* still, Mother Earth ?
Thou wert warming thy fingers old
O'er the embers covered and cold
Of that most fiery spirit, when it fled—
What, Mother, dost thou laugh now he is dead ?

" Who has known me of old," replied Earth,
" Or who has my story told ?
It is thou who art over bold."
And the lightning of scorn laughed forth
As she sung, " To my bosom I fold
All my sons when their knell is knolled ;
And so with living motion all are fed,
And the quick spring like weeds out of the dead.

" Still alive and still bold," shouted Earth,
" I grow bolder and still more bold.
The dead fill me ten thousand fold
Fuller of speed, and splendour, and mirth,
I was cloudy, and sullen, and cold,
Like a frozen chaos uprolled,
Till by the spirit of the mighty dead
My heart grew warm.   I feed on whom I fed.

" Ay, alive, and still bold," muttered Earth,
" Napoleon's fierce spirit rolled,
In terror and blood and gold,
A torrent of ruin to death from his birth.
Leave the millions who follow to mould
The metal before it be cold ;
And weave into his shame, which like the dead
Shrouds me, the hopes that from his glory fled."

———◆———

TO THE MOON.

ART thou pale for weariness
Of climbing heaven, and gazing on the earth,
Wandering companionless
Among the stars that have a different birth,—
And ever changing, like a joyless eye
That finds no object worth its constancy ?

SONG FOR TASSO.

I LOVED—alas! our life is love;
But when we cease to breathe and
move
I do suppose love ceases too.
I thought, but not as now I do,
Keen thoughts and bright of linked
lore,
Of all that men had thought before,
And all that nature shows, and more.

And still I love and still I think,
But strangely, for my heart can drink
The dregs of such despair, and live,
And love; [   ]
And if I think, my thoughts come fast,
I mix the present with the past,
And each seems uglier than the last.

Sometimes I see before me flee
A silver spirit's form, like thee,
O, Leonora, and I sit
[   ] still watching it,
Till by the grated casement's ledge
It fades, with such a sigh, as sedge
Breathes o'er the breezy streamlet's
edge.

THE WANING MOON.

AND like a dying lady, lean and pale,
Who totters forth, wrapt in a gauzy
veil,
Out of her chamber, led by the insane
And feeble wanderings of her fading
brain,
The moon arose upon the murky earth,
A white and shapeless mass.

EPITAPH.

THESE are two friends whose lives
were undivided,
So let their memory be, now they have
glided
Under the grave; let not their bones
be parted,
For their two hearts in life were single
hearted.

INVOCATION TO MISERY.

COME, be happy!—sit by me,
Shadow-vested Misery:
Coy, unwilling, silent bride,
Mourning in thy robe of pride,
Desolation—deified!

Come, be happy!—sit near me:
Sad as I may seem to thee,
I am happier far than thou,
Lady, whose imperial brow
Is endiademed with woe.

Misery! we have known each other,
Like a sister and a brother
Living in the same lone home,
Many years—we must live some
Years and ages yet to come.

'Tis an evil lot, and yet
Let us make the most of it;
If love lives when pleasure dies,
We will love, till in our eyes
This heart's Hell seem Paradise.

Come, be happy!—lie thee down
On the fresh grass newly mown,
Where the grasshopper doth sing
Merrily—one joyous thing
In a world of sorrowing!

There our tent shall be the willow,
And thine arm shall be my pillow;
Sounds and odours sorrowful
Because they once were sweet, shall
lull
Us to slumber, deep and dull.

Ha! thy frozen pulses flutter
With a love thou darest not utter.

*   *   *   *

Thou art murmuring, thou art weeping,
Whilst my burning bosom's leaping.

Kiss me;—oh! thy lips are cold:
Round my neck thine arms enfold—
They are soft, but chill and dead;
And thy tears upon my head
Burn like points of frozen lead.

Hasten to the bridal bed—
Underneath the grave 'tis spread:
In darkness may our love be hid,
Oblivion be our coverlid—
We may rest, and none forbid.

Clasp me till our hearts be grown
Like two lovers into one;
Till this dreadful transport may
Like a vapour fade away,
In the sleep that lasts alway.

We may dream, in that long sleep,
That we are not those who weep;
E'en as pleasure dreams of thee,
Life-deserting Misery,
Thou mayst dream of her with me.

Let us laugh, and make our mirth,
At the shadows of the earth,
As dogs bay the moonlight clouds,
That, like spectres wrapt in shrouds,
Pass o'er night in multitudes.

All the wide world beside us
Are like multitudinous
Shadows shifting from a scene—
What but mockery may they mean.
Where am I ?—Where thou hast been.

AN ARIETTE FOR MUSIC.

TO A LADY SINGING TO HER ACCOMPANIMENT ON THE GUITAR.

As the moon's soft splendour
O'er the faint cold starlight of heaven
Is thrown,
So thy voice most tender
To the strings without soul has given
Its own.

The stars will awaken,
Though the moon sleep a full hour later
To-night:
No leaf will be shaken
Whilst the dews of thy melody scatter
Delight.

Though the sound overpowers,
Sing again, with thy sweet voice revealing
A tone
Of some world far from ours,
Where music and moonlight and feeling
Are one.

ARIEL TO MIRANDA.

WITH A GUITAR.

ARIEL to Miranda ;—Take
This slave of music, for the sake
Of him, who is the slave of thee ;
And teach it all the harmony
In which thou canst, and only thou,
Make the delighted spirit glow,
Till joy denies itself again,
And, too intense, is turned to pain.
And by permission and command
Of thine own Prince Ferdinand,
Poor Ariel sends this silent token
Of more than ever can be spoken ;
Your guardian spirit, Ariel, who
From life to life must still pursue
Your happiness, for thus alone
Can Ariel ever find his own ;
From Prospero's enchanted cell,
As the mighty verses tell,
To the throne of Naples he
Lit you o'er the trackless sea,
Flitting on, your prow before,
Like a living meteor.

When you die the silent moon,
In her interlunar swoon,
Is not sadder in her cell
Than deserted Ariel ;
When you live again on earth,
Like an unseen star of birth,
Ariel guides you o'er the sea
Of life from your nativity.
Many changes have been run
Since Ferdinand and you begun
Your course of love, and Ariel still
Has tracked your steps and served
your will.
Now in humbler, happier lot
This is all remembered not ;
And now, alas ! the poor sprite is
Imprisoned for some fault of his
In a body like a grave—
From you, he only dares to crave,
For his service and his sorrow,
A smile to-day, a song to-morrow.

The artist who this idol wrought,
To echo all harmonious thought,
Felled a tree, while on the steep

The woods were in their winter sleep,
Rocked in that repose divine
On the wind-swept Apennine ;
And dreaming some of Autumn past,
And some of Spring approaching fast,
And some of April buds and showers,
And some of songs in July bowers,
And all of love ; and so this tree,—
O that such our death may be !
Died in sleep, and felt no pain,
To live in happier form again ;
From which, beneath Heaven's fairest
        star,
The artist wrought this loved Guitar,
And taught it justly to reply,
To all who question skilfully,
In language gentle as its own,
Whispering in enamoured tone
Sweet oracles of woods and dells,
And summer winds in sylvan cells ;
For it had learnt all harmonies
Of the plains and of the skies,
Of the forests and the mountains,
And the many-voicèd fountains ;
The clearest echoes of the hills,
The softest notes of falling rills,
The melodies of birds and bees,
The murmuring of summer seas,
And pattering rain, and breathing dew,
And airs of evening ; and it knew
That seldom-heard mysterious sound,
Which, driven in its diurnal round,
As it floats through boundless day,
Our world enkindles on its way—
All this it knows, but will not tell
To those who cannot question well
The spirit that inhabits it.
It talks according to the wit
Of its companions ; and no more
Is heard than has been felt before,
By those who tempt it to betray
These secrets of an elder day :
But sweetly as its answers will
Flatter hands of perfect skill,
It keeps its highest, holiest tone,
For our belovèd friend alone.

THE MAGNETIC LADY TO HER PATIENT.

SLEEP on! sleep on! forget thy pain:
    My hand is on thy brow,
My spirit on thy brain ;
My pity on thy heart, poor friend ;
    And from my fingers flow

The powers of life, and like a sign,
    Seal thee from thine hour of woe ;
And brood on thee, but may not blend
        With thine.

Sleep on ! sleep on ! I love thee not ;
    But when I think that he
Who made and makes my lot
As full of flowers as thine of weeds,
    Might have been lost like thee ;
And that a hand which was not mine,
    Might then have chased his agony
As I another's—my heart bleeds
        For thine.

Sleep, sleep, and with the slumber of
    The dead and the unborn,
Forget thy life and woe ;
Forget that thou must wake for ever ;
    Forget the world's dull scorn ;
Forget lost health, and the divine
    Feelings that die in youth's brief
        morn ;
And forget me, for I can never
        Be thine.

Like a cloud big with a May shower,
    My soul weeps healing rain,
On thee, thou withered flower ;
It breathes mute music on thy sleep ;
    Its odour calms thy brain !
Its light within thy gloomy breast
    Speaks like a second youth again.
By mine thy being is to its deep
        Possest.

The spell is done.   How feel you now ?
    Better—Quite well, replied
The sleeper.—What would do
You good when suffering and awake?
    What cure your head and side ?—
'Twould kill me what would cure my
        pain ;
    And as I must on earth abide
Awhile, yet tempt me not to break
        My chain.

TO THE QUEEN OF MY HEART.*

SHALL we roam, my love,
To the twilight grove,

----

* This poem is considered doubtful; but
it was published by Captain Medwin as
Shelley's.

When the moon is rising bright?
Oh, I'll whisper there
In the cool night-air,
    What I dare not in broad daylight!

I'll tell thee a part
Of the thoughts that start
    To being when thou art nigh;
And thy beauty, more bright
Than the stars' soft light,
Shall seem as a weft from the sky.

When the pale moonbeam
On tower and stream
    Sheds a flood of silver sheen,
How I love to gaze
As the cold ray strays
    O'er thy face, my heart's throned
        queen!

Wilt thou roam with me
To the restless sea,
    And linger upon the steep,
And list to the flow
Of the waves below
    How they toss and roar and leap?

Those boiling waves
And the storm that raves
    At night o'er their foaming crest,
Resemble the strife
That, from earliest life,
    The passions have waged in my
        breast.

Oh, come then and rove
To the sea or the grove
    When the moon is rising bright,
And I'll whisper there
In the cool night-air
    What I dare not in broad daylight.

GINEVRA.*

WILD, pale, and wonder-stricken, even as one
Who staggers forth into the air and sun
From the dark chamber of a mortal fever
Bewildered, and incapable, and ever
Fancying strange comments in her dizzy brain
Of usual shapes, till the familiar train
Of objects and of persons passed like things
Strange as a dreamer's mad imaginings,
Ginevra from the nuptial altar went;
The vows to which her lips had sworn assent
Rung in her brain still with a jarring din,
Deafening the lost intelligence within.

And so she moved under the bridal veil,
Which made the paleness of her cheek more pale,
And deepened the faint crimson of her mouth,
And darkened her dark locks, as moonlight doth,—
And of the gold and jewels glittering there
She scarce felt conscious,—but the weary glare
Lay like a chaos of unwelcome light,
Vexing the sense with gorgeous undelight.
A moonbeam in the shadow of a cloud
Was less heavenly fair—her face was bowed,
And as she passed, the diamonds in her hair
Were mirrored in the polished marble stair
Which led from the cathedral to the street;
And ever as she went her light fair feet
Erased these images.

    The bride-maidens who round her thronging came,
Some with a sense of self-rebuke and shame,

* This fragment is part of a poem which Shelley intended to write, founded on a story
to be found in the first volume of a book entitled "L'Osservatore Fiorentino."

Envying the unenviable; and others
Making the joy which should have been another's
Their own by gentle sympathy; and some
Sighing to think of an unhappy home:
Some few admiring what can ever lure
Maidens to leave the heaven serene and pure
Of parents' smiles for life's great cheat; a thing
Better to taste sweet in imagining.

But they are all dispersed—and, lo! she stands
Looking in idle grief on her white hands,
Alone within the garden now her own;
And through the sunny air, with jangling tone,
The music of the merry marriage bells,
Killing the azure silence, sinks and swells;
Absorbed like one within a dream who dreams
That he is dreaming, until slumber seems
A mockery of itself—when suddenly
Antonio stood before her, pale as she.
With agony, with sorrow, and with pride,
He lifted his wan eyes upon the bride,
And said—" Is this thy faith?" and then as one
Whose sleeping face is stricken by the sun
With light like a harsh voice, which bids him rise
And look upon his day of life with eyes
Which weep in vain that they can dream no more,
Ginevra saw her lover, and forbore
To shriek or faint, and checked the stifling blood
Rushing upon her heart, and unsubdued
Said—" Friend, if earthly violence or ill,
Suspicion, doubt, or the tyrannic will
Of parents, chance, or custom, time or change,
Or circumstance, or terror, or revenge,
Or wildered looks, or words, or evil speech,
With all their stings [   ] can impeach
Our love,—we love not:—if the grave which hides
The victim from the tyrant, and divides
The cheek that whitens from the eyes that dart
Imperious inquisition to the heart
That is another's, could dissever ours,
We love not."—" What, do not the silent hours
Beckon thee to Gherardi's bridal bed?
Is not that ring"——a pledge, he would have said
Of broken vows, but she with patient look
The golden circle from her finger took,
And said—" Accept this token of my faith,
The pledge of vows to be absolved by death;
And I am dead or shall be soon—my knell
Will mix its music with that merry bell;
Does it not sound as if they sweetly said
' We toll a corpse out of the marriage bed?'
The flowers upon my bridal chamber strewn
Will serve unfaded for my bier—so soon
That even the dying violet will not die
Before Ginevra." The strong fantasy
Had made her accents weaker and more weak,
And quenched the crimson life upon her cheek,

And glazed her eyes, and spread an atmosphere
Round her, which chilled the burning noon with fear,
Making her but an image of the thought
Which, like a prophet or a shadow, brought
News of the terrors of the coming time
Like an accuser branded with the crime
He would have cast on a beloved friend,
Whose dying eyes reproach not to the end
The pale betrayer— he then with vain repentance
Would share, he cannot now avert, the sentence—
Antonio stood and would have spoken, when
The compound voice of women and of men
Was heard approaching; he retired, while she
Was led amid the admiring company
Back to the palace,—and her maidens soon
Changed her attire for the afternoon,
And left her at her own request to keep
An hour of quiet and rest:—like one asleep
With open eyes and folded hands she lay,
Pale in the light of the declining day.

　　Meanwhile the day sinks fast, the sun is set,
And in the lighted hall the guests are met;
The beautiful looked lovelier in the light
Of love, and admiration, and delight
Reflected from a thousand hearts and eyes
Kindling a momentary Paradise.
This crowd is safer than the silent wood,
Where love's own doubts disturb the solitude;
On frozen hearts the fiery rain of wine
Falls, and the dew of music more divine
Tempers the deep emotions of the time
To spirits cradled in a sunny clime :
How many meet, who never yet have met,
To part too soon, but never to forget.
How many saw the beauty, power and wit
Of looks and words which ne'er enchanted yet;
But life's familiar veil was now withdrawn,
As the world leaps before an earthquake's dawn,
And unprophetic of the coming hours,
The matin winds from the expanded flowers,
Scatter their hoarded incense, and awaken
The earth, until the dewy sleep is shaken
From every living heart which it possesses,
Through seas and winds, cities and wildernesses,
As if the future and the past were all
Treasured i' the instant;—so Gherardi's hall
Laughed in the mirth of its lord's festival,
Till some one asked—" Where is the Bride?"　And then
A bridesmaid went,—and ere she came again
A silence fell upon the guests—a pause
Of expectation, as when beauty awes
All hearts with its approach, though unbeheld;
Then wonder, and then fear that wonder quelled;
For whispers passed from mouth to ear which drew
The colour from the hearer's cheeks, and flew
Louder and swifter round the company;
And then Gherardi entered with an eye

Of ostentatious trouble, and a crowd
Surrounded him, and some were weeping loud.

    They found Ginevra dead ! if it be death,
To lie without motion, or pulse, or breath,
With waxen cheeks, and limbs cold, stiff, and white,
And open eyes, whose fixed and glassy light
Mocked at the speculation they had owned.
If it be death, when there is felt around
A smell of clay, a pale and icy glare,
And silence, and a sense that lifts the hair
From the scalp to the ankles, as it were
Corruption from the spirit passing forth,
And giving all it shrouded to the earth,
And leaving as swift lightning in its flight
Ashes, and smoke, and darkness: in our night
Of thought we know thus much of death,—no more
Than the unborn dream of our life before
Their barks are wrecked on its inhospitable shore.
The marriage feast and its solemnity
Was turned to funeral pomp—the company
With heavy hearts and looks, broke up; nor they
Who loved the dead went weeping on their way
Alone, but sorrow mixed with sad surprise
Loosened the springs of pity in all eyes,
On which that form, whose fate they weep in vain,
Will never, thought they, kindle smiles again.
The lamps which half extinguished in their haste
Gleamed few and faint o'er the abandoned feast,
Showed as it were within the vaulted room
A cloud of sorrow hanging, as if gloom
Had passed out of men's minds into the air.
Some few yet stood around Gherardi there,
Friends and relations of the dead,—and he,
A loveless man, accepted torpidly
The consolation that he wanted not,
Awe in the place of grief within him wrought.
Their whispers made the solemn silence seem
More still—some wept, [   ]
Some melted into tears without a sob,
And some with hearts that might be heard to throb
Leant on the table, and at intervals
Shuddered to hear through the deserted halls
And corridors the thrilling shrieks which came
Upon the breeze of night, that shook the flame
Of every torch and taper as it swept
From out the chamber where the women kept;
Their tears fell on the dear companion cold
Of pleasures now departed ; then was knolled
The bell of death, and soon the priests arrived,
And finding death their penitent had shrived,
Returned like ravens from a corpse whereon
A vulture has just feasted to the bone.
And then the mourning women came.

*   *   *   *   *

THE DIRGE.

Old winter was gone
In his weakness back to the mountains hoar,
And the spring came down
From the planet that hovers upon the shore
Where the sea of sunlight encroaches
On the limits of wintry night;
If the land, and the air, and the sea
Rejoice not when spring approaches,
We did not rejoice in thee,
Ginevra !

She is still, she is cold
On the bridal couch,
One step to the white deathbed,
And one to the bier,
And one to the charnel—and one, O where?
The dark arrow fled
In the noon.

Ere the sun through heaven once more has rolled,
The rats in her heart
Will have made their nest,
And the worms be alive in her golden hair,
While the spirit that guides the sun,
Sits throned in his flaming chair,
She shall sleep.

*　　　*　　　*　　　*　　　*

Pisa, 1821.

CHARLES THE FIRST.

FRAGMENTS.

ACT I.

SCENE I.—*The Pageant to [celebrate] the arrival of the Queen.*

A PURSUIVANT.

PLACE, for the Marshal of the Masque !

FIRST SPEAKER.

What thinkest thou of this quaint masque, which turns,
Like morning from the shadow of the night,
The night to day, and London to a place
Of peace and joy ?

SECOND SPEAKER.

And Hell to Heaven.
Eight years are gone,
And they seem hours, since in this populous street
I trod on grass made green by summer's rain,
For the red plague kept state within that palace
Where now reigns vanity—in nine years more
The roots will be refreshed with civil blood;

And thank the mercy of insulted Heaven
That sin and wrongs wound as an orphan's cry,
The patience of the great avenger's ear.

THIRD SPEAKER (*a youth*).

Yet, father, 'tis a happy sight to see,
Beautiful, innocent, and unforbidden
By God or man;—'tis like the bright procession
Of skiey visions in a solemn dream
From which men wake as from a paradise,
And draw new strength to tread the thorns of life.
If God be good, wherefore should this be evil?
And if this be not evil, dost thou not draw
Unseasonable poison from the flowers
Which bloom so rarely in this barren world?
O, kill these bitter thoughts which make the present
Dark as the future!—

    *   *   *   *

When avarice and tyranny, vigilant fear,
And open-eyed conspiracy lie sleeping
As on Hell's threshold; and all gentle thoughts
Waken to worship him who giveth joys
With his own gift.

SECOND SPEAKER.

How young art thou in this old age of time!
How green in this grey world!   Canst thou not think
Of change in that low scene in which thou art
Not a spectator but an actor?   [   ]
The day that dawns in fire will die in storms,
Even though the noon be calm.   My travel's done;
Before the whirlwind wakes I shall have found
My inn of lasting rest, but thou must still
Be journeying on in this inclement air.

    *   *   *   *   *

FIRST SPEAKER.

That
Is the Archbishop.

SECOND SPEAKER.

              Rather say the Pope.
London will be soon his Rome: he walks
As if he trod upon the heads of men.
He looks elate, drunken with blood and gold;
Beside him moves the Babylonian woman
Invisibly, and with her as with his shadow,
Mitred adulterer! he is joined in sin,
Which turns Heaven's milk of mercy to revenge.

ANOTHER CITIZEN [*lifting up his eyes*].

Good Lord! rain it down upon him. [   ]
Amid her ladies walks the papist queen,
As if her nice feet scorned our English earth.
There's old Sir Henry Vane, the Earl of Pembroke,

Lord Essex, and Lord Keeper Coventry,
And others who make base their English breed
By vile participation of their honours
With papists, atheists, tyrants, and apostates.
When lawyers mask 'tis time for honest men
To strip the vizor from their purposes.

*   *   *   *   *

FOURTH SPEAKER (*a pursuivant*).

Give place, give place !
You torch-bearers advance to the great gate,
And then attend the Marshal of the Masque
Into the Royal presence.

FIFTH SPEAKER (*a law student*).

                         What thinkest thou
Of this quaint show of ours, my aged friend ?

FIRST SPEAKER.

I will not think but that our country's wounds
May yet be healed—The king is just and gracious,
Though wicked counsels now pervert his will:
These once cast off—

SECOND SPEAKER.

                         As adders cast their skins
And keep their venom, so kings often change;
Councils and counsellors hang on one another,
Hiding the loathsome [   ]
Like the base patchwork of a leper's rags.

THIRD SPEAKER.

O, still those dissonant thoughts—List ! loud music
Grows on the enchanted air !   And see, the torches
Restlessly flashing, and the crowd divided
Like waves before an Admiral's prow.

*   *   *   *   *

ANOTHER SPEAKER.

Give place—
To the Marshal of the Masque !

THIRD SPEAKER.

How glorious !   See those thronging chariots
Rolling like painted clouds before the wind:
                         Some are
Like curved shells dyed by the azure depths
Of Indian seas; some like the newborn moon;
And some like cars in which the Romans climbed
(Canopied by Victory's eagle wings outspread)
The Capitolian—See how gloriously
The mettled horses in the torchlight stir
Their gallant riders while they check their pride,
Like shapes of some diviner element !

Second Speaker.

Ay, there they are—
Nobles, and sons of nobles, patentees,
Monopolists, and stewards of this poor farm,
On whose lean sheep sit the prophetic crows.
Here is the pomp that strips the houseless orphan,
Here is the pride that breaks the desolate heart,
These are the lilies glorious as Solomon,
Who toil not, neither do they spin,—unless
It be the webs they catch poor rogues withal.
Here is the surfeit which to them who earn
The niggard wages of the earth, scarce leaves
The tithe that will support them till they crawl
Back to its cold hard bosom.   Here is health
Followed by grim disease, glory by shame,
Waste by lank famine, wealth by squalid want,
And England's sin by England's punishment.
And, as the effect pursues the cause foregone,
Lo, giving substance to my words, behold
At once the sign and the thing signified—
A troop of cripples, beggars, and lean outcasts,
Horsed upon stumbling shapes, carted with dung,
Dragged for a day from cellars and low cabins
And rotten hiding-holes to point the moral
Of this presentiment, and bring up the rear
Of painted pomp with misery !

Speaker.

Tis but
The anti-masque, and serves as discords do
In sweetest music.   Who would love May flowers
If they succeeded not to Winter's flaw;
Or day unchanged by night; or joy itself
Without the touch of sorrow ?

*   *   *   *   *

SCENE II.—*A Chamber in Whitehall.*

Enter the King, Queen, Laud, Wentworth, *and* Archy.

King.

Thanks, gentlemen, I heartily accept
This token of your service: your gay masque
Was performed gallantly.

Queen.

And, gentlemen,
Call your poor Queen your debtor.   Your quaint pageant
Rose on me like the figures of past years,
Treading their still path back to infancy,
More beautiful and mild as they draw nearer
The quiet cradle.   I could have almost wept
To think I was in Paris, where these shows
Are well devised—such as I was ere yet
My young heart shared with [   ] the task,
The careful weight of this great monarchy.

There, gentlemen, between the sovereign's pleasure
And that which it regards, no clamour lifts
Its proud interposition.

   *   *   *   *

KING.

My lord of Canterbury.

ARCHY.

            The fool is here.

LAUD.

I crave permission of your Majesty
To order that this insolent fellow be
Chastised, he mocks the sacred character,
Scoffs at the stake, and—

KING.

            What, my Archy !
He mocks and mimics all he sees and hears,
Yet with a quaint and graceful licence—Prithee
For this once do not as Prynne would, were he
Primate of England.
He lives in his own world; and, like a parrot,
Hung in his gilded prison from the window
Of a queen's bower over the public way,
Blasphemes with a bird's mind:—his words, like arrows
Which know no aim beyond the archer's wit,
Strike sometimes what eludes philosophy.

QUEEN.

Go, sirrah, and repent of your offence
Ten minutes in the rain: be it your penance
To bring news how the world goes there.   Poor Archy !
He weaves about himself a world of mirth
Out of this wreck of ours.

LAUD.

I take with patience, as my master did,
All scoffs permitted from above.

KING.

            My Lord,
Pray overlook these papers.   Archy's words
Had wings, but these have talons.

QUEEN.

            And the lion
That wears them must be tamed.   My dearest lord,
I see the newborn courage in your eye
Armed to strike dead the spirit of the time.

   *   *   *   *

Do thou persist: for, faint but in resolve,
And it were better thou hadst still remained

The slave of thine own slaves, who tear like curs
The fugitive, and flee from the pursuer;
And Opportunity, that empty wolf,
Flies at his throat who falls.   Subdue thy actions,
Even to the disposition of thy purpose,
And be that tempered as the Ebro's steel;
And banish weak-eyed Mercy to the weak
Whence she will greet thee with a gift of peace,
And not betray thee with a traitor's kiss,
As when she keeps the company of rebels,
Who think that she is fear.   This do, lest we
Should fall as from a glorious pinnacle
In a bright dream, and wake as from a dream
Out of our worshipped state.

     *   *   *   *   *

LAUD.

* * And if this suffice not,
Unleash the sword and fire, that in their thirst
They may lick up that scum of schismatics.
I laugh at those weak rebels who, desiring
What we possess, still prate of Christian peace,
As if those dreadful messengers of wrath,
Which play the part of God 'twixt right and wrong,
Should be let loose against innocent sleep
Of templed cities and the smiling fields,
For some poor argument of policy
Which touches our own profit or our pride,
Where it indeed were Christian charity
To turn the cheek even to the smiter's hand :
And when our great Redeemer, when our God
Is scorned in his immediate ministers,
They talk of peace !
Such peace as Canaan found, let Scotland now.

     *   *   *   *   *

QUEEN.

My beloved lord,
Have you not noted that the fool of late
Has lost his careless mirth, and that his words
Sound like the echoes of our saddest fears ?
What can it mean ?   I should be loth to think
Some factious slave had tutored him.

KING.

It partly is,
That our minds piece the vacant intervals
Of his wild words with their own fashioning ;
As in the imagery of summer clouds,
Or coals in the winter fire, idlers find
The perfect shadows of their teeming thoughts :
And partly that the terrors of the time
Are sown by wandering Rumour in all spirits
And in the lightest and the least, may best
Be seen the current of the coming wind.

N N

QUEEN.

Your brain is overwrought with these deep thoughts ;
Come, I will sing to you ; let us go try
These airs from Italy,—and you shall see
A cradled miniature of yourself asleep,
Stamped on the heart by never-erring love ;
Liker than any Vandyke ever made,
A pattern to the unborn age of thee,
Over whose sweet beauty I have wept for joy
A thousand times, and now should weep for sorrow,
Did I not think that after we were dead
Our fortunes would spring high in him, and that
The cares we waste upon our heavy crown
Would make it light and glorious as a wreath
Of heaven's beams for his dear innocent brow.

KING.

Dear Henrietta !

*   *   *   *   *

SCENE III.

HAMPDEN, PYM, CROMWELL, *and the younger* VANE.

HAMPDEN.

England, farewell ! thou, who hast been my cradle,
Shalt never be my dungeon or my grave !
I held what I inherited in thee,
As pawn for that inheritance of freedom
Which thou hast sold for thy despoiler's smile :
How can I call thee England, or my country ?
Does the wind hold ?

VANE.

The vanes sit steady
Upon the Abbey towers.   The silver lightnings
Of the evening star, spite of the city's smoke,
Tell that the north wind reigns in the upper air.
Mark too that flock of fleecy winged clouds
Sailing athwart St. Margaret's.

HAMPDEN.

Hail, fleet herald
Of tempest ! that wild pilot who shall guide
Hearts free as his, to realms as pure as thee,
Beyond the shot of tyranny !   And thou,
Fair star, whose beam lies on the wide Atlantic,
Athwart its zones of tempest and of calm,
Bright as the path to a beloved home,
O light us to the isles of th' evening land !
Like floating Edens, cradled in the glimmer
Of sunset, through the distant mist of years
Tinged by departing Hope, they gleam !   Lone regions,
Where power's poor dupes and victims, yet have never
Propitiated the savage fear of kings
With purest blood of noblest hearts ; whose dew

Is yet unstained with tears of those who wake
To weep each day the wrongs on which it dawns ;
Whose sacred silent air owns yet no echo
Of formal blasphemies ; nor impious rites
Wrest man's free worship from the God who loves
Towards the worm, who envies us his love,
Receive thou young [   ] of Paradise,
These exiles from the old and sinful world !
This glorious clime, this firmament, whose lights
Dart mitigated influence through the veil
Of pale blue atmosphere ; whose tears keep green
The pavement of this moist all-feeding earth,
This vaporous horizon ; whose dim round
Is bastioned by the circumfluous sea,
Repelling invasion from the sacred towers,
Presses upon me like a dungeon's grate,
A low dark roof, a damp and narrow vault :
The mighty universe becomes a cell
Too narrow for the soul that owns no master.
                              While the loathliest spot
Of this wide prison, England, is a nest
Of cradled peace built on the mountain tops,
To which the eagle-spirits of the free,
Which range through heaven and earth, and scorn the storm
Of time, and gaze upon the light of truth,
Return to brood over the [   ] thoughts
That cannot die, and may not be repelled.

    *   *   *   *   *

---◆---

PROLOGUE TO HELLAS—A FRAGMENT.

HERALD OF ETERNITY.

IT is the day when all the Sons of God
Wait in the roofless senate-house whose [place]
Is chaos and the immovable abyss
Frozen by his steadfast word to hyaline.

    *   *   *   *   *

The shadow of God, and delegate
Of that before whose breath the universe
Is as a print of dew.
                              Hierarchs and kings,
Who from your thrones pinnacled on the past
Sway the reluctant present, ye who sit
Pavilioned on the radiance or the gloom
Of mortal thought, which, like an exhalation
Steaming from earth, conceals the * * of heaven
Which gave it birth, * * * assemble here
Before your Father's throne.   The swift decree
Yet hovers, and the fiery incarnation
Is yet withheld, clothed in which it shall
    *   *   *   *   annul
The fairest of those wandering isles that gem
The sapphire space of interstellar air,—
That green and azure sphere, that earth enwrapped
Less in the beauty of its tender light

Than in an atmosphere of living spirit
Which interpenetrating all the * * *
* * * it rolls from realm to realm
And age to age, and in its ebb and flow
Impels the generations
To their appointed place,
Whilst the high Arbiter
Beholds the strife, and at the appointed time
Sends his decrees veiled in eternal * * *
Within the circuit of this pendent orb
There lies an antique region, on which fell
The dews of thought, in the world's golden dawn,
Earliest and most benign; and from it sprung
Temples and cities and immortal forms,
And harmonies of wisdom and of song,
And thoughts, and deeds worthy of thoughts so fair.
And, when the sun of its dominion failed,
And when the winter of its glory came,
The winds that stripped it bare blew on, and swept
That dew into the utmost wildernesses
In wandering clouds of sunny rain that thawed
The unmaternal bosom of the North.
Haste, Sons of God, * * for ye beheld,
Reluctant or consenting or astonished,
The stern decrees go forth which heaped on Greece
Ruin and degradation and despair.
A fourth now waits. Assemble, Sons of God,
To speed or to prevent or to suspend
(If, as ye dream, such power be not withheld)
The unaccomplished destiny.

     *   *   *   *   *

CHORUS.

The curtain of the universe
    Is rent and shattered,
The splendour-wingèd worlds disperse
    Like wild doves scattered.

    Space is roofless and bare,
And in the midst of a cloudy shrine,
    Dark amid thrones of light.
In the blue glow of hyaline
Golden worlds revolve and shine.
In   *   *   * flight
From every point of the Infinite,
Like a thousand dawns on a single night
    The splendours rise and spread.
    And through thunder and darkness dread
Light and music are radiated,
And, in their pavilioned chariots led
By living wings, high overhead
    The giant Powers move,
Gloomy or bright as the thrones they fill.

  *   *   *   *   *

    A chaos of light and motion
    Upon that glassy ocean.

    *   *   *   *   *

The senate of the Gods is met,
Each in his rank and station set;
    There is silence in the spaces—
Lo ! Satan, Christ, and Mahomet,
    Start from their places !

*   *   *

CHRIST.

Almighty Father !
Low-kneeling at the feet of Destiny

*   *   *   *   *

There are two fountains in which spirits weep
When mortals err, Discord and Slavery named;
And with their bitter dew two Destinies
Filled each their irrevocable urns.   The third,
Fiercest and mightiest, mingled both, and added
Chaos and death, and slow oblivion's lymph,
And hate and terror, and the poisoned rain

*   *   *   *   *

The Aurora of the nations.   By this brow
Whose pores wept tears of blood; by these wide wounds;
By this imperial crown of agony;
By infamy and solitude and death,
(For this I underwent); and by the pain
Of pity for those who would * * for me
The unremembered joy of a revenge,
(For this I felt); by Plato's sacred light,
Of which my spirit was a burning morrow;
By Greece, and all she cannot cease to be,
Her quenchless words, sparks of immortal truth,
Stars of all night—her harmonies and forms,
Echoes and shadows of what Love adores
In thee; I do compel thee, send forth Fate,
Thy irrevocable child !   Let her descend,
A seraph-wingèd victory [arrayed]
In tempest of the omnipotence of God
Which sweeps through all things.
From hollow leagues, from Tyranny which arms
Adverse miscreeds and emulous anarchies
To stamp, as on a wingèd serpent's seed,
Upon the name of Freedom ; from the storm
Of faction, which like earthquake shakes and sickens
The solid heart of enterprise; from all
By which the holiest dreams of highest spirits
Are stars beneath the dawn *   *   *
*   *   *   She shall arise
Victorious as the world arose from chaos !
And, as the heavens and the earth arrayed
Their presence in the beauty and the light
Of thy first smile, O Father; as they gather
The spirit of thy love, which paves for them
Their path o'er the abyss, till every sphere
Shall be one living spirit; so shall Greece—

SATAN.

Be as all things beneath the empyrean,
Mine !   Art thou eyeless like old Destiny,

Thou mockery-king, crowned with a wreath of thorns—
Whose sceptre is a reed, the broken reed
Which pierces thee, whose throne a chair of scorn !
For seest thou not beneath this crystal floor
The innumerable worlds of golden light
Which are my empire, and the least of them
* * * which thou wouldst redeem from me ?
Know'st thou not them my portion ?
Or wouldst rekindle the * * strife
Which our great Father then did arbitrate
When he assigned to his competing sons
Each his apportioned realm ?

             Thou Destiny,
Thou who art mailed in the omnipotence
Of Him who sends thee forth, whate'er thy task,
Speed, spare not to accomplish ! and be mine
Thy trophies, whether Greece again become
The fountain in the desert whence the earth
Shall drink of freedom, which shall give it strength
To suffer, or a gulf of hollow death
To swallow all delight, all life, all hope.
Go, thou vicegerent of my will, no less
Than of the Father's. But, lest thou shouldst faint,
The bloodhounds famine and pestilence
Shall wait on thee; the hundred-forked snake
Insatiate superstition still shall * * *
The earth behind thy steps; and war shall hover
Above, and fraud shall gape below, and change
Shall flit before thee on her dragon wings,
Convulsing and consuming. And I add
Three phials of the tears which demons weep
When virtuous spirits through the gate of death
Pass triumphing over the thorns of life,—
Sceptres and crowns, mitres and swords and snares
Trampling in scorn, like Him and Socrates.
The first is anarchy; when power and pleasure,
Glory and science and security,
On freedom hang like fruit on the green tree,
Then pour it forth, and men shall gather ashes.
The second, tyranny—

CHRIST.

             Obdurate spirit !
Thou seest but the past in the to-come.
Pride is thy error and thy punishment.
Boast not thine empire, dream not that thy worlds
Are more than furnace-sparks or rainbow-drops
Before the power that wields and kindles them.
True greatness asks not space; true excellence
Lives in the Spirit of all things that live,
Which lends it to the worlds thou callest thine.

     *   *   *   *   *

MAHOMET.

     *   *   *   *   *

      Haste thou, and fill the waning crescent
With beams as keen as those which pierced the shadow

Of Christian night rolled back upon the West
When the orient moon of Islam rode in triumph
From Tmolus to the Acroceraunian snow.

   *   *   *   *   *
                      Wake, thou word
Of God, and from the throne of Destiny
Even to the utmost limit of thy way
May triumph—

   *   *   *   *   *
           Be thou a curse on them whose creed
Divides and multiplies the most high God!

1821.

      ◆────────◆

SONG OF PROSERPINE,

WHILST GATHERING FLOWERS ON THE PLAIN OF ENNA.

SACRED Goddess, Mother Earth,
   Thou from whose immortal bosom
Gods and men and beasts have birth,
   Leaf and blade, and bud and blossom,
Breathe thine influence most divine
On thine own child, Proserpine.

If with mists of evening dew
   Thou dost nourish these young flowers
Till they grow in scent and hue
   Fairest children of the Hours,
Breathe thine influence most divine
On thine own child, Proserpine.

      ◆────────◆

OTHO.

THOU wert not, Cassius, and thou couldst not be,
   "Last of the Romans,"—though thy memory claim
From Brutus his own glory, and on thee
   Rests the full splendour of his sacred fame;
Nor he who dared make the foul tyrant quail
   Amid his cowering senate with thy name;
Though thou and he were great, it will avail
To thine own fame that Otho's should not fail.

'Twill wrong thee not: thou wouldst, if thou couldst feel,
   Abjure such envious fame.   Great Otho died
Like thee: he sanctified his country's steel,
   At once the tyrant and tyrannicide,
In his own blood.   A deed it was to wring
   Tears from all men—though full of gentle pride,
Such pride as from impetuous love may spring
That will not be refused its offering.

Dark is the realm of grief: but human things
   Those may not know who cannot weep for them.

1817.

FRAGMENTS.

SILENCE! Oh well are Death and Sleep and Thou
Three brethren named, the guardians gloomy-winged
Of one abyss, where life and truth and joy
Are swallowed up. Yet spare me, Spirit, pity me!
Until the sounds I hear become my soul,
And it has left these faint and weary limbs,
To track along the lapses of the air
This wandering melody until it rests
Among lone mountains in some * * * *

1818.

———

MY head is wild with weeping for a grief
   Which is the shadow of a gentle mind.
I walk into the air (but no relief
   To seek,—or haply, if I sought, to find;
It came unsought);—to wonder that a chief
   Among men's spirits should be cold and blind.

1818.

———

THE fierce beasts of the woods and wildernesses
Track not the steps of him who drinks of it;
For the light breezes, which for ever fleet
Around its margin, heap the sand thereon.

1818.

———

FLOURISHING vine, whose kindling clusters glow
   Beneath the autumnal sun, none taste of thee;
For thou dost shroud a ruin, and below
   The rotting bones of dead antiquity.

1818

Sonnets.

I.

OZYMANDIAS.

I MET a traveller from an antique land
  Who said : " Two vast and trunkless legs of stone
Stand in the desert.   Near them on the sand,
  Half sunk, a shattered visage lies, whose frown
And wrinkled lip and sneer of cold command
Tell that its sculptor well those passions read
  Which yet survive, stamped on these lifeless things,
The hand that mocked them and the heart that fed.
And on the pedestal these words appear:
  ' My name is Ozymandias, king of kings:
Look on my works, ye mighty, and despair !'
  Nothing beside remains.   Round the decay
Of that colossal wreck, boundless and bare,
  The lone and level sands stretch far away."

II.

POLITICAL GREATNESS.

NOR happiness, nor majesty, nor fame,
  Nor peace, nor strength, nor skill in arms or arts,
Shepherd those herds whom tyranny makes tame;
  Verse echoes not one beating of their hearts,
History is but the shadow of their shame,
  Art veils her glass, or from the pageant starts
As to oblivion their blind millions fleet,
  Staining that Heaven with obscene imagery
Of their own likeness.   What are numbers knit
  By force or custom ?   Man who man would be,
Must rule the empire of himself; in it
  Must be supreme, establishing his throne
On vanquished will, quelling the anarchy
  Of hopes and fears, being himself alone.

III.

TO A REVIEWER.

ALAS ! good friend, what profit can you see
  In hating such an hateless thing as me?
There is no sport in hate where all the rage
  Is on one side.   In vain would you assuage
Your frowns upon an unresisting smile,
  In which not even contempt lurks, to beguile
Your heart, by some faint sympathy of hate.
  O conquer what you cannot satiate !

For to your passion I am far more coy
Than ever yet was coldest maid or boy
In winter noon.   Of your antipathy
If I am the Narcissus, you are free
To pine into a sound with hating me.

IV.

LIFT not the painted veil which those who live
Call Life; though unreal shapes be pictured there,
And it but mimic all we would believe
With colours idly spread: behind, lurk Fear
And Hope, twin destinies; who ever weave
The shadows, which the world calls substance, there.

I knew one who lifted it—he sought,
For his lost heart was tender, things to love
But found them not, alas ! nor was there aught
The world contains, the which he could approve.
Through the unheeding many he did move,
A splendour among shadows, a bright blot
Upon this gloomy scene, a Spirit that strove
For truth, and like the Preacher found it not.

V.

FEELINGS OF A REPUBLICAN ON THE FALL OF BONAPARTE.

I HATED thee, fallen Tyrant !   I did groan
To think that a most unambitious slave,
Like thou, should dance and revel on the grave
Of Liberty.   Thou mightst have built thy throne
Where it had stood even now : thou didst prefer
A frail and bloody pomp, which Time has swept
In fragments towards oblivion.   Massacre,
For this, I prayed, would on thy sleep have crept,
Treason and Slavery, Rapine, Fear, and Lust,
And stifled thee their minister.   I know
Too late, since thou and France are in the dust,
That Virtue owns a more eternal foe
Than Force or Fraud : old Custom, Legal Crime,
And bloody Faith, the foulest birth of Time.

VI.

YE hasten to the dead : what seek ye there,
Ye restless thoughts and busy purposes
Of the idle brain, which the world's livery wear ?
O thou quick heart, which pantest to possess
All that anticipation feigneth fair—
Thou vainly curious mind which wouldest guess
Whence thou didst come and whither thou mayst go,
And that which never yet was known wouldst know—
Oh ! whither hasten ye, that thus ye press
With such swift feet life's green and pleasant path,
Seeking alike from happiness and woe
A refuge in the cavern of grey death ?
O heart and mind and thoughts ! what thing do you
Hope to inherit in the grave below ?

VII.

SONNET TO BYRON.

[I AM afraid these verses will not please **you, but**]
If I esteemed you less, Envy would kill
   Pleasure, and leave to Wonder and Despair
The ministration of the thoughts that fill
   The mind which, like a worm whose life may share
A portion of the unapproachable,
   Marks your creations rise as fast and fair
As perfect worlds at the Creator's will.
But such is my regard that nor your power
   To soar above the heights where others [climb],
Nor fame, that shadow of the unborn hour
   Cast from the envious future on the time,
   Move one regret for his unhonoured name
   Who dares these words :—the worm beneath the sod
May lift itself in homage of the God.

1821.

Translations.

HYMN TO MERCURY.

TRANSLATED FROM THE GREEK OF HOMER.

I.

Sing, Muse, the son of Maia and of Jove,
The Herald-child, king of Arcadia
And all its pastoral hills, whom in sweet love
Having been interwoven, modest May
Bore Heaven's dread Supreme—an antique grove
Shadowed the cavern where the lovers lay
In the deep night, unseen by Gods or Men,
And white-armed Juno slumbered sweetly then.

II.

Now, when the joy of Jove had its fulfilling,
And Heaven's tenth moon chronicled her relief,
She gave to light a babe all babes excelling,
A schemer subtle beyond all belief;
A shepherd of thin dreams, a cow-stealing,
A night-watching, and door-waylaying thief,
Who 'mongst the Gods was soon about to thieve
And other glorious actions to achieve.

III.

The babe was born at the first peep of day;
He began playing on the lyre at noon,
And the same evening did he steal away
Apollo's herds;—the fourth day of the moon
On which him bore the venerable May,
From her immortal limbs he leaped full soon,
Nor long could in the sacred cradle keep,
But out to seek Apollo's herds would creep.

IV.

Out of the lofty cavern wandering
He found a tortoise, and cried out—"A treasure!"
(For Mercury first made the tortoise sing)
The beast before the portal at his leisure
The flowery herbage was depasturing,
Moving his feet in a deliberate measure
Over the turf.   Jove's profitable son
Eyeing him laughed, and laughing thus begun:—

V.

" A useful godsend are you to me now,
King of the dance, companion of the feast,
Lovely in all your nature !   Welcome, you
Excellent plaything !   Where, sweet mountain beast,
Got you that speckled shell ?   Thus much I know
You must come home with me and be my guest ;
You will give joy to me, and I will do
All that is in my power to honour you.

VI.

" Better to be at home than out of door ;
So come with me, and though it has been said
That you alive defend from magic power,
I know you will sing sweetly when you're dead."
Thus having spoken, the quaint infant bore,
Lifting it from the grass on which it fed,
And grasping it in his delighted hold,
His treasured prize into the cavern old.

VII.

Then scooping with a chisel of grey steel
He bored the life and soul out of the beast—
Not swifter a swift thought of woe or weal
Darts through the tumult of a human breast
Which thronging cares annoy—not swifter wheel
The flashes of its torture and unrest
Out of the dizzy eyes—than Maia's son
All that he did devise hath featly done.

VIII.

And through the tortoise's hard strong skin
At proper distances small holes he made,
And fastened the cut stems of reeds within,
And with a piece of leather overlaid
The open space and fixed the cubits in,
Fitting the bridge to both, and stretched o'er all
Symphonious cords of sheep-gut rhythmical.

IX.

When he had wrought the lovely instrument,
He tried the chords, and made division meet
Preluding with the plectrum, and there went
Up from beneath his hand a tumult sweet
Of mighty sounds, and from his lips he sent
A strain of unpremeditated wit
Joyous and wild and wanton—such you may
Hear among revellers on a holiday.

X.

He sung how Jove and May of the bright sandal
Dallied in love not quite legitimate ;
And his own birth, still scoffing at the scandal,
And naming his own name, did celebrate ;

His mother's cave and servant maids he planned all
In plastic verse, her household stuff and state,
Perennial pot, trippet, and brazen pan,—
But singing he conceived another plan.

XI.

Seized with a sudden fancy for fresh meat,
He in his sacred crib deposited
The hollow lyre, and from the cavern sweet
Rushed with great leaps up to the mountain's head,
Revolving in his mind some subtle feat
Of thievish craft, such as a swindler might
Devise in the lone season of dun night.

XII.

Lo ! the great Sun under the ocean's bed has
Driven steeds and chariot—the child meanwhile strode
O'er the Pierian mountains clothed in shadows,
Where the immortal oxen of the God
Are pastured in the flowering unmown meadows,
And safely stalled in a remote abode—
The archer Argicide, elate and proud,
Drove fifty from the herd, lowing aloud.

XIII.

He drove them wandering o'er the sandy way,
But, being ever mindful of his craft,
Backward and forward drove he them astray,
So that the tracks which seemed before, were aft;
His sandals then he threw to the ocean spray,
And for each foot he wrought a kind of raft
Of tamarisk, and tamarisk-like sprigs,
And bound them in a lump with withy twigs.

XIV.

And on his feet he tied these sandals light,
The trail of whose wide leaves might not betray
His track; and then, a self-sufficing wight,
Like a man hastening on some distant way,
He from Piera's mountain bent his flight;
But an old man perceived the infant pass
Down green Onchestus heaped like beds with grass.

XV.

The old man stood dressing his sunny vine:
" Halloo ! old fellow with the crooked shoulder !
You grub those stumps? before they will bear wine
Methinks even you must grow a little older:
Attend, I pray, to this advice of mine,
As you would 'scape what might appal a bolder—
Seeing, see not—and hearing, hear not—and—
If you have understanding—understand."

XVI.

So saying, Hermes roused the oxen vast;
O'er shadowy mountain and resounding dell,
And flower-paven plains, great Hermes past;
Till the black night divine, which favouring fell

Around his steps, grew grey, and morning fast
Wakened the world to work, and from her cell
Sea-strewn, the Pallantean Moon sublime
Into her watch-tower just began to climb.

XVII.

Now to Alpheus he had driven all
The broad-foreheaded oxen of the Sun;
They came unwearied to the lofty stall
And to the water-troughs which ever run
Through the fresh fields—and when with rushgrass tall,
Lotus and all sweet herbage, every one
Had pastured been, the great God made them move
Towards the stall in a collected drove.

XVIII.

A mighty pile of wood the God then heaped,
And having soon conceived the mystery
Of fire, from two smooth laurel branches stript
The bark, and rubbed them in his palms,—on high
Suddenly forth the burning vapour leapt,
And the divine child saw delightedly—
Mercury first found out for human weal
Tinder-box, matches, fire-irons, flint and steel.

XIX.

And fine dry logs and roots innumerous
He gathered in a delve upon the ground—
And kindled them—and instantaneous
The strength of the fierce flame was breathed around:
And whilst the might of glorious Vulcan thus
Wrapt the great pile with glare and roaring sound,
Hermes dragged forth two heifers, lowing loud,
Close to the fire—such might was in the God.

XX.

And on the earth upon their backs he threw
The panting beasts, and rolled them o'er and o'er,
And bored their lives out.   Without more ado
He cut up fat and flesh, and down before
The fire, on spits of wood he placed the two,
Toasting their flesh and ribs, and all the gore
Pursed in the bowels; and while this was done
He stretched their hides over a craggy stone.

XXI.

We mortals let an ox grow old, and then
Cut it up after long consideration,—
But joyous-minded Hermes from the glen
Drew the fat spoils to the more open station
Of a flat smooth space, and portioned them; and when
He had by lot assigned to each a ration
Of the twelve Gods, his mind became aware
Of all the joys which in religion are.

XXII.

For the sweet savour of the roasted meat
Tempted him though immortal.   Natheless

He checked his haughty will and did not eat,
Though what it cost him words can scarce express,
And every wish to put such morsels sweet
Down his most sacred throat, he did repress;
But soon within the lofty portalled stall
He placed the fat and flesh and bones and all.

XXIII.

And every trace of the fresh butchery
And cooking, the God soon made disappear,
As if it all had vanished through the sky;
He burned the hoofs and horns and head and hair,
The insatiate fire devoured them hungrily;
And when he saw that everything was clear,
He quenched the coals and trampled the black dust,
And in the stream his bloody sandals tossed.

XXIV.

All night he worked in the serene moonshine—
But when the light of day was spread abroad
He sought his natal mountain peaks divine.
On his long wandering, neither man nor god
Had met him, since he killed Apollo's kine,
Nor house-dog had barked at him on his road;
Now he obliquely through the keyhole past,
Like a thin mist, or an autumnal blast.

XXV.

Right through the temple of the spacious cave
He went with soft light feet—as if his tread
Fell not on earth; no sound their falling gave;
Then to his cradle he crept quick, and spread
The swaddling-clothes about him; and the knave
Lay playing with the covering of the bed
With his left hand about his knees—the right
Held his beloved tortoise-lyre tight.

XXVI.

There he lay innocent as a newborn child,
As gossips say; but though he was a god,
The goddess, his fair mother, unbeguiled
Knew all that he had done being abroad:
" Whence come you, and from what adventure wild,
You cunning rogue, and where have you abode
All the long night, clothed in your impudence?
What have you done since you departed hence?

XXVII.

" Apollo soon will pass within this gate
And bind your tender body in a chain
Inextricably tight, and fast as fate,
Unless you can delude the God again,
Even when within his arms—ah, runagate !
A pretty torment both for gods and men
Your father made when he made you !"—" Dear mother,"
Replied sly Hermes, " wherefore scold and bother?

XXVIII.

"As if I were like other babes as old,
And understood nothing of what is what;
And cared at all to hear my mother scold.
I in my subtle brain a scheme have got,
Which whilst the sacred stars round Heaven are rolled
Will profit you and me—nor shall our lot
Be as you counsel, without gifts or food,
To spend our lives in this obscure abode.

XXIX.

"But we will leave this shadow-peopled cave
And live among the Gods, and pass each day
In high communion, sharing what they have
Of profuse wealth and unexhausted prey;
And from the portion which my father gave
To Phœbus, I will snatch my share away,
Which if my father will not—natheless I,
Who am the king of robbers, can but try.

XXX.

"And, if Latona's son should find me out,
I'll countermine him by a deeper plan;
I'll pierce the Pythian temple-walls, though stout,
And sack the fane of everything I can—
Cauldrons and tripods of great worth no doubt,
Each golden cup and polished brazen pan,
All the wrought tapestries and garments gay."
So they together talked;—meanwhile the Day

XXXI.

Ethereal born arose out of the flood
Of flowing Ocean, bearing light to men.
Apollo past toward the sacred wood,
Which from the inmost depths of its green glen
Echoes the voice of Neptune,—and there stood
On the same spot in green Onchestus then
That same old animal, the vine-dresser,
Who was employed hedging his vineyard there.

XXXII.

Latona's glorious Son began:—"I pray
Tell, ancient hedger of Onchestus green,
Whether a drove of kine has past this way,
All heifers with crooked horns? for they have been
Stolen from the herd in high Pieria,
Where a black bull was fed apart, between
Two woody mountains in a neighbouring glen,
And four fierce dogs watched there, unanimous as men.

XXXIII.

"And, what is strange, the author of this theft
Has stolen the fatted heifers every one,
But the four dogs and the black bull are left:
Stolen they were last night at set of sun,

Of their soft beds and their sweet food bereft—
   Now tell me, man born ere the world begun,
Have you seen any one pass with the cows?"—
To whom the man of overhanging brows :

XXXIV.

" My friend, it would require no common skill
   Justly to speak of everything I see :
On various purposes of good or ill
   Many pass by my vineyard,—and to me
'Tis difficult to know the invisible
   Thoughts, which in all those many minds may be:
Thus much alone I certainly can say,
I tilled these vines till the decline of day.

XXXV.

" And then I thought I saw, but dare not speak
   With certainty of such a wondrous thing,
A child, who could not have been born a week,
   Those fair-horned cattle closely following,
And in his hand he held a polished stick:
   And, as on purpose, he walked wavering
From one side to the other of the road,
And with his face opposed the steps he trod."

XXXVI.

Apollo hearing this, past quickly on—
   No winged omen could have shown more clear
That the deceiver was his father's son.
   So the God wraps a purple atmosphere
Around his shoulders, and like fire is gone
   To famous Pylos, seeking his kine there,
And found their track and his, yet hardly cold,
And cried—" What wonder do mine eyes behold !

XXXVII.

" Here are the footsteps of the horned herd
   Turned back towards their fields of asphodel;
But these ! are not the tracks of beast or bird,
   Grey wolf, or bear, or lion of the dell,
Or maned Centaur—sand was never stirred
   By man or woman thus ! Inexplicable !
Who with unwearied feet could e'er impress
The sand with such enormous vestiges ?

XXXVIII.

" That was most strange—but this is stranger still !"
   Thus having said, Phœbus impetuously
Sought high Cyllene's forest-cinctured hill,
   And the deep cavern where dark shadows lie,
And where the ambrosial nymph with happy will
   Bore the Saturnian's love-child, Mercury—
And a delightful odour from the dew
Of the hill pastures, at his coming, flew,

XXXIX.

And Phœbus stooped under the craggy roof
    Arched over the dark cavern:—Maia's child
Perceived that he came angry, far aloof,
    About the cows of which he had been beguiled,
And over him the fine and fragrant woof
    Of his ambrosial swaddling-clothes he piled—
As among firebrands lies a burning spark
Covered, beneath the ashes cold and dark.

XL.

There, like an infant who had sucked his fill
    And now was newly washed and put to bed,
Awake, but courting sleep with weary will,
    And gathered in a lump hands, feet, and head,
He lay, and his beloved tortoise still
    He grasped and held under his shoulder-blade.
Phœbus the lovely mountain-goddess knew,
Not less her subtle, swindling baby, who

XLI.

Lay swathed in his sly wiles. Round every crook
    Of the ample cavern, for his kine, Apollo
Looked sharp; and when he saw them not, he took
    The glittering key, and opened three great hollow
Recesses in the rock—where many a nook
    Was filled with the sweet food immortals swallow,
And mighty heaps of silver and of gold
Were piled within—a wonder to behold

XLII.

And white and silver robes, all overwrought
    With cunning workmanship of tracery sweet—
Except among the Gods there can be naught
    In the wide world to be compared with it.
Latona's offspring, after having sought
    His herds in every corner, thus did greet
Great Hermes:—" Little cradled rogue, declare
Of my illustrious heifers, where they are !

XLIII.

"Speak quickly ! or a quarrel between us
    Must rise, and the event will be, that I
Shall haul you into dismal Tartarus,
    In fiery gloom to dwell eternally:
Nor shall your father nor your mother loose
    The bars of that black dungeon—utterly
You shall be cast out from the light of day,
To rule the ghosts of men, unblest as they."

XLIV.

To whom thus Hermes slily answered:—" Son
    Of great Latona, what a speech is this !
Why come you here to ask me what is done
    With the wild oxen which it seems you miss?

I have not seen them, nor from any one
  Have heard a word of the whole business;
If you should promise an immense reward,
  I could not tell more than you now have heard.

XLV.

"An ox-stealer should be both tall and strong,
  And I am but a little newborn thing,
Who, yet at least, can think of nothing wrong:
  My business is to suck, and sleep, and fling
The cradle-clothes about me all day long,
  Or, half asleep, hear my sweet mother sing,
And to be washed in water clean and warm,
And hushed and kissed and kept secure from harm.

XLVI.

"O, let not e'er this quarrel be averred!
  The astounded Gods would laugh at you, if e'er
You should allege a story so absurd,
  As that a newborn infant forth could fare
Out of his home after a savage herd.
  I was born yesterday—my small feet are
Too tender for the roads so hard and rough:
And if you think that this is not enough,

XLVII.

"I swear a great oath, by my father's head,
  That I stole not your cows, and that I know
Of no one else, who might, or could, or did.
  Whatever things cows are, I do not know,
For I have only heard the name."—This said,
  He winked as fast as could be, and his brow
Was wrinkled, and a whistle loud gave he,
Like one who hears some strange absurdity.

XLVIII.

Apollo gently smiled and said :—"Ay, ay,—
  You cunning little rascal, you will bore
Many a rich man's house, and your array
  Of thieves will lay their siege before his door,
Silent as night, in night ; and many a day
  In the wild glens rough shepherds will deplore
That you or yours, having an appetite,
Met with their cattle, comrade of the night !

XLIX.

"And this among the Gods shall be your gift,
  To be considered as the lord of those
Who swindle, housebreak, sheepsteal, and shoplift ;
  But now if you would not your last sleep doze,
Crawl out !"—Thus saying, Phœbus did uplift
  The subtle infant in his swaddling-clothes,
And in his arms, according to his wont,
A scheme devised the illustrious Argiphont.

L.

*   *   *   *   *

  *   *   *   *   *

And sneezed and shuddered—Phœbus on the grass
  Him threw, and whilst all that he had designed
He did perform—eager although to pass,
  Apollo darted from his mighty mind
Towards the subtle babe the following scoff :—
" Do not imagine this will get you off,

LI.

" You little swaddled child of Jove and May !"
  And seized him :—" By this omen I shall trace
My noble herds, and you shall lead the way."
  Cyllenian Hermes from the grassy place,
Like one in earnest haste to get away,
  Rose, and with hands lifted towards his face
Round both his ears—up from his shoulders drew
His swaddling clothes, and—" What mean you to do

LII.

" With me, you unkind God?"—said Mercury :
  " Is it about these cows you tease me so ?
I wish the race of cows were perished !—I
  Stole not your cows—I do not even know
What things cows are. Alas ! I well may sigh,
  That since I came into this world of woe,
I should have ever heard the name of one—
But I appeal to the Saturnian's throne."

LIII.

Thus Phœbus and the vagrant Mercury
  Talked without coming to an explanation,
With adverse purpose. As for Phœbus, he
  Sought not revenge, but only information,
And Hermes tried with lies and roguery
  To cheat Apollo—but when no evasion
Served—for the cunning one his match had found—
He paced on first over the sandy ground.

LIV.

He of the Silver Bow the child of Jove
  Followed behind, till to their heavenly Sire
Came both his children—beautiful as Love,
  And from his equal balance did require
A judgment in the cause wherein they strove.
  O'er odorous Olympus and its snows
A murmuring tumult as they came arose,—

LV.

And from the folded depths of the great Hill,
  While Hermes and Apollo reverent stood
Before Jove's throne, the indestructible
  Immortals rushed in mighty multitude ;

And whilst their seats in order due they fill,
  The lofty Thunderer in a careless mood
To Phœbus said :—" Whence drive you this sweet prey,
This herald-baby, born but yesterday ?

LVI.

" A most important subject, trifler, this
  To lay before the Gods !"—" Nay, father, nay,
When you have understood the business,
  Say not that I alone am fond of prey.
I found this little boy in a recess
  Under Cyllene's mountains far away—
A manifest and most apparent thief,
A scandal-monger beyond all belief.

LVII.

" I never saw his like either in heaven
  Or upon earth for knavery and craft :
Out of the field my cattle yester-even,
  By the low shore on which the loud sea laughed,
He right down to the river-ford had driven ;
  And mere astonishment would make you daft
To see the double kind of footstep strange
He has impressed wherever he did range.

LVIII.

" The cattle's track on the black dust, full well
  Is evident, as if they went towards
The place from which they came—that asphodel
  Meadow, in which I feed my many herds—
His steps were most incomprehensible—
  I know not how I can describe in words
Those tracks—he could have gone along the sands
Neither upon his feet nor on his hands ;

LIX.

" He must have had some other stranger mode
  Of moving on : those vestiges immense,
Far as I traced them on the sandy road,
  Seemed like the trail of oak-toppings :—but thence
No mark or track denoting where they trod
  The hard ground gave :—but, working at his fence,
A mortal hedger saw him as he past
To Pylos, with the cows, in fiery haste.

LX.

" I found that in the dark he quietly
  Had sacrificed some cows, and before light
Had thrown the ashes all dispersedly
  About the road—then, still as gloomy night,
Had crept into his cradle, either eye
  Rubbing, and cogitating some new sleight.
No eagle could have seen him as he lay
Hid in his cavern from the peering day.

LXI.

" I taxed him with the fact, when he averred
   Most solemnly that he did neither see
Or even had in any manner heard
   Of my lost cows, whatever things cows be ;
Nor could he tell, though offered a reward,
   Not even who could tell of them to me."
So speaking, Phœbus sate ; and Hermes then
Addressed the Supreme Lord of Gods and Men :

LXII.

" Great Father, you know clearly beforehand
   That all which I shall say to you is soothe ;
I am a most veracious person, and
   Totally unacquainted with untruth.
At sunrise, Phœbus came, but with no band
   Of Gods to bear him witness, in great wrath,
To my abode, seeking his heifers there,
And saying that I must show him where they are,

LXIII.

" Or he would hurl me down the dark abyss.
   I know, that every Apollonian limb
Is clothed with speed and might and manliness,
   As a green bank with flowers—but unlike him
I was born yesterday, and you may guess
   He well knew this when he indulged the whim
Of bullying a poor little newborn thing
That slept, and never thought of cow-driving.

LXIV.

" Am I like a strong fellow who steals kine
   Believe me, dearest Father, such you are,
This driving of the herds is none of mine ;
   Across my threshold did I wander ne'er,
So may I thrive !   I reverence the divine
   Sun and the Gods, and I love you, and care
Even for this hard accuser—who must know
I am as innocent as they or you.

LXV.

" I swear by these most gloriously-wrought portals—
   (It is, you will allow, an oath of might)
Through which the multitude of the Immortals
   Pass and repass for ever, day and night,
Devising schemes for the affairs of mortals—
   That I am guiltless ; and I will requite,
Although mine enemy be great and strong,
His cruel threat—do thou defend the young !"

LXVI.

So speaking, the Cyllenian Argiphont
   Winked, as if now his adversary was fitted :
And Jupiter according to his wont,
   Laughed heartily to hear the subtle-witted

Infant give such a plausible account,
   And every word a lie. But he remitted
Judgment at present—and his exhortation
Was, to compose the affair by arbitration.

LXVII.

And they by mighty Jupiter were bidden
   To go forth with a single purpose both,
Neither the other chiding nor yet chidden:
   And Mercury with innocence and truth
To lead the way, and show where he had hidden
   The mighty heifers.—Hermes, nothing loth,
Obeyed the Ægis-bearer's will—for he
Is able to persuade all easily.

LXVIII.

These lovely children of Heaven's highest Lord
   Hastened to Pylos and the pastures wide
And lofty stalls by the Alphean ford,
   Where wealth in the mute night is multiplied
With silent growth. Whilst Hermes drove the herd
   Out of the stony cavern, Phœbus spied
The hides of those the little babe had slain,
Stretched on the precipice above the plain.

LXIX.

" How was it possible," then Phœbus said,
   " That you, a little child, born yesterday,
A thing on mother's milk and kisses fed,
   Could two prodigious heifers ever flay ?
Even I myself may well hereafter dread
   Your prowess, offspring of Cyllenian May,
When you grow strong and tall."—He spoke, and bound
Stiff withy bands the infant's wrists around.

LXX.

He might as well have bound the oxen wild;
   The withy bands, though starkly interknit,
Fell at the feet of the immortal child,
   Loosened by some device of his quick wit.
Phœbus perceived himself again beguiled,
   And stared—while Hermes sought some hole or pit,
Looking askance and winking fast as thought,
Where he might hide himself and not be caught.

LXXI.

Sudden he changed his plan, and with strange skill
   Subdued the strong Latonian, by the might
Of winning music, to his mightier will;
   His left hand held the lyre, and in his right
The plectrum struck the chords—unconquerable
   Up from beneath his hand in circling flight
The gathering music rose—and sweet as Love
The penetrating notes did live and move

LXXII.

Within the heart of great Apollo—he
    Listened with all his soul, and laughed for pleasure.
Close to his side stood harping fearlessly
    The unabashed boy; and to the measure
Of the sweet lyre, there followed loud and free
    His joyous voice; for he unlocked the treasure
Of his deep song, illustrating the birth
Of the bright Gods and the dark desert Earth :

LXXIII.

And how to the Immortals every one
    A portion was assigned of all that is ;
But chief Mnemosyne did Maia's son
    Clothe in the light of his loud melodies ;
And as each God was born or had begun
    He in their order due and fit degrees
Sung of his birth and being—and did move
Apollo to unutterable love.

LXXIV.

These words were winged with his swift delight:
    " You heifer-stealing schemer, well do you
Deserve that fifty oxen should requite
    Such minstrelsies as I have heard even now.
Comrade of feasts, little contriving wight,
    One of your secrets I would gladly know,
Whether the glorious power you now show forth
Was folded up within you at your birth,

LXXV.

" Or whether mortal taught or God inspired
    The power of unpremeditated song?
Many divinest sounds have I admired,
    The Olympian Gods and mortal men among;
But such a strain of wondrous, strange, untired,
    And soul-awakening music, sweet and strong,
Yet did I never hear except from thee,
Offspring of May, impostor Mercury !

LXXVI.

" What Muse, what skill, what unimagined use,
    What exercise of subtlest art, has given
Thy songs such power ?—for those who hear may choose
    From three, the choicest of the gifts of Heaven,
Delight, and love, and sleep,—sweet sleep, whose dews
    Are sweeter than the balmy tears of even:
And I, who speak this praise, am that Apollo
Whom the Olympian Muses ever follow:

LXXVII.

" And their delight is dance, and the blithe noise
    Of song and overflowing poesy;
And sweet, even as desire, the liquid voice
    Of pipes, that fills the clear air thrillingly;

But never did my inmost soul rejoice
   In this dear work of youthful revelry,
As now I wonder at thee, son of Jove;
   Thy harpings and thy song are soft as love.

LXXVIII.

" Now since thou hast, although so very small,
   Science of arts so glorious, thus I swear,
And let this cornel javelin, keen and tall,
   Witness between us what I promise here,-
That I will lead thee to the Olympian Hall,
   Honoured and mighty, with thy mother dear,
And many glorious gifts in joy will give thee,
And even at the end will ne'er deceive thee."

LXXIX.

To whom thus Mercury with prudent speech:—
   " Wisely hast thou inquired of my skill:
I envy thee no thing I know to teach
   Even this day:—for both in word and will
I would be gentle with thee; thou canst reach
   All things in thy wise spirit, and thy sill
Is highest in heaven among the sons of Jove,
Who loves thee in the fulness of his love.

LXXX.

" The Counsellor Supreme has given to thee
   Divinest gifts, out of the amplitude
Of his profuse exhaustless treasury;
   By thee, 'tis said, the depths are understood
Of his far voice; by thee the mystery
   Of all oracular fates,—and the dread mood
Of the diviner is breathed up, even I—
A child—perceive thy might and majesty—

LXXXI.

" Thou canst seek out and compass all that wit
   Can find or teach;—yet since thou wilt, come take
The lyre—be mine the glory giving it—
   Strike the sweet chords, and sing aloud, and wake
Thy joyous pleasure out of many a fit
   Of tranced sound—and with fleet fingers make
Thy liquid-voiced comrade talk with thee,
It can talk measured music eloquently.

LXXXII.

" Then bear it boldly to the revel loud,
   Love-wakening dance, or feast of solemn state,
A joy by night or day—for those endowed
   With art and wisdom who interrogate
It teaches, babbling in delightful mood
   All things which make the spirit most elate,
Soothing the mind with sweet familiar play,
Chasing the heavy shadows of dismay.

LXXXIII.

"'To those who are unskilled in its sweet tongue,
 Though they should question most impetuously
Its hidden soul, it gossips something wrong—
 Some senseless and impertinent reply.
But thou who art as wise as thou art strong
 Can compass all that thou desirest.   I
Present thee with this music-flowing shell,
Knowing thou canst interrogate it well.

LXXXIV.

" And let us two henceforth together feed
 On this green mountain slope and pastoral plain,
The herds in litigation—they will breed
 Quickly enough to recompense our pain,
If to the bulls and cows we take good heed;
 And thou, though somewhat over fond of gain,
Grudge me not half the profit."—Having spoke,
The shell he proffered, and Apollo took.

LXXXV.

And gave him in return the glittering lash,
 Installing him as herdsman;—from the look
Of Mercury then laughed a joyous flash.
 And then Apollo with the plectrum strook
The chords, and from beneath his hands a crash
 Of mighty sounds rushed up, whose music shook
The soul with sweetness, as of an adept
His sweeter voice a just accordance kept.

LXXXVI.

The herd went wandering o'er the divine mead,
 Whilst these most beautiful Sons of Jupiter
Won their swift way up to the snowy head
 Of white Olympus, with the joyous lyre
Soothing their journey; and their father dread
 Gathered them both into familiar
Affection sweet,—and then, and now, and ever,
Hermes must love Him of the Golden Quiver,

LXXXVII.

To whom he gave the lyre that sweetly sounded,
 Which skilfully he held and played thereon.
He piped the while, and far and wide rebounded
 The echo of his pipings; every one
Of the Olympians sat with joy astounded,
 While he conceived another piece of fun,
One of his old tricks—which the God of Day
Perceiving, said:—" I fear thee, Son of May;

LXXXVIII.

" I fear thee and thy sly chameleon spirit,
 Lest thou should steal my lyre and crooked bow;
This glory and power thou dost from Jove inherit,
 To teach all craft upon the earth below;

Thieves love and worship thee—it is thy merit
   To make all mortal business ebb and flow
By roguery:—now, Hermes, if you dare,
   By sacred Styx a mighty oath to swear

LXXXIX.

" That you will never rob me, you will do
   A thing extremely pleasing to my heart."
Then Mercury sware by the Stygian dew,
   That he would never steal his bow or dart,
Or lay his hands on what to him was due,
   Or ever would employ his powerful art
Against his Pythian fane.   Then Phœbus swore
There was no God or man whom he loved more.

XC.

" And I will give thee as a goodwill token,
   The beautiful wand of wealth and happiness;
A perfect three-leaved rod of gold unbroken,
   Whose magic will thy footsteps ever bless;
And whatsoever by Jove's voice is spoken
   Of earthly or divine from its recess,
It, like a loving soul to thee will speak,
And more than this, do thou forbear to seek.

XCI.

" For, dearest child, the divinations high
   Which thou requirest, 'tis unlawful ever
That thou, or any other deity,
   Should understand—and vain were the endeavour;
For they are hidden in Jove's mind, and I
   In trust of them, have sworn that I would never
Betray the counsels of Jove's inmost will
To any God—the oath was terrible.

XCII.

" Then, golden-wanded brother, ask me not
   To speak the fates by Jupiter designed;
But be it mine to tell their various lot
   To the unnumbered tribes of human kind.
Let good to these, and ill to those be wrought
   As I dispense—but he who comes consigned
By voice and wings of perfect augury
To my great shrine, shall find avail in me.

XCIII.

" Him will I not deceive, but will assist;
   But he who comes relying on such birds
As chatter vainly, who would strain and twist
   The purpose of the Gods with idle words,
And deems their knowledge light, he shall have mist
   His road—whilst I among my other hoards
His gifts deposit.   Yet, O Son of May,
I have another wondrous thing to say.

XCIV.

"There are three Fates, three virgin Sisters, who
  Rejoicing in their wind-outspeeding wings,
Their heads with flour snowed over white and new,
  Sit in a vale round which Parnassus flings
Its circling skirts—from these I have learned true
  Vaticinations of remotest things.
My father cared not. Whilst they search out dooms,
They sit apart and feed on honeycombs.

XCV.

" They, having eaten the fresh honey, grow
  Drunk with divine enthusiasm, and utter
With earnest willingness the truth they know,
  But if deprived of that sweet food, they mutter
All plausible delusions;—these to you
  I give;—if you inquire, they will not stutter:
Delight your own soul with them:—any man
You would instruct, may profit, if he can.

XCVI.

"Take these and the fierce oxen, Maia's child—
  O'er many a horse and toil-enduring mule,
O'er jagged-jawed lions, and the wild
  White-tusked boars, o'er all, by field or pool,
Of cattle which the mighty Mother mild
  Nourishes in her bosom, thou shalt rule—
Thou dost alone the veil of death uplift—
Thou givest not—yet this is a great gift."

XCVII.

Thus king Apollo loved the child of May
  In truth, and Jove covered them with love and joy.
Hermes with Gods and men even from that day
  Mingled, and wrought the latter much annoy,
And little profit, going far astray
  Through the dun night. Farewell, delightful Boy,
Of Jove and Maia sprung,—never by me,
Nor thou, nor other songs shall unremembered be.

HYMN TO CASTOR AND POLLUX.

YE wild-eyed Muses, sing the Twins of Jove,
Whom the fair-ankled Leda mixed in love
With mighty Saturn's heaven-obscuring child,
On Taygetus, that lofty mountain wild,
Brought forth in joy ; mild Pollux void of blame,
And steel-subduing Castor, heirs of fame.
These are the Powers who earth-born mortals save,
And ships, whose flight is swift along the wave.
When wintry tempests o'er the savage sea
Are raging, and the sailors tremblingly
Call on the Twins of Jove with prayer and vow,
Gathered in fear upon the lofty prow,

And sacrifice with snow-white lambs, the wind
And the huge billow bursting close behind,
Even then beneath the weltering waters bear
The staggering ship—they suddenly appear,
On yellow wings rushing athwart the sky,
And lull the blasts in mute tranquillity,
And strew the waves on the white ocean's bed,
Fair omen of the voyage; from toil and dread
The sailors rest, rejoicing in the sight,
And plough the quiet sea in safe delight.

TO THE MOON.

DAUGHTER of Jove, whose voice is melody,
Muses, who know and rule all minstrelsy!
Sing the wide-wingèd Moon.   Around the earth,
From her immortal head in Heaven shot forth,
Far light is scattered—boundless glory springs
Where'er she spreads her many beaming wings,
The lampless air glows round her golden crown.

But when the Moon divine from Heaven is gone
Under the sea, her beams within abide,
Till, bathing her bright limbs in Ocean's tide,
Clothing her form in garments glittering far,
And having yoked to her immortal car
The beam-invested steeds, whose necks on high
Curve back, she drives to a remoter sky
A western Crescent, borne impetuously.
Then is made full the circle of her light,
And as she grows, her beams more bright and bright,
Are poured from Heaven, where she is hovering then,
A wonder and a sign to mortal men.

The Son of Saturn with this glorious Power
Mingled in love and sleep—to whom she bore
Panderá, a bright maid of beauty rare
Among the Gods, whose lives eternal are.

Hail, Queen, great Moon, white-armed Divinity,
Fair-haired and favourable, thus with thee,
My song beginning, by its music sweet
Shall make immortal many a glorious feat
Of demi-gods, with lovely lips, so well
Which minstrels, servants of the Muses, tell.

TO THE SUN.

OFFSPRING of Jove, Calliope, once more
To the bright Sun thy hymn of music pour,
Whom to the Child of star-clad Heaven and Earth,
Euryphæssa, large-eyed nymph, brought forth;
Euryphæssa, the famed sister fair,
Of great Hyperion, who to him did bear

A race of loveliest children; the young Morn,
Whose arms are like twin roses newly born;
The fair-haired Moon, and the immortal Sun,
Who, borne by heavenly steeds, his race doth run
Unconquerably, illuming the abodes
Of mortal men and the eternal Gods.

Fiercely look forth his awe-inspiring eyes
Beneath his golden helmet, whence arise
And are shot forth afar, clear beams of light;
His countenance with radiant glory bright,
Beneath his graceful locks far shines around,
And the light vest with which his limbs are bound
Of woof etherial, delicately twined,
Glows in the stream of the uplifting wind.
His rapid steeds soon bear him to the West,
Where their steep flight his hands divine arrest,
And the fleet car with yoke of gold, which he
Sends from bright heaven beneath the shadowy sea.

TO THE EARTH, MOTHER OF ALL.

O UNIVERSAL Mother, who dost keep
From everlasting thy foundations deep,
Eldest of things, Great Earth, I sing of thee;
All shapes that have their dwelling in the sea,
All things that fly, or on the ground divine
Live, move, and there are nourished—these are thine;
These from thy wealth thou dost sustain; from thee
Fair babes are born, and fruits on every tree
Hang ripe and large, revered Divinity!

The life of mortal men beneath thy sway
Is held; thy power both gives and takes away!
Happy are they whom thy mild favours nourish,
All things unstinted round them grow and flourish.
For them endures the life-sustaining field
Its load of harvest, and their cattle yield
Large increase, and their house with wealth is filled.

Such honoured dwell in cities fair and free,
The homes of lovely women, prosperously;
Their sons exult in youth's new-budding gladness,
And their fresh daughters, free from care or sadness,
With bloom-enwoven dance and happy song
On the soft flowers the meadow grass among,
Leap round them sporting—such delights by thee
Are given, rich Power, revered Divinity!

Mother of Gods, thou wife of starry Heaven,
Farewell! be thou propitious and be given
A happy life for this brief melody,
Nor thou, nor other songs shall unremembered be.

TO MINERVA.

I sing the glorious Power with azure eyes,
Athenian Pallas! tameless, chaste, and wise;
Tritogenia, town-preserving maid,
Revered and mighty; from his awful head
Whom Jove brought forth, in warlike armour drest,
Golden, all radiant! wonder strange possessed
The everlasting Gods that shape to see,
Shaking a javelin keen, impetuously
Rush from the crest of Ægis-bearing Jove;
Fearfully Heaven was shaken and did move
Beneath the might of the Cerulean eyed;
Earth dreadfully resounded, far and wide,
And lifted from its depths, the sea swelled high
In purple billows, the tide suddenly
Stood still, and great Hyperion's son long time
Checked his swift steeds, till where she stood sublime,
Pallas from her immortal shoulders threw
The arms divine; wise Jove rejoiced to view.
Child of the Ægis bearer, hail to thee,
Nor thine nor others' praise shall unremembered be.

THE CYCLOPS:

A SATYRIC DRAMA.

TRANSLATED FROM THE GREEK OF EURIPIDES.

SILENUS.	ULYSSES.
CHORUS OF SATYRS	THE CYCLOPS.

Sil. O BACCHUS, what a world of toil, both now
And ere these limbs were overworn with age,
Have I endured for thee ! First, when thou fled'st
The mountain-nymphs who nurst thee, driven afar
By the strange madness Juno sent upon thee;
Then in the battle of the sons of Earth,
When I stood foot by foot close to thy side,
No unpropitious fellow combatant,
And driving through his shield my winged spear,
Slew vast Enceladus. Consider now,
Is it a dream of which I speak to thee?
By Jove it is not, for you have the trophies !
And now I suffer more than all before.
For when I heard that Juno had devised
A tedious voyage for you, I put to sea
With all my children quaint in search of you,
And I myself stood on the beaked prow
And fixed the naked mast, and all my boys
Leaning upon their oars, with splash and strain
Made white with foam the green and purple sea, —
And so we sought you, king. We were sailing
Near Malea, when an eastern wind arose,
And drove us to this wild Ætnean rock;
The one-eyed children of the Ocean God,
The man-destroying Cyclopses inhabit,
On this wild shore, their solitary caves,
And one of these, named Polypheme, has caught us
To be his slaves; and so, for all delight
Of Bacchic sports, sweet dance and melody,
We keep this lawless giant's wandering flocks.
My sons indeed, on far declivities,
Young things themselves, tend on the youngling sheep,
But I remain to fill the water casks,
Or sweeping the hard floor, or ministering
Some impious and abominable meal
To the fell Cyclops. I am wearied of it !
And now I must scrape up the littered floor
With this great iron rake, so to receive
My absent master and his evening sheep
In a cave neat and clean. Even now I see
My children tending the flocks hitherward.

Ha! what is this? are your Sicinnian measures
Even now the same, as when with dance and song
You brought young Bacchus to Athæa's halls?

    *   *   *   *   *

CHORUS OF SATYRS.

STROPHE.

Where has he of race divine
Wandered in the winding rocks?
Here the air is calm and fine
For the father of the flocks;
Here the grass is soft and sweet,
And the river-eddies meet
In the trough beside the cave,
Bright as in their fountain wave.
Neither here, nor on the dew
Of the lawny uplands feeding.
Oh, you come!—a stone at you
Will I throw to mend your breeding;
Get along, you horned thing,
Wild, seditious, rambling!

EPODE.*

An Iacchic melody
To the golden Aphrodite
Will I lift, as erst did I
Seeking her and her delight
With the Mænads, whose white feet
To the music glance and fleet.
Bacchus, O beloved, where,
Shaking wide thy yellow hair,
Wanderest thou alone, afar?
To the one-eyed Cyclops, we,
Who by right thy servants are,
Minister in misery,
In these wretched goatskins clad,
Far from thy delights and thee.

Sil. Be silent, sons; command the slaves to drive
The gathered flocks into the rock-roofed cave.
   Chorus. Go! But what needs this serious haste, O father?
   Sil. I see a Greek ship's boat upon the coast,
And thence the rowers with some general
Approaching to this cave. About their necks
Hang empty vessels, as they wanted food,
And water-flasks. O, miserable strangers!
Whence come they, that they know not what and who
My master is, approaching in ill hour
The inhospitable roof of Polypheme,
And the Cyclopian jawbone, man-destroying?
Be silent, Satyrs, while I ask and hear
Whence coming, they arrive the Ætnean hill.

-----

* The Antistrophe is omitted.

Uly. Friends, can you show me some clear water spring,
The remedy of our thirst? Will any one
Furnish with food seamen in want of it?
Ha! what is this? We seem to be arrived
At the blithe court of Bacchus. I observe
This sportive band of Satyrs near the caves.
First let me greet the elder. Hail!

Sil.   Hail thou
O, Stranger! tell thy country and thy race.

Uly. The Ithacan Ulysses and the king
Of Cephalonia.

Sil.   Oh, I know the man,
Wordy and shrewd, the son of Sisyphus.

Uly. I am the same, but do not rail upon me.

Sil. Whence sailing do you come to Sicily?

Uly. From Ilion, and from the Trojan toils.

Sil. How, touched you not at your paternal shore?

Uly. The strength of tempests bore me here by force.

Sil. The self-same accident occurred to me.

Uly. Were you then driven here by stress of weather?

Sil. Following the Pirates who had kidnapped Bacchus.

Uly. What land is this, and who inhabit it?

Sil. Ætna, the loftiest peak in Sicily.

Uly. And are there walls, and tower-surrounded towns?

Sil. There are not;—These lone rocks are bare of men.

Uly. And who possess the land? the race of beasts?

Sil. Cyclops, who live in caverns, not in houses.

Uly. Obeying whom? Or is the state popular?

Sil. Shepherds: no one obeys any in aught.

Uly. How live they? do they sow the corn of Ceres?

Sil. On milk and cheese, and on the flesh of sheep.

Uly. Have they the Bromian drink from the vine's stream?

Sil. Ah! no; they live in an ungracious land.

Uly. And are they just to strangers?—hospitable?

Sil. They think the sweetest thing a stranger brings
Is his own flesh.

Uly.   What! do they eat man's flesh?

Sil. No one comes here who is not eaten up.

Uly. The Cyclops now—Where is he? Not at home?

Sil. Absent on Ætna, hunting with his dogs.

Uly. Knowst thou what thou must do to aid us hence?

Sil. I know not: we will help you all we can.

Uly. Provide us food, of which we are in want.

Sil. Here is not anything, as I said, but meat.

Uly. But meat is a sweet remedy for hunger.

Sil. Cow's milk there is, and store of curdled cheese.

Uly. Bring out:—I would see all before I bargain.

Sil. But how much gold will you engage to give?

Uly. I bring no gold, but Bacchic juice.

Sil.   O, joy!
Tis long since these dry lips were wet with wine.

Uly. Maron, the son of the God, gave it me.

Sil. Whom I have nursed a baby in my arms.

Uly. The son of Bacchus, for your clearer knowledge.

Sil. Have you it now?—or is it in the ship?

Uly. Old man, this skin contains it, which you see.

Sil. Why this would hardly be a mouthful for me.

Uly. Nay, twice as much as you can draw from thence.

Sil. You speak of a fair fountain, sweet to me.

Uly. Would you first taste of the unmingled wine?

Sil. 'Tis just—tasting invites the purchaser.

Uly. Here is the cup, together with the skin.

Sil. Pour: that the draught may fillip my remembrance

Uly. See!

Sil.   Papaiapæx! what a sweet smell it has!

Uly. You see it then?—

Sil.   By Jove, no! but I smell it.

Uly. Taste, that you may not praise it in words only.

Sil. Babai!   Great Bacchus calls me forth to dance!
Joy! joy!

Uly.   Did it flow sweetly down your throat?

Sil. So that it tingled to my very nails.

Uly. And in addition I will give you gold.

Sil. Let gold alone! only unlock the cask.

Uly. Bring out some cheeses now, or a young goat.

Sil. That will I do, despising any master.
Yes, let me drink one cup, and I will give
All that the Cyclops feed upon their mountains.

*   *   *   *

Chorus. Ye have taken Troy and laid your hands on Helen?

Uly. And utterly destroyed the race of Priam.

Sil. * * The wanton wretch! she was bewitched to see
The many-coloured anklets and the chain
Of woven gold which girt the neck of Paris,
And so she left that good man Menelaus.
There should be no more women in the world
But such as are reserved for me alone.
See, here are sheep, and here are goats, Ulysses,
Here are unsparing cheeses of pressed milk;
Take them; depart with what good speed ye may;
First leaving my reward, the Bacchic dew
Of joy-inspiring grapes.

Uly.   Ah me! Alas!
What shall we do? the Cyclops is at hand!
Old man, we perish! whither can we fly?

Sil. Hide yourselves quick within that hollow rock.

Uly. 'Twere perilous to fly into the net.

Sil. The cavern has recesses numberless;
Hide yourselves quick.

Uly.   That will I never do!
The mighty Troy would be indeed disgraced
If I should fly one man.   How many times
Have I withstood, with shield immovable,
Ten thousand Phrygians!—if I needs must die,
Yet will I die with glory;—if I live,
The praise which I have gained will yet remain.

Sil. What, ho! assistance, comrades, haste assistance!

The CYCLOPS, SILENUS, ULYSSES; CHORUS.

Cyc. What is this tumult?   Bacchus is not here,
Nor tympanies nor brazen castanets.
How are my young lambs in the cavern?   Milking
Their dams or playing by their sides?   And is

The new cheese pressed into the bulrush baskets?
Speak! I'll beat some of you till you rain tears—
Look up, not downwards when I speak to you.

Sil. See! I now gape at Jupiter himself,
I stare upon Orion and the stars.

Cyc. Well, is the dinner fitly cooked and laid?

Sil. All ready, if your throat is ready too.

Cyc. Are the bowls full of milk besides?

Sil.   O'er-brimming;
So you may drink a tunful if you will.

Cyc. Is it ewe's milk or cow's milk, or both mixed?

Sil. Both, either; only pray don't swallow me.

Cyc. By no means.   *   *   *
What is this crowd I see beside the stalls?
Outlaws or thieves? for near my cavern-home,
I see my young lambs coupled two by two
With willow bands; mixed with my cheeses lie
Their implements; and this old fellow here
Has his bald head broken with stripes.

Sil.   Ah me!
I have been beaten till I burn with fever.

Cyc. By whom? Who laid his fist upon your head?

Sil. Those men, because I would not suffer them
To steal your goods.

Cyc.   Did not the rascals know
I am a God, sprung from the race of heaven?

Sil. I told them so, but they bore off your things,
And ate the cheese in spite of all I said,
And carried out the lambs—and said, moreover,
They'd pin you down with a three-cubit collar,
And pull your vitals out through your one eye,
Torture your back with stripes, then binding you,
Throw you as ballast into the ship's hold,
And then deliver you, a slave, to move
Enormous rocks, or found a vestibule.

Cyc. In truth? Nay, haste, and place in order quickly
The cooking knives, and heap upon the hearth,
And kindle it, a great faggot of wood—
As soon as they are slaughtered, they shall fill
My belly, broiling warm from the live coals,
Or boiled and seethed within the bubbling cauldron.
I am quite sick of the wild mountain game,
Of stags and lions I have gorged enough,
And I grow hungry for the flesh of men.

Sil. Nay, master, something new is very pleasant
After one thing for ever, and of late
Very few strangers have approached our cave.

Uly. Hear, Cyclops, a plain tale on the other side.
We, wanting to buy food, came from our ship
Into the neighbourhood of your cave, and here
This old Silenus gave us in exchange
These lambs for wine, the which he took and drank,
And all by mutual compact, without force.
There is no word of truth in what he says,
For slily he was selling all your store.

Sil. I? May you perish, wretch—

Uly.   If I speak false!

Sil. Cyclops, I swear by Neptune who begot thee,

By mighty Triton and by Nereus old,
Calypso and the glaucous Ocean Nymphs,
The sacred waves and all the race of fishes—
Be these the witnesses, my dear sweet master,
My darling little Cyclops, that I never
Gave any of your stores to these false strangers;
If I speak false may those whom most I love,
My children, perish wretchedly !

    Chorus.   There stop !
I saw him giving these things to the strangers.
If I speak false, then may my father perish,
But do not thou wrong hospitality.

  Cyc. You lie ! I swear that he is juster far
Than Rhadamanthus—I trust more in him.
But let me ask, whence have ye sailed, O strangers ?
Who are you ? And what city nourished ye ?

  Uly. Our race is Ithacan—having destroyed
The town of Troy, the tempests of the sea
Have driven us on thy land, O Polypheme.

  Cyc. What, have ye shared in the unenvied spoil
Of the false Helen, near Scamander's stream ?

  Uly. The same, having endured a woful toil.

  Cyc. O, basest expedition ! sailed ye not
From Greece to Phrygia for one woman's sake ?

  Uly. 'Twas the Gods' work—no mortal was in fault.
But, O great offspring of the ocean-king,
We pray thee and admonish thee with freedom,
That thou dost spare thy friends who visit thee,
And place no impious food within thy jaws.
For in the depths of Greece we have upreared
Temples to thy great father, which are all
His homes. The sacred bay of Tænarus
Remains inviolate, and each dim recess
Scooped high on the Malean promontory,
And aery Sunium's silver-veined crag,
Which divine Pallas keeps unprofaned ever,
The Gerastian asylums, and whate'er
Within wide Greece our enterprise has kept
From Phrygian contumely ; and in which
You have a common care, for you inhabit
The skirts of Grecian land, under the roots
Of Ætna and its crags, spotted with fire.
Turn then to converse under human laws,
Receive us shipwrecked suppliants and provide
Food, clothes, and fire, and hospitable gifts ;
Nor fixing upon oxen-piercing spits
Our limbs, so fill your belly and your jaws.
Priam's wide land has widowed Greece enough ;
And weapon-winged murder heaped together
Enough of dead, and wives are husbandless,
And ancient women and grey fathers wail
Their childless age ;—if you should roast the rest,
And 'tis a bitter feast that you prepare,
Where then would any turn ? Yet be persuaded ;
Forego the lust of your jawbone ; prefer
Pious humanity to wicked will :
Many have bought too dear their evil joys.

  Sil. Let me advise you, do not spare a morsel

Of all his flesh. If you should eat his tongue
You would become most eloquent, O Cyclops!

Cyc. Wealth, my good fellow, is the wise man's God,
All other things are a pretence and boast.
What are my father's ocean promontories,
The sacred rocks whereon he dwells, to me?
Stranger, I laugh to scorn Jove's thunderbolt,
I know not that his strength is more than mine.
As to the rest I care not:—When he pours
Rain from above, I have a close pavilion
Under this rock, in which I lie supine,
Feasting on a roast calf or some wild beast,
And drinking pans of milk, and gloriously
Emulating the thunder of high heaven.
And when the Thracian wind pours down the snow,
I wrap my body in the skins of beasts,
Kindle a fire, and bid the snow whirl on.
The earth, by force, whether it will or no,
Bringing forth grass, fattens my flocks and herds,
Which, to what other God but to myself
And this great belly, first of deities,
Should I be bound to sacrifice? I well know
The wise man's only Jupiter is this,
To eat and drink during his little day,
And give himself no care. And as for those
Who complicate with laws the life of man,
I freely give them tears for their reward.
I will not cheat my soul of its delight,
Or hesitate in dining upon you:
And that I may be quit of all demands,
These are my hospitable gifts;—fierce fire
And yon ancestral cauldron, which o'er bubbling
Shall finely cook your miserable flesh.
Creep in!—

    *   *   *   *   *

Uly. Ay! ay! I have escaped the Trojan toils,
I have escaped the sea, and now I fall
Under the cruel grasp of one impious man.
O Pallas, mistress, Goddess, sprung from Jove,
Now, now, assist me! Mightier toils than Troy
Are these;—I totter on the chasms of peril;
And thou who inhabitest the thrones
Of the bright stars, look, hospitable Jove,
Upon this outrage of thy deity,
Otherwise be considered as no God!

CHORUS [*alone*].

For your gaping gulf, and your gullet wide
The ravine is ready on every side,
The limbs of the strangers are cooked and done,
There is boiled meat, and roast meat, and meat from the coal,
You may chop it, and tear it, and gnash it for fun,
An hairy goat's-skin contains the whole.
Let me but escape, and ferry me o'er
The stream of your wrath to a safer shore.

The Cyclops Ætnean is cruel and bold,
      He murders the strangers

That sit on his hearth,
And dreads no avengers
To rise from the earth.

He roasts the men before they are cold,
He snatches them broiling from the coal,
And from the cauldron pulls them whole,
And minces their flesh and gnaws their bone
With his cursed teeth, till all be gone.

Farewell, foul pavilion !
Farewell, rites of dread !
The Cyclops vermilion,
With slaughter uncloying,
Now feasts on the dead,
In the flesh of strangers joying !

Uly. O Jupiter ! I saw within the cave
Horrible things ; deeds to be feigned in words,
But not believed as being done.
  Chorus. What sawest thou the impious Polypheme
Feasting upon your loved companions now ?
  Uly. Selecting two, the plumpest of the crowd,
He grasped them in his hands.
  Chorus.   Unhappy man

          *   *   *   *   *

Uly. Soon as we came into this craggy place,
Kindling a fire, he cast on the broad hearth
The knotty limbs of an enormous oak,
Three waggon loads at least, and then he strewed
Upon the ground, beside the red firelight,
His couch of pine leaves ; and he milked the cows,
And pouring forth the white milk, filled a bowl
Three cubits wide and four in depth, as much
As would contain four amphoræ, and bound it
With ivy wreaths ; then placed upon the fire
A brazen pot to boil, and made red hot
The points of spits, not sharpened with the sickle,
But with a fruit-tree bough, and with the jaws
Of axes for Ætnean slaughterings.*
And when this God-abandoned cook of hell
Had made all ready, he seized two of us
And killed them in a kind of measured manner;
For he flung one against the brazen rivets
Of the huge cauldron, and seized the other
By the foot's tendon, and knocked out his brains
Upon the sharp edge of the craggy stone :
Then peeled his flesh with a great cooking knife
And put him down to roast.   The other's limbs
He chopped into the cauldron to be boiled.
And I, with the tears raining from my eyes,
Stood near the Cyclops, ministering to him ;
The rest, in the recesses of the cave,
Clung to the rock like bats, bloodless with fear.
When he was filled with my companion's flesh,

---

* I confess I do not understand this.—*Note of the Author.*

He threw himself upon the ground and sent
A loathsome exhalation from his maw.
Then a divine thought came to me. I filled
The cup of Maron, and I offered him
To taste, and said :—" Child of the Ocean God,
Behold what drink the vines of Greece produce,
The exultation and the joy of Bacchus."
He, satiated with his unnatural food,
Received it, and at one draught drank it off,
And taking my hand, praised me :—" Thou hast given
A sweet draught after a sweet meal, dear guest."
And I perceiving that it pleased him, filled
Another cup, well knowing that the wine
Would wound him soon and take a sure revenge.
And the charm fascinated him, and I
Plied him cup after cup, until the drink
Had warmed his entrails, and he sang aloud
In concert with my wailing fellow-seamen
A hideous discord—and the cavern rung.
I have stolen out, so that if you will
You may achieve my safety and your own.
But say, do you desire, or not, to fly
This uncompanionable man, and dwell
As was your wont among the Grecian Nymphs
Within the fanes of your beloved God ?
Your father there within agrees to it,
But he is weak and overcome with wine,
And caught as if with birdlime by the cup,
He claps his wings and crows in doting joy.
You who are young escape with me, and find
Bacchus your ancient friend ; unsuited he
To this rude Cyclops.
   Chorus.   Oh, my dearest friend,
That I could see that day, and leave for ever
The impious Cyclops.
        *   *   *   *   *

   Uly. Listen, then, what a punishment I have
For this fell monster, how secure a flight
From your hard servitude.
   Chorus.   Oh, sweeter far
Than is the music of an Asian lyre
Would be the news of Polypheme destroyed.
   Uly. Delighted with the Bacchic drink he goes
To call his brother Cyclops—who inhabit
A village upon Ætna not far off.
   Chorus. I understand, catching him when alone
You think by some measure to despatch him,
Or thrust him from the precipice.
   Uly.   O no ;
Nothing of that kind ; my device is subtle.
   Chorus. How then ? I heard of old that thou wert wise.
   Uly. I will dissuade him from this plan, by saying
It were unwise to give the Cyclopses
This precious drink, which if enjoyed alone
Would make life sweeter for a longer time.
When vanquished by the Bacchic power, he sleeps,
There is a trunk of olive wood within,
Whose point having made sharp with this good sword

I will conceal in fire, and when I see
It is alight, will fix it, burning yet,
Within the socket of the Cyclops' eye
And melt it out with fire—as when a man
Turns by its handle a great auger round,
Fitting the framework of a ship with beams,
So will I, in the Cyclops' fiery eye
Turn round the brand and dry the pupil up.

 Chorus. Joy! I am mad with joy at your device.
 Uly. And then with you, my friends, and the old man,
We'll load the hollow depth of our black ship,
And row with double strokes from this dread shore.
 Chorus. May I, as in libations to a God,
Share in the blinding him with the red brand?
I would have some communion in his death.
 Uly. Doubtless: the brand is a great brand to hold.
 Chorus. Oh! I would lift an hundred waggon loads,
If like a wasp's nest I could scoop the eye out
Of the detested Cyclops.
 Uly.   Silence now!
Ye know the close device—and when I call,
Look ye obey the masters of the craft.
I will not save myself and leave behind
My comrades in the cave: I might escape
Having got clear from that obscure recess,
But 'twere unjust to leave in jeopardy
The dear companions who sailed here with me.

CHORUS.

Come! who is first, that with his hand
Will urge down the burning brand
Through the lids, and quench and pierce
The Cyclops' eye so fiery fierce?

SEMICHORUS I.

Song within.

Listen! listen! he is coming,
A most hideous discord humming,
Drunken, museless, awkward, yelling,
Far along his rocky dwelling;
Let us with some comic spell
Teach the yet unteachable.
By all means he must be blinded,
If my counsel be but minded.

SEMICHORUS II.

Happy those made odorous
With the dew which sweet grapes weep,
To the village hastening thus,
Seek the vines that soothe to sleep,
Having first embraced thy friend,
There in luxury without end,
With the strings of yellow hair,
Of thy voluptuous leman fair,
Shalt sit playing on a bed!
Speak what door is opened?

CYCLOPS.

Ha ! ha ! ha ! I'm full of wine,
Heavy with the joy divine,
With the young feast oversated,
Like a merchant's vessel freighted
To the water's edge, my crop
Is laden to the gullet's top.
The fresh meadow grass of spring
Tempts me forth thus wandering
To my brothers on the mountains,
Who shall share the wine's sweet fountains.
Bring the cask, O stranger, bring !

CHORUS.

One with eyes the fairest
Cometh from his dwelling ;
Some one loves thee, rarest,
Bright beyond my telling.
In thy grace thou shinest
Like some nymph divinest,
In her caverns dewy :
All delights pursue thee,
Soon pied flowers, sweet-breathing,
Shall thy head be wreathing.

Uly. Listen, O Cyclops, for I am well skilled
In Bacchus, whom I gave thee of to drink.
Cyc. What sort of God is Bacchus then accounted ?
Uly. The greatest among men for joy of life.
Cyc. I gulped him down with very great delight.
Uly. This is a God who never injures men.
Cyc. How does the God like living in a skin ?
Uly. He is content wherever he is put.
Cyc. Gods should not have their body in a skin.
Uly. If he gives joy, what is his skin to you ?
Cyc. I hate the skin, but love the wine within.
Uly. Stay here, now drink, and make your spirit glad.
Cyc. Should I not share this liquor with my brothers ?
Uly. Keep it yourself, and be more honoured so.
Cyc. I were more useful, giving to my friends.
Uly. But village mirth breeds contests, broils, and blows.
Cyc. When I am drunk none shall lay hands on me.
Uly. A drunken man is better within doors.
Cyc. He is a fool, who drinking, loves not mirth.
Uly. But he is wise, who drunk, remains at home.
Cyc. What shall I do, Silenus ?   Shall I stay ?
Sil. Stay—for what need have you of pot companions ?
Cyc. Indeed this place is closely carpeted
With flowers and grass.
Sil.   And in the sun-warm noon
'Tis sweet to drink.   Lie down beside me now,
Placing your mighty sides upon the ground.
Cyc. What do you put the cup behind me for ?
Sil. That no one here may touch it.
Cyc.   Thievish one !
You want to drink;—here place it in the midst.
And thou, O stranger, tell how art thou called ?

Uly. My name is Nobody. What favour now
Shall I receive to praise you at your hands?
 Cyc. I'll feast on you the last of your companions.
 Uly. You grant your guest a fair reward, O Cyclops.
 Cyc. Ha! what is this? Stealing the wine, you rogue!
 Sil. It was this stranger kissing me because
I looked so beautiful.
 Cyc.   You shall repent
For kissing the coy wine that loves you not.
 Sil. By Jupiter! you said that I am fair.
 Cyc. Pour out, and only give me the cup full.
 Sil. How is it mixed? let me observe.
 Cyc.   Curse you!
Give it me so.
 Sil.   Not till I see you wear
That coronal, and taste the cup to you.
 Cyc. Thou wily traitor!
 Sil.   But the wine is sweet.
Ay, you will roar if you are caught in drinking.
 Cyc. See now, my lip is clean and all my beard.
 Sil. Now put your elbow right and drink again.
As you see me drink— * * * * *
 Cyc. How now?
 Sil.   Ye Gods, what a delicious gulp!
 Cyc. Guest, take it;—you pour out the wine for me.
 Uly. The wine is well accustomed to my hand.
 Cyc. Pour out the wine!
 Uly.   I pour; only be silent.
 Cyc. Silence is a hard task to him who drinks.
 Uly. Take it and drink it off; leave not a dreg.
O, that the drinker died with his own draught!
 Cyc. Papai! the vine must be a sapient plant.
 Uly. If you drink much after a mighty feast,
Moistening your thirsty maw, you will sleep well;
If you leave aught, Bacchus will dry you up.
 Cyc Ho! ho! I can scarce rise. What pure delight!
The heavens and earth appear to whirl about
Confusedly. I see the throne of Jove
And the clear congregation of the Gods.
Now if the Graces tempted me to kiss
I would not, for the loveliest of them all
I would not leave this Ganymede.
 Sil.   Polypheme,
I am the Ganymede of Jupiter.
 Cyc. By Jove you are; I bore you off from Dardanus.

ULYSSES *and the* CHORUS.

Uly. Come boys of Bacchus, children of high race,
This man within is folded up in sleep,
And soon will vomit flesh from his fell maw;
The brand under the shed thrusts out its smoke,
No preparation needs, but to burn out
The monster's eye;—but bear yourselves like men.
 Chorus. We will have courage like the adamant rock,
All things are ready for you here; go in,
Before our father shall perceive the noise.
 Uly. Vulcan, Ætnean king! burn out with fire
The shining eye of this thy neighbouring monster!

And thou, O Sleep, nursling of gloomy night,
Descend unmixed on this God-hated beast,
And suffer not Ulysses and his comrades,
Returning from their famous Trojan toils,
To perish by this man, who cares not either
For God or mortal; or I needs must think
That Chance is a supreme divinity,
And things divine are subject to her power.

CHORUS.

Soon a crab the throat will seize
    Of him who feeds upon his guest,
Fire will burn his lamp-like eyes
    In revenge of such a feast!
A great oak stump now is lying
In the ashes yet undying.
    Come, Maron, come!
Raging let him fix the doom,
Let him tear the eyelid up,
Of the Cyclops—that his cup
    May be evil!
O, I long to dance and revel
With sweet Bromian, long desired,
In loved ivy-wreaths attired;
    Leaving this abandoned home—
    Will the moment ever come?

Uly. Be silent, ye wild things! Nay, hold your peace,
And keep your lips quite close; dare not to breathe,
Or spit, or e'en wink, lest ye wake the monster,
Until his eye be tortured out with fire.
    Chorus. Nay, we are silent, and we chaw the air.
    Uly. Come now, and lend a hand to the great stake
Within—it is delightfuly red hot.
    Chorus. You then command who first should seize the stake
To burn the Cyclops' eye, that all may share
In the great enterprise.
    Semichorus I.   We are too few,
We cannot at this distance from the door
Thrust fire into his eye.
    Semichorus II.   And we just now
Have become lame; cannot move hand or foot.
    Chorus. The same thing has occurred to us—our ankles
Are sprained with standing here, I know not how.
    Uly. What, sprained with standing still?
    Chorus.   And there is dust
Or ashes in our eyes, I know not whence.
    Uly. Cowardly dogs! ye will not aid me then?
    Chorus. With pitying my own back and my backbone,
And with not wishing all my teeth knocked out,
This cowardice comes of itself—but stay,
I know a famous Orphic incantation
To make the brand stick of its own accord
Into the skull of this one-eyed son of Earth.
    Uly. Of old I knew ye thus by nature; now
I know ye better.—I will use the aid
Of my own comrades—yet though weak of hand

Speak cheerfully, that so ye may awaken
The courage of my friends with your blithe words.
  Chorus. This I will do with peril of my life,
And blind you with my exhortations, Cyclops.
                    Hasten and thrust,
                    And parch up to dust,
                    The eye of the beast,
                    Who feeds on his guest,
                    Burn and blind
                    The Ætnean hind!
                    Scoop and draw,
                    But beware lest he claw
                    Your limbs near his maw.

  Cyc. Ah me! my eyesight is parched up to cinders.
  Chorus. What a sweet pæan! sing me that again!
  Cyc. Ah me! indeed, what woe has fallen upon me!
But wretched nothings, think ye not to flee
Out of this rock; I, standing at the outlet,
Will bar the way and catch you as you pass.
  Chorus. What are you roaring out, Cyclops?
  Cyc.   I perish!
  Chorus. For you are wicked.
  Cyc.   And besides miserable.
  Chorus. What, did you fall into the fire when drunk?
  Cyc. 'Twas Nobody destroyed me.
  Chorus.   Why then no one
Can be to blame.
  Cyc.   I say 'twas Nobody
Who blinded me.
  Chorus.   Why then you are not blind.
  Cyc. I wish you were as blind as I am.
  Chorus.   Nay,
It cannot be that no one made you blind.
  Cyc. You jeer me; where, I ask, is Nobody?
  Chorus. Nowhere, O Cyclops * * *
  Cyc. It was that stranger ruined me:—the wretch
First gave me wine and then burnt out my eye,
For wine is strong and hard to struggle with.
Have they escaped, or are they yet within?
  Chorus. They stand under the darkness of the rock
And cling to it.
  Cyc.   At my right hand or left?
  Chorus. Close on your right.
  Cyc.   Where?
  Chorus.   Near the rock itself.
You have them.
  Cyc.   Oh, misfortune on misfortune!
I've cracked my skull.
  Chorus.   Now they escape you there.
  Cyc. Not there, although you say so.
  Chorus.   Not on that side.
  Cyc. Where then?
  Chorus. They creep about you on your left.
  Cyc. Ah! I am mocked! They jeer me in my ills.
  Chorus. Not there! he is a little there beyond you.
  Cyc. Detested wretch! where are you?

Uly.   Far from you
I keep with care this body of Ulysses.
   Cyc. What do you say? You proffer a new name.
   Uly. My father named me so; and I have taken
A full revenge for your unnatural feast;
I should have done ill to have burned down Troy
And not revenged the murder of my comrades.
   Cyc. Ai! ai! the ancient oracle is accomplished;
It is said that I should have my eyesight blinded
By you coming from Troy, yet it foretold
That you should pay the penalty for this
By wandering long over the homeless sea.
   Uly. I bid thee weep—consider what I say,
I go towards the shore to drive my ship
To mine own land, o'er the Sicilian wave.
   Cyc. Not so, if whelming you with this huge stone
I can crush you and all your men together;
I will descend upon the shore, though blind,
Groping my way down the steep ravine.
   Chorus. And we, the shipmates of Ulysses now,
Will serve our Bacchus all our happy lives.

TRANSLATIONS FROM MOSCHUS.

I.

WHEN winds that move not its calm surface sweep
   The azure sea, I love the land no more.
The smiles of the serene and tranquil deep
   Tempt my unquiet mind.—But when the war
Of ocean's grey abyss resounds, and foam
   Gathers upon the sea, and vast waves burst,
I turn from the drear aspect to the home
   Of earth and its deep woods, where interspersed,
When winds blow loud pines make sweet melody.
Whose house is some lone bark, whose toil the sea,
   Whose prey the wandering fish, an evil lot
Has chosen.—But I my languid limbs will fling
Beneath the plane, where the brook's murmuring
   Moves the calm spirit but disturbs it not.

II.

PAN loved his neighbour Echo—but that child
   Of Earth and Air pined for the Satyr leaping;
The Satyr loved with wasting madness wild
   The bright nymph Lyda,—and so the three went weeping.
As Pan loved Echo, Echo loved the Satyr;
   The Satyr, Lyda—and thus love consumed them.
And thus to each—which was a woful matter—
   To bear what they inflicted, justice doomed them;
For inasmuch as each might hate the lover,
   Each loving, so was hated.—Ye that love not
Be warned—in thought turn this example over,
   That when ye love, the like return ye prove not.

SONNET.

From the Italian of Dante.

DANTE ALIGHIERI TO GUIDO CAVALCANTI.

GUIDO, I would that Lappo, thou, and I,
Led by some strong enchantment, might ascend
A magic ship, whose charmed sails should fly
With winds at will where'er our thoughts might wend,
And that no change, nor any evil chance,
Should mar our joyous voyage; but it might be,
That even satiety should still enhance
Between our hearts their strict community.
And that the bounteous wizard then would place
Vanna and Bice and my gentle love,
Companions of our wandering, and would grace
With passionate talk wherever we might rove
Our time, and each were as content and free
As I believe that thou and I should be.

———◆———

SCENES FROM THE "MAGICO PRODIGIOSO" OF CALDERON.

CYPRIAN *as a Student;* CLARIN *and* MOSCON *as poor Scholars, with books.*

 Cyp. In the sweet solitude of this calm place,
This intricate wild wilderness of trees
And flowers and undergrowth of odorous plants,
Leave me; the books you brought out of the house
To me are ever best society.
And whilst with glorious festival and song
Antioch now celebrates the consecration
Of a proud temple to great Jupiter,
And bears his image in loud jubilee
To its new shrine, I would consume what still
Lives of the dying day, in studious thought,
Far from the throng and turmoil. You, my friends,
Go and enjoy the festival; it will
Be worth the labour, and return for me
When the sun seeks its grave among the billows,
Which among dim grey clouds on the horizon
Dance like white plumes upon a hearse;—and here
I shall expect you.
 Mos.   I cannot bring my mind,
Great as my haste to see the festival
Certainly is, to leave you, sir, without
Just saying some three or four hundred words.
How is it possible that on a day
Of such festivity, you can bring your mind
To come forth to a solitary country
With three or four old books, and turn your back
On all this mirth?
 Cla.   My master's in the right;
There is not anything more tiresome

Than a procession day, with troops of men,
And dances, and all that.

    Mos.   From first to last,
Clarin, you are a temporizing flatterer ;
You praise not what you feel but what he does ;
Toadeater !

    Cla.   You lie—under a mistake—
For this is the most civil sort of lie
That can be given to a man's face.   I now
Say what I think.

    Cyp. Enough, you foolish fellows.
Puffed up with your own doting ignorance,
You always take the two sides of one question.
Now go, and as I said, return for me
When night falls, veiling in its shadows wide
This glorious fabric of the universe.

    Mos. How happens it, although you can maintain
The folly of enjoying festivals,
That yet you go there ?

    Cla.   Nay, the consequence
Is clear:—who ever did what he advises
Others to do ?

    Mos.   Would that my feet were wings,
So would I fly to Livia.   [*Exit.*

    Cla.   To speak truth,
Livia is she who has surprised my heart ;
But he is more than half way there.—Soho !
Livia, I come ; good sport, Livia, Soho !   [*Exit.*

    Cyp. Now, since I am alone, let me examine
The question which has long disturbed my mind
With doubt ; since first I read in Plinius
The words of mystic import and deep sense
In which he defines God.   My intellect
Can find no God with whom these marks and signs
Fitly agree.   It is a hidden truth
Which I must fathom.   [*Reads.*

    Enter the DEVIL, *as a fine Gentleman.*

    Demon. Search even as thou wilt,
But thou shalt never find what I can hide.

    Cyp. What noise is that among the boughs ? Who moves ?
What art thou ?

    Demon.   'Tis a foreign gentleman.
Even from this morning I have lost my way
In this wild place, and my poor horse at last
Quite overcome, has stretched himself upon
The enamelled tapestry of this mossy mountain,
And feeds and rests at the same time.   I was
Upon my way to Antioch upon business
Of some importance, but wrapt up in cares
(Who is exempt from this inheritance ?)
I parted from my company, and lost
My way, and lost my servants and my comrades.

    Cyp. 'Tis singular, that even within the sight
Of the high towers of Antioch, you could lose
Your way.   Of all the avenues and green paths
Of this wild wood there is not one but leads

As to its centre, to the walls of Antioch;
Take which you will you cannot miss your road.

Demon. And such is ignorance! Even in the sight
Of knowledge it can draw no profit from it.
But as it still is early, and as I
Have no acquaintances in Antioch,
Being a stranger there, I will even wait
The few surviving hours of the day,
Until the night shall conquer it. I see
Both by your dress and by the books in which
You find delight and company, that you
Are a great student;—for my part, I feel
Much sympathy with such pursuits.

Cyp.   Have you
Studied much?

Demon.   No,—and yet I know enough
Not to be wholly ignorant.

Cyp.   Pray, sir,
What science may you know?

Demon.   Many.

Cyp.   Alas!
Much pains must we expend on one alone,
And even then attain it not;—but you
Have the presumption to assert that you
Know many without study.

Demon.   And with truth.
For in the country whence I come, sciences
Require no learning,—they are known.

Cyp.   Oh, would
I were of that bright country! for in this
The more we study, we the more discover
Our ignorance.

Demon.   It is so true that I
Had so much arrogance as to oppose
The chair of the most high Professorship,
And obtained many votes, and though I lost,
The attempt was still more glorious, than the failure
Could be dishonourable: if you believe not,
Let us refer it to dispute respecting
That which you know best, and although I
Know not the opinion you maintain, and though
It be the true one, I will take the contrary.

Cyp. The offer gives me pleasure. I am now
Debating with myself upon a passage
Of Plinius, and my mind is racked with doubt
To understand and know who is the God
Of whom he speaks.

Demon.   It is a passage, if
I recollect it right, couched in these words:
"God is one supreme goodness, one pure essence,
One substance, and one sense, all sight, all hands."

Cyp. 'Tis true.

Demon.   What difficulty find you here?

Cyp. I do not recognise among the Gods
The God defined by Plinius; if he must
Be supreme goodness, even Jupiter
Is not supremely good; because we see
His deeds are evil, and his attributes

Tainted with mortal weakness; in what manner
Can supreme goodness be consistent with
The passions of humanity?
  Demon.   The wisdom
Of the old world masked with the names of Gods,
The attributes of Nature and of Man;
A sort of popular philosophy.
  Cyp. This reply will not satisfy me, for
Such awe is due to the high name of God
That ill should never be imputed. Then,
Examining the question with more care,
It follows, that the gods should always will
That which is best, were they supremely good.
How then does one will one thing—one another?
And you may not say that I allege
Poetical or philosophic learning:
Consider the ambiguous responses
Of their oracular statues; from two shrines
Two armies shall obtain the assurance of
One victory. Is it not indisputable
That two contending wills can never lead
To the same end? And being opposite,
If one be good is not the other evil?
Evil in God is inconceivable;
But supreme goodness fails among the gods
Without their union.
  Demon.   I deny your major.
These responses are means towards some end
Unfathomed by our intellectual beam.
They are the work of providence, and more
The battle's loss may profit those who lose,
Than victory advantage those who win.
  Cyp. That I admit, and yet that God should not
(Falsehood is incompatible with deity)
Assure the victory; it would be enough
To have permitted the defeat; if God
Be all sight,—God, who beheld the truth,
Would not have given assurance of an end
Never to be accomplished; thus, although
The Deity may according to his attributes
Be well distinguished into persons, yet
Even in the minutest circumstance,
His essence must be one.
  Demon.   To attain the end
The affections of the actors in the scene
Must have been thus influenced by his voice.
  Cyp. But for a purpose thus subordinate
He might have employed genii, good or evil,—
A sort of spirits called so by the learned,
Who roam about inspiring good or evil,
And from whose influence and existence we
May well infer our immortality:
Thus God might easily, without descending
To a gross falsehood in his proper person,
Have moved the affections by this mediation
To the just point.
  Demon.   These trifling contradictions
Do not suffice to impugn the unity

Of the high gods; in things of great importance
They still appear unanimous; consider
That glorious fabric—man,—his workmanship,
Is stamped with one conception.

Cyp.   Who made man
Must have, methinks, the advantage of the others.
If they are equal, might they not have risen
In opposition to the work, and being
All hands, according to our author here,
Have still destroyed even as the other made?
If equal in their power, and only unequal
In opportunity, which of the two
Will remain conqueror?

Demon.   On impossible
And false hypothesis there can be built
No argument.   Say, what do you infer
From this?

Cyp.   That there must be a mighty God
Of supreme goodness and of highest grace,
All sight, all hands, all truth, infallible,
Without an equal and without a rival;
The cause of all things and the effect of nothing,
One power, one will, one substance, and one essence.
And in whatever persons, one or two,
His attributes may be distinguished, one
Sovereign power, one solitary essence,
One cause of all cause.   [*They rise.*

Demon.   How can I impugn
So clear a consequence?

Cyp.   Do you regret
My victory?

Demon.   Who but regrets a check
In rivalry of wit?   I could reply
And urge new difficulties, but will now
Depart, for I hear steps of men approaching,
And it is time that I should now pursue
My journey to the city.

Cyp.   Go in peace!

Demon. Remain in peace!   Since thus it profits him
To study, I will wrap his senses up
In sweet oblivion of all thought, but of
A piece of excellent beauty; and as I
Have power given me to wage enmity
Against Justina's soul, I will extract
From one effect two vengeances.   [*Exit.*

Cyp.   I never
Met a more learned person.   Let me now
Revolve this doubt again with careful mind.   [*He reads.*

Enter LELIO *and* FLORO.

Lel. Here stop.   These toppling rocks and tangled boughs,
Impenetrable by the noonday beam,
Shall be sole witnesses of what we——

Flo.   Draw!
If there were words, here is the place for deeds.

Lel. Thou needest not instruct me ; well I know
That in the field the silent tongue of steel
Speaks thus.   [*They fight.*

Cyp.   Ha ! what is this ?   Lelio, Floro,
Be it enough that Cyprian stands between you,
Although unarmed.
    Lel.   Whence comest thou, to stand
Between me and my vengeance?
    Flo.   From what rocks
And desert cells ?

Enter MOSCON *and* CLARIN.

    Mos. Run, run ! for where we left my master
We hear the clash of swords.
    Cla.   I never
Run to approach things of this sort, but only
To avoid them.   Sir ! Cyprian ! sir !
    Cyp. Be silent, fellows !   What ! two friends who are
In blood and fame the eyes and hope of Antioch;
One of the noble men of the Colatti,
The other son of the Governor, adventure
And cast away, on some slight cause no doubt,
Two lives the honour of their country?
    Lel.   Cyprian !
Although my high respect towards your person
Holds now my sword suspended, thou canst not
Restore it to the slumber of its scabbard.
Thou knowest more of science than the duel;
For when two men of honour take the field,
No [   ] or respect can make them friends,
But one must die in the pursuit.
    Flo.   I pray
That you depart hence with your people, and
Leave us to finish what we have begun
Without advantage.
    Cyp.   Though you may imagine
That I know little of the laws of duel,
Which vanity and valour instituted,
You are in error.   By my birth I am
Held no less than yourselves to know the limits
Of honour and of infamy, nor has study
Quenched the free spirit which first ordered them;
And thus to me, as one well experienced
In the false quicksands of the sea of honour,
You may refer the merits of the case;
And if I should perceive in your relation
That either has the right to satisfaction
From the other, I give you my word of honour
To leave you.
    Lel.   Under this condition then
I will relate the cause, and you will cede
And must confess the impossibility
Of compromise; for the same lady is
Beloved by Floro and myself.
    Flo.   It seems
Much to me that the light of day should look
Upon that idol of my heart—but he——
Leave us to fight, according to thy word.
    Cyp. Permit one question further: is the lady
Impossible to hope or not ?
    Lel.   She is

So excellent, that if the light of day
Should excite Floro's jealousy, it were
Without just cause, for even the light of day
Trembles to gaze on her.
 Cyp.   Would you for your
Part marry her?
 Flo.   Such is my confidence.
 Cyp. And you?
 Lel.   O, would that I could lift my hope
So high? for though she is extremely poor,
Her virtue is her dowry.
 Cyp.   And if you both
Would marry her, is it not weak and vain,
Culpable and unworthy, thus beforehand
To slur her honour? What would the world say
If one should slay the other, and if she
Should afterwards espouse the murderer?
> [*The rivals agree to refer their quarrel to* CYPRIAN ; *who in consequence visits* JUSTINA, *and becomes enamoured of her: she disdains him, and he retires to a solitary seashore.*

SCENE II.

CYPRIAN.

Oh, memory! permit it not
That the tyrant of my thought
Be another soul that still
Holds dominion o'er the will,
That would refuse, but can no more,
To bend, to tremble, and adore.
Vain idolatry!—I saw,
And gazing, became blind with error;
Weak ambition, which the awe
Of her presence bound to terror!
So beautiful she was—and I,
Between my love and jealousy,
Am so convulsed with hope and fear,
Unworthy as it may appear;
So bitter is the life I live,
That, hear me, Hell! I now would give
To thy most detested spirit
My soul, for ever to inherit,
To suffer punishment and pine,
So this woman may be mine.
Hear'st thou, Hell! dost thou reject it?
My soul is offered!

Demon [*unseen*].   I accept it.
> [*Tempest, with thunder and lightning.*

CYPRIAN.

What is this? ye heavens for ever pure,
At once intensely radiant and obscure!
 Athwart the ethereal halls
The lightning's arrow and the thunder-balls
 The day affright.
 As from the horizon round,
 Burst with earthquake sound,

In mighty torrents the electric fountains;
Clouds quench the sun, and thunder smoke
Strangles the air, and fire eclipses heaven.
Philosophy, thou canst not even
Compel their causes underneath thy yoke,
From yonder clouds even to the waves below
The fragments of a single ruin choke
    Imagination's flight;
For, on flakes of surge, like feathers light,
The ashes of the desolation cast
    Upon the gloomy blast,
Tell of the footsteps of the storm.
And nearer see the melancholy form
Of a great ship, the outcast of the sea,
    Drives miserably !
And it must fly the pity of the port,
Or perish, and its last and sole resort
Is its own raging enemy.
The terror of the thrilling cry
Was a fatal prophecy
Of coming death, who hovers now
Upon that shattered prow,
That they who die not may be dying still.
And not alone the insane elements
Are populous with wild portents,
But that sad ship is as a miracle
Of sudden ruin, for it drives so fast
It seems as if it had arrayed its form
With the headlong storm.
It strikes—I almost feel the shock,—
It stumbles on a jagged rock,—
Sparkles of blood on the white foam are cast.

A Tempest—All exclaim within,

We are all lost !
    Demon [*within*]. Now from this plank will I
Pass to the land and thus fulfil my scheme.
    Cyp. As in contempt of the elemental rage
A man comes forth in safety, while the ship's
Great form is in a watery eclipse
Obliterated from the Ocean's page,
And round its wreck the huge sea-monsters sit,
A horrid conclave, and the whistling wave
Are heaped over its carcass, like a grave.

The DEMON *enters, as escaped from the sea.*

    Demon [*aside*]. It was essential to my purposes
To wake a tumult on the sapphire ocean,
That in this unknown form I might at length
Wipe out the blot of the discomfiture
Sustained upon the mountain, and assail
With a new war the soul of Cyprian,
Forging the instruments of his destruction
Even from his love and from his wisdom.   Oh !
Beloved earth, dear mother, in thy bosom
I seek a refuge from the monster who
Precipitates itself upon me.
    Cyp.   Friend.

Collect thyself; and be the memory
Of thy late suffering, and thy greatest sorrow
But as a shadow of the past,—for nothing
Beneath the circle of the moon, but flows
And changes, and can never know repose.

    Demon. And who art thou, before whose feet my fate
Has prostrated me?

    Cyp.   One who moved with pity,
Would soothe its stings.

    Demon.   Oh! that can never be!
No solace can my lasting sorrows find.

    Cyp. Wherefore?

    Demon.   Because my happiness is lost.
Yet I lament what has long ceased to be
The object of desire or memory,
And my life is not life.

    Cyp.   Now, since the fury
Of this earthquaking hurricane is still,
And the crystalline heaven has reassumed
Its windless calm so quickly, that it seems
As if its heavy wrath had been awakened
Only to overwhelm that vessel,—speak,
Who art thou, and whence comest thou?

    Demon.   Far more
My coming hither cost, than thou hast seen
Or I can tell. Among my misadventures
This shipwreck is the least. Wilt thou hear?

    Cyp.   Speak.

    Demon. Since thou desirest, I will then unveil
Myself to thee;—for in myself I am
A world of happiness and misery;
This I have lost, and that I must lament
For ever. In my attributes I stood
So high and so heroically great,
In lineage so supreme, and with a genius
Which penetrated with a glance the world
Beneath my feet, that won by my high merit
A king—whom I may call the King of Kings,
Because all others tremble in their pride
Before the terrors of his countenance,
In his high palace roofed with brightest gems
Of living light—call them the stars of Heaven—
Named me his counsellor. But the high praise
Stung me with pride and envy, and I rose
In mighty competition, to ascend
His seat and place my foot triumphantly
Upon his subject thrones. Chastised, I know
The depth to which ambition falls; too mad
Was the attempt, and yet more mad were now
Repentance of the irrevocable deed:
Therefore I chose this ruin with the glory
Of not to be subdued, before the shame
Of reconciling me with him who reigns
By coward cession.—Nor was I alone,
Nor am I now, nor shall I be alone;
And there was hope, and there may still be hope,
For many suffrages among his vassals
Hailed me their lord and king, and many still

Are mine, and many more, perchance shall be.
Thus vanquished, though in fact victorious,
I left his seat of empire, from mine eye
Shooting forth poisonous lightning, while my words
With inauspicious thunderings shook Heaven,
Proclaiming vengeance, public as my wrong,
And imprecating on his prostrate slaves
Rapine, and death, and outrage. Then I sailed
Over the mighty fabric of the world,
A pirate ambushed in its pathless sands,
A lynx crouched watchfully among its caves
And craggy shores ; and I have wandered over
The expanse of these wide wildernesses
In this great ship, whose bulk is now dissolved
In the light breathings of the invisible wind,
And which the sea has made a dustless ruin,
Seeking ever a mountain, through whose forests
I seek a man, whom I must now compel
To keep his word with me. I came arrayed
In tempest, and although my power could well
Bridle the forest winds in their career,
For other causes I forebore to soothe
Their fury to Favonian gentleness,
I could and would not ; (thus I wake in him   [Aside.
A love of magic art). Let not this tempest,
Nor the succeeding calm excite thy wonder ;
For by my art the sun would turn as pale
As his weak sister with unwonted fear.
And in my wisdom are the orbs of Heaven
Written as in a record ; I have pierced
The flaming circles of their wondrous spheres
And know them as thou knowest every corner
Of this dim spot. Let it not seem to thee
That I boast vainly ; wouldst thou that I work
A charm over this waste and savage wood,
This Babylon of crags and aged trees,
Filling its leafy coverts with a horror
Thrilling and strange? I am the friendless guest
Of these wild oaks and pines—and as from thee
I have received the hospitality
Of this rude place, I offer thee the fruit
Of years of toil in recompense ; whate'er
Thy wildest dream presented to thy thought
As object of desire, that shall be thine.

*   *   *   *   *

And thenceforth shall so firm an amity
'Twixt thou and me be, that neither fortune,
The monstrous phantom which pursues success,
That careful miser, that free prodigal,
Who ever alternates with changeful hand,
Evil and good, reproach and fame ; nor Time.
That loadstar of the ages, to whose beam
The winged years speed o'er the intervals
Of their unequal revolutions ; nor
Heaven itself, whose beautiful bright stars
Rule and adorn the world, can ever make
The least division between thee and me,
Since now I find a refuge in thy favour.

SCENE III.

The DEMON *tempts* JUSTINA, *who is a Christian.*

DEMON.

Abyss of Hell! I call on thee,
Thou wild misrule of thine own anarchy!
From thy prison-house set free
The spirits of voluptuous death,
That with their mighty breath
They may destroy a world of virgin thoughts;
Let her chaste mind with fancies thick as motes
Be peopled from thy shadowy deep,
Till her guiltless fantasy
Full to overflowing be!
And with sweetest harmony,
Let birds, and flowers, and leaves, and all things move
    To love, only to love.
Let nothing meet her eyes
But signs of Love's soft victories;
Let nothing meet her ear
But sounds of love's sweet sorrow,
So that from faith no succour she may borrow,
But, guided by my spirit blind
And in a magic snare entwined,
She may now seek Cyprian.
Begin, while I in silence bind
My voice, when thy sweet song thou hast began.

A VOICE (*within*).

What is the glory far above
All else in human life?

ALL.

Love! love!

[*While these words are sung, the* DEMON *goes out at one
door, and* JUSTINA *enters at another.*

THE FIRST VOICE.

There is no form in which the fire
Of love its traces has impressed not.
Man lives far more in love's desire
Than by life's breath, soon possessed not.
If all that lives must love or die,
All shapes on earth, or sea, or sky,
With one consent to Heaven cry
That the glory far above
All else in life is—

ALL.

Love! O love!

JUSTINA.

Thou melancholy thought which art
So fluttering and so sweet, to thee
When did I give the liberty
Thus to afflict my heart?

What is the cause of this new power
Which doth my fevered being move,
Momently raging more and more ?
What subtle pain is kindled now
Which from my heart doth overflow
Into my senses ?—

ALL.

Love ! O love !

JUSTINA.

'Tis that enamoured nightingale
Who gives me the reply ;
He ever tells the same soft tale
Of passion and of constancy
To his mate, who rapt and fond
Listening sits, a bough beyond.

Be silent, Nightingale—no more
Make me think, in hearing thee
Thus tenderly thy love deplore,
If a bird can feel his so,
What a man would feel for me.
And, voluptuous vine, O thou
Who seekest most when least pursuing,—
To the trunk thou interlacest
Art the verdure which embracest,
And the weight which is its ruin,—
No more, with green embraces, vine,
Make me think on what thou lovest,—
For whilst thou thus thy boughs entwine,
I fear lest thou shouldst teach me, sophist,
How arms might be entangled too.

Light-enchanted sunflower, thou
Who gazest ever true and tender
On the sun's revolving splendour !
Follow not his faithless glance
With thy faded countenance,
Nor teach my beating heart to fear,
If leaves can mourn without a tear,
How eyes must weep ! O Nightingale,
Cease from thy enamoured tale,—
Leafy vine, unwreathe thy bower,
Restless sunflower, cease to move,—
Or tell me all, what poisonous power
Ye use against me—

ALL.

Love ! love ! love !

Jus. It cannot be !—Whom have I ever loved ?
Trophies of my oblivion and disdain,
Floro and Lelio did I not reject ?
And Cyprian ?—   [*She becomes troubled at the name of* CYPRIAN
                Did I not requite him
With such severity, that he has fled
Where none has ever heard of him again ?

Alas! I now begin to fear that this
May be the occasion whence desire grows bola,
As if there were no danger.   From the moment
That I pronounced to my own listening heart,
Cyprian is absent, O me miserable!
I know not what I feel!   [*More calmly.*

            It must be pity
To think that such a man, whom all the world
Admired, should be forgot by all the world,
And I the cause.   [*She again becomes troubled.*

            And yet if it were pity,
Floro and Lelio might have equal share,
For they are both imprisoned for my sake.   [*Calmly.*
Alas! what reasonings are these? it is
Enough I pity him, and that, in vain,
Without this ceremonious subtlety.
And woe is me! I know not where to find him now,
Even should I seek him through this wide world.

Enter DEMON.

Demon. Follow, and I will lead thee where he is.

Jus. And who art thou, who hast found entrance hither,
Into my chamber through the doors and locks?
Art thou a monstrous shadow which my madness
Has formed in the idle air?

Demon.   No.   I am one
Called by the thought which tyrannizes thee
From his eternal dwelling; who this day
Is pledged to bear thee unto Cyprian.

Jus. So shall thy promise fail.   This agony
Of passion which afflicts my heart and soul
May sweep imagination in its storm,
The will is firm.

Demon.   Already half is done
In the imagination of an act.
The sin incurred, the pleasure then remains,
Let not the will stop half way on the road.

Jus. I will not be discouraged, nor despair,
Although I thought it, and although 'tis true,
That thought is but a prelude to the deed:
Thought is not in my power, but action is:
I will not move my foot to follow thee.

Demon. But far a mightier wisdom than thine own
Exerts itself within thee, with such power
Compelling thee to that which it inclines
That it shall force thy step; how wilt thou then
Resist, Justina?

Jus.   By my free-will.

Demon.   I
Must force thy will.

Jus.   It is invincible;
It were not free if thou hadst power upon it.

                    [*He draws, but cannot move her.*

Demon. Come, where a pleasure waits thee.

Jus.   It were bought
Too dear.

Demon. 'Twill soothe thy heart to softest peace.

Jus. 'Tis dread captivity.

Demon.   'Tis joy, 'tis glory.

Jus. 'Tis shame, 'tis torment, 'tis despair.

Demon.   But how
Canst thou defend thyself from that or me,
If my power drags thee onward?

Jus.   My defence
Consists in God.

> [*He vainly endeavours to force her, and at last
> releases her.*

Demon. Woman, thou hast subdued me
Only by not owning thyself subdued.
But since thou thus findest defence in God,
I will assume a feigned form, and thus
Make thee a victim of my baffled rage.
For I will mask a spirit in thy form
Who will betray thy name to infamy,
And doubly shall I triumph in thy loss,
First by dishonouring thee, and then by turning
False pleasure to true ignominy.   [*Exit.*

Jus.   I
Appeal to Heaven against thee; so that Heaven
May scatter thy delusions, and the blot
Upon my fame vanish in idle thought,
Even as flame dies in the envious air,
And as the flowret wanes at morning frost,
And thou shouldst never—But, alas! to whom
Do I still speak?—Did not a man but now
Stand here before me?—No, I am alone,
And yet I saw him.   Is he gone so quickly?
Or can the heated mind engender shapes
From its own fear? Some terrible and strange
Peril is near.   Lisander! father! lord!
Livia!—

> *Enter* LISANDER *and* LIVIA.

Lis.   O, my daughter! What?

Liv. What?

Jus.   Saw you
A man go forth from my apartment now?—
I scarce sustain myself!

Lis.   A man here!

Jus. Have you not seen him?

Liv.   No, Lady.

Jus. I saw him.

Lis.   'Tis impossible; the doors
Which led to this apartment were all locked.

Liv. [*aside*]. I daresay it was Moscon whom she saw,
For he was locked up in my room.

Lis.   It must
Have been some image of thy fantasy.
Such melancholy as thou feedest, is
Skilful in forming such in the vain air
Out of the motes and atoms of the day.

Liv. My master's in the right.

Jus.   O, would it were
Delusion; but I fear some greater ill.
I feel as if out of my bleeding bosom
My heart were torn in fragments; ay,
Some mortal spell is wrought against my frame

So potent was the charm, that had not God
Shielded my humble innocence from wrong,
I should have sought my sorrow and my shame
With willing steps.—Livia, quick bring my cloak,
For I must seek refuge from these extremes
Even in the temple of the highest God
Which secretly the faithful worship.

Liv. Here.

Jus. [*putting on her cloak*]. In this, as in a shroud of snow, may I
Quench the consuming fire in which I burn,
Wasting away!

Lis. And I will go with thee.

Liv. When I once see them safe out of the house
I shall breathe freely.

Jus. So do I confide
In thy just favour, Heaven!

Lis. Let us go.

Jus. Thine is the cause, great God! turn for my sake,
And for thine own, mercifully to me!

SCENES FROM THE FAUST OF GOETHE.

Prologue in Heaven.

The Lord and the Host of Heaven.   Enter three Archangels.

Raphael.

The sun makes music as of old
   Amid the rival spheres of Heaven,
On its predestined circle rolled
   With thunder speed: the Angels even
Draw strength from gazing on its glance,
   Though none its meaning fathom may:
The world's unwithered countenance
   Is bright as at creation's day.

Gabriel.

And swift and swift, with rapid lightness,
   The adorned Earth spins silently,
Alternating Elysian brightness
   With deep and dreadful night; the sea
Foams in broad billows from the deep
   Up to the rocks; and rocks and ocean,
Onward, with spheres which never sleep,
   Are hurried in eternal motion.

Michael.

And tempests in contention roar
   From land to sea, from sea to land;
And, raging, weave a chain of power,
   Which girds the earth, as with a band.
A flashing desolation there,
   Flames before the thunder's way;
But thy servants, Lord, revere
   The gentle changes of thy day.

CHORUS OF THE THREE.

The Angels draw strength from thy glance,
　Though no one comprehend thee may;
Thy world's unwithered countenance
　Is bright as on creation's day.*

Enter MEPHISTOPHELES.

Mep. As thou, O Lord, once more art kind enough
To interest thyself in our affairs—
And ask, " How goes it with you there below?"
And as indulgently at other times
Thou tookedst not my visits in ill part,
Thou seest me here once more among thy household.
Though I should scandalize this company,
You will excuse me if I do not talk
In the high style which they think fashionable;
My pathos would certainly make you laugh too,
Had you not long since given over laughing.
Nothing know I to say of suns and worlds;
I observe only how men plague themselves;
The little god o' the world keeps the same stamp,
As wonderful as on creation's day:
A little better would he live, hadst thou
Not given him a glimpse of heaven's light
Which he calls reason, and employs it only
To live more beastlily than any beast.
With reverence to your Lordship be it spoken,

---

* *Raphael.* The sun sounds, according to ancient custom,
In the song of emulation of his brother-spheres.
And its fore-written circle
Fulfils with a step of thunder.
Its countenance gives the Angels strength
Though no one can fathom it.
The incredible high works
Are excellent as at the first day.
　Gabriel. And swift, and inconceivably swift
The adornment of earth winds itself round,
And exchanges Paradise-clearness
With deep dreadful night.
The sea foams in broad waves
From its deep bottom, up to the rocks,
And rocks and sea are torn on together
In the eternal swift course of the spheres.
　Michael. And storms roar in emulation
From sea to land, from land to sea,
And make, raging, a chain
Of deepest operation round about.
There flames a flashing destruction
Before the path of the thunderbolt.
But thy servants, Lord, revere
The gentle alternations of thy day.
　Chorus. Thy countenance gives the Angels strength,
Though none can comprehend thee :
And all thy lofty works
Are excellent as at the first day.

Such is a literal translation of this astonishing Chorus ; it is impossible to represent in another language the melody of the versification ; even the volatile strength and delicacy of the ideas escape in the crucible of translation, and the reader is surprised to find a caput mortuum.—*Author's Note.*

He's like one of those long-legged grasshoppers,
Who flits and jumps about, and sings for ever
The same old song i' the grass. There let him lie,
Burying his nose in every heap of dung.
 The Lord. Have you no more to say? Do you come here
Always to scold, and cavil, and complain?
Seems nothing ever right to you on earth?
 Mep. No, Lord! I find all there, as ever, bad at best.
Even I am sorry for man's days of sorrow;
I could myself almost give up the pleasure
Of plaguing the poor things.
 The Lord.   Knowest thou Faust?
 Mep. The Doctor?
 The Lord. Ay; my servant Faust.
 Mep.   In truth
He serves you in a fashion quite his own;
And the fool's meat and drink are not of earth.
His aspirations bear him on so far
That he is half aware of his own folly,
For he demands from Heaven its fairest star,
And from the earth the highest joy it bears,
Yet all things far, and all things near, are vain
To calm the deep emotions of his breast.
 The Lord. Though he now serves me in a cloud of error,
I will soon lead him forth to the clear day.
When trees look green full well the gardener knows
That fruits and blooms will deck the coming year.
 Mep. What will you bet?—now I am sure of winning—
Only, observe you give me full permission
To lead him softly on my path.
 The Lord.   As long
As he shall live upon the earth, so long
Is nothing unto thee forbidden—Man
Must err till he has ceased to struggle.
 Mep.   Thanks.
And that is all I ask; for willingly
I never make acquaintance with the dead.
The full fresh cheeks of youth are food for me,
And if a corpse knocks, I am not at home.
For I am like a cat—I like to play
A little with the mouse before I eat it.
 The Lord. Well, well! it is permitted thee. Draw thou
His spirit from its springs; as thou find'st power,
Seize him and lead him on thy downward path;
And stand ashamed when failure teaches thee
That a good man, even in his darkest longings,
Is well aware of the right way.
 Mep.   Well and good.
I am not in much doubt about my bet,
And if I lose, then 'tis your turn to crow;
Enjoy your triumph then with a full breast.
Ay; dust shall he devour, and that with pleasure,
Like my old paramour, the famous Snake.
 The Lord. Pray come here when it suits you; for I never
Had much dislike for people of your sort.
And, among all the Spirits who rebelled,
The knave was ever the least tedious to me.
The active spirit of man soon sleeps, and soon

He seeks unbroken quiet; therefore I
Have given him the Devil for a companion,
Who may provoke him to some sort of work,
And must create for ever.—But ye, pure
Children of God, enjoy eternal beauty;
Let that which ever operates and lives
Clasp you within the limits of its love;
And seize with sweet and melancholy thoughts
The floating phantoms of its loveliness.

        [*Heaven closes; the Archangels* **exeunt**.

   Mep. From time to time I visit the old fellow,
And I take care to keep on good terms with him.
Civil enough is this same God Almighty,
To talk so freely with the Devil himself.

MAY-DAY NIGHT.

SCENE.—*The Hartz Mountain, a desolate Country.*

FAUST, MEPHISTOPHELES.

   Mep. Would you not like a broomstick? As for me,
I wish I had a good stout ram to ride;
For we are still far from th' appointed place.

   Fau. This knotted staff is help enough for me,
Whilst I feel fresh upon my legs. What good
Is there in making short a pleasant way?
To creep along the labyrinths of the vales,
And climb those rocks, where ever-babbling springs
Precipitate themselves in waterfalls,
Is the true sport that seasons such a path.
Already Spring kindles the birchen spray,
And the hoar pines already feel her breath:
Shall she not work also within our limbs?

   Mep. Nothing of such an influence do I feel.
My body is all wintry, and I wish
The flowers upon our path were frost and snow.
But see, how melancholy rises now,
Dimly uplifting her belated beam,
The blank unwelcome round of the red moon,
And gives so bad a light, that every step
One stumbles 'gainst some crag. With your permission,
I'll call an Ignis-Fatuus to our aid:
I see one yonder burning jollily.
Halloo, my friend! may I request that you
Would favour us with your bright company?
Why should you blaze away there to no purpose?
Pray be so good as light us up this way.

   Ignis-Fatuus. With reverence be it spoken, I will try
To overcome the lightness of my nature;
Our course, you know, is generally zigzag.

   Mep. Ha, ha! your worship thinks you have to deal
With men. Go strait on, in the Devil's name,
Or I shall puff your flickering life out.

   Ignis-Fatuus.   Well,
I see you are the master of the house;
I will accommodate myself to you.
Only consider, that to-night this mountain
Is all enchanted, and if Jack-a-Lantern

Shows you his way, though you should miss your own,
You ought not to be too exact with him.

FAUST, MEPHISTOPHELES, *and* IGNIS-FATUUS, *in alternate Chorus.*

The limits of the sphere of dream,
    The bounds of true and false, are past.
Lead us on, thou wandering Gleam,
    Lead us onward, far and fast,
    To the wide, the desert waste.

But see, how swift advance and shift,
    Trees behind trees, row by row,—
How, cliff by cliff, rocks bend and lift
    Their frowning foreheads as we go.
    The giant-snouted crags, ho! ho!
    How they snort, and how they blow!

Through the mossy sods and stones
Stream and streamlet hurry down
A rushing throng! A sound of song
Beneath the vault of Heaven is blown!
Sweet notes of love, the speaking tones
Of this bright day, sent down to say
That Paradise on Earth is known,
Resound around, beneath, above.
All we hope and all we love
Finds a voice in this blithe strain,
Which wakens hill and wood and rill,
And vibrates far o'er field and vale,
And which Echo, like the tale
Of old times, repeats again.

To whoo! to whoo! near, nearer now
The sound of song, the rushing throng!
Are the screech, the lapwing, and the jay,
All awake as if 'twere day?
See, with long legs and belly wide,
A salamander in the brake!
Every root is like a snake,
And along the loose hill side,
With strange contortions through the night,
Curls, to seize or to affright;
And, animated, strong, and many,
They dart forth polypus-antennæ,
To blister with their poison spume
The wanderer. Through the dazzling gloom
The many-coloured mice, that thread
The dewy turf beneath our tread,
In troops each other's motions cross,
Through the heath and through the moss;
And, in legions intertangled,
The fireflies flit, and swarm, and throng,
Till all the mountain depths are spangled.

Tell me, shall we go or stay?
Shall we onward? Come along!

Everything around is swept
Forward, onward, far away!
Trees and masses intercept
The sight, and wisps on every side
Are puffed up and multiplied.

Mep. Now vigorously seize my skirt, and gain
This pinnacle of isolated crag.
One may observe with wonder from this point,
How Mammon glows among the mountains.
  Fau.   Ay—
And strangely through the solid depth below
A melancholy light, like the red dawn,
Shoots from the lowest gorge of the abyss
Of mountains, lightning hitherward: there rise
Pillars of smoke, here clouds float gently by;
Here the light burns soft as the enkindled air,
Or the illumined dust of golden flowers;
And now it glides like tender colours spreading;
And now bursts forth in fountains from the earth;
And now it winds, one torrent of broad light,
Through the far valley with a hundred veins;
And now once more within that narrow corner
Masses itself into intensest splendour.
And near us, see, sparks spring out of the ground,
Like golden sand scattered upon the darkness;
The pinnacles of that black wall of mountains
That hems us in, are kindled.
  Mep.   Rare, in faith!
Does not Sir Mammon gloriously illuminate
His palace for this festival—it is
A pleasure which you had not known before.
I spy the boisterous guests already.
  Fau.   How
The children of the wind rage in the air!
With what fierce strokes they fall upon my neck!
  Mep. Cling tightly to the old ribs of the crag.
Beware! for if with them thou warrest
In their fierce flight towards the wilderness,
Their breath will sweep thee into dust, and drag
 Thy body to a grave in the abyss.
 A cloud thickens the night.
Hark! how the tempest crashes through the forest!
 The owls fly out in strange affright;
The columns of the evergreen palaces
 Are split and shattered;
 The roots creak, and stretch, and groan;
 And ruinously overthrown,
 The trunks are crushed and shattered
 By the fierce blast's unconquerable stress.
Over each other crack and crash they all
 In terrible and intertangled fall;
And through the ruins of the shaken mountain
 The airs hiss and howl—
It is not the voice of the fountain,
 Nor the wolf in his midnight prowl.
Dost thou not hear?
 Strange accents are ringing

Aloft, afar, anear;
    The witches are singing !
The torrent of a raging wizard song
Streams the whole mountain along.

CHORUS OF WITCHES.

The stubble is yellow, the corn is green,
Now to the Brocken the witches go ;
The mighty multitude here may be seen
Gathering, wizard and witch, below.
Sir Urean is sitting aloft in the air ;
Hey over stock ! and hey over stone !
'Twixt witches and incubi, what shall be done ?
Tell it who dare ! tell it who dare !

A VOICE.

Upon a sow-swine, whose farrows were nine,
Old Baubo rideth alone.

CHORUS.

Honour her to whom honour is due,
Old mother Baubo, honour to you !
An able sow, with old Baubo upon her,
Is worthy of glory, and worthy of honour !
The legion of witches is coming behind,
Darkening the night, and outspeeding the wind—

A VOICE.

Which way comest thou ?

A VOICE.

                    Over Ilsenstein ;
The owl was awake in the white moonshine ;
I saw her at rest in her downy nest,
And she stared at me with her broad, bright eye.

VOICES.

And you may now as well, take your course on to He
Since you ride by so fast, on the headlong blast.

A VOICE.

She dropt poison upon me as I past.
Here are the wounds——

CHORUS OF WITCHES.

                    Come away ! come along !
The way is wide, the way is long,
But what is that for a Bedlam throng ?
Stick with the prong, and scratch with the broom.
The child in the cradle lies strangled at home,
And the mother is clapping her hands.

SEMICHORUS OF WIZARDS I.

                    We glide in
Like snails when the women are all away ;
And from a house once given over to sin
Woman has a thousand steps to stray.

SEMICHORUS II.

A thousand steps must a woman take,
Where a man but a single spring will make.

VOICES ABOVE.

Come with us, come with us, from Felunsee.

VOICES BELOW.

With what joy would we fly, through the upper sky!
We are washed, we are 'nointed, stark naked are we;
But our toil and our pain, is for ever in vain.

BOTH CHORUSES.

The wind is still, the stars are fled,
The melancholy moon is dead;
The magic notes, like spark on spark,
Drizzle, whistling through the dark.
        Come away!

VOICES BELOW.

        Stay, oh stay!

VOICES ABOVE.

Out of the crannies of the rocks,
Who calls?

VOICES BELOW.

        Oh, let me join your flocks!
I, three hundred years have striven
To catch your skirt and mount to Heaven,—
And still in vain.   Oh, might I be
With company akin to me!

BOTH CHORUSES.

Some on a ram and some on a prong,
On poles and on broomsticks we flutter along;
Forlorn is the wight, who can rise not to-night.

A HALF-WITCH BELOW.

I have been tripping this many an hour;
Are the others already so far before?
No quiet at home, and no peace abroad!
And less methinks is found by the road.

CHORUS OF WITCHES.

Come onward away! aroint thee, aroint!
A witch to be strong must anoint—anoint—
Then every trough, will be boat enough;
With a rag for a sail we can sweep through the sky,
Who flies not to-night, when means he to fly?

BOTH CHORUSES.

We cling to the skirt, and we strike on the ground;
Witch-legions thicken around and around:
Wizard-swarms cover the heath all over.   [*They descend.*

Mep. What thronging, dashing, raging, rustling;
What whispering, babbling, hissing, bustling;

What glimmering, spurting, stinking, burning,
As Heaven and Earth were overturning.
There is a true witch element about us,
Take hold on me, or we shall be divided:—
Where are you?

    Fau. [*from a distance*].   Here!
    Mep.   What
I must exert my authority in the house.
Place for young Voland! pray make way, good people.
Take hold on me, doctor, and with one step
Let us escape from this unpleasant crowd:
They are too mad for people of my sort.
Just there shines a peculiar kind of light—
Something attracts me in those bushes. Come
This way: we shall slip down there in a minute.

    Fau. Spirit of Contradiction! Well, lead on—
'Twere a wise feat indeed to wander out
Into the Brocken upon May-day night,
And then to isolate oneself in scorn,
Disgusted with the humours of the time.

    Mep. See yonder, round a many-coloured flame
A merry club is huddled altogether:
Even with such little people as sit there
One would not be alone.

    Fau.   Would that I were
Up yonder in the glow and whirling smoke,
Where the blind million rush impetuously
To meet the evil ones; there might I solve
Many a riddle that torments me!

    Mep.   Yet
Many a riddle there is tied anew
Inextricably. Let the great world rage!
We will stay here safe in the quiet dwellings.
'Tis an old custom. Men have ever built
Their own small world in the great world of all.
I see young witches naked there, and old ones
Wisely attired with greater decency.
Be guided now by me, and you shall buy
A pound of pleasure with a dram of trouble.
I hear them tune their instruments—one must
Get used to this damned scraping. Come, I'll lead you
Among them; and what there you do and see,
As a fresh compact 'twixt us two shall be.
How say you now? this space is wide enough—
Look forth, you cannot see the end of it—
An hundred bonfires burn in rows, and they
Who throng around them seem innumerable;
Dancing and drinking, jabbering, making love,
And cooking, are at work. Now tell me, friend,
What is there better in the world than this?

    Fau. In introducing us, do you assume
The character of wizard or of devil?

    Mep. In truth, I generally go about
In strict incognito; and yet one likes
To wear one's orders upon gala days.
I have no ribbon at my knee; but here
At home, the cloven foot is honourable.
See you that snail there?—she comes creeping up,

And with her feeling eyes hath smelt out something;
I could not, if I would, mask myself here.
Come now, we'll go about from fire to fire:
I'll be the pimp, and you shall be the lover.

[*To some Old Women, who are sitting round a heap of glimmering coals.*

Old gentlewomen, what do you out here?
You ought to be with the young rioters
Right in the thickest of the revelry—
But every one is best content at home.

General. Who dare confide in right or a just claim?
So much as I had done for them! and now—
With women and the people 'tis the same,
   Youth will stand foremost ever,—age may go
To the dark grave unhonoured.

Minister. Now-a-days
People assert their rights: they go too far;
   But as for me, the good old times I praise;
Then we were all in all, 'twas something worth
   One's while to be in place and wear a star;
That was indeed the golden age on earth.

*Parvenu.** We too are active, and we did and do
What we ought not perhaps; and yet we now
Will seize, whilst all things are whirled round and round,
A spoke of Fortune's wheel, and keep our ground.

Author. Who now can taste a treatise of deep sense
And ponderous volume? 'tis impertinence
To write what none will read, therefore will I
To please the young and thoughtless people try.

Mep. [*Who at once appears to have grown very old*]. I find
         the people ripe for the last day,
Since I last came up to the wizard mountain;
And as my little cask runs turbid now,
So is the world drained to the dregs.

Pedlar-Witch. Look here,
Gentlemen; do not hurry on so fast
And lose the chance of a good pennyworth.
I have a pack full of the choicest wares
Of every sort, and yet in all my bundle
Is nothing like what may be found on earth;
Nothing that in a moment will make rich
Men and the world with fine malicious mischief—
There is no dagger drunk with blood; no bowl
From which consuming poison may be drained
By innocent and healthy lips; no jewel,
The price of an abandoned maiden's shame;
No sword which cuts the bond it cannot loose,
Or stabs the wearer's enemy in the back;
No——

Mep. Gossip, you know little of these times.
What has been, has been; what is done, is past.
They shape themselves into the innovations
They breed, and innovation drags us with it.
The torrent of the crowd sweeps over us,
You think to impel, and are yourself impelled.

---

* A sort of fundholder.

Fau. Who is that yonder?

Mep.   Mark her well.   It is
Lilith.

Fau.   Who?

Mep.   Lilith, the first wife of Adam.
Beware of her fair hair, for she excels
All women in the magic of her locks;
And when she winds them round a young man's neck,
She will not ever set him free again.

Fau. There sit a girl and an old woman—they
Seem to be tired with pleasure and with play.

Mep. There is no rest to-night for any one:
When one dance ends another is begun;
Come, let us to it; we shall have rare fun.

[FAUST *dances and sings with a Girl, and* MEPHISTOPHELES
    with an Old Woman.

Procto-Phantasmist. What is this cursed multitude about?
Have we not long since proved to demonstration
That ghosts move not on ordinary feet?
But these are dancing just like men and women.

The Girl. What does he want, then, at our ball?

Fau.   Oh! he
Is far above us all in his conceit:
Whilst we enjoy, he reasons of enjoyment;
And any step which in our dance we tread,
If it be left out of his reckoning,
Is not to be considered as a step.
There are few things that scandalize him not:
And when you whirl round in the circle now,
As he went round the wheel in his old mill,
He says that you go wrong in all respects,
Especially if you congratulate him
Upon the strength of the resemblance.

Procto-Phan.   Fly !
Vanish ! Unheard of impudence ! What, still there !
In this enlightened age too, since you have been
Proved not to exist !—But this infernal brood
Will hear no reason and endure no rule.
Are we so wise, and is the *pond* still haunted?
How long have I been sweeping out this rubbish
Of superstition, and the world will not
Come clean with all my pains !—it is a case
Unheard of !

The Girl.   Then leave off teasing us so.

Procto-Phan. I tell you, spirits, to your faces now,
That I should not regret this despotism
Of spirits, but that mine can wield it not.
To-night I shall make poor work of it,
Yet I will take a round with you, and hope
Before my last step in the living dance
To beat the poet and the devil together.

Mep. At last he will sit down in some foul puddle;
That is his way of solacing himself ;
Until some leech, diverted with his gravity,
Cures him of spirits and the spirit together.

[*To* FAUST, *who has seceded from the dance.*
Why do you let that fair girl pass from you,
Who sung so sweetly to you in the dance?

Fau. A red mouse in the middle of her singing
Sprung from her mouth.
    Mep.   That was all right, my friend,
Be it enough that the mouse was not grey.
Do not disturb your hour of happiness
With close consideration of such trifles.
    Fau. Then saw I——
    Mep.   What?
    Fau.   Seest thou not a pale
Fair girl, standing alone, far, far away ?
She drags herself now forward with slow steps,
And seems as if she moved with shackled feet :
I cannot overcome the thought that she
Is like poor Margaret
    Mep.   Let it be—pass on—
No good can come of it—it is not well
To meet it—it is an enchanted phantom,
A lifeless idol ; with its numbing look,
It freezes up the blood of man; and they
Who meet its ghastly stare are turned to stone,
Like those who saw Medusa.
    Fau.   Oh, too true !
Her eyes are like the eyes of a fresh corpse
Which no beloved hand has closed, alas !
That is the heart which Margaret yielded to me—
Those are the lovely limbs which I enjoyed !
    Mep. It is all magic, poor deluded fool;
She looks to every one like his first love.
    Fau. Oh, what delight ! what woe ! I cannot turn
My looks from her sweet piteous countenance.
How strangely does a single blood-red line,
Not broader than the sharp edge of a knife,
Adorn her lovely neck !
    Mep.   Ay, she can carry
Her head under her arm upon occasion;
Perseus has cut it off for her. These pleasures
End in delusion.—Gain this rising ground,
It is as airy here as in a [   ]
And if I am not mightily deceived,
I see a theatre—What may this mean ?
    Attendant. Quite a new piece, the last of seven, for 'tis
The custom now to represent that number.
'Tis written by a Dilettante, and
The actors who perform are Dilettanti;
Excuse me, gentleman; but I must vanish,
I am a Dilettante curtain-lifter.

Posthumous Poems.

TO MARY,

ON HER OBJECTING TO THE "WITCH OF ATLAS" UPON THE SCORE OF
ITS CONTAINING NO HUMAN INTEREST.

How, my dear Mary, are you critic-bitten
  (For vipers kill though dead) by some review,
That you condemn these verses I have written
  Because they tell no story, false or true?
What though no mice are caught by a young kitten?
  May it not leap and play as grown cats do,
Till its claws come?   Prithee for this one time
Content thee with a visionary rhyme.

What hand would crush the silken-wingèd fly,
  The youngest of inconstant April's minions,
Because it cannot climb the purest sky,
  Where the swan sings amid the sun's dominions?
Not thine.   Thou knowest 'tis its doom to die
  When day shall hide within her twilight pinions
The lucent eyes and the eternal smile,
Serene as thine, which lent it life awhile.

To thy fair feet a wingèd Vision came,
  Whose date should have been longer than a day,
And o'er thy head did beat its wings for fame,
  And in thy sight its fading plumes display ;
The watery bow burned in the evening flame,
  But the shower fell, the swift sun went his way—
And that is dead.——O let me not believe
That anything of mine is fit to live !

Wordsworth informs us he was nineteen years
  Considering and retouching Peter Bell ;
Watering his laurels with the killing tears
  Of slow, dull care, so that their roots to hell
Might pierce, and their wide branches blot the spheres
  Of heaven with dewy leaves and flowers ; this well
May be, for heaven and earth conspire to foil
The over-busy gardener's blundering toil.

My Witch indeed is not so sweet a creature
  As Ruth or Lucy, whom his graceful praise
Clothes for our grandsons—but she matches Peter,
  Though he took nineteen years and she three days
In dressing.   Light the vest of flowing metre
  She wears ; he, proud as dandy with his stays,
Has hung upon his wiry limbs a dress
Like King Lear's "looped and windowed raggedness."

If you strip Peter, you will see a fellow
  Scorched by hell's hyperequatorial climate
Into a kind of a sulphureous yellow ;
  A lean mark, hardly fit to fling a rhyme at ;
In shape a Scaramouch, in hue Othello.
  If you unveil my Witch, no priest nor primate
Can shrive you of that sin—if sin there be
In love, when it becomes idolatry.

TO CONSTANTIA.

The rose that drinks the fountain dew
  In the pleasant air of noon
Grows pale and blue with altered hue
  In the gaze of the nightly moon ;
For the planet of frost, so cold and bright,
Makes it wan with her borrowed light.

Such is my heart—roses are fair,
  And that at best a withered blossom ;
But thy false care did idly wear
  Its withered leaves in a faithless bosom !
And fed with love, like air and dew,
Its growth——

TO F. G.

Her voice did quiver as we parted,
  Yet knew I not that heart was broken
From which it came, and I departed,
  Heeding not the words then spoken.
    Misery—O Misery,
  This world is all too wide for thee.

THE AZIOLA.

  " Do you not hear the Aziola cry ?
    Methinks she must be nigh,"
  Said Mary, as we sate
In dusk ere the stars were lit or candles brought ;
    And I, who thought
This Aziola was some tedious woman,
  Asked, " Who is Aziola ?" How elate
I felt to know that it was nothing human,
  No mockery of myself to fear and hate !
    And Mary saw my soul,
And laughed and said, " Disquiet yourself not ;
  'Tis nothing but a little downy owl."

  Sad Aziola ! Many an eventide
    Thy music I had heard
By wood and stream, meadow and mountain side,
    And fields and marshes wide—
Such as nor voice nor lute nor wind nor bird
    The soul ever stirred ;
  Unlike and far sweeter than they all :
  Sad Aziola ! from that moment I
    Loved thee and thy sad cry.

TO ———

THE serpent is shut out from Paradise,
The wounded deer must seek the herd no more
    In which its heart-cure lies ;
The widowed dove must cease to haunt a bower
Like that from which its mate with feignèd sighs
    Fled in the April hour.
I, too, must seldom seek again
Near happy friends a mitigated pain.

Of hatred I am proud,—with scorn content ;
Indifference that once hurt me, now is grown
    Itself indifferent.
But, not to speak of love, pity alone
Can break a spirit already more than bent.
    The miserable one
Turns the mind's poison into food—
Its medicine is tears—its evil good.

Therefore, if now I see you seldomer,
Dear friends, dear *friend !* know that I only fly
    Your looks because they stir
Griefs that should sleep, and hopes that cannot die ;
The very comfort that they minister
    I scarce can bear ; yet I,
So deeply is the arrow gone,
Should quickly perish if it were withdrawn.

When I return to my cold home, you ask
Why I am not as I have ever been.
    You spoil me for the task
Of acting a forced part on life's dull scene,
Of wearing on my brow the idle mask
    Of author great or mean
In the world's Carnival.   I sought
Peace thus, and but in you I found it not.

Full half an hour to-day, I tried my lot
With various flowers, and every one still said,
    "She loves me——loves me not."
And if this meant a vision long since fled,
If it meant fortune, fame, or peace of thought,
    If it meant—but I dread
To speak what you may know too well ;
Still there was truth in the sad oracle.

The crane o'er seas and forests seeks her home ;
No bird so wild but has its quiet nest
    When it no more would roam :
The sleepless billows on the ocean's breast
Break like a bursting heart and die in foam,
    And thus, at length, find rest ;
Doubtless there is a place of peace
Where my weak heart and all its throbs will cease.

I asked her yesterday if she believed
That I had resolution. One who had
    Would ne'er have thus relieved
His heart with words—but what his judgment bade
Would do, and leave the scorner unreprieved.
    These verses are too sad
To send to you, but that I know,
Happy yourself, you feel another's woe.

SUMMER AND WINTER.

IT was a bright and cheerful afternoon
Towards the end of the sunny month of June,
When the north wind congregates in crowds
The floating mountains of the silver clouds
From the horizon, and the stainless sky
Opens beyond them like eternity.
All things rejoiced beneath the sun, the weeds,
The river, and the cornfields, and the reeds ;
The willow-leaves that glanced in the light breeze,
And the firm foliage of the larger trees.

It was a winter such as when birds die
In the deep forests, and the fishes lie
Stiffened in the translucent ice which makes
Even the mud and slime of the warm lakes
A wrinkled clod as hard as brick ; and when
Among their children comfortable men
Gather about great fires and yet feel cold :
Alas ! then, for the homeless beggar old !

———

THE TOWER OF FAMINE.*

AMID the desolation of a city
    Which was the cradle and is now the grave
Of an extinguished people, so that pity
    Weeps o'er the shipwrecks of oblivion's wave,
There stands the Tower of Famine.   It is built
Upon some prison-homes, whose dwellers rave
For bread and gold and blood ; pain linked to guilt
    Agitates the light flame of their hours
Until its vital oil is spent or spilt ;
    There stands the pile, a tower amid the towers
And sacred domes ; each marble-ribbèd roof,
    The brazen-gated temples, and the bowers
Of solitary wealth ! the tempest-proof
    Pavilions of the dark Italian air
Are by its presence dimmed—they stand aloof
    And are withdrawn—so that the world is bare,
As if a spectre wrapt in shapeless terror
    Amid a company of ladies fair
Should glide and glow, till it became a mirror
    Of all their beauty, and their hair and hue,
The life of their sweet eyes with all its error
    Should be absorbed till they to marble grew.

———

TO ——

HERE, my dear friend, is a new book for you ,
I have already dedicated two
To other friends, one female and one male.
What you are is a thing that I must veil ;
What can this be to those who praise or rail ?
I never was attached to that great sect

---

* At Pisa there still exists the prison of Ugolino, which goes by the name of " La Torre della Fame ; " in the adjoining building the galley slaves are confined.   It is situated near the Ponte al Mare, on the Arno.

Whose doctrine is that each one should select
Out of the world a mistress or a friend,
And all the rest, though fair and wise, commend
To cold oblivion—though it is the code
Of modern morals, and the beaten road
Which those poor slaves with weary footsteps tread
Who travel to their home among the dead,
By the broad highway of the world—and so,
With one sad friend and many a jealous foe,
The dreariest and the longest journey go.

Free love has this, different from gold and clay,
That to divide is not to take away:
Like ocean which the general north wind breaks
Into ten thousand waves, and each one makes
A mirror of the moon ; like some great glass,
Which did distort whatever form might pass,
Dashed into fragments by a playful child,
Which then reflects its eyes and forehead mild,
Giving for one, which it could ne'er express,
A thousand images of loveliness.

If I were one whom the loud world held wise,
I should disdain to quote authorities
In the support of this kind of love :—
Why, there is first the God in heaven above,
Who wrote a book called Nature ('tis to be
Reviewed, I hear, in the next *Quarterly*) ;
And Socrates, the Jesus Christ of Greece,
And Jesus Christ Himself did never cease
To urge all living things to love each other,
And to forgive their mutual faults, and smother
The devil of disunion in their souls.

* * * * * *

It is a sweet thing, friendship, a dear balm,
A happy and auspicious bird of calm,
Which rides o'er life's ever tumultuous ocean ;
A god that broods o'er chaos in commotion ;
A flower which, fresh as Lapland's roses are,
Lifts its bold head into the world's pure air,
And blooms most radiantly when others die—
Health, hope, and youth, and brief prosperity ;
And with the light and odour of its bloom
Shining within the dungeon and the tomb ;
Whose coming is as light and music are
'Mid dissonance and gloom—a star
Which moves not 'mid the moving heavens alone—
A smile among dark frowns—a gentle tone
Among rude voices, a beloved light,
A solitude, a refuge, a delight.

If I had but a friend ! Why, I have three,
Even by my own confession ; there may be
Some more, for what I know ; for 'tis my mind
To call my friends all who are wise and kind,
And these, Heaven knows, at best are very few ;
But none can ever be more dear than you.
Why should they be ? My Muse has lost her wings,
Or like a dying swan who soars and sings

I should describe you in heroic style ;
But as it is—are you not void of guile ?
A lovely soul, formed to be blessed and bless ;
A well of sealed and secret happiness ;
A lute, which those whom love has taught to play
Make music on to cheer the roughest day.

*   *   *   *   *   *

FRAGMENTS.

I.

WAKE the serpent not, lest he
    Should not know the way to go.
Let him crawl which yet lies sleeping
Through the deep grass of the meadow.
Not a bee shall hear him creeping,
Not a mayfly shall awaken
From its cradling bluebell shaken ;
Not the starlight as he's sliding
Through the grass with silent gliding.

II.

I WOULD not be a king—enough
    Of woe it is to love ;
The path to power is steep and rough,
    And tempests reign above.

I would not climb the imperial throne ;
'Tis built on ice which fortune's sun
    Thaws in the height of noon.
Then farewell, king ; yet were I one,
    Care would not come so soon.
Would he and I were far away,
Keeping flocks on Himalay.

III.

I AM drunk with the honey wine
Of the moon-unfolded eglantine,
Which fairies catch in hyacinth buds :—
The bats, the dormice, and the moles
Sleep in the walls or under the sward
    Of the desolate Castle yard ;
And when 'tis spilt on the summer earth
Or its fumes arise among the dew,
Their jocund dreams are full of mirth,
They gibber their joy in sleep ; for few
Of the fairies bear those bowls so new.

IV.

IN the cave which wild weeds cover
Wait for thine ethereal lover ;
For the pallid moon is waning
O'er the spiral cypress hanging,
And the moon no cloud is staining.

It was once a Roman's chamber,
    Where he kept his darkest revels,
And the wild weeds twine and clamber ;
    It was then a chasm for devils.

V.

A GENTLE story of two lovers young,
  Who met in innocence and died in sorrow,
And of one selfish heart whose rancour clung
  Like curses on them ;—are ye slow to borrow
    The lore of truth from such a tale?
    Or in this world's deserted vale,
    Do ye not see a star of gladness
    Pierce the shadows of its sadness,
  When ye are cold, that love is a light sent
From heaven, which none shall quench, to cheer the innocent?

VI.

  ROME has fallen ; ye see it lying
  Heaped in undistinguished ruin ;—
  Nature is alone undying.

VII.

TO WILLIAM SHELLEY.

THY little footsteps on the sands
  Of a remote and lonely shore ;
The twinkling of thine infant hands
  Where now the worm will feed no more ;
    Thy mingled look of love and glee
    When we returned to gaze on thee.

VIII.

MY dearest Mary, wherefore hast thou gone
And left me in this dreary world alone?
Thy form is here indeed—a lovely one—
But thou art fled, gone down the dreary road
That leads to Sorrow's most obscure abode ;
Thou sittest on the hearth of pale despair,
          Where,
For thine own sake, I cannot follow thee.

July 1819.

IX.

  THE world is dreary,
  And I am weary
Of wandering on without thee, Mary ;
  A joy was erewhile
  In thy voice and thy smile,
And 'tis gone, when I should be gone too, Mary.

X.

AND where is truth? On tombs? For such to thee
Has been my heart, and thy dead memory
Has lain from childhood, many a changeful year—
Unchangingly preserved and buried there.

XI.

WHEN a lover clasps his fairest,
Then be our dread sport the rarest ;
  Their caresses were like the chaff
  In the tempest, and be our laugh
His despair—her epitaph.

When a mother clasps her child,
Watch till dusty Death has piled
His cold ashes on the clay ;
She has loved it many a day,
She remains—it fades away.

XII.

AND who feels discord now or sorrow?
  Love is the universe to-day—
These are the slaves of dim to-morrow,
  Darkening Life's labyrinthine way.

XIII.

ONE sang of thee who left the tale untold,
  Like the false dawns which perish in the bursting ;
Like empty cups of wrought and dædal gold,
  Which mock the lips with air when they are thirsting

XIV.

YE gentle visitations of calm thought—
Moods like the memories of happier earth,
Which come arrayed in thoughts of little worth,
Like stars in clouds by the wild winds enwrought,
But that the clouds depart and stars remain,
While they remain, and ye, alas ! depart.

XV.

How sweet it is to sit and read the tales
  Of mighty poets, and to hear the while
Sweet music, which, when the attention fails,
  Fills the dim pause——

XVI.

THE fitful alternations of the rain
When the chill wind, languid as if with pain
Of its own heavy moisture, here and there,
Drives through the grey and beamless atmosphere.

XVII.

THERE is a warm and gentle atmosphere
About the form of one we love, and thus
As in a tender mist our spirits are
Wrapt in the —— of that which is to us
The health of life's own life.

XVIII.

WHAT men gain fairly—that they should possess,
And children may inherit idleness
From him who earns it. This is understood,
Private injustice may be general good.
But he who gains by base and armèd wrong,
Or guilty fraud or base compliances,
May be despoiled ; even as a stolen dress
Is stript from a convicted thief, and he
Left in the nakedness of infamy.

XIX.

O THOU immortal deity
Whose throne is in the depth of human thought,
I do adjure thy power and thee
By all that man may be, by all that he is not,
By all that he has been and yet must be !

XX.

ON KEATS,

WHO DESIRED THAT ON HIS TOMB SHOULD BE INSCRIBED—

" HERE lieth One whose name was writ on water,"
But, ere the breath that could erase it blew,
Death, in remorse for that fell slaughter,
Death, the immortalising winter, flew
Athwart the stream, and Time's monthless torrent grew
A scroll of crystal, blazoning the name
Of Adonais !——

XXI.

HE wanders, like a day-appearing dream,
    Through the dim wildernesses of the mind ;
Through desert woods and tracts, which seem,
    Like ocean, homeless, boundless, unconfined.

XXII.

WHERE art thou, Presumptuous, who profanest
    The wreath to mighty poets only due,
Even whilst like a forgotten moon thou wanest ?
    Touch not those leaves which for the eternal few
Who wander o'er the paradise of fame
    In sacred dedication ever grew ;—
One of the crowd thou art without a name.
    Ah ! friend, 'tis the false laurel that I wear ;
Bright though it seem, it is not the same
    As that which bound Milton's immortal hair ;
Its dew is poison, and the hopes that quicken
    Under its chilling shade, though seeming fair,
Are flowers which die almost before they sicken.

XXIII.

THE rude wind is singing
    The dirge of the music dead,
The cold worms are clinging
    Where kisses were lately fed.

XXIV.

THE babe is at peace within the womb,
The corpse is at rest within the tomb—
    We begin in what we end.

XXV.

WHEN soft winds and sunny skies
With the green earth harmonise,
And the young and dewy dawn,
Bold as an unhunted fawn,
Up the windless heaven is gone—
Laugh—for ambushed in the day,
Clouds and whirlwinds watch their prey.

XXVI.
TO CONSTANTIA SINGING.

MY spirit like a charmed bark doth swim
  Upon the liquid waves of thy sweet singing,
Far away into the regions dim
  Of rapture—as a boat with swift sails winging
Its way adown some many-winding river.

XXVII.
TO MUSIC.

No, Music, thou art not the God of Love,
  Unless Love feeds upon his own sweet self
Till it becomes all music murmurs of.

XXVIII.

THE silver key of the fountain of tears
  Where the spirit drinks till the brain is wild ;
Softest grave of a thousand fears
  Where their mother, Care, like a drowsy child,
    Is laid asleep in flowers.

XXX.

To thirst and find no fill—to wail and wander
With short unsteady steps—to pause and ponder—
To feel the blood run through the veins and tingle
Where busy thought and blind sensation mingle ;
To nurse the image of unfelt caresses
Till dim imagination just possesses
The half-created shadow.

XXX.

WEALTH and dominion fade into the mass
  Of the great sea of mingled right and wrong,
When once from our possession they must pass ;
  But love, though misdirected, is among
The things which are immortal, and surpass
All that frail stuff which will be or which was.

XXXI.

MY thoughts arise and fade in solitude,
The verse that would invest them melts away
Like moonlight in the heaven of spreading day.
How beautiful they were ! how firm they stood,
Flecking the starry sky like woven pearl !

XXXII.
FRAGMENT OF A SONG.
AN EARLY POEM.

YET look on me—take not thine eyes away
  Which feed upon the love within mine own,
Which is indeed but the reflected ray
  Of thine own beauty from my spirit thrown.
Yet speak to me—thy voice is as the tone
  Of my heart's echo, and I think I hear
That thou yet lovest me ; yet thou alone
  Like one before a mirror without care
Of aught but thine own features imaged there ;
  And yet I wear out life in watching thee ;
A toil so sweet at times, and thou indeed
  Art kind when I am sick, and pity me.

EPIGRAMS TRANSLATED FROM THE GREEK.

SPIRIT OF PLATO.

EAGLE, why soarest thou above that tomb?
    To what sublime and star-y-paven home
        Floatest thou?
I am the image of swift Plato's spirit,
Ascending heaven—Athens does inherit
        His corpse alone.

FROM THE GREEK.

A MAN who was about to hang himself,
    Finding a purse, then threw away his rope.
The owner, coming to reclaim his pelf,
    The halter found, and used it. So is Hope
Changed for Despair—one laid upon the shelf,
    We take the other. Under heaven's high cope,
Fortune is God—all you endure and do
Depends on circumstance as much as you.

TO STELLA. (FROM PLATO.)

THOU wert the morning star among the living
    Ere thy fair light had fled ;—
Now, having died, thou art as Hesperus giving
    New splendour to the dead.

FROM PLATO

KISSING Helena, together
With my kiss my soul beside it
Came to my lips, and there I kept it—
For the poor thing had wandered thither
To follow where the kiss should guide it,
O, cruel I, to intercept it.

THE PINE FOREST

OF THE CASCINE, NEAR PISA.

THIS poem has already appeared at page 496; but, in Mrs. Shelley's edition of her husband's poems, so many changes, insertions, and omissions appear in it, that we think it well to reproduce it in the form thus presented to us.

THE INVITATION.

BEST and brightest, come away,
Fairer far than this fair day,
Which, like thee to those in sorrow,
Comes to bid a sweet good-morrow
To the rough year just awake
In its cradle on the brake.
The brightest hour of unborn spring,
Through the winter wandering,
Found, it seems, the halcyon morn,
To hoar February born ;
Bending from heaven, in azure mirth,
It kissed the forehead of the earth,
And smiled upon the silent sea,
And bade the frozen streams be free ;
And waked to music all their fountains,
And breathed upon the frozen mountains,
And like a prophetess of May,
Strewed flowers upon the barren way,
Making the wintry world appear
Like one on whom thou smilest, dear.

Away, away, from men and towns,
To the wild woods and the downs—
To the silent wilderness
Where the soul need not repress
Its music, lest it should not find
An echo in another's mind,
While the touch of Nature's art
Harmonises heart to heart.
I leave this notice on my door
For each accustomed visitor :—
" I am gone into the fields
To take what this sweet hour
        yields ;—
Reflection, you may come to-mor-
        row,
Sit by the fireside of Sorrow.—
You with the unpaid bill, Despair,
You tiresome verse-reciter, Care,
I will pay you in the grave,
Death will listen to your stave.—
Expectation too, be off !
To-day is for itself enough ;
Hope, in pity mock not woe
With smiles, nor follow where I go ;
Long having lived on thy sweet food,
At length I find one moment good

After long pain—with all your love,
This you never told me of."

Radiant Sister of the Day,
Awake ! arise ! and come away !
To the wild woods and the plains,
To the pools where winter rains
Image all their roof of leaves ;
Where the pine its garland weaves
Of sapless green, and ivy dun,
Round stems that never kiss the sun ;
Where the lawns and pastures be,
And the sandhills of the sea ;
Where the melting hoar-frost wets
The daisy star that never sets,
And wind-flowers and violets,
Which yet join not scent to hue,
Crown the pale year weak and new ;
When the night is left behind
In the deep east, dun and blind,
And the blue noon is over us,
And the multitudinous
Billows murmur at our feet,
Where the earth and ocean meet ;
And all things seem only one,
In the universal sun.

THE RECOLLECTION.

Now the last day of many days,
All beautiful and bright as thou,
The loveliest and the last is dead,
Rise, Memory, and write its praise !
Up to thy wonted work ! come, trace
The epitaph of glory dead,
For now the Earth has changed its
        face,
A frown is on the Heavens' brow.

I.

We wandered to the pine-forest
    That skirts the ocean foam,
The lightest wind was in its nest,
    The tempest in its home ;
The whispering waves were half asleep,
    The clouds were gone to play,
And on the bosom of the deep
    The smile of Heaven lay ;
It seemed as if the hour were one
    Sent from beyond the skies,
Which scattered from above the sun
    A light of Paradise.

II.

We paused amid the pines that stood
    The giants of the waste,
Tortured by storms to shapes as rude
    As serpents interlaced ;
And soothed by every azure breath
    That under heaven is blown,
To harmonies and hues beneath,
    As tender as its own ;
Now all the tree-tops lie asleep,
    Like green waves on the sea,
As still as in the silent deep
    The ocean woods may be.

III.

How calm it was !—the silence there
    By such a chain was bound,
That even the busy woodpecker
    Made stiller by her sound
The inviolable quietness ;
    The breath of peace we drew,
With its soft motion made not less
    The calm that round us grew.

There seemed from the remotest seat
  Of the wide mountain waste,
To the soft flower beneath our feet,
  A magic circle traced,—
A spirit interfused around
  A thrilling silent life,
To momentary peace it bound
  Our mortal nature's strife ;—
And still I felt the centre of
  The magic circle there,
Was one fair form that filled with love
  The lifeless atmosphere.

IV.

We paused beside the pools that lie
  Under the forest bough,
Each seemed as 'twere a little sky
  Gulfed in a world below ;
A firmament of purple light,
  Which in the dark earth lay,
More boundless than the depth of
    night
  And purer than the day—
In which the lovely forests grew,
  As in the upper air,

More perfect both in shape and hue
  Than any spreading there.
There lay the glade and neighbouring
    lawn,
  And through the dark green wood
The white sun twinkling like the dawn
  Out of a speckled cloud.
Sweet views which in our world above
  Can never well be seen
Were imaged in the water's love
  Of that fair forest green.
And all was interfused beneath
  With an Elysian glow,
An atmosphere without a breath,
  A softer day below.
Like one beloved the scene had lent
  To the dark water's breast
Its every leaf and lineament
  With more than truth exprest,
Until an envious wind crept by,
  Like an unwelcome thought,
Which from the mind's too faithful eye
  Blots one dear image out.
Though thou art ever fair and kind,
  The forests ever green,
Less oft is peace in S——'s mind
  Than calm in waters seen.

TO ——.

THE keen stars were twinkling,
And the fair moon was rising among
    them,
        Dear * * * * !
The guitar was tinkling,
But the notes were not sweet till you
    sang them
        Again.
As the moon's cold splendour
O'er the faint cold starlight of heaven
  Is thrown,
So your voice most tender
To the strings without soul had then
    given
        Its own.

The stars will awaken   [later,
Though the moon sleep a full hour
    To-night ;
No leaf will be shaken
Whilst the dews of your melody
    scatter
        Delight.
Though the sound overpowers,
Sing again, with your dear voice re-
    vealing
        A tone
Of some world far from ours,
Where music and moonlight and
    feeling
        Are one.

TO THE LORD CHANCELLOR.

THY country's curse is on thee, darkest Crest
  Of that foul, knotted, many-headed worm,
Which rends our Mother's bosom—Priestly Pest,
  Masked Resurrection of a buried form ! *

---

* The Star Chamber.

Thy country's curse is on thee ! Justice sold,
  Truth trampled, Nature's landmarks overthrown,
And heaps of fraud-accumulated gold
  Plead, loud as thunder, at Destruction's throne ;

And, whilst that slow, sure Angel which aye stands,
  Watching the beck of Mutability,
Delays to execute her high commands,
  And, though a nation weeps, spares thine and thee ;

O let a father's curse be on thy soul,
  And let a daughter's hope be on thy tomb,
Be both on thy grey head a leaden cowl,
  To weigh thee down to thine approaching doom !

I curse thee by a parent's outraged love,
  By hopes long cherished and too lately lost,
By gentle feelings thou couldst never prove,
  By griefs which thy stern nature never crost ;

By those infantine smiles of happy light,
  Which were a fire within a stranger's hearth,
Quenched even when kindled, in untimely night,
  Hiding the promise of a lovely birth ;

By those unpractised accents of young speech,
  Which he who is a father thought to frame
To gentlest lore, such as the wisest teach ;
  Thou strike the lyre of mind, O grief and shame !

By all the happy see in children's growth,
  That undeveloped flower of budding years,
Sweetness and sadness interwoven both,
  Source of the sweetest hopes and saddest fears ;

By all the days under an hireling's care,
  Of dull constraint and bitter heaviness,—
O wretched ye, if ever any were,
  Sadder than orphans, yet not fatherless !

By the false cant which on their innocent lips
  Must hang like poison on an opening bloom,
By the dark creeds which cover with eclipse
  Their pathway from the cradle to the tomb ;

By thy most impious Hell, and all its terrors,
  By all the grief, the madness, and the guilt
Of thine impostures, which must be their errors,
  That sand on which thy crumbling power is built ;

By thy complicity with lust and hate,
  Thy thirst for tears —thy hunger after gold,
The ready frauds which ever on thee wait,
  The servile arts in which thou hast grown old ;

By thy most killing sneer, and by thy smile,
  By all the arts and snares of thy black den,
And—for thou canst outweep the crocodile
  By thy false tears—those millstones braining men ;

By all the hate which checks a father's love,
  By all the scorn which kills a father's care,
By those most impious hands which dared remove
  Nature's high bounds—by thee—and by despair!—

Yes, the despair which bids a father groan,
  And cry, "My children are no longer mine;
The blood within those veins may be mine own,
  But, tyrant, their polluted souls are thine—"

I curse thee, though I hate thee not; O slave!
  If thou couldst quench the earth-consuming Hell
Of which thou art a demon, on thy grave
  This curse would be a blessing.   Fare thee well!

————————

TO WILLIAM SHELLEY.

The billows on the beach are leaping around it,
  The bark is weak and frail,
The sea looks black, and the clouds that bound it
  Darkly strew the gale.
Come with me, thou delightful child;
Come with me, though the wave is wild
And the winds are loose; we must not stay,
Or the slaves of law may rend thee away.

They have taken thy brother and sister dear,
  They have made them unfit for thee,
They have withered the smile and dried the tear
  Which should have been sacred to me.
To a blighting faith and a cause of crime
They have bound them slaves in youthly time,
And they will curse my name and thee
Because we fearless are and free.

Come thou, belovèd as thou art,
  Another sleepeth still
Near thy sweet mother's anxious heart,
  Which thou with joy shalt fill;
With fairest smiles of wonder thrown
On that which is indeed our own,
And which in distant lands will be
The dearest playmate unto thee.

Fear not the tyrants will rule for ever,
  Or the priests of the evil faith;
They stand on the brink of that raging river
  Whose waves they have tainted with death.
It is fed from the depth of a thousand dells,
Around them it foams and rages and swells;
And their swords and their sceptres I floating see,
Like wrecks on the surge of eternity.

Rest, rest, shriek not, thou gentle child!
  The rocking of the boat thou fearest,
And the cold spray and the clamour wild?—
  There, sit between us two, thou dearest;

Me and thy mother—well we know
The storm at which thou tremblest so,
With all its dark and hungry graves,
Less cruel than the savage slaves
Who hunt us o'er these sheltering waves.

This hour will in thy memory
Be a dream of days forgotten ;
We soon shall dwell by the azure sea
Of serene and golden Italy,
Or Greece, the mother of the free.
And I will teach thine infant tongue
To call upon those heroes old
In their own language, and will mould
Thy growing spirit to the flame
Of Grecian lore, that by such name
A patriot's birthright thou mayst claim.

FRAGMENT.

ALAS ! this is not what I thought life was.
I knew that there were crimes and evil men,
Misery and hate ; nor did I hope to pass
Untouched by suffering through the rugged glen.
In mine own heart I saw as in a glass
The hearts of others * * * * and when
I went among my kind, with triple brass
Of calm endurance my weak breast I armed,
To bear scorn, fear, and hate, a woeful mass.

Poems.

FROM ST. IRVYNE; OR, THE ROSICRUCIAN.

I.

'TWAS dead of the night when I sat in my dwelling,
    One glimmering lamp was expiring and low;
Around, the dark tide of the tempest was swelling,
    Along the wild mountains night ravens were yelling,
        They bodingly presaged destruction and woe.

'Twas then that I started!—the wild storm was howling,
    Nought was seen save the lightning which danced in the sky;
Above me the crash of the thunder was rolling,
    And low, chilling murmurs the blast wafted by.

My heart sank within me—unheeded the war
    Of the battling clouds on the mountain-tops broke,
Unheeded the thunder-peal crashed in mine ear—
This heart, hard as iron, is stranger to fear,
    But conscience in low, noiseless whisperings spoke.

'Twas then that her form on the whirlwind upholding,
    The ghost of the murdered Victoria strode;
In her right hand a shadowy shroud she was holding—
    She swiftly advanced to my lonesome abode.

I wildly then called on the tempest to bear me—

    *   *   *   *   *   *

II.

GHOSTS of the dead! have I not heard your yelling
    Rise on the night-rolling breath of the blast,
When o'er the dark ether the tempest is swelling,
    And on eddying whirlwind the thunder-peal past?

For oft have I stood on the dark height of Jura,
    Which frowns on the valley that opens beneath;
Oft have I braved the chill night tempest's fury,
    Whilst around me, I thought, echoed murmurs of death.

And now, whilst the winds of the mountain are howling,
    O father! thy voice seems to strike on mine ear;
In air, whilst the tide of the night storm is rolling,
    It breaks on the pause of the elements' jar.

On the wing of the whirlwind which roars o'er the mountain,
    Perhaps rides the ghost of my sire who is dead,
On the mist of the tempest which hangs o'er the fountain,
    Whilst a wreath of dark vapour encircles his head.

III.

A BALLAD.

THE death-bell beats !—
The mountain repeats
The echoing sound of the knell,
  And the dark monk now
  Wraps the cowl round his brow,
As he sits in his lonely cell.

And the cold hand of death
Chills his shuddering breath
As he lists to the fearful lay
  Which the ghosts of the sky,
  As they sweep wildly by,
Sing to departed day.
And they sing of the hour
When the stern fates had power
To resolve Rosa's form to its clay.

But that hour is past,
And that hour was the last
Of peace to the dark monk's brain,
  Bitter tears from his eyes gushed
    silent and fast,
And he strove to suppress them in
  vain.

Then his fair cross of gold he dashed
  on the floor
When the death-knell struck on his
  ear,
  " Delight is in store
  For her evermore,
But for me is fate, horror, and fear."

Then his eyes wildly rolled
When the death-bell tolled,
And he raged in terrific woe,
  And he stamped on the ground,
  But when ceased the sound,
Tears again began to flow ;

And the ice of despair
  Chilled the wild throb of care,
And he sat in mute agony still,
  Till the night stars shone through
    the cloudless air,
And the pale moonbeam slept on the
  hill.

Then he knelt in his cell,
And the horrors of hell
Were delights to his agonised pain,
  And he prayed to God to dissolve
    the spell,
Which else must for ever remain,

And in fervent prayer he knelt on
  the ground
Till the abbey bell struck one ;
  His feverish blood ran chill at the
    sound ;
  A voice hollow and horrible mur-
    mured around—
" The term of thy penance is done."

Grew dark the night,
The moonbeams bright
Waxed faint on the mountains
  high ;
  And from the black hill
  Went a voice, cold and chill,—
" Monk, thou art free to die."

Then he rose to his feet
And his heart loud did beat,
And his limbs they were palsied with
  dread ;
  Whilst the grave's clammy dew
  O'er his pale forehead grew,
And he shuddered to sleep with the
  dead.

And the wild midnight storm
Raved around his tall form,
As he sought the chapel's gloom ;
  And the sunk grass did sigh
  To the wind bleak and high
As he searched for the new-made tomb.

And forms dark and high
Seemed around him to fly,
And mingle their yells with the blast ;
  And on the dark wall
  Half-seen shadows fall,
As enhorrored he onward passed.

And the storm-fiends wild rave
O'er the new-made grave,
And dread shadows linger around ;
  The monk called on God his soul
    to save,
And in horror sank on the ground.

Then despair nerved his arm
To dispel the charm,
And he burst Rosa's coffin asunder,
  And the fierce storm did swell
  More terrific and fell,
And louder pealed the thunder.

And laughed in joy the fiendish
    throng
  Mixed with ghosts of the moulder-
    ing dead ;
And their grisly wings, as they floated
    along,
  Whistled in murmurs dread.

And her skeleton form the dead nun
    reared,
  Which dripped with the chill dew
    of hell ;
In her half-eaten eyeballs two pale
    flames appeared,
And triumphant their gleam on the
    dark monk glared,
  As he stood within the cell.

And her lank hand lay on his shudder-
    ing brain,
  But each power was nerved by fear :
" I never, henceforth, may breathe
    again,
Death now ends mine anguished
    pain—
  The grave yawns—we meet there."

And her skeleton lungs did utter the
    sound
  So deadly, so lone, and so fell,
That in long vibrations shuddered
    the ground,
And, as the stern notes floated around,
  A deep groan was answered from
    hell.

IV.

How swiftly through heaven's wide expanse
  Bright day's resplendent colours fade !
How sweetly does the moonbeam's glance
  With silver tint St. Irvyne's glade !

No cloud along the spangled air
  Is borne upon the evening breeze.
How solemn is the scene ! how fair
  The moonbeams rest upon the trees !

Yon dark gray turret glimmers white,
  Upon it sits the mournful owl ;
Along the stillness of the night
  Her melancholy shriekings roll.

But alone on Irvyne's tower
  The silver moonbeam pours her ray ;
It gleams upon the ivied bower,
  It dances in the cascade's spray.

Ah ! why do darkening shades conceal
  The hour when man must cease to be ?
Why may not human minds unveil
  The dim mists of futurity ?

The keenness of the world hath torn
  The heart which opens to its blast ;
Despised, neglected, and forlorn,
  Sinks the wretch in death at last.

V.

How stern are the woes of the desolate mourner
  As he bends in still grief o'er the hallowèd bier,
As enanguished he turns from the laugh of the scorner,
  And drops to perfection's remembrance a tear ;
When floods of despair down his pale cheek are streaming,
When no blissful hope on his bosom is beaming,
Or, if lulled for a while, soon he starts from his dreaming,
  And finds torn the soft ties to affection so dear.

Ah ! when shall day dawn on the night of the grave,
  Or summer succeed to the winter of death?
Rest awhile, hapless victim, and Heaven will save
  The spirit that faded away with the breath.
Eternity points to its amaranth bower,
Where no clouds of fate o'er the sweet prospect lower,
Unspeakable pleasure, of goodness the dower,
  When woe fades away like the mist of the heath.

VI.

Ah ! faint are her limbs, and her footstep is weary,
  Yet far must the desolate wanderer roam ;
Though the tempest is stern and the mountain is dreary,
  She must quit at deep midnight her pitiless home.
I see her swift foot dash the dew from the whortle
As she rapidly hastes to the green grove of myrtle,
And I hear, as she wraps round her figure the kirtle,
  "Stay thy boat on the lake, dearest Henry ; I come."

High swelled in her bosom the throb of affection
  As lightly her form bounded over the lea,
And arose in her mind every dear recollection—
  "I come, dearest Henry ; I wait but for thee."
How sad when dear hope every sorrow is soothing,
When sympathy's swell the soft bosom is moving,
And the mind the mild joys of affection is proving,
  Is the stern voice of fate that bids happiness flee !

Oh ! dark lowered the clouds on that horrible eve,
  And the moon dimly gleamed through the tempested air.
Oh ! how could fond visions such softness deceive?
  Oh ! how could false hope rend a bosom so fair?
Thy love's pallid corse the wild surges are laving,
O'er his form the fierce swell of the tempest is raving ;
But, fear not, parting spirit ; thy goodness is saving
  In eternity's bowers a seat for thee there.

Posthumous Fragments.

By MARGARET NICHOLSON.

THESE burlesque fragments were written by Shelley during his first term at University College. They were published by him under the assumed name of John Fitz-Victor, and were, in fact, a practical joke on the public, in which he was aided by his friend Mr. Hogg.

Margaret Nicholson was a madwoman—a laundress—who attempted to kill George III. in 1786. She was shut up in Bedlam at the time the "Fragments" appeared. They have no claim to republication except that of the interest attaching to the early literary efforts of a great poet.

To the "Fragments" the following Advertisement is prefixed :—

"The energy and native genius of these 'Fragments' must be the only apology which the Editor can make for thus intruding them on the public notice. The first I found without title, and have left it so. It is intimately connected with the dearest interests of universal happiness; and much as we may deplore the fatal and enthusiastic tendency which the ideas of this poor female had acquired, we cannot fail to pay the tribute of unequivocal regret to the departed memory of genius, which, had it been rightly organised, would have made that intellect which has since become the victim of frenzy and despair a most brilliant ornament to society.

"In case the sale of these 'Fragments' evinces that the public have any curiosity to be presented with a more copious collection of my unfortunate Aunt's poems, I have other papers in my possession which shall in that case be subjected to their notice. It may be supposed they require much arrangement; but I send the following to the press in the same state in which they came into my possession.—J. F."

FRAGMENTS.

AMBITION, power, and avarice now have hurled
Death, fate, and ruin on a bleeding world.
See, on yon heath what countless victims lie !
Hark, what loud shrieks ascend through yonder sky !
Tell then the cause—'tis sure the avenger's rage
Has swept these myriads from life's crowded stage.
Hark to that groan ; an anguished hero dies ;
He shudders in death's latest agonies.
Yet does a fleeting hectic flush his cheek,
Yet does his panting breath essay to speak—

"O God ! my wife, my children ! Monarch thou
For whose support this fainting frame lies low,
For whose support in distant lands I bleed,
Let his friends' welfare be the warrior's meed.

He hears me not—ah, no !—kings cannot hear,
For passion's voice has dulled their listless ear.
To thee, then, mighty God, I lift my moan ;
Thou wilt not scorn a suppliant's anguished groan.
Oh ! now I die—but still is death's fierce pain—
God hears my prayer—we meet, we meet again."
He spake, reclined him on death's bloody bed,
And with a parting groan his spirit fled.

Oppressors of mankind, to *you* we owe
The baleful streams from whence these miseries flow !
For you how many a mother weeps her son
Snatched from life's course ere half his race was run !
For you how many a widow drops a tear
In silent anguish on her husband's bier !

" Is it then thine, Almighty Power," she cries,
" Whence tears of endless sorrow dim these eyes?
Is it this system which thy powerful sway
Which else in shapeless chaos sleeping lay
Formed and approved?—It cannot be,—but oh !
Forgive me, Heaven, my brain is warped by woe."
'Tis not—He never bade the war-note swell ;
He never triumphed in the work of hell.
Monarchs of earth ! thine is the baleful deed,
Thine are the crimes for which thy subjects bleed.
Ah ! when will come the sacred fated time
When man, unsullied by his leaders' crime,
Despising wealth, ambition, pomp, and pride,
Will stretch him fearless by his foeman's side?
Ah ! when will come the time when o'er the plain
No more shall death and desolation reign?
When will the sun smile on the bloodless field,
And the stern warrior's arm the sickle wield?
Not whilst some King, in cold ambition's dreams,
Plans for the field of death his plodding schemes ;
Not whilst for private pique the public fall,
And one frail mortal's mandate governs all,
Swelled with command, and mad with dizzying sway,
Who sees unmoved his myriads fade away,
Careless who lives or dies—so that he gains
Some trivial point for which he took the pains.
What, then, are kings?—I see the trembling crowd,
I hear their fulsome clamours echoed loud ;
Their stern oppressor pleased appears awhile,
But April sunshine is a monarch's smile.
Kings are but dust—the last eventful day
Will level all, and make them lose their sway ;
Will dash the sceptre from the monarch's hand,
And from the warrior's grasp wrest the ensanguined brand.

O Peace, soft Peace ! art thou for ever gone?
Is thy fair form indeed for ever flown?
And love and concord hast thou swept away
As if incongruous with thy parted sway?
Alas ! I fear thou hast, for none appear.
Now o'er the palsied earth stalks giant Fear,

With War, and Woe, and Terror in his train ;
List'ning he pauses on the embattled plain,
Then speeding swiftly o'er the ensanguined heath,
Has left the frightful work to hell and death.
See ! gory Ruin yokes his blood-stained car ;
He scents the battle's carnage from afar ;
Hell and destruction mark his mad career.
He tracks the rapid step of hurrying Fear,
Whilst ruined towns and smoking cities tell
That thy work, Monarch, is the work of hell.
" It is thy work," I hear a voice repeat ;
Shakes the broad basis of thy blood-stained seat ;
And at the orphan's sigh, the widow's moan,
Totters the fabric of thy guilt-stained throne.
" It is thy work, O Monarch !"—now the sound,
Fainter and fainter yet, is borne around ;
Yet to enthusiast ears the murmurs tell
That Heaven, indignant at the work of hell,
Will soon the cause, the hated cause, remove,
Which tears from earth peace, innocence, and love.

FRAGMENT,

Supposed to be an Epithalamium of Francis Ravaillac and Charlotte Cordé.

'Tis midnight now—athwart the murky air
    Dark lurid meteors shoot a livid gleam ;
From the dark storm-clouds flashes a fearful glare,
    It shows the bending oak, the roaring stream.
I pondered on the woes of lost mankind,
    I pondered on the ceaseless rage of kings-
My rapt soul dwelt upon the ties that bind
    The mazy volume of commingling things,
        When fell and wild misrule to man stern sorrow brings.
I heard a yell—it was not the knell
    When the blasts on the wild lake sleep,
That floats on the pause of the summer gale's swell
    O'er the breast of the waveless deep.
I thought it had been death's accents cold
    That bade me recline on the shore ;
I laid mine hot head on the surge-beaten mould,
    And thought to breathe no more.

            But a heavenly sleep
            That did suddenly steep
                In balm my bosom's pain,
            Pervaded my soul,
            And free from control
                Did mine intellect range again.

Methought, enthroned upon a silvery cloud,
    Which floated 'mid a strange and brilliant light,
My form upborne by viewless æther rode,
    And spurned the lessening realms of earthly night.

What heavenly notes burst on my ravished ears !
   What beauteous spirits met my dazzled eye !
Hark ! louder swells the music of the spheres,
   More clear the forms of speechless bliss float by,
   And heavenly gestures suit æthereal melody.

But fairer than the spirits of the air,
   More graceful than the sylph of symmetry,
Than the enthusiast's fancied love more fair,
   Were the bright forms that swept the azure sky.
Enthroned in roseate light, a heavenly band
   Strewed flowers of bliss that never fade away ;
They welcome virtue to its native land,
   And songs of triumph greet the joyous day
   When endless bliss the woes of fleeting life repay

Congenial minds will seek their kindred soul
   E'en though the tide of time has rolled between ;
They mock weak matter's impotent control,
   And seek of endless life the eternal scene.
At death's vain summons *this* will never die,
   In Nature's chaos *this* will not decay—
These are the bands which closely, warmly, tie
   Thy soul, O Charlotte, 'yond this chain of clay,
   To him who thine must be till time shall fade away.

Yes, Francis ! thine was the dear knife that tore
   A tyrant's heart-strings from his guilty breast ;
Thine was the daring at a tyrant's gore,
   To smile in triumph, to contemn the rest ;
And thine, loved glory of thy sex ! to tear
   From its base shrine a despot's haughty soul,
To laugh at sorrow in secure despair,
   To mock with smiles, life's lingering control,
   And triumph 'mid the griefs that round thy fate did roll.

Yes ; the fierce spirits of the avenging deep
   With endless tortures goad their guilty shades ;
I see the lank and ghastly spectres sweep
   Along the burning length of yon arcades ;
And I see Satan stalk athwart the plain,
   He hastes along the burning soil of hell :
" Welcome, thou despots, to my dark domain ;
   With maddening joy mine anguished senses swell
   To welcome to their home the friends I love so well."

    *   *   *   *   *   *

Hark to those notes ! how sweet, how thrilling sweet
They echo to the sound of angels' feet !

    *   *   *   *   *   #

Oh ! haste to the bower where roses are spread,
For there is preparèd thy nuptial bed.
Oh haste—hark ! hark !—they're gone.

CHORUS OF SPIRITS.

Stay, ye days of contentment and joy,
 Whilst love every care is erasing !
Stay, ye pleasures that never cloy,
 And ye spirits that can never cease pleasing !
And if any soft passion be near,
 Which mortals, frail mortals, can know,
Let love shed on the bosom a tear,
 And dissolve the chill ice-drop of woe.

SYMPHONY.

Francis.

" Soft, my dearest angel, stay ;
 Oh ! you suck my soul away !
 Suck on, suck on ; I glow, I glow !
 Tides of maddening passion roll,
 And streams of rapture drown my soul.
 Now give me one more billing kiss,
 Let your lips now repeat the bliss ;
 Endless kisses steal my breath,
 No life can equal such a death."

Charlotte.

" Oh ! yes, I will kiss thine eyes so fair,
 And I will clasp thy form ;
 Serene is the breath of the balmy air,
  But I think, love, thou feelest me warm.
 And I will recline on thy marble neck
  Till I mingle into thee ;
 And I will kiss the rose on thy cheek,
  And thou shalt give kisses to me.
 For here is no morn to flout our delight,
  Oh ! dost thou not joy at this?
 And here we may lie an endless night,
  A long, long night of bliss."

Spirits ! when raptures move,
Say what it is to love,
 When passion's tear stands on the cheek,
When bursts the unconscious sigh ;
 And the tremulous lips dare not speak
What is told by the soul-felt eye.
 But what is sweeter to revenge's ear
Than the fell tyrant's last expiring yell?
 Yes ! than love's sweetest blisses 'tis more dear
To drink the floatings of a despot's knell.
 I wake—'tis done—'tis o'er.

  * * * * * *

DESPAIR.

AND canst thou mock mine agony, thus calm
 In cloudless radiance, Queen of silver night?
Can you, ye flow'rets, spread your perfumed balm,
 'Mid pearly gems of dew that shine so bright?

And you, wild winds, thus can you sleep so still
   Whilst throbs the tempest of my breast so high?
Can the fierce night-fiends rest on yonder hill,
   And, in the eternal mansions of the sky,
   Can the directors of the storm in powerless silence lie?

Hark! I hear music on the zephyr's wing,
   Louder it floats along the unruffled sky;
Some fairy sure has touched the viewless string—
   Now faint in distant air the murmurs die,
Awhile it stills the tide of agony.
   Now—now it loftier swells,—again stern woe
Arises with the awakening melody;
   Again fierce torments, such as demons know,
   In bitterer, feller tide, on this torn bosom flow.

Arise, ye sightless spirits of the storm,
   Ye unseen minstrels of the aërial song,
Pour the fierce tide around this lonely form,
   And roll the tempest's wildest swell along.
Dart the red lightning, wing the forkèd flash,
   Pour from thy cloud-formed hills the thunder's roar ·
Arouse the whirlwind—and let ocean dash
   In fiercest tumult on the rocking shore,
   Destroy this life or let earth's fabric be no more.

Yes, every tie that links me here is dead;
   Mysterious fate, thy mandate I obey;
Since hope, and peace, and joy for aye are fled,
   I come, terrific power, I come away.
Then o'er this ruined soul let spirits of hell
   In triumph, laughing wildly, mock its pain;
And though with direst pangs my heartstrings swell,
   I'll echo back their deadly yells again,
   Cursing the power that ne'er made aught in vain.

FRAGMENT.

YES! all is past—swift time has fled away,
   Yet its swell pauses on my sickening mind;
How long will horror nerve this frame of clay?
   I'm dead, and lingers yet my soul behind.
O powerful fate, revoke thy deadly spell!
   And yet that may not ever, ever be;
Heaven will not smile upon the work of hell,
   Ah no! for Heaven cannot smile on me;
   Fate, envious fate, has sealed my wayward destiny.

I sought the cold brink of the midnight surge,
   I sighed beneath its wave to hide my woes,
The rising tempest sang a funeral dirge,
   And on the blast a frightful yell arose.
Wild flew the meteors o'er the maddened main,
   Wilder did grief athwart my bosom glare;
Stilled was the unearthly howling, and a strain
   Swelled 'mid the tumult of the battling air,
   'Twas like a spirit's song, but yet more soft and fair.

I met a maniac ; like he was to me ;
    I said, " Poor victim, wherefore dost thou roam ?
And canst thou not contend with agony,
    That thus at midnight thou dost quit thine home ?
Ah, there she sleeps ! Cold is her bloodless form,
    And I will go to slumber in her grave ;
And then our ghosts, while raves the maddened storm,
    Will sweep o'er the wildered wave.
    Wilt thou our lowly beds with tears of pity lave ? "

" Ah no ! I cannot shed the pitying tear ;
    This breast is cold, this heart can feel no more ;
But I can rest me on thy chilling bier,
    Can shriek in horror to the tempest's roar. "

    *   *   *   *   *

THE SPECTRAL HORSEMAN.

WHAT was the shriek that struck fancy's ear
As it sate on the ruins of time that is past ?
Hark ! it floats on the fitful blast of the wind,
And breathes to the pale moon a funeral sigh.
It is the Benshie's moan on the storm,
Or a shivering fiend that, thirsting for sin,
Seeks murder and guilt when virtue sleeps,
Winged with the power of some ruthless king,
And sweeps o'er the breast of the prostrate plain.
It was not a fiend from the regions of hell
That poured its low moan on the stillness of night ;
It was not a ghost of the guilty dead,
Nor a yelling vampire reeking with gore ;
But aye at the close of seven years' end
That voice is mixed with the swell of the storm,
And aye at the close of seven years' end
A shapeless shadow that sleeps on the hill
Awakens and floats on the mist of the heath.
It is not the shade of a murdered man,
Who has rushed uncalled to the throne of his God,
And howls in the pause of the eddying storm.
This voice is low, cold, hollow, and chill ;
'Tis not heard by the ear, but is felt in the soul.
'Tis more frightful far than the death-demon's scream,
Or the laughter of fiends when they howl o'er the corpse
Of a man who has sold his soul to hell.
It tells the approach of a mystic form,
A white courser bears the shadowy sprite ;
More thin they are than the mists of the mountain
When the clear moonlight sleeps on the waveless lake.
More pale *his* cheek than the snows of Nitbona
When winter rides on the northern blast,
And howls in the midst of the leafless wood.
Yet when the fierce swell of the tempest is raving,

And the whirlwinds howl in the caves of Inisfallen,
Still secure 'mid the wildest war of the sky,
The phantom courser scours the waste,
And his rider howls in the thunder's roar.
O'er him the fierce bolts of avenging heaven
Pause, as in fear, to strike his head.
The meteors of midnight recoil from his figure,
Yet the wildered peasant that oft passes by
With wonder beholds the blue flash through his form ;
And his voice, though faint as the sighs of the dead,
The startled passenger shudders to hear,
More distinct than the thunder's wildest roar.
Then does the dragon, who, chained in the caverns
To eternity, curses the champion of Erin,
Moan and yell loud at the lone hour of midnight,
And twine his vast wreaths round the forms of the demons,
Then in agony roll his death-swimming eyeballs,
Though wildered by death, yet never to die !
Then he shakes from his skeleton folds the nightmares
Who, shrieking in agony, seek the couch
Of some fevered wretch who courts sleep in vain.
Then the tombless ghosts of the guilty dead
In horror pause on the fitful gale ;
They float on the swell of the eddying tempest,
And, scared, seek the caves of gigantic . . . .
Where their thin forms pour unearthly sounds
On the blast that sweeps the breast of the lake,
And mingles its swell with the moonlight air.

MELODY TO A SCENE OF FORMER TIMES.

ART thou, indeed, for ever gone ?
For ever, ever lost to me ?
Must this poor bosom beat alone,
Or beat at all if not for thee ?
Ah ! why was love to mortals given
To lift them to the height of heaven,
Or dash them to the depths of hell ?
Yet I do not reproach thee, dear.
Ah, no ! the agonies that swell
This panting breast, this frenzied brain,
Might wake my ——'s slumbering tear.
Oh ! Heaven is witness I did love,
And Heaven does know I love thee still—
Does know the fruitless, sick'ning thrill
When reason's judgment vainly strove
To blot thee from my memory—
But which might never, never be.
Oh ! I appeal to that blest day
When passion's wildest ecstasy
Was coldness to the joys I knew,
When every sorrow sank away.
Oh ! I had never lived before,
But now these blisses are no more.

And now I cease to live again,
I do not blame thee, love; ah, no!
The breast that feels this anguished woe
Throbs for thy happiness alone.
Two years of speechless bliss are gone,
I thank thee, dearest, for the dream.

'Tis night—what faint and distant scream
Comes on the wild and fitful blast?
It moans for pleasures that are past,
It moans for days that are gone by.
Oh! lagging hours, how slow you fly!
I see a dark and lengthened vale,
The black view closes with the tomb;
But darker is the lowering gloom
That shades the intervening dale.
In visioned slumber for a while
I seem again to share thy smile,
I seem to hang upon thy tone;
Again you say, "Confide in me,
For I am thine, and thine alone,
And thine must ever, ever be."
But oh! awakening still anew,
Athwart my enanguished senses flew
A fiercer, deadlier agony!

ALPHABETICAL INDEX TO POEMS.

INDEX OF FIRST LINES.

PRINTED BY BALLANTYNE, HANSON AND CO.
EDINBURGH AND LONDON

THE
CHANDOS
CLASSICS